ABSENCE OF LIGHT—
CRAWFORD HILL

A Novel

MARSHA J. MACDONALD

ISBN: 978-1-4834-6789-4 (sc)
ISBN: 978-1-4834-6791-7 (hc)
ISBN: 978-1-4834-6790-0 (e)

Library of Congress Control Number: 2017904861

Lulu Publishing Services rev. date: 08/01/2018

This novel is dedicated to the many friends I met while working at the Medical University of South Carolina in Charleston; the memories of my travels in the region of Sheffield, England; and to my father, who taught me that darkness is merely the absence of light.

Contents

Author's Note

Rice plantations of All Saints Parish, Georgetown District in South Carolina once provided one of three major cash crops—including indigo and cotton—that supplied the city of Charleston and the region with its foundation of wealth. When the market for indigo shifted to the ports of India and the West Indies in the mid-eighteenth century, Georgetown District's rice exports superseded indigo as the king of crops in the region. Accordingly, rice earned the title Carolina Gold.

Built upon the backs of African slaves, the All Saints Parish rice plantations boasted some of the wealthiest planters in the region. Impressive plantation mansions with expansive lawns, tea gardens, lily ponds, and tree-lined drives draped in Spanish moss—called "allées"—punctuated the landscape. Such wealth was only possible due to the extensive human labor of thousands of slaves—both in terms of growing and harvesting the Carolina Gold rice, and in terms of maintaining the luxurious environs and lifestyles of the plantation owners.

The rice banks—engineered and built by the African slaves—rivaled, if not surpassed, the Egyptian pyramids in impressiveness and scale. Slaves brought with them from Africa their comprehensive knowledge of growing rice—the April planting, opening sluice gates for the May sprout-flow flooding, hoeing, the long-water flooding, cultivating to promote growth, the final hoeing and July harvest flow, threshing to separate the heads from their stalks, and the pounding to remove outer husks and inner cuticles from the rice grains. Growing and harvesting rice required strenuous labor, made all the more arduous by the oppressive heat and humidity of the South's late-spring and summer months. Without the expertise and stamina of the

African slave, the enormous wealth of All Saints Parish would never have been realized.

Enslaved Africans from various ethnic groups of West and Central Africa had been brought to the colonies to work on plantations in coastal South Carolina. Their descendants gave birth to the Gullah culture and language that still exists. Gullah language is a creole tongue, formed by the amalgam of various African languages and English, that was originally created by the enslaved Africans. It is said that the Gullah speech of today is likely no more than a pale reflection of antebellum slave speech. Gullah culture remains evident in South Carolina among those descendants, known as Gullah Geechee people, who weave sweetgrass baskets, share Gullah folktales, perform spiritual folk-tradition concerts such as the call-and-response ring shout, enjoy time-honored cuisine at festivals—for example, smoked mullet, shrimp n' grits, and sweet potato pie—and pass down numerous other rich traditions of their ancestors.

It was the expert labor of the Gullah slaves on the All Saints Parish, Georgetown District rice plantations that contributed to the vast wealth of South Carolina. And it was that wealth that supplied much of the leadership removing South Carolina from the Union on December 20, 1860. Shortly after the state's secession from the Union, the first volleys of shelling on Union-held Fort Sumter in Charleston's harbor—fired on April 12, 1861—ignited the Civil War. Ultimately, slavery would be abolished, and the South would never be the same. Before long, Carolina Gold would cease to be the major commercial crop of the state's Georgetown District.

CHAPTER I

Loxley House

"But we must have a tree, Benjamin, we simply must!" Alexandra implored her husband. "After all—"

"Yes, yes, my dear. I know. Prince Albert and Queen Victoria are having a tree brought over from Germany," he commented dryly, and finished, "My, but you are an impetuous thing!" Benjamin said no more about the matter and resumed reading his copy of the morning paper.

Alexandra approached her husband, and daring to fold down the top of his paper, she asserted timidly, "But how can we *not* have a tree when we are expecting a houseful of people for Christmas?"

Benjamin hesitated a moment before looking over his wife's hand upon the paper. "You have covered the article I am reading." He dropped his eyes, but Alexandra kept her hand stubbornly on the folded edge. Benjamin cleared his throat to suggest she remove her hand, which she did. He gave the paper a defiant shake and resumed his reading.

Alexandra had all but surrendered the matter. Dejectedly she began to walk away, but she decided that the issue was simply too important to let rest. She turned sharply. "But it is the very first Christmas the queen shall have a tree, and I don't understand why we cannot have one also!"

Benjamin lowered his paper and noted the agitation on his young wife's brow that matched her upset voice. For a moment, he steadily eyed Alexandra who, by now, seemed on the verge of tears.

Ever since Alexandra had received word from friends in London about the purported royal Christmas tree, her imagination had run circles around the idea. Now she felt her hopes all but dashed by Benjamin's apparent obstinacy.

"I've already informed household staff and the head gardener that we *are* to have a tree," he remarked, and resumed reading the newspaper before him.

Alexandra required a moment to comprehend her husband's words. "We ... we *are* to have a tree?"

"Yes, dear," Benjamin acknowledged, from behind his lifted paper.

Alexandra scarcely knew whether to succumb to gathering tears or laugh. She did neither of these. Instead, she picked up a small brocaded pillow from an adjacent sofa and flung it at her husband. "You *tease!*" she cried, with a stomp of her foot.

The flung pillow struck the newspaper hard, whereupon Benjamin thrust it aside as though angry. "You, my darling, are in trouble now!" he threatened, his eyes narrow.

Before Alexandra could utter a sound, Benjamin rose from his chair and darted toward her.

Alexandra shrieked and fled his impending chase. "You devil!" she shouted as she ran, dodging him this way and that around the furniture. "You knew all along! It isn't fair!" she panted, nimbly avoiding his grasp.

Benjamin laughed heartily as he moved deftly to one side, trapping Alexandra between the papered wall and a round cherrywood table. She stood poised for escape, panting and flushed, but with nowhere to go.

"Ha! I've got you cornered!" Benjamin triumphed.

Alexandra's eyes darted, but she could see no way out. Her eyes fixed on her husband's, she nervously wafted aside a stray wisp of golden hair.

"Now you're all mine!" Benjamin menaced playfully.

"No!" Alexandra shrieked, and backed into the corner as Benjamin closed in toward her.

In an instant, Benjamin's arms flew around her.

Alexandra writhed to free herself ... but to no avail.

"Be still!" he admonished. "And take your due!"

"I won't!" She averted her face downward.

"Come on, now," he coaxed. "Look at me when I talk to you!"

"No!" Alexandra writhed harder in his grasp.

"Look at me, my darling—"

"No! I won't kiss you!"

"Just one kiss, Rose—"

"No! I'll never kiss you again—ever!"

But her words grew muffled as Benjamin raised her chin and pressed his lips tenderly against hers. She fought him off, but he held her fast, sweetly planting a second kiss on her upturned mouth.

"Never again?" he murmured.

"Never," she uttered unconvincingly, and succumbed to the pleasures of his kisses.

Benjamin chuckled jubilantly to himself, even as they kissed. His victory was cut short, however, as Alexandra mischievously bit down on his lower lip. Benjamin drew back.

"Ooow! *Rose!*" Astonished, he held one hand held to the wounded lip.

"Ha! That will teach you." She laughed gleefully and darted past him, fleeing the corner, nearly toppling the cherrywood table.

Benjamin ran quickly after her. "No kiss, no tree!"

Their merriment echoed through the main hall and many rooms of Loxley House as Benjamin gave chase, close on Alexandra's heels. In the end, Benjamin again won his kiss, Alexandra had been promised her tree, and the household staff's tongues began to wag and wonder at such frivolous behavior at the otherwise staid country estate.

———◊———

Loxley House was as any other English country house in the Derbyshire countryside—stone, impressive in size, and situated on endless acres of open land. This particular house was quite plain, although nonetheless grand for its simplicity. Approached from the broad front drive, one could count numerous windows set with dull uniformity along its sprawling gray stone facade. The house resembled nothing more than a rectangle—with the exception of a cupola boasting seven gables; a lone arched door at the east wing; and several brickwork chimneys protruding skyward, adding unnecessary height to the three-story affair.

A broad staircase of stone led from the regal circular drive up to the front entrance of Loxley House. Stone banisters flanked the staircase more as a point of architecture than of practicality. The massive front doors to Loxley House stood doublewide but otherwise as simple as any other aspect of the place. Even the door-knockers hung without particular distinction, although they served their purpose.

Similarly, the landscaping about the house lacked particular adornment. The front lawns spread as flat green seas upon either side of the wide drive. Characteristic of the surrounding Derbyshire countryside, the nearby grounds consisted mainly of rambling open lands punctuated by undulating hills and inclines.

Some distance behind the house stood a thick wood of beech, pine, and elm trees. Near this woodland glimmered a modest lake fed by a shallow, yawning river at the lake's north end. An enchanting stone footbridge spanned the demarcation between the river and lake in three arched tiers. Collectively, these woodlands and the northern grounds, including the river and lake, comprised the Pleasure Garden.

This title—Pleasure Garden—had been conferred upon the grounds owing to the leisure and sport that could be conducted there, and the misnomer of "Garden" was an obvious understatement. In autumn, the woodland was ripe for hunting. In winter, ice-skating and ice-sledding occupied the frozen lake. Late spring was ideal for rowing upon the river, gliding beneath the arches of the stone footbridge and emerging upon the rippling lake. Summertime invited picnics, kite flying, and strolls along the lake's edge.

In actuality, the only true garden at Loxley House was a maze-like, ornamental expanse of tall hedgerows a short distance from the front of the house. At the center of this labyrinth grew a small rose garden, and at the heart of it was a low sundial cast in bronze. Benjamin Fairfield presumed that perhaps the sundial's placement there functioned to time contests on how long it took one to find their way to the center of the garden. Alexandra insisted its purpose was purely aesthetic, although her younger sisters, Allison and Annabelle, surmised that the sundial was symbolic. "It means that one should take time from the maze that life is to sit a while and enjoy the roses," they would say. Nonetheless, in England the sun was generally either quenched by rain or cloaked in gray clouds, rendering the sundial useless.

Benjamin Fairfield had inherited the whole of Loxley Estate from his father, and the Fairfield lineage of ownership dated back to the mid-seventeenth century when the house had first been built. Now, in 1846, the house was nearly two hundred years old, although its sturdy stonework had endured none the worse for wear. Similarly, the interior of Loxley House had been constructed solidly and practically, weathering several generations of occupants and houseguests with hardly a scratch. Benjamin Fairfield and his staff determined that the house should remain well-maintained for future occupants, despite the fact that he and Alexandra seemed unable to conceive an heir to their country estate.

As it was, Loxley House remained populated more by household staff and groundskeepers than by family, although Benjamin Fairfield and his wife Alexandra treated their various workers—domestic personnel, gardeners, coachmen, grooms, and so on—as if they *were* family. A steward and housekeeper supervised the populous staff of housemaids and butlers, capably assuring that the house continued running in smooth working order at all times.

Several grooms and coachmen cared for the housed carriages and stabled horses behind the west wing of Loxley House, and exactly twenty men labored as gardeners and groundskeepers upon the estate. A few of the latter held the additional responsibility for the upkeep of the canoes, ice-sleds, and ice-skates housed in a quaint stone edifice near the south end of the lake.

Indoors, elegant simplicity best described the décor at Loxley House. Benjamin believed that too much clutter or fuss made it difficult for one to think. Alexandra and her sisters were like-minded, having grown up in modest middleclass surroundings. Similarly, the household staff did not seem to mind the paucity of crystal chandeliers, antique baubles, or carved gold-gilt frames to clean. Light dusting, sweeping, carpet beating, and disrupting cobwebs provided plenty of housekeeping to occupy them on a weekly basis.

Together, austerity and practicality constituted the essence of the Loxley estate—its house and grounds. What lent the place its charm, however, was not the understated style of architecture, the neatly manicured grounds, the whimsical stone footbridge spanning the Pleasure Garden's river, or even the front yard's labyrinthine garden with its unique sundial. The charm of

Loxley House lay in its chief occupants; among these, it could be said—and heartily agreed to by Benjamin himself—that the charm of Loxley House rested in the presence of the three sisters: Alexandra, Allison, and Annabelle.

———◇———

Alexandra Rosalynn was the eldest of the three sisters. She had wed Benjamin Fairfield just three years previously, in 1843, at the age of twenty. Because Benjamin was eight years older than Alexandra, she regarded him not only as husband and best friend but also as a surrogate older brother and somewhat as a father figure. The sudden, untimely death of the sisters' parents had thrust Alexandra into a maternal role at age eighteen, looking after Allison, age fourteen, and Annabelle, age twelve. The three young women's parents had been acquainted with a member of the Loxley House staff. When word had reached Benjamin in the spring of 1841 of the three girls' tragic loss, he took it upon himself to journey the short distance to their home in Sheffield to inquire as to their needs.

Benjamin located their address upon a bustling street of modest row houses. Finding the door-knocker in disrepair, he rapped upon the door with his gloved hand. After a moment, he heard footsteps from within, and the door creaked open upon its hinges.

Allison stood facing him on the threshold. They spoke briefly, all the while her wide-eyed, innocent face looking solemnly up at him. Uncertainly she let him inside and ushered him into the front parlor where she and her sisters had been occupied that day sorting through their parents' belongings—which to sell and which to keep.

The three women were dressed in mourning, the black of their attire setting off the pale of their fair skin and blond hair, seeming to further dramatize their grief. Upon meeting Alexandra, Benjamin again briefly explained the reason for his visit: that he was the owner of Loxley House, staff had informed him of the tragedy that had befallen the young Summers girls, and he wanted to be of assistance to them.

The four sat quietly in the parlor. Alexandra apologized distractedly for the room's disarray. Benjamin politely declined Alexandra's offer to make him some tea. He reiterated the purpose of his visit.

Initially, Alexandra politely refused his offers of monetary assistance and advised Allison and Annabelle to do the same. Once more, Benjamin pleaded with them to take advantage of his concern for them, but again, Alexandra steadfastly refused. Benjamin sighed heavily, and a pregnant silence settled between the four.

Annabelle, only twelve, her eyes welling, looked from Mr. Fairfield to Alexandra. She ventured timidly, "But … whatever shall we do now Momma and Poppa are … are in heaven?" Her voice ended in a tremulous squeak.

Benjamin looked anxiously at Alexandra, who only stared, blinking back tears, at her younger sister.

Allison surveyed the three others, and blurted forlornly, "Alexandra, we shall have to go to the poorhouse!" All eyes turned to Allison. "I … I'm afraid of the poorhouse! *Please* Alexandra. I don't *want* to go to the poorhouse!" And with that, Allison bowed her face in her hands and sobbed as if all the world's sorrows issued from her heart.

It was more than Benjamin could bear, and he would have insisted on the spot that they accept his help, but Allison's outburst sent her two sisters into helpless fits of tears as well. Benjamin had little to do at the moment but try to calm and console the three young women, their blond heads bent weeping before him. When at last the three pairs of round blue eyes looked at Benjamin, he sighed and leaned forward in his chair. "Dear girls, please be sensible. Let me help you," he entreated.

A long silence passed between them, and Benjamin studied their innocent young faces. On each visage, high cheekbones tapered to a neat little chin that neither receded nor protruded too much. Above this, each girl possessed a most exquisite mouth, the lips neither too generous nor too spare, yet the lines of their curves an enchantment—almost an invitation. Beneath each intelligent brow, the nose was finely rendered and in delightful proportion to the surrounding features. Each countenance possessed enough character to disqualify it from being regarded as classic beauty; however, it was this very quality that not only attracted but sustained one's interest. Although the three sisters appeared strikingly similar in looks, there was a subtle, individual quality to each lovely face. Alexandra's features, finely chiseled and rather more angular than her sisters', lent her a regal, aristocratic quality. Annabelle, while decidedly pretty, was somewhat more ordinary in appearance, with perhaps a hint of plainness. Allison's attributes could only be described as angelic. Beneath Allison's thick cascades of golden tresses, she possessed a softness, a sort of fragile femininity; when older, she would decidedly be the most alluring of the three.

"Please." Benjamin implored the three sisters one last time to accept his financial assistance.

The two younger sisters looked at Alexandra through red-rimmed eyes, over dampened cheeks. Allison applied a handkerchief to the tip of her nose and swallowed hard, feeling certain Alexandra would decline.

Downcast that his journey had been made in vain, Benjamin rose to leave.

"I … I accept your offer," Alexandra said quietly, then stood modestly to face Benjamin.

Benjamin turned. "My dear Miss Summers, you have no idea how happy you have made me!"

With details of the financial assistance quickly worked out, Benjamin further insisted on checking in on the three young women from time to time to see how they were faring.

In a short while, Benjamin Fairfield's visits to the modest house in Sheffield increased as he had grown increasingly fond of Alexandra Rosalynn Summers. Before long, he began courting Alexandra and bestowed upon her the pet name of Rose, which he derived from her middle name and which he said suited her sweet nature.

Alexandra and Benjamin married in 1843, when Alexandra was just twenty and Benjamin was twenty-eight. Allison and Annabelle—ages sixteen and fourteen—served as bridesmaids for the ceremony held at Loxley House. Since that day, Allison and Annabelle lived with Benjamin and Alexandra at the estate.

This Christmas, the winter of 1846, would be their fourth together at Loxley—and it promised to be the most grand because of the promised tree.

CHAPTER 2

Christmas at Loxley—1846

Numerous carriages of holiday guests began arriving at Loxley House a week or so before Christmas. Bleak, frozen London was a social wasteland at this time of year, and those who could afford it journeyed to their families' and friends' country houses to enjoy their gaiety, warmth, and snow-laden bucolic settings. Each year, Benjamin and Alexandra invited several of their friends to Loxley House to celebrate the Christmas holidays. This year they had planned such a holiday with the initial intent of keeping the guestlist conservative, but once Benjamin had promised Alexandra that they would have a tree like Queen Victoria's, their invitations began to multiply.

Sentimentality, sympathy, and various other excuses were the main culprits in the extension of the guestlist. It was: "We simply must invite the Bergins!" or "The Harrisons will feel left out if we don't ask them!" and "But the Wights are such good friends of the Edgertons; we must have them come as well." In addition, Alexandra, Allison, and Annabelle each clamored to invite former school friends whom they had known in Sheffield. Benjamin's younger brother, Todd, also wanted to add another name to the swelling guestlist. Todd was home, visiting for the holidays, and hoped to invite a good friend of his, Jeremy Stewart, to join them at Christmas.

"It is *only* one more guest, Benjamin," Alexandra prompted.

Benjamin agreed, and the invitation to Jeremy Stewart was granted. In turn, Jeremy Stewart inquired whether he could extend the invitation to include his younger brother as well. This invitation was also granted, and Benjamin noted, "If need be, Jeremy Stewart and his brother, Brandon, can share Todd's room." The guestlist had indeed grown beyond anyone's expectations.

Upon his arrival home to Loxley House, Todd informed Benjamin that Jeremy and Brandon would be delayed a few days in London before they could travel to Loxley. Initially, Todd said only that the two brothers had some business to attend to in London. Later, he confided that the business they had to conduct was the burial of their father and the settling of his estate. Their father, a prominent university professor and chairman of the Department of Literature, had suddenly contracted a brief illness and died just days before. "There are to be at least one hundred carriages in the funeral procession," Todd said, adding, "Jeremy insisted I return home, not wishing to spoil my holiday on his account. They will both come as soon as they're able. Their father's death is the reason Jeremy hoped his younger brother might be invited here too. Their mother died a few years ago, as well. So, with all the students gone for the Christmas holiday, and with no parents, Brandon would have been quite alone."

Benjamin, as well as Alexandra and her two sisters, felt immediately sympathetic toward the two brothers upon hearing this. Allison felt particularly compassionate toward Brandon who, at nearly nineteen, was her same age, as she remembered how it felt to lose one's parents while still young.

Meanwhile, as the rooms of Loxley House began to fill with holiday guests, Todd spoke glowingly of his two friends, Jeremy and Brandon. Jeremy was twenty-one, would graduate from the university at the end of the spring term, and then advance to post-graduate military school. Brandon was a student of the university's Literature, Journalism, and Art & Illustration courses. Todd had been in several classes with Jeremy, although Brandon, being younger, had only been acquainted with Todd through Jeremy when socializing at London pubs and university gatherings.

Allison discreetly inquired about both young men from Todd in order to learn more about Brandon—and the more Allison heard about the two brothers, the more anxious she grew to meet him.

Brandon Jonathan Stewart was reported by Todd to be studious, yet adventuresome; intelligent and well-read; amiable, with a pleasant sense of humor; and possessing an unassuming nature that was at the heart of all his attributes and charms. Brandon aspired to be a writer and illustrator, and perhaps to travel. This latter ambition Allison found romantic, and the other two, she surmised, indicated a thoughtful, sensitive nature. Todd further informed Allison that Brandon was a gentleman, considerate, and somewhat reserved, though tending at times to be pensive and quiet. All she heard fascinated Allison immensely, and she grew increasingly anxious for the arrival of Brandon and Jeremy to Loxley House.

Yet with Christmas only days away, Allison worried, and asked more than once, "Todd, are you sure they will come after all?" Todd replied that he saw no reason for the brothers *not* to arrive, and Allison felt somewhat reassured.

Perhaps the only element of disappointment for Allison was that Todd regarded Brandon as only somewhat handsome, punctuating his assessment with a dismissive shrug. Ever so briefly crestfallen, Allison reminded herself that looks were not everything. That Brandon might be considered only average in looks deterred her imagination not one wit from conjuring pleasant images of how they would first meet upon his arrival.

———◇———

Missing their first train from London to Sheffield, then traveling by hired carriage over icy snow-laden roads westward to Loxley House, the two brothers arrived several hours later than expected. A house servant ushered them through the entryway's large double doors where they stood all but unnoticed for some time. There, Jeremy and Brandon found a number of the Fairfield's guests milling about the enormous front hall, eagerly awaiting the positioning of the promised Christmas tree. Cold, tired, and hungry due to their journey from London, the two looked in vain about the sea of meandering guests for any sign of Todd Fairfield. The huge evergreen tree that lay stretched upon the marble floor had caused such commotion, even among the household staff, that no one had noticed to announce the brothers' arrival.

Descending the sweeping staircase to the right of where the tree lay, Alexandra spotted two young men standing idly near the front door and looking a bit lost beside the chattering crowd of visitors. Alexandra assumed these two must be Todd's friends. Wending her way through the crowd below, she happened upon Allison and Annabelle visiting amiably with a few of their friends from Sheffield. "Allison, Annabelle—I believe Todd's guests have arrived," Alexandra noted as she passed by. Upon this revelation, Allison quickly excused herself from the company of her friends, giving Annabelle's arm an urgent tug to hurry and follow her and Alexandra.

Alexandra had just made the two young men's acquaintance when Allison and Annabelle approached demurely, emerging from the gathering of guests. Her eyes fixed on Brandon, Allison was instantly smitten—her heart melted upon her first sight of him.

Brandon Jonathan Stewart was strikingly handsome, his looks suggesting a stoic vulnerability. He was tall, but not overly so; square shouldered; and of strong, slender build. His deep-set, expressive brown eyes glanced at Allison from beneath a smooth, intelligent brow and the most delicious waves of thick dark-brown hair she had ever seen. She noted his high cheekbones and a handsome nose that complemented, rather than detracted from, his appearance. His chin was strong but not obtrusive, and it helped set off his fine, sensitive mouth—the lower lip slightly fuller than the upper—that concealed a broad, easy smile. Already, Allison yearned to see Brandon smile; but for the moment, weary from travel and feeling ill at ease in his unfamiliar surroundings, Brandon remained polite but somber.

Alexandra introduced the two young men to her sisters. Allison shyly stammered her hello, then finding her tongue, interjected a heartfelt condolence on behalf of their father's untimely death. Brandon nodded his thank you with a sad smile. His brown eyes suddenly grew wet, and he glanced away from Allison, grateful for a sudden boisterous commotion near the foot of the staircase that commanded everyone's attention.

Benjamin was on the staircase, orchestrating from above the erection of the unwieldy evergreen. Several of the estate's gardeners strained to right the tree into position, but its size obligated several of the guests to rush forward and help. Brandon, glad for the distraction, eagerly pitched in to assist in the effort, followed quickly by Jeremy.

Allison looked on, her heart full; she had noticed the tears in Brandon's eyes and suspected his reason for so quickly rushing to help raise the tree.

Annabelle knowingly tucked her arm around her sister's waist, gave her a gentle squeeze, and whispered into Allison's golden locks, "But Allison, you've only just met him!"

Allison returned her sister's confidential smile, then turned her attention back to Brandon; Jeremy; the guests; and the towering, wavering evergreen.

From high atop the staircase, Benjamin called down to the men struggling amidst the prickly green branches, "A bit closer to the stairs. A bit more *this* way. Yes, that's it ... you have it!"

But the tree began to sway, and it seemed to everyone, for a moment, that it would topple.

"*Careful!*" Benjamin threw his hands up anxiously and gesticulated.

Alexandra held her breath, her hands to her lips, until the tree was at last righted and towered majestically in its place before the admiring guests. The front hall was filled with hushed "—Oohs!" and "—Aahs!" However, for the moment, Allison did not care one fig for the tree. On tiptoe she strained to locate Brandon in the thick cluster of guests—she was hopelessly captivated, and it was clearly not the tree that had won her attention. She eagerly anticipated the chance to become better acquainted with Brandon during his holiday stay at Loxley House.

Because Allison was a bit shy, and Brandon was relatively reserved as well as somewhat brooding as of late, it was up to Todd to contrive situations in which Allison and Brandon might become better acquainted. This task proved difficult, as Brandon was still feeling out of sorts and not of good company. Brandon had noticed Allison but did not feel at his best to socialize or converse much with any of those about him. He declined numerous invitations to spend time with Jeremy, Todd, Allison, her younger sister, and their friends, regretting that his current mood was not conducive to sharing in the festive holiday agenda. In the few days before Christmas, both Brandon and Jeremy had their somber moments together to mourn the loss of their father; they took long morning walks in the snow and retired early in the evenings to talk quietly, alone in their shared room.

Since the brothers' arrival at Loxley House, Jeremy Stewart proved the more gregarious of the two—Brandon only assumed a more sociable nature when not at his older brother's side. Brandon's grief over his father's death was far more apparent in his demeanor than Jeremy's. Because Jeremy was older, he felt he must repress his sorrows and behave as a lighthearted participant in the holiday festivities to help cheer his younger brother. Both in his grief and in the massive country estate surrounded by strangers, Brandon felt quite out of place and alone. Although Jeremy's efforts at boisterousness and good cheer seemed at times contrived and transparent, they served, nonetheless, to console Brandon and prevent him from brooding alone. The two brothers had always been close, and now they were all the other had in the world—hence, each silently vowed to look after the other.

This aloof behavior of Brandon's did not escape Allison's notice, and the brothers' absences pained her greatly. This was not only because Allison missed Brandon's presence but because she wished she could help console him. She wanted ever so much to tell him that she knew what he was enduring, that she too had recently lost her parents. She imagined ways whereby she might seek him out alone to talk, but the holiday agenda was too full for any such impromptu rendezvous between the two. Tree trimming, dances, dinners, parlor games, sleigh rides, ice-skating, and ice-sledding all occupied Allison's time with the other guests; as she shared hostess duties with her sisters, she could not easily engage her attention with any one single person. Allison felt such increasing concern for Brandon's happiness that she scarcely wondered whether he even cared for her as much as she cared for him.

On a crisp, clear day the week before the new year, Allison, Annabelle, Alexandra, and Benjamin set out with several of their guests for a small ice-sledding party on the Pleasure Garden's lake, beyond the east wing of Loxley House. Benjamin and two of the estate staff had previously contrived several wooden ice-sleds—wooden chairs fastened upon sled rails to be propelled from behind by ice-skaters. For the women, it was a great thrill to be a passenger aboard an ice-sled, to sit and be glided over the slick ice with the rhythmic whoosh and clatter of the men's skates from behind. It was the decision of the skaters where one would be propelled and how fast. The men, bundled in their winter coats, and the women, in their warmest winter dresses, cloaks, bonnets, scarves, and muffs, eagerly set out from the front doors of Loxley House toward the frozen lake.

Allison had hoped that Brandon and Jeremy might join the ice-sledding party, but neither they nor Todd could be located that afternoon. The sledding party had made their plans and set off without them. To her chagrin, Allison was paired with a fourteen-year-old boy, the son of one of the visitors. How she wished he could have been Brandon instead. She worried that perhaps Brandon and Jeremy were off together brooding over the loss of their father, although their spirits had lifted somewhat during their stay at Loxley. As Allison navigated the icy walkway along the front of the house, unenthusiastically trailing after the others, she could not have guessed that Jeremy and Brandon were engaged nearby with Todd and several other young men in some light-hearted roughhousing in the snow.

As the little ice-sledding party rounded the east corner to the side of the house, Allison dutifully trudged along with the young boy in tow, then realized she had forgotten to bring her muff. Her fingers were already beginning to feel chilled through her woolen gloves. "I forgot my muff," she informed her fourteen-year-old escort and turned abruptly back, nearly slipping on the ice. The boy began to follow, but Allison waved him on, "Go ahead with the others. I'll catch up. Tell Alexandra."

The boy looked puzzled and stood uncertainly, staring after Allison.

"Tell Mrs. *Fairfield!*" Allison clarified with an element of exasperation.

The boy nodded and ran after the others.

Allison surmised that the day was not turning out at all right: Brandon had been absent since breakfast; she had been assigned to a mere boy for ice-sledding—an embarrassing disgrace to be so paired at the worldly age of eighteen—and now she had forgotten her muff. Treading the icy walkway proved too tedious, and so Allison clomped, with little improvement in speed, through the low drifts bordering the walk. At last she reached the house, retrieved her muff, and hurriedly set out once again for the frozen lake.

As Allison emerged around the east corner of the house, she was struck in the face with a hard, stinging blow. Her right eye was the unsuspecting target of a round frozen ball hurled by one among the group of young men roughhousing nearby. Several young men had been rambunctiously hailing snowballs between their two warring factions; they stopped short when they realized one snowball had gone sadly amiss and struck Allison. Upon impact, Allison lost her footing and tumbled backward, falling hard upon the icy walkway. Her head missed the downy bank of snow alongside the house and struck, instead, the frozen stone footpath. Momentarily dazed, she lay in pain, afraid to move, her blue eyes wide and gazing absently up at the cloud-dappled sky overhead. In an instant she began to cry. She scarcely knew what had occurred, only that the pains emanating from the back of her head and her wounded eye were overwhelming. She let her tears flow hot and unchecked.

At once the young men stopped their play and rushed gravely toward Allison. Although Todd was among them, he instead ran pell-mell through the drifts to fetch Benjamin from the ice-sledding party now assembled at the lake's edge. Brandon Stewart was the first one of the group to reach Allison.

Blinded by tears, aching, and cold, Allison was only dimly aware of someone kneeling at her side. Gradually the other young men clustered around, hushed and speculating among themselves whether or not she was seriously hurt. Embarrassed by so many young men gathered around her, Allison blinked back tears. The first person she identified was Brandon, who knelt beside her. Brandon's face was drained of color, save for the flush of cold upon his cheeks. Overcome with concern, he was scarcely able to ask Allison if she was badly hurt. Allison imagined Brandon looking down at her just then—her nose red with cold and crying, eyes puffy and one bruised, cheeks tear-stained, hair matted, and bonnet disheveled in the damp snow. At once she concluded that Brandon Jonathan Stewart must think her a ridiculous spectacle of a young woman, and she promptly burst into tears all over again. Allison felt so beside herself, she had not even summoned the wherewithal to respond to Brandon's concerned inquiry.

Brandon interpreted Allison's tearful reaction to his concern as proof that she knew it was he who had hurled the errant snowball. He concluded that, now, she must loathe him. Disheartened, he knelt idly by her side, crushed that his own careless act had sabotaged his plans to finally ask Allison out on a sleigh ride that evening.

The crowd of young men collected about Allison parted as Benjamin, followed by Alexandra and Todd, strode briskly forward. Benjamin knelt beside Allison, took her hands in his, and speaking gently, ascertained that she could try to stand and venture into the house. As Benjamin helped Allison to rise, Brandon remained kneeling on the cold, hard walkway, gazing at the place where Allison had lain and inwardly cursed his carelessness.

No sooner had Benjamin helped Allison to her feet, than she uttered a sharp cry of pain and fainted dead away, caught swiftly up in Benjamin's arms. Her right ankle had been sorely turned in her fall, and with searing pain, it had failed to support her as she stood.

Benjamin carried Allison hurriedly around the corner of the house with Alexandra and the others following anxiously behind. Brandon stared after the concerned procession that rushed along the front walkway, Allison's limp frame borne away with urgency in Benjamin's arms, her golden curls dangling loose from her pretty bonnet. Inwardly, Brandon was consumed with remorse. Sullenly he stalked off alone through the snowfields behind Loxley House toward the woods.

Brandon's spirits, which Jeremy had tried so very hard to lift, seemed all at once to crash down around him as he trudged sullenly through the drifts. Threatening a snowstorm, the sky gathered dark clouds overhead as Brandon reached a low stone wall at the edge of the north wood. In the distance, he saw the ice-sledding party upon the frozen lake and heard their laughter echo across the drifts, but he could only think of Allison. Although he surmised that he should return to the house to check on her, he imagined the unkind reception he would undoubtedly receive—by now, *everyone* at Loxley House must know it was he who had hurled the errant snowball that struck Allison. And so, he lingered for some time near the low stone wall, staring darkly at the frozen winter woods beyond and brooding.

As his thoughts spiraled downward, a sudden flood of longing for his father seized Brandon, and he emitted several uncontrolled sobs, burying his face in his coat-sleeve upon the wall. Brandon would have hurled himself headlong into the drifts and wept disconsolately, but he reminded himself that at nearly age nineteen he must be stoic in both his grief for his departed father and his remorse for having injured Allison. Struggling to contain his emotions, he swallowed the lump in his throat and dried his eyes on his sleeve. Sniffling in the darkening cold, he turned and slowly ascended the hill toward the house as a light flurry of snow began to fall. Beyond, the frozen lake lay silent, the ice-sledding party having long since departed.

The late-afternoon sky had turned nearly black as evening as Brandon reached the house. Squinting in the gloom and swirling flakes, he spied a small dark bundle lying along the footpath at the side of the house. Drawing nearer, he recognized it was Allison's muff and stooped to pick it up. Dusting snow from the damp fur, Brandon rounded the corner to the front of the house where he encountered Jeremy.

"*There* you are!" Jeremy called out from the front steps.

Brandon looked up, his set jaw belying his feelings of forlorn sorrow.

Jeremy drew near to where Brandon stood. "The Fairfields had begun to worry. It seems there is a sudden storm brewing. They sent me out to look for you." Jeremy paused, then asked with some concern, "Are you all right?"

Brandon shrugged and looked down at the muff in his hands.

"What have you got there?" Jeremy asked.

"It's Allison's muff. She must have dropped it when she fell."

"Well, we'd best be getting inside," Jeremy prompted, shivering in his wool coat. "It's getting bloody cold out."

As the two ascended the stone steps toward the front door, Jeremy noted, "They know who caused Allison's fall."

Brandon stopped dead in his tracks, certain he would never again set foot inside Loxley House. Yet he was less concerned for his own fate than he was for Allison's. "How is she? ... Will she be all right?" he asked, a note of trepidation in his voice.

Jeremy smiled and clapped his brother on the back. "She is faring well enough. No true harm done."

This did not assure Brandon, and he stood hesitantly upon the lower steps looking up at Jeremy and the doors to Loxley House.

Jeremy turned. "She's doing quite well—*really.*"

Brandon remained uncertain and, looking downward, toyed nervously with the fur bundle in his gloved hands.

Jeremy trod down the steps to where his brother stood and grasped his arm. "Look here—"

Brandon glanced up to meet his brother's eyes.

"They know you struck her with a snowball, but no one is blaming you. They know it was an accident."

"I hadn't meant it." Brandon's voice trailed.

"Of course not. Why, even Allison hasn't blamed you—"

"Allison?!" Brandon's eyes widened. "Does *she* know it was I who—" He could not finish and felt more crestfallen than before. It had been one thing for him to imagine that she knew her injuries were his fault—quite another to actually hear it first-hand.

"Allison doesn't blame you. Again, *no one* blames you. In fact, she was the first to suggest that someone go and look for you. She was worried."

Brandon looked doubtful, and his expression grew slightly wounded. "She ... she knows I hadn't meant it?"

"She wanted to go look for you herself, in spite of her injured ankle, until I assured her that I was on my way."

Brandon looked thoughtful, blew on his numbing fingers through his knit gloves, and said quietly, "I suppose we'd best go inside."

Jeremy smiled encouragingly, clapped his brother on the shoulder, and the two ascended the steps as great downy flakes of snow fell silently about them. It was indeed growing bitterly cold outside. Jeremy opened the front door, and they entered the warmth and lamplight of Loxley House.

"Brandon, Allison has been asking for you," Alexandra said as she met Jeremy and Brandon in the front hall.

Brandon felt at once eager and reluctant to see Allison. Alexandra took Allison's muff from Brandon and escorted him up to her sister's room.

Allison lay upon her bed propped up on several plump pillows, her ankle elevated at the foot of the bed on a small cushion. A thick feather-down quilt was drawn over her for warmth. It had hurt Allison excruciatingly to have her hair combed where her head was bruised, her face washed where her eye had been struck, and her stockings and frock changed due to her sprained ankle—but she had been determined to look her best for Brandon, once he was found.

Brandon's profuse apologies were absorbed by Allison's limitless forgiveness, and soon they began talking and laughing together as good friends. Before long, they both felt in enough humor to make light of the mishap and tease each other about it. They were so engaged for nearly two hours when a housemaid, accompanied by Alexandra, brought Allison's dinner up on a tray.

"But I wanted to be downstairs with the others!" Allison implored. She looked so woebegone that Alexandra relented, and Brandon chivalrously offered to carry Allison downstairs to the dining room.

———— ⸸ ————

Relieved of her hostess duties due to her sprained ankle, Allison now could afford much more leisure time to spend with her friends from Sheffield and, even more importantly, with Brandon. However, she also— albeit reluctantly—encouraged Brandon to spend some time outdoors with Jeremy, Todd, and the others. Brandon did so on occasion but used his sense of guilt over her injuries as an excuse to stay indoors and entertain her. "I would like to stay with you, if you will have me," he would say. As the days passed, the two spent afternoons by the fireside engaged with games of chess or cards, or reading to one another from books of poetry and volumes of literature. In the evenings, Allison would play piano for Brandon; he adored hearing her play, watching her slender fingers flit over the keys. They talked together for hours about all manner of things and, most significantly, about the respective loss of their parents. By the eve of Brandon's departure for London, a close bond had formed between them—though neither spoke of this to the other.

Allison's injured ankle had mended somewhat by the last day of Brandon and Jeremy's stay at Loxley House. Together, Annabelle and Alexandra helped Allison on with her boots so that Brandon could take her out on an early-evening sleigh ride. The process hurt her so much that she gasped with pain and began to cry.

"Perhaps we'd best not try, Allison," Alexandra gently advised, and she began to withdraw the boot.

"No! No, please. I simply *must* go!" Allison entreated, and promptly checked her tears. It was the last day before Brandon's departure for London, and she could not imagine missing the chance of him escorting her on a starlit-evening sleigh ride.

Annabelle, her hand upon the withdrawn boot, glanced at Alexandra for her decision.

"It really doesn't hurt too terribly," Allison said, as much to convince herself as to convince her sisters.

Alexandra nodded at Annabelle. "One more try."

At last the boot was on, though unfastened, and Allison limped down the staircase supporting herself along the banister. Brandon met her at the foot of the stairs.

"Are you able to walk on it?" he asked with concern.

"Yes ... I think so." Allison, however, felt doubtful.

Brandon stood poised to help as Allison let go of the banister and ventured to alight from the bottom stair. Immediately upon stepping down, Allison drew in a sharp breath of pain, and for lack of the banister she clung to Brandon for support. His arm was instantly about her waist, and his other hand held tight to hers.

"Perhaps this was a foolhardy idea. I dare say, we should stay in," he suggested.

Allison considered that maybe Brandon was right, but the idea of not going sleighing with him was too dismal a thought. "No ... I'll be all right ... really."

"If you're quite sure," Brandon cautioned, his arm still fast about her.

Allison looked up at him and nodded. "I've been shut indoors for too long. And tomorrow, you will return to London."

Brandon carried Allison down the front steps of Loxley House to the waiting sleigh attended by a coachman. Both helped Allison to board the open sleigh, then the coachman handed the reins to Brandon as he took his place on the seat beside Allison. A solitary white horse was harnessed to the graceful curves of the sleigh, its breath clouding in the chilly early-evening air.

With a gentle slap of the riding whip and a shake of the reins, Brandon and Allison glided over the snow-covered drive in a sweeping arc. The horse stepped jauntily, pulling them effortlessly over the shallow drifts. Allison drew closer to Brandon upon the plush seat cushion and tucked her gloved hand about the crook of his arm. He smiled contentedly and gave the whip another gentle crack.

The two hardly spoke as they coursed over the drifts and into the woods behind Loxley House—both were savoring memories of the times they had spent together during the Christmas holiday, relishing the present moment, and thinking sorrowfully of Brandon's imminent departure for

London the next morning. As they reached the heart of the woods, Brandon let the horse slow its pace so that Allison and he could enjoy the stillness and fairytale beauty of the snow-laden trees around them.

Here, the road diverged. "Shall we see what is this way?" Brandon indicated the road to the left. Allison nodded, and Brandon guided the sleigh toward the west and the setting sun.

"It seems we've only just become acquainted, and now you're leaving for London," Allison noted quietly, as they embarked along the left fork of the road.

Brandon slowed the sleigh to a near stop. "Am I only an acquaintance, then?" He pondered her gloved hand tucked securely about his coat-sleeve.

"Of course not. We are more than mere acquaintances. I regard you as a friend, and I shall miss your company." At once Allison regretted that her words had sounded too matter of fact and formal. On the other hand, she had wanted to say more but thought better of it—perhaps saying more would sound too forward.

"And I shall miss your company as well," Brandon reciprocated. "*Simpleton!*" he silently chided himself; could he really manage no more inventive or demonstrative a reply than this? There seemed so much more he had wanted to tell Allison just then, but he had let the moment slip away.

The two rode in awkward silence for some time as the left road directed them up a low incline through the trees to a clearing on the crest of a hill. The sun was nearly set, turning the glistening white drifts about them to hues of rose and amber. In the distance stood Loxley House, its six proud chimneys billowing the promise of cozy hearths inside.

"Stop the sleigh a moment, please ... if you don't mind," Allison requested. "The view is so pleasant here."

Brandon pulled back on the reins until the horse brought the sleigh to a gentle stop. Allison, still close at Brandon's side, looked out upon the scenery below. The rose-stained drifts had nearly faded to gray as the sky above revealed freckles of pale starlight.

Allison sighed. "It is so beautiful here, so peaceful and still." Then, in spite of herself, she blurted, "I wish you weren't going back to London, Brandon. I shall miss you far too much. I don't *want* you to go!" Instantly her cheeks flushed with her bold admission, and she quickly looked away as her gloved fingers toyed nervously upon her lap.

"Truth be told, Allison ... I've grown quite fond of you," Brandon admitted.

Allison's eyes met his.

"We are more than mere acquaintances ... more than just friends ... aren't we?" he asked.

"Yes ... I believe we are." She looked into his rich brown eyes earnestly.

"I feel we've grown ... quite close, actually ... these past days together."

"Brandon, I—" She paused uncertainly, then declared softly, in the ebbing twilight, "I care for you more than I dare say. From ... from the moment I first saw you."

"Allison—" Brandon turned to her and caught up both her gloved hands in his own. "I adore you. My heart is *beside* itself with affection for you." He nearly blushed upon his own admission.

"Oh, Brandon ... can it really be so? Can you *really* care for me?" Allison's pale-blue eyes beseeched him.

"Dear, sweet Allison—how can it be otherwise?" He bent his head and impulsively kissed her gloved fingers, then lifted his eyes to meet hers, and whispered, "I care for you beyond all earthly expression."

Allison pressed his gloved hands in hers. "My every heartbeat speaks my love for you," she murmured, and promptly punctuated her words in little kisses upon his gloved fingers.

"Allison, my dear one," Brandon sighed, embracing her to him.

"My sweet," Allison breathed, and nestled warmly in his arms.

Brandon kissed Allison's cheek, then studied the soft blue of her eyes as the last vestiges of daylight receded into night. "How unfortunate that we must part tomorrow," he lamented.

Allison flung her arms about Brandon's neck. He held her close, his cheek pressed against hers. Above, the ivory sliver of moon smiled down upon them as Allison's eyes welled with the untimeliness of their parting. She swallowed hard and could say no more.

"Dear one," Brandon coaxed softly, "don't be sad, not in our final hours together." Gently Brandon loosened her arms from about him, and cajoled,

"Come now, chin up. We had best head back, or everyone will begin to worry."

Allison nodded and settled back in her seat, her arm linked through Brandon's, wondering how she could ever let him return to London.

———◇———

Todd, Jeremy, and Brandon had planned to take the first train from Sheffield to London. Their carriage was scheduled to leave Loxley House shortly after sunrise and stood ready on the icy front drive as the coachman deposited the young men's luggage inside.

Upstairs, alone in her room, Allison watched from the window as Todd, Jeremy, and then Brandon disappeared inside the waiting carriage. After a moment, the carriage moved slowly down the long drive. Allison gazed after it until it shrank to the size of a lump of coal, all but lost in the snowy landscape. She turned from the window, leaned against the papered wall, and sighed.

"I will come to visit you every spare moment I can," Brandon had promised her the night before. Now Allison wondered whether Brandon would soon forget her altogether as he returned to his world of the university, his studies, and his friends. Abruptly she turned to the window once more and searched for any sign of the carriage, but the view was empty. She bit her lip and vowed not to cry.

"He won't be back," she whispered. "I'll never see him again." And with that, she bent her head and wept.

CHAPTER 3

Crawford Hill

Dim starlight and bright fireflies emerged in the ebbing twilight that settled hushed and weary over Crawford Hill plantation. Springtime rains had swollen the rice fields with the first flooding of the planting season. This year, 1853, promised to be a bountiful one. As the sky overhead darkened, the Crawford Hill slaves sopped homeward, exhausted and famished from working the rice fields. Cooking fires and lantern light illuminated the neighborhoods of slave cabins. Sounds of babies wailing, food preparation, children playing, men and women talking in Gullah, and the singing of spiritual hymns filled the air. In the nearby woods and salt marshes, crickets chirped, and toads chorused guttural grunts.

Inside the Big House at Crawford Hill, Annabelle sat at her writing table after dinner to compose a long letter to her older sister.

"Dearest Allison,

"After you and Brandon married in the spring of 1847 and moved to Castleton, I saw so little of you. We had visited often, but it was never the same as having you under the same roof at Loxley House. After I sailed for South Carolina three years ago, and William and I married, I feared I should never see you again. Now I am so anxious to have both you and Brandon—and little Barry—come to live with us. My dear sister, it all seems far too good to be true!

"Poor Alexandra! I do fear for her now that she will be all alone at Loxley House. I still mourn Benjamin since his unfortunate hunting accident the autumn of 1849. He was still quite young, and it was so

sudden and tragic for all of us. I can't think how Alexandra shall endure with us both an ocean apart from her. Although you have written that she has assured you that you must come, and I know you would not leave her if you thought it unwise. She understands that *The Illustrated London News* is sending Brandon to South Carolina as a foreign correspondent and tells me she could not conceive of you staying behind in England. How dreadful to think that she and Benjamin were unable to conceive children; what a comfort they would have been to her now.

"We are all so anxious to meet little Barry. I can hardly believe he will soon be five! Where has the time flown? Our own little Carolina is three, and Ashley is now one. Carolina takes after her father, and Ashley resembles us Summers women—somewhat fair and blue-eyed. I must confess I feel a little awkward boasting about my little ones to you whenever I write. I know how very much you and Brandon have wanted more children in addition to little Barry, and I've worried so each time you have written of another miscarriage. That your second-born died of fever within her first year grieved us so. It was as if we had lost our own. Allison, I pray so much for you and Brandon to be granted just one more child!

"Dear sister, I am digressing from my real purpose in writing. Since you and Brandon will be arriving within the next few months, I wanted to tell you more about Crawford Hill. You will find the climate, people, culture, politics—everything—quite different from England. Much has changed about Crawford Hill since I first arrived here in 1850, and you have probably forgotten quite a bit of what I had written then. Forgive me if I repeat anything of which you are already aware, but I do have a dual purpose in writing this as well—I hope to maintain a journal of our family's history for Carolina and Ashley to keep when they are older. To that end, please keep the pages I send to you.

"The Big House of Crawford Hill Plantation faces south. To the east, the Waccamaw River spills into Winyah Bay, which in turn empties into the Atlantic. An extensive network of rice fields stretches northward of here in the plantation region known as All Saints Parish in Georgetown District. To the west is somewhat higher ground and woods. We are at as great a distance from the neighboring plantations as they are from each other. Directly behind the Big House is a large pond with a willow tree *at its edge that reminds me of the lake at Loxley, although this pond is smaller. An expanse of lawn extends from behind the house in a gentle westward slope. It is here that the slaves' quarters begin.*

"The neighborhoods of slave cabins seem nearly to comprise townships of sorts. First, there are a number of four-room two-story brick houses for the more highly skilled of our slaves. (Dear Allison, I am still uncomfortable referring to another human being as one of my slaves. If William was not such a kind, decent, gentle man, and a humane slaveholder—although I do wonder whether the latter two terms are not mutually exclusive—I should never have married a slaveholder!) Behind these rows of brick houses are neighborhoods of simple wooden cabins for the field laborers and less-skilled help. These cabins consist generally of only one or two rooms. Farther from these are villages of mud huts with thatched roofs that I am told resemble the traditional huts of Africa; here, they are situated along symmetrical lines to form regular neighborhoods.

"Extending northward and westward from the perimeter of these neighborhoods are the provisional crops of vegetables and fields for livestock—fowl, sheep, dairy cattle, and such. Eastward are the rice fields. (The rice fields provide our main commercial crop. We grow a small bit of cotton as well.) Beyond these fields are the woods, which are deeper and darker than any I can recall in England. The woods here seem impenetrable in places. Our lands extend on either side of the Waccamaw River and its tributaries, and include a portion of woodland.

"This region in Georgetown District in South Carolina holds the richest rice plantations in all the South. Wealth and its resultant power flourish among the All Saints Parish plantation owners. (Power has not been to William's benefit, however, when he pushes for slavery-reform measures. Financial power does not necessarily beget political power, I'm afraid.) William prides himself that Crawford Hill is one of the largest and richest tracts of land in lower All Saints Parish.

"Oh, dear! Allison, I must stop now. Little Ashley is crying, and Ester is preoccupied with some other task at the moment. I shall write more later."

Crawford Hill plantation had been held by the Crawford family for generations. Currently, it was owned by William Crawford, a deceptively sharp young business man. He was tall, of substantial build, and was considered attractive in an ordinary sense, although he was not particularly handsome. He was jovial, gregarious, down-to-earth, and practical. William demonstrated both a big heart and a brilliant mind for business. Well-liked and respected by most of the All Saints Parish plantation owners, he possessed many good friends.

When William had inherited Crawford Hill from his father in 1843, the neighboring plantation owners were eager to guide him in managing the operations of the plantation. Even though William had learned much from his father, it was a great responsibility to be suddenly thrust into the position of sole owner at the age of twenty-one. Nonetheless, within five years he had acquired more land for rice fields and expanded his holdings southward as well as inland of the Waccamaw River and Winyah Bay. These holdings were used as additional cropland and grazing land to enhance the plantation's self-sufficiency. Now—as William celebrated his thirty-first birthday—Crawford Hill was one of the wealthiest rice plantations in the region, if not in the South, and everyone agreed that William's father would have been proud of his son's burgeoning success.

"Success is all very well and good," William's friends would say, "but don't delay things that really matter in life."

"I have all I need. I'm happy enough as things are," William would reply.

Nonetheless, his friends persisted that he worked too hard and should marry, have a family, and live a full life. Inwardly William had to admit that his friends were right, although he would affably retort to the contrary. William was lonely for companionship, for someone with whom to share his bounty. Despite his gregarious nature, William was a private individual; and so, he kept his secret longings to himself and continued to make light of his friends' concerns. He vowed that he was satisfied with the success of the plantation, his many friendships, and the advantages that had been placed on both of these and on his good health; however, seeing his two younger sisters marry in recent years and move away to other places in the Deep South heightened his growing sense of aloneness.

Without a family of his own to care for, William immersed himself in the profitable running of Crawford Hill. But most importantly, after he established financial stability and the expansion of his holdings, he worked tirelessly to create as salubrious, humane, and comfortable an environment for his slaves as was possible. He felt a profound sense of responsibility to the nearly one thousand slaves that labored in his fields and to the many enslaved servants who worked in his house, and dreamed of the day when all plantation owners would be held to certain legal standards regarding the way in which they provided for and treated their slaves.

"As long as slavery is an institution in these Southern states, there need to be certain standards of ownership adhered to," he would urge. "Reforms are needed not only for the benefit of the slaves, but I can tell you by my own experience that the proper care of one's property, including one's slaves, proves to be most profitable in the long run."

A number of like-minded neighbors were inclined to agree but would not actively support William in advocating for the enactment of slavery-reform measures. The majority of slaveholders shook their heads with amusement at such propositions. "William Crawford is a decent enough fellow," they gossiped, "but where does he come up with such ideas? Ridiculous!" Some feared that reforms would be the first step toward eventual abolition. Others asserted that legal standards would render slaveholding a privilege instead of a right. To others, the notion of slavery reform was simply beyond them. "Leave well enough alone, William," they cajoled. William could only sigh, shrug, and issue a wry smile in response to their apathy.

The majority of Southern slaveholders seemed either unable or unwilling to invest significantly in their slaves' welfare beyond the most basic and sparest necessities of life. They attributed William's reported success exclusively to other factors, claiming that he had simply inherited the richest rice fields in the district and that the lack of a family and a wife to encumber him allowed him to work harder than they could.

It was ironic that these same neighbors encouraged William to meet a suitable young woman and marry—and how they could tailor any aspect of an issue to suit their own particular needs in an argument. After a time, William began to question whether their interests in his matrimonial status were genuine or whether they secretly wished his success to wane as a result of marrying. As someone who sought harmony in all things in life, William was loath to allow such petty incongruities in his neighbors' logic about his personal matters spoil his friendships with them.

Nonetheless, there was one slaveholder in All Saints Parish whom very few could tolerate. Jack Davenport owned a modest and struggling plantation southwest of Crawford Hill. "Wicked" and "Loathsome" were the terms most often used to describe this man. Others asserted that he wasn't a man at all but the devil incarnate, due to all the abhorrent atrocities he committed against his slaves. Davenport's piercing gray eyes, fiery red hair, wiry build, and acerbic nature supported the label of "devil."

"It's a wonder that man ever found a wife!" the neighbors would say.

"Poor Sara Davenport!" the women would remark.

Privately William Crawford mused that if Jack Davenport, of all people, had found a wife, then it was simply a matter of time until he too would marry.

None of the women in All Saints Parish captivated William's attention enough for him to court them for very long, let alone marry them. It wasn't that All Saints Parish lacked intelligent, attractive women, but none seemed practical or down-to-earth enough for William's taste. As refined ladies of their fathers' wealthy estates, Southern women generally seemed too caught up in high society. Their lives seemed to William little more than a social whirl of frivolities and affected, coy pretenses, all designed to snare unsuspecting bachelors into their webs of high-society concerns. On the whole, that was how young women of well-to-do households were socialized into Southern life. Talk of slavery reform and politics induced little but yawns from such women.

City women whom William had met in Charleston impressed him as little else than urban versions of plantation women. In the city of Charleston, upper-class women were even more intensely caught up in high society than their rural counterparts. The only advantage William discerned initially was that the Charlestonian women seemed more tolerant of political discussion—that is, until he discovered a good many of them merely parroted what they had read in the newspapers or heard gossiped about in governing circles without giving such matters any analytical thought. Women such as these only feigned interest in matters of substance, as they knew this image was what attracted wealthy young men such as William Crawford.

Disheartened by such superficiality and contrived pretense, William plunged into his work with a renewed fervor. Besides, he had once suffered a disillusioning courtship with a woman to whom he had nearly proposed when it became evident that she was not only simply interested in his wealth but had been unfaithful during their brief courtship as well.

William, downhearted and his pride wounded, believed he would be a single man for the remainder of his days. In the aftermath of his ruined courtship, neighbors joked that he was married to Crawford Hill. Indeed, for a short while William became a man obsessed with his work. He contemplated expanding into the cotton trade with England and considered purchasing a vast tract of cotton fields south of All Saints Parish. In order to educate himself on his plan, he traveled to England to learn a bit about the cotton trade and the British textile industry. Besides, after his failed courtship he needed some time away.

It was midsummer, 1848, when William Crawford found himself at Loxley House in Derbyshire, England. He had been invited there by a friend of Benjamin's who owned a number of textile factories in Manchester.

"I don't wish to intrude on the Fairfields," William had cautioned.

"Not to worry," the other assured. "Benjamin Fairfield is a good friend of mine, and in his wire he said that he would be delighted to hear all about America firsthand from a Southern plantation owner. He will be happy to have you visit."

Ten days of English country-house living allowed William ample diversion and relaxation from his concerns about having left Crawford Hill for so many weeks. Although he had left his plantation in the capable hands of his overseers, he still worried that some unforeseen disaster might befall his lands or his slaves while he was away. Midsummer was the period between planting and harvesting time, and with the exception of his respite at Loxley House, William felt anxious to conclude his business in England and return home.

It was not only the bucolic setting of Loxley House that took William's mind off his plantation matters, however. Annabelle Summers caught his immediate fancy. The attraction between them was mutual and virtually instantaneous. William had never met a woman like Annabelle. She was intelligent and charming, but not affectedly so. She seemed both sensible and unassuming, and William was further impressed that she came from common middleclass roots. He found in Annabelle Summers a refreshingly modest, genuine nature—decidedly a rare quality among the Southern women he had known. From the first moment he met her, William discerned that she would make someone a good wife and be a good mother.

Initially, Annabelle was fascinated by William Crawford. She had never met an American before, and she was as entranced by his unique Charlestonian accent as he was by the lilt of her English one. She found William—with his wealth, independence, yet unaffected manner—to be the most intriguing man she had ever met. Ample glances and smiles were exchanged between the two. But in short order, as Annabelle learned more about William Crawford, she began to realize her attraction for him was futile—perhaps even regrettable.

Annabelle was shocked and dismayed to learn that William Crawford was a slaveholder. Upstairs in her bedroom, Annabelle exchanged hushed words with Alexandra over the issue.

"My God!" Annabelle exclaimed. "The man *owns* other people!" Annabelle had heard of slavery and knew what it entailed; like most British, she abhorred slavery.

"He *is* from the South—," Alexandra began, hoping to placate her younger sister's agitation.

"But he owns people and forces them to work for him, and most likely whips and beats them, and ... and heaven knows *what!*" Annabelle paced furiously, then exploded, "And he is under our very roof!"

"Shhh!" Alexandra cautioned. "He might hear you."

"Maybe he *should.* Good Lord! The audacity to steal another's freedom, to buy and sell another human being as though they were property—like livestock!"

"In the South they *are* property," Alexandra reminded.

"I don't care. No one should be mere chattel to another. It isn't right. It isn't moral!" Annabelle shuddered with disdain. "And to *think* that I fancied I might *like* him!"

"Well, we all would be more pleased if we had learned he was only involved in the business of the cotton trade. That he is a slaveholder cannot be helped, and as long as he is a guest in our house, we will treat him cordially."

"Oh, very well," Annabelle sighed with a distinct edge of reluctance. Her arms folded before her, she paced a few steps, turned, and impatiently tapped her foot on the floor. "So, how much longer is Mr. Crawford to be here?"

"Just over a week, from what Benjamin tells me."

Annabelle sighed again, then sat, shoulders slumped, resignedly on her bed. "I suppose there is little to do about it, then."

Alexandra reflected a moment, then ventured, "He is here on business to look into the cotton trade with our country, and if it were not for our country's textile industry and dependence on cotton from the American South, their need for slavery would quickly diminish."

Annabelle looked up sharply. "So, you are implicating our country in all of this?"

"Well ... yes. Indirectly, it is true. We need cotton from the South, and the South needs slaves to produce the cotton." Alexandra surmised the logic of her argument was not air tight, but the hour was late, and she did not want Mr. Crawford's stay at Loxley House to be unpleasant on account of her sister's heated sociopolitical views on the matter.

Annabelle mulled over Alexandra's points briefly, then pointed out, "Well, we in England certainly do not depend on slaves to work our textile mills; and besides, Mr. Crawford grows rice!"

Clearly the hour was late, and the two sisters wisely let the matter drop. Alexandra held her tongue on the issue of Britain's dependence on child labor.

The next morning, at breakfast, Annabelle hardly spoke. Her aloof silence did not go unnoticed, as the textile-mill owner from Manchester and William Crawford were the only guests occupying the breakfast table at Loxley House. Both Alexandra and Benjamin suspected what was bothering Annabelle. William, with his penchant for harmony and goodwill, could not help but notice that Annabelle was troubled. She shied away from talking with him and was tersely polite in response to his conversing with her.

Throughout breakfast, Benjamin and Alexandra cast Annabelle admonishing glances. These warning glances only served to make Annabelle increasingly nervous and agitated. Midway through breakfast she accidentally knocked a bowl of berry preserves onto the carpet with her elbow. Whereas she might normally have exclaimed "Oh, dear!" and apologized for her clumsiness, she did not do so this time. Instead, she inwardly blamed William's presence for making her so careless, whereupon she shot up from her chair, her fists clenched at her sides, and blurted, "Don't worry—we shall have one of our *slaves* clean it up!" Instantly she blushed scarlet, realizing the crude harshness of her words. Too embarrassed to apologize to the horrified faces seated about her, she strode quickly from the room.

Alexandra had little choice but to disclose to their guests the cause of Annabelle's annoyance.

"If I could free every slave, I would!" William sputtered, feeling marked concern for the unpleasantness his presence at Loxley had inadvertently caused. "But I can't accomplish such a thing … and if I were to free my own slaves—good Lord!—where on earth would they go? What would they do? They need me as much as I need them; I'm afraid that is how the system is. Clearly, it is an abominable system by its very definition, but it is a system that I inherited. All I *can* do is the very best I am able to by my own slaves and encourage humane treatment for those slaves belonging to others. Every time I espouse the institution of slavery reforms, everyone turns a deaf ear. No one wants anything at all to do with a reformed system of slavery with humane, regulated standards set for its implementation." William sighed in an attitude of defeat. "I am sorry; I did not mean to disrupt your household by my presence here." He sighed again and watched—feeling rather at loose ends—as one of the Fairfield's domestic staff worked to clean up the spilled bowl of preserves upon the carpet. In truth, William felt partly responsible for the spilled preserves and felt compelled to help the young aproned woman clean it up; but it was not the socially accepted custom to do so, and so he sat uncomfortably in his chair and watched as she scrubbed.

Annabelle had not been seen for the remainder of the morning. By early afternoon, Allison noted to the others that she had spied Annabelle through an upstairs window. "She's out walking in the Pleasure Garden, near the lake," she informed.

"I think I'd better try to have a word with her, if I might—try to set things right," William said. No one argued his suggestion; certainly the lack of rapport between the two could not worsen further.

William found Annabelle standing upon the crest of the stone footbridge that spanned the river's flow into the lake. She was leaning on the stone parapet, daydreaming into the reflected clouds that sailed upon the water below. She did not notice William approach upon the bridge. He stood a few paces from Annabelle before he spoke.

"Miss Summers—"

Annabelle jumped, startled. "How long have you been here?" she asked, feeling somewhat flustered.

"I'm sorry, Miss Summers … I didn't mean to alarm you."

Annabelle knew not what to say and simply stood facing him, wishing he would go away, yet oddly wishing that he would stay. Her confusion made her cross. She demanded, "Well, what *is* it then, Mr. Crawford?"

William had intended to apologize for offending her sensibilities regarding slavery due to his mere presence at Loxley House. Instead, he noticed how the breeze softly ruffled her blond tresses and observed how the blue skies above intensified the delicate pale-blue of her eyes.

The way William studied Annabelle just then disarmed her, and she knit her pretty brow in consternation. Her tone now softer, she asked, "Mr. Crawford? …"

William hesitated, then enunciated words even he had not expected to utter. "You are perhaps the most remarkable woman I have ever met." Upon this, he turned away slowly and began to descend the curve of the footbridge.

Annabelle stared after him for some moments, perfectly nonplussed. "Mr. Crawford!" she called out, and gathering her skirts up in her hands she dashed quickly after him as he strode across the lawn.

William and Annabelle talked at length as they wandered the Pleasure Garden and sat a while beneath the shade of an elm. When they returned to the house, Annabelle announced that she planned to go for a row with William upon the lake that afternoon. Clearly, William and Annabelle had reconciled their differences.

The remaining days of William's visit at Loxley House had passed all too quickly. An ocean apart, William and Annabelle courted by correspondence. In the autumn of 1849 Annabelle wrote to William of the tragic hunting accident that had claimed Benjamin's life. Their correspondence intensified afterward; and by the following year, William proposed to Annabelle in a letter. In 1850, Annabelle said tearful goodbyes to her elder sister Alexandra and to Allison and Brandon in nearby Castleton, then she set sail for South Carolina to become Mrs. Annabelle Crawford.

In preparation for Annabelle's arrival at Crawford Hill, William began building a new Big House in which they could live and raise a family. The previous year's profits from the rice crop were ample enough to allow for a large Victorian-style house to replace the plain and rather careworn Big House that had preceded William by generations. Construction of the new house took several months of careful labor, the slaves ceasing their work only during times of inclement weather.

The new Big House was not yet finished when Annabelle arrived at Crawford Hill. After William and Annabelle married—exchanging vows in the simple whitewashed clapboard church in northern All Saints Parish— they inhabited the old house while the new one was being completed. Despite the incessant hammering and sawing nearby, William and Annabelle managed enough peace and privacy to conceive their first child the winter of 1850.

By the spring of 1853 William and Annabelle were comfortably settled in the new Big House with their two daughters, Carolina age three and Ashley age one; however, the first few years of married life had been quite an adjustment for Annabelle. She had first to adjust to being married and having a husband but also, in short order, to the ordeals of pregnancy and raising children. Often, she wondered if she had not taken on too much too quickly. If Annabelle could have summarized her first three years of married life at Crawford Hill in a single word, she would have said "joyful." But this was not to imply that she found the transition into her new life easy; when she first set foot in the South, it was not only William who greeted her but also profound culture shock.

Everything about the South seemed vastly different from life in Derbyshire, England. The food, climate, surroundings, and people, were all distinctly foreign to Annabelle. Most immediately striking was the composition of the population of All Saints Parish—slaves outnumbered whites by nine to one. Being surrounded by so many dark-skinned faces speaking in Gullah intimidated Annabelle at first. Furthermore, she was awestruck by the vastness of Crawford Hill and had not gleaned from William's letters the plantation's actual immensity. The slaves' neighborhoods west of the Big House consisted of over two hundred dwellings, each one housing roughly five slaves. William assured her, however, that his was only the second-largest plantation in All Saints Parish—the estate of Joshua J. Ward held roughly one thousand one hundred and twelve slaves at last count.

Alligators, fireflies, boiled peanuts, Gullah language, stifling humidity, mosquitoes, and a new husband, among other adjustments, increasingly served to unnerve Annabelle. By the end of her third week at Crawford Hill, she suddenly burst into tears at dinner and fled wordlessly upstairs to the bedroom. William quickly followed and found her flounced upon the bed crying.

"My dear, what is it?" he asked with alarm.

Annabelle wailed piteously, "I miss my sisters. I miss England. I want to go *home!*" whereupon she fell into disconsolate sobbing.

William comforted her the best he could; and in the end, Annabelle apologized for her childlike outburst and vowed to try harder to adjust to her new surroundings. Sniffling and dabbing her eyes with William's pocket-square, she quavered, "Are you sure we are in America and not Africa?"

William chuckled at this. He gave his young bride a consoling squeeze and kissed her cheek. "Of course we are in America."

In time, Annabelle adjusted to living in All Saints Parish, and the Gullah tongue grew more intelligible to her. Although plagued by intermittent bursts of homesickness, she kept busy raising their daughters and helping

William to run the plantation. In time, Crawford Hill became home, and her initial homesickness for England faded into a distant memory.

Now, in the spring of 1853, as William and Annabelle expected Brandon; Allison; and their five-year-old son, Barry, to come to live with them, they anticipated the utter foreignness that All Saints Parish would present to them. To help prepare her sister and brother-in-law for their transition, Annabelle resumed her letter to Allison, which had been interrupted by little Ashley's crying.

"Dearest Allison, fate willing, I shall have this letter to you posted before your departure from England! I realize that I have not yet described to you in any detail about the Big House in which you, Brandon, and little Barry shall be living. The house is about three years old, and outside, the trees, flowers, and shrubs are all quite attractively grown up about it. In the front, there is the long tree-lined drive (called an 'allée') that curves before the front porch in a roundabout, and there is a broad expanse of lawn surrounding the house. I adore the front porch—a verandah that actually runs about the entire perimeter of the house, bordered by a charming low wooden rail. William's carpenters and builders—all slaves—worked with him on the design of the house, and it is a dream! The porch is shaded all about by an awning of roof supported by slender white columns.

"The front door is reached by several wooden steps leading from the drive to the porch, and it is a handsome double-door of solid oak. A peaked gable is centered over the door, and above this is a rounded turret with a charming half-conical, half-peaked roof above a small curved balcony.

"There are plenty of windows throughout. The southeast corner of the house is accented by a three-storied turret, the top story of which is octagonal— it reminds me of a tower in a fairytale's castle.

"The entire effect of the wooden house—which is all painted a sun-kissed white, except for the gray front steps and porch floor—is that of a cozy, enchanting doll's house. The roof is comprised of subtly mottled dusty-red shingles—not the usual deep-gray or moss-green seen in these parts. It is a

quite striking house. I believe William opted to build the house in an eclectic Romantic-era style for my sake because I was coming all the way from England to live at Crawford Hill. Soon after I came to All Saints Parish, this house became my refuge—just as soon as it was built and fit to move in to.

"Inside, the house is spacious—but with no shortage of rooms, many closets, and all sorts of wonderful nooks, doors, windows, and charming little touches. There is an enormous third-story attic that is not only fit for storage but serves as added living space for our two foremost house servants who otherwise occupy the main turret as their quarters. The whole of the attic is really a third floor to the house with many rooms and a cathedral ceiling—quite comfortable and charming in its own way. The upper story of the southeast turret is accessed by the attic and, as mentioned, serves as the main part of the two lead house servants' chambers.

"The second floor of the house consists of baths, water closets, bedchambers, guest rooms, and the children's nursery.

"Downstairs, in the southwest corner, is the kitchen and adjoining dining room. Behind these rooms is the west sitting room. Here I have arranged in front of the windows several shelves of brightly colored glass vases, bowls, pitchers, and plates—all hand-blown glass from Charleston. When the sun sets through this window, a beautiful rainbow of colors is cast upon the white walls and hardwood floor. As the room is light and airy, sparsely furnished—a settee, some wing-back and rocking chairs, and an antique dark-wood hutch—it is my favorite room of the house in spring and summer. There are a few rather nondescript rooms at the back of the house; we have not settled in well enough yet to give them a defined purpose—even after three years. It is truly a very large house!

"In the front southeast corner of the house is the formal sitting room, which we call the 'east sitting room'—although it is as cozy and lived in as any. This room is by no means as grand as its counterparts at Loxley House. It is too comfortable and boasts a large yawning hearth where we enjoy sitting and sipping brandy on cold winter evenings. It is my favorite room in late autumn and winter—so cozy and warm!

"But be forewarned, Allison—the seasons in South Carolina are far less predictable than in England, with the exception of summer. Summer in the South feels as hot and humid as putting your face before a tea kettle's steam, *and the season lasts that way for roughly four or five months. Many of our neighbors at All Saints Parish flee for the summer to properties far eastward and northward of here to avoid the 'sickly season.' (Ship captains will simply not sail up the Waccamaw River in summer!) Some neighbors flee to Charleston, some to Columbia, some go to Flat Rock in the mountains, and others travel to Europe to avoid summer here. We, however, and several other of our neighbors do stay. (We did stay one summer in Charleston, but William worried so about the plantation and business that he kept returning by carriage to visit home.) William once told me that he could not see leaving his slaves, servants, and field hands for places such as Charleston or Flat Rock when they could not come along also——it was not fair to them that we should escape at least some shred of the summer's stifling heat and humidity when they could not. William had thought of sending me to cooler climes in summer, but we decided that it would not do for him to travel to and fro so much in the summer to visit, nor did I want to be apart from him for the duration of the summer months with our children. The only true scourges of summer are the mosquitoes, which one learns to handle in various ways."*

Annabelle paused from her writing and thought a moment, then decided it would simply not do to tell Allison of summer's malarial season ... or hurricanes—she did not want to unnecessarily worry her sister or dissuade her from coming. One simply had to get used to a place in order to inhabit it comfortably and properly. Picking up her pen she resumed.

"I am nearly finished describing the house, Allison, so please bear with me. The front hall is all hardwood floors—as are all the floors in the house. There is no fancy marble or stonework here as at Loxley. The staircase inside ascends to the left, at right angles to the front hall.

"It really is a very sweet house, comfortable and inviting despite its grand size and numerous rooms. You will feel quite at home here, Allison, and I'm sure Brandon and little Barry shall as well. I can scarcely wait until you, Brandon, and Barry have arrived!

"Dear sister, I had best close and dispatch this letter to you. With deep affection,

"Love, Annabelle"

CHAPTER 4

The Stewarts Arrive at Crawford Hill

Annabelle busied herself supervising the household servants in preparing the Big House for the Stewart's arrival at Crawford Hill. William had left two days earlier to conduct business in Charleston and to meet the Stewarts when their ship sailed into Charleston harbor.

Brandon and Allison had dismissed their domestics, closed up their modest house in Castleton, England, and with their son Barry in tow, bid Alexandra a tearful goodbye at Sheffield station, then set sail for Charleston, South Carolina. Any discomforts of the voyage were outweighed by Allison's anticipation of her reunion with Annabelle, Brandon's excitement over his first assignment as a foreign correspondent for *The Illustrated London News*, and Barry's wide-eyed curiosity and innate sense of adventure.

William had traveled by carriage with two of his coachmen to the city of Charleston. The coachmen, vis-à-vis carriage, and wagon waited near the Cooper River docks as William scanned the early-morning crowd of new arrivals for any sign of the Stewarts. Annabelle had described them well enough: *"Barry is five and has brown hair and eyes like his father. Brandon is tall, trim, and exceedingly handsome. Allison looks quite like me, only prettier."* Here, she had playfully pouted before pronouncing in ink upon the page, *"She looks like an angel."* William quickly reviewed Annabelle's note and tucked it in his coat pocket. Among the disembarking passengers, William spotted the three new arrivals in short order and greeted them warmly.

The Stewarts politely refused William's hospitable suggestion that they all spend a night in Charleston so that they could rest before setting out on their journey northward. Because the distance—"as the crow flies," as William put it—from Charleston's harbor to Winyah Bay, just south of All Saints Parish in Georgetown District, was roughly thirty miles, the journey could be made comfortably enough in one day. "The roads are fair enough ... some uphill, some downhill, and with the horses pacing at about five miles per hour, it will be approximately six hours, perhaps seven—not counting taking breaks for food or rest along the way," William calculated. It was promptly agreed to set out as soon as possible. Although somewhat tired from their voyage, Brandon and Allison were anxious to see Annabelle and their new surroundings at Crawford Hill. William did persuade them, however, to first have a quick bite to eat before embarking on the northbound road. And, of course, there were the necessary provisions to see to—arranging for their trunks, carpetbags, and other luggage to be transported to Crawford Hill. The bulk of their belongings would be taken by small ship up the coast to Winyah Bay, then up the Waccamaw River to be deposited at the Crawford Hill plantation's dock in two days' time. William's second coachman would follow their vis-à-vis carriage by wagon, transporting their luggage containing clothes and items of more immediate usefulness.

While William and the Stewarts were attending to these matters and preparing to embark by midmorning on their journey northward, Annabelle was busy with Ester in readying the Stewart's rooms—one for Barry and the other for Allison and Brandon.

"There is still so much to do, and William said they may arrive even today. How will I ever be ready in time?" Annabelle fretted. Just then she noticed Ester struggling to reposit a large bureau against the wall. "Ester, let's wait and let Jacob help us with that later."

"Yes'm, Miss Annabelle; 'cept dat he done been gone fo' hours now. I ain' seen Jacob since early dis mo'nin."

"Oh, darn...," Annabelle worried, then sighed. "Well, as soon as we see him, he needs to help us with the bureau and with the bed in Barry's room."

"Yes'm," Ester said, with a nod of her kerchiefed head.

———◇———

Ester and Jacob, along with their son Quash, lived in the Big House with Annabelle and William. They comprised the Crawford's main household servants and were the only slaves at Crawford Hill who lived in the Big House. Annabelle had written about them to Allison—the servants and their son who occupied the main turret and part of the attic space as their living quarters. At twenty-eight, Jacob was just three years younger than William, and Ester was twenty-three, just one year younger than Annabelle. Their son, Quash, was one-and-a-half, not much older than the Crawford's own little Ashley. William and Annabelle regarded Ester, Jacob, and Quash as part of their own family. Indeed, William had known Ester and Jacob for as long as he could remember, and Annabelle had quickly grown fond of them as well. She had written to Allison and Brandon of Ester and Jacob in glowing terms while the Stewarts were still in England.

"...Jacob and Ester are both well-suited to each other. Both are admirably bright, sensible, and possess a wealth of common sense and wisdom beyond their years. Jacob is calm and steady, quiet but good-natured. Ester is only marginally more prone to emotion and is a very warm, caring person. I believe it is partly our proximity in ages that has helped us all to get along as family. Ester and I have weathered together our recent pregnancies, and that brought us closer still.

"I care for Ester and Jacob so, I shudder to imagine their fates had they been born into an abusive plantation-family's home. Jacob is rather tall and lanky, yet of good build—much the way I remember Brandon to be. He is a handsome man in an ordinary sort of way. Ester is of ample, womanly figure. Her eyes are large and round as a doe's. Her features are so finely rendered that one could easily imagine her as an African princess—she is that exquisitely beautiful. Both are very capable and responsible, and they are ever impressing me by their character, judgement, and kindliness. We are truly fortunate to have them here with us.

"Ester and Jacob both speak Gullah, which is essentially a blend *of African tongues and English. When you first arrive, you will find Gullah is a completely different language than English, although it shares the same vocabulary as English—do not trifle about this; in time you will grow to understand it. I believe Gullah and other Creole tongues are partly responsible for whites erroneously thinking their African slaves are of inferior intelligence—it is an abhorrent mistake! My goodness, after all, it is each and every African slave brought to this country who has learned to assimilate a myriad of African tongues and English into one intelligible language in order to survive here. I am hard-pressed to imagine that I would have been capable of devising the same hybrid language. Nonetheless, as Jacob and Ester are household slaves, you will find their Gullah very mild and should have little trouble understanding them. The same is true of a number of our other domestic slaves and cooks."*

Now, while Annabelle and Ester unfolded sheets to make up the bed in Allison and Brandon's room, they heard Jacob running up the stairs, shouting, "Miss Annabelle! Miss Annabelle!"

"In here, Jacob!" Annabelle called. She and Ester exchanged concerned glances. Jacob appeared in the doorway out of breath and panting. "Miss Annabelle," he gasped, "you gotta come quick. Der be trouble on de Davenport plantation!"

Annabelle trusted Jacob and wasted no time by asking what the matter was. On occasion, news of trouble would spread from slave to slave by word of mouth, across the fields of one plantation to another. All too often, word would reach Crawford Hill of illness or a punishment carried too far on the neighboring Davenport plantation; and whenever Jacob brought such news to Annabelle, her heart was invariably moved to try to help.

As Annabelle dashed from the room, she told Ester, "Please look after the children while I'm out."

As Jacob and Annabelle rushed downstairs, Jacob hurriedly explained what the matter was. Annabelle quickly grabbed a bottle of brandy, some linens, and a few medicinal supplies from the kitchen, and tossed them in a canvass bag. "I hope we're not too late," she said as she rushed after Jacob down the verandah steps to the carriage waiting out front.

Horrific stories of Jack Davenport and the atrocities he committed against his slaves were legendary throughout All Saints Parish. It was well-known that he was both a drunkard and a cruel, callous man who beat both his slaves and his wife often. Now Jacob had heard that a young slave woman lay bruised and bleeding in her ramshackle cabin—beaten nearly to death by Jack Davenport.

A particularly close network of communication had developed between the field slaves of Crawford Hill and the Davenport plantation. The two plantations shared a common boundary, and news spread rapidly by word of mouth—especially when there was trouble. Disturbances often originated on the Davenport property, and it was quickly learned that William Crawford's benevolence could be relied upon.

Jacob and Annabelle raced down the drive in the two-seat carriage, then headed west, Jacob conveying the carriage at breakneck speed.

"Do you know why she was beaten?" Annabelle asked.

"Davenport done had his way wit' her long time ago. She done gib him a female chil, but he want'd a male chil', so he done beat her. Dey say he jez 'bout nearly kill'd her."

Annabelle's eyes stung with tears, and she fretted silently that they would not arrive in time to help the young woman. Jacob cracked the whip harder, and the carriage jostled roughly down the rutted road.

"What about the baby girl?"

"Don' know," Jacob said plainly, and concentrated solemnly on the road ahead. He didn't have the heart to tell Annabelle that Jack Davenport had ordered the infant to be drowned.

In the distance, as the Davenport's plantation house came into view, Jacob slowed the horses until they came to a stop beneath a small grove of trees bordering the Davenport's property. They left the carriage some distance away and, guided by one of the Davenport slaves, discreetly made their way through a short span of cotton fields to the woman's cabin. It was a risk coming in broad daylight, for both knew that Jack Davenport forbade *anyone* from tending to a slave who had been beaten. Indeed, the slaves knew they had also taken a great risk by merely summoning outside assistance for the battered woman.

Annabelle and Jacob found the slave woman alone, unattended, in a dirty tumbledown one-room cabin. She lay on her stomach upon a makeshift mattress of carded-lint cotton and straw upon the floor. The flesh on her back had been lacerated in countless crosshatches by Jack Davenport's bullwhip. Her blood soaked the bedding beneath her.

"Lord have mercy," Annabelle breathed, a catch in her voice. She quickly knelt beside the woman, Jacob fast at her side. "She's barely conscious," Annabelle noted.

Jacob set about helping Annabelle to dress the woman's wounds, his jaw set firmly. The woman flinched and moaned in her delirium as healing salve and gentle strips of linen were applied to her wounds.

"Poor thing," Annabelle said quietly, her eyes welling.

"Damn Davenport!" Jacob cursed under his breath. "*Damn* him!"

They worked quietly for some moments, gently cleansing and dressing the young woman's wounds, each praying silently that she would survive.

Suddenly the cabin door thrust open with a bang.

Annabelle and Jacob nearly leapt out of their skins. Instantly they turned to see Jack Davenport framed in the doorway of the darkened cabin, his fists clenched about a hunting rifle held squarely before him.

"You got no business here!" Davenport menaced, his eyes piercing Annabelle's.

Jacob stood poised to defend Annabelle, if need be.

Annabelle remained kneeling and turned back to the slave woman upon the crude bed. "This woman is in need of medical attention," she asserted.

"Get the *hell* out!" Davenport thundered, and strode forward, his hands tensed about the rifle. "*Now!*"

Frightened, Annabelle rose uncertainly and stood facing Jack Davenport, trying in vain not to tremble. "*Leave* us!" she spat, scarcely finding her tongue.

Jacob glanced at Annabelle, and in that instant Davenport wheeled the rifle about by its barrel, swinging the butt of the gun with full force toward Jacob. Annabelle's eyes widened in horror.

"*No!*" she cried, darting quickly between Davenport and Jacob.

In mid-swing Davenport angrily hurled the rifle aside. "*Move*, bitch!"

Annabelle remained protectively in front of Jacob, whose eyes shot daggers at Davenport.

In an instant, Davenport grabbed Annabelle by the shoulders and roughly thrust her aside. "Meddling bitch!" he hissed.

Annabelle stumbled sideways and fell, striking her temple hard against the dirt floor.

Jacob raised a clenched fist and lunged forward.

"Jacob—*no!*" Annabelle cried out. A trickle of warm blood coursed down the curve of her cheek, and she felt slightly dazed as she struggled to rise to her feet.

Jacob remained poised to attack, his clenched fist raised, but he heeded Annabelle's wishes.

On her feet once again, her eyes flashing, Annabelle said tersely, "We are leaving." She mopped the blood from her cheek with the back of her hand and faltered as she stepped toward Jacob. Quickly Jacob moved forward and steadied Annabelle, consumed both with concern for her and with rage at Davenport.

Jack Davenport retrieved the rifle from the cabin floor, his eyes narrowed with disdain for Annabelle Crawford and her slave.

Jacob and Annabelle walked slowly out of the cabin, a cluster of frightened and curious dark faces hovering nearby, watching and waiting. Jacob supported Annabelle protectively. "You's aw'right, Miss Annabelle?" he asked quietly.

"I ... I think so," she said as she fought back tears.

Behind them, they heard the rifle cock.

"Only nigger that's any good is a *dead* one!" Davenport spat on the ground.

Annabelle felt her blood run cold. Jacob's heart pounded in his throat, but he nudged Annabelle steadfastly forward.

A rifle shot rang out.

Annabelle froze, fearing Jacob would collapse dead at her side. "My God—*Jacob!*" she uttered.

Behind them, Jack Davenport fired again.

"It's aw'right, Miss Annabelle," Jacob whispered. "De bastard's jus' firin' in de air t' frighten us."

Annabelle nearly swooned in Jacob's arms, but he steadily guided her forward, his arm securely about her waist, his hand held tightly upon hers. "No need to fear, Miss Annabelle. We's gonna be aw'right."

"I'll kill *both* of you, if I ever see you on my property *again!*" Davenport shouted.

At last Jacob and Annabelle reached their carriage sheltered beneath the grove of trees. Jacob helped Annabelle climb up into the carriage. "Miss Annabelle, you is tremblin' so," he noted with concern.

Annabelle, consumed with a myriad of emotions and her head aching, said nothing and leaned back against the carriage seat as Jacob climbed in beside her and took up the reins, sending the carriage toward home.

Jacob cast a sidelong glance at Annabelle, and soothed, "Jus' don' you fear 'bout dat man Davenport. We is safe now."

Instantly Annabelle buried her face in her hands and sobbed. Jacob tenderly hooked his arm about her shoulders and drew her close beside him. Annabelle rested her head gratefully against Jacob's shoulder and wept, her tears mingling with the blood that seeped from the wound at her temple. As the carriage rolled forward, the horses gently ambling, Annabelle's tears subsided as she remained nestled securely against Jacob, his arm protectively about her. They rode like this the remainder of their short journey homeward to Crawford Hill.

Ester had been out sweeping the front verandah when Jacob and Annabelle returned from the Davenport Plantation. She did not realize anything was wrong until she saw Jacob help Annabelle, trembling and unsteady, down from the carriage and noted the rivulets of blood that stained her cheek and had matted her hair. "Good Lawd!" Ester uttered. Setting her broom aside, she quickly descended the verandah steps, her eyes fixed on Annabelle and Jacob as they approached the house.

Ester helped Annabelle inside and upstairs to her room, all the while pumping both Jacob and Annabelle with questions and punctuating their narration with curses against Jack Davenport.

"Dat man, he got de devil in his soul," she muttered.

"He ain' *got* no soul," Jacob spat.

Annabelle winced as Ester cleansed and dressed the wound to her temple.

"Don' need no stichin', anyhow," Ester said.

This comforted Annabelle, but in her mind's eye she could only see a vision of the young slave woman, bloodied and half-dead, lying prostrate before her. Somehow, Annabelle knew that the woman had not survived, that her tragic soul had been mercifully delivered from its torment. A few generous sips of brandy administered by Jacob's steady hand helped to ease Annabelle's trembling and quiet her mind.

"Thank you Ester. Thank you Jacob," Annabelle said, and added hesitantly, "I hope you don't mind; I need to lie down a while. Yet there is still so much to do before my sister and her family arrives."

"Don' you fret none 'bout dat Miss Annabelle," Ester said. "Jacob an' I c'n look after de house 'til den. You go an' res' a while, long as you like."

Annabelle reclined on her bed. "Thank you both."

"You sure we ain' best git de doctor?" Jacob asked.

Annabelle shook her head. "I'm sure," she yawned. "I'll be all right. I just need to rest a while." In an instant, her eyelids fluttered closed, and she was fast asleep.

Jacob and Ester tiptoed from the room, gingerly closing the door behind them, and resumed preparations for the Stewart's arrival.

"Today's spring weather is so beautiful, I came down in the vis-'a-vis." William indicated the handsome open carriage fitted with two opposing plush seats behind the driver's elevated seat. "Besides, the seating makes conversation and getting acquainted easier."

He crossed the street toward the carriage with Brandon and Allison, little Barry trudging behind with his hand clasped tightly in his mother's. There, they boarded the vis-à-vis as William's coachmen and the available hired labor from the wharves loaded the Stewarts' carpetbags, trunks, and satchels, along with William's luggage, into the plantation wagon.

"This seems like a bit of an effort, I know," William said. "I could have arranged for you to sail up the coast and the Waccamaw, but I figured you already had enough of sailing, having just crossed the Atlantic. Plus you would have had to spend the night on the ship—besides which, I wanted to show you the scenery between Charleston and Crawford Hill. It's spectacular; there's nothing like springtime in South Carolina!"

In the vis-'a-vis, William and Brandon took the seat facing the rear to afford Allison and Barry the better view of the road ahead. The second coachman followed the vis-à-vis in the plantation wagon.

As they journeyed northward, Brandon and Allison drank in the lush green landscape surrounding them. It was late April, and the weather that greeted them was undeniably the finest that South Carolina had to offer. A slight breeze carried with it the sweet scents of grasses and wild flowers. The air was mildly humid and soothing. Galleons of white clouds drifted overhead in the crisp blue sky, their shadows tracing the subtle contours of the land below. Meandering waterways and rivers threaded the landscape, glinting in the sun. To the west, there stood a deep wood of leaves glittering in the gentle gusts. All around them the land was rich and green.

Weary from traveling, lulled by the rhythmic motion of the carriage, and softly fanned by the sweet warm breeze upon their faces, Allison and Barry soon drifted off to sleep. The best seat in the vis-à-vis had been lost to Allison and Barry dozing, but Brandon did not mind. He and William were pleasantly engaged in conversation, and consequently, the view had receded into secondary importance.

"Now, Annabelle was never quite clear on just what your journalistic assignment *is* here," William was saying. "All she's mentioned is that *The Illustrated London News* wants you to write about the South as a foreign correspondent."

"The paper wants me to report on the interrelationship of Southern politics, society, and economics, as well as—" Brandon stopped short, then finished tentatively, "... the ... antislavery movement." Brandon studied William's expression, but the latter seemed unruffled by his mention of abolition. "My assignment is to report on Southern culture, plantation life—anything noteworthy or of interest I might find while I'm here— and how each of these aspects of the South intertwine and influence each other, as well as any specific newsworthy stories that might arise. Initially, my editors were dubious about my living in the country rather than in the city of Charleston, but when I told them we would be living on one of the wealthiest and most influential rice plantations in the South, they consented." Brandon chuckled.

William beamed with pride, yet noted humbly, "I could not have accomplished all I have if it weren't for what my father had left to me *and* if it weren't for the expertise and labor of my field hands and various specialized workers." Then, to divert attention from himself and get to know his new acquaintance better, he added, "Annabelle always speaks of you in glowing terms. She tells me that you graduated near the top of your class at the university in London."

Brandon smiled modestly. "Oh, it was nothing really."

"Still, Annabelle said you were only about twenty when you went to London to interview Queen Victoria for *The Illustrated London News.*"

"Twenty-two or twenty-three," Brandon corrected. "The paper wanted me to interview the Prime Minister of Nepal, Jung Bahadur Kunwar Rana—"

"Good Lord—that is a larger mouthful than some of our slaves' African basket names! Akouassiba, Bungoh, Quacco, Aminaba!" William laughed.

Brandon grinned affably. "Quite!" Yet he could not help but wonder whether those from other lands found names such as William's and his equally tongue-twisting and foreign to their ears—William Cornelius Archibald Crawford and Brandon Jonathan Stewart. "At any rate," he continued, "the Nepalese Prime Minister, Jung Bahadur, was on a trip to Europe and England along with his seven brothers and a number of cooks. I was granted an interview with both Queen Victoria and Jung Bahadur. Some say, arguably, that the Prime Minister was more resplendent than the queen. He wore velvet robes trimmed in lace and studded with jewels and pearls, and he wore a plumed cap of white silk also glittering with jewels. Of course, I had to sketch the queen and Jung Bahadur together for an illustration to accompany the article." Brandon paused and sighed at the fond memory, still so vivid in his mind. "It was just three years ago and quite a daunting experience for me, as it was one of my first assignments for the *News.*"

William was duly impressed. "Your editors must have thought highly of you."

Brandon shrugged and grinned in a blend of satisfaction and modesty. "In 1851, I covered the Crystal Palace Exhibition at the London World's Fair—a far more routine sort of assignment. In fact," Brandon suddenly remembered, "it seems to me there was a new large strain of rice developed from a plantation in All Saints Parish that was on display at the Crystal Palace Exhibition that year."

"That would be Joshua John Ward. Every year, we have a fair of the Winyah and All Saints Agricultural Society. It seems that Ward's slaves have brought him silver medals for at least the past few years. A fellow named Tucker wins nearly each year as well. Which isn't to say *I've* never won!" William winked and laughed.

As the carriage proceeded northward toward the rice-plantation region of All Saints Parish and Crawford Hill, Brandon and William continued to converse about their respective professions and various relevant subjects.

A brief stop enroute, just south of the Santee River near the Hopswee Plantation, allowed everyone to stretch their legs and have a quick bite to eat. Because William was only loosely acquainted with the plantation's owner, John Hume Lucas, they stopped along the banks of a tributary of the nearby Santee River to picnic rather than calling on Mr. Lucas. There, beneath the shade of moss-draped trees, they spread out quilt blankets and opened baskets of fruit, sandwiches, cider, and wine.

"John's property is modest." William gestured in the direction of the Hopswee Plantation. "In 1850, the Georgetown Census showed that Hopswee Plantation had only about one hundred eighty slaves and produced three hundred sixty thousand pounds of rice."

"That seems rather impressive, given the number of workers," Brandon surmised.

"Yes ... not too bad, really. But his is a much smaller operation than mine or several others in All Saints Parish. He owns, if I'm not mistaken, about three thousand acres—a decent amount of land for that number of slaves."

Keeping an eye on Barry to be sure he would not wander off too far, Allison listened to her husband and William talk of the Hopswee and other nearby rice plantations; she knew it would take some time—if ever—to get used to hearing the word "slave." As Barry began to scamper off toward the tributary's banks, Allison called out, "Stay near us, Barry. We may be leaving soon."

Shrugging his disappointment, Barry turned and trudged back to the picnic blanket.

"Matter o' fact, we bes' pack up an' head out," the vis-à-vis coachman said as he squinted upward to determine the position of the sun.

William shielded his eyes with his hand and noted the sun was reclined farther than he had anticipated at that point in their journey. He pulled out his pocket watch. "Yes, he's right," he said to Brandon and Allison. "We'd best pack up and get going. We're only about halfway there."

After the coachmen, William, Brandon, and Allison gathered up the picnic belongings, they headed back to the wagon and carriage to continue along the northbound road.

After a time, the vis-'a-vis, followed by the wagon, rolled onto a bridge spanning the Santee River.

"It's not much farther now," William noted.

Having dozed off from their lunch, the jostling of the carriage onto the Santee River's bridge roused both Allison and Barry from their sleep.

"Ummmm ... are we there?" Allison inquired drowsily, and stretched her arms pleasantly before her.

Barry sat up, rubbed his eyes, and yawned, "Where are we?"

"Just a little farther to go," William assured.

"You're missing all the scenery," Brandon chided playfully.

Allison concealed a yawn, then observed, "It seems quite green, as in England, but much more wild than what we are used to in Derbyshire."

William agreed with her assessment and told them all about the mosquitoes, bats, palmetto bugs—"enormous flying cockroaches the size of one's thumb"—raccoons, deer, and alligators that abounded in South Carolina's Lowcountry, the region of All Saints Parish.

"Alligators?" Barry asked.

William explained all about alligators that lived in the rivers, lagoons, and near the salt marshes. Barry's eyes grew wide.

As they neared the southern tip of All Saints Parish, William instructed the coachman to detour the vis-à-vis off the main route and onto a short jaunt along the spare dirt tracks of a country road. They rolled along a mild ascent, stopping near a grassy knoll. The wagon with their luggage waited behind on the main road.

"From here, we can see Crawford Hill, All Saints Parish, and the Waccamaw River," William said. He suggested they get out of the carriage for a short break and to admire the view before completing their trip. William then helped Allison down from the vis-'a-vis, and Brandon lifted Barry down.

"This is known as Picnic Hill," William said, referring to the grassy knoll where they stood. "It's a pretty spot for travelers to stop and rest a while."

Barry looked with grave consternation at the tall grass all about them. "Are there any alligators here?" he asked.

"No, no!" William laughed. "No alligators here; you are perfectly safe."

Barry looked greatly relieved and grinned. Allison smiled in amusement, and Brandon affectionately tousled his son's hair.

The coachman waited by the vis-à-vis as William and the Stewarts ascended the knoll. Barry, tugging at his mother's hand, trudged along dutifully, looking all about him at the new and wild country that was now his home. The four stopped at the hill's crest and looked out upon the land beyond.

William, his arm outstretched, pointed out particular aspects of the landscape and various points of interest as Allison and Brandon listened with rapt attention. Inland, were low hills, woodlands, and fields planted in cotton and provisional crops. Eastward lay the expansive rice fields flanking the banks of the Black, Pee Dee, and Waccamaw Rivers. Adjoining the rice fields, farther to the east, was a long strip of higher land where the plantation estates stood. This stretch of land reclined into a narrow coastal strip of salt marshes demarcated from the Atlantic Ocean by three thin strips of land generously referred to as islands—North Island, Du Bourdieu, and Pawley's Island.

"Now, you can see there," William pointed, "the waterways networking the rice fields are bordered by rice banks, the higher land. The rice banks were all built by hand, mostly in the last century, by the slaves of All Saints Parish. The banks stand about eight feet high and are roughly fifteen feet across at their base and about five feet across at the top. The slaves used shovels, hoes, and baskets to clear and drain the fields for rice planting, filling the baskets with mud and depositing the mud on the rice banks to build them up. It was a tremendous amount of work, if you stop to think about it. It is said that all the rice banks in the South Carolina Lowcountry and Georgia, combined, rival the pyramids in Egypt in the scope of their engineering and construction."

"That is quite impressive," Brandon marveled. Clearly, this was an engineering feat that he had never read about in his World History course at the university in London.

"This month, April, is the planting month for rice," William continued. "We call our rice Carolina Gold. The slaves drop rice seeds into the trenches and cover the seeds with their heel. After the fields are planted, we open the sluice gates along the rice banks at high tide to flood the fields—this is what we call 'the sprout flow.' After about three to seven days, the rice begins to sprout, and the fields are drained. Then we flood the fields again to submerge the rice—this kills insects as well as young grasses that opportunistically sprout along with the rice. This second flooding, called 'the long water,' is then drained to about one-half the plant's height to support the young rice plants until they are strong enough to stand erect. This is the stage you can see now." William made a sweeping gesture over the swollen rice fields. "In three or four weeks we begin cultivation. Not as pleasant for the slaves as planting time a few weeks ago, owing to the change in weather. By cultivation time, in mid- to late May, the weather will be quite hot, damp, and miserable to labor in, I'm afraid. In July, we have the last flooding, 'the harvest flow.' Harvesting the rice begins in September, but meanwhile, we contend with migratory rice birds that swoop down and threaten to pluck the rice fields clean—yellow-and-black bobolinks mostly."

"How do you prevent the birds from ruining the crops?" Allison asked.

"Mainly by shooting at them or making noise to scare them … but they keep coming anyway." William pointed farther north, along the horizon. "Now, up there … Upper All Saints Parish, in Horry District, is mainly planted by yeoman rice farmers." William lowered his arm, indicating land in the near distance. "The wealthiest rice plantations are at the southern end, in Lower All Saints Parish, in Georgetown District."

Brandon scanned the horizon. "Where are the borders of All Saints Parish?"

"All Saints Parish extends from the Waccamaw River's mouth at Winyah Bay, just there," William pointed, "and continues northward, paralleling the rivers up to just beyond Murrell's Inlet. It's … oh … about twenty miles end to end and roughly ten miles wide."

They gazed out upon the Waccamaw River glistening in the spring sun; the deep emerald woods of cypress, magnolia, pine, and oak; Winyah Bay; and the flooded rice fields. Cranes, egrets, and woodducks abounded along the low salt marshlands. Plantation houses, steam-powered rice mills, and villages of slave cabins dotted the landscape before them.

"Do you think you can be happy here?" Brandon whispered to Allison.

"Why, it seems a *lovely* place to live," she assured, and returned her gaze to the land below.

At last restless, Barry furtively tugged his mother's hand signaling that he wanted to wander off and explore. Allison granted Barry permission to do so, and he scampered off through the tall grass.

"Don't go too far, Barry," Brandon called. "Stay where you can see us!" This was just barely possible, as the grass was nearly as tall as Barry.

"Yes, Father. I will," Barry returned, in an obedient sing-song.

Barry ran and skipped through the grass—his arms outstretched as a gliding rice bird, he swooped and wheeled. His sun-kissed brown locks could be seen bobbing and circling about the hilltop, pausing here and there so that he could examine a bug, capture a butterfly, or squint overhead at a circling hawk. Insects buzzed in the tall grass around him, all but unseen among the blades and thickets.

William Crawford was no less exuberant about the land than Barry, and he had found yet another landmark to point out to Allison and Brandon.

"Can we see Crawford Hill from here?" Brandon squinted into the near distance.

This question cued William to point out nearly every plantation in Lower All Saints Parish, beginning with his own twenty-five thousand acre Crawford Hill boasting approximately nine hundred and fifty to one thousand slaves. Farther north were William Alston's sixteen thousand acres and five hundred and sixty slaves, then Joshua John Ward's Oryzantia and Aderly plantations, and beyond these, Oak Hill, Crow Field, Waterford, Hagley, Willbrook, and others.

"The plantations have such romantic names," Allison mused.

"Romantic like 'Hopswee'?" Brandon teased.

"Stop! They *are* romantic, as if from out of a book."

"Hopswee is *also* known as 'Hopsewee-on-the-Santee,' " William put in.

Both Brandon and Allison agreed that latter name was far more pleasing to be sure.

"All Saints Church is about five miles north of Crawford Hill. I don't know if you can see it from here," William said as he extended his arm in the general direction. "It's where we attend church each Sunday." William concluded, "Well, I suppose we had best collect Barry and start for home. I've probably bored you both to tears."

"No, not at *all*. Not in the *least*, William," Brandon and Allison chorused.

As they turned to go, Allison noted what appeared to be a modest plantation house at the southwest edge of All Saints Parish that William had neglected to mention. The house and surrounding fields stood just at the border of Crawford Hill. "William," she asked, pointing out the rather austere house and fields, "is that your neighbor's place? Whose house and lands are there?"

"That is Jack Davenport's plantation. He lives there with his wife, Sara, and their son, Tom. Tom is two or three years older than Barry, I believe."

"How many acres does Davenport own?" Brandon asked.

"He has about nine thousand acres, and he owns about two hundred and fifty to three hundred slaves, on average. His is one of the smallest and least-profitable plantations in Lower All Saints Parish."

"Why is his plantation so small?" Allison wondered.

"His lands run farther inland, leaving little land suitable for growing rice. The provisional crops are only to keep food on his table and keep the operation self-sufficient. He relies on cotton crops, mainly; and in these parts, that's far less profitable. But there's more to it than that." William continued, "You see, generations ago, the Davenport holdings were reputed to be some of the richest in the region, but Jack Davenport—as his father, and his father before him—drinks away most of the profits. What I mean is, they spent more time with the bottle than managing their holdings, as does Jack Davenport. They've all made some poor investments, mismanaged their lands and operations. In the end, they have each had to sell off sections of the plantation. Some years ago, I purchased some of Davenport's rice fields ... I only wish I could have purchased some of his slaves too." William shook his head and sighed. "Jack Davenport treats his slaves abominably. A poor cotton harvest with a scant rice harvest to fall back on strikes dread into the hearts of Davenport's slaves. He works them mercilessly. Whatever slaves he's had that didn't run off or die of illness, he has probably beaten or worked to death—or tortured."

"Tortured?" Allison felt sure that she must have misunderstood.

"Yes, tortured. For example, he took one slave woman of his and had her shut into a barrel through which he had driven rows of nails. Then he ordered the barrel, with the woman shut inside of it, to be rolled down a hill."

Allison gasped, her hand to her mouth.

"*Christ!*" Brandon breathed.

"That's not all," William said. "Afterward, he left the woman inside the barrel, bleeding but still alive, in the woods. She either bled or starved to death. No one really knows which."

"That ... that's *horrible!*" Allison was stunned that such punishment could be allowed to occur. Her eyes stung, imagining the sheer atrocity of it.

"I'm afraid that is mere sport compared to some of what Davenport is capable of."

"What do you mean?" Brandon asked, not really sure he actually wanted to hear.

"Last spring we had a cholera epidemic in these parts. Now, most plantation owners employ physicians and medical nurses on a contractual basis. The physicians handle all sorts of ills, from extracting teeth to minor surgery. The nurses look after the plantation hospitals and immediate needs of the sick. But Jack Davenport refuses to invest in this system of medical care. When his slaves are ailing he generally lets them rely on local plantation conjurers or plantation priests."

"What are *they*, exactly?" Allison asked, intrigued.

"Basically they are medicine men of the old religion, of traditional African practices. They use spells, curses, brew teas, and the like. The slaves call these so-called practitioners 'conjure doctors.' Sadly, most slaves still put their faith in these people and remain wary of what they call 'white man's medicine.' They use pokeberry tea, gypsum weed, clumps of dirt." William shook his head, then looked steadily at Brandon and Allison.

"Would you believe a common diagnosis for a number of ailments is that the poor sufferer has a lizard in his head?" He enunciated these last several words carefully.

"A ... lizard?" Allison was not sure she had heard right.

"Good Lord," Brandon uttered. Indeed, he *would* have quite a lot to write about for *The Illustrated London News!*

"I don't mean to paint too dismal a picture of conjure doctors," William said. "They do have some folk remedies that seem to help, even heal. But they are a sad match for an epidemic of cholera—such as we've had before."

"What happened to the Davenport slaves during the epidemic?" Brandon asked.

"Well ... his slaves started dying ... dropping like flies. Some medical nurses even volunteered to help his slaves, free of charge. Some say it was Jack's pride and obstinacy; others say it was his drunkenness. Hell, I don't know ... but he refused any help *at all*. His slaves dropped dead in the fields as they worked. In the end there were too many bodies to be dealt with properly, so he had his surviving slaves dig a mass grave. They dug the grave with shovels and hoes, filling baskets with mud as if they were building a rice bank. It's been said that nearly one hundred bodies were heaped in that mass grave."

"My God, William, are you serious?" Allison's eyes teared, and she squeezed Brandon's hand for comfort.

"I wish I could tell you I wasn't." William pointed toward the Davenport lands. "See that barren patch of land there, just to the right of that large oak tree?"

Wordlessly Brandon and Allison nodded.

"That's where the mass grave was dug. Men, women, children, little babies, all heaped in, one atop the other and filled over with dirt." William sighed and shook his head. "Nothing, not one blade of grass has grown on that spot since. Some of the slaves think the conjure doctors put a spell on the land."

"What kind of man *is* he?" Allison uttered, in stunned disbelief.

"Some of the slaves say he's no man at all but the devil incarnate. Others say he was born without a soul. I think they're closer to the truth than we all realize."

The tale had visibly upset Allison far more than William had anticipated. Brandon tucked a protective arm about Allison's waist and kissed her temple, although he too felt deeply unsettled by what William had just relayed.

"I didn't mean to upset you," William said. "We are all so familiar with the tale by now. It must sound utterly shocking to you."

Allison nodded. "Yet it is always good to know the truth, to understand what one is dealing with." She was glad, however, that Barry had been out of earshot for this particular narration of William's.

Brandon called for Barry to join them in the carriage. Barry's innocent face, framed by chestnut waves of hair, popped up from the tall grass, and he happily scampered to his parents' side.

Seated in the vis-à-vis carriage once again, they descended the grassy knoll and embarked northward along the main road, the wagon of trunks, carpetbags, and satchels following dutifully behind. All the while, Barry prattled on about the insects, butterflies, and rabbits that he had discovered in the grass, including the skeleton of a fallen hawk.

Allison sat close beside Brandon, half listening to her son and half thinking about Jack Davenport and the atrocities he committed, the wanton neglect and mass carnage. Allison now ached to see her sister Annabelle and wondered if she would find her very much changed.

———◆———

Live oaks draped in Spanish moss shaded the long drive leading to the Big House at Crawford Hill. At a distance, the white Victorian-style house gleamed in the early-evening sun as a beacon at the end of the tree-lined drive. Before the house, the drive turned around an oval of lawn, forming a roundabout, and branched off to the right, leading to the stables and carriage houses a distance away.

The vis-à-vis emerged from the canopy of live oaks and slowed to a halt before the Big House. The wagon laden with the Stewart's belongings drew up behind and stopped.

Ester stepped out onto the front verandah and called back through the open door, "Miss Annabelle! Miss Annabelle! Dey is here! Dey is here!"

Jacob appeared from inside the house, and he and Ester descended the front porch steps to meet the Stewarts. William commenced the introductions as Annabelle at last appeared upon the verandah.

"Allison!" she cried, a joyful catch in her voice.

The two sisters rushed forward and met in a heartfelt embrace.

"Annabelle! Oh, Annabelle!" Allison wept with joy.

"Dear Allison!" Annabelle let her tears fall unchecked.

Brandon strode forward and embraced Annabelle in turn.

"It is so good to see you again, Brandon. I'm *so* happy you are all finally here," Annabelle gushed, brushing at gleeful tears. Then she drew back from Brandon's embrace and leaned down to meet Barry. "And who might you be?" she asked sweetly.

Barry retreated uncertainly behind Allison's skirts.

"Dat be Massa Barry!" Ester announced, and she too leaned down to smile at the boy.

"What a handsome young man you are," Annabelle exclaimed, and then she straightened. "Why, I haven't seen little Barry since he was just a baby. He certainly takes after his father." Annabelle sighed contentedly and looked at the new arrivals—her sister, Brandon, and Barry—once more. "I can't believe you are all really here," she said, her eyes brimming.

"Nor can I," Allison beamed as she swept aside another tear.

Jacob had summoned a few of the house servants to help with the Stewarts' luggage as well as William's trunk and carpetbags. "We bes' git de trunks an' things into de house," he advised.

Brandon stepped forward to help unload the trunks and other luggage from the wagon.

William touched Brandon on the arm. "They'll take care of it."

"I don't mind," Brandon said, whereupon he quickly doffed his tan cotton jacket and slung it over the side of the wagon to help.

"Massa Brandon," Jacob said hesitantly, "you ... you don' need t'."

"It's all right." Brandon began to roll up his sleeves.

Jacob was nonplussed. "Massa Willem? ..." he queried.

William smiled in amusement. "It's all right, Jacob." He watched a moment as Brandon and a house servant began to hoist down a small trunk from the wagon bed. "Oh, what the hell," William laughed good-naturedly, then removed his jacket and turned up his shirt cuffs.

Only Allison fully understood. Both she and Brandon had felt uncomfortable being referred to as "Miss" and "Massa" as means of deferral by Ester and Jacob. Although Brandon and Allison had hired domestics to help run their house in England, they had never felt comfortable being served beyond what was absolutely necessary. Furthermore, Brandon's numerous articles for *The Illustrated London News* reporting on the disparity between the upper and serving classes in English society had piqued their social consciences all the more.

"Here, let me give you a hand," William offered, enthusiastically stepping forward.

"Well, *I'll be*," Ester breathed. Then she announced for all to hear, "I'll see dat de tea be ready in 'bout an hour."

"That will be fine, Ester. Thank you." Annabelle said. Turning to Allison and Barry, she invited, "Well! Let's go inside. I want you to see the house, and we are anxious to hear all about your voyage and the drive up from Charleston."

After tea, a tour of the house, and then dinner—followed by berry pie and peach wine for dessert—the household retired for the evening. The children—Carolina, Ashley, Quash, and Barry—had long since been carried upstairs and tucked into their beds. Allison and Annabelle lingered in the darkened upstairs hallway a moment, each holding an oil lamp for light. They talked quietly a while, then hugged fondly once more and bade each other a good night.

Annabelle quietly entered her and William's bedroom and set her oil lamp upon the bureau. "It's like a dream," she said as her fingers worked nimbly to unpin her long waves of hair.

"I'm glad your sister is here for you," William said, and crossing the room to Annabelle, he slipped his arm about her waist beneath her flowing tresses. He smoothed back a stray lock from her forehead and bent to kiss her—but stopped short. "What's this?" he asked, noting the wound to her temple. He knit his brow in consternation and lifted the oil lamp to inspect the injury. "What on *earth*?" he uttered.

"It's nothing, really," Annabelle answered quickly. She dared not tell him of the harrowing visit earlier that day to the Davenport plantation. Pinning her hair up had concealed the wound, and her sister's arrival at Crawford Hill had made her quite forget about the incident.

"But what happened?" William pressed.

"I ... I tripped," Annabelle began. "You see ... Ester and I were arranging Allison and Brandon's room, and I simply tripped and struck my head. It was quite silly of me, really." It was a story she had worked out earlier with Ester and Jacob; she swore them not to tell of the episode at Jack Davenport's plantation. It was a secret easily kept, for all three knew that William would have certainly confronted Davenport; and as a result, the slaves on his plantation would all have had hell to pay.

William tenderly kissed Annabelle's temple. "Poor dear," he soothed. "Does it hurt?"

"Not anymore," Annabelle smiled, and masked an inner sigh of relief. It was one of many such tales regarding the Davenport plantation that William would never hear about. She extinguished her oil lamp, and William blew out his bedside taper.

The Big House grew dark and quiet but for one room. Allison stood in her white cotton-lace nightgown carefully brushing her long blond hair that fell in thick, shining waves below her waist. Brandon, reclining on the bed, watched her reflection in the mirror. The oil lamp burned softly beside her atop the bureau, casting a halo about both itself and Allison.

"I thought you would be asleep by now," Allison said. "It's been a long day."

"You were talking with Annabelle for quite a while," Brandon noted.

"I stopped by the nursery afterward to look in on little Ashley and Carolina."

"They *are* little treasures, aren't they?" Brandon remarked.

"Absolutely adorable!" She threaded the brush through her tresses languidly, and sighed, "Simply adorable."

Brandon sat up upon the bed and gazed at Allison in the low lamplight. "Your parents should have named you 'Angela.'"

Allison glanced at her husband's reflection in the mirror. "And why is that?" she asked with amusement.

"'Angela' starts with the letter 'A' as does 'Annabelle' and 'Alexandra.'"

"My name, 'Allison,' begins with an 'A,'" she returned, and resumed attention to her hair, working her brush patiently through a stubborn tangle.

"Yes, however, 'Angela' is more suited to you."

"How so?"

"Because, dear one ... you *look* like an angel." He was no longer light-hearted but serious and filled with sentiment.

"And have you ever seen an angel?" Allison's tone was quiet, although coyly challenging.

Brandon studied his wife's reflection in the mirror, the soft halo of lamplight about her. "Yes, every day of my life since we were married."

Setting down her hair brush, Allison's eyes filled, and she turned to look at Brandon. "You always know just what to say."

Brandon gave a modest shrug. "I'm a writer," he quipped, and broke into a jovial grin.

"Writers and actors are *never* to be believed," Allison teased, and extinguished the oil lamp.

"Come here," Brandon beckoned her, his arms outstretched.

Allison slipped under the cotton coverlets and snuggled close beside him. They lay together, sharing a pleasant silence for a moment; then, Allison spoke. "I was thinking," she began, "perhaps we can try again one day. We've always wanted a little girl, a sister for Barry."

"I ... I'm not sure. Do you want to risk another miscarriage? Can we put ourselves through that again?"

"I want to try again, just once more ... for you ... for both of us—not right away, of course. We've only just arrived here, and we must settle in for a while first. But I thought perhaps we should try ... another chance in our new home, a new beginning."

Brandon heard the longing and determination in his wife's voice. "Are you quite sure you really want this, Allison?" he asked quietly.

She nodded her head upon the pillow. "Yes," she whispered, "if you want it as well."

Brandon hesitated a moment, then kissed the smooth arc of her cheek. "I *do* love you so, dear one," he whispered.

Allison knew by this gesture and these words that he had consented. She kissed him gratefully on the cheek and nestled warmly in his arms.

"I love you, dear one." Brandon murmured, and worn from the journey, quickly drifted off to sleep.

Days stretched into weeks and weeks into months. Initially, the South proved a strange and foreign place to the Stewarts; but in time, they adjusted to their new home. There was much to learn about plantation life and Southern society. As quickly as Brandon wrote articles about their new surroundings for *The Illustrated London News*, Allison dispatched letters to her sister Alexandra at Loxley House in Derbyshire, England.

Allison wrote one such letter to her sister one sunny afternoon in September, 1853.

"*Dear Alexandra,*

"*The oppressive heat of summer is waning, and we are now, at long last, blessed by a cool breeze now and again. William and Brandon are already enthusiastically discussing their plans for autumn hunting in the nearby woods. Even hunts are conducted quite differently here than in England.*

"*It is September, and the slaves are toiling to bring in the rice harvest. My heart breaks for them when I see them working so hard in this intolerable heat.*

"*Slavery seems a monstrous system, even here at Crawford Hill. I don't mean to suggest that William and Annabelle are not exceptionally kind, solicitous, and humane. Only, the system's ills are inherent, I fear, despite an owner's best intentions. Please never breathe a word of this to William or our dear sister Annabelle, but I believe slavery is the South's sorrow.*

"*On summer days, when we and our neighbors sit on the verandah sipping cool drinks, the field hands are in the fields laboring in the hot sun for up to fourteen hours a day—sometimes longer. It is a system that degrades both the slave and the owner. I have mentioned in an earlier letter to you about William's interest in instituting enforceable slavery reforms;*

it is to his credit that he both advocates and works toward this ... but it falls on deaf—even cynical and ridiculing—ears.

"William has his Africans work the plantation according to the 'task system.' Each worker and field hand has individual work assignments that they are expected to accomplish each day. The faster and stronger slaves are allowed to help those who are weaker and slower, those who struggle to keep up with their work. All in all, it is a team effort. Before dawn each day, except Sunday, the slaves are already out in the fields working. They take a break at midday to eat and rest a while, and then they continue, working until twilight and often until well after dark. Annabelle says they work like this all year round with a few days off at Christmas and Easter. The slaves work in sweltering heat, drenching rains, hail, and the bitter cold of winter. (Annabelle says that winters in South Carolina can be quite unpredictable—some quite warm, others nearly cold enough to snow!)

"Now it is September, and the rice fields are drained for harvest. The slaves move in droves across the fields, wielding rice hooks to cut the long stalks. The rice is dried, tied in sheaves, and transported on river boats to the threshing yards. (William owns one of the few plantation threshing and pounding mills in the region.) Some rice is mill processed; however, much is processed by hand. The slaves mostly employ great flailing sticks to thresh. Women weave broad, shallow baskets of pine and sweet grass for winnowing the rice. This labor is far more arduous and tedious than it sounds; yet the actual harvesting of the rice from the drained fields is the most grueling. Jacob says that the rice on the stalks is quite coarse and abrasive to the slave's hands. Their hands are often quite blistered, chaffed, and callused during harvest time.

"It is true—as you had asked—that the slaves do sing as they labor, but it is to my ears a terribly mournful sound, an expression of fragile hope in the midst of despair. I have seen happiness upon the plantation here, it is true. But it is not a thorough happiness; it's as though it is a happiness born of profound necessity as opposed to an easy, natural inclination.

"In the fields, the slaves are supervised by the slave drivers and by overseers. These men are either African or white, as it is on many plantations. But ultimately, everyone answers to William.

"The plantation seems a constant hive of activity and a world

unto itself. There are house servants and field workers (supervised by Ester and Jacob, as well as by the field hands and overseers) including cooks, seamstresses, prime hands, coopers, carpenters, ditchmen, drivers, plowmen, coachmen, cattle minders, hog minders, shepherds, stablemen, poultry minders, gardeners, cloth weavers, basket weavers, blacksmiths— butchers, bakers, and candlestick makers! It is an overwhelming number of workers, and I dare say, the quite large staff at Loxley House pales in comparison.

"When Brandon, Barry, and I first arrived at Crawford Hill, so many dark-skinned faces in such a foreboding landscape seemed quite intimidating at first. It is said that in All Saints Parish there is one white person for every nine or ten Africans. But living on the plantation, one has the feeling that it is really one white for every one hundred Africans. There is absolutely no rational reason I can surmise that this ratio should intimidate me so . . . except that all the Africans on the place mostly speak Gullah.

"Brandon and I are finally beginning to develop an intelligible ear for the slaves' Gullah language. As Annabelle has explained it, Gullah is an amalgam of many diverse African languages incorporating the vocabulary of English. It is very much like trying to understand a very thick Scottish brogue! Ultimately, it makes sense, but it takes considerable effort to get used to it. Fortunately, most of the house servants' and cooks' Gullah is quite mild and, to extend the metaphor, is more as a Cockney accent is to proper English than pure Gullah. (To our amusement and dismay, Barry is trying to imitate the way the house servants talk!)

"Poor little Barry. He complains, at times quite plaintively, that there are no boys his age to play with. He and Carolina are very close in age, and they get along together quite pleasantly—but he tells me, 'Yes, Mother, but she is a girl!' He is only five and too young for school, and none of the house servants' children are of suitable age. William suggested Tom Davenport who is seven years old, but I've heard such tales of horror about the Davenport plantation. The owner, Jack Davenport, is of ill repute and a drunkard as well. Perhaps when Barry is a little older and we have been here longer we can reconsider regarding Tommy as a potential companion.

"Now, Alexandra, I must tell you of this summer's heat so you will not be so envious of our weather this winter when you are all but snowbound. In the South, dear sister, horses sweat, men perspire, and woman 'glow,'—the latter being a romantic euphemism for what horses do! Intermittent summer rains and early mornings provide some relief from the heat, but the dampness is relentless. After one bathes and dresses, one feels the immediate need to repeat bathing! At midday, the slightest exertion produces an outpouring of 'glow' from every brow and pore. One gets used to going about in dampish clothes—there is no other recourse. Women here remind me that the humidity is good for the skin, although that seems of small consolation. Our books, shoes—anything leather—grow spoiled with mildew from the constant damp. In fact, no sooner do the laundresses complete the day's wash of bed clothes and bath linens than these folded goods begin to sprout mildew while stored upon their closet shelves. Can you believe it? All the laundered things must be rewashed to get rid of the mildew before they can be used again!

"Nights are frequently too hot to allow for a proper sleep. The bedclothes themselves feel quite hot, as if one has just removed a hot iron from them. We let Barry sleep on a cotton rug on the floor downstairs near the window where it is less hot. (It would be an error to say it is cooler.)

"During the day, thank heaven for mint juleps, peach wine, and whiskey sours—the latter mostly imbibed by the men. The alcohol has an immediate, soothing effect against the heat, although I believe it ultimately compounds the misery, leaving one feeling somewhat parched.

"Day and night, we remain ever vigilant against the ubiquitous mosquitoes that thrive in this hot, damp climate. Ester has taught us the trick to dab a handkerchief soaked in whiskey or brandy against a bite to relieve the itching. Bless her heart! (One tries not to think about malaria!)

"One also wishes that one did not have to think about palmetto bugs. Palmetto bugs, despite the rather endearing name ascribed to them, are really nothing more than enormous flying cockroaches, about the full size of your thumb. Barry, of course, finds the scuttling creatures fascinating, as small boys are prone to do. (Dear Alexandra, I hope you are not dining or sipping tea while I tell you this.) One night, I woke up to a gentle scratching sound. Brandon and I searched the room with oil lamps trying to discern where the sound was coming from. We had nearly surrendered our search when I saw upon my bureau a huge black palmetto bug gnawing on the varnish. He had carved out quite a nice little spot down to the bare wood! Brandon and I could hardly believe it. My God, Alexandra. It was ghastly. I still shudder to think of it. We had been awakened by the sound of an insect eating our furniture! Brandon deftly swatted at it with the closest object at hand—my hair brush! He missed, and the offensive creature flew about the room nearly entangling itself in my hair. I shrieked and nearly cried! For a moment, I thought Brandon would strike me on the head with the brush by accident! In the end, Brandon was victorious. The palmetto was decapitated, its head impaled on the bristles of my brush, its body—legs twitching—lay in the corner on the floor. Can you guess how much I missed England that night?

"Not all of summer has been pure misery, however, dear sister. Fireflies, which I told you of earlier, are enchanting, especially as they emerge at twilight. These creatures are not our land-bound glowworms— fireflies emerge at night and actually fly! (They are, I suppose, nature's apology for palmettos.)

"And there have been elegant afternoon socials, formal dinners at neighboring plantations, Sunday church services and picnics, and rowing upon the river. (Barry finally saw his first alligator when we were out rowing; I've never seen his eyes so round!)

"Annabelle and I particularly enjoy ample leisure time, although we ultimately are in charge of managing the house servants. Most of the house servants at Crawford Hill are young women, even though we have several men about as well. Most of the female house servants are recruited on an as-needed basis. Annabelle will assign them to various household tasks when extra help is required, and then later dispatch them back to the fields or wherever they had been chosen from.

"Ester, Jacob, and all the other house servants attend to menus and cooking, cleaning, washing, ironing, mending, nursing, looking after the children, polishing silver, and various other tasks—much the way it is at Loxley House. However, at Crawford Hill, I often wonder if there are not too many house servants—maids, cooks, waiters, laundresses, and so on—as I am afraid I am becoming spoiled! Our tea and meals are prepared for us, baths drawn for us, personal maids and servants to help us dress if we wish. The intensely attentive degree of servitude is much greater than in a typical English country estate, I wager. And the degree of attentiveness by the house servants at Crawford Hill far exceeds that of the spare domestic help whom Brandon and I had hired while living in Castleton.

"If field hands and house servants live worlds apart from each other, then we, the landed gentry, so to speak, live in a world even further removed from these—and the plantation-owner men further still removed even from us. I am still not entirely sure what constitutes William's work, except that he is kept perpetually busy each day. He spends hours in his study upstairs dealing with the finances and business of running Crawford Hill. Occasionally he consults with lawyers, bankers, and accountants in Charleston. He confers with his overseers and drivers. He sees to the purchasing of provisions and the selling of rice. Nothing is done without his approval, and little escapes his notice.

"Brandon keeps busy with his writing and illustrating for The Illustrated London News. His editors are quite pleased so far. Of course, I need not tell you about the articles he has written, for you are able to read them yourself in the News. Brandon is accomplishing everything he had set out to do so far—writing about Southern society, plantation life, politics, economics, and the issue of abolition.

"Alexandra, I had best close, as I believe I have written all there is to tell, and I fear my hand is beginning to fail. Write to us soon. I miss you so! Brandon sends his deepest affection, and Barry blows you a kiss! We miss you, and Loxley, and England terribly. Stay well.

"All my love,

"Allison"

CHAPTER 5

Three Babies

A number of months earlier, it had been a point of amusement that Annabelle, Allison, and Ester had each announced they were with child. Now they dreaded enduring the summer heat for the remaining months of their pregnancies. It was difficult enough for a woman to patiently suffer the discomforts of a pregnancy, let alone compound the unwieldy ordeal with a humid, hot South Carolina summer. And this particular summer, in 1855, seemed especially hot and damp.

All women knew they risked their lives to bear children and that, once born, their babies' lives could very well be claimed by disease within the first five years of childhood. And so, as many women did, Annabelle, Allison, and Ester had each prayed and made a pact with destiny to see themselves and their children safely through. However, their pacts and prayers seemed somewhat superfluous because they had each discerned divine omens that boded well for them. Ester fretted little over her pregnancy, for Quash had been born easily and was now a strong, healthy boy. Annabelle had given birth to two fine, healthy girls, and she had no reason to expect complications this time. Allison's fears of miscarriage had diminished with each passing month, and now that her belly had grown round and plump beneath her maternity frock, she joyfully knew that fate would absolutely grant her one more child. Sealing the three women's confidences was the fact that they had each conceived at very nearly the same time and now shared their pregnancies together—it was a sign that their babies were each meant to be.

The women had made a ritual of taking late-afternoon tea together in the west sitting room. Here, they would work on embroidery and knitting, and visit together, discussing things that only women shared with one another. Annabelle, Allison, and Ester would sit in a semicircle in wooden rocking chairs facing the window where the sunlight streamed in, illuminating the colored glass items placed on the shelves before it. There were pitchers, jars, bowls, vases, and plates of all hues, giving the effect of a church's stained-glass window. The rays of late-afternoon sun cast rainbows of color across the room, spilling against the white walls and dappling the hardwood floor. As the women attended to their needlework, rocking in their chairs and talking, they would occasionally look up, past the rows of colored glass, at the trees and green lawn beyond. When the sun grew too low and bright, Ester would rise and draw the sheer curtains closed.

On this particular summer afternoon, the women were so assembled, sharing a pot of tepid tea with lemon while waiting for Dr. Fletcher to arrive and look in on them.

"If'n it be a girl chil', we is gonna call her 'Cinda,'" Ester was saying. "An' if'n it be a boy, we is gonna call him 'Cudjo' … o' m'be 'Joe.' Jacob, he like d' name 'Cudjo' bes'." She turned to Allison, "Has you d'cided on a name yet, Miss Allison?"

"If we have a girl, Brandon and I want to continue my family's tradition of beginning her name with an 'A.' We will name the baby 'Amelia,' but we aren't sure of a middle name. Oh, well," Allison beamed, "there is still time to decide."

"An' if'n you have a boy chil', Miss Allison?"

"If we have a boy, Brandon favors naming him 'Charles,' but that is so plain."

"Still, it sounds fine with 'Stewart,'" Annabelle mused. "Charles Stewart," she pronounced. The name had a pleasant ring.

"Yes, it would be a fine name," Allison said, "but it invariably becomes reduced to 'Charlie' or 'Chuck' in everyday use, and soon 'Charles' would be forgotten altogether. I had thought 'Charlton Stewart' might be nice, but I will leave the decision up to Brandon."

"Well, you know our William!" Annabelle declared. "He must of course name a boy after the Cooper River, since Carolina was named after the state and Ashley was named after the river west of Charleston. So now,

'Cooper,' if we have a boy, for the river east of Charleston." Annabelle thought a moment, then cautioned, "Allison, if you and Brandon *do* want to name your baby Charles—if it is a boy—don't be at all surprised if William urges you to change the name to 'Charleston,'" Annabelle giggled.

Allison laughed and shook her head. "There is no way on this *earth* that Brandon and I will name our baby 'Charleston!' Although—..." Allison paused, then looked thoughtful. "'Charleston Stewart' ... Annabelle, that's actually quite nice. And if your baby is a girl?" asked Allison.

"Well! I asked William just this morning what names are left, if we have another girl; should we name her after a mountain or a valley? William responded quite seriously. He said to me—" and here, Annabelle imitated her husband, lowering her voice and knitting her brow thoughtfully, "'Well, my dear ... there's the Waccamaw.'" Annabelle shook her head. "Can you imagine?"

"Waccamaw Crawford?" Allison and Ester each exclaimed.

The three women laughed heartily at this.

"Miss Annabelle, Massa Willem mus' be foolin' wit' you," Ester chuckled.

"Oh, he is. He's only teasing, I'm sure." Annabelle giggled, shook her head, and all but rolled her eyes. "At least I *hope* so! But he had best make up his mind soon, or I'll name her 'Amber' and that will be that."

"'Amber' ... Oh, what a sweet name," Allison cooed, wishing she had thought of it first.

"But 'Amelia' is *so* pretty," Annabelle said, "I wish I had thought of 'Amelia.'"

"Brandon has his heart set on 'Amelia,' if it's a girl," Allison noted.

"Well, if William and I have a girl I am sure she will be little Columbia or Waccamaw or Winyah—heaven knows!"

"Den we bes' pray de Lawd gib you a boy chil'!" Ester teased; it seemed like sound advice nonetheless.

At that moment, little Carolina wandered in and pulled a footstool over to sit upon so that she could join her mother, Aunt Allison, and Ester. The moment the three women saw Carolina, they burst into laughter— Carolina had stuffed a feather pillow beneath her frock, over her stomach, and declared she wanted to be like the grownup ladies. The three were still giggling and exclaiming over little Carolina's "round belly" when a house servant announced that Dr. Fletcher had arrived.

Dr. Fletcher was ushered into the west sitting room and offered a cup of tepid tea, for which he was grateful. He was quite pleased to find his three maternity patients in such merry spirits, despite the oppressive summer heat and the inconvenience of their conditions.

Dr. Fletcher was of excellent repute, especially in matters of pregnancy and childbirth. He was not the general physician whom William Crawford had contracted out to on a regular basis, but William and Brandon wanted the best obstetric care for their wives and for Ester as well. They all felt extremely fortunate to have secured Dr. Fletcher's services—he boasted many years of experience.

Seated, and beginning to sip his tea, the doctor spied little Carolina sitting near her mother and noticed her plump belly. "Why! My goodness, ladies, I did not realize I have a fourth patient to check on!" He winked at little Carolina who, hiding a shy smile behind a damp thumb, ducked behind her mother's chair. Dr. Fletcher chuckled his amusement.

Upstairs, the doctor examined Ester first and declared that she was doing just fine.

Next, he examined Annabelle. "Don't be surprised if you and William have twins!" he winked.

"Twins!" Annabelle exclaimed. "No *wonder* I've grown so big."

"Yes, twins," Dr. Fletcher smiled, "and don't worry about anything; the *three* of you are doing just fine."

Annabelle was elated and could not wait to tell William the unexpected news that evening.

Lastly, Dr. Fletcher ascended the stairs with Allison to examine her. Allison was quite accustomed to the doctor's visits by now, although she still felt shy as he poked, probed, and inspected. The doctor always carried out a more thorough examination of Allison due to his concern for her history of miscarriages.

Dr. Fletcher removed the unwieldy speculum from his black medical bag. The speculum had looked daunting to Allison upon the doctor's first visit, but now she was all too familiar with it. The speculum had two elongate spoon-like appendages that were flat where a spoon's bowl would have been. One appendage was stationary and the other movable by means of a long threaded drill-like piece. Turning the threaded drill-like piece caused the spoon-like appendages to move apart, extending the gap between them. To be certain that the metal speculum was never too cold for Allison before its insertion, Dr. Fletcher always made a practice of first warming the device in his hands.

Lying on the bed with her knees bent and legs wide apart, Allison waited self-consciously and patiently as the doctor probed and prodded. Dr. Fletcher noted that Allison's cervix had dilated somewhat more than expected for so early a stage in her pregnancy. Because Dr. Fletcher seemed to be taking a longer time than usual, Allison lifted her head to try to see the doctor from over her round belly, but she could only manage a glimpse of his furrowed brow as it promptly disappeared downward to reconfirm the dilation of her cervix.

At last, Dr. Fletcher had finished. Allison felt him attenuate the speculum and slide it gently out. "You are doing fine Allison, but you must have more bed rest." Allison listened attentively as he explained about the widening of her cervix and other observations about her general condition.

"Doctor ... I ... I'm so far along," she stammered. "I ... I can't possibly miscarry *now*, can I?" Her eyes filled, and she suddenly felt frightened.

"No, no, Allison!" he assured. "Everything is progressing very well ... really. You are healthy, and the baby will be just fine."

His soothing tone and words consoled her, but she looked anxiously up at him, nonetheless. "Are you quite sure?"

The doctor smiled. "Quite sure. Only, you will need to rest more, not exert yourself. I'm afraid that means stairs are out. Plenty of bed rest is the prescription." He continued to explain that she was of delicate physical constitution, and any unnecessary stairs or exertions could cause a miscarriage or premature birth. "You just take good care of yourself, rest, and do everything I told you, and everything will be just fine as can be." He squeezed her hand reassuringly, and Allison bravely promised to follow his instructions to the letter. At least he had ultimately relented a little, allowing her to come downstairs once a day for tea with Annabelle and Ester. How could he not, since he had seen how joyful she had been that afternoon when he first arrived?

The doctor took his leave, and Allison remained upstairs in her room. The sun had reclined over the fields, its rays spilling in through the curtain lace, gilding everything copper. Allison sat upon her bed, bit her lip, and blinked back tears. All at once she felt downhearted and failed, and she wondered how she could tell Brandon what the doctor had said.

Downstairs, William and Brandon had just returned home from an errand to a neighboring plantation as Dr. Fletcher was leaving. The doctor relayed his good news about each of their wives' conditions, then he drew Brandon aside in private in order to more fully explain his advice for Allison's confinement.

Allison, determining to be strong for Brandon, turned her thoughts to cheery imaginings of the baby's birth and all the happiness and promise a second child, a new life in their midst, would bring to them. "Silly goose!" she silently scolded herself for worrying over what the doctor had said. She only needed to follow Dr. Fletcher's orders, and all would be well. She smiled to herself and hugged her plump belly.

A quiet creak of the bedroom door interrupted Allison's serene reverie, and she turned her head to see Brandon. "Hello, dearest," she smiled, happy to see him home.

Brandon smiled and greeted her but could not conceal his concern for her. "I spoke with Dr. Fletcher downstairs, just as he was leaving," he began. In an instant, Brandon studied his wife's fair complexion, her robin's-eggs eyes, the soft blush of her lips, the exquisite arc of her cheekbones, and the delicately chiseled curve of her chin. "I do adore you so," he whispered as he sat alongside her on the bed.

In his expression and tone of voice, Allison discerned the depth of his concern for both her and their unborn child stirring gently inside her. "Everything will be fine," she reassured softly, and lovingly placed his hand upon her rounded tummy.

"I love you, Allison. . . . I fear for you and our baby."

Allison turned and embraced him. Brandon held her close.

"I'm a little frightened too," Allison confided.

They drew apart, and Brandon smiled encouragingly. "We've only to do as Dr. Fletcher says, and all will work out just fine." He said this as much to convince himself as to convince her.

Allison broke into a smile and nodded. "I am so anxious for our new baby," she said, her eyes shining.

———◇———

Dr. Fletcher called upon the women at Crawford Hill again in early July. He was primarily interested in looking in on Allison. After examining Allison, he met with both her and Brandon. "The baby does not appear to be positioned quite right," he said. But the doctor was optimistic, assuring them that the baby still had plenty of time to "cooperate and align itself properly."

Allison was told to rest even more and to refrain from taking tea downstairs. "You must lie quietly in bed as much as possible," the doctor warned her.

Before he left, he reassured Allison and Brandon in no uncertain terms, "You will have your baby, I am absolutely sure of that." And he smiled and winked to comfort them both.

Allison's baby was due in early September, roughly three weeks after Ester's and a few weeks before Annabelle's twins were to be born. Throughout the remaining two months of Allison's confinement, Brandon stayed home to look after her and wrote no more than a handful of short articles for the paper.

The summer weeks wore on, and the heat was stifling, adding to the tedium and discomfort of Allison's confinement. Her slender frame and need for rest made her appear pale and fragile; even so, her face radiated joy—it was certain that she and Brandon would indeed have their baby. Nothing else mattered.

———◇———

Late one afternoon in early September, Allison's water broke, and her contractions began. Jacob was at once dispatched to north All Saints Parish to summon Dr. Fletcher. By the time the doctor arrived at Crawford Hill, Allison was already in considerable pain and was being cared for by an

African midwife. As William, Annabelle, and Brandon waited anxiously downstairs, Dr. Fletcher hurried to Allison's room to attend to her labor.

Immediately upon inspection, it was clear that the baby's position in the womb had not improved—in fact, it was worse than before. The baby was breech, its tiny legs askew. In addition, the muscles of Allison's uterus did not provide sufficiently strong or regular contractions to allow for an easy birth.

Allison drifted in and out of labor throughout the night. Downstairs, in the east sitting room, Brandon scarcely slept, until by sheer exhaustion from worry he at last drifted into a sound sleep upon the sofa. Hours earlier, Annabelle and William had at last retired to their rooms for the night; William had insisted that Annabelle get some rest given her own delicate condition. A second African midwife had been summoned shortly before dawn to relieve the first attending midwife of her vigil at Allison's bedside. Dr. Fletcher caught what sleep he could between Allison's spells of labor pains.

Early the next morning, in the predawn hours, an acutely painful contraction thrust Allison awake, whereupon she gasped, then moaned in sheer agony. Her cries roused the entire household.

Instantly awakened, Brandon stumbled from the sofa and rushed to the foot of the staircase. He stood poised at the bottom step, his heart pounding and his hand upon the banister. His presence at Allison's side would only complicate matters, and knowing this, he did not go up. Through the closed bedroom door upstairs, Brandon could hear his wife's tearful moans and pleas, and the doctor's low, reassuring voice.

"Damn it! *Christ!*" Brandon uttered as his eyes welled.

Upstairs, Allison's cries grew more desperate, and she called Brandon's name in a plaintive, heartfelt wail.

Brandon raced up the stairs, hesitated only a moment, then thrust open the bedroom door.

"You had best leave!" Dr. Fletcher ordered.

Immediately the African midwife sent Brandon away, then closed the bedroom door and locked it. Brandon paced the hallway and struck his fist against the wall in frustration.

"Oh, God—*please!*" Allison moaned from behind the closed bedroom door, and she fell to weeping.

There was nothing Brandon could do. He went downstairs to wait.

As the sun began to rise over the nearby rice fields, Barry, Carolina, Quash, and Ashley were only told that Allison was not feeling well, that the doctor was with her, and they were all to spend a day or two at a neighbor's plantation until Allison felt better and her baby was born. A house servant and coachman left with the children before breakfast.

Annabelle paced in her night-robe and wrung her hands, wishing that her sister's delivery could be as easy and progress as quickly as Ester's had just three weeks before when little Cinda was born. But she knew it was too late for such a wish. As little Cinda's healthy cries emanated from the third-floor turret that early morning, the clatter of kitchenware punctuated the tense quiet of the house while the plantation cooks prepared breakfast. Annabelle stopped her pacing, placed both hands upon her own plump belly, and felt her babies kick. Her joy in this was short-lived as another painful moan arose from Allison's room.

Just then William entered their room. "Don't worry, Annabelle," he comforted, encircling his arms about his wife's round middle. "Allison will be just fine," he soothed, trying to foster a positive outlook for his wife's sake. He kissed her on the cheek, and Annabelle nodded. She did not want William to know how upset she was, and she forced a smile.

Throughout the morning, the atmosphere at Crawford Hill's Big House was tense and quiet, punctuated only by Allison's intermittent moans, plaintive wails, and cries. Breakfast was served as usual, and Ester noted, "We all bes' eat n' keep up our stren'th." But Brandon had no stomach for food—only black coffee. Annabelle and William tried their best to comfort Brandon, assuring him that Allison and the baby would be fine, although both were on edge, and Annabelle had to fight to conceal her mounting worry for her sister.

By early afternoon, Allison's labor subsided—perhaps due to sheer physical exhaustion. Allison drifted in and out of a nightmarish sleep, murmuring and tossing her head languidly upon her pillow, her pale complexion beaded with perspiration.

Dr. Fletcher summoned Brandon upstairs by midafternoon. The doctor and African midwife remained nearby as Brandon took a simple wooden chair at Allison's bedside. He tenderly clasped her frail hand in both his and pressed it to his lips. "Dear one," he murmured, the lump in his throat swelling.

Allison's eyelids fluttered open, and she focused hazily on Brandon. Two tears ran out from the corners of her eyes. "We'll be fine," she whispered, her voice barely audible.

Brandon swallowed hard and forced a smile. "Of course, we will," he managed. He kissed her hand once more before letting go. "You will be just fine," he said, his voice strained.

Yet Allison had been in labor for twenty-four hours with no result in sight.

Allison sensed Brandon's profound concern, and she would have broken down in cleansing sobs, but she had not the strength. Her eyelids fluttered closed over her pale-blue eyes, and she drifted off once more into restless sleep.

Dr. Fletcher placed a gentle hand on Brandon's shoulder. "I'd like to have a word with you," he said, indicating the hallway.

Brandon followed the doctor out, and the midwife closed the bedroom door behind them. Here, the doctor explained that he had tried without success to reposition the baby, confessing that such manipulation only rarely ever worked. He had further tried forceps, but Allison's contractions were both too weak and too irregular to allow for an assisted birth. In between such efforts, Allison needed to rest. Now there was only one alternative remaining.

"We will have to perform a cesarean," he said. "There is, of course, a risk with any surgery; but at this point, it is unavoidable and imperative that we do the procedure."

Brandon's mouth went dry and his head seemed to swim. "Yes, of course. Do whatever needs to be done," he said quietly, as if caught up in a terrible dream.

"William and Annabelle have sent for a plantation nurse to assist me...," the doctor was saying, but Brandon was scarcely able to absorb his words. He could only think of Allison.

The doctor clapped Brandon on the shoulder and told him not to worry.

"Your wife is in good care," he assured. Then he left Brandon's side and disappeared into Allison's room to prepare for the surgery and wait for the nurse to arrive.

An hour later, in the dimly lit upstairs bedroom, Allison was given chloroform by the plantation nurse who then instructed the African midwife on how to administer it as the surgery progressed. The nurse worked carefully to assist the doctor and intermittently mopped beads of perspiration from his forehead.

Downstairs, Brandon was beside himself with fear and worry. He paced and nursed a large glass of brandy, which impaired his overwrought sobriety not one wit. Each minute that passed seemed an eternity. Annabelle, William, Ester, and Jacob all clustered together to lend Brandon and each other support. Brandon felt that he could not have endured the ordeal without them.

After some time, a newborn baby's first cries rang out, and Brandon bolted up the stairs. He met the doctor who, looking quite wan and exhausted, emerged from Allison's room, closing the door behind him.

"Mr. Stewart," Dr. Fletcher announced, "you have a beautiful little daughter!" Brandon's heart felt a tremendous sense of relief.

"And Allison—... how is she?" Brandon asked anxiously, a profound note of trepidation in his voice.

"Your wife is just fine. She's been through quite an ordeal, but she is resting comfortably—she is asleep just now. She can only get stronger from here on out."

"She ... she's really all right, then?" Brandon stammered.

"Yes, just fine," Dr. Fletcher reassured.

"... May I see her?"

"By all means, though only for a short while ... then let her sleep," he cautioned.

Allison lay pale and motionless upon her bed, except for the subtle rise and fall of her chest. Despite the late-afternoon September heat, a soft white quilt was drawn up about her.

The plantation nurse stood near Allison's bed cradling the newborn infant in her arms. The nurse was in her mid-forties and seemed kind and capable. "Your wife is doing just fine," she said to Brandon, her tone hushed as she nodded toward the bed. "Come, hold your new baby girl," she urged, and smiled.

Brandon took the warm, tiny bundle into his arms as the nurse looked on. He gazed down at the infant fast asleep in its swaddling of white linens. This very first sight and feel of his baby girl safe and warm in his arms touched his heart deeply. His eyes welled once more—this time, out of joy.

"What's her name?" the nurse asked quietly.

"Amelia," Brandon said softly. "Amelia Satira."

"Amelia Satira Stewart," the nurse pronounced, savoring the poetic sound. "That's a lovely name."

Allison stirred slightly and murmured quietly in her sleep. Brandon gingerly transferred the sleeping infant back into the nurse's arms and went to Allison's side. Sitting on the edge of the bed, he gazed down at Allison, his heart full. "Dear one...," he whispered tenderly.

Allison's eyes opened slowly to see Brandon near, at her side. She was too weak to move or speak; yet she felt so very comforted by his presence, so very happy to see him. A faint smile crossed her lips.

Brandon gathered her hands in his and bent to kiss her forehead. "We have a little girl."

"Amelia," Allison murmured, then contentedly closed her eyes to sleep as grateful tears crept down her pale cheeks.

Brandon remained at her side until the descending sun shone crimson through the curtain lace, and an oil lamp had been lit in answer to the first evening star.

———◊———

Over the following couple of days, it was decided to let Barry, Carolina, Ashley, and Quash remain at the neighbor's plantation house for an extended time in order to allow for a quiet household at Crawford Hill as Allison recovered and regained her strength. Brandon scarcely left Allison's side, helping to nurse her back to health. By the end of the second day, the color had at last begun to return to her cheeks, and Allison confirmed that she was definitely beginning to feel stronger, just as Dr. Fletcher had promised.

"It is so very kind of the neighbors to look after the children while I recover," Allison said. But she missed Barry terribly, and his absence from Crawford Hill gave her added incentive to get well as quickly as possible. Allison's consolation was in nursing Amelia while she sat propped up on pillows that Brandon and the midwife would plump behind her, helping her to sit upright.

Before dawn the next morning—the third morning after Amelia's birth—the African midwife assigned to watch over Allison during the night rushed from her room and called anxiously for Annabelle and William. She knocked frantically at their bedroom door, rousing them from a sound sleep. "Miss Annabelle! Miss Annabelle! Massa Willem!" she called in a loud whisper, through the closed bedroom door.

At last Annabelle and William opened the door.

"Come quick. Der be trouble," the midwife said, her eyes wide with alarm, the oil lamp she held quivering in her hand.

William strode with her swiftly down the hallway, and Annabelle followed as quickly as she possibly could, given the twins stirring within her plump belly.

"I think she got de fever," the midwife said as they reached Allison's room.

Annabelle moved to her sister's bedside, holding her oil lamp aloft. Allison's complexion was wan as candle wax and damp with perspiration. Annabelle placed her hand tenderly on Allison's pale brow. "Dear God!" she gasped. "She's burning up with fever!"

Within minutes, the household was alerted as to Allison's condition. Jacob was dispatched to fetch the doctor, and Ester was summoned to sit with Allison and look after her. The midwife was encouraged to get some rest, having been up most the night to attend to Allison; and so, reluctantly, she went out, shaking her kerchiefed head and praying in Gullah. William rushed to summon Brandon who was sleeping down the hall in his son Barry's room.

William knocked lightly upon the bedroom door and hesitated a moment before entering. Brandon lay sound asleep upon the bed. William quietly crossed the darkened room and gently shook his brother-in-law's shoulder. "Brandon . . . Brandon, wake up."

Brandon roused himself sleepily. "Ummm … William? … What is it?" Brandon squinted in the darkness.

William's voice was low and calm—but deliberate. "Allison has a fever, she seems quite ill. You had best come and be with her."

Brandon shot awake and left his bed to follow William to Allison's room.

"Jacob's gone to summon Dr. Fletcher," William informed as the two men strode down the hall.

The sun had been up for hours by the time Jacob had returned to Crawford Hill. Dr. Fletcher had been unavailable, away on an emergency call in north Horrey District. Jacob did, however, bring with him a young doctor by the name of Langford, recommended to him by Dr. Fletcher's wife.

Upon first impressions, Dr. Langford—not quite thirty and boyish-faced beneath waves of sandy hair—presented a dubious appearance to the anxious household. After a brief conference with Annabelle and William, he easily bounded up the stairs by twos, his black medical bag in hand. Once in Allison's bedroom, Dr. Langford introduced himself to Brandon, then summarily dismissed him and Ester from the room, closing the door behind them. Turning to Allison's bedside, Dr. Langford surmised immediately that his examination of Allison would be a mere formality; upon first sight, he knew she had contracted childbed fever.

William, Annabelle, Ester, Jacob, and Brandon all waited anxiously downstairs in the west sitting room. Brandon paced and fretted silently as the others sat tensely by. After a time, Dr. Langford entered the sitting room and explained quite plainly what the problem was.

Dr. Langford addressed Brandon. "Your wife has childbed fever—puerperal infection."

"I don't quite understand." Brandon was vaguely aware of the condition but knew little about it.

Dr. Langford invited Brandon to take a seat, whereupon he explained the matter to Brandon and the others. "Since the last century, it has been known that the incidence of postpartum infection can be reduced through personal cleanliness—changing or cleaning of bed linens, limiting vaginal inspections during labor, and not only scrubbing hands in soap and water but soaking them in a chlorinated lime solution before and after examining women who are with child. Yet even to this day, few doctors follow this simple practice. Childbed fever—the result of postpartum infection—has clearly been shown to be transmitted to the woman from her obstetrician, but most doctors scoff at this notion. Your Dr. Fletcher is of the old school in this regard; he, like most doctors, does not acknowledge the validity of this practice, dismissing it as impractical theorizing without proof." Dr. Langford paused thoughtfully, then continued, "And as a result, his patients, I'm afraid, do not always profit by his practices. In Allison's particular case, the baby was breech and a certain amount of vaginal inspection was unavoidable during her pregnancy and labor. I would rule out her cesarean as a source of infection. Unfortunately, her present ill condition could have been avoided; I attribute her childbed fever to the methods that Dr. Fletcher employs in his obstetrical work."

To those assembled before the doctor, it was clear that the tone of his words was not that of a cocky young physician out to besmirch the reputation of a fellow practitioner; his words had been sincere, knowledgeable, and genuine.

"What ... what can be done for my wife?" Brandon inquired soberly.

Dr. Langford spoke confidently. "I will stay with her today and keep a watch on her. It will be a while before I can accurately assess the severity of her infection. Her condition may be more serious than it appears now, but she is young and strong. Try not to worry." His words were mildly reassuring to those seated before him.

Brandon rose from his chair. "I would like to be with Allison, if I may."

Dr. Langford held him off. "I think it would be best for your wife just now if she is not to be disturbed." His tone was gentle and sympathetic.

Brandon nodded his reluctant consent, and feeling somewhat at a loss, resumed his chair.

The doctor addressed Annabelle. "It is particularly important that you do not look in on her, Mrs. Crawford. Current medical theories hold that you could, in your present condition, contract childbed fever from your sister. It's best that you keep away for your own protection."

Annabelle nodded, and William squeezed her hand consolingly. "She will be fine," he encouraged gently.

"Ester, be sure that you, too, remain away from Allison's room, for the same reasons. It is imperative," the doctor cautioned.

Ester nodded, her eyes full. Jacob cupped a protective arm about his wife's shoulders.

Brandon, William, Annabelle, Ester, and Jacob remained gravely quiet as Dr. Langford ascended the stairs to keep his vigil at Allison's bedside. He nursed her as best he could to reduce her fever and more thoroughly assessed her condition by examination. Now and again throughout the morning hours, Allison would drowsily murmur Brandon's name, whereupon the doctor would caress her beaded brow and soothe her back to sleep.

By noon, Dr. Langford descended the stairs and assembled Brandon, William, and Annabelle, once again, in the west sitting room. Streams of sunlight cast a pattern of colors across the hardwood floor beyond the palette of glass objects lining the window's shelves. The three sat attentively before the doctor who paced a moment before them, collecting his thoughts. Then, at once, he faced them, his expression grave.

"I'm afraid Allison is having a rather tough time of it," he said. "The infection of the placental site had begun mildly and asymptomatically over the course of the last two or three days. Initially, despite Allison's fever, I believed the infection might still be localized and manageable. With infections such as this, you see, they begin unsuspected and therefore untended; that is their rather insidious nature." Dr. Langford hesitated and studied the anxious faces before him. He sighed heavily, and concluded, "Allison's infection has spread through the uterine wall, and I'm afraid it has spread into her bloodstream."

A moment of stunned silence pervaded the room. Dr. Langford offered no further prognosis, except to tell Brandon, "Perhaps you should be with your wife now. We shall want to keep her as comfortable as possible until the infection runs its course." With this pronouncement, the doctor had left the prognosis open.

Brandon, Annabelle, and William clung to hope. As the afternoon hours crept past, Brandon stayed attentively at Allison's side. He bathed her forehead with cool water and calmed her with caresses as she writhed weakly in feverish deliriums. Now and again, she murmured his name, lost in some troubling dream. Brandon lifted her hand and pressed the tender, curved fingertips to his lips. "Mend quickly, dear one," he murmured, choking back tears.

By late afternoon Dr. Langford encouraged Brandon to take a break. "Go and take some tea, have a little to eat, and rest a while. You need your strength too," he advised.

Brandon nodded and reluctantly rose to leave. He hesitated a moment and lovingly caressed Allison's damp cheek with the backs of his fingers. "Call me the moment there is any change," Brandon whispered.

Dr. Langford nodded, and Brandon went quietly out.

Brandon descended the stairs to find Annabelle and William sitting worriedly upon the settee in the west sitting room. The late afternoon sun cast stained-glass patterns upon the white walls and hardwood floor. Brandon entered through the open doorway looking weary and solemn.

"Is she——" William did not finish.

Brandon shook his head and managed a faint smile, "No, she's all right. The doctor is with her." Somewhat absently Brandon took a chair.

"I've asked the servants to bring in tea and a bit to eat," Annabelle said.

Brandon nodded distractedly. Though feeling famished, he had no appetite; but he would eat to satisfy the doctor and for Allison's sake.

Footsteps were heard upon the stairway, and in a moment, Dr. Langford appeared in the sitting-room doorway. Instantly Brandon, Annabelle, and William saw in the doctor's expression the news he had to tell.

"I am sorry," Dr. Langford pronounced solemnly. "Allison had acute puerperal infection. ... There was nothing we could do."

His words echoed incomprehensibly to those seated around him. He turned to Brandon, and announced softly, "I am so sorry, Brandon; your wife ... is dead."

Upon this pronouncement Annabelle broke down in great heaving sobs in William's arms.

Brandon rose calmly, and said quietly to Dr. Langford, "I would like to see her now."

"By all means," the doctor allowed softly, and the two went up together to Allison's room. There, the doctor left Brandon some moments alone in his wife's room.

Allison lay still upon the bed, the white quilt drawn up about her. The sun shone through the curtain lace, glinting golden on Allison's waves of hair. Her complexion was smooth and pale as ivory, her blue eyes closed peacefully, permanently.

Brandon sat upon the edge of her bed and cradled her limp hand in his. He bent and tenderly, reverently pressed his lips to hers. The rose blush and warmth of life had not yet ebbed from her sweet lips. Brandon studied his wife's angelic countenance as if to etch it into memory. Wordlessly he replaced her hand upon the bed, letting his fingers linger a moment before relinquishing her hand altogether. He rose from her bedside and walked from the room, passing the doctor, unnoticed, in the hallway.

Reality pervaded Brandon's senses in a confused, bewildered haze. He wondered idly where Allison was—she should be with him at a time such as this.

Within an hour, Brandon could not be found anywhere at Crawford Hill. The coachmen and stable hands reported a horse and carriage missing.

———◇———

Oil lamps were lit in the Big House to ward off the night as it descended upon the land. As evening fell, the news of Allison's passing pervaded the house with a solemnity that touched each heart profoundly. Annabelle wept as a child in William's arms amidst the darkening shadows of the west sitting room. Upstairs, in the attic's turret, Jacob and Ester mourned Allison's passing in a flood of tears and utter heartbreak, even as little Cinda slept peacefully nearby. The midwife, no longer needed to watch over Allison in the night, returned tearfully to her shared slave-cabin quarters near the edge of the woods. Downstairs, the house servants set about their evening duties with grave expressions as they spoke in hushed tones of "poor Miss Allison."

Dinner was perfunctorily prepared that evening, though no one had the desire to swallow but a few bites.

Annabelle ate nothing, but instead retired to her chambers early. She did not look in upon Allison's body; she could not bear to do so. No sooner had Annabelle retired to her room, however, than the first signs of her own labor began. She cried out for William and asked him to send for

Dr. Langford, and to fetch their new house servant, Cotta, to sit with her until the plantation midwife could be once again summoned. Grief over her sister's death had produced the effect upon Annabelle of inducing premature labor, and the unexpectedness of the event frightened her. "Please William," she implored, her eyes swollen with grief yet wide with fear, "send Cotta to me, quickly."

Cotta had been recruited from the fields to come and live in the Big House a few months earlier to help Ester in her final months of her confinement before she gave birth to Cinda. She was young—her age presumed to be little more than twenty, although her exact age was uncertain. A decidedly pretty slip of a young woman with a wide-eyed innocence about her features, Cotta had seemed, at first, as a frightened deer upon being brought to live in the Big House.

Several young slave women had been considered by Annabelle and Ester before Cotta was chosen. She proved to be pleasant, conscientious, quick, and bright; however, it was not only these qualities that won her a place in the Crawford household. It had also been a matter of her conduct during her interview that brought her into residence in the Big House.

Cotta, looking poised to flee at any moment, had stood upon the hardwood floor of the west sitting room before Annabelle and Ester. Asked her name, Cotta begrudgingly muttered, "Cotta," beneath her breath and fidgeted uncertainly. Annabelle asked her to repeat her name more clearly. "Cotta," she repeated angrily, and looked hard at Annabelle. Before Annabelle could begin her next question, Cotta blurted, "Don't wanna be no nigger t' some fancy house servant!" Her eyes flashed defiantly at Ester and Annabelle. The latter two sat in stunned silence. Annabelle, finding her tongue, was about to remonstrate Cotta for her uncooperative, if not rebellious, attitude, but she was interrupted by Cotta. "I is happy workin' in de fiel's," Cotta asserted with enhanced defiance.

"I see…," Annabelle said evenly, a trace of disappointment in her voice.

Annabelle and Ester exchanged dismayed glances, and the atmosphere grew heavy.

At once Cotta regretted her rebellious tongue, and she colored, trembling where she stood. The truth was, Cotta was intrigued by the Crawford Hill Big House and had often fantasized about what it must be like to live in it, with all its comforts and finery. In spite of that, the idea of actually coming to live in the Big House now intimidated Cotta; she felt out of her element and hid her fears of inadequacy behind a rebellious front. Nonetheless, Cotta repeated, albeit with diminished conviction, "I is happy in de fiel's, an' I ain' gonna lib in de Big House." She punctuated her words with a stomp of her foot.

Then, to Annabelle's and Ester's complete surprise, Cotta bent her face in her hands and wept, visibly trembling from head to toe. "I is so *sorry!*" she quavered, her words muffled in her hands.

It was some time before Annabelle and Ester were able to calm Cotta. She sat tearfully before them, and asked timidly, "If'n I come to lib in de Big House, would I get t' wear dem good dresses an' eat better?" She looked damp-eyed from Ester to Annabelle.

Annabelle broke into a warm maternal smile. "Of course, you would."

Cotta looked uncertainly at the two women seated before her. She swallowed hard, feeling as if her very fate now hung in the balance. "Does you … still want me t' come an' … lib here? …"

Annabelle turned to Ester. "What do you think?"

With a knowing smile, Ester responded, "I think she's gonna do jus' fine, Miss Annabelle."

Cotta, unable to believe her good fortune, was rendered all but speechless, scarcely able to utter her gratitude.

"You will take a room in the attic, down the hall from Ester and Jacob's room," Annabelle said, adding, "You may move in today, if you like."

"Yes, Miss Annabelle," Cotta said shyly. "Dat be fine wit' me, thank you."

As the following weeks passed, the entire household fell in love with Cotta. She proved to be a bright presence in the Big House—eager to please; ever grateful for her good fortune; always ready with a smile; and happy as a lark, often humming or singing melodically as she worked.

Now, as Annabelle began her labor to deliver her twins into the world, it was Cotta whom she wanted with her to comfort her in her physical distress, unease, and sorrow. Cotta remained steadfastly by Annabelle's side until both the African midwife and Dr. Langford had arrived to attend to the birth.

By early morning Annabelle's twins were born healthy and squalling, oblivious to the sorrows of Allison's death that pervaded the house at Crawford Hill.

Barry had been sent for the morning after his mother's death, the morning that his Aunt Annabelle had given birth to twins. A coachman had been dispatched to bring Barry home from the neighbor's plantation estate. The plantation owners were instructed that Carolina and Ashley would remain in their care an extra day or two until Annabelle felt more recovered from her labor and her grief.

Barry was excited about returning to Crawford Hill to see his new baby sister and to be reunited with his mother and father. He had missed his parents over the past several days and was eager to tell them all about his adventures on the neighbor's estate—pony rides, chasing geese, flying kites, and much, much more.

Arriving at the Crawford Hill Big House, Barry clambered down from the vis-à-vis and scampered up the front steps of the verandah. He let himself in through the front door to find no one downstairs but Cotta and a few of the household cooks preparing a late morning breakfast. Upstairs the sounds of babies crying stirred the air in the otherwise still house.

Momentarily forgetting proper decorum in his enthusiasm to be home, Barry gaily called out for his parents, "Mother! Father!—I'm home!" His happy announcement was lost in the din of the infants' cries upstairs.

"Massa Barry," Cotta said, "yer father be upstairs, chil'." But Cotta was mistaken. She was unaware that Brandon had not yet returned to Crawford Hill since his sudden, unexpected departure the night before.

Barry climbed the stairs. "Father? I'm home!"

Cotta watched him ascend the stairs, sadly shook her kerchiefed head, and sighed. Barry had just turned seven years of age, and she imagined the impact the news of his mother's death would have on the boy.

Barry knocked softly on his parents' closed bedroom door, and called out, "Mother? Father?" No one answered. After waiting a moment, he slowly opened the door and in the muted morning light discerned his mother's form upon the bed. "Mother? Are you awake?" Barry called out, his voice hushed. There came no reply but for the quiet ticking of a clock in the stale bedroom air. Letting go of the doorknob Barry slowly entered his parents' room. "Mother? . . ." he whispered.

"Barry!" His Uncle William called to him sharply from the open doorway.

Barry turned abruptly to face his uncle, his young mouth agape.

"Barry, come here and close the door," William instructed.

"You'll wake Mother!" Barry cautioned in a concerned whisper.

"Barry—now!" William ordered.

Barry walked from the room and closed the door.

William's manner softened somewhat, and he apologized to the boy for his gruff tone.

"Where is my father?" Barry looked up at his uncle quizzically.

William paused uncertainly, then said, "Your father will be home soon. . . . Now, why don't you go downstairs and have some breakfast?"

"But, Uncle—"

"Let your mother sleep; she needs her rest. After breakfast, I want you to go straight to your room."

Barry hesitated—his homecoming was not at all as he had imagined.

"Can you do that for me, Barry?" William prodded.

"Yes, sir," Barry answered quietly. He dutifully trudged down the hall to do as his Uncle William had asked, wondering why his uncle was so cross with him.

After breakfast, William looked in on Annabelle and the twins, then retired to his study to work on funeral arrangements for Allison.

Barry went up to his room after breakfast as instructed and tried to amuse himself with his toys, games, and picture books. He wanted his father and did not know why he had not come home yet. He wished his mother would wake up and look in on him so he could see his new baby sister.

Outside the Big House, on Crawford Hill plantation, it was business as usual. The field hands had been at work attending to the rice harvest since dawn. Hundreds of slaves were busy shoveling basketfuls of muck and mire, standing thigh deep in mud to drain the fields by opening the rice banks. It was harsh, exhausting work made all the more miserable by the suffocating humidity and the stench of the stagnant fields.

Barry stood at his bedroom window and looked out upon the rich green fields and workers. Above, the sky was a brilliant blue, and the clouds were large and billowing that day. "Dem is cauliflower clouds," Ester would say to the children, "an' when it rains, dat be cauliflower juice!" Barry, Quash, Carolina, and Ashley would giggle. But Barry was not giggling now; something seemed terribly wrong, but he knew not what. With a dejected sigh he turned from the window.

It had been decided that Ester and Jacob would break the news to Barry of his mother's death. They entered his room at midday to tell him his mother had been taken by God up into heaven. They spoke in hushed, gentle tones, coming to the point gradually.

"You ... you mean my mother is ... dead?" Barry quavered, not quite willing to believe the news.

"Yes, chil'," Ester pronounced softly.

Barry saw the truth in their expressions and heard the affirmation in Ester's voice. His lower lip quivered, and his brown eyes welled deep. Never before in his young life had he felt so lost and alone. He said nothing but fell sobbing against Ester, burying his face in her aproned skirts. The boy was inconsolable, and cried plaintively, "I want my father! I want my father!" between piteous wails and gulps.

Later, when he was calmer, Ester and Jacob sat with him quietly, gave him a bit of cake to eat, and told him of the beautiful angels in heaven and how his mother was now with the angels and God.

———————————

Allison was buried in the cemetery adjoining All Saints Church. Because Allison was British, it had been decided that the verses to be read would be derived from the English *Book of Common Prayer*. The minister read from a small black-bound book with gold-gilt pages, "… for as much as it has pleased the Divine of his great mercy to take unto himself the soul of our dear Allison, here departed, we therefore commit her body to the ground—earth to earth, ashes to ashes, dust to dust—in sure and certain hope of her resurrection to eternal life."

Barry's mind had wandered, and he shifted where he stood. His Aunt Annabelle, Uncle William, and his cousins Carolina and Ashley stood nearby. Ester, Jacob, Quash, and Cotta were also in attendance, as were numerous neighbors and friends from the surrounding plantation estates. Barry looked up at the gathering clouds overhead and wondered how much higher heaven was.

"… and she shall dwell in the House of the Lord forever," the minister concluded.

With a gentle reminder from his Uncle William, Barry dutifully stepped forward and cast the first fistful of earth upon the casket. A light rain began to fall, the droplets one by one spattering and beading upon the polished wood. "Cauliflower juice," Barry thought absently, and he gazed upward as if searching the slate-bellied clouds for some sign of his mother. He stepped back from the grave as two great tears spilled from his eyes. Silently he wondered where his father was and why he had not yet come home.

CHAPTER 6

An Odyssey of Mourning

Brandon's denial of Allison's death was absolute. Reality had sifted from his perceptions, leaving only the urgent need to seek out Allison. His thoughts did not seem to run clear—he only knew that he must travel northward to be with her as he had so often done from London to Loxley House while they were courting, and then after their marriage as he had done from London to Castleton. He needed Allison now, for without her he felt an unutterable aloneness—he needed her with him to feel whole.

Brandon left the Crawford's borrowed horse and carriage unattended on the street near Charleston's North Eastern Rail Road depot. Here, he purchased a northbound ticket and boarded the evening train with nothing but a modest sum of money for the journey and the clothes on his back.

Traveling northward, the train stations' schedules guided Brandon through the cities of York, Derby, and finally to Castleton. Brandon comprehended these schedule listings to be the familiar English towns he knew so well; instead, that York was rather York, Pennsylvania; that Derby was but a small town in Connecticut; and that Castleton was actually a place called Castleton-on-Hudson in New York State did not penetrate his bereaved consciousness. Throughout his journey, Brandon ate and slept little. There was but one sustaining force guiding him—he would soon be with Allison.

At last arrived in Castleton-on-Hudson, Brandon took a second-floor room in a dim and musty roadside inn on the edge of town. He spent his days walking the town's streets in the hope of seeing Allison somewhere amidst the bustling crowds. Each day, he returned to his room with some new present he had spied in a store window, then purchased to give to her—a new hat, lace gloves, scented soaps, a pale-blue silk frock to complement her eyes, and a ribbon for her hair. Yet with each passing day, swelling in his heart was the growing realization that Allison would not be found here, in this remote town; he began ever so slowly to doubt if he would ever find her.

By the week's end, Brandon, feeling weary and downhearted, unlocked the door of his rented second-floor room and set out as he had the previous morning. He found no presents for Allison that day and returned to his room at the inn empty-handed. The abject futility of his search and his long, fruitless journey from Crawford Hill seemed to mock him; hope was replaced by a growing, haunting emptiness. His hand quivered as he worked the key into the lock and entered the desolate foreignness of the small hired room.

Brandon surveyed the spare quarters—the yellowed, fading wall paper; the tattered tapestry rug on the scuffed wood floor; the dim, sputtering gaslamps; the stale, musty air; the forlorn, misshapen bedstead. All at once he felt utterly alone. In an instant, reality rushed back to him in a flood of vivid, stark images. The color drained from his face and his heart pounded wildly as he stood transfixed. Images of Allison's lifeless body upon their bed leapt to his mind. His thoughts reeled and he swayed slightly. Allison was dead. His wife, his soulmate, his dear one was dead. *Dead.* The realization was absolute; and yet, Brandon felt strangely bewildered. Why did he not cry? Where was his anguish? His sorrow? He felt unnaturally numb to the loss and went calmly out from the room.

Brandon purchased a bottle of brandy from a shop that sold spirits across the road from the inn. While on his brief errand, Brandon was no longer fooled by slender golden-haired women whom he saw at a distance or in passing. None of these were Allison—she was dead.

As Brandon headed back to his room at the inn with the bottle of brandy, his movements seemed trivial, mechanical, as if oddly detached from himself. "Allison is dead," he ruminated, as he crossed the road toward the inn, climbed the stairs, and again slipped the key in the lock. "Allison is dead," he repeated silently, in an effort to fully comprehend the cruel truth of her passing and impart some glimmer of feeling to the stark realization that she was no more.

Sitting in a worn, overstuffed chair beside the bed, Brandon opened the bottle of brandy and placed it upon the bedside table next to him. Rising, he retrieved a drinking glass from the washstand. The glass in his hand, Brandon caught a glimpse of his reflection in the washstand's mirror. He had scarcely eaten in days and was unshaven. Darkly circled eyes stared back at him, past his pale complexion. "Allison is dead," he thought, whereupon his blood ran cold. Involuntarily he trembled, his hand shaking so that the drinking glass slipped from his grasp, shattering upon the floor. The indelible image of Allison's still body upon her deathbed flashed in his mind. "Dear God," he breathed as his eyes, brimming with tears, reflected back at him. At once the stark reality of her passing overcame him.

Turning abruptly, Brandon strode to the bedside table, hoisted the bottle of brandy to his lips, and drank in great gulps. The alcohol tasted smooth as he swallowed, felt good in his empty stomach, and its effects gradually pervaded his perceptions. Brandy would serve as the antidote to a devastating, heartbreaking reality that seemed all but intent on robbing him of his sanity. Hoisting the bottle upward again, he drank in generous swigs.

With one quarter of the bottle consumed, Brandon extinguished the sputtering gaslamps and sat upon the floor in the darkness at the foot of the bed. Only the sallow glow from the street lamps outside illuminated the room with a dim, somber light casting haunting and misshapen shadows. All at once tears flooded Brandon's eyes and spilled silently down his cheeks. He bent his head and wept brokenly, his face in his hands. Sorrow tore at his heart, and he implored God through his tears, "Why didn't you take me instead? Why didn't you take *me?*" He sobbed bitterly, feeling abject grief would utterly consume him.

After a time, Brandon's sobs subsided, and he sipped from the bottle of brandy in the darkness as stray tears coursed their way downward. Suddenly it occurred to Brandon that Allison must have been long since buried, that he had not been at Crawford Hill to attend her funeral. He elicited an anguished moan of self-reproach and fell again to disconsolate weeping. "I'm so sorry, Allison. *So sorry,*" he murmured brokenly.

Unsteadily Brandon stood as the room spun crazily about him. He blotted his descending tears on his shirt cuffs, lifted the bottle to his mouth, tilted his head back, and swallowed. Desultory self-blame plagued his tortured thoughts. *He* had wanted another child. *He* had encouraged William to use Dr. Fletcher's services. *He* had not been at Allison's side in her final moments. And lastly, he had not been home to bury Allison, to bury his own wife. That the first few self-accusations were distorted beyond truth mattered not—Brandon was convinced that he was at fault for all that had come to pass.

"Damn it! *Damn it!*" he cursed himself, his hand clenched tight about the neck of the bottle. Brandon's grief was immeasurable, unbearable, and his guilt and self-disdain all consuming.

In an instant, his rage exploded, and he hurled the bottle hard against the wall where it splintered in rough shards. Brandy flowed downward in amber stains upon the sallow papered wall.

The bottle of brandy had been but the first victim of his wrath. For nearly an hour, Brandon raged in a drunken torment that left the room a piteous ruin. Amidst the spilled furniture, Brandon at last lay prostrate upon the floor in a helpless fit of weeping. Beside him, the washstand was overturned, its bowl and pitcher shattered on the floor. Upon the wall, the mirror hung wildly askew, its glass fractured. Bedclothes and the down pillow, torn and shredded, were strewn aside in a disheveled heap. The room's heavy bureau had been toppled, and the small bedside table lay smashed to bits in the corner. Brandon was too drunk with brandy and filled with self-pity to feel remorse for his destruction. He only felt beyond hope. What did any of it matter? Existence had become devoid of meaning, as though his very soul had been plunged into a dark, infinite abyss.

Slowly Brandon righted himself and sat upon the floor mopping at his tears with his shirt cuffs as the darkened room swirled about him. Drying his eyes, he half staggered and half crept toward the bed. Drunkenly he clambered to his feet, stood a moment, wavered, then collapsed upon the bare mattress, all but unconscious from drink. The bed spun and shifted wildly beneath him.

"I miss you so, Allison," he murmured tearfully. He vowed, however, not to cry any longer but to sleep. His hazy resolve to do so swiftly crumbled with renewed remorse for having missed Allison's funeral and for his assumed hand in her death. "Forgive me, dear one," he uttered as a fresh outpouring of sorrow wetted his cheeks. "Allison, please come back, *please...,"* he murmured. *"Please* come back to me, *please* come back." Upon this final utterance, Brandon's consciousness ebbed. Darkness eclipsed his grief, and Brandon succumbed to a deep, consuming, drunken sleep.

In the predawn hours, Brandon awoke and slowly opened his eyes to find the room illuminated by a soft golden light. He turned and sat up on the bed to see what produced the strange muted glow. There, at the foot of his bed, was an apparition of Allison holding a slender lit taper.

"Allison!" Brandon whispered. He might have started at the vision, but he felt oddly serene. Cautiously he extended his hand toward her. "Dear one," he uttered as his eyes welled and his heart pounded with joy. Had fate *really* sent her back to him?

Allison did not reach to touch his hand but only smiled. "Brandon," she said gently, "our children need you. Look after them for me."

Brandon moved his lips as if to speak, but he knew not what to say.

"I will always be with you," Allison vowed softly. Her figure receded into the darkness as the golden glow of candlelight ebbed from the room. A profound drowsiness swept over Brandon, and he reclined on the mattress to sleep. Just before he drifted off, he felt the familiar, gentle warmth of Allison's lips press against his cheek in a tender kiss. At once Brandon was at peace.

Brandon did not stir again until late in the afternoon. When he awoke, his head ached and his stomach felt hollow. The room smelled of stale brandy, and the light of day offended his eyes. He sat up on the bed, rubbed his hands over his face, and immediately felt queasy. Bolting from the bed, he nearly missed reaching the bath in time to be violently ill. Waves of racking heaves purged his stomach of its contents but did little to expel the vestiges of alcohol that coursed through his veins. Brandon emerged from the bath feeling haggard and lightheaded, with a gnawing emptiness at the pit of his stomach. He stood a moment and surveyed the wreckage of his room.

Brandon raked an unsteady hand through his hair and ran his fingers over his unshaven chin. The knock sounded again, and Brandon went to open the door a crack to see who was there. In the hallway, he saw the chambermaid with the day's fresh linens and a new pitcher of water. At first, Brandon could not find his tongue—his mouth felt dry, his mind clouded.

The chambermaid, dressed in her prim, starched uniform, surveyed him critically. "I knocked earlier," she said as she surveyed his rumpled attire from head to toe. She looked him straight in the eye. "But I suppose you were ... out."

Brandon took her meaning, but said nothing. For a moment he wavered slightly and looked as if he might faint.

"Are you ill, sir?" the chambermaid inquired, suddenly solicitous.

Brandon steadied himself against the door frame, shook his head, and forced his tongue to heed his will. "No ... I'm all right," he managed.

"I brought your water and fresh linens." She moved as if wanting to enter the room.

"No. It's all right. I'll take them," Brandon said. He opened the door just far enough to take the things inside.

The chambermaid gave a compliant shrug and handed the items over.

"Thank you," Brandon said, his words more slurred than enunciated.

"Sure you're all right?" she asked.

Brandon only nodded, repeated his "thank you," and closed the door.

Brandon carried the pitcher to the bedside and sat a moment, then raised the pitcher to his lips to drink. He swallowed the cool water in slow, cautious sips, feeling he was drinking as much to replenish his tears as to remedy the harsh effects of drink. His tongue felt revived, but the water had the effect of making him feel slightly inebriated once again. The room shifted and spun slightly, and he carefully placed the pitcher on the floor, then lay upon the bed.

He stared up at the discolored ceiling and reflected on the vision of Allison that had visited him the night before. Feeling miserable and wretched, tears again crept from his eyes. As he slept, Allison's words echoed in his dreams: "Our children need you. ... Look after them for me. ... I will always be with you."

———————◊———————

Reparations for the damaged room left Brandon with barely enough money to travel home. The manager of the inn had been furious and all but threw Brandon out; however, the chambermaid was placated as Brandon had given her all of the charming presents he had bought for Allison. Brandon's remaining cash allowed for train tickets and one spare meal a day but not for further accommodation. This hardship seemed not to matter, as he had but one immediate purpose—to return home to his son and new baby daughter.

By the time Brandon reached Wilmington, Virginia, his pocketbook was empty. Consequently, he relied on the kindness of southbound travelers to convey him by carriage the remaining one hundred miles home. The last of these deposited him at the end of the half-mile oak-lined drive to Crawford Hill. Here, Brandon finished his journey on foot.

"Massa Brandon!" Cotta exclaimed. She had been busy tidying the west sitting room and was startled by Brandon's sudden, unexpected appearance. No sooner had Cotta voiced her surprise, however, than she peered uncertainly at the gaunt, disheveled man who stood across the room. "Massa Brandon? ... Dat really be you?"

Brandon appeared pale and unshaven. His rumpled clothes hung loose on his thin frame, dark circles shadowed his eyes, and he wavered slightly where he stood. "Cotta...," he acknowledged as an affirmation of his identity.

It was nearly tea time, and Brandon had half expected to find William, Annabelle, and the children downstairs, yet the house was uncannily quiet, and only he and Cotta occupied the sitting room.

Cotta stood uncertainly with her feather duster in her hands. "Massa Willem, he be out on business. Annabelle an' Ester, dey is up wit de litt'l uns," she said, then hesitated. "An' ... an' yer son Barry, he be at school wit' de other chil'un."

Brandon nodded, too weary and weak to enunciate a response. Momentarily nauseous with hunger, Brandon's complexion turned ashen, and he felt as if he might faint.

"Massa Brandon, is you aw'right?" Cotta asked as she nervously toyed with the duster.

Brandon nodded, and the feeling passed. "I'll be all right. I ... I've hardly eaten these past several days."

"Well, you jus' set yerself down here, an' I'll fetch you some eats," Cotta said, her voice infused with concern. She put aside her feather duster and scurried off to the kitchen.

Brandon did not sit but, instead, went upstairs to seek Annabelle and announce his return home. He found her alone with two infants in the nursery. Brandon stood in the open doorway and watched as Annabelle cooed and cradled one small bundle in her arms. From the angle at which she stood, she looked very much like Allison; but now Brandon's mind was clearer, and he knew it was not his wife who stood before him. Annabelle's black mourning frock confirmed this.

Annabelle did not notice Brandon standing at the nursery door. After a moment, he said tentatively, "Annabelle? . . ."

Startled, Annabelle turned and faced Brandon, the swaddled infant snug in her arms. "Brandon!" she exclaimed, her mouth agape.

"I've come home," he said quietly.

Annabelle's eyes teared with relief to see Brandon home again; and yet, she was troubled at seeing him in such a world-weary state. She crossed the floor to him, and inquired softly, "Where have you been? We've all been so worried."

Brandon knew not what to say, and all he could manage was an enigmatic, "I was away."

"Barry is convinced you would never return, that he would never see his father again."

Brandon looked downward, consumed with guilt.

"He shall be overjoyed to see you," Annabelle assured.

Brandon raised his eyes and glanced at the sleeping infant tucked in Annabelle's arms. "You've had your twins, I see." He managed a faint glimmer of a smile.

"Yes . . . yes, I did." Annabelle's expression turned joyful for a moment, then grew melancholy once again.

"Where is my daughter, Amelia? Is she with Ester?" Brandon was suddenly anxious to see his new baby girl.

An awkward moment passed between them, then Annabelle turned and walked to the middle of the room. As there were only two infants in the nursery, Brandon naturally assumed that Ester must be nursing his daughter upstairs, tending to her elsewhere. Annabelle only stood quietly in the center of the nursery, her back turned to him.

Something about Annabelle's strange silence and manner frightened him. Brandon entered the room from the doorway, and asked sharply, an edge of panic in his voice, "Annabelle, where is Amelia?" He suddenly feared that she had died while he was away.

Annabelle turned and smiled sadly, offering Brandon the warm, precious bundle in her arms. "She is right here, Brandon. Do not worry—she was not taken from you. She has been here, safe with us." Annabelle's eyes brimmed as they sparkled, and the corners of her mouth turned upward ever so slightly as she held little Amelia out to her father.

Brandon received the sleeping baby into his arms, and his voice caught with emotion, "I was afraid that." But he did not finish. He swallowed hard and looked with overwhelming wonderment and joy at the tiny infant asleep in his arms.

Whereupon Annabelle bent her face in her hands and wept.

Alarmed, Brandon stepped forward. "Annabelle! What is it? What is wrong?"

"Oh, Brandon," Annabelle wept mournfully, "our twins ... our little boy ... he died."

"I'm so sorry, Annabelle. When?"

Annabelle looked up at Brandon, her eyes streaming tears. "Several nights ago. He died in his sleep. We found him dead in his crib the next morning. ... We had named him Charleston." Annabelle's tears flowed in earnest; her dead infant son had been given the name that Allison had favored should Annabelle give birth to a boy—it had been a small way to keep her sister's memory alive in the child—but now, he too was gone forever.

Brandon was moved beyond words; nothing spoken could deliver Annabelle's and William's dead baby back into the world. Their loss tugged on his heart as if the loss had been his own. "I'm so very sorry," he at last whispered, his eyes welling.

Annabelle dabbed at her eyes with her handkerchief and brightened somewhat. "But fate has been kind. You have Amelia. And look here, we have little Cooper." Annabelle lovingly indicated the tiny infant asleep in his crib.

"You had best take Amelia," Brandon said, feeling momentarily dizzy from hunger and exhaustion.

Annabelle carefully transferred the baby, as it yawned and stirred, from Brandon's arms to the crib beside Cooper's. Brandon looked down at his daughter and seemed, to Annabelle, to be holding the crib's rail for support.

Annabelle walked slowly to the foot of Amelia's crib and stood close at Brandon's side. "I *should* be angry with you," she said quietly. "We all should. But I am *not* angry with you." She placed a consoling hand upon his. "We were afraid we might never see you again—" Annabelle's voice caught, and she stopped abruptly.

In an instant, Brandon turned to Annabelle and embraced her. Her arms flew fast about him, and the two held each other, drawing strength and comfort from one another. As the two parted, Annabelle insisted that Brandon eat something before washing up and resting.

Downstairs, Cotta served Brandon a modest plate of food to eat and poured some tea into his cup. Annabelle sat across the table's corner as Brandon was served and began to eat. As Brandon lifted his water glass, his hands shook so with hunger that he could scarcely hold the glass to his lips to drink. Annabelle reached out a guiding hand to help him sip. Gradually Brandon's quivering subsided as he ate the hot rice, corn muffins, roasted chicken, and breaded okra upon his plate. He ate slowly, feeling weak and weary. Annabelle looked on in concerned silence. How haggard and aged beyond his twenty-eight years Brandon looked just then. Annabelle's heart went out to him.

Cotta offered to serve a second plate, but Brandon declined, feeling only profoundly tired and in need of a bath and sleep. Nonetheless, Brandon remained at the table some moments to rest as the welcome effects of nourishment began to pervade his limbs.

"I had best check on Carolina and Ashley," Annabelle said. "They are playing on the back verandah. Will you be all right?"

Brandon nodded. "Yes, go on. I'm feeling much better now."

Annabelle pressed his hand in hers and departed to see to her children.

Cotta cleared the table, then she planted herself solicitously at Brandon's side. "Massa Brandon, you sho' dere ain' nothin' mo' I c'n git fo' you?"

"Thank you, Cotta, no," Brandon said quietly.

Cotta hesitated a moment, then she left to resume her dusting of the adjacent sitting room. No sooner had Cotta departed than the front door was opened, then shut hard, followed by the sound of small feet trudging across the hardwood floor. Barry had returned from school.

Barry paused at the open door of the dining room and stared at the rumpled, gaunt-looking man seated at the head of the dining-room table. "Father? ..." he asked uncertainly.

Brandon looked up to see his son.

"Father!" Barry cried, promptly dropping his school books and running to greet him.

Brandon relinquished his chair and knelt to embrace his son who rushed into his waiting arms. The two enclasped one another in a joyous reunion.

"Father! You're home. I'm so glad your home!" Barry greeted, his words muffled against Brandon's shirt.

Brandon held the boy close, filled with remorse for having abandoned his son to face his mother's death alone.

Barry squirmed slightly and pulled away. He looked up at his father, and asked, "Will you be going away again, Father?" Doubt and trepidation filled his young voice.

Brandon's heart was consumed with tenderness. "No, no I won't, Barry. I'm home to stay," he promised quietly.

But Barry looked doubtful, and his brow darkened. A sudden flurry of anger seized the boy. "Then, why did you go away at all?" Barry remonstrated, his tiny voice strained.

Brandon sought to respond, but Barry would not be placated. "Why did you go?" he cried. "Mother died and you didn't care! You didn't even *care!*" he shouted as great tears began to spill down his innocent cheeks. "You left me and mother, and you didn't even care! I hate you! *I hate you!*" Barry wailed.

Brandon caught his son in his arms and held him fast. "No, Barry, *no!* I care about you!"

"No you don't! You don't care *at all*, and I *hate* you!" Barry wailed, squirming desperately to free himself from his father's embrace. "*I hate you!*" he shouted.

Brandon's eyes filled. "No, Barry ... *please* ... you're wrong. I care. I *love* you!"

"No you don't. You're lying!" Barry asserted venomously. He wriggled harder in an effort to extract himself from his father's hold. "Let me go!"

Barry shouted, and angrily pummeled his father with clenched fists. "Let me go! Let me go! I hate you! *I hate you!*" Barry shrilled.

Defeated, Brandon relaxed his hold about the boy. "Barry, please," he whispered, but he did not let the boy go.

"My mother is dead, and I *hate* you!" Barry cried.

The volley of clenched blows and sharp kicks wounded, but the words broke Brandon's heart. Brandon felt that he deserved this condemning reception by his son—perhaps without quite realizing it, Brandon did not turn the boy loose in order to sustain further the vows of loathing and punishing blows hailed against him.

Annabelle rushed into the room, alarmed at the sound of Barry's wails and vindictive shouts. "Barry, what *is* all of this?!" she cried. "Stop this at once!"

But Barry remained in his father's hold, pummeling him mercilessly while tears streamed down his young face. "I hate you! I hate you!" he wailed. "Mother died, and you don't care!"

A loud crash was heard in the adjacent west sitting room. Cotta, jitterily dusting the colored glass items on the window shelves, could hear everything that transpired between father and son; as a result, she had dropped a favorite crimson vase. Nervously she set about picking up the broken glass. "Lawdy, Lawdy," she sighed, her eyes misting, then spilling over.

"Brandon, let him be," Annabelle implored.

In a moment, Brandon set the boy free.

Barry quickly ran away, but stopped at the open door. Turning his tearstained face to look at his father from across the room, he declared angrily, "I hope you go away again and *never* come back! I *hate* you!" With that, Barry scampered up the stairs to his room where his door shut with a resounding bang. There, Barry flung himself upon his bed and sobbed.

Barry's muffled sobs could be heard downstairs. Slowly Brandon rose, then resumed his chair at the head of the table. He leaned his elbows upon the table, his head in his hands, in an attitude of utter defeat.

Annabelle drew near, and offered quietly, "Don't worry, Brandon. I will have a talk with Barry later, if you like."

Brandon looked up at Annabelle and nodded his consent with a heavy sigh.

Annabelle took a chair beside Brandon. "But before I can talk to Barry, you must tell me where you were."

Brandon swallowed hard and stared darkly at the empty table before him.

Annabelle laid a gentle hand upon his arm. "Brandon, how can I explain anything to Barry when none of us knows why you were gone so long or where you were? Please, Brandon, tell me."

Brandon hesitated, and then he looked at Annabelle, his eyes welling. "I had gone to search for Allison," he confessed quietly.

"Oh—Brandon!" Annabelle gasped, then gently pressed his hands in hers upon the table.

Brandon's eyes welled deep. "Without Allison I ... I'm not quite sure where I belong anymore—" He broke off and swallowed hard.

Annabelle took his meaning at once, and she secured his hands more firmly in hers. "Brandon, this is your home; it always will be. You are our family. You are like a brother to William, and to me." Annabelle gave Brandon's hands a reassuring squeeze. "You will always have a place in our hearts and in our lives—" Her voice broke, and she bit her lip to keep from breaking down.

A tear crept down Brandon's cheek as his eyes met Annabelle's, her hands now enfolded in his. "Thank you," he said softly.

"You see, Barry, your father *does* love you very much indeed, only ... he was not quite himself after your mother died." Annabelle was seated alongside Barry on the edge of his bed and spoke in quiet, reassuring tones. She had allowed the boy a short time alone in his room, then went in to talk with him as she had promised Brandon.

"But ... why did he go away?" Barry asked plaintively, sniffling.

"Your father...," Annabelle began, but hesitated a moment. How could she explain it to a boy just turned seven? "Your father," she continued, "was so very sad that your mother had gone up to heaven. Because your father loved her so, he still wanted her here with him, with you, and with your new baby sister, Amelia. Your father could not quite believe that your mother was dead." Annabelle paused as Barry listened attentively. "He went to look for her. That is why he went away."

"But he didn't find mother, because she is dead," Barry offered thoughtfully, seeking confirmation.

"That is right, Barry." Annabelle tucked her arm about Barry's shoulders and gave him a little hug. "Now," she whispered, "your father *does* love you, and he is *very* sorry to have gone away and left you. You really must try very hard to forgive him. Do you think you can?"

Barry looked up at his Aunt, his eyes brimming, and nodded.

"There's a good lad." Annabelle smiled encouragingly and gently tousled the boy's dark locks. She kissed him on the temple, and then rose, and reminded, "Dinner will be ready soon." Annabelle went out, closing the door quietly behind her.

Barry sat in the gathering darkness, his tears silently rolling down in streams. He felt profoundly sorry for telling his father he hated him; the harshness of his words echoed starkly in his young mind. Nonetheless, he summarily checked his tears, washed his face, and readied himself for dinner—he was not about to have his Uncle William, Jacob, and Ester, or particularly his cousins, Carolina and Ashley, see that he had been crying.

William was absent from dinner, as he had not yet concluded his day's business. Brandon's place was unoccupied as well. After a warm bath, he collapsed into bed and slept until the following morning. It had been the first night in many that Brandon had drifted off to sleep without surrendering to grief. Here, at Crawford Hill, in the bed he had once shared with Allison, Brandon felt her presence. And although he lay upon the bed in which she had died, he took comfort in sensing her nearness.

Plates of white china, cut crystal, and polished silver glinted in the midmorning light that bathed the dining-room table. Corn muffins and preserves were served as Cotta moved about the table pouring tea. William, Annabelle, Carolina, Ashley, and Barry, as well as Ester, Jacob, and Quash, were assembled about the table for breakfast. Only Allison's place and chair remained empty.

"Good morning, everyone," Brandon said quietly. He stood near the open dining-room door surveying the breakfast scene before him, noting especially Allison's unoccupied place, then studied his son, Barry, a moment. Brandon did not yet know the result of Annabelle's talk with Barry the previous evening. Now Barry looked up at his father, his eyes wide, but he said nothing.

William broke the silence. "It's good to see you, Brandon. Good to have you home." Brandon nodded and met his brother-in-law's eyes.

Although rested and shaved, Brandon's countenance seemed fragile. No one missed the paleness of his complexion, the dark shadows about his eyes, the way his fresh white shirt and dark trousers hung loosely on his gaunt frame. Yet Brandon's eyes remained on Barry—had his son forgiven him, he wondered.

"Barry's in trouble!" Carolina sang gleefully to her younger sister.

Ashley responded to this assertion with widened eyes.

"Shush!" Annabelle scolded sharply. "Be still!"

At that moment, Barry thrust himself up from his chair and ran to his father who knelt down and received him with open arms. Barry clung to his father and wept. Brandon held his son close, his eyes brimming. He ran a hand through Barry's chestnut locks and soothed, in a voice fraught with emotion, "It's all right, Barry. I'm sorry. I love you."

"I love you too," Barry squeaked, his words muffled against his father's shirt.

"I know you do," Brandon whispered, and held his son tighter.

The eyes of those seated about the table glistened as the morning sunlight glinted upon the tableware. Setting down the teapot, Cotta fled to the kitchen, bowed her head in her apron's skirt and wept.

CHAPTER 7

Dispositions and Churchyards

Two letters arrived at Crawford Hill, both addressed to Brandon. One of these was from Alexandra and contained a note of condolence inside for Annabelle and William that expressed her sorrow over the loss of their newborn twin as well as commiseration over the shared loss of their dear sister Allison.

Alexandra was hard-hit by her sister's death; however, in her letter to Brandon she put a brave face on her own mourning for his sake. "*My dear brother,*" she wrote, "*No matter what sorrows life sends our way, we must remember that in all things there is a purpose greater than ourselves.*" The tone of her letter was philosophical yet deeply sympathetic; all that she conveyed comforted Brandon greatly. Finishing Alexandra's letter, Brandon deposited it carefully back inside its envelope and saved it in the top drawer of his bureau.

The second letter sent to Brandon had been dispatched from his brother Jeremy, now living in Delhi in northern India where he was currently serving as captain of a British military unit. Mail between India and England was interminably slow; consequently, news of Allison's death had not yet reached Jeremy. His letter to Brandon was, therefore, quite ordinary although its content included some special, good news to share with everyone at Crawford Hill.

"*. . . Ranjana is fair skinned and an exquisite beauty, if I may boast. She is one quarter Euro-Asian, her mother being one-half British, one-half Punjabi. First and foremost, she considers herself Indian—from her traditional 'salwar kamis' dress and nose-ring to her long plait of* *dark-brown hair. Had she not helped to nurse me back to health during my bout of dysentery and fever, I doubt very much I should be writing to you now.*

"But better than this, dear brother, Ranjana consented to be my wife. We married in July at the hill station in Darjeeling. We are so very much in love—I am grateful to have ever so perfect a companion in India and in my life.

"Because Ranjana is mostly of East Indian blood, our marriage met with some opposition, as you might suppose; however, we were determined, and, suffice it to say, in result of the matter, military command did not wish to lose one of its most promising young captains. Ranjana is so fair that one day we shall pass quite easily as a proper couple in London society. Euro-asian marriages are not as common as they once were, but I've never had patience with the uncharitable thoughts of small-minded people.

"Regretfully, I must close and attend to drills. With mail so slow— traveling halfway around the world—it seems better to write shorter letters more frequently. Give my best to all at Crawford Hill, and kiss Allison for me. I am supposing that little Barry now has a new sister or brother. We are anxious to hear the news!

"With affection,

"Jeremy"

Brandon finished the letter, neatly folded it, and slowly placed it atop Alexandra's letter in his bureau drawer. How terribly alone he felt just then and wished his brother was not half a world away. Still, Jeremy's good news of his marriage cheered Brandon somewhat, and he resolved to begin a letter to his brother that night after dinner.

———◇———

Annabelle did not approach Brandon about the disposition of Allison's personal effects. She and William had decided that when Brandon was ready, he would pose the suggestion. Meanwhile, neither they nor Ester and Jacob were sure whether it had been difficult or a comfort for Brandon to have retained a wardrobe and roomful of reminders of Allison. Closeted discussions and concerned whispers always resulted in the same conclusion among the four: Brandon should be the one to mention the matter of the disposition of Allison's belongings.

William paused one afternoon from a review of his plantation accounts when a light knocking sounded on his study door. "Yes? Come in," he called, looking up from his papers.

Brandon entered. "I'm sorry to interrupt your work—"

"Quite all right," William broke in.

"I wondered if I might speak with you a moment."

"Of course," William nodded, and solicitously put his work aside as he waited for Brandon to continue.

Brandon desultorily paced a moment, then took a chair opposite William's desk.

Outside, a late-autumn storm blew rain in sheets against the windows. The oil lamp upon William's desk filled the cozy room with a soft golden glow.

"It's about the matter of Allison's personal effects ... her things. ... I'm not quite sure ..." Brandon left off uncertainly. He glanced downward momentarily, then once more met William's eyes. "I had rather hoped that you and Annabelle could help me sort through—" Brandon swallowed hard, unable to finish.

"Of course, we will help," William said softly.

"Perhaps tomorrow afternoon, if it is convenient," Brandon suggested.

"Tomorrow should be fine," William agreed, adding, "I will speak to Annabelle."

"Thank you," Brandon said, his voice so quiet as to be barely audible. He rose to go out but hesitated at the door.

William stood and went to him. Placing a gentle hand on Brandon's shoulder, he offered, "We needn't do this tomorrow, if you aren't ready."

Brandon shook his head. "No ... it's all right" he assured, his eyes damp. "Tomorrow."

The following afternoon, on a wet and blustery late-November day, Annabelle, Brandon, Ester, and Cotta began the task of sorting through Allison's clothes and various other personal effects, deciding what to keep and what to discard or give away. The task would prove difficult and lengthy, not owing to the sheer scale of Allison's belongings but due to the sentiment and memories attached to each item. They had assembled in Brandon's bedroom at noon, quickly realizing they would not finish sorting until dinnertime—if then. Yet this was not a task to be rushed; indeed, it was less a task than a solemn ritual. Each precious item of Allison's demanded its due measure of attention as its fate was being considered. As the hours passed, the four sorted, bundled, and remembered. Memories spilled forth in both tears and fond smiles until, item by item, recollections finally led back to Brandon and Allison's first meeting at Loxley house nine years before.

As the afternoon hours waned, Brandon managed to persuade Annabelle to keep for herself several of Allison's favorite dresses. Cotta inherited three pairs of shoes, which she delighted in—both for their fineness and because they had been Miss Allison's. Ester was equally touched to be given an elegant black woolen coat.

Among Allison's belongings were hats and bonnets, petticoats, dressing gowns, pantalets, two black riding habits, carriage dresses, silk-taffeta walking dresses, evening dresses, shawls, corsets and corset covers, and her several maternity gowns. Inside Allison's bureau drawer were brooches, hair ribbons, silk stockings, three fans, numerous lace-edged handkerchiefs, and an oval locket of silver. Atop the bureau were bottles of scent, a hand mirror, and a wooden boar bristle hairbrush.

Brandon parted with the brooches, ribbons, fans, and other contents of the bureau drawer, but he retained the silver locket; it had been his first present to Allison when they were courting. As Brandon reviewed the contents of the bureau top, he decided to keep the three bottles of scent as well. He had not the heart to pour them out; even so, he knew he could not dispose of them otherwise, for anyone else wearing Allison's particular scents would be too unsettling for him. Most likely, the three bottles would remain as they were, sealed and untouched for some time to come.

Brandon lifted the wooden hair brush and found several strands of Allison's golden hair intertwined in the dark bristles. Immediately his eyes welled, and he tenderly ran his fingers along the slender strands threading the brush's tufts.

"Brandon?" Annabelle studied him from across the room. "What is it?"

Ester and Cotta paused from their folding and boxing, and turned their attention to Brandon.

At first, Brandon could not answer. His eyes threatened to spill over, but he swallowed hard and found his voice. "It is Allison's hair brush ... there are stands of her hair." He could say no more and replaced the brush, with a trembling hand, back on top of the bureau.

Annabelle's eyes filled, and she quickly dashed the tears from her cheeks. Ester and Cotta, with bowed heads, quietly resumed their solemn work.

At that moment, William entered the bedroom. He stood near the doorway, for the room was so strewn with clothes and trunks as to prevent easy navigation once inside. In his hands, he held a small wooden box with a hinged lid. He had come across it in a desk drawer while reviewing the account books in his study, then suddenly remembered that he and Annabelle had meant to give its contents to Brandon. "Brandon, we kept these for you," he said, and crossed the room, carefully stepping about the small heaps of clothes and shoes.

Brandon met William at the center of the room and eyed the small box with some curiosity.

"I'd forgotten until now, since you had been away ... and after all that has happened, well ... Annabelle and I weren't sure," William explained. "We thought you would want to have them."

Annabelle, Cotta, and Ester looked on as William emptied the contents of the box into his hand. Brandon extended his upturned palm to receive what William's hand concealed. William opened his fingers, and Brandon felt two small objects deposited upon his palm. Looking down, Brandon saw Allison's wedding and engagement rings lying in the hollow of his hand.

The wholly unexpected appearance of these two objects seemed strangely out of context. Brandon glanced up at William unable to speak— his lips moved as if to utter a sound, but none came. Brandon slowly, deliberately tightened his fist about the two rings, then he broke down and wept. William's arms immediately encompassed Brandon, and he clasped him firmly in a consoling embrace. Annabelle sank into a chair weeping, comforted by Ester and Cotta. Outside, the autumn storm sent rain in streams upon the window glass.

———◇———

Christmas, 1855, arrived beneath a thick cloak of gray storm clouds. William and Annabelle did their best to put a cheerful face on the occasion. A tree was cut and set in the east sitting room before the wide front window, and the usual preparations were made to distribute gifts among the house servants and slaves on Christmas morning.

As was the tradition each Christmas, virtually all of the Crawford Hill slaves gathered about the front lawn and drive of the Big House to receive special holiday gifts of appreciation from William and Annabelle. There were smoked meats, tobacco, gingerbread, apples, molasses, new shoes, knitted gloves, and scarves. The gifts included portions of rum, as Christmas was one of the few times, as well as weddings, that the slaves were permitted to imbibe. As William and Annabelle dispensed gifts—with the help of Ester, Jacob, their son Quash, and Cotta—there was caroling, dancing, fiddling, and drumming among the slaves yet waiting to receive their portion. Although dispensing the gifts to roughly one thousands slaves usually required three hours to complete, Annabelle and William always made a practice of remaining afterward to watch the celebration on their front lawn.

Annabelle unfailingly took a moment to study each dark face that filed past and was always ready with a warm smile and word of gratitude for each worker's labors. Some of the expressions were hard and bitter in return, while some were timid; however, most were grateful, smiling back warmly and politely thanking "Massa Willem" and "Miss Annabelle." Nonetheless, all of the slaves were grateful, regardless of their exact circumstances, that they belonged to William Crawford and not to Jack Davenport.

"Dere be one Chris'mas dat Davenport, he git drunk, an' he crucify one o' de slaves. Anyhow, he neber gib nothin' on Chris'mas to his workers but de whip," Ester had noted to Annabelle one Christmas. From that time on, Annabelle vowed to spare no effort to give the Crawford Hill slaves a truly prosperous and happy Christmas, as if her singular efforts could somehow compensate for the plight of the Davenport slaves.

This year, the celebration at Crawford Hill lasted until late afternoon, when at last the heavens cracked, and rain began to pour down. Hurriedly the slaves began to retreat to the shelter of their cabins with their gifts of food, rum, and new articles of clothing. Annabelle, William, and the household staff rushed indoors where they would remain for the rest of the day.

"You should have come out with us, Brandon," Annabelle said, shaking the rain from her coat and entering the east sitting room.

Brandon stood at the front window looking out at the windswept torrents. He was lost in thought about previous Christmases and when he first met Allison at Loxley House. Consequently, Brandon did not acknowledge Annabelle but remained gazing out upon the gray and damp—a scene that seemed to mirror his spirit.

"The fire's nearly gone out," William noted as he entered the room. Embers glowed upon the hearth as the vestiges of flames flickered, casting sporadic shadows across the room.

Annabelle looked meaningfully from her husband to Brandon, her expression wrought with worry. William took her meaning; he sighed, gave his head a slight shake, and his brow similarly troubled, tended to the dying hearth.

———— ◊ ————

Brandon had not been quite the same since Allison's death. With each passing day, he seemed to grow more apathetic and aloof. In his work for *The Illustrated London News*, Brandon's artistic endeavors invariably turned to charcoal drawings of Allison. Many evenings, Brandon would sit alone in the dim light of his room producing sketch after sketch of his departed wife as if in hopes of somehow resurrecting her to life through his renderings. No matter how lifelike the drawings, the familiar contours of Allison's cheeks tapering to her neat little chin remained flat on paper, her smiling eyes could not see, and her lips remained silent. In the end, each rendering would be shelved, and the exercise would end in more brandy and another flood of tears.

A month after Allison's death, Brandon had dispatched a letter to his editors in London requesting an unsalaried leave of bereavement. The reply had come by wire that his employers were deeply sympathetic, and they consented kindly, adding that Brandon should not push himself to work again until he felt rested and ready. His position as foreign correspondent would be waiting when he returned to his work again. In the interim, his editors said that they would make temporary use of their Northern correspondents in the states, assigning them to also report on Southern matters, and that Brandon was not to worry.

Although temporarily released from his work obligations, Brandon had little heart for any endeavor. All that seemed to give him happiness was the time he spent with Barry—helping his son with school lessons, or roughhousing together on an occasional afternoon. Nothing, however, fulfilled Brandon more than his Sunday visits to Allison's grave at the All Saints Churchyard.

Throughout the autumn and winter weeks, except in severe weather, Brandon would accompany Barry to church on Sundays with the Crawfords. On these blustery, crisp days, while all the parishioners were warm inside the church, Brandon would spend his weekly vigil alongside Allison's grave. Brandon, cloaked in his black winter coat and black hat, standing alone beneath the bare-limbed trees, presented a piteous scene to the congregation as they filed out of church each Sunday. As the church bells rang the conclusion of Sunday services, Brandon would join the others, treading up the grassy slope—his fingertips numb, lips pale, and shivering with cold. Each Sunday, Annabelle and William would entreat Brandon to come into the church with them and the children, but Brandon would unfailingly decline; this was his time to spend with Allison, and he preferred his solitude at her graveside.

What troubled Annabelle and William most about these bleak months of mourning was that Brandon wholly neglected little Amelia. He could not bring himself to even look in on her in the nursery, let alone hold her—it was quite as though she had never been born. At the start of her young life,

Amelia knew best the hands and voices of Ester and Annabelle—her father was all but unknown to her.

———◇———

Now, on this dreary Christmas afternoon, Brandon remained fixed at the east sitting room's front window longing only to be at Allison's grave. It was his first Christmas since her death, and he felt he must, somehow, be with her on this day.

"I'll go and ask Cotta to make some tea," Annabelle said, and she went out from the room.

William turned a log on the fire, sending up sparks and crackling flames. "Will you take tea with us, Brandon?" William asked, turning toward the window. But Brandon was gone, and the only answer was the sound of the front door closing.

Brandon set off on horseback from the stables for All Saints Churchyard. He rode a cloud-gray horse, which Annabelle had given him, named Endeavor. Overhead, the sky was almost black as night despite the nearly full moon, and all about, a fierce wind battered the trees, stripping away leaves and felling limbs. Rain lashed in violent waves against the Big House and quickly soaked Brandon through. As Brandon turned onto the north road, thunder cracked as if to split the heavens, and lightning scorched the ground. Endeavor spooked, wheeled about, then reared perilously. Quickly Brandon settled the horse and spurred it on northward.

Soon the woods loomed deep along both sides of the narrow road, and lightning flashed eerily in the darkness. The rain pelted so hard that it was difficult for Brandon to see the road ahead of him. Undaunted and determined, Brandon prodded Endeavor to do his bidding. The horse adjusted nervously and uncertainly to the tempest that whipped about them and pressed onward, its hooves splashing along the muddied road.

Suddenly another horse and rider overtook Brandon, abruptly crossing the road a short distance in front of him. Startled, Endeavor reared up noisily, nearly losing its footing—almost throwing Brandon. Twice more Endeavor reared and snorted, hooves raking the air. Brandon held on as if for dear life, all the while cursing and trying to calm the steed. The intruder remained poised steadfastly before Brandon in the pelting rain, blocking the roadway.

Once Endeavor was calmed somewhat, Brandon shielded his eyes from the downpour and squinted in the darkness to see who was there before him. The other rider moved forward to meet Brandon. A hand reached out and stroked Endeavor's neck as a low, familiar voice soothed the horse.

"God *damn it*, William!" Brandon shouted angrily, through the spattering rain and crashes of thunder. His shout unsteadied Endeavor, and William quickly grabbed the reins, holding them fast. Shaken by anger and fright, Brandon cursed William furiously, "*Damn* it! What the *hell* are you *doing?!*"

The storm flailed wildly about them, fierce cold cutting through their wet clothes. Before William could reply, the wind ripped at a huge limb that suddenly tore loose and hurled toward them.

"*Down!*" cried William. He ducked quickly, simultaneously pulling Brandon's coat-sleeve downward, sending him out of harm's way. The limb narrowly missed Brandon and struck a nearby tree with a resounding *thwack*. William let go of Brandon's sleeve. "Brandon, you *must* come back with me to the house!" William warned, shouting to be heard above the din of the storm. He regained his hold of Endeavor's reins.

Infuriated, Brandon spat, "No! I *must* visit Allison!"

The two men's horses pranced agitatedly beneath their riders and hooved the mired road.

"That branch nearly struck you. You might have been killed!" William shouted.

Lightning flashed, and the horses maneuvered nervously.

"Let me go!" Brandon hollered. Defiantly he commanded his horse to turn and gallop off, but William held fast to Endeavor's reins. Brandon's eyes narrowed and shot daggers at William. "Let me pass!" he threatened tersely.

William did not retort, nor did he relinquish the reins; rather, he looked steadily at Brandon through the downpour and dim light with a mixture of frustration and concern. Had Annabelle not so plaintively beseeched William to venture out into the storm to search for Brandon and fetch him home, William might have let Brandon go; instead, William retained a firm hold of Endeavor's reins.

"Let me *pass*, damn you!" Brandon cried out, his voice a blend of anger and anguish. "I'm going to visit Allison. Now, let me be!"

"Allison is *dead!* William hurled meanly. In an instant, William blanched, regretting his harsh, careless words.

Brandon's eyes flashed rage and hurt. "*Bastard!*" he spat. But he was wounded to the quick, and his voice was all but muted by the storm that raged about them.

William's eyes stung. Reluctantly he let go of Endeavor's reins. In an instant, Brandon turned and galloped off, disappearing into the black of the storm.

Annabelle heard footsteps on the verandah and the sound of the front door. She looked up anxiously from her chair by the hearth to see William alone, drenched through and shivering, at the open door of the east sitting room.

"William!" Annabelle rushed forward. "Where is Brandon? Didn't you find him? Come near the fire," she prompted, her words tumbling forth one after the other.

William sat near the fire as Annabelle took his wet coat and laid it aside. "Ester! Cotta!" she called.

Straightaway, the two women appeared.

"Ester, have a hot bath drawn for William. Cotta, hot tea please, quickly."

"Yes, Miss Annabelle," each answered, and scurried off.

William sat shivering near the fire.

"I'll bring some wool blankets for you," Annabelle said. "You should get out of your wet things."

William shrugged. "I'm all right," he said, hugging himself for warmth.

Shortly, Annabelle returned and placed the blankets snugly about William's shoulders.

"You didn't find Brandon, then?" Annabelle asked anxiously. "We knew that he kept wishing he could visit Allison's gravesite today, as it is Christmas Day."

William hesitated, then reluctantly admitted, "Yes, I did find him … not far off along the north road."

"Then, where is he? What happened?"

The logs on the fire sparked and crackled, and William stared somewhat guiltily into the flames.

"William...," Annabelle entreated.

Sheepishly William admitted, "We had an argument."

"What do you mean ... an argument?"

But at precisely that moment Cotta entered the room with a tray of hot tea.

"I done brought de whiskey too, Miss Annabelle," Cotta offered timidly. "Ester say dat whiskey be de bes' thing fo' a chill."

"Thank you, Cotta. That will be fine," Annabelle said.

Cotta set the tray down on the sofa table and went out.

Annabelle turned her attention back to William. "Now, please tell me exactly what happened."

William sighed. "I passed Brandon along the north road intending to cut him off and talk some reason into him, but it's so damn hard to see in the rain and wind. I misjudged the distance and cut him off too abruptly. Endeavor reared and nearly threw him."

"Oh, William!" Annabelle exclaimed.

"Brandon was furious! And rightly so. But I would not let him continue; it was foolhardy for him to go. He cursed me and said he was going to visit Allison." William paused and glanced downward, ashamed. "I shot back at him ... 'Allison is dead!'"

For an instant, Annabelle was speechless. Then, her eyes misting, she scolded, "My God, William—how could you?!"

"I hadn't meant it," he said, his expression filled with regret. He sighed, "Then I let him go."

"Oh, honestly, William!" Annabelle rose and paced briefly. Then she stopped, knelt before him, and laid a caring hand on his cold fingers. "It's all right, William. It went badly. There is nothing to be done about it now. We can only wait and hope Brandon returns soon."

William nodded, took a shot of whiskey, and then sipped the hot tea that Cotta had prepared. Inwardly, he cursed his careless tongue and quick temper.

Ester entered the room. "Massa Willem, Jacob say der be a hot bath fo' you now."

"Thank you, Ester," William replied, whereupon he rose from his chair, and cursed, "*Damn it!* I should go to look for him again"

"William, no!" Annabelle chided. "He's gone too far by now to be found. It won't do any good with *both* of you catching your death in this storm."

Reluctantly William conceded to his wife's common sense. "Brandon is like a brother to me," William said quietly. "If anything happens to him—" He didn't finish.

Annabelle prompted, "Go up to your bath while it is still hot. Don't worry; he will return safely." She said this as much to convince herself as to assure William.

After his altercation with William upon the north road, Brandon had sped off at a furious pace. In his haste and anger, Brandon missed a fork in the road that would have carried him to All Saints Churchyard. Instead, he soon found himself on an unfamiliar route that carried him northwest, into the thick of the woods. Dusk had nearly receded into night, and Brandon could only discern the shadowy blackness of the forest looming about him—the narrow road, rutted and strewn with a wind-torn debris of branches, was barely visible. Blinded by rain and blowing leaves and twigs, Brandon was obliged to slow Endeavor's pace. Half-frozen with cold, and all but lost in the falling darkness, Brandon decided to double back to find the main road. As evening threatened to settle pitch upon the woods, Brandon wondered if he would not soon lose his way altogether.

Thunder crashed deafeningly overhead. Lightning split an oak tree not one hundred feet away at the edge of the wood. Slapping the reins and spurring Endeavor with his heels, Brandon wheeled the horse about and sped perilously southward toward the main road.

A sharp blow struck Brandon's temple hard. Endeavor reared. Momentarily dazed, Brandon lost his grip on the reins and was thrown. He fell squarely on his back upon the road, the breath knocked soundly out of him. Gasping for air, blood flowing hot from his brow, Brandon struggled in vain to rise. Endeavor, neighing shrilly and snorting wildly, continued to rear, hooves slicing the air. Each time Endeavor reared, its hooves descended closer to Brandon as he lay upon the road struggling for breath. At last

Brandon gulped a shallow breath and rolled aside just as Endeavor's hooves came crashing down.

Staggering to his feet, Brandon approached Endeavor and caught hold of the horse's reins. After several uncertain minutes, he calmed the horse enough to gingerly remount, all the while speaking to it through lips numb with cold in soothing, reassuring tones. All but frozen through, his fingers so stiff with cold as to scarcely handle the reins, Brandon guided Endeavor slowly southward through the pitch of night toward Crawford Hill.

More than one hour had passed since William's return to the house, and still Brandon was not home. Christmas dinner would be delayed further—except for the children, who were summoned from their upstairs play for a bite to eat.

"Where is my father?" Barry asked.

"He is ... out on an errand," Annabelle presented. "He will be home soon, Barry."

The boy looked doubtful.

Annabelle stooped down to Barry's level. "He *will* be home, Barry. Now, run along and have dinner with the other children. It's nearly bedtime."

Obediently Barry did as his aunt said.

Annabelle and William waited nervously by the fire as the minutes ticked by, while the storm lashed violently against the house. A crash of thunder seemed to shake the very earth upon which the Big House stood. Spasms of lightning flashed eerily in the surrounding darkness.

"*Damn it!*" William shot up from his chair. "I can't just keep sitting here by the fire. I'm going out to look for Brandon and bring him back!"

"There is no need," a quiet, unsteady voice said.

At once Annabelle and William turned to see Brandon. He stood at the threshold of the east sitting room, trembling and pale with cold, his teeth chattering so that he could hardly speak. Rain dripped from his clothes in pools at his feet.

Immediately Annabelle flew to him and led him over to the fire where she helped him to sit in her overstuffed wingback chair.

William clasped Brandon's shoulder. "Are you all right?"

Brandon nodded uncertainly, his teeth chattering uncontrollably.

"My God, you're frozen through," Annabelle said.

William wasted not one second further in setting out to retrieve warm blankets and asking Cotta to bring more hot tea and whiskey.

Brandon reclined wearily in the chair, too cold, tired, and hungry to speak.

Annabelle knelt before him, gathered up both his hands in hers and rubbed his fingers to warm them.

"Poor thing," she comforted as she reached up to smooth aside a stray lock of wet hair that had fallen over Brandon's right eye. "You've been hurt!" she cried, upon seeing the wounding gash that had caused Brandon to fall from his horse.

Annabelle's expression of utter consternation prompted Brandon to raise his stiffened fingers to his temple to assess the damage. "A branch struck me," he said. But his fingers were numb and clumsy, and he only succeeded in reopening the wound. Fresh blood flowed liberally downward.

Annabelle gasped and blanched. Her expression of horror unnerved Brandon, and he felt momentarily lightheaded.

"Does it hurt?" Annabelle asked nervously as she pulled out a white-linen handkerchief from her skirt pocket and pressed it gently to the wound.

Brandon winced.

"I'm sorry," she said softly, dabbing and gently pressing to stem the stubborn flow of blood.

William returned to the sitting room with an armful of blankets. "Cotta has the tea nearly ready," he announced, but stopped short, seeing Annabelle's reddened handkerchief placed against Brandon's brow.

"He's been hurt!" Annabelle said, her voice sounding tearful.

"I'll be fine...," Brandon said uncertainly.

William draped a wool blanket around Brandon's shoulders. "Let me have a look," he advised gently.

Annabelle moved back as William examined the wound.

"Here's the oil lamp," she said, holding it aloft for William to see better.

"It is more of a scrape and a nasty bruise ... not a cut. I don't believe it should require stitches," he pronounced carefully.

"Let me see," Annabelle said, a note of urgency to her voice. "No, it's not very deep. You won't need stitches." She dabbed the handkerchief upon the wound twice more. "The bleeding has nearly stopped," she informed with relief.

Brandon shivered beneath the blankets. His lips were no longer quite so numb, but his teeth still chattered. He noted Annabelle pouring the tea, and interjected, "I think I could use some whiskey."

"Of course," Annabelle nodded, and decanted some whiskey into a glass, but Brandon's fingers were still too stiff and cold to manage it properly. "Here, let me," Annabelle said, and kneeling at the side of his chair, she fed the whiskey to him in small sips.

William paced a moment, then addressed Brandon, "Are you *sure* you'll be all right?"

Brandon nodded, and said between sips, "No harm done."

William sat in the chair opposite Brandon's and looked across at him with a regret that spoke volumes. "I'm sorry," he said. "I had no right to—"

"It's all right, William. I ... I lost my head. You were right to try and stop me from going."

William glanced downward, nonetheless sorry for his earlier thoughtless words—how cruel and heartless they had sounded!

Annabelle said quietly, "You *do* realize, Brandon, that Allison would never have wanted you to venture out in such a storm."

"No. No, she would not have," Brandon conceded quietly. He took another grateful sip of whiskey and, his eyes growing damp, finished softly, "It's just that Christmas Day was very special to us, to Allison and me." He gazed into the firelight, and the flames blurred before him.

CHAPTER 8

The Studio

"But who will look after Amelia and Barry while you are working? And how will you meet expenses in the city as a freelance writer?" Annabelle pointed out.

Brandon had just announced his plans to leave Crawford Hill with the children and move to the city of Charleston. Still unable to concentrate on his work for *The Illustrated London News*, he had written to his editors in London seeking an extension of his leave of bereavement—he requested a one-year non-salaried leave of absence. It was now mid-February of the year 1856, and in the five months following Allison's death Brandon had scarcely produced a single article for his employer. He planned, instead, to write freelance articles for the Charleston newspapers, *The Mercury* and *Charleston Daily Courier*, explaining to William and Annabelle that living in the city in new surroundings would stimulate him to write again while not having to contend with the pressure of regular deadline-based assignments.

"A boardinghouse room should be affordable enough," Brandon said. "I will hire someone to look after Amelia when I am working, and Barry will be at school. Finances will not be a problem, as I can always find positions as an art tutor to the young women of Charleston society as well as paint portraits for extra money." Brandon presented his plan with confidence to William and Annabelle, although even he doubted its viability.

"You ... don't *really* mean to raise Amelia and Barry in a boardinghouse ... do you?" Annabelle queried. Her opposition was not due to any pretense about social-class differences, but cramped city life seemed a less salubrious environment practically as well as recreationally for raising children.

Brandon sighed and looked from William to Annabelle. "We really can't impose on you any longer," he said, then added soberly, "and ... if I am forced to write in order to earn my way in the world, then perhaps I *shall* be able to write again."

Beyond this, Brandon offered no further explanation.

"It's a foolhardy plan, Brandon," William cautioned, "and wholly unnecessary. You are welcome to stay here at Crawford Hill as long as you like—you *know* that."

A long silence passed between the three before Annabelle asked, "Your mind is quite set, then?"

Brandon nodded. "Yes," he said, his voice solemn and low.

"It just doesn't seem practical—" William began.

"It is for the best," Brandon interjected with finality.

"But you are family," Annabelle asserted, growing agitated with apprehension. "We want you to stay here with us. If you go to Charleston with the children—" Annabelle could not finish. Tears had caught in her throat, and she could not tell him how much he and the children would be missed. Her jaw set, she strode quickly from the room. A minute later the light staccato of her footsteps could be heard rushing up the staircase.

"I'd best go to her," William said, and moved to leave the room. At the door he hesitated, then turned. "Brandon?"

"Yes?"

"Why Charleston?"

"I don't understand." Brandon looked puzzled.

"Why not return to England with the children?" William asked pointedly.

William's insight brought Brandon to the realization of something he had kept buried in his heart all these months, and William's words had the impact of a revelation. Brandon did *not* want to go to Charleston; he wanted to stay at Crawford Hill—yet he said nothing.

William drew near Brandon and clasped his shoulder. "You belong here, with us," he encouraged.

Brandon issued a wry smile. "I suppose maybe we do," he conceded.

"I'd better go and tell Annabelle the good news." William smiled warmly. "No more foolish ideas now? You *are* staying?" he asked with pronounced fondness.

Brandon's smile broadened into a grin. "No more foolish ideas," he confirmed, then asked softly, "William?"

The latter hesitated.

"Thank you," Brandon uttered meaningfully.

William, touched by Brandon's heartfelt gratitude, nonetheless jested, "Maybe now I'll be back in Annabelle's good graces since letting you go out in that storm on Christmas Day."

Brandon smiled at William's jest, then suddenly remembered, "I had best tell Barry we are staying here after all. He has been sulking all morning about our leaving Crawford Hill."

After dinner that evening, William, Annabelle, and Brandon sat sipping brandies before the fire in the east sitting room, which was their habit during the autumn and winter months. William and Annabelle sat together on the sofa facing the hearth, and Brandon assumed his customary wingback chair to the left of the fireplace.

"Since you have decided to stay at Crawford Hill," William was saying, "Annabelle and I were talking about making some provisions for you."

"Provisions?" Brandon looked puzzled.

"What William means," Annabelle put in, "is that we want to give you that old carriage house, the one just behind the Big House. Since it is no longer used, William and I decided you should have it." She smiled pleasantly, pleased with their offer.

Brandon felt mildly perplexed. "I see...," he said slowly, although he did not really understand at all.

William explained, "We had thought long ago of converting it into a guest house one day, but we really haven't the need. So, under the circumstances, we thought it just the thing for you."

"For your birthday, actually," Annabelle put in. "Your birthday is about a week off, but we couldn't wait to tell you—and tonight seemed the perfect time."

Brandon smiled politely; his expression, however, was filled with apprehension. "So ... you are giving me ... the empty carriage house ... for my birthday? ..."

"Yes, you know the one—right behind the house here, to the east of the pond out back," William explained, gesturing vaguely in the direction of the carriage house. "Of course, it will require substantial work to fix it up, but as soon as the weather improves!" He beamed with enthusiasm, and added, "Don't worry, we can always build a fireplace or install a cast-iron furnace—whichever you prefer—for heat in winter."

"And a stove," Annabelle put in quickly, "a cast-iron stove for tea will be no problem, really."

Brandon endeavored to sustain a polite smile, but he gazed downheartedly into his brandy glass. He reflected a moment on all that William and Annabelle had said and idly traced the rim of the brandy glass with his finger. "Perhaps I *should* return to England," he thought—after all, it seemed that William and Annabelle were moving to banish him and his children from the Big House. Their news was all so sudden, he scarcely knew what to think.

"The carriage house is really too small to serve as a guest house anyway," Annabelle noted, "but it should provide ample space for you."

Brandon looked from Annabelle to William. "Thank you both. ... It really is a most generous gift. I'm sure there will be adequate room for me and the children." The veneer of politeness about his words concealed the deep misgivings he felt about the plan.

"You and the children?" William was puzzled.

"Yes, Amelia and Barry," Brandon said, looking from William to Annabelle, then back again.

All at once William burst into laughter, and Annabelle, realizing the misunderstanding, followed in kind.

"Oh no! Oh, Brandon!" William roared.

Annabelle laughed so that tears ran down her cheeks. "Poor Brandon!" was all she could utter.

Brandon was dumbfounded. "I ... I don't understand. ..."

Gradually William's and Annabelle's laughter subsided, and they clarified the matter.

"I'm afraid we got a bit ahead of ourselves," William apologized.

"We haven't put it very clearly, have we?" Annabelle noted to William.

"We don't mean for you and the children to *live* in the carriage house!" William chuckled, his eyes twinkling with amusement.

Brandon looked vastly relieved, yet he could only repeat, "But ... I don't understand."

"We want to convert the carriage house into an art studio for you," Annabelle explained, "your own place where it is quiet for you to paint, sketch, and write—without children running about underfoot and babies crying."

"An art studio?" Brandon's eyes widened as visions of the completed studio piqued his imagination.

"It will take in a lot of good northern light, once we put in more windows," William noted. "That *is* what artists prefer isn't it? Northern light?"

Brandon was all but speechless. "Yes, yes ... northern light."

"And skylights overhead, if you like!" Annabelle enthused.

Brandon was overwhelmed, and stammered, "I ... don't know what to say." He felt he wanted to jump up and hug them both. "It's far too generous."

"Nonsense!" William returned.

"Then, thank you. Thank you both!" Brandon exclaimed heartily.

It was the most animated and enthused Brandon had felt about anything since the death of his wife. William and Annabelle noted this with no small consideration, and it pleased them deeply to see this buoyant change in him.

Renovations to the carriage house were completed ahead of schedule, and the studio was ready for use by mid-May. The north wall was finished in three sets of bay windows with window seats. Overhead, in the high ceiling, were the promised skylights, above which white clouds sailed in a sea of brilliant blue. In the east wall, a handsome stonework fireplace had been constructed, flanked by built-in bookshelves. At the opposite end of the studio stood a cast-iron stove for boiling water for tea and for added warmth in winter. The walls were white, the floor of dark hardwood. A single sturdy desk was installed opposite the hearth, the only additional furniture consisting of two wooden chairs. The remainder of the studio was kept spare, save for painting supplies and a large easel. A single door, flanked by two slender windows, allowed entrance at the south side of the studio. From this door, a footpath led across the upward-sloping lawn toward the back verandah of the Big House.

Upon Ester's suggestion, several slave children of the plantation carpenters collected baskets of smooth round stones from about the plantation grounds and placed them in neat rows along either side of the footpath as borders.

Barry and Quash eagerly volunteered when Annabelle commented that the stones along the path might look better painted white—and, as Ester had noted, would be less likely for someone to trip over. Painting the stones was an afternoon task that soon became a contest between the two boys to see whose row would be finished first. Each supplied with a pail of white paint and a brush, the two boys worked their way steadily down the long rows of stones. At nearly seven years of age, Barry had the advantage over Quash, who was barely five. However, it was Quash who soon realized that he could more quickly paint each rock by dunking it into his paint pail rather than applying his brush. Barry, intent on his own work, did not notice for some time that Quash was now far ahead of him along the path.

"Hey! That's not fair!" Barry asserted, looking up to see little Quash dunking a stone into his pail.

"Is *too* fair!" Quash countered, quickly dunking another stone.

"It *is* not!" Barry fumbled to more quickly slap paint on his stone with a sopping brush. "You have to use the brush, or it isn't fair!"

"Who says?!" Quash retorted, gleefully dunking another stone.

"*I* say!" Barry stood, staring in dismay as Quash worked nimbly along his row.

Quash ignored his older playmate. He had fewer than a dozen stones left and was intent on winning.

"You're cheating!" Barry complained.

Quash did not look up.

Suddenly a foot kicked aside one of Quash's stones just as he reached for it.

"Hey!" Quash stood defiantly and faced Barry.

"You have to play fair!" Barry asserted. "We're supposed to use brushes."

"You kicked my stone!" Quash shouted.

"*So?!*"

In a single motion, without quite thinking what he was about, Quash dashed the remainder of his white paint upon Barry. Both boys stood transfixed in horror, Quash uncertain about what he had just done and Barry in utter disbelief, dripping wet with paint. On impulse, Quash pointed, and laughed, "*Ha!*"

"I'll *get* you!" Barry threatened. But before he could douse Quash with paint, the latter turned and fled with a loud, high-pitched shriek. Barry chased after Quash—his brush held threateningly aloft and paint sloshing out of his pail as he ran. Quash screeched and ran helter-skelter about the lawn, dodging trees and shrubs. At last Barry tackled Quash, and both boys tumbled, panting, to the ground. Barry's paint pail spilled upon the grass.

"Lemme go!" Quash screamed as Barry straddled him, pinning him to the ground. "Lemme go!" he wailed.

Barry plunged his brush into the thick pool of spilled paint upon the lawn and held it menacingly aloft. "Let's see how *you* like it!" he threatened.

"Massa Barry!" An angry, authoritative voice caused Barry to freeze. He looked with alarm to see Ester charging across the lawn, her skirts billowing in long angry strides.

"Massa Barry! You git up dis ins'ant!"

Reluctantly, obediently, Barry did so.

"Good Lor', look at de bot' o' you!" Ester scolded.

"Quash started it!" Barry accused.

Quash scrambled to his feet. "Did not!" Quash said tearfully.

"Did so!"

"Shush-up, de bot' o' you!" Ester shouted. "I don' care *who* start'd *what!*"

"But—" Barry began to protest, but Ester shot him a threatening glare.

"You bot' be quiet, o' I is gonna gib you thrashin's you ain' neber gonna fo'git. Ya hear me?"

Immediately both boys fell silent.

"Now, bot' you behave, o' I is gonna whup you so hard you is gonna think Jack Davenport is a *saint!*"

On first sight of Barry and Quash covered in paint, Brandon had burst out laughing. Using an ample supply of rags and turpentine, it took nearly an hour for Jacob and him to clean both boys. It was decided that the paint in their hair would eventually grow out; so Ester, with a sigh and shaking her head, carried the scissors back into the house—much to both boys' relief.

Once the boys were clean and bathed, it was Ester who saw to it that they apologized and shook hands. And although both boys still smelled faintly of turpentine when they sat down to dinner that evening, Brandon nonetheless allowed Barry a slice of berry pie for dessert, whereupon Ester was obliged to extend the same privilege to Quash.

No one begrudged Brandon his amusement over the unruly episode, each silently noting that it was good to see him in cheerful spirits—whatever the cause. In the long months since Allison's death, Brandon generally remained aloof and somber, and he was frequently prone to brooding. To see a smile on his face and a sparkle in his eye was a rare and welcome sight.

<hr />

No one was permitted to visit the studio once Brandon began his work there. Unable to concentrate on his writing for the paper, he instead began work straightaway on a large oil painting of Allison. It was for this reason that he allowed no one into the studio; he wanted no one to see the work until it was completed. One day, in the near future, he intended to present it as a gift of gratitude to the Crawfords for all they had done for him and his children. But more than this, the studio quickly became a place where Brandon could be alone with his memories of Allison—he wanted no outside intrusions to disrupt his contemplations.

Throughout the summer months, Brandon spent hour upon hour at work in his studio. There, in solitude and quiet, his thoughts invariably turned to Allison. He reflected somberly on the life they had once shared and how terribly alone he felt now that she was gone. He missed having her to talk to, the touch of her hand, the sweet lilt of her voice, the laughter they once shared—her companionship.

Attempts to somehow resurrect her through countless artistic endeavors, each painstakingly rendered in charcoal or pen-and-ink, adorned the walls in frames and stood piled in low stacks upon the window seats. From memory, Brandon had drawn portrait after portrait of Allison—his dear one. He often worked late into the night as the oil lamps flickered low, the charcoal sticks he used dwindling to mere stubs. In one drawing after the next, Allison's eyes looked lovingly up from the smudges of black upon white on each broad page. With tenderness and passion, Brandon captured and preserved her likeness on endless sheets of drawing paper—a particular tilt of her head, the high arc of her cheekbones tapering to her tidy chin, a certain familiar smile or bashful glance. When longing for the pale blue of her eyes, the crimson blush of her lips, the soft cream of her skin, and her fragrant golden tresses, he turned to his brushes, canvas, and oils, rendering Allison in delicate pastels. Her image cast in these soft hues came to be as her very flesh, her spirit, and her warmth. When the various drawings Brandon had produced grew far too real to gaze upon, he would put them sorrowfully aside—Allison's image blurring before his welling eyes. But the one image he could not hide away was the nearly completed oil painting of Allison that occupied the easel in the center of the studio.

An early autumn chill chased away summer's sultry nights, and the calendars were turned to September. September marked two events at Crawford Hill: the first birthdays of little Cooper and Amelia as well as the first anniversary of Allison's death from childbed fever. Amelia's birthday passed unacknowledged by Brandon. The approaching anniversary of his wife's untimely death eclipsed any joy he might have felt over little Amelia's milestone. Brandon's mourning for Allison particularly deepened at this time, such that he could not even bear to look upon Amelia; she took after her mother so—the same blond hair, the color of sunlit wheat; the same pale-blue eyes, reminiscent of England's mist-laden skies; and the same delicate skin, as pure as fresh cream. To look upon her nearly always resurrected Brandon's grief. He had seldom held her or had much to do with her since her birth—and now he all but denied her existence. "If it weren't for Amelia," he brooded silently, "Allison would be alive." It was a thought that haunted him beyond his will to be rid of it, although it sickened him with guilt to think it. If he blamed Amelia, he need not, at least so heavily, blame himself.

———◇———

On the eve of the anniversary of Allison's death, Brandon stole away to the solitude of his studio. He left the Big House after dinner without a word and carried with him a full bottle of brandy. He did not have the heart to join William and Annabelle in the sitting room after dinner for their customary glass of brandy together—he needed to be alone.

"Tomorrow, we will drive up to the churchyard together and take flowers to Allison," Annabelle had said at dinner. Her words echoed starkly in Brandon's mind as he walked the stone-lined path across the back lawn that led from the Big House to his studio. The two rows of smooth white stones, so exuberantly painted by Barry and Quash, seemed to glow in the bright moonlight. All about, crickets chorused unseen in the shadows, and a night-bird sang a low, mournful tune.

Once inside the studio, curtains drawn and door closed, Brandon lit a single oil lamp and set a low fire upon the hearth. Together, the lamplight and flickering firelight illuminated the numerous charcoal and pen-and-ink renderings of Allison that hung framed upon the studio walls. In the center of the room, beneath the skylights overhead, stood the large unfinished oil painting of Allison upon its easel. On a tarpaulin, spread upon the floor beside the easel, lay scattered a collection of brushes, paints, jars of linseed oil, and a palette. Brandon stood before the canvass, uncapped the bottle of brandy, and placing it to his lips swallowed several draughts in quick succession. He knew that neither sleep nor diversion would serve to remedy the hollowness and sorrow that welled inside him on this night. He knew only that he wanted to let the bottle of brandy numb and obliterate the pain of his loss.

Upon the canvas before him, Allison stood posed in her favorite gown of forest-green taffeta. It was the dress Brandon had given to her at Christmas the year before her death. Behind Allison, Brandon had painted flowering hedgerows and the low stone wall at Loxley house. In her hands, Allison held a single long-stemmed rose of pale pink. A faint smile played upon her lips, and her eyes gazed contentedly out from the gentle brushstrokes and canvas as if she could see those who looked upon her.

Allison's image had been captured upon the canvas with such tenderness and loving detail that she seemed all but real, even when viewed in the full stream of daylight that washed down upon her from the skylights above. Now, in the low golden glow of the dim lamplight, Allison's image seemed hauntingly incarnate, as if she had stepped forth from the flickering shadows. Brandon had only to attend to the details of the flowers upon the hedgerow and better match the pale of Allison's cheek to the rose that she held, and he would deem the painting completed. In a number of days, when the oil paint would have at last dried, he would present it to William and Annabelle.

Brandon drank again from the bottle of brandy, and then sat upon the floor, reclining against the wall. There, he sat for some time sipping brandy, all the while gazing up at the painting of Allison. As the long minutes stretched into nearly half an hour, the effects of the alcohol pleasantly clouded his mind, and Allison's image grew ever more real to him in the glimmering lamplight.

Bottle in hand, Brandon rose and stood once more before the portrait. As he did so, he felt the floor shift a moment beneath his feet—the brandy was having its desired effect, its pleasant warmth and numbing pervading his limbs and senses. Brandon swallowed heartily from the bottle, then blotted his lips on the cuff of his shirtsleeve. Allison looked on, smiling tenderly at him from the shadows.

Brandon's eyes welled deep as he gazed at her lifelike image. His heart ached for her to actually be there, to be real and near to him. The brandy warmed him from within and taunted his vulnerable perceptions. Perhaps Allison *was* real ... perhaps all he must do is simply utter her name and she would mystically transform from paint and canvas to whole, warm, and real before him. The play of shadow and flickering light upon the canvas teased his clouded mind as his welling eyes blurred her image, and he let the delusion of drink have its way with him.

"Allison? ..." Brandon whispered tentatively, "... Allison?" There came no answer, and Allison remained motionless and silent upon the canvas.

Languidly two rivulets of tears traced the arcs of Brandon's cheeks. How could she not have answered him? How could she not come to him?

Despite his haze of intoxication, Brandon realized the hollow error of his delusion. His eyes welled deeper, and he brushed a tear aside with the back of his hand. Allison was dead. "Tomorrow, we will drive up to the churchyard together...," Annabelle had said. Nothing would ever bring Allison back to him—nothing.

Brandon lifted the bottle once more. The brandy was nearly half-finished, and the room seemed to whirl uncertainly about him as he tilted his head back and swallowed several more draughts. Blotting his wet lips on his shirt cuff and standing somewhat waveringly before the easel, Brandon surveyed the lifeless portrait before him.

Hazily Brandon remembered that the pale of Allison's cheek did not quite complement the hue of the rose in her hands. With great concern, Brandon determined to correct the error. Setting the bottle unsteadily on the hardwood floor, he retrieved from his disarray of supplies at the easel's base his palette and a slender tapered brush. Carefully drawing near the canvas, Brandon wetted the tip of the fine brush in linseed and a smudge of pale pink. "I must fix this, dear one," he slurred. Ever so tenderly he traced the arc of Allison's cheek with the wetted tip. As he did so, his eyes flooded with tears, obliging him to withdraw the brush and put aside both it and the palette. He stood trembling before Allison's image now clouded by his welling eyes.

"Oh! ... Allison!" he uttered brokenly, and sank to his knees, letting his sorrow pour forth in a flood of hot tears. He lifted his eyes to the canvas. "Allison, why? Dear one—*why*?" he beseeched the darkness. "Why did you leave me? Why did you have to die?" Brandon sobbed disconsolately, mopping his hot flood of tears upon his shirtsleeves. "I love you. ... I *love* you, Allison. And what of our children? ... How could you leave us? ..." he wept. He felt unspeakably lost and alone. The stark, bleak reality of Allison's death profoundly overwhelmed him to his very core, and he gave himself over to anguished, racking wails.

Consumed by grief, Brandon knelt upon the floor sobbing. He possessed neither the strength nor will for anything but abject mourning, as his heart felt shattered into unsalvageable bits. All seemed hopelessness and utter desolation, as if all meaning had been torn from his existence. Suddenly he longed to be dead too—to pass beyond his world of emptiness and sorrow, to dwell with Allison in the unseen reality beyond. He yearned for her so—all else was emptiness and despair.

After a time, weeping quietly and mopping at his tears, Brandon looked up once more at the painting upon its stand. "Why did you *leave* us?" he pleaded.

But Allison did not answer. She merely smiled down at him contentedly, oblivious to his grief.

Stemming his tears, Brandon rose to his feet and stood quietly before the painting. Before he quite knew what he was about, he lifted an unsteady hand and slowly raked his fingers through the wet oil paint, obliterating Allison's image. "Don't look at me, Allison," he uttered brokenly. "Don't look at me. Please don't see me like this." Again and again, he raked his fingers through the paint as his eyes welled deeper and deeper, until Allison's image was rendered nothing more than a blurred smear of muddied oils. "I don't want you to see me like this," he wept. He staggered backward and blinked through damp lashes to view Allison's image once more.

Only then did Brandon comprehend the horror of his destruction of the beloved painting. His heart pounded wildly and his blood turned to ice in his veins. Trembling so that he could scarcely stand, Brandon felt that his senses hung by a slender thread, and he knew not what prevented his mind from flying hopelessly into bits.

Then, in an instant, his grief transformed to anger. "Damn you! *Damn* you, Allison! Why did you leave?!" Brandon cried out in anguish. He swallowed once more in generous gulps from the bottle of brandy. "You had *no* right to leave! *Damn* you!" he cursed.

Brandon looked about him at the array of Allison's portraits upon the walls. All were smiling with placid unconcern, as if mocking his torment. She had abandoned him, and now she did not care. From every wall, Allison's unconcerned images silently taunted him in the glimmering firelight.

"Bloody *hell*, Allison! To bloody *hell* with you!" he shouted as he angrily hurled the bottle of brandy toward the far wall, nearly losing his footing as he did so. The bottle shattered against a portrait, splintering the glass pane within its frame, the amber fluid running in rivulets down the wall.

In that instant, Brandon's tortured sensibilities also shattered. In a blind rage, Brandon lunged at the portraits, pulling them from the walls, splintering the glass, breaking the frames, and tearing each image to bits. Cursing Allison and weeping, he charged wildly about the studio, smashing and shredding one portrait after another, oblivious to the sharp fragments of glass cutting his hands. Torn and crumpled bits of paper, stained red with blood, lay strewn across the hardwood floor alongside the twisted, splintered remnants of frames. Broken glass crunched underfoot, glittering in the firelight. At last the walls were bare—not a single image of Allison remained.

Drunk and anguished beyond reasoning, scarcely aware of the bleeding lacerations across his hands and wrists, Brandon gathered up the remaining stacks of charcoal and ink renderings from the window seats. Weeping and sniffling, he carried them in a disheveled armload toward the hearth. "I'm glad you're dead, Allison! May you burn in *hell!*" he wailed, cursing Allison bitterly and casting the drawings upon the lapping flames. Brandon stood trembling before the swelling inferno, watching the edges of the paper curl and blacken as the fire consumed them. "I wish you were *me*, Allison. I wish you were *me!*" For her to bear forever, with full force, his grief and wretched torment was what she deserved. "I wish you were *me* and I was *dead!*" he wept.

Yet no sooner had Brandon so venomously uttered these words than his heart all at once melted with remorse. How could he *ever* wish such torment upon Allison—upon his dear one?

In an instant, the plain realization of what he had just done clutched at Brandon's heart, whereupon he elicited an anguished sob and dropped to his knees before the hearth. Hot tears spilled down unchecked. Brandon bowed his head and clutched at his chestnut locks with bloodied hands. "Oh, God! Oh, *Allison!* Allison, please forgive me. I didn't mean it, dear one. I didn't mean it," Brandon sobbed haltingly. "Please forgive me, Allison—I love you so *very* much. I love you," he murmured through his tears, his voice scarcely audible. Upon that utterance, he lay prostrate upon the floor in racking sobs until he could cry no more.

At once Brandon knew he could not be alone any longer—he could not endure it. Mopping his eyes and sniffling, he slowly struggled to his feet as the room spun wildly, the floor undulating beneath him. Brandon careened out of the studio, stumbling over the neat row of glowing white stones along the footpath. As he crossed the lawn toward the shadow of the Big House, the stars overhead madly circled and spun, then dropped from the sky. Brandon's legs turned to water, and he sank unconscious upon the grass.

"Massa Willem! Massa Willem!" Cotta pounded urgently upon William and Annabelle's closed bedroom door. "Miss Annabelle! Massa Willem! Come quick, der be trouble!"

William appeared at the door, bleary eyed and dressed in his robe and nightclothes. Annabelle was fast behind him.

"What is it, Cotta? What's wrong?" William asked.

"It be Massa Brandon. Der be somethin' dreadful wrong!" Cotta's manner was fearful and grave, and she wrung her hands with worry. "Come wit' me—quick!" she said, and turned, William and Annabelle following close behind.

Cotta led them downstairs to the back verandah where she paused and pointed to a place a short distance across the lawn. Fear clutched her heart as she did so, and her arm quivered as she indicated the place where Brandon's body lay supine and pale upon the grass.

Annabelle gasped, her hand to her mouth, as she rushed down the steps of the verandah and across the grass, her robe flowing behind her. William and Cotta followed close at her heels.

The early-morning sun streamed amber across the dew-beaded lawn, and there, among the damp, tender blades, lay Brandon—pale and motionless.

"Oh, sweet Jesus, don' let Massa Brandon be dead," Cotta uttered, and stood with her folded hands pressed to her lips, her young brow furrowed with worry.

Annabelle and William knelt down in the damp grass beside Brandon.

"Is ... is he all right?" Annabelle asked, her voice fraught with alarm. Secretly she feared Cotta's prayer was too late, and she looked at William anxiously.

William said nothing but in a moment determined that Brandon—despite all appearances—was indeed alive. Annabelle sighed with profound relief, and Cotta, glancing upward, whispered her fervent gratitude.

"Cotta, run back to the house and boil water for tea—lots of it. Tell Jacob to send for the plantation physician, Dr. Langford."

"Yessuh, Massa Willem!" Cotta turned and ran quick as she could back to the Big House.

At that moment, Brandon moaned quietly and blearily opened his eyes. The ground beneath him was unsteady, and the morning sun, gleaming golden, sought to blind him. Brandon's lips moved as if to speak but formed no words. His eyelids fluttered closed, and with a low moan, he slipped again into unconsciousness.

William lifted Brandon up to carry him into the house, and as he did so, Annabelle cried out, "My God! His hands!" Her eyes were wide with horror, and she clasped her hands to her mouth. "William, his ... his hands!"

"Jesus!" William breathed, noting the limp, curled fingers of Brandon's hands crusted in dried blood and swollen with innumerable lacerations, and splotches of red staining the white cloth of his shirt cuffs. "Jesus!" he uttered, his expression wrought with unease. He strode swiftly, carrying Brandon across the lawn toward the house, Annabelle fast at his side.

By afternoon, Brandon had awakened. He lay propped up on three plump pillows, beneath the coverlets of his bed. His injured hands were wrapped thick in bandages of white gauze. Annabelle sat on the edge of the bed and fed Brandon sips of hot tea as William paced, then sat upon a wooden chair and issued a heavy sigh.

Dr. Langford snapped his black medical bag closed. "It is a miracle that only ten stitches were required. You were fortunate, Brandon." He paused for a moment, then asked, "Are you *sure* you don't recall how this accident to your hands occurred?"

Brandon felt as if his body had been resurrected from death. His head ached in dull, pulsing throbs, and Annabelle's tea did little to calm his hollow, angry stomach. Brandon hazily recollected only vague, nightmarish images—the reality of which seemed uncertain. "No, I ... I don't remember how it happened," he answered the doctor quietly.

"Well, then." Dr. Langford took his medical bag in hand and moved to leave. "I will be back in a number of days to remove the stitches. Meanwhile, keep the dressings clean, dry, and changed often." He indicated Brandon's swaddled hands that lay idle and useless atop the coverlets.

Annabelle put the teacup upon the side table and rose to escort the doctor out. Once they had left the room, William rose and paced thoughtfully, stopping at the foot of the bed. He surveyed Brandon in concerned silence. The latter gazed absently at his bandaged, useless hands as his head pounded, his stomach felt raw, and his body thirsted for more tea.

"An *entire* bottle of brandy?" William asked.

Brandon looked up and met his brother-in-law's eyes. "Nearly so," he uttered, his tongue thick, "three quarters, I think. I don't remember." Brandon's eyes fell once again to his bandaged hands.

William sighed. He walked to the side of the bed and sat on its edge. "Brandon—" He hesitated, then admonished quietly, "Dr. Langford said that if you were trying to kill yourself, it was considerate of you to attend to your own embalming in the process."

Brandon looked up from his swaddled hands. "He said that, did he?" he enunciated softly.

William nodded, his brow knit with deep concern. A brief silence passed between them, then he asked, "Were you trying to—"

"No, of course not." Brandon's voice was a hushed whisper. He glanced down at his bandaged hands, then his eyes met William's. "It's just that...," he faltered, and swallowed the lump welling in his throat. "It's just that it's been so hard," he managed, his voice strained with emotion, "all these months ... without Allison ... and now it's been one year since—"

With that Brandon broke down and wept. William held him close, and his own eyes grew damp.

"There, there, now," William consoled, his voice low and gentle. He knew of no words—no adequate words—for Brandon's utter heartbreak and loss. "There, there ... everything will be all right ... everything will be all right," he soothed as Brandon wept, his bandaged hands held fast around William.

"Soon de weather be too col' fo' flowers," Cotta said, placing a vase—tall, with white blossoms—on a window seat in the studio. Cotta had already placed one vase of flowers on the hearthstone and another on Brandon's desk. Cotta stood back and surveyed her adornments to the studio with satisfaction, not really minding that no one seemed to notice her efforts. Jacob was busy cleaning the ashes from the fireplace while Ester worked to scrub the blood stains from the floor with a shallow basin of peroxide.

But Annabelle looked up from sweeping the bits of broken glass into a heap on the hardwood floor. "The flowers are lovely, Cotta. Brandon will be quite pleased."

Cotta smiled modestly, her hands clasped behind her back, imagining how cheered Massa Brandon would be to see the studio made tidy once again—and brightened with fresh flowers.

"Cotta? Please come hold the dustpan for me."

"Yes'm" Cotta said, and left her pleasant reverie to help her mistress. She stooped to hold the metal dust pan.

Be careful not to cut your hands," Annabelle cautioned.

"Yes'm."

Annabelle carefully swept the straw bristles forward, depositing a small heap of broken glass into the pan. This, Cotta dutifully deposited in the wooden waste barrel.

Although it was only three days since Brandon had been found by Cotta, unconscious upon the back lawn, he had announced that he intended to begin writing again—and so, the studio was being made ready.

"It is what Allison would have wanted, and I believe it is what I must do," Brandon had told William. He yearned to feel productive once again, to illustrate and write, to immerse himself in his work. He yearned for a healthy sense of normalcy to return to his life and missed his familiar routine of contribution and accomplishment through work. Even with bandaged hands, Brandon found he could manage a pen well enough to write. "I must let go of the past. It's time I return to work," he had announced, this time with a conviction in his tone not heard before.

Brandon's harrowing night of inebriated near madness had served to waken him from a year of sorrow and brooding. For the first time since

Allison's death, Brandon began to feel whole again. He felt possessed of a new inner strength and calm. He resolved that he must live mindful of Allison's spirit always with him, at his side. The future no longer loomed threateningly bleak and empty before him. It was the joy and light that Allison had once brought him that would sustain him now—he would cling to that.

Brandon stood before his bureau and, with bandaged hands, opened the top drawer. From inside he withdrew Allison's silver locket in which he had carefully tucked away several fine strands of her hair. Cradling the oval locket in the white gauze of his bandaged fingers, Brandon murmured, "I shall always love you, dear one." His eyes misted. He kissed the locket and slipped its long silver chain about his neck where he silently vowed to wear it always near his heart and until his death. He slid the bureau drawer closed and fingered the locket beneath his shirt, feeling its metal casing warm against his skin.

With that, Brandon went out of the room, out of the house, and walked down the back footpath, neatly bordered with smooth white stones, to the studio.

CHAPTER 9

Mutiny

"There exists a tenuous balance of power between North and South that signifies a system of symbiosis—the living together of two dissimilar organisms in close association or union, particularly where this is advantageous to both. In the case of a fungus and an alga, their symbiotic relationship together forms the lichen. In the case of North and South, their union synergistically forms America and all her essential power as one nation among many. However, this symbiosis between North and South is not a strict mutualism, for in point of fact, it omits over twenty percent of the nation's population—a disadvantaged portion of the American population.

"This disadvantaged population is that of the African-American slave. With two such disparate socioeconomic entities—namely, North and South—in cohabitation, many speculate as to how much longer such a mutual tolerance can endure. Already, there are signs surfacing of nasty divorce. An integral element of this growing rift between Northern and Southern socioeconomic ideologies and systems is, in fact, the America slave population. Northern abolitionists contend that the institution of slavery is essentially morally wrong. Yet the Southern slaveholder contends that the institution of slavery remains, at best, a regrettable but inextricable cog in their largely agrarian socioeconomic way of life. To a Northern abolitionist writing in, perhaps, William Lloyd Garrison's paper—*The Liberator*—the issue of slavery distills down to a moral imperative. To a staunch Southern slaveholder, the issue of slavery is purely one of economics, culture, and social class.

"Still, it must be remembered abroad that not all Southerners and

Northerners are overzealous extremists; more temperate views are to be found on both sides of the ideological fence. It must be emphasized that some Southern slaveholders do view slavery as an unfortunate-but-necessary evil—albeit, a view of little practical consolation to the African slave. And there is at least one slave holder in All Saints Parish, Georgetown District in South Carolina who believes that slavery, in all its aspects, should be federally regulated by a system of humanitarian reform measures and gradually phased out over time while assimilating the slave to independence through education and occupational training. Needless to say, such rather more patient and temperate views as this latter one receive little if any contemplation by either the majority of Southerners or by abolitionists. Meanwhile, the rift between North and South—ideological, socioeconomic, and political—continues to stretch wider.

"That North and South, in at least some respects, are approaching a parting of the ways is not an entire surprise. Since 1820 to date, the South has been growing increasingly apart from the North. Many fear that, as with all things, what is stretched too far will eventually and inevitably sever. Some further believe that this severing of the ways is growing close at hand as the ever-widening rift takes on political overtones. To find evidence of this, one only needs to read John C. Calhoun's *The Southern Carolina Exposition and Protest*, which purports that states should have the right to reject federal laws that they deem unconstitutional. One can easily see the purpose behind a political push for such legislation: the South is determined to preserve its way of life, its society and culture, its largely agrarian economy, and—vitally important to these—its system of slavery. The South depends on slave labor to produce agricultural surpluses for sale abroad and to the Northern states. In the South, moral imperatives have little or no currency when it comes to the issue of slavery.

"Indeed, it seems that the South itself has become a slave to the system of slaveholding that it has created and preserved for generations. One may ask, at what cost will the South continue to defend and preserve this system? Equally difficult to envision is how the South would ever extricate itself from either its system of slavery or, as many predict, its arguably inevitable political divorce from the North. As the tenuous balance of power between

North and South continues to be tested, one can only speculate. Is theirs a symbiosis that can last?

"Brandon Jonathan Stewart—1857, for *The Illustrated London News*"

"Well, here it is." Brandon paused and leaned back in his chair. "Now, remember, it is only the first draft," he cautioned, handing William the two handwritten pages.

William took the proffered article and stood reading it with interest. As William read, Brandon waited anxiously, toying idly with his pen. Finishing the article, William bore a quizzical expression. "So ... which are we?" William repeated the question, tapping the top half of the paper with his finger.

Brandon rose, pen in hand, and stood beside William. "I'm sorry, I don't take your meaning."

"Here, you see? In this first paragraph. Which is the South? Fungus or alga?"

Brandon issued an amused sigh and, shaking his head, snatched the pages out of William's hand. "This is serious!" he said, although he too broke into a grin at least as broad as William's.

William chuckled. "And so, do you mean to imply that you want my opinion again?"

Playing gamely along, Brandon sat wearily upon his desk chair, feigned a labored sigh, and bemoaned, "The effort we journalists must go through to preserve the integrity of our work!" His tone and expression were those of mock martyrdom.

William laughed and retrieved the papers from Brandon's grasp. "All right, seriously," he said, and began to quickly review the article. As he scanned the pages, he jested, "You know you will have to put me on salary soon."

"—Ummm, I'll check with my editors," Brandon replied dryly.

William looked up from the rough draft. "Why should you need editors when you have me and my esteemed opinion?"

"Get out!" Brandon laughed, and hurled his pen at William.

"Hey!" William warned playfully, all but ignoring the pen that struck him and clattered to the floor.

With that, Brandon sat quietly and let William review the paper.

"Your article seems fair enough," William pronounced, when he was through. "It seems an accurate enough representation of both the abolitionist and proslavery views ... though you might want to mention escalating political tensions and controversy over expanding slavery into the Western territories," he noted, then thought a moment. "But I take it, this is to be a short article?"

Brandon retrieved his pen from the floor. "Or I may extend it. But it is one of a series, and I don't believe it would be suited to being a front-page piece."

"I see." William looked thoughtful, then suggested, "There is one problem I see with it. Perhaps it overly portends an ultimate rift between North and South."

Brandon considered this a moment. "Do you think I am sensationalizing, embellishing upon the situation?"

Glancing upward, William reflected briefly, then shook his head. "No, no ... I suppose not. You do have a solid foundation upon which to build your premise of an increasing disparateness." William shrugged. "In truth, who *can* see what the future will hold. And I am sure you're correct in your assessment of the true purpose behind John C. Calhoun's paper—a preparative measure of legislation to preserve the status quo of the South."

"No glaring inaccuracies, then? A fair representation?"

"Quite good!" William handed the pages back to Brandon. "Quite good, I *must* say!"

"Why, *thank* you!" Brandon returned in mock politeness.

"At least," William noted, "a balanced view can be found in the newspapers from time to time. I find the majority of more vocal abolitionists to be mainly a lot of rabble-rousers—a fringe element of their movement."

"People like John Brown?" It was common knowledge that Brown advocated and practiced armed insurrection as a means to abolish slavery; he and his supporters had killed five proslavery Southerners just the year before, in May of 1856, in what became known as the Pottawatomie Massacre.

"Yes, I suppose so. Versus those abolitionists of Garrison's caliber. Either way, whether we are considering either a more central or a fringe element of the abolitionist movement, their cause is, nonetheless, a threat to the South."

Brandon sat thoughtfully and drummed his pen on the desktop. "Meanwhile, the Democratic Party struggles to maintain unity between its Northern and Southern wings—despite their rift growing wider—in an effort to preserve their party's power in Congress. The South needs to keep enough representation in Congress to garner sufficient votes to block any undesirable legislation—be it political, ideological, social, or economic. Even power within the Democratic Party is, by definition, divided."

"Between North and South."

"Exactly," Brandon nodded.

William sighed and grew serious. "The rift is growing; you are right."

"And the abolitionists—though I *do* believe morally right—fuel the growing division," Brandon noted, "as you often say, by demagoguing the issue."

William shook his head dejectedly. "And here I am, caught in the middle between staunch slavery-at-any-cost Southerners as one extreme and over-zealous abolitionists as the other extreme."

"Yes, and the majority of abolitionists seem to believe that all slaveholders are like Jack Davenport—cruel and merciless, treating their slaves as less than human, as mere commodities to be used and abused, and bought and sold like mere chattel, then at death to be discarded as cheaply as possible." Brandon's expression darkened with marked disdain.

"There are, however, far too many slaveholders like Jack Davenport, though heaven knows—or I *should* say, Satan knows—that Davenport is an extremist."

"He *is* that—a *wretched* extremist." Brandon shook his head and sighed.

A reflective silence passed between the two men.

Brandon rose from his chair. "And what of this recent Supreme Court verdict over the Dred Scott case? Scott lived as a *free* man under the ruling of the Missouri compromise. Then the Kansas-Nebraska Act was pushed through Congress, giving territories the right to choose unilaterally whether to be free or slaveholding. Under this new act, Dred Scott lost his status as a free man and was legislatively deemed a slave. He sued to reclaim his freedom and lost to a Southern-dominated Supreme Court." He placed his hands on his hips, shook his head, and finished, "In short, owning slaves has become a constitutional right—while the slave in America is guaranteed no constitutional rights whatsoever."

William paced and grew agitated. These occasional discussions of slavery, while of benefit in some respects, only served to stir up frustration on both their parts. William was a reluctant slaveholder through his inheritance of Crawford Hill plantation from his father. He cared for his hundreds of slaves as best he could and treated his household servants as family. Furthermore, he advocated the unpopular notion of humane reform measures to regulate slavery at every possible opportunity. "Reform slavery now," William would say, "then gradually phase it out with a concerted program of incremental assimilation, education, and occupational training to grant slaves ultimate self-sufficient independence as equals. Allow time for social and economic adjustment for both the South and the slave. Evolution, not revolution."

Brandon championed this view. "One must be sensible and practical; there are no instant remedies," he would concede. As a British foreigner in America, Brandon—although definitely pro-abolition—was more even-minded and even-tempered about the issue than the Northern abolitionists. "Was there ever a movement to prevent slavery?" he would rhetorically posit, "Yet now these abolitionists demagogue the issue, expecting to abruptly uproot a system that has existed for countless generations."

Now, while William paced and brooded, Brandon scowled thoughtfully and fidgeted with his pen. The two men's frustrations sufficiently piqued, they both fell silent.

Finally, William stopped his pacing. "There is one other problem with your article, now that I think about it."

"What is that?" Brandon asked, attentive once again.

"You mentioned an *anonymous* All Saints Parish slaveholder who advocates regulation of slavery through federal reform." William grinned.

Brandon understood the jest; William's name had been left out of the article. He broke into a smile, and joked, "Well, I *had* thought of submitting a pen-and-ink portrait of you to *The Illustrated London News* to be made into an engraving to illustrate the article!"

Laughing heartily, William said, "I'd best let you get back to your writing." He turned to leave but stopped at the door of the studio before going out, feeling for something folded in his coat pocket. "I almost forgot!" he announced, and extracted a rather worn and battered envelope from his pocket. "It's a letter from Jeremy, from India." He strode back to Brandon at his desk. "It came with the mail a short time ago. Annabelle asked me to bring it to you."

Rising, Brandon took the letter with an anxious hand. "Oh, good! I hear from Jeremy so seldomly, the mail between here and India is so interminably slow. Since the news of the Sepoy mutiny in Northern India, I've been hoping to hear *something*."

Immediately William felt bad and apologized. "I'm sorry Brandon, I should have remembered to give you Jeremy's letter first thing."

"Oh, that's all right. Besides, the letter must have taken over two months to reach here; another hour or so is of no matter." Brandon smiled reassuringly.

"Well, I'm sure your brother is fine," William offered.

"Of course." Although, Brandon could only hope this was so. He opened the envelope, drew out the several pages, and began to read.

"Let us know how Jeremy and Ranjana are doing," William said.

Brandon glanced up and nodded. "Of course."

William went out, and Brandon resumed his chair. He laid Jeremy's letter upon the polished wood of his desk and continued to read his brother's familiar hand.

"*Dear Brandon,*

"*I trust all is well with you. I keep you in my thoughts, and I wish—still—that I could have been of some consolation to you in your loss when Allison passed on. It did ease my mind to find your last letter to me sounding somewhat brighter, and I am relieved to hear you are back at your writing and illustrating again. In fact, on occasion, I receive a copy of a back issue of The Illustrated London News, and I am always pleased and proud to find your illustrations and articles among its pages once again—particularly when on the front page!*

"*By now you must have read of the Sepoy Mutiny that has only just begun here—it erupted on May 10, 1857. (The mail is so slow!) If you were here now, you would be foreign correspondent for The*

Illustrated London News covering the *Sepoy Mutiny*. The sepoys are the British-commanded Army of Bengal comprised of indigenous East Indians. Currently, there are about 200,000 sepoys in the army versus only about 50,000 British. Apparently, many issues culminated in this current rebellion: caste issues in the ranks, annexation of lands by the East India Company consequently disinheriting Indians, rumors of Muslims and Hindus being forced to become Christian, high-caste sepoys fearing that the General Service Enlistment Act of July 1856 would prevent sons from following fathers (within a culture of traditionally strong family service) into the same army, et cetera. But have you yet learned what is thought to be the main cause ultimately precipitating this rebellion? I shall tell you, dear brother, in case you have not heard by the time this letter reaches you.

"The sepoys had been issued a new type of rifle called the *Enfield*. To load the rifle, one must bite the cartridges with one's teeth to open them. (Never mind what our mothers tell us about not using our teeth to open things!) Well, it was rumored, in short order, that the cartridge casings had been coated with animal fat (to repel water and keep the powder dry). Can you imagine? Muslims, believing the pig to be unclean, and Hindus, believing the cow to be sacred, refused to use the rifles due to the coatings on the cartridges! All of those who refused orders to use the Enfields were promptly imprisoned. As a result, the Sepoy regiments at Meerut rebelled, killing their British superiors. Fortunately, I had not been posted to serve at Meerut!

"I am to receive orders very soon. We are at Lucknow for the time being. Some believe the mutiny will be short-lived, that it is spurious and will be easily put down. However, others believe the matter of the cartridges was simply the final straw to a host of grievances among the sepoy regiments and will take months to suppress. Apparently, a British sergeant-major's wife was told by a sepoy in the Cawnpore market place, 'You will none of you come here much oftener. You will not be alive another week.' My own feeling is that whether organized or disorganized, the rebellion is in its infancy and will be brief. I suppose that by the time you receive this letter, the mutiny will be well over with and forgotten.

Nonetheless, we officers are on alert to stand by for orders, at least as a precaution.

"Ranjana; our baby, Sonia; and I were about to leave for the Simla hill station for the summer months, but the mutiny has prevented our departure. Instead, I am sending Ranjana and Sonia into the British Residency here at Lucknow as a precaution. I had wanted to send them ahead to Simla without me, but Ranjana would not hear of it. (You should see our little Sonia. She is just half a year old and so precious. She is so like Ranjana—a pretty thing to be sure!) Ranjana insists on staying at the Residency, where many other officers are also sending their wives and children for protection. Whether the mutiny is short-lived or not, I think it unwise to have my wife and baby girl in tow in a climate of such rebellion and anger, but Ranjana was absolutely despondent at the prospect of our parting. She tells me that because she is part Indian she would be spared, that I should not fret for her or Sonia's safety. She may be right, although it is a rough scenario to have to even consider! Yet how can I send her away to Simla? Ranjana is such a sweet child, really; she also believes, quite firmly, that as long as she is near me I cannot be wounded or killed in battle! And so, I have reluctantly given in, and she and Sonia will move into the British Residency at Lucknow today. I pray it is the right decision.

"Ranjana is packing her clothes as I write, and she wishes me to convey to you the following: you had written that little Amelia is by now a year and a half old and still learning to talk, and that she pronounces her name as May-la. This pronunciation in the Hindi language is spelled 'Mela' and is often used as a girl's name. Ranjana informed me that 'Mela' means 'religious gathering' or 'festival,' and she believes it is an auspicious sign. (Ranjana wanted me to be very sure to tell you that!)

"I shall miss Ranjana while she is in the Lucknow Residency, but at least we shall be close as circumstances and duty call. It can't be avoided. Another thing that can't be avoided—little Sonia is beginning to fuss and cry as Ranjana packs things for them to take to the Residency, so I must close and attend to little Sonia. Circumstance and duty can be sweet!

"Keep well, and I will write again as soon as this ugly rebellion blows over.

"With love, your brother, Jeremy"

Brandon carefully refolded the letter, placed it in its envelope, and tucked it into his top desk drawer. There was nothing left to do about the matter but follow the news in the papers, wait for Jeremy's next letter, and hope the rebellion would soon end.

———◇———

Throughout the summer months and spilling into autumn, the Indian Mutiny raged on. Violence spread from Meerut to Delhi, Gwalior, Jhansi, Bareilly, Cawnpore, Allahabad, Benares, and even Lucknow. In the wake of the violence were tales of unutterable atrocities committed by the sepoys against British soldiers and civilian women and children. Women were raped and infants were, reportedly, tossed on bayonets for sport. In retaliation, the British carried out such barbarism as tying sepoys to the mouths of their cannons and blowing them into bits of flesh and bone while, at the very least, other sepoys were shot and hanged. British troops soon were sacking whole towns—setting fires, breaking into houses, and killing Indian women as well as men. It seemed there were no rules of war, or if there were, they were all being violated. The *London Times* wrote, "This blind and indiscriminate exasperation is resolving itself into the mere hatred of dark skin."

Brandon worried about Jeremy; his wife, Ranjana; and their baby daughter, Sonia. Still, there was nothing to be done but hope and wait for word. Despite Brandon's concern, it was difficult for him or for anyone at Crawford Hill to imagine the bloodshed and violence sweeping across the North of India. Comparatively, life at Crawford Hill continued serenely and civilly.

As the sweltering summer faded from the South Carolina Lowcountry, the season's rice harvest was commenced along the Waccamaw's swollen fields. All the while shooing away hungry, swooping yellow-and-black bobolinks, the Crawford Hill field slaves worked tirelessly to harvest the shoulder-high rice plants with sickles. By mid-September, the harvested grain was dried and trussed into sheaves, then loaded onto shallow boats for transport to the threshing yards.

In early autumn—as the rice was threshed, winnowed, and milled—the fields were prepared for the next planting. Oxen pulling plows turned under roots and stubble. Strong dark hands wielding hoes broke clods of earth and raked the ground smooth. Then, before the winter frost, rows were formed in anticipation of seeding and left fallow until spring.

Months had passed, and Brandon soon began to wonder whether he would receive any word of his brother's fate before springtime. One afternoon, however, in midwinter, two letters arrived at Crawford Hill for Brandon—both from India. That neither envelope was addressed in Jeremy's familiar hand did not bode well. One letter appeared to have been sent by a Mrs. K. Bartrum in Calcutta, of whom Brandon knew nothing. Perhaps more fearful than anxious to learn both letters' contents, Brandon decided to wait until evening to read them in William and Annabelle's company.

Brandon bid Barry goodnight at his bedroom door, and cautioned, "No reading now. Lamp out; it's bedtime."

"Yes, Father," Barry conceded without protest, and he yawned soundly. "Goodnight, Father."

Brandon carried Amelia, fast asleep in his arms, into her room and laid her down upon her bed, tucking the bedclothes up warmly about her. He kissed Amelia's forehead and whispered, "Goodnight, Mela," then gazed down at her a moment in the dim lamplight. How very much she would look like her mother one day, he reflected. He then thought of Jeremy; Ranjana; and their baby girl, Sonia; and felt for the two letters tucked in his jacket pocket wondering what news their contents held. "Sleep tight, Mela," Brandon whispered once more to Amelia, and then he went out.

Downstairs, Brandon met Annabelle and William in the east sitting room. The latter two sat facing the hearth and sipping brandy together as Brandon took his familiar wingback chair to the left of the low, crackling fire.

"Are the little ones asleep?" Annabelle asked.

"Umm ... yes ... I believe so," Brandon answered somewhat distractedly.

"There is a glass of brandy for you." William indicated the glass at Brandon's chair-side table.

"Thank you." Brandon fell silent a moment and did not touch the brandy left for him. "I've received two letters from India today," he said.

"From Jeremy?" William sat forward with surprise.

"We haven't heard from Jeremy in over six months!" Annabelle interjected.

"The letters are not from Jeremy." Brandon withdrew the letters from his jacket pocket. "I haven't opened them yet, however. I thought … I thought I would wait and open them when you both are here." Slowly Brandon opened the first envelope and withdrew its contents. He then rose, crossed to the sofa, and held the folded letter out to William. The page shook slightly in Brandon's hand. "Perhaps you could read it for me."

William nodded, and said quietly, "Of course."

"Surely, it can't be bad news." Annabelle commented.

Brandon resumed his chair as William cleared his throat and began to read the letter's contents in the still of the fire-lit room,

> "Dear Mr. Brandon Jonathan Stewart:
> "We regret to inform you that your brother—Captain Jeremy Randolph Stewart—was …"

William hesitated and glanced up at Brandon a moment, then continued,

> "… was killed … at the siege of Lucknow … in the latter days of October."

Annabelle gasped, and William cleared his throat, his eyes misting, before reading further.

"Go on," Brandon urged quietly.

William resumed reading.

> "Captain Stewart was engaged in the heroic defence of the British Residency under the Commander-in-Chief of the Indian Army, Sir Colin Campbell. He led his regiment well and fought bravely to sustain the honor and principles of the British Crown, his nation, and empire.
> "We extend our deepest condolences."

William did not bother to read the closure; it was a standard letter written in an unfamiliar hand at an office somewhere in Delhi.

Brandon sat quietly gazing downward, his face ashen. "Jeremy...," he uttered quietly, then bit his lip hard as his eyes filled.

"I'm sorry," William offered solemnly, his voice thick with emotion.

Annabelle withdrew her handkerchief, dabbed liberally at her eyes, and sniffled. "Poor Jeremy."

Brandon rose and took the letter from William. He hesitated a moment, then held out the second envelope. "Perhaps if you could read this other letter as well; there may be some further news."

William nodded and took the second letter.

"Maybe it contains some word of Jeremy's wife and child," Annabelle suggested, her voice strained with emotion.

"This second letter is from a Mrs. Kathryn Bartrum," William informed, then commenced to read. Kathryn Bartrum wrote that she— the wife of Surgeon Robert Henry Bartrum—had been reluctant to leave her husband at an outstation and go into protection with her child at the Residency at Lucknow. She had done so, nonetheless, and was trapped inside the Residency for months as the mutiny raged on about it. There, Kathryn Bartrum had met Ranjana Stewart and her baby girl, Sonia.

"*... Ranjana Stewart and I were both officers' wives who reluctantly conceded to sequestering ourselves within the walls of Lucknow's Residency. We became well-acquainted throughout the long hard months of the siege. Ranjana often told me that if anything were to happen to Jeremy, she was not sure what she would do.*

"*Campbell's troops broke through the siege upon the Residency, ending the battle and freeing us at last from inside. As we all made ready to leave, word got through that my husband and Jeremy had both been killed in battle just as they were reaching the safety of the Residency. Ranjana and Sonia occupied the room next to mine. After the news of Captain Stewart's death, several of us heard a muffled gunshot nearby, inside the Residency.*

"*My dear Mr. Stewart, I regret so much to tell you this ... but I feel I must. Ranjana was found with Sonia held in her arms, both dead—killed from a single pistol shot that Ranjana had fired through both their hearts."*

William stopped and swallowed hard. Annabelle gasped audibly, her hands clutched to her lips.

Brandon's eyes brimmed and spilled over. "Dear God," he murmured, stunned, and shook his head sadly. The news was almost too much to take in. Kathryn Bartrum's account of Ranjana's and little Sonia's deaths seemed nearly surreal, but then, so did most of what she or anyone had written about the mutiny.

"There is another paragraph…," William offered hesitantly.

Brandon nodded for him to continue as he brushed the tears from his eyes with the back of his hand. "Go on, please."

Reluctantly William recommenced reading.

"Upon emerging from the Residency, we found that the cannonading and musket fire had nearly ruined it. The walls were pocked, and brickwork had fallen and was strewn on the ground. Skeletons—those of Indians and British alike—littered the yard in front of the crumbling Residency. It is said that a cemetery will be established near the Residency at Lucknow to accommodate the two thousand or so British killed these past several months. I believe your brother, Jeremy, is to be buried in that cemetery. General Havelock's grave is to be built specially in Alambagh near Lucknow.

"I have lost my husband, and my young son lies dying due to his deprivations during the siege. I am left alone and friendless, hoping only to sail for England soon. Believe me when I tell you that I share in your loss, and I regret having to write such dreadful words about the fate of your brother, your brother's wife, and their baby daughter.

"May God comfort us both in our losses,

"Kathryn Bartrum"

William concluded the letter, his voice gruff with emotion. The room fell silent. William carefully refolded the letter from Kathryn Bartrum and replaced it in its worn envelope, all the while a knot swelling tight in his throat and his eyes misting.

Brandon rose slowly and stood gazing down at the flames upon the hearth. "Jeremy … Jeremy was only thirty-three," he said quietly as the bright hue of the firelight melted before his welling eyes. Horrific images of the mutiny swirled in his mind—images of Jeremy felled in battle; of Ranjana holding the barrel of a pistol against Sonia's breast and her own, then, with a trembling hand, squeezing the trigger; images of the reported atrocities and barbarism; blood, streams of blood, everywhere. Brandon bit the inside of his lip hard to keep from breaking down, but it was of no use. All at once Brandon bent his head in his hands and let his tears flow. "Jeremy…," he wept.

Rising from the sofa, Annabelle went to Brandon's side and tucked her hand consolingly about his arm. She swallowed hard, fighting back tears, then said softly, "I remember when … when I first met you and Jeremy at Loxley House at Christmas—" Abruptly Annabelle stopped and flung her arms about Brandon. "Oh, Brandon! I am *so* sorry!" she wept, in a flood of hot tears. Brandon enveloped Annabelle in his embrace and kissed the soft waves of her hair, his tears wetting the tender strands. Wordlessly Brandon and Annabelle clung fast to one another and wept, letting cherished memories of days long since gone unleash torrents of sorrow from within each their hearts.

———※———

Annabelle wrote to Alexandra in England some days later.

"… *Poor Brandon. First he suffered the loss of his wife, our dear Allison—that all but destroyed him, poor dear!—and now there is the tragic news of his brother's death, killed in the mutiny in India. I fear we have all had far more than our share of loss in recent years—your Benjamin (How we continue ever to miss him!) and our newborn, Charleston (Cooper's twin brother) two years ago. Ester says that death simply comes in waves, that one is afflicted by a loss of loved ones for a time, but then death grows weary and moves on—I pray that death will at last let us be for a time. Alexandra, I look about me—at my loved ones (and I think of you so far away)—and I hope and pray for fate to spare us all a while longer. Life is so precious and yet so tenuous, it seems. I implore death to move on and let us be! Nonetheless, I would gladly sacrifice my life for any of these children here among our family at Crawford Hill.*

"*The children, Alexandra, what blessings they all are. I must tell you about each one—they all grow so very fast—and the news will help cheer us. When there seems ever so much sorrow in the world, it is the hope and promise of our little ones that gives us cheer.*

"*Carolina is now seven and is the very image of her father. She has grown into a very sweet little girl and is quite pretty—if I may say so—with glossy brown locks and bright brown eyes. Although Carolina is reserved, she is not shy . . . rather, poised. Can you believe she is already learning to sew and do needlework? She is inquisitive, well-behaved, and dotes on reading. Brandon says that Carolina shall grow up to be quite the Southern belle, and many men's hearts will be at her mercy one day. I dare say he may be right. The same, I fear, could be said for little Ashley.*

"*Ashley is now five, and despite her blond curls and blue eyes, she could be described in the same terms as her sister Carolina, except that Ashley is, indeed, a very shy child.*

"*Now, I must tell you, Alexandra, that our baby Cooper is nothing like his two older sisters. He is only two and a half, but already he is such a handful! William will say that Cooper is adventurous and curious; however, Ester says that Cooper is mischievous and rambunctious. I believe Ester is right! Cooper is constantly in motion, forever up and about doing—never sitting quietly—until he has quite exhausted himself. Good heavens, he even seems to sleep fitfully! William only laughs and says that he was the same as a baby. Can you imagine? Yet William is, admittedly, quite gregarious and jocular (he loves to tease!). Perhaps these qualities blossomed out of a rather more wild nature as a child. The apple does not usually fall far from the tree, as they say.*

"*On the contrary, Ester and Jacob's little ones are of even temperament and predictability. Quash is nearly six. He is tall for his age and lanky, but a handsome boy who takes after his father in every way. Already, he is quite good with his hands and is a remarkably clever child. He follows*

Jacob about as Jacob works, and he pretends to be building or fixing things as his father does. He is an adorable child, as is his baby sister Cinda.

"Cinda is a treasure! She is nearly two and a half, as is Amelia, and such a bright-eyed, pretty thing. She has inherited her mother's exquisite African-princess looks and shares the same quality of wide-eyed innocence about her. She and Amelia play together and are at times quite inseparable.

"Most of the children at the Big House are well-suited by gender and age to be each other's playmates except for poor Barry. Barry will be nine this year, and only Carolina is near enough in age to be his companion. In earlier years, Barry reluctantly agreed to play house on occasion with Carolina, Ashley, and Quash, but now he really is too old to put up with such nonsense. (Similarly, Carolina's tolerance of boys has waned, and she promptly wrinkles her nose at the mere mention of 'boys.')

"Barry has grown into such a handsome boy. He looks so very much like Brandon, with chestnut waves of hair and beautiful brown eyes. If Carolina will one day have all the men's hearts at her mercy, then Barry shall one day break all the young women's hearts. Allison would have been so pleased and proud to know the young man Barry is becoming. Barry is as clever and intelligent as his father, and he seems to rather enjoy schoolwork. But Barry also loves exploring the woods and plantation grounds as well as horseback riding, and he is beginning to learn about guns and hunting. He also delights in building all sorts of 'inventions' out of bits of wood and odd nails and such.

"Brandon is concerned, however, that Barry has no children his age to play with except those at the All Saints Parish school. So, often, Barry is off by himself playing alone. He does, however, dote on Amelia; he is a good, attentive big brother to her. It is as if he has tried to compensate for Brandon's apparent neglect of them the year after Allison died—and in recent months, for Brandon's being so absorbed in his work for The Illustrated London News in his studio.

"Now, Alexandra, I must tell you of our dear little niece, Amelia. She is such a precious thing! Like Ashley, Amelia has our blond curls and blue eyes. Just as Barry shall grow up to look just like Brandon, Amelia shall grow up one day to look just like Allison—although, I can't help but wonder if she might not take a bit more after me in her manner

than Allison. She is a good child, well behaved generally, though endlessly curious. With no mother, and with Brandon so preoccupied for the better part of her young life, Amelia has grown to be quite shy and starved for attention. She is quite an affectionate child. There remains a waiflike quality about her because of Brandon's aloofness for much of these past years. Ester says Amelia will grow to be quite an independent spirit, and I dare say she is right.

"I should add that we no longer call Amelia by her Christian name, but rather, we call her 'Mela,' a permutation of Amelia. This is how she is able to pronounce her name, and Jeremy's wife, Ranjana, had written that 'Mela' is a girl's name in India—it drives from the Sanskrit, meaning 'festival' or 'religious gathering.' In the days since the news of Jeremy's and Ranjana's tragic deaths, and that of their baby Sonia's, we have all come to call Amelia only by 'Mela.' This has been Brandon's wish, I believe, to keep some memory of his brother, Ranjana, and Sonia alive through his child.

"Poor Brandon, he is too young to have suffered such losses in his life. He only turned thirty-one last week, on February twenty-fifth. We prepared a special dinner and baked a spice cake—his favorite—but after the news from India, there was little cheer or appetite to be had. There is perhaps one grace to have emerged from this latest tragedy—Brandon is now more attentive and closer to his children, particularly Mela. At long last, he no longer seems to blame himself or Mela for Allison's death from childbed fever. There is no more precious sight than to see Brandon with little Mela—his 'little dear one,' as he calls her—gathered up and held snug in his arms. Brandon is, after all, becoming quite the doting father these past few weeks. It is such a refreshing joy to see him this way with the children!

"Oh, dear! The most dreadful disturbance has just begun downstairs, and I wager Cooper is at the center of it. Ester and Cotta are with the children in the sitting room, but I had best go see what the matter is.

"Dear Alexandra, do write soon and keep well. William and Brandon send their best.

"Your loving sister, Annabelle"

CHAPTER 10

Resilience and Remembrance

For her fifth birthday, on September fourth in 1860, Mela received a pretty porcelain doll that stood nearly her own height. Her Aunt Annabelle and Uncle William had purchased the doll for her on a recent trip into the city of Charleston. It was a splendid doll that Mela promptly christened "Amanda." Her name—Amelia—started with the letter "A" as did her mother's name and her two aunts' names; and so, she decided her favorite doll should be named Amanda. Amanda arrived at Crawford Hill dressed in a sunny yellow frock trimmed with lace and a broad straw sunbonnet that was tied with a wide bow under her chin. Beneath the broad brim of her hat spilled down thick spirals of brown ringlets. Mela adored Amanda, and the doll became her most favorite playmate—second only to Cinda, of course.

For days, Mela doted on Amanda, taking the doll with her everywhere. A special place had to be set at the dining table for breakfast, the midday meal, and at dinner. Mela even invited her new doll to afternoon tea with the grownups in the west sitting room. "Shhh!" Mela would admonish Amanda during tea, "It's not nice to talk when other people are talking!" Amanda would sit obediently and silently by as Brandon, William, Annabelle, Ester, and Jacob exchanged amused smiles and winks. Insistently Mela even ensured that Amanda shared her tub at bath time.

Days passed, and Mela and Amanda remained inseparable. "Whenever will the novelty of her new doll wear thin, I wonder?" Annabelle would remark, though obviously delighted that the gift had been such a success.

Mela had scarcely let Amanda out of her sight until one afternoon nearly a month after her birthday. Cinda and Mela had set about playing dress-up on the back verandah. Costuming themselves in outsized frocks that cousin Carolina had long since outgrown, their own church gloves, and necklaces fashioned by Ester out of threaded cranberries, the two girls prattled happily upon the porch. Cinda trudged about in a pair of her mother's work shoes, and Mela shuffled noisily in a pair of her Aunt Annabelle's high-button boots. To and fro, the two little girls traipsed along the wooden verandah, holding their dragging hemlines high in front so as not to trip. All the while, they chattered gaily, inventing conversations that they imagined fine ladies engaged in. Once in a while, bonneted heads held proudly, they stopped to admire their reflections in the window glass.

"Someday we is gonna be grow'd ladies o' de house like yer aunt, Miss Annabelle," Cinda proclaimed.

Mela nodded with decision at her reflection in the square panes of glass, but declared, "I'm gonna grow up to be just like my father!"

Just then Cotta emerged from the back door of the house carrying a small tray of various teacups and accoutrements and set it down on a low wicker table. "I done brought you girls a bit o' tea," she offered, and smiled at the girls in their too-big dresses.

"We ain' girls. We is *ladies!*" Cinda corrected—her expression radiant, her mouth a beaming crescent of white.

"So, you *is!*" Cotta grinned at the two little ones. "An' I ain' neber afo' seen two such pret'y lil ladies."

Mela curtsied unsteadily in her outsized shoes. "Why thank you, Miss Cotta."

Cinda curtsied in turn and parroted Mela.

"You bes' drink yer tea b'fo' it gits col'," Cotta advised. Chuckling to herself, Cotta went inside the house and left the two girls to their play.

Mela and Cinda sat on the wicker verandah chairs and began to pour their "tea," which was really only water with a spoonful of molasses added to give it color and flavor.

"Do you think we should invite Amanda?" Mela asked, then sipped her "tea" with a crooked finger.

"Ummm—" Cinda playacted intent contemplation of the proposal. "Sho' we should. We ain' seen Miss Amanda in eber so long," she intoned, mimicking an upper-society Charleston drawl over her thick Gullah. This sent both girls into a fit of laughter that did not subside until their sides ached.

"Well, I shall go and fetch Miss Amanda, then." Mela rose from her chair. "Wait right here."

Cinda sipped her "tea," and Mela disappeared, shuffling in her outsized boots into the house. At the foot of the stairs, Mela left her aunt's boots behind, and humming to herself, happily climbed the staircase. Half running and half skipping, barefoot, along the upstairs hallway, Mela called out her doll's name, "Amanda! Amanda!" She knew she would find poor Amanda just where she had left her in her bedroom and now felt sorry she had not invited Amanda to play dress-up with her and Cinda from the start. "Amanda!" Mela called in a singsong as she neared her bedroom door.

Abruptly Mela stopped inside the doorway of her room and stood transfixed, her little mouth agape, mute in horror. Cooper sat in the middle of her bedroom floor, a round white stone clutched in his hands. Mela recognized that the stone was one of the painted ones from the footpath to her father's studio. But it was not the stolen rock that was the object of Mela's distress. Amanda lay supine upon the floor beside Cooper, her pretty porcelain face shattered into bits from a single blow of Cooper's white stone.

Unaware of Mela's stunned presence in the doorway, Cooper sat holding the stone in his hand and peering intently into the gaping hollow of Amanda's porcelain skull.

All at once Mela shrilled and lunged forward at Cooper. Flailing wildly, she fell upon him and screamed. "How dare you?! How *dare* you?!" she cried, pummeling him with clenched fists.

Cooper fought back with sharp kicks and slaps, trying to push Mela away from him. "Get off me! Get *off* me!"

"How dare you?! How *dare* you?!" Mela shrieked, and pummeled blindly. "She was my doll! Amanda was *my doll!*" Mela wept, kicking and hitting at Cooper with all her might.

"Get *off* me!" Cooper yelled. He struck the hard toes of his shoes at Mela's shins in quick succession.

"She was my doll!" Mela wept, punching Cooper hard in the shoulder.

She returned Cooper's kicks in quick staccato blows, but her bare feet were no match for Cooper's leather shoes.

Suddenly Cooper yanked hard on Mela's hair, and she cried out shrilly in pain.

"Stop this! Stop this *at once!*" Brandon strode purposefully through the doorway, Annabelle fast behind him.

"Children! Please!" Annabelle admonished.

"Stop this *right now!*" Brandon commanded, and pulled Mela—weeping, flailing, and kicking—off of her cousin.

Upon sight of his mother, Cooper began to cry—if for no other reason than to win her sympathy. "She *hit* me!" he lamented, turning to the protection of his mother as she knelt in her skirts beside him upon the hardwood floor.

Mela struggled to free herself from her father's hold, sending out desultory kicks and blows that only lashed at the air. All the while she sobbed and emitted anguished shrieks.

"*Amelia!* Stop this *instant!*" Brandon shouted over the pitch of her wails and cries.

"No! I *won't!* I *won't* stop!" she yelled, then all at once collapsed sobbing into her father's arms. "He ruined my doll! He ruined my doll!" She sobbed in small convulsions against her father's chest. "I want my Amanda!" she mourned piteously.

Brandon held Mela close, gently shushing and rocking her. His eyes fell upon the ruined doll, the shattered bits of porcelain scattered upon the floor, and the white-painted rock.

Cooper cried with feigned innocence in his mother's embrace and did not dare to even glance in his Uncle Brandon's direction.

"I want my doll ... I want my doll ...," Mela wept brokenly. "Father ...— I want ...— Amanda ...—" she hiccupped as her tears wet her father's shirt.

Brandon's eyes met Annabelle's. She scarcely knew what to say. There was simply no excuse for her son's behavior. She and William would have to confer later as to a suitable punishment for the boy.

"She hit me first," Cooper bemoaned, sniffling quietly.

No one paid Cooper's allegations any heed.

Mela could do nothing but sob in her father's arms.

"It's all right now. It will be all right," Brandon soothed. "We will buy you a new doll."

"But … I want *Amanda*," Mela wept, her heart feeling as shattered as the porcelain bits that lay strewn across the floor.

Brandon was beside himself. He hardly knew what to say or do to console his little girl. He rose up, Mela bundled in his arms. "Maybe we can fix Amanda," he soothed, although he knew the task would be impossible.

This tentative promise, however, consoled Mela somewhat, and she laid her head on her father's shoulder, a silent stream of hot tears wetting his shirt through.

"I had best take Mela to my room," Brandon said to Annabelle, glancing momentarily downward to indicate the ruined doll.

Annabelle nodded. "I'll have Ester or Cotta sweep …" She didn't finish but, instead, sighed. Cooper was fast becoming more than she could contend with.

Cooper, by now, decided he had cried enough—at least for sympathetic effect—and sat up, rubbing his eyes with damp fists.

Brandon turned to go, Mela whimpering in his arms, but stopped short when Annabelle suddenly gasped.

"Brandon!"

He turned back to see her eyes wide with alarm.

Even little Cooper removed his damp fists from his eyes to see where his mother was pointing.

"Amelia's feet!"Annabelle uttered.

Brandon adjusted Mela in his arms and looked down to see the bottoms of Mela's feet crisscrossed in rivulets of blood and droplets of red splashing down onto the hardwood floor.

"*Christ!*" Brandon gasped.

"She must have cut her feet on the bits of porcelain," Annabelle said.

Brandon kissed Mela's blond curls, and said to Annabelle, "I'm taking her to my room. Send Ester to us."

Annabelle nodded. "I'm so *sorry* Brandon—"

But he was gone.

Cooper sat guiltily on the floor before his mother. "She hit me first," he said, then hesitated. "Besides, I only wanted to see what was inside," he pronounced, as if to summarily justify his smashing Amanda.

Annabelle sighed. She sent Cooper to his room, then she went to fetch Cotta and Ester to see to the broken doll and to Mela's injured feet.

Mela's feet were not as badly cut as they had first appeared, although they remained bandaged for several days until they healed.

For her part, Cinda vowed never to talk to Cooper again, "... long as I lib!" adding vehemently, "I *hates* him!"

Mela only wanted Amanda back, but over time, she realized this could never be. She imagined that now she understood, at least a little, about the loss her father felt since her mother, Allison, had gone to heaven.

"Maybe Amanda be in he'ven wit' yer mother," Cinda consoled.

"Maybe...," Mela nodded solemnly.

The earth spun round and round in a frantic blur of grass, sky, and clouds. Mela shrieked with delight, both her hands held firm in her father's as he wielded her in great circles through the air.

"Up we fly!" Brandon soared Mela higher as he turned with quick steps upon the small patch of lawn.

"Faster, Father!" Mela giggled, and then shrieked with apprehension and delight as Brandon obliged her. He whirled her faster, round and round, up and down.

"Up and down we fly!" Brandon cried, though growing winded. Three circles more, then Brandon announced, "It's time to land!"

Panting and dizzy, Brandon slowed his pace and eased Mela to the ground. Mela's feet touched the ground with desultory steps, and Brandon let go her hands. Both tumbled dizzily upon the grass. Mela lay giggling as pregnant white clouds circled madly overhead.

"You're nearly getting too big for flying," Brandon laughed.

"I want to fly again!" Mela giggled, "Like a bird!"

Brandon groaned, then laughed.

The clouds overhead had stopped circling.

"I want to fly again!" Mela repeated expectantly.

"Mela!" Brandon admonished playfully, "Didn't you hear what I just said?" He turned his head upon the grass to see Mela's pale-blue eyes looking at him longingly across the short green blades.

"But you only said I's *nearly* too big!" Mela persisted.

"'Am,'" Brandon corrected. "You must say 'I am,' not 'I is.' And it is 'did not'; you mustn't say 'di'n't.'" He hoped the slave-children's Gullah language would not permanently leave its mark on Mela's proper English.

"I am. Did not," Mela enunciated carefully, to please her father.

"That's better."

"Well? ..."

"Well what?"

Mela crawled across the short span of lawn in her skirts to where her father lay and sat upon her heels. "I want to fly again!" Mela hesitated, then remembered her manners. "Can I, *please?*" she sang.

"Maybe later, Mela."

"*Please*, Father?"

Brandon sighed and sat up upon the grass. "Mela, Mela, Mela," he recited in his whatever-am-I-going-to-do-with-you? tone, and shook his head.

"Please, please, *please?*" Mela sang.

Brandon chuckled. "My little dear one, do you know what a century is?"

Mela hesitated. "A very long time?"

Brandon nodded. "Yes, it is a *very* long time. One hundred years, to be precise."

"So? ..." Mela asked timidly.

"So, I am one third of a century old, and you are nearly too big for flying."

"So?"

"So, your father needs a short rest. We can fly again later, after the picnic."

Mela's eyes lit up. "Promise?"

Brandon chuckled with amusement and ruffled her golden curls. "I promise."

"Oh, goody!" Mela squealed, and clapped her hands.

"Hey," Brandon remembered, "let's look at those feet of yours. Let's see how well they are healing."

Mela shifted her position upon the grass and stuck her feet out from beneath her skirts. Brandon lifted one bare foot, and then the other, to inspect the cuts that had all but healed upon her tender soles.

"They are nearly all better now," Brandon smiled. He was glad there would be no scars left from the shards of porcelain that had once been Amanda. "Where did you leave your shoes and stockings?"

Mela turned and pointed down the sloping lawn. "With Aunt Annabelle on the pignic blanket."

" 'Picnic,' " Brandon corrected.

" 'Pig-nic,' " Mela enunciated carefully, and nodded.

Brandon chuckled and shook his head.

"So? ..." Brandon lifted a small unshod foot and peered intently.

"So? ..." Mela mimed, her heel cradled in her father's palm.

"Does this hurt?" He tickled the sole of Mela's foot with nimble fingers.

"*Aaah!*" Mela shrieked wildly and yanked her foot from her father's hand.

"What? Are you ... *ticklish?*" Brandon teased, feigning disbelief.

Giggling, Mela scampered backward on the grass to make her escape. Instantly Brandon caught her and began tickling her ribs. Mela shrieked with laughter until her ribs grew overwhelmed, and—half giggling, half in tears—she begged for her father to stop.

Brandon stopped and raised his hands. "All right. It's all right, little dear one—you're free."

Mela sat up laughing and panting, holding her sides. Yet, in an instant, she dove headlong upon her father, knocking him backward onto the grass. Sitting upon his stomach in her rumpled skirts, she tickled him mercilessly until he laughed so hard tears ran from the corners of his eyes.

"Mela, stop!" He pleaded for mercy. "Please, *stop!* Mela!"

Mela only giggled and tickled harder.

"Mela—*now!*"

Mela stopped tickling and sat up tall, triumphantly giggling with delight.

Brandon caught his breath. "Mela, come now. You must get off me."

"Why?"

"You're sitting on my stomach."

"So?" Mela chirped.

"So, I can't breathe." Brandon's tone was measured but nonetheless good-natured.

"So?" Mela giggled.

Brandon coughed slightly. "Come now, Mela. Get off me." In an instant he would become annoyed.

Mela realized she had played her game long enough. "I'll let you go, but you have to say the magic words."

Brandon was about to retort when Ester approached across the gentle slope of lawn, Quash and Cinda close behind. "Ain' no one is ebber let go wit'out gibben r'pentance an' thanks to de A'mighty!" Ester admonished playfully.

Startled, Mela jumped up, and Brandon smoothed the disheveled skirt of her Saturday frock.

Shaking her head, hands on her hips, Ester clicked her tongue, then warned, "You *chillun* bes' come fo' de picnic, o' dere'll be no chickun o' peach pie lef' fo' y'all t' eats." Ester had emphasized the word 'chillun' to include Brandon.

"Yes, *Mam!*" Brandon teased.

In return, Ester shot Brandon an admonishing glance, belied by the glimmer of a grin.

Ester, Brandon, and the three children trudged down the grassy slope—Mela's hand tucked into her father's, Ester leading the way.

Shortly, Barry ran to meet them. "Father?" he asked in an exasperated voice, while keeping stride at his father's side.

Brandon noticed his son's agitation. "Yes, Barry? What is it?"

"I let Carolina fly my kite, and it went down in the pond," he reported peevishly.

"I see." Brandon's tone was sympathetic but measured.

"I spent a whole week making it—each day after lessons—and now it's ruined!"

Brandon felt his son's disappointment, but prodded gently, "And what did I tell you about the kite today?"

"That it needed a longer tail due to the wind." Barry's voice trailed downward, then he shrugged. "But it worked fine for me, and I flew it just before Carolina—" Barry wanted to say "—ruined it!" but he refrained.

"Well, I am sorry about it, Barry," Brandon sympathized. "I can help you make another kite tomorrow, a special one. How will that be?"

Barry shrugged dejectedly. "All right, I suppose."

Brandon nearly reprimanded Barry for his ill tone, but thought better of it.

Sensing his father's displeasure with his attitude, Barry said, "I'm sorry, Father. I *would* like your help."

"That's fine, then. Tomorrow, it is." Brandon smiled and clapped his son on the shoulder.

"It's just that I told Carolina not to fly it too near the pond, but she let out more string, the wind caught it up, then it crashed straight into the water!" Barry hesitated, then added with due humiliation, "I might have saved it still, but the ducks swam over and began pecking at it."

Brandon laughed out loud at this as Mela, Quash, and Cinda giggled, and Ester grinned and shook her head.

"It's not *funny!*" Barry shot, wounded.

Brandon sobered, though his eyes twinkled. "No, of course not," he conceded. "I suppose Carolina was very sorry for the mishap? . . ."

Barry nodded. "Yes, she was quite sorry about it," he admitted.

"Well, here you are at last!" Annabelle announced as Brandon, Ester, and the children approached the picnic blankets, wicker hampers, and plates of food.

"We were playing up there," Mela piped gaily, pointing in the direction of the Big House.

"Were you, now?" Annabelle smiled and cast Mela a playful wink. "I never would have guessed!" she jested, surveying with amusement the grass stains and wrinkles on Mela's frock. A stubborn edge of Mela's hem remained upturned above her bare feet, and a lace flounce on her pantalets was torn. "*Honestly*, Brandon!" Annabelle upbraided with tongue-in-cheek disapproval.

Brandon smoothed Mela's upturned hem, then asked, "Where are William and Ashley?"

"Dey be comin', Massa Brandon." Cotta extended a slender arm to indicate William jogging up a low hill, carrying Ashley piggyback. "From dem fiel's down yonder."

Mela tugged furtively at her father's sleeve. "I want to go piggyback too! I want to go piggyback too!" She looked expectantly up at her father.

"Maybe later, after we have eaten," Brandon replied absently.

Somewhat winded, William reached the blankets and knelt upon the grass to let Ashley clamber down.

"Can I have pie, Mother?" Ashley piped, her fair curls in an unruly mass, her cheeks ruddy with sun and laughter.

"After lunch, Ashley. And it is 'May I?' not 'Can I?'"

"May I?"

"You may have pie after you've eaten your lunch," William stated. "And that goes for you too, Carolina."

"C'n we eats pie now?" Quash asked Ester.

"Yeah, c'n we?" Cinda piped.

"You twos behave, or I's gonna git your daddy to give you a whoopin' like you ain' neber seen," Ester replied in mock seriousness. Even so, her two children knew she meant business—pie would wait until after lunch.

"Can we play tree tag later?" Mela asked.

With amusement, Brandon chuckled, "Before or after your piggyback ride?"

"After! No ... —before! ...—*Both!*" Mela chirped.

"Those are little children's games." Carolina all but rolled her eyes—although, deep down, she hoped that maybe they *would* play tree tag.

"Might as well play tree tag. I can't fly my kite," Barry brooded.

William laughed, "I remember a day when picnics were relaxing!"

Brandon chuckled. "Indeed!"

"Yes, it once *was* relaxing—when *we* were children!" Annabelle joked.

Everyone laughed heartily at this, even the little ones.

The late afternoon picnic fare consisted of cornbread, rice, chicken, black-eyed peas, and peach pie for dessert. Cups and glasses were amply refilled with either iced tea, wine, or water. Mint juleps were promised for later, in the relative cool of the evening upon the verandah. By then, all the children would be asleep upstairs—only the distant sounds of crickets chirping and frogs croaking would interrupt the quiet.

"Cooper! Cooper Crawford! Get your hands out of that pie this instant!" Annabelle darted to her feet, all but overturning her plate as she stood. "Cooper! Now! I mean it!"

"I want my pie *now!*" Cooper yelled, his small hands dripping and sticky with pie filling.

Annabelle snatched Cooper up from the blanket where he sat and pulled him aside by a sticky hand. His little feet tripped after her. "I want my pie now!" he half pleaded and half insisted.

Annabelle parted her lips, about to shoot back, "You won't have any pie at all!" But instead, her cheeks turned scarlet, and her eyes welled. Annabelle looked helplessly at William, oblivious that Cooper was wiping pie filling from his free hand onto her skirt. "He's been like this all day," she said, her voice thin. "Can you manage him a while?" She broke off abruptly for fear of giving in to tears.

William was already on his feet. All the while, Cooper squirmed and licked his sticky fist.

"Cooper's in trouble now!" one of the children whispered.

"He's *always* in trouble," said another.

As William led Cooper off near the edge of the pond for a firm talking to, Annabelle struggled to regain her composure and make light of the ruined pie and her son's dismal behavior. "Little boys can be such a handful."

Ester rose and tucked her arm affectionately around Annabelle's shoulders. "Neber you mind, Miss Annabelle. Neber you mind 'bout de pies. We done got plen'y more up in de kitch'n."

Annabelle smiled and gave Ester's hand a warm squeeze. "Thank you, Ester. I'm all right now. It's just that Cooper—" Her voice trailed and she looked downward.

"Lil' Cooper *is* a han'ful. Yes, m!" Ester nodded emphatically and grinned.

Annabelle broke into a broad smile that chased away her impending tears. Sitting once again upon the picnic blanket, Annabelle resumed her plate.

The remainder of the picnic passed uneventfully, and no one found any complaint in this whatsoever. The adults discussed the latest news of their neighbors, politics, and rice prices, while the children predictably picked at their food and giggled with one another in hushed whispers. After a while, lunch was over, and it was time for dessert. Cotta poured iced tea as Ester served slices of the two peach pies that Cotta had fetched from the kitchen—pies that had escaped Cooper's wanton unruliness.

"Where does tea come from?" Carolina asked, surveying the green liquid in her glass.

"Tea first came to South Carolina in 1799 by way of a French botanist named Francois Andre Michaux who planted it near Charleston at Middleton Barony," William said as Cotta poured his serving of iced tea. "In fact, South Carolina is the only state where it has been grown." His voice held an edge of pride.

"However," Brandon put in, "I believe the most recent attempt to grow tea commercially in South Carolina was in 1848. A retired London physician attempted to produce it. And that effort failed when he was shot to death ... I believe in 1853. Currently, much of our black tea is grown in British-run tea plantations in Eastern India and Ceylon and is imported. Much of our green tea is imported from China."

"Still, we do have tea grown on plantations in the South," William added, "but it is not sold commercially."

"And where do we get the ice from?" Barry was intrigued, as the weather in South Carolina was rarely cold enough to produce a hail storm let alone a shred of snow.

"Our ice is shipped from the North," William explained. "The ice is sent down the Mississippi River from ice ponds in the upper Midwest and delivered to our plantation ice-house. It is packed in sawdust to help prevent it from melting."

Barry was fascinated as he examined the chunk of ice in his glass.

"I would have thought our ice was transported by sea to the Waccamaw—" Brandon began, until he felt a tugging on his sleeve.

"I've finished my plate," Mela whispered.

Brandon surveyed her plate. "What about those black-eyed peas?"

Mela scrunched her nose and looked apprehensively down at the small mound of black-spotted tan morsels on her plate.

"It seems to me," Brandon said, "that you've hardly touched them at all. You should try to eat your peas."

"I really don't like peas." Mela frowned.

"You should say, 'I don't care for peas'; that is more proper," Brandon corrected.

"I don't care for peas," Mela recited dully, then brightened. "Do you mean I don't *have* to eat them?" She grinned expectantly up at her father.

Brandon cast her a you-know-better-than-that glance, and Mela frowned once again.

"I really *don't* care for peas, Father," she pleaded.

"Black-eyed peas are really only beans," Brandon explained.

"I don't care. Then, I don't like beans either," Mela pouted.

"Three bites," he coaxed.

Mela frowned and looked at her plate as if she might cry.

"Mela, Mela, Mela," Brandon sighed. "Whatever am I going to do with you, my little dear one?"

Mela shrugged. "... Can I ... May I have ... *pie?*"

"*Pie?!*" Brandon teased, affecting an aristocratic air. "Pie without black-eyed peas, young lady? ... Hmmm ... I don't think so." He thought a moment. "I'll tell you what. You may have peach pie if you trade each bite of pie with a spoonful of peas. The pie and peas can take turns. Does that sound fair?"

Brightening somewhat, Mela smiled and nodded. Father's idea did make the thought of swallowing the black-eyed peas more palatable. Mela hated the way peas felt in her mouth—soft and mushy, slimy from bits of bacon fat, and the way they squished between her teeth. She imagined they were small legless insects whose innards squirted out as she chewed. But Father's idea was fair, and she *did* want to please him—she adored him. She would try very hard not to think about chewing on insects.

"When I grow up, I want to be just like you!" Mela pronounced.

"You do, do you?" Brandon grinned with affection and amusement.

Mela nodded and, smiling bravely, took a spoonful of her black-eyed peas.

After dessert, Ester, Cotta, and Annabelle began to pack things up as William orchestrated the children in a game of hide-and-go-seek, and Brandon set off with Mela upon his back for a leisurely piggyback ride around the pond.

"We should have brought cornbread to feed the ducks!" Mela piped.

"Yes, we should have." Brandon said. "Although, I wager they've had their fill of Barry's kite."

Mela giggled at this, although she was sorry about Barry's kite and his earlier upset over it. She tugged her father's shirtsleeve. "Can we go over the bridge?"

"I don't see why not."

Once they reached the crest of the wooden footbridge, Brandon stopped at the railing. A small fleet of ducks appeared from beneath the bridge, quacking and paddling.

Mela giggled, "I'm too high up, Father. Can I get down now?"

"Of course." Brandon knelt down so that Mela could stand upon the bridge.

Mela was not yet tall enough to see over the top rail, but she stood on tiptoe, her hands over the middle rail, and watched the flotilla of ducks glide in a perfect "V" on the water's smooth surface. The sun would set soon, and even now its rays cast a soft amber light forming lengthening shadows.

"Can we come here tomorrow and feed the ducks?"

"I'm afraid not, Mela." Brandon felt bad about telling her no, but explained, "In the morning we have church, in the afternoon I have promised your brother to help him build a new kite, and then I must finish an article I am writing for the paper."

"After that, can we feed the ducks?" Mela looked up at her father expectantly.

Brandon shook his head. "By then it will be dinnertime, besides which, your Uncle William and I have planned to go up to Georgetown for business—we won't be home until evening, after dinner."

"Oh." Mela looked dejectedly at the water below. "May I come by myself?"

"Mela, you know the rule about that. You are not to come to the pond at all unless an adult is with you."

"But I'm bigger now. Even you said I am nearly too big for flying."

"That is different."

"Why?"

"It just is. It is not safe for you to be at the pond alone."

"But why?" Mela's tone bordered on a whine.

"Mela! ..." Brandon warned.

"*Please*, Father?" Mela sing-songed, hoping earnest charm would change his mind.

"Mela, no! Absolutely *not*. You know better. You are never to come here unless either I am with you or unless Jacob, Ester, Cotta, or your Aunt Annabelle or Uncle William are with you." Brandon was losing his patience. "Is that understood?"

Mela pouted. "Yes—" Her tone sounded more defiant and spoiled than she had intended. She looked sorrowfully at the water and at the ducks paddling in happy circles at the pond's far shore, expecting her father's firm reprimand. She wanted to cry without knowing quite why.

In the quiet around them, the sun cast a warm, glowing hue upon the early evening. Brandon knelt down to Mela's height, and said gently, "Do you know what I think?"

Mela shook her head, impending tears clutched in her throat.

"I think it has been a very long day, and you are tired. What do you think?"

Mela felt sleepy and unhappy, but shrugged and rubbed desultorily at one eye. The corners of her mouth dipped downward in a pronounced frown.

"Do you know what else I think?"

Looking at her father sorrowfully, Mela shook her head.

"I think that if you stood on your head just now, you would be smiling." Brandon's eyes twinkled and he gave Mela an affectionate, gentle pinch upon her cheek at a corner of her frown. "Don't you think so?" he smiled.

Mela could not help but brighten at this, and she nodded. Father was not so very angry with her after all, and everything would be all right, she decided.

Brandon gently tousled Mela's golden curls. "Shall we go back now?"

Mela nodded and climbed up on her father's back. "Can we go once more around the pond?" she asked timidly.

"Of course," Brandon answered gently.

By the time they returned to the picnic blanket, Mela was fast asleep. Her arms dangled, loosely encircling her father's neck; her cheek rested upon his shoulder; and her bare feet hung limp beneath the flounces of her pantalets. Tree tag would have to wait for another day.

"Too much picnic?" Annabelle asked, with a knowing smile.

"I believe so," Brandon nodded.

"Here, let me," William said. He stepped forward and helped to lay Mela, as she slept, upon the picnic blanket.

"Yes, too much picnic." Brandon smiled down at his sleeping daughter. "I'd best carry her up to the house and put her to bed."

Annabelle nodded. "It is nearly dark out already."

"Nearly autumn," William noted.

"Ester, Jacob, and Cotta have already taken the other children up to the house to get them ready for bed, and the kitchen servants have already cleared away the picnic things." Annabelle breathed in the sweet twilight air. "It is such a pleasant evening, and there's a full moon. William and I decided to enjoy the quiet and wait for you and Mela."

"It *was* a rather boisterous afternoon," Brandon chuckled.

"Good Lord!" William laughed, "Did you see the way Cooper dove into that pie?!"

Brandon grinned. "All in all, it *was* rather funny."

"Hush now, you two. You'll wake Mela," Annabelle warned.

But Mela had not stirred. She lay peacefully dozing upon the blanket.

"It is amazing how Mela has all but forgotten her doll, Amanda—how, just days ago, Cooper dove into ..." Brandon didn't finish—he did not want to upset Annabelle over the conduct of her, at times, wayward son.

Nonetheless Annabelle looked up at him apologetically. "Yes, she certainly enjoyed the picnic today. Why, she had taken Amanda with her nearly *everywhere* until ..." She sighed, and said, somewhat wistfully, "The resiliency of youth ..."

William squeezed his wife's hand affectionately. "What is past, my dear, is past. Mela and the other children had a very spirited day, today, and now she is asleep—probably having pleasant dreams of the picnic. *That is what is important now.*"

"Of course. Quite right." Annabelle managed a smile.

Brandon gazed down at his little dear one. "I imagine this is how Allison looked at Mela's age."

Annabelle reflected a moment. "Alexandra would remember Allison best at that age; but yes, I believe Mela does quite take after her mother."

Gazing affectionately at Mela, Brandon's eyes misted. "I still miss Allison." Then he brightened. "Mela told me she wants to be just like me when she grows up."

"Like Father, like daughter," William quipped.

Annabelle's eyes twinkled. "She told me, 'I want to *marry* Father one day.'"

"Did she?" Brandon grinned and shook his head.

"Tsk-tsk. *Poor* thing!" William intoned with mock concern.

Brandon cast William a playfully admonishing glance. Then he knelt and gathered Mela up in his arms. "Well, it's far past bedtime."

"Father?" Mela murmured groggily as her eyes closed once more.

"Shhh, now. Time for bed," Brandon whispered.

As Brandon carried Mela snugly in his arms, up the sloping lawn toward the Big House, he thought of Annabelle's words—"The resiliency of youth." Amanda would soon be long forgotten and Barry would soon have a new kite; only the days ahead would matter. Yet Allison would never be forgotten, or his brother, Jeremy—no matter how resilient Brandon's heart had become throughout the passage of time.

CHAPTER II

Mela

Mela's shoes issued a low sucking sound as she strode across the back lawn toward the Big House. Her taffeta skirts—sopping and muddy—clung to her legs, impeding her gait. Mud spatters freckled her face and hair. Her forehead and chin each bore a broad, muddy smudge. Cinda, in only slightly better condition, plodded quickly along, close at her friend's heels.

"Hurry, Cinda, before anyone sees us!" Mela warned, her voice hushed.

"I *is* hurry'n!" Cinda complained in a loud whisper.

At last both girls reached the back-verandah steps.

"Tiptoe!" Cinda reprimanded.

Mela nodded.

A loose board creaked as they crept across the wood-slat floor of the verandah. Mela and Cinda exchanged wide-eyed glances.

Ever so carefully, Mela turned the brass knob of the back door and slipped quietly inside the house, followed closely by Cinda. Hand in hand, the two girls tiptoed down the long hallway—eyes watchful, ears keen for the slightest sound. After a heart-pounding eternity, they reached the end of the back hallway where it opened to the broad atrium of the front hall. From where the girls stood, the staircase was but a stone's throw away. The only sounds in the house were that of the front-hall clock and the servants bustling to and fro in the kitchen preparing the evening dinner. All else was still. Mela's nose tickled, and she rubbed at it hard with a soiled fist so she would not sneeze.

Cinda tugged Mela's hand and looked at her anxiously. Mela nodded.

In unison, the two girls tiptoed quickly across the hardwood floor to the foot of the stairs. No sooner had each girl placed her hand upon the banister than a stern voice froze them in their tracks.

"Mela! Cinda!" Annabelle exclaimed. "Where on *earth* have you two been?!"

Neither Cinda nor Mela dared speak or move, though their hearts plummeted.

"Turn and look at me when I speak to you!" Annabelle scolded.

Reluctantly the two girls turned and looked up at Annabelle, their expressions rendered with forged innocence. The latter drew up just short of the two damp, mud-spattered girls.

"Just look at you!" Annabelle admonished. "Where on earth have you been?! And in your best Sunday clothes!"

Mela and Cinda cast their eyes downward and shrugged imperceptibly. There was nothing they could say, there was no excuse for where they had been or that they had ruined their Sunday frocks with mud.

"Where have you been? Answer me!" Annabelle demanded sternly.

Mela swallowed hard. "Nowhere," she mumbled, her eyes downcast.

"Nowhere, *indeed!*" But no sooner had Annabelle spoken than she guessed the apparent truth. "You were both down at the pond, *weren't* you?"

"No, Aunt Annabelle," Mela said, her voice tremulous, horrified at the charge waged against her.

"Don't lie to me, either of you!" Annabelle shot. "How dare you both stand there, wet and muddy, and lie to me!"

Mela's mouth fell open, but she could not utter a syllable. Cinda's eyes welled, and she looked down at the hardwood floor.

"Mela!" Annabelle's voice was like ice. "Only this morning your father mentioned how much you had wanted to go to the pond today, that you had pleaded to go, and he was sorry that he could not take you."

"But I *didn't!*" Mela's voice was thin with emotion.

Annabelle stomped her foot on the hardwood floor. "*Don't* interrupt, young lady." Annabelle pursed her lips, then added, "Apparently, you are not quite the good girl your father believes you to be!" Annabelle stopped at this, realizing her words were far harsher than she had ever intended. She would have measured her words and tone more carefully, but Cooper had been misbehaving just moments before, and Annabelle's patience was wearing thin.

Cinda fidgeted nervously. "But … we di'n't go—"

"Not another word!" Annabelle glowered at the two girls. How *dare* they both talk back to her!

For a moment, a dreadful silence passed between the three. Even the kitchen servants had fallen still, anxious as to what all the commotion was about.

When Annabelle spoke again, her voice was firm and uncompromising. "Cinda! You are to go to your mother at once. *Now!*"

Obediently Cinda turned, scarcely venturing a worried glance at her muddy companion, then she trudged, sniffling, up the stairs to the attic.

"Mela. Go up to your room, and stay there until your father gets here. There will be no dinner for you tonight until we see just what your father has to say about all of this!"

But Mela did not move. "We didn't *go* to the pond," she insisted, her tone plaintive.

"Go! *Now!*" Annabelle ordered, punctuating her command with another stomp of her foot.

Mela turned defiantly, her head held high, and ascended the staircase with hard steps. After a moment, Mela's bedroom door all but slammed. Annabelle shut her eyes, sighed, and shook her head. First Cooper, and now Mela and Cinda—would the day never end?

"I did not go to the pond," Mela stated matter-of-factly. She stood before her father in the west sitting room. All evidence of her afternoon misadventure with Cinda was now confined to a wicker hamper in the laundry shed. Scrubbed clean and dressed for bed in a white cotton gown and pantalets, she looked, in fact, angelic. The spatters of mud had been washed from her hair, and her golden curls were pulled back with a shiny silk ribbon.

"Your Aunt Annabelle tells me differently," Brandon said. "She says that you disobeyed me and that you lied to her." He glanced from Mela to Annabelle seated nearby upon the settee. "She also told me that you talked back to her. I cannot have that," he concluded firmly.

"I don't care *what* she says," Mela declared. "I didn't go to the *pond!*"

"I saw your clothes in the hamper. They are wet and muddy. If you and Cinda were not at the pond, then I suppose you have a better answer."

Mela bit her lip thoughtfully and glanced down at the floor. Fidgeting nervously with the gathers of her nightgown, she decided she must confess. "We … we went to the slave cabins by the creek, and—" Mela paused, guiltily considering her ruined Sunday clothes.

"And what?" Brandon prompted evenly.

"And … we made mud pies." Mela raised her eyes to meet her father's gaze.

"Go upstairs to your room, Mela, and do not come out again until you can tell me the truth." Brandon's tone was unyielding.

Mela's jaw dropped. "I *am* telling the truth!"

"Mela!"

"But father! …"

"Go upstairs!"

"But it's not *fair*. I *didn't* lie!" Surely, of anyone, her father should believe her.

"You heard me, Mela. Now, *go!*"

"I didn't lie, and I didn't go to the pond!" Mela's pale-blue eyes flashed defiantly.

Brandon rose from his chair, seeming to tower above her. "Amelia, go up to your room this minute!"

"*No!*" Mela stomped her foot.

Brandon extended his arm, pointing in the direction of the stairs. "*Now, Amelia! Go!*"

Mela wanted to blurt, "I won't! It's not fair!" But her father's anger was so absolute, she knew it was of little use to argue further. Instead, she turned on her heel and strode out of the sitting room.

"I've never known her to lie before," Annabelle remarked with concern and puzzlement.

Brandon sighed. "I'd best go and talk to her." Something about the entire matter did not seem quite right. What if Mela *had* been telling the truth?

Brandon caught up to Mela halfway up the stairs. "Mela, stop a moment. I need to talk to you."

Mela turned, her lips pursed and fists clenched at her sides. Her eyes looked hard into her father's.

Hesitating a moment, Brandon stood just beneath her on the stairs. He began carefully, "You see, I don't know whether you were at the pond today or not—"

"I *wasn't!*" Mela's eyes teared, but she remained defiant. Then, in an instant, Mela lashed out—her fist striking her father's shoulder with a sharp, stinging blow.

The force of the unexpected blow caused Brandon to wince.

"It's *not* fair!" Mela pronounced as if to justify her punch. Yet she froze, and her heart pounded with fear—she dared not imagine her father's anger now.

Brandon's jaw was set firm, but his eyes had welled deep.

Mela was instantly sorry. She knew it was not the blow of her hand to her father's shoulder that had caused his tears but the wound to his heart.

For a moment neither one spoke.

"Go up to your room," Brandon said quietly.

Mela hesitated, wanting to apologize, but her sense of feeling sorely misjudged and unfairly punished won out. Her head held high, she turned and marched forthrightly up the stairs. Brandon watched her ascend, noting the defiant bounce of her curls with each hard step, and sighed.

"Massa Brandon? ..." Cotta called up the stairs.

Brandon turned to see Cotta poised below him on the steps with a small tray of dinner in her hands.

"Miss Annabelle done tol' me t' bring dis plate o' food up t' Mela. She say dat de littlun' ain' et' nothin' yet t'night."

Brandon moved aside to let Cotta pass. "Sorry," he mumbled. He felt weary, and his eyes still glistened from the sting of Mela's hand.

Cotta moved past, then hesitated with her tray. "You ... you be feelin' awright, Massa Brandon?"

Managing a smile, Brandon nodded.

"M'be ... m'be you woul' like t' take dis on up t' yer lil chil'," Cotta offered shyly, then immediately flushed, hoping Brandon would not mistake her meaning as impertinence regarding her duties as house servant.

Brandon shook his head. "No, Cotta, it's all right. You go on up." His tone was gentle and appreciative.

Cotta proceeded on her way.

Amends with Mela would have to wait until the next day.

———————

Fingers of sunlight poked through the curtain lace as a choir of birds twittered softly beyond the window panes. Slowly Mela opened her eyes to the dim rosy hue of her room. Upon sitting up in her bed, Mela suddenly felt peculiar and was obliged to lie back down on her pillows. Still, she felt oddly weak and hollow. Scared and uncertain as to why she felt so utterly peculiar, she slipped out from beneath her covers to seek her father.

Outside her father's bedroom door, Mela reached up, turned the knob, and entered. Somewhat dizzy, she stood ... feeling for a moment ... as if the hardwood floor was not ... quite beneath her.

"Father? ... Father, wake up," she whispered.

But Brandon did not stir. Only the clock on the bureau ticked as the morning sun bathed the room in a low golden light.

Mela wavered where she stood as if the floor was shifting underneath her. Her lips and skin felt oddly chilled, and her legs scarcely wanted to support her. She dared not venture even one step closer to her father's bed to rouse him lest her legs fail her altogether. "Father ... please ... *wake up!*" she called out plaintively. Great black splotches began to appear and fade in erratic pulses before her eyes, affecting her sight. "Father! ..." she pleaded.

Brandon stirred and sat up, squinting in the dim morning light to see Mela standing in the middle of his bedroom floor. "What is it Mela?" he yawned. "Are you all right?"

Unable to answer, Mela issued a low moan and crumpled, unconscious, upon the floor.

Darting from his bed, Brandon quickly knelt at her side. "Mela? ... *Mela! ...*"

Pale and still as death, Mela did not respond.

Brandon placed a quivering hand on her forehead but felt no signs of fever. "*Mela! ...*" he called to her again, his voice tremulous with fright.

There was no response.

"Dear Lord!" he breathed. Gathering her up gently into his arms, he bore her limp frame to the bed and laid her down upon the coverlets. He felt her forehead and cheek again. "Mela— ... Mela— ... can you hear me?"

While Brandon's own heart raced, it seemed that Mela's heart was still—she lay wan and motionless, scarcely breathing.

Within seconds, Brandon stood pounding frantically at Ester and Jacob's closed bedroom door.

"Good Lor'! What is it?" Jacob exclaimed as he opened the door. Close behind him, Ester was pulling a robe on over her night clothes.

"It's Mela," Brandon uttered, pale with fright, his voice fraught with urgency. "Ester, can you come? Something is wrong. Something is terribly wrong!"

"Yes, o' course." Ester brushed past Jacob and followed hurriedly behind Brandon's long anxious strides.

"She's in my room," Brandon directed, his voice edged with panic. He led Ester down the attic stairs and through the hallway to his room where he ushered her inside. He dared to hope that they would find Amelia awake and sitting up, but instead she remained as he had left her—pale and still.

Ester sat on the edge of the bed and felt Mela's forehead.

"I don't know what's wrong—if she is ill or fainted or what—but she won't wake up or move. I ... I didn't know what to do!" Brandon's words tumbled agitatedly one after the other.

Ester calmly took up Mela's hands in both of hers and waited a long moment, her expression serious. Watching Ester, Brandon's heart leapt against his chest, and he feared the worst. Presently, Ester rose and indicated the bedside. "Stay wit' her now. I's gonna fetch de smellin' salts." She added gently, "Don' fret so, Massa Brandon. Yer chil', Miss Mela, she gonna be fine, jus' fine." She gave Brandon's arm an assuring squeeze and went out.

Sitting on the edge of the bed, Brandon held his daughter's pale hand in his and kissed the limp fingers. "*Jesus,*" he breathed.

Seconds stretched into an eternity, but at last Ester returned with a vial of smelling salts in her hand. Occupying the opposite side of the bed, Ester uncorked the glass vial of salts and passed its pungent odor beneath Mela's nose. At once Mela was roused; she murmured something, then her eyelids fluttered opened. Somewhat disoriented, Mela's pale-blue eyes looked up at Ester, then at Brandon.

"She gonna be jus' fine now, you'll see," Ester reassured, with a comforting smile.

"Father? ..." Mela murmured.

"Yes, Mela, I'm here," Brandon whispered, his voice fraught with emotion. He pressed Mela's little hands tenderly in his.

"What ... what ... happened ? ..."

Brandon swallowed hard, and Ester answered for him. "You jus' had a faintin' spell, chil', an' giben yer father a *mos'* awful fright!" She smiled warmly, and her dark eyes twinkled assurance.

"I'm so ... hungry." Mela felt as if she might faint again.

Brandon caressed Mela's cheek with the backs of his fingers. "Shhh—lie still now, my little dear one," he soothed.

Ester rose from the bed. "I's gonna fetch some food fo' Mela. She be fine now, don' you worry none, Massa Brandon."

As Ester left the room, Brandon called to her, "Ester? ..."

"Yessuh." She paused at the doorway.

"Thank you, Ester," he said as his eyes filled with heartfelt gratitude.

Ester smiled. "I ain' done so terrible much, Massa Brandon," she said modestly, and went out.

Turning to Mela, Brandon asked gently, "Didn't you eat any of the dinner that Cotta brought up to you last night?"

Mela shook her head no upon the pillow.

"Why ever not?"

Mela shrugged. She looked up at him sadly, as if she might cry.

Brandon gathered her in his arms and hugged her to him. "There, there...," he whispered, "I'm sorry, my little dear one. We're all right now. We're all right."

Mela forgave her father for his unfair disbelief about the mud pies, and Brandon forgave her for making mud pies in her best Sunday clothes—but only after a stern lecture on the matter.

The following Saturday, Brandon specially escorted Mela to the pond to feed the ducks. It would be their last such outing for some time, as the overhead skies had turned to slate, and autumn began to chill the air. But the threat of inclement weather and saying her farewells to the ducks was now of little importance to Mela. Mela was once again—and she felt forevermore—in her father's good graces, and that was all that mattered to her. Once again the apple of her father's eye, Mela was bound and determined not to fall far from the tree.

September faded into the chill of October, which ebbed into the children's celebration of All Hallow's Eve—replete with jack o' lanterns, frightful costumes, bobbing for apples, apple cider, and pumpkin pie. On the cusp of autumn, Barry, with his father's help, made more than one new kite to fly in the howling winds, and he even made one for Carolina. Meanwhile, storms came and went with flashes of lightning, crashes of thunder, and driving rain, alternating between days of warm, bright skies, as the innately erratic season could not yet decide which it truly wanted to be—summer or fall. Early November cast a palette of crisp gold, fiery red, brilliant yellow, and rust-brown leaves upon the ground heralding the onset of winter, which was now only weeks away. Throughout this time, Mela endeavored quite successfully to be the well-behaved girl she knew her father wanted her to be as she sought more and more to emulate him. She loved him so.

"Like father, like daughter," William would chuckle, finding Mela frequently seated beside her father at his studio desk. Seated there, she would "write" and "illustrate" on sheet after sheet of scrap paper. Mela's increasing emulation of her father concerned him at times. "She should be playing with the other children or with her dolls," Brandon would say. But Annabelle and William always reassured him, "She will grow out of it with time."

On this particular mid-November morning, Mela was not seated near her father at his studio desk diligently "working" but was at play somewhere in the Big House. Brandon rather missed her company, although he was glad she had apparently found some other activity with which to busy herself. In a while, he would take a break from his writing and go up to the Big House to check on Mela and see what sort of play she was engaged in. Perhaps she and Cinda were playing tea-party or dress-up.

It seemed a shame that nearly all the other children at the Crawford Hill Big House were school age except Mela, Cinda, and Cooper. This meant that on weekdays there was little diversion for Mela and Cinda except to play together or alone. Although the two little girls were endlessly fond of each other, and at times inseparable, Brandon wished they also had the company of other children to play with. The rambunctious little Cooper was clearly too troublesome for the two girls to handle—if he was not stumbling headlong into mischief on his own, then he was busy ruining their play. Lack of ample playmates fostered Cinda's inherently quiet nature, fueled Cooper's mischievous behavior, and encouraged Mela all the more to emulate and keep company with her father. Brandon reflected on this, then lifted his eyes upward from his writing paper, and whispered longingly, "Allison, dear one, if only you were here to be with our little one."

Annabelle, while somewhat of a surrogate mother to Mela, was too busy attending to Cooper and helping run the plantation to spend much time with the child. (And it was debatable which of her duties—attending to Cooper or the demands of the plantation—presented the greater challenge!)

Since Mela's birth, Ester had served as Mela's nursemaid; but now, even Ester's household duties had expanded in proportion to the household's growth, leaving little free time to devote specially to Mela. At least Ester found time to read to the children each afternoon from various children's books. In the South, teaching a favorite slave or house-servant to read was at times tolerated; and so, the practice of doing this at Crawford Hill had been carried out by William's father and his father before him. Now Ester spent an hour or two each afternoon before tea teaching Mela, Cinda, Quash, and Cooper to read. Annabelle made a point that Cotta should be in attendance as well. While Brandon was pleased that his daughter had this opportunity for a head-start on her education, he worried about the influence of Ester's Gullah. Brandon could only hope that Mela would learn to translate the printed words from Ester's spoken Gullah into proper English; otherwise, he feared, she would forevermore read in Gullah.

One more year, Brandon consoled himself, and then Mela could attend school in Upper All Saints Parish with the other children. Upon first arriving at Crawford Hill, Brandon was grateful to learn that the children's school in All Saints Parish was adequately, if not lavishly, provided for. He was further relieved to learn that the religious moral teachings that infused the curriculum were moderate and not overbearing. Such moral teachings often disseminated the Southern religious culture's distinctive gender conventions—conventions that Brandon did not wholeheartedly agree with, to say the very least. Men and women of the South tended far more to live their lives as members of a gender than as individuals. Slaveholders generally saw to it that their daughters received an education appropriate to their social station; however, even now, in 1860, no Southern women shared equal access to education as did men. Ultimately, Brandon wanted more than this for Mela. While Southern women were increasingly attending academies sponsored by the churches, Brandon ultimately envisioned a university education for his daughter. Accordingly, Brandon had to smile at his fear that Mela would ever grow subservient to stifling Southern gender conventions; after all, Mela was always, except for this mid-November morning, huddled over sheets of paper "writing" and "illustrating"—emulating Father.

Lost in thought, imagining Mela's future, Brandon did not hear William enter the studio.

"Hard at work, I see," William teased.

"I *knew* I should have locked the door," Brandon shot back, with a grin.

"So, where is your assistant this morning?" William closed the studio door behind him and went over to stand near the hearth."

"My assistant?" Brandon chuckled, and looked across his desk at William. "Oh, I dispatched her to Charleston. She's going to be my city correspondent—investigative reporting, politics . . . that sort of thing."

"I see!" William smiled broadly. He shivered and briskly rubbed his hands together. "Brrrr! It's *cold* in here. Your fire's almost died out."

"I'm all right," Brandon said casually, but admitted, ". . . although my fingers *are* feeling a bit stiff."

"Hmmm. . . ," William mused. "Stiff fingers might improve your drawing!"

Grinning at William's teasing banter, Brandon leaned back in his desk chair and stretched. "Don't you have anything better to do this morning, William, other than bothering people who are trying to earn their daily bread?"

"Do you mean to tell me this is *work?*!" William feigned incredulity, his eyes sparkling mischievously beneath arched eyebrows.

" 'Hard at work, I see,' " Brandon said, repeating William's first words to him upon entering the studio.

"I was being *sarcastic,*" William deadpanned.

Brandon laughed and threw a pen at him. "Either make yourself useful or go away!"

"Don't worry, I'm going. I've got plenty to do today. *Real* work! Not writing stories and drawing pictures—that's child's play!" William smirked.

"Ummm," Brandon nodded. "Yes, it is child's play; and Mela would do a much better job at it than *you* ever could," Brandon shot, and laughed heartily at his jest.

"What?!" Mela better than *me?*" William pretended offense.

"Absolutely!"

"Well! I am *highly* insulted! The *audacity!*"

"Go!" Brandon grinned at his friend from across his desk.

William remained by the hearthside. "I still say it's too damn cold in here."

Brandon shot him a warning glance.

"All right, I'm leaving!" With a broad smile that belied his mock indignation, William strode toward the door.

"Good!"

"Fine!"

William went out of the studio just as Brandon turned and hurled a second pen at him. As the door closed, the pen struck the doorframe and clattered to the floor.

"Blast!" Brandon exclaimed under his breath, then retrieved the pen. While he was up, he placed another log on the fire, then he returned to his desk. Settling down to work, he mumbled to himself, "Now, where was I? ..." As he absorbed himself in the article before him, Brandon made a mental note to check on Mela in a short while and see what play she had found to be engaged in this morning. He would go up to the Big House after the new log on the hearth was consumed.

Mela stood upon a low wooden footstool before her father's bedroom washstand. She knew her father was at work in his studio and would not return to the Big House for quite some time. Alone in her father's room, the bedroom door shut carefully behind her, Mela decided she should begin the day as Father did. Poised on the foot stool, she studied her reflection a moment in the lower portion of the washstand mirror. Then she spied her father's shaving brush, still damp from his early-morning shave, and the shallow porcelain mug of shaving soap. Carefully she decanted a bit of water from the stand's pitcher into the bowl, wet the brush, and worked the soap in the mug into a froth with the bristles. Studying her reflection once again, Mela lathered her cheeks and chin. She would not lather her upper lip, because Father kept a mustache.

Facing the mirror, Mela tilted her head slowly every which way, deciding how to begin her shave. She would start with her cheeks first and finish with her chin. Mela scanned the washstand's table top for her father's razor, but it was not there. She frowned—how could she shave without Father's razor? Then she remembered. Momentarily stepping down from the footstool, Mela opened a shallow drawer at the front of the stand. There it was. Cautiously Mela picked up the razor by its gleaming handle and closed the drawer. Back atop the footstool, Mela puffed her cheeks with air and drew the razor near.

But Mela was a deliberate and thoughtful child. Pausing a moment, she remembered how Father had always told her never to play with knives and to never even go near the kitchen bread knife as "it is sharp as a razor." How sharp *was* a razor? Mela wondered. It couldn't be *that* bad; after all, her father *did* use a razor to shave, and he never even cut himself. Nonetheless, Mela decided that she had better test the blade first, before beginning.

Deflating her puffed cheeks, Mela set the razor aside, next to the washstand bowl. She picked up her father's linen towel from the bar on the stand, folded it several times, and draped it over her left hand. She doubted the razor could even cut through the towel. Lifting the razor once more, she applied the blade to the towel and began gently sawing it back and forth. Eyes squinting above lathered cheeks, she strained to see any effect of the blade on the white linen. Apparently the blade was not cutting at all, and she sawed four more times. At last Mela stopped and shrugged. What was all the fuss about sharp knives and razors? Parents were silly; they worried too much.

Nonetheless, Mela decided to unfurl the towel to see if it bore even one cut or at least a slight fray. Certainly the razor had not penetrated at all; if it had, she would have felt it—and she had felt nothing. Still clutching the razor, Mela unfurled the linen towel with both hands and held it up to the light of the window. At once her lathered jaw fell open and her eyes gaped round. The cloth was cut clean through in numerous slashes—it was positively crosshatched with cuts! Mela's eyes immediately darted to the place on her hand where the towel had been folded. Her heart skipped a beat. Blood ran in a torrent down her arm, dripping to the floor. Razor slashes crosshatched her fingers and palm. The blade of the razor was so sharp that it had cut her hand painlessly. Mela could only stand gaping open-mouthed at the blood and linen towel lacerated with cuts. Brandon's razor, all but forgotten, was still clutched tight in her right hand—the late morning sunlight glinting on its blade. Mela was so stunned at the results of her experiment that she did not even hear her father enter the room behind her.

There Mela stood, perched precariously upon the wooden footstool, blood flowing down her thin little arm, the shining razor held aloft in her right hand. Brandon's heart stopped.

"Mela...," he enunciated quietly, "put the razor down." The calm authority of his command was fraught with anxiousness. His heart pounded.

"Father!" Mela turned abruptly in surprise. Quite literally, she had been caught red-handed, and she scarcely knew what to say. Her eyes stared at her father with a wide frightened innocence above her lathered cheeks.

His anger rising, Brandon strode toward Mela and extracted the razor from her hand. He snatched the ruined towel out of her grasp and tossed it roughly aside.

"Jesus *Christ*, Mela!" Brandon shouted. "What in God's name possessed you?!"

Mela's eyes welled deep and, before Brandon could grasp her bloodied hand to tend to it, she put both small fists to her eyes to wipe away the tears. Blood ran down her lathered left cheek, turning the foam pink. With her other hand, Mela managed to get soap in her right eye, and it began to sting.

Brandon took her wounded hand in his and began to inspect the cuts. "Jesus Christ!" he uttered under his breath.

"Oooww!" Mela whined.

"Hold still!"

"I have soap in my eye!" Mela whimpered.

Brandon ignored this. He was far more concerned with gashes across her hand. "Be still!" he warned.

"My eye hurts." Mela stomped her foot.

"Well, you will have to *wait*, Mela. I must bandage your hand first." Brandon's tone was uncompromising and rough.

Instantly Mela began to cry in earnest.

Brandon submerged her hand in the soapy water of the washstand bowl to rinse it, and the water stung horribly—searing into each and every cut. Mela cried out and tried to pull her hand back, but Brandon held it fast beneath the water. Mela wailed piteously. Mercifully, her tears cleansed the offending soap from her eye, but this did little to quell the misery of her slashed hand.

"It hurts! Father, it hurts!" Mela wailed as if her heart would break.

Her pleas were so woeful that Brandon felt his own eyes sting with tears, but he did not extract her hand from the bowl of reddened water until he had thoroughly cleansed away the blood and washed the cuts.

Once he removed Mela's hand from the water, she calmed down considerably. All the while that Brandon bandaged her hand in a clean pocket-square, Mela wept and whimpered. Still, Brandon's anger was far stronger than his sympathy. He wiped the lather and tears from her face with a fresh towel in hard strokes. Mela whimpered and sniffled. At last he held a handkerchief to her nose, and commanded her sharply, "Blow!"

After a time, Mela sat upon the edge of her father's bed, her left hand swathed in the clean white pocket-square, her tearstained cheeks scrubbed clean. That is where Brandon had ordered her to sit and not to cry. The lump in Mela's throat was so enormous, she felt she could hardly breathe. Desperately she tried not to cry. She looked up with round eyes at her father who paced angrily, then stood fixed before her.

"Don't you ever disobey me, *ever*! Do you hear?!"

Mela scarcely dared nod her head.

Brandon sighed. "Haven't I told you before that knives and sharp things are not toys?"

"Y ... yes," Mela quavered, her eyes filling.

"You might have lost a finger, or *worse!*"

"I ... I'm sorry, Father." Mela's voice was barely audible, and a great tear slipped silently down her cheek.

"You had better be sorry!" Brandon admonished, although the anger had all but gone from his voice.

Mela could not utter another sound but bent her head of ruffled curls and wept, blotting her tears with the thick swathe of her bandaged hand.

All at once Brandon's heart melted. He sat beside Mela on the bed and hugged her close. "Mela," he sighed, and kissed the top of her head. "What am I going to do with you?"

Mela shrugged in her father's arms and wept, her cheek against his shirt.

"I'm sorry I yelled so, Mela. I didn't mean to yell at you, but you might have cut yourself badly. *Anything* might have happened, something terrible. Do you understand?"

Mela nodded her cheek against her father's shirt dampened with tears.

"You know I love you, Mela," he said gently, "but I scold you because you absolutely must do what I say. You simply *must* obey me. You *must.*"

Mela wept silently, yet all the harder, in her father's arms. Brandon kissed her curls once again and rocked her gently to and fro to comfort her. "Shhh ... shhh, now; it's all right," he soothed.

After a time, Mela calmed down and remained huddled in her father's embrace.

"Why on earth did you ever try to shave, Mela?" Brandon asked gently.

Mela hesitated, then answered quietly, her words muffled in her father's shirt, "I ... I want to be like you."

This admission touched Brandon as it never had before. "I see...," he said quietly, and his eyes filled.

CHAPTER 12

Secession

"In his first issue of *The Liberator*, in 1831, abolitionist leader William Lloyd Garrison wrote, 'I do not wish to think, speak, or write with moderation. No! No! Tell a man whose house is on fire to give a moderate alarm; tell him to moderately rescue his wife from the hands of a ravisher; tell the mother to gradually extricate her babe from the fire into which it has fallen;—but urge me not to use moderation in a case like the present. I am in earnest—I will not equivocate—I will not excuse—I will not retreat a single inch—AND I WILL BE HEARD.' As if to further emphasize these words, Garrison burnt a copy of the United States Constitution during one July fourth celebration in 1844 in protest of slavery.

"Since the November sixth election of Republican Abraham Lincoln to the office of the presidency of America, slaveholders and government leaders across the South are echoing Garrison's words and sentiment—*not* with regard to abolition but with regard to secession! Southern proponents of secession are determined not only to be heard but to act!

"Indeed, South Carolina metaphorically burned the American Constitution upon Lincoln's election on November sixth: South Carolina lowered the American flag at Charleston and raised her own Palmetto flag. It remains to be seen whether South Carolina will also metaphorically—and perhaps literally—burn the American Constitution when she votes on the issue of secession from the Union just days from now. The Convention of the People of South Carolina will be held in Saint Andrew's Hall in the peninsula city of Charleston on December 20, 1860 to decide the fate of South Carolina. The state may very well vote to free herself from bondage to the Union in order to maintain the bondage of slavery and preserve the Southern way of life."

Brandon paused from his writing and set his pen aside—he had not slept well the night before and found it difficult to concentrate. In three days' time, he and William would depart by carriage for Charleston to attend the convention at Saint Andrew's Hall. While Brandon looked forward to attending what could very well be a historic event, he was concerned about leaving the children for nearly a week—particularly Mela.

Brandon stretched, yawned, leaned back in his desk chair, and gazed absently across his studio.

"At a loss for words?" William asked. Sitting upon a window seat in Brandon's studio, he looked up a moment from his copy of the *Charleston Mercury*.

"No, not really," Brandon yawned. "Just tired."

"I didn't sleep well either." William folded his newspaper and set it aside. "Cotta's pecan pie."

Brandon nodded. "I dare say, you're right. Best pecan pie ever made, but it is far too rich."

"Well," William noted, "it isn't Cotta's fault that we each had three slices after dinner."

"Two and a half," Brandon admitted.

Grinning, William conceded, "Two and a half." Upon that, he rose and crossed the studio to Brandon's desk. "Let's see what you've got so far."

Handing the page to William, Brandon shook his head doubtfully. "The ink isn't flowing yet this morning,"

"That's because the studio is so damn cold!" William jested. "The ink is frozen!"

"Get out!" Brandon grinned.

"Not until I've finished reading," William chuckled, then turned his attention to the unfinished article. William read in silence. Knitting his brow thoughtfully, he handed the page back to Brandon. "It's a good start ... but I suppose it could use some 'punching up.'"

About to nod in agreement, Brandon instead narrowed his eyes thoughtfully. "You think it needs punching up?"

William shrugged and nodded. "Yes, 'punching up.'"

"Well!" Brandon insinuated playfully, "That's not *all* that needs 'punching up'! ..."

William laughed heartily, and Brandon joined in until he was interrupted by another broad yawn.

"Damn!" Brandon uttered, punctuating his yawn. Reaching out a hand to the freshly inked page upon his desk, he crumpled the unfinished article in a ball. "Blast!" he muttered, and hurled it across the room onto the flickering hearth.

"Hey! What did you do that for?!"

"It wasn't any good."

"It was fine!"

"It needed 'punching up,'" Brandon mocked.

The crumpled ball of writing quickly ignited and was engulfed in flames.

"'Punching,' not 'burning,'" William chuckled, then shrugged, and added, "Well, never mind. There will be plenty to write about at the convention in Charleston."

"Definitely, there should be."

"Where is Mela this morning?" William indicated the empty chair beside Brandon's desk. "Is she having her morning shave?" he teased.

The night before, while Brandon slept, Cotta's pecan pie had elicited yet another nightmare about the matter of Mela's "shaving." The starkly vivid nightmare woke him abruptly before dawn, his heart pounding and his nightclothes bathed in a cold sweat. Brandon shuddered as he recalled the dream. "No, she's not 'shaving'—she's had one '*close shave*' enough, if you get my drift."

William grinned. "Excellent play on words!"

"Well, I *am* a *journalist*, after all...," Brandon boasted jokingly. Then, to answer William's question as to Mela's whereabouts, Brandon explained, "You see, Mela has decided that since I am going away soon, she wants to start getting used to the idea of my being gone. Since yesterday morning I have ceased to exist."

"Ah ... I see." William frowned thoughtfully. "Poor thing ... she *will* miss you. At least Carolina, Ashley, and Cooper are all used to me coming and going for days at a time while away on business."

Brandon nodded.

It was true that William was gone now and again on local business about Upper and Lower All Saints Parish or occasionally to Charleston. Although William's children were accustomed to his frequent absences and had their mother at home when he was away, Brandon's children were seldom without their father, and they had no mother to be there for them should he be absent.

"Mela won't even talk to me, except in the most cursory manner," Brandon grumbled as he toyed with his pen. "I don't think she is truly angry with me for going away but is only insulating herself from me ... I suppose, so that she won't miss me quite so terribly." He sighed. "I looked in on her this morning to invite her to keep me company in the studio, but she responded the same as yesterday morning. She barely glanced up at me, and when she did, her eyes were hard and cold. 'No, thank you, Father,' she said perfunctorily, and resumed her play alone."

"Ah, you British!" William chided playfully. "The stoic stiff-upper-lip nonsense."

Brandon smiled knowingly, and then sobered. "I hope Mela will be all right while I'm gone. I hate to leave her for so many days. She doesn't quite understand ... but I absolutely must go."

"And what about Barry?"

"Barry, naturally, wants to come along with us. *He* is angry with me because I won't let him. We had quite a discussion the other night— an argument, more like. Barry is twelve now and reaching that difficult age between boyhood and becoming an adventurous, independent young man—willful. He says that he *is* old enough to come along. I tried to explain that you and I have work to do, that he will likely be bored and left alone in a hotel room with little to do." Brandon rolled his eyes, and shook his head. "Then I made the mistake of telling Barry I needed him at Crawford Hill to help look after Mela. That went over *quite* well, I must say!" Brandon finished, an edge of sarcasm in his voice.

William chuckled, then observed, "I suppose with Barry twelve years old and Mela only five, the two are reaching a parting of age."

"Yes, it *is* becoming more difficult lately." Brandon fell silent. Looking downward, toying with the pen in his hands, his eyes misted, and he uttered quietly, "How I wish Allison were here."

"We will be home again no later than Christmas Eve Day," William had promised Annabelle and the children. The Convention of the People of South Carolina was scheduled to meet on December 20, 1860. If the convention's Ordinance of Secession passed, then William and Brandon would return by December twenty-fourth. If the ordinance did not pass, then they would likely return home sooner.

The morning of December seventeenth—the day of William and Brandon's departure—dawned crisp but not unpleasantly so. Overhead, skies promised a clear, warm day. Winter weather along South Carolina's coast was seldom predictable. Winter one year might prompt outdoor picnics and visits to the seaside, whereas other winters were beset with chill winds, rain or hail, or even the rare occasion of a light falling of snow. On this particular day, the weather could not have cooperated better for a journey to Charleston.

Annabelle, Carolina, Ashley, and Cooper, along with Ester, Cinda, and Quash, as well as Cotta, all stood upon the front verandah of the Big House to see William and Brandon off. Jacob had driven their carriage onto the roundabout, stopping it before the verandah steps. Servants loaded the trunks, carpetbags, and satchels for the two men's journey as William boarded the carriage. Brandon, meanwhile, had briefly returned inside the Big House to say his final goodbyes to Barry and Mela, each of whom were playing alone in their respective rooms.

Standing in the doorway of his son's bedroom, his hand resting on the brass knob, Brandon said, "I'm leaving now, Barry. I should be home by Christmas Eve day."

Barry sat at his desk working intently on a charcoal drawing of a horse. He glanced up at his father briefly, and nearly spat, "So? Who cares!" But instead, he bit his tongue, shrugged, and busied himself with the details of the horse's mane.

His son's aloofness and surly attitude stung. "Well," Brandon said quietly, "goodbye, then, Barry." He wanted to say something more but refrained.

Without looking up, Barry forced a monosyllabic, "Bye," and using his fingertips, shaded the charcoal contours of the horse's back and legs. His cold indifference to his father's leaving was meant to wound.

Silently Brandon watched his son a moment, then went out, closing the door behind him. Barry's aloof dismissal of his father had wounded as intended. His heart somewhat heavy, Brandon walked down the hall to Mela's room. Tapping on her bedroom door, he called tentatively, "Mela?" Silence. He tapped again. "Mela? It's Father." Still, no answer came. Opening the door, Brandon found Mela seated upon the middle of her floor, a tin cup of soapy water beside her and a reed in her hand, desultorily blowing bubbles into the air.

"Mela, your Uncle William and I are leaving now. . . . I hoped you might want to come downstairs and see us off along with the others."

Mela did not look up. She went on blowing bubbles as if her father was not even there, as if he had already long since gone.

Brandon entered the room and knelt upon one knee opposite Mela. "Don't I at least get one hug goodbye, then?" he asked softly.

If Mela considered this at all, she did not show it. She only continued to blow gently through the reed, then she shook it to free the hollow sphere, marveling at its iridescent surface as it glided through the air.

Brandon rose. Pausing at the door, he added quietly, "Be good for your Aunt Annabelle and Ester."

Mela scarcely shrugged in response, gazing at the floating bubble.

Heavy hearted, standing at his daughter's doorway, Brandon offered, "I shall miss you, even if you shan't miss me." He sighed and turned to leave.

Mela listened as her father's footsteps faded down the hall and descended the stairs, whereupon she heard the sound of the front door closing. The house was still. Mela kept blowing bubbles, though her eyes welled, melting the shimmering hues before her.

William, having said his goodbyes to Annabelle and the children, was seated in the carriage waiting. He occupied the driver's side, the reins held loosely, yet ready, in his hands. William enjoyed driving and did not bother about social pretenses of requiring a coachman to chauffeur him on business trips. Driving afforded him quiet time alone to ponder and reflect or to think about the future. On this trip, however, he looked forward to Brandon's company—the two men had long since grown as close as brothers and as comfortable sharing a silence between them as with any topic of conversation.

Brandon stepped up into the carriage and sat on the passenger's side. "Sorry to keep you waiting."

"Mela and Barry are not coming down to see you off, then?"

Brandon glanced toward the Big House and everyone gathered out front, save for his own two children. "No ... no, they're not coming down," he said quietly.

William hesitated.

"We'd best be off," Brandon said.

Final goodbyes were sung out gaily between William and the others as he guided the carriage across the roundabout and set off down the long oak-lined drive. Gradually the carriage grew smaller, obscured by the shadows cast by the canopy of moss-draped branches overhead.

Suddenly the front door opened, and Mela darted past all those gathered on the verandah. She bounded down the verandah steps and stood upon the rutted dirt of the roundabout. Her eyes wide with panic, she scanned the empty roundabout for her father and Uncle William in their carriage—but they were not there. "Where is my father?" Mela asked, her voice sounding thin and anxious.

Annabelle hurried down the verandah steps and knelt at Mela's side to explain that her father had already gone and to comfort her—but it was too late. Mela saw the mere speck of the carriage in the distance, nearing the end of the long drive.

"Father!" Mela burst into tears and scampered down the drive, chasing after the receding carriage. "Father! *Father!*" Mela wailed, tears streaming down her cheeks as she ran as fast as her legs would carry her.

Annabelle rushed after Mela and caught her gently by the arm. "Father!" Mela cried plaintively, then fell sobbing in her Aunt's arms. "I want my father—I want my *father!*" she wept, her words muffled against the lace of Annabelle's bodice.

In the distance, the carriage rounded the corner onto the main road and slipped from view.

"I want my father!" Mela bawled.

"He will be home again soon, Mela," Annabelle whispered, rocking the distraught child held close against her. "It's all right," she soothed. "He will return home soon."

"I want my father!" Mela sobbed inconsolably. Her heart had broken.

———◇———

Slate-colored chimney smoke drifted upward in lazy plumes tingeing the blue marbled sky. Morning's last blush had long since faded from view. Risen well before dawn, Brandon had already bathed and dressed for breakfast—an unfamiliar bed and new surroundings had seen to that. Nonetheless, Brandon had slept soundly enough and felt rested, eager to begin the day. He stood at his hotel window and looked northeastward over the Charleston rooftops. Although old-lineage Charlestonians preferred to think of their city as quite sophisticated, even cosmopolitan, Brandon thought of Charleston as simply a small provincial harbor town. Assuredly, however, Charleston was not without its unique Southern charms, and these were not lost on Brandon's artistic eye. Even the steeple-pierced panorama of rooftops—peaked and flat, chimney-studded and gabled—possessed a charm all its own. What a picturesque view his hotel window offered! Perhaps later, he would sketch the city's rooflines against the backdrop of the sky, punctuated by ship masts that hovered over the Cooper River, to show to Mela and Barry upon his return home.

William and Brandon had obtained top, fifth-floor, rooms at the regal and much-touted Mills House Hotel. First opened just seven years earlier, in 1853, the hotel was still considered quite new. A local newspaper had billed the hotel as "one of the largest, most commodious buildings in the city!" During this particular week of the Convention of the People of South Carolina, Charleston could be especially thankful to the Hotel's financier that the Mills House had been built at all—all one hundred twenty-five rooms had been booked for the event; the hotel was filled to capacity! Brandon was thankful for William's foresight to reserve their adjacent top-floor rooms well in advance. The minute William had heard that the convention site had been moved from Columbia to Charleston due to a sudden smallpox epidemic, he arranged for two rooms at the elegant Mills House Hotel. Less expensive accommodations could have been had at any one of the other three hotels in Charleston—the Charleston and Pavilion Hotels or Waverly House—but William decided that he and Brandon may as well be comfortable and have the best. While the Charleston Hotel had always been considered the most fashionable accommodation, fashion did not equate to comfort as William had said. He and Brandon agreed on the understated elegance of the Mills House. Of course, Brandon had shuddered to suppose what their hotel rooms would cost, but William had jovially insisted on paying for both of them, saying, "My treat! Consider it my Christmas gift for you!" Brandon did not argue.

"Christmas," Brandon mused as he gazed out over the Charleston rooftops. How unlike Christmas in England the holiday was in the South. Brandon fondly recalled London cloaked in snow and the gentle, rolling hills of Derbyshire hidden beneath a blanket of sparkling white. Then, with a tender pang of sentimentality, he remembered that one special Christmastime years earlier—his errant snowball that had accidentally struck Allison at Loxley House and their sleigh ride together at dusk, when they first dared profess their love to one another. How long ago it all seemed—and yet as if it were only yesterday. For a moment, Brandon imagined the Charleston skyline patched with white, the chill air dappled with great downy flakes. He missed snow, even with its myriad of inconveniences. He hoped he would be able to see Mela's first frolic in the snow while she was still a little girl, while snow would still hold a special enchantment for her as it once had for Barry back in England—as it always seemed to for most little ones.

Brandon glanced at his pocket watch: eight-thirty. If William did not rise soon, Brandon would go down to the dining room alone; he was famished.

Looking out again upon the Charleston skyline, Brandon tried to recall the many distinguishing features of the city pointed out to him by William the evening before. It seemed that William knew the city as intimately as his own plantation. To the east, Saint Philip's church steeple soared heavenward, dwarfing the plumes of gray chimney smoke swirling about it. William had joked that there was at least one church per city block in Charleston. Brandon doubted this was true, although even he noted there were at least a dozen in the immediate vicinity of the Mills House Hotel alone. Moreover, most of the churches had been built in recent years, from 1800 to 1850. One exception to this was Saint Michael's Protestant Episcopal Church, one block south of the Mills House. It had stood on the corner of Broad and Meeting Streets since 1761, erected nearly one hundred years earlier. "George Washington worshipped here when visiting Charleston," William had informed. "I'm impressed!" Brandon had issued a sly grin in return, a touch of sarcasm to his voice. "Still sore because your side lost the war?" William had jested. Brandon could only grin sheepishly and shrug in concession. Upon this, William had promised that while in Charleston they would ascend St. Michael's steeple for a full, panoramic view of the city, the harbor, and both the Ashley and Cooper rivers. Brandon had agreed that he would bring his sketching material.

Now, as Brandon scanned the rooftops, there was only one other building he recognized: the U.S. Custom House—a low, white-columned building, stately and dignified, perched on the water's edge along the Cooper River's waterfront. The names of the many other distinctive buildings, landmarks, steeples, and parks escaped Brandon since William's window-view tour the evening before. There would be much to see in Charleston. Several years earlier, upon their arrival in the city, neither Brandon nor Allison had taken the time to tour—they had only been anxious to travel onward to Crawford Hill. Now Brandon wished that they had taken the time, and more so, he wished Allison were here now to enjoy the sites with him.

Glancing at his pocket watch once again, his stomach issuing a low rumble of hunger, Brandon noted that it was nearly nine o'clock. Precisely then, a knock sounded at his hotel-room door. It was William, at last. After greeting each other, the two men headed downstairs to breakfast.

Cut crystal, silver place settings, cloths of white linen, gleaming tea and coffee services, high ceilings, dark wood paneling, thick carpets, and crisply attired servants all lent the dining room of the Mill's House an unmistakable air of elegance and formality. Amidst these fine surroundings, William and Brandon were soon seated comfortably before generous plates of poached eggs, slices of ham, berry muffins, jam, and fresh orange wedges.

They shared their table with two other gentlemen who had been similarly served. One was just finishing his breakfast while the other wrote busily in a notebook far more than he bothered with eating, alternatively brushing muffin crumbs from his fingers and taking up his pen to write. The former gentleman finished his plate, dusted the crumbs from his beard and mustache with his napkin, and then rose. "Don't forget to eat," he said to his companion. "I'm sure Uncle Billy can wait!" he joked. "Besides, if you starve, what'll Uncle Billy have left to do?" He chuckled at his own humor.

His fellow journalist scarcely stopped writing and glanced upward. "Don't you have a paper to run?"

With a good-natured twinkle in his eye, the former laughed, then turned and threaded his way through the crowded dining room toward the door.

The writer shook his head with a grin and put his pen aside. "Never mind him," he said to William and Brandon. "*I* certainly don't! He's only the managing editor of the *Charleston Mercury*."

"And you are? ..." Brandon asked.

The writer extended his free hand across the table. "Alfred Cooke, lowly local writer for the *Charleston Daily Courier*." He studied Brandon a moment. "You're not local are you?"

"I write and sketch for *The Illustrated London News*," Brandon explained.

"Ah! A foreign correspondent!" Alfred noted. "Well, let us hope the convention proves worth the excursion from London."

"Actually," William put in, "Brandon has been living in South Carolina at my plantation for the past six or so years now."

"Oh, I *see*! ..." Alfred Cooke laughed, "Practically a native South Carolinian! And ... you are?"

"William Crawford. I own Crawford Hill rice plantation in Lower All Saints Parish." He extended his hand across the table.

"Well—William, Brandon—I'm pleased to meet both of you." Alfred thought a moment. "Crawford Hill ... isn't that one of the largest rice plantations in the region?"

"Nearly so." William shrugged modestly.

"Who is Uncle Billy?" Brandon interjected. "Is he the managing editor of the *Charleston Daily Courier*?"

Alfred erupted in laughter. "Heavens, no," he grinned. "Uncle Billy is a carrier for the *Courier* in Charleston, a Negro. He's been delivering the paper to our fellow Charlestonians for ... oh, must be twenty, twenty-five years or more. Everyone knows Uncle Billy," he explained, ending with a note of fondness.

Alfred Cooke struck Brandon and William as a pleasant man, intelligent but without scholarly pretense. He was down-to-earth, genuine, warm, and cordial. Alfred was perhaps ten years older than Brandon, in his early forties. Although decidedly attractive, his face was distinguished more by character than by handsomeness. He possessed an element of charisma, but not overpoweringly so, humble rather than domineering. Affable and bright, he was evidently—as his breakfast had long since grown cold—stock of a strong work ethic. Butter stains and muffin crumbs spotted Alfred's open notebook.

Conversation between the three men soon turned to the newspaper business. Only then did Alfred Cooke put away his pen and resume his cold breakfast, commenting briefly between bites. Brandon explained that he was working as a foreign correspondent covering issues pertaining to the Southern economy, society, culture, slavery versus abolition, and politics. Alfred informed William and Brandon that he had been a writer for the *Charleston Daily Courier* for over ten years and, prior to that, he had written for a paper in Washington, D.C.

"... I once lived in Washington for nearly ten years, but it was never home to me," Alfred continued, upon finishing a bite of orange. "I missed the South. Some wondered how I could be satisfied leaving the country's political hub and a major Washington publication, but Charleston is home. Besides, the *Courier* had begun publication in 1803 and was, by then, well-established as the leading commercial paper of the South. My choice to leave Washington really wasn't as misguided a decision as my Northern colleagues had thought. In my estimation, the *Courier* rivals any major paper this country has! The *Charleston Mercury*, on the other hand, is mainly a political vehicle of extreme viewpoints. Our paper, the *Courier*, is considered far more mainstream. We aim to serve as an intelligent representative of the property holders of Charleston and the state. Our property holders *are* our city and state, and our paper stands by their best interests," Alfred concluded.

"Should South Carolina secede, how will the *Courier* respond?" Brandon asked, although he supposed he could have guessed the answer.

"Mr. Stewart," Alfred smiled kindly, "we are a *Southern* paper—in fact, *the* Southern paper!" He did not need to elaborate further.

Brandon grinned. "Of course," he conceded good-naturedly. He took Alfred's meaning: the *Courier*, as any Southern paper, would support a vote to secede.

"Indeed," William added, "any Southerner worth his salt should support secession. Or I *should* say that any Southerner worth his *rice* or *cotton* should support secession!"

"Nonetheless," Alfred cautioned, "a modest number of our fellow Southerners think it is madness to secede. Admittedly, there are a couple of people on the *Courier* staff who adhere to a more moderate view—they believe war will be inevitable should there be a vote to secede."

"In spite of that, the vast majority favors secession," Brandon put in.

"Yes, the majority does," Alfred agreed.

"And I must say, I am among them," William noted. "I am in full support of secession. The Southern economy and social system will only improve, granting a higher standard of living for everyone in the South, should South Carolina and her sister states secede from the Union."

Alfred wanted to interject, "Unless there is war," but William had continued speaking, expounding his views.

"In fact," William said, "I believe secession with political autonomy will ameliorate the Southern economy to the degree that there will be a trickle-down effect benefiting the poor and the Negro, even within the institution of slavery. Independence will allow prosperity, and all—white and Negro—should benefit as a result. Of course, ideally, I would prefer a system in which all men could be free; however, even if all Southerners abruptly agreed to free the slaves all at once, utter chaos would be the inevitable result."

"Which is why the abolitionists are too extreme; they haven't thought anything through," Alfred put in.

"Absolutely," William agreed. "Take All Saints Parish, for example, which is about nine tenths African slaves, most of whom are illiterate. Do the abolitionists really believe we can free them in a *day*? How would they fare? What would they do? Is it so moral to set free a people all of a sudden, when they have no means to fend for themselves? Little, if any, education? No land, no property?" William shook his head and poked his fork into a bit of egg and ham as if to punctuate his words.

"The sins of the fathers cannot be erased in a single day," Brandon reflected as William chewed, savoring his ham and eggs.

Alfred heartily nodded his agreement.

William swallowed, and stated, "To stay in the Union while upholding and enforcing the institution of slavery will only insidiously disrupt and tangibly strain the Southern way of life, her society and economy. Any further hopes for a gradual but steady improvement for the South—and *all* her people—will be deterred, if not shaken. Only political and economic autonomy, as well as declaring independence from the abolitionist's incendiary moral outrage, can ensure a bright and constructive future for the South—both slave and free."

"Do you think other Southern states will follow South Carolina's lead if it secedes?" Brandon asked.

William nodded, savoring another bite of ham, then swallowed. "I believe it is highly likely!"

"And," Brandon posed, "... do you think war would follow?"

William shrugged easily. The possibility of war had not eluded his imagination, but the probability seemed remote, even unwarranted. "I can't say. ... I would *hope* not! The North would be foolish to embark on such a plan." He left it at that. No one wanted war, it was plain. Indeed, many Southerners—while willing to secede at any cost—had not entertained the possibility of war.

After a pause, Alfred offered, "I wouldn't rule war out altogether."

This turn of conversation to a possibility of war lent an air of solemnity to the table. Each of the three men fell silent as they ate their breakfasts.

Sunlight streamed through the window panes, glinting upon the polished silver and crystal ware, and spotlighting crumbs and forgotten napkins upon the thick carpet. A white-gloved hand tilted a tea spout over Brandon's cup and filled it; above the white glove peered a dark-skinned wrist. "Thank you," Brandon said, meeting the African servant's eyes. But given the turn of conversation, his appetite was now less keen for tea or the muffin spread with berry jam that he bit into. What upon the table, he wondered, was not the product of slave labor—even if indirectly so?

As William ate, he reflected further on his hopes for an independent South and a series of slavery-reform measures that would pave the way for eventual abolition. Through independence, he believed, the South could grow stronger and focus on reforming and regulating the conditions of slavery until the practice could be phased out entirely. He hoped for reforms to cease the inhumane abuses wrought upon the African by the likes of Jack Davenport. He yearned for the cessation of breaking up African families upon the auction block; better living conditions; improved medical care; reasonable work hours; ample food; proper burials; humane disciplinary actions; abolition of the bull whip; legal marriages; and one day, perhaps, literacy and education for all Africans. For as long as the institution of slavery was to prevail, William determined that it *must* be reformed—until it could be phased out in such a way as to advantage the former slave. The issue was, for William, both a moral and practical imperative.

"Well," Alfred Cooke broke the silence, "today is December eighteenth. We have only two days before we learn the vote—whether we secede or not. But I'm betting we do."

"And the other Southern states will follow," Brandon offered.

Alfred nodded. "And," he added soberly, "the possibility of war."

"I'm not convinced," William put in, although Alfred's assertions had piqued his concerns.

Brandon remained silent, his brow knit in consternation.

Only time would tell whether the South would secede and if war would ensue.

⸺◇⸺

"It is, indeed, a breathtaking view," William noted.

"Quite," Brandon agreed, duly impressed.

The two men had ascended the steeple of Saint Michael's Church as high as the spiraling stairs could carry them.

"This steeple is one hundred and eighty-six feet tall to its tip." William leaned over the railing and peered upward.

"And the steeple across the way there," Brandon asked, pointing northeast, "would that one be St. Phillips?"

"Yes, and beyond it, the Cooper River."

Brandon's gaze traced the Cooper River's swell to Charleston's harbor at the peninsula's tip. Sunlight glinted on the water in flecks of silver as a crisp breeze wafted whitecaps across the harbor's surface. Here and there, the shadow of a stray cloud or two lumbered across the land and sea. Brandon turned the collar of his black wool frock coat up about his neck to ward off the chill.

"It *is* rather cold up here," William noted, and similarly adjusted his coat collar.

"Without this morning's breeze, the view would not be as clear," Brandon observed, and then pointed to a low island of masonry in the harbor. "There ... that is Fort Sumter, isn't it?"

"Yes, it is. The fort is named for General Thomas Sumter, a Revolutionary War hero. It is said that seventy-thousand tons of granite were imported from New England to build up the sandbar in the entrance to Charleston Harbor that Fort Sumter dominates."

"Seventy-thousand *tons?*" Brandon exclaimed. He let out a low whistle to punctuate his utter amazement. Surely he had not heard right.

"Yes, seventy-thousand. Oh, and Sumter's construction was begun about thirty years ago. It is said that the structure is not yet complete."

"I think Alfred Cooke said Fort Sumter was about two or three miles from the city, near the harbor's mouth."

William squinted, estimating the distance. "Yes, I believe it is about two and one-half miles. The distance makes the fort look quite small from here, but I think it covers about two and one-half acres." Then William extended his arm to point to a venue along the city's shore. "And over there, that area of green and trees at the tip of the peninsula is White Point Gardens."

"White Point? Why 'White'?" It seemed an odd name for such a lush green expanse of public property.

"Long ago, it was called Oyster Point, due to all the oyster shells covering the ground. Sun-bleached oyster shells and white sands ultimately gave way to the park's current name," William explained.

"Much more poetic than 'Oyster Point,' I'd say."

"I suppose." William laughed. "You writers—always thinking about words."

Brandon, lost in thought, smiled absently, all but ignoring William's jest. He rounded the steeple landing—first, looking northward toward the railroad lines that led into the northern end of the city; next, scanning the ship masts that lined the Cooper River's banks; and finally gazing, once again, upon the harbor's mouth and Fort Sumter. "Should South Carolina secede, and *should* war follow, it seems Charleston would be considered a strategic city with its sea and rail access."

William shrugged. "There won't be a war," he said easily. It was less a matter of his being sure—although he believed it would be foolhardy for the North to instigate such a conflict—and more a matter that he simply could not afford to consider the possibility of war.

Brandon let the issue drop.

Strolling clockwise about the steeple's upper landing, the two stopped at each arched window to admire the view and note the various Charleston landmarks. At last they faced north again, where the city's northern boundary of houses and streets dwindled into a seemingly infinite stretch of bare land dotted with woods. Somewhere beyond the horizon was Crawford Hill plantation—and Mela and Barry. Already, Brandon missed his children and wondered if they were missing him too. Upon that thought, he scoffed silently, recalling their stolid expressions upon his departure. Missing him, *indeed!* Brandon sighed.

"What did Alfred say the population of Charleston is? Forty thousand, five hundred or so?" William asked, interrupting Brandon's thought.

"That sounds about right...," Brandon agreed idly, then confirmed, "Yes, that is what Alfred said ... and that about seventy-five percent of all South Carolina's people live here, in Charleston." He reflected a moment. "It just does not seem a large enough city to contain such a large population."

"Well," William began to explain, "you see, Charleston has a special way of fitting so many people into such a small land mass."

"Reclaimed land?" Brandon already knew that much of Charleston had been built on landfill. Bogs and harbor shores were filled and built up with anything from storm debris and palmetto logs to sawdust and wood chips in order to extend the city's living space.

"Reclaimed land?!" William feigned surprised. "*No, no!* You see, unique to Charleston—if you've noticed—most houses are built one room wide and two deep with the narrow width facing the street and the front entrance of the house to the side."

Brandon looked dubious. "And? . . ."

"And that is how they can fit more houses on the same amount of land that way," William concluded, matter-of-factly—despite the tell-tale mischievous twinkle in his eye.

"I think we had best head back down," Brandon prompted.

"Why?"

"The thin air up here has obviously compromised your thinking." Brandon grinned.

William laughed, "All right, all right, I was only joking." Just then he remembered one more building he had meant to point out to Brandon. "The telegraph office! I can point it out to you before we go down." He led Brandon to the southeast face of the steeple. "It is just over there, near the corner of East Bay and Broad streets. It's not far at all from Saint Andrew's Hall on Broad Street."

"That will be convenient tomorrow, after the vote is taken at Saint Andrew's," Brandon noted. "Whether the vote is to secede or not, there's bound to be a throng of journalists and others at the telegraph office eager to spread the news. Perhaps we can keep near the doors of Saint Andrew's during the convention in order to escape early and beat the crowds to the telegraph."

William nodded. "That sounds like a good strategy to me."

"Alfred Cooke offered to meet us at Saint Andrew's tomorrow and furnish me with whatever background information I may need to write my articles for *The Illustrated London News.*"

"That was generous of him."

"He seems quite a decent chap—likable."

"Perhaps we can treat him to dinner afterwards, at the Mills House," William suggested.

"My idea exactly."

Upon that, the two men descended from St. Michael's spire and their steeple-view tour of the city, all the while talking animatedly about what the next day might bring.

BANG! BANG! A gavel pounded sharply to call the convention to order. Muted by a din of shuffling feet, scraping chairs, and anxious voices, the gavel was pounded yet again.

"The Convention of the People of South Carolina is now called to order!" a rather distinguished-looking man at the head of the hall, gavel in hand, called out over the sea of attendees. Two more claps of the gavel silenced the hall.

Brandon stood—along with William and their new acquaintance, Alfred Cooke—just inside, near the front doors to Saint Andrew's Hall. Many others stood near them, and many more stood along the rear of the hall because seating capacity was insufficient to accommodate everyone in attendance. One hundred and sixty-nine delegates, who sat before the throngs of attendees, waited to hear the Ordinance of Secession read aloud and vote. As the proceedings commenced, Brandon took up his notepad and began to write.

"Saint Andrew's Society of Charleston, South Carolina, is Charleston's oldest benevolent society," Brandon wrote, "established to assist all people in distress. However, today, it is South Carolina herself who is distressed. Since the Republican election of Abraham Lincoln to the presidency, South Carolina and her Southern Sister States fear a radicalized new government in Washington. Above all, they fear the loss of their 'property'—their slaves—and economic ruin! The assistance South Carolina seeks is nothing short of independence from the newly elected Republican government and from the Republican-dominated Northern States. Indeed, South Carolina has already coined her mottos: 'Southern Rights,' 'Equality of the States,' and 'Don't Tread on Me.'" Brandon lifted his pen to reflect a moment, and then he wrote a note in parentheses in the margin, "How odd that rights, equality, and being treaded upon should only be of concern with regard to the states and not with regard to the slave!" Deep in thought, his pen's tip poised above his pad, Brandon felt a nudge on his arm.

"They're about to read the ordinance," William whispered.

Turning his attention to the distinguished gentleman presiding over the hall, Brandon put aside his notes and pen. Alfred Cooke did the same. The three men, as all those assembled in that great hall, centered their full attention on each word that was read. If a pin had dropped in that hall that day, its clatter would surely have been noticed. Hardly a person stirred throughout the reading of the ordinance, and at its conclusion came the announcement, "The voting will now commence!"

"History is about to be made, I wager," Brandon commented to his companions.

"Yes, it is!" Alfred returned.

A quiet air of excitement filled the hall as the voting began. Alphabetically the delegates cast their ballots by a voice vote of "Yea!" or "Nay!" beginning with John H. Adams of Richland District. At last Henry C. Young of Laurens District finalized the voting by declaring a unanimous, "Yea!"

Instantly the hall filled with the swell of excited voices. BANG! BANG! BANG! The gavel pounded. "Order! *Order!*" someone shouted above the din. "*Order!*" Slowly the hall quieted. All eyes returned to the gentleman holding the gavel as he waited for the assembly to be still. At last he spoke, a note of triumph in his voice belying his otherwise dignified composure. "The union now subsisting between South Carolina and other states under the name of the 'United Sates of America' is hereby dissolved." With a final clap of the gavel, the convention was concluded.

"The Union is dissolved!" one man hollered. With that, the hall erupted in shouts of rejoicing. Handshakes and hearty embraces were exchanged, hats were tossed in the air—the hall was a clamor of jubilation.

Quickly Brandon darted for the door, William and Alfred Cooke close on his heels. Once outside the hall, they found the sidewalk below thronged with anxious citizens. "What's the outcome?" someone in the crowd called out. Others echoed the eager cry. "What's the decision? What's the vote?" they shouted, then gradually fell quiet to hear the news.

"The Union is dissolved!" Brandon pronounced, from atop the front steps of Saint Andrew's Hall.

"We have seceded!" Alfred confirmed.

A great cheer arose among the throngs of onlookers lining Broad Street.

Rushing down the front steps of Saint Andrew's Hall, Brandon pressed through the crush of people clustered along the front walkway. At last he reached a clearing in the crowd at the center of Broad Street where he stopped and looked back to see William and Alfred emerging from the throngs, not far behind him.

As William caught up to Brandon, Alfred called to them, "I'll meet you at the Mills House later for dinner." Then he bounded off down Broad Street for the *Charleston Daily Courier* office. Despite Alfred Cooke's concerns about the prospect of war, the excitement over secession was infectious even to him. Alfred simply had to return to his office to share the news with his colleagues and begin writing about the convention's revolutionary vote— news to be spread throughout the South.

In no time, Brandon and William reached the telegraph office. They were the first to arrive there with the news of secession. Brandon hastily finished writing his brief copy of the news to be telegraphed, first to a New York correspondent, and then wired overseas to London and *The Illustrated London News* office. As quickly as Brandon wrote, the telegraph operator excitedly clicked the news over the wire—first northward, then across the Atlantic. No sooner had the telegrams been dispatched than a breathless young man stumbled into the telegraph office. "The signing of the ordinance is to be held at Saint Andrew's Hall at six-thirty tonight!" he announced, then departed as quickly as he had come to spread the word elsewhere.

Brandon looked blankly at William. "The *signing*?!" he blurted, aghast. His eyes darted to the telegraph, now silent, having carried his last words of the secession northward and to London. "What does he mean 'the signing'? Isn't it settled?" He looked anxiously at William, feeling as if all the blood had suddenly drained to his feet. What a blunder to have sent the wire so prematurely!

"The voice vote isn't legally binding," William explained.

"Holy *Christ*!" Brandon blurted, his eyes darting again to the telegraph as if to will that his words could be retrieved, but the news was well on its way. What a blunder! He would have to issue a statement of correction—*immediately!*

"Excuse me!" an impatient voice gruffed as an elbow all but pushed Brandon aside.

"But—," Brandon began to protest, only to be cut off by a plume of pipe smoke and to find a throng of men pressing into the telegraph office behind him and William.

"It's all right," William said, and taking Brandon's arm, began to leave.

"But … but it's only a voice vote. It's not legal! I … I've sent the wire!" Brandon stammered.

"The signing is just a formality—ceremony," William assured.

"Are you certain?" Brandon felt beside himself with worry.

"Absolutely certain." William smiled, and declared, "We *have* seceded!" He gave Brandon's shoulder a sound, celebratory clap.

At that moment, the bells of Saint Michael's church began to peal.

"Do you hear?" William asked. "Even the church bells are announcing secession."

Brandon heaved a sigh of relief. His wire of the news had been accurate after all.

As the bells of Saint Michael's steeple clanged jubilation for all the citizens of Charleston, the happy news of secession ignited the crowds with excitement and quickly spread to nearby homes and businesses. In no time, all of Charleston was transformed. Shops began to close for the day as people flooded the streets, grog shops, and taverns to celebrate. Hats were hurled into the air as exuberant citizens whooped and cheered, hugged and clapped. Flags of celebration were hung colorfully from piazza rails and balconies. People sang and danced in the streets. Speeding down Broad Street on horseback, a man fired his pistol in the air, several blasts in quick succession. A group of boys on the corner set off a flurry of firecrackers. Elsewhere, a fiddler played a lively tune to the accompaniment of a mouth-harp as others danced a jig. Cascading down from the windows of the *Charleston Mercury* were quickly printed sheets proclaiming, "The Union is dissolved!"

In his office at the *Charleston Daily Courier*, Alfred Cooke had already begun his news article: "The tea has been thrown overboard; the revolution of 1860 has been initiated."

CHAPTER 13

Juliana

Juliana was a young slave woman of no more than eighteen years of age. She and her older brother were household slaves on the forlorn and troubled Davenport plantation. As Juliana emerged into womanhood, she had grown increasingly uncomfortable under the watchful eyes of her owner, Jack Davenport. Increasingly she voiced her fears to her brother, and she wished to run away with him someday, to flee north.

Davenport's plans for Juliana, however, did not include any allowance for her escape; he had other intensions for her in mind. The very day that Charleston erupted in jubilation over the vote of secession, Davenport visited the simple wooden cabin behind the Big House that Juliana shared with her brother. Sending her brother off on some pretext of an errand, Jack Davenport then closed the cabin door behind him and locked it with its wooden latch. Juliana's eyes flashed defiance at her owner, but defiance quickly dissolved into fear as Davenport's eyes traced her head to foot, penetrating her worn cotton skirt and blouse. He moved slowly toward her until she had nowhere to turn for escape. Her back to the wall, Jack Davenport, quite literally, had her cornered.

Juliana struggled to find her voice. "What ... what does you want?" she quavered.

Davenport wasted no time with words. In an instant he was upon her. His wet, slimy mouth and breath reeking of stale alcohol smothered the young woman's lips, cheeks, and neck. Instantly Juliana resisted—kicking, pushing, and scratching, and at last delivering a sharp bite to Davenport's arm. Davenport slapped her for this and forced her downward, hard upon the floor. All the while, Juliana cried out, but not one slave came to her aid for fear of Davenport's inevitable reprisals. So fearful of their master's wrath were they that they took to their cabins and shut their doors upon hearing her cries—there was simply too much risk in taking on the burden of another; it was safer to remain shut away from any trouble.

His full weight upon her, Davenport muffled Juliana's screams with the rough scratch of his beard and foul whiskey-laden breath. With one hand, he pinned her wrists above her head against the floor as he tore at her clothes with the other. Running his tongue up her neck, he grunted his hot rank breath into her flaring nostrils. Juliana averted her head furtively this way and that to avoid Davenport's assaults to her cheeks, neck, and lips, but it was to no avail. Her eyes wide with fright, tears coursed down her cheeks.

After a time Juliana's strength gave out, and she could struggle no more beneath her assailant. Why hadn't her brother returned? Why was there no one to help her? Juliana wept in earnest as Davenport's saliva, thick with alcohol, mingled with her tears upon her cheeks and neck. Silently weeping, Juliana prayed for deliverance. She struggled again, but it was of no use. Her delicate, thin frame was no match for Davenport's as he lay upon her, his free hand straying downward, tearing the undergarments from about her thighs and fumbling to open the front of his trousers.

At once a searing pain consumed Juliana, and she cried out a shriek so piercing, even Davenport stopped a moment—yet her cry piqued his lust all the more, and he continued in increasingly hard, rhythmic thrusts against her. With each thrust, Juliana felt only helpless terror and searing pain. Davenport finished violently, with spasmodic grunts of his hot, foul breath upon her.

Then, as quickly as he had begun, Davenport rolled off Juliana and lay satisfied, prone upon the floor. Juliana lay upon the floor heaving with sobs. She could scarcely think save for her awareness of the brutal pain above her thighs that rendered her too frightened to move. A small viscous pool of blood mingled with ejaculate stained the hard-plank floor where Juliana lay.

All at once Juliana felt Davenport's rough hands upon her, and she nearly fainted with the fear that he would rape her again. But Davenport had no designs to take her again; instead, he would teach the young slave woman a lesson for resisting him. Pulling Juliana to her feet, he forced her from the cabin and led her to the smokehouse nearby. There, he would teach her the consequences of disobedience, of daring to fend him off. The small row of teeth marks, swollen and red upon his arm, still smarted as a reminder of her waywardness. It was in the smokehouse that he would mete out her punishment. The next time that he wanted to have his way with her, perhaps she would comply more readily!

At the open smokehouse door, Davenport brutally pushed Juliana inside. "You ain' never gonna resist me again, nigger bitch!"

Juliana stumbled and fell as Davenport pushed her forward. Violently he yanked her to her feet once more. Juliana wrestled to break free from Davenport's grasp, but he caught her once again and shook her so hard that her teeth rattled. At once Davenport slapped her, knocking her down. Crying out, Juliana clasped a hand to the blood that gushed from her stinging lower lip. Trembling and whimpering, Juliana unsteadily tried to rise to her feet, but Davenport pushed her down to her knees. Juliana knelt on the smokehouse floor in her torn, blood-stained frock. Her head hung low, Juliana sobbed as if for dear life, wishing her brother would come to rescue her—surely he would come to save her, *surely* he would.

Roughly Davenport fastened a sturdy rope about Juliana's wrists, binding them tightly. Pulling Juliana to her feet, he led her to a meat hook suspended by a chain from the high ceiling of the smokehouse. After fastening the rope that bound her wrists to the hook, he turned a creaking geared wheel, raising her up until she hung suspended by her wrists, her bare toes scarcely touching the smokehouse floor. Juliana feared that her arms would rip from her body; the floor ever so slightly brushing the tips of her toes taunted her with the illusion that she might be able to stand and relieve the terrible racking strain upon her arms. Juliana instinctively writhed to free herself as she desperately felt for a foothold on the floor below—but as it was, she could only dangle helplessly, suspended from the hook and chain above. Satisfied that he had Juliana where he wanted her, Davenport went out.

Left in the dark smokehouse, the rope cutting into her wrists, Juliana wept and prayed silently for deliverance, believing that this was her punishment.

Suddenly Davenport flung open the smokehouse door. He had returned to the smokehouse with a bottle of whiskey in one hand and a riding whip in the other. Juliana's eyes flashed abject fear. She realized what further evil Davenport intended to deliver upon her, and she prayed only for freedom or death. Shutting the smokehouse door and latching it, Davenport gulped thirstily from the bottle of whiskey. Then, setting the bottle aside, he set about his task.

With the first lash of the riding whip, Juliana convulsed and shrieked in agony. "Dear Jesus!" she uttered, then bent her head and wept. With each successive lash, Juliana's body convulsed against the searing blows. Pausing only for gulps of whiskey, Davenport raised the whip again and again, losing count—if he had bothered to count at all—of the number of lashes that ribboned Juliana's back. Rivers of blood seeped through, then thoroughly soaked, the white cotton fabric of her torn blouse and dripped in puddles upon the smokehouse floor.

Upon the next lash of the whip, Juliana's body went limp, and upon the succeeding three blows, Juliana no longer convulsed with pain. Satisfied, Davenport lowered her limp body to the ground and unbound her wrists. He would have had his way with her again, there and then, as he had in her cabin, but he had grown too intoxicated to adequately perform his conquest. Neither too little nor too much whiskey would do when he determined to have his way with a young slave woman—and he held the same rule regarding his wife, Sara.

Jack Davenport took a final swig of whiskey and looked down upon Juliana's motionless form upon the floor. He noted the contours of her breasts beneath her blouse and the full swell of her hips below the narrow waist. His mouth twisted into a sneer between his hellfire-red mustache and beard. "Next time, you'll think twice about resisting me," he slurred beneath his breath. "Next time!" he menaced, and staggered out.

For now, Jack Davenport would leave Juliana in the smokehouse. Later, maybe, he would send his wife's personal house servant, Hetty, to the smokehouse to tend to Juliana's wounds—maybe. Meanwhile, Jack Davenport wanted only the comfort of his bed, to sleep off the ill effects of too much whiskey and the pleasures of his sex act. Little did his inebriated senses comprehend that Juliana was dead, that she had died even before he had finished whipping her.

———⋄———

Annabelle sat at the little writing table in her upstairs bedroom before a half-finished letter to her elder sister, Alexandra, at Loxley House. So much had happened that she hardly knew where to begin. With a short sigh, determined, she set pen to paper and continued writing.

". . . Alexandra, there has been such a whirlwind of excitement the last two days, I simply have not had the chance to resume my letter to you until now. I am sure you will read of South Carolina's vote to secede from the Union far before this letter reaches Loxley House. Indeed, it was the very return of William and Brandon from Charleston with news of secession that obliged me to interrupt my writing to you. Above, I had hardly finished telling of their departure, and now they have returned!

"I had fretted so over Barry's anger and Mela's upset at being left behind at Crawford Hill when their father went to Charleston without them. Mela gave way to tears when Brandon and William's carriage disappeared from view because she had not even told her father goodbye. And Barry was still sulking at being considered too young to go along with his father. (Young Barry is only twelve!)

"Poor Brandon! Upon his return, he expected to be met with a reception to match his send-off. But Barry had quite forgiven him and, bounding out of the house, ran to Brandon beaming and shouting, 'Father's home! Father's home!' Mela, poor little one, literally—I dare say—flew into her father's arms off the front verandah's steps. Brandon caught her up in his arms and held her fast, asking, 'How is my little dear one?' Mela only burst into tears of joy and clung to her dear father. Brandon gave Barry a sound hug and tousled his hair—as is his way of affection with Barry. All was quite forgiven! Mela has scarcely left Brandon out of her sight these past few days. She missed him so. Every day she would ask me, 'Aunt Annabelle, when will Father come home?'

"Our children are ever so much more used to William being away

on business. They would have hardly heralded his return except that they were eager to hear every detail of the secession and of Charleston. One would think the children have forgotten all about Christmas, which is tomorrow!

"We shall all go up to All Saints Church for Christmas service, and then, in the afternoon, give out gifts to our dear house servants, field hands, and overseers on the front lawn as we do every year. In the evening, we shall have our family Christmas and open presents in the front parlor by the fire and our decorated tree. Alexandra, do you remember our first Christmas tree at Loxley House? Wherever has the time flown?

"William and Brandon would have returned home sooner from Charleston, but the city is only now winding down from its celebration of the vote. The mayor of Charleston issued a proclamation on the twenty-second forbidding the shooting of fireworks within the city except in times of official public rejoicing. Anyone caught shooting off fireworks otherwise shall have to pay a fine of ten dollars! Can you imagine, Alexandra? Although you live at Loxley House and I at Crawford Hill, I dare say we have not forgotten our humble beginnings; ten dollars is nothing to scoff at! Perhaps the mayor is concerned about the possibility of fire breaking out about the city as well as the noisy disruption of fireworks late at night—in which case a ten-dollar fine should have served as an apt deterrent. Nonetheless, many ignored the mayor's ruling and set off fireworks all night for several nights! The city coffers are prospering, although the citizens' pockets are growing emptier! Bonfires were lit, and rockets and Roman candles were set off at night.

"Oh, Alexandra, how I wish I could have been there! Yet I feel nearly as though I have been. Brandon—our resident writer—paints pictures with his telling and brings everything so vividly to life! Brandon has been hard at work these last two days since his return from Charleston. He has hardly eaten or slept, spending hours in his studio writing and sketching while the events of the last week are still fresh in his mind—he is anxious to rush his stories to The Illustrated London News offices. Soon you shall see his articles published in the paper. You must write and tell me what you think, Alexandra.

"These are exciting times and, I fear, a bit uncertain. But William feels assured that there is no need for concern, and I lean on his word. Nonetheless, this America is such a young country. And now, with secession, I feel a dose of uncertainty in our crisp winter breeze ... I long now for the established homelands and traditions of England—the solid familiarity of Loxley House.

"Dear Alexandra, I do not mean to upset you with my concerns; however, the joy and excitement of the past few days has been sorely marred in my heart by the news of yet another sorrowful event upon the neighboring Davenport Plantation.

"Where our fields meet Davenport's land, the field slaves exchange news and talk. Ultimately, our Jacob passes on whatever news he hears to William and to me. Alexandra, it is especially this last bit of news that troubles my heart and has me longing for England. I hesitate to tell you ... but if I don't, I can't say what shall happen if I leave it bottled up inside me. Alexandra, Jack Davenport violated a young African woman, then hung her by her wrists in his smokehouse and beat her to death with a riding whip. He left her body on the smokehouse floor where she was not found for two days until servants went to put up some pork. Jacob relays that she was called Juliana—such a pretty name—and was only about eighteen years of age. Davenport had her body buried in an unmarked plot near the woods and sent her brother to the auction block in Charleston—it is said that Davenport is afraid of what revenge Juliana's brother might visit upon him and that Davenport wanted the auction money for alcohol. Juliana died the day the Ordinance of Secession was signed. Upon her violation and death, Roman candles and rockets were fired off the tip of Charleston's White Point Gardens, flaring gaily over the harbor. Alexandra! What kind of a civilization is this?

"Again, dear sister, do not breathe a word of this to anyone as you have promised before. I simply cannot have William know that I used to go with Jacob to the Davenport plantation to administer aid to the slaves toward whom Davenport was violent. I have not dared set foot on the Davenport place since that time some five years ago when that devil drove Jacob and me from his lands with a shotgun—I have been too afraid; even so, I regret not being able to venture there to help those such as poor

Juliana. It brings tears to my eyes just to think of her plight and her torturous final hours upon this earth.

"I turned to the Bible for some comfort and to better understand God's nature and purpose in the face of this sorrowful tragedy. As if providentially, I opened the book to the passage that instructs us to live as free men, and to not use our freedom as a covering for evil but to use it as bondslaves of God. Alexandra, it seems that those free men who willingly enslave others without regret are not bondslaves to God at all. I pray for our slaves—really, I do. Do you remember how defiant I was at Loxley House years ago when William and I first met there? How antislavery I was? Alexandra, in my heart of hearts I still am, and sometimes . . . I wonder what I am doing here at all.

"Dear sister—how I long for my elder sister just now!—I had best close before I take to dampening all of my handkerchiefs over the sad fate of poor Juliana. We are anxious to open the Christmas packages you sent, and we thank you for them. How early we must prepare to send gifts across the ocean! I hear the dinner bell ringing—now I must close, or I shall be late for Christmas Eve dinner!

"Do write again soon, Alexandra. I miss you dearly. Love always,

"—Annabelle"

Candlelight and lamplight illuminated the dining room. Aromas of stuffed goose and plumb pudding dominated the scents wafting in from the kitchen as Ester, Cotta, and several other house servants bustled to and fro with heavy platters and serving dishes. The goose, trimmed in berries, was set before William at the head of the table for him to carve. Bored with waiting for dinner to commence, the children began to fidget, and Cooper grew contrary.

"I'm not hungry!" Cooper protested. "I want to open presents!"

"Presents are tomorrow," Annabelle reminded her son gently as she entered the dining room. She smoothed Cooper's blond hair with one hand and cast a quick glance at William. She had hoped that William would not see that she had been crying again.

"I want to open presents!" Cooper insisted plaintively.

Annabelle sighed and bent to whisper in her son's ear. "We can each open one present tonight after dinner, but there won't be any more presents until tomorrow," she soothed.

"Why?" Cooper challenged.

"Because tomorrow is Christmas Day," Annabelle explained, her tone patient and melodic.

"So?" Cooper blurted. He only knew that he was not hungry, especially not for the spoonful of stewed okra Cotta had just served upon his plate. He wanted everyone to open presents, and that was that!

"Cooper, please behave," Annabelle pleaded, a note of distress edging her voice.

"I *hate* okra!" Cooper's face twisted into an expression of sheer disdain.

"Cooper! . . . That's enough!" William warned sternly from the head of the table, his carving implements poised over the goose.

"Cooper's in trouble . . . Cooper's in trouble," Ashley sing-songed, then giggled quietly.

Carolina hushed her little sister with a jab of her elbow. "You'll be in trouble next," she warned.

Ashley fell silent.

"I hate okra!" Cooper grumbled flatly, pushing his plate away.

Annabelle looked apologetically from Cooper to Cotta, who, by now, was serving the offending okra to Carolina, seated beside her father at the table's corner. There was simply no excuse for her son's insolent, rude behavior. "Cooper, apologize to Cotta for your ill manners at once," Annabelle stated firmly, though her emotions were piqued.

Cooper stared disdainfully at the heap of stewed okra upon his plate. "No!" He shook his head vehemently.

"Cooper! . . ." William warned. "Apologize *now!*"

"No! I hate Cotta too! She's *nobody!*" Cooper declared.

Annabelle looked from Cooper to Cotta. "I . . . I'm sorry," Annabelle stammered, then she flushed scarlet. "Excuse me," she uttered quietly, her voice nearly breaking as she fled from the room.

In an instant, Cooper slipped down off his seat and disappeared below the table.

William did not bother to retrieve Cooper from beneath the table to issue any stern reprimand; his first concern was Annabelle. Setting down the carving utensils with a clatter, he strode after Annabelle.

"Ouch! *Cooper!*" Carolina yelled as her brother pinched her on the ankle.

"Stop it!" Ashley cried, and kicked her feet beneath the table.

Ester, Cotta, and Jacob were left to restore order and carve the Christmas goose.

William found Annabelle in the west sitting room. She stood in the darkness near the window shelves of colorful glass items, her head bowed in her hands weeping.

"Annabelle! Sweetheart!" William strode up to her from behind and held her about the shoulders. "What's all of this?" he asked gently, his voice edged with alarm.

Annabelle only turned, rested her cheek upon William's shirt, and let him embrace her.

"Is it Cooper?" he asked, then immediately apologized. "I'm sorry, dear. I haven't been attentive enough helping with the children since I returned home, have I?"

"No … no, it's not the children," Annabelle said as she wiped at her tears.

"Then, whatever is it?" William let go his embrace and tilted Annabelle's chin up with a gentle hand. "Tell me what's troubling you," he entreated. He searched her glistening eyes in the stream of moonlight that glowed through the window.

Annabelle swallowed hard. "How can our son say Cotta is a '*nobody*'? Oh, William!" Annabelle bit her lip to stave off more tears, then continued, "It's Juliana. I looked at Cotta, and I thought, what if she had met the same fate as Juliana? Or what if Ester had? Or one day, little Cinda? Or any of our—" She broke off, unable to utter the final syllable: slaves. Annabelle looked up into her husband's eyes. "What are our children learning, William? How could Cooper say Cotta is a '*nobody*'?" Her voice quavered with distress, and a tear coursed down her cheek.

William tucked Annabelle safe in his embrace. "Shhh, shhh, now," he soothed. "I'm sure Cooper is only angry with Cotta because of the okra and nothing else. He is blaming her for his own misbehavior." William knew not what else to say. With regard to Juliana, what consolation was there for such an atrocity committed against *any* human being? Still, Annabelle wept quietly, her cheek against William's shirtfront.

"There, there, sweetheart," William soothed. "Don't cry so. Cotta, Cinda, and Ester are safe here with us and always will be."

Annabelle nodded and worked to stem her flow of tears. "I know," she sniffled.

Kissing the top of her head, William offered Annabelle his pocket-square. "Now, then," he said, his voice taking on a note of parental cheer, "tomorrow is Christmas, and tonight we have a Christmas Eve goose to carve."

Taking her husband's pocket-square, Annabelle mopped her damp cheeks and applied it to her reddened nose. "I'll be all right now," she said, and managed a smile.

"That's my love," William encouraged.

They walked together toward the dining-room door, whereupon William hesitated. "If Cooper does not behave, then we will send him to his room without dinner, even if it *is* Christmas Eve," he declared.

Annabelle laughed, "Except for a plateful of okra!"

"I wager he *will* behave upon *that* threat!" William chortled.

Together, William and Annabelle entered the dining room in good spirits, their eyes—even if Annabelle's were a bit damp—twinkling gaily. Cooper, under a stern threat of Ester's, was well-behaved once again. Jacob had finished carving and was now serving the goose. As they took their seats at the table, Annabelle and William noticed that Brandon, Barry, and Mela were not yet present.

"Is Brandon working late again?" William asked, although his question was more perfunctory than otherwise.

"He really mustn't miss dinner." Annabelle rose from the table. "I'll go and see if he is still in the studio."

Interrupting, Carolina jumped up. "I'll go, Mother," she offered eagerly. Carolina all but idolized her Uncle Brandon. Although only ten, she surmised he was—second to her father, of course—the handsomest, smartest, kindest man she could ever imagine. Surely there were none like her Uncle Brandon in the whole of All Saints Parish—or perhaps anywhere!

"Just look from the back verandah to see if the studio windows are dark," Annabelle directed.

But no sooner had Carolina turned to set off on her special errand than Brandon entered the dining room from the hall doorway with Mela in his arms and Barry in tow.

"Sorry we are so late. Time got away from me, I'm afraid," Brandon said. "I hope you didn't wait dinner on my account."

William assured Brandon they were just about to start. Brandon let Mela scamper down from his arms to take her seat beside Annabelle. Brandon then took his seat next to Mela, and Barry drew out a chair beside his father.

"I was just about to fetch you, Uncle Brandon," Carolina offered timidly.

"Were you now?" Brandon smiled. "That was very thoughtful of you," he commended.

Carolina smiled shyly, then looked downward.

"Have you much more work to do?" Annabelle asked Brandon.

"No, I'm nearly done—" He yawned broadly, in spite of himself. "I'm sorry, I've been staying up too late the last two nights." He stifled another yawn.

Indeed, Brandon looked tired, and Annabelle was concerned for him. "You really should make an early evening of it tonight, though I hope you will open presents with us this evening after dessert."

"Yes, presents—absolutely," Brandon said, though his eyelids and stifled yawns were telling him otherwise.

"Father brought me a present from Charleston!" Mela beamed.

"You don't say?" William grinned, and cast a knowing wink at Brandon. "And what about Father Christmas? He is bound to bring you lots of presents that you can open tomorrow—won't that be fun?"

"Yes!" Mela nodded to agree with her Uncle, but secretly she knew a million presents from Father Christmas would never compare to just *one* present from her own dear father. Nothing in the world would ever be as special as anything he might have to give her.

After dinner, the family gathered in the east sitting room by the fireside. There, Ester and Jacob lit the candles on the decorated tree that stood before the front window. Cooper, less interested in opening presents than he had declared at dinner, now divided his rambunctious attention between the candles upon the tree and the crackling fire upon the hearth. Scampering to and fro between the tree and hearth, Cooper was quickly underfoot—if not a downright hazard. In one fell swoop, William caught Cooper up, flounced him onto his lap, and held him fast in a bear hug. "Settle down, now," he whispered in the boy's ear. Resigned to his fate, Cooper did so.

With the tree's candles lit, Annabelle distributed presents to the children—each to be opened one by one. Ashley received a new doll, and Carolina, a new holiday dress of velvet and satin. Cooper got a cast-iron toy-train set with brightly painted cars and a track to push them on. There was a new kite for Quash, crafted by Jacob, and a rag doll for Cinda that Ester had made. In fact, Cinda's rag doll was so fine and commanded so many exclamations that poor Ashley was envious, in spite of her new store-bought doll. Next, Brandon gave Mela her gift—a bright-red wool coat with a hooded collar trimmed in fur and a fur muff to match. Immediately Mela wanted to dress up in her new gift. Brandon helped her on with the coat and fastened the buttons for her. Climbing up into her father's lap, Mela kissed him on the cheek and sat contentedly as Barry opened his present.

"Your present is last because it is the best!" William confided to Barry, and then winked secretly at Brandon.

Barry's gift was wrapped in a box far larger and heavier than any of the others. Inside the wrappings and ribbons, Barry found only a large straw basket of apples and carrots. Looking puzzled, Barry hardly knew what to say. He managed a polite, "Thank you," but any thought of asking about his unusual gift was promptly cut off by William admonishing that Father Christmas would not come if the children stayed up too late—it was time for bed.

Amidst both grumbling about bedtime and talking excitedly about what tomorrow would bring, the children clambered up the stairs to bed.

William, Annabelle, and Brandon remained in the sitting room to take their customary evening brandy together by the hearth. Pouring them each a brandy, Brandon then took his usual wingback chair to the left of the hearth as William and Annabelle occupied the sofa before the fire.

"Are you feeling better now?" William asked Annabelle.

She nodded. "Yes, better." Her tone was measured—her earlier upset over the young slave woman Juliana would not quickly fade.

"Had you been feeling unwell, Annabelle?" Brandon asked. "I thought perhaps you seemed a bit out of sorts earlier."

"I was only feeling upset again over Juliana." She shook her head. "It's too much to dwell on just now."

Swirling the amber liquid in the bowl of his glass, Brandon took a sip and gazed into the fire. Sometimes reality—especially when next door—could be overwhelming when dwelt upon too intensely. He did not blame Annabelle for her upset or for wishing the topic dismissed. Indeed, Brandon's own eyes had welled upon first hearing from Jacob the account of Juliana's unconscionable abuse and her untimely death at the hands of Jack Davenport.

Changing the subject, for Annabelle's sake, William let out a chuckle. "Did you see Barry's expression when he opened that basket of apples and carrots?" He laughed and shook his head.

Brandon grinned. "Wait until he sees the horse tomorrow—imagine his expression then!"

"His eyes will be like saucers!" William grinned.

"'Lightning' seems the perfect name for the horse—he seems so spirited. I'm sure Barry will be ecstatic!" Annabelle said.

"He will be, I'm sure," Brandon nodded. "I only hope Mela's red coat and muff from Charleston compensate for Barry's new horse—" Brandon broke into a broad yawn before continuing. "Actually, I'm hoping the children's gifts will compensate for the fact that I will be going away again soon."

This was news to William and Annabelle. "Going away? Where? Why?" they asked.

"I've decided to go to Washington, D.C. for perhaps two or three weeks—possibly longer. It depends upon what I learn when I'm there. Since the vote to secede, I want to investigate Washington's political climate firsthand and President Buchannan's policies regarding the potential dissolution or salvaging of the Union." Brandon paused, then added, "In fact, I anticipate that I shall be traveling quite a lot over the next several months between Washington and Charleston, and possibly to other Southern states as well." Brandon gazed reflectively down at the brandy in his glass for a moment. "I don't relish leaving the children for so long, or so frequently, but I must. Whatever the outcome, history is being made in this country. I really must cover it firsthand. I'd prefer not to rely solely on collaborations with our Northern correspondents or on trading information with other paper's writers such as the *London Times*. Besides, there are aspects of a story I might find of importance that another journalist would not, and I've learned to trust my own instincts. The only exception I would make is to share information with Alfred Cooke of the *Charleston Daily Courier* in Charleston."

The matter seemed settled. William and Annabelle thought to argue the point, to somehow dissuade Brandon, but the news was quite sudden and caught them off guard. Besides, all of Brandon's reasoning was quite sound. Hence, they let the matter rest and allowed the conversation to turn to other things, particularly their anticipation of Christmas Day.

As Annabelle and William talked together, Brandon sat quietly by the fire imagining his trip northward as he nursed his brandy. After a time, the effects of the late hour, the brandy, and the warm hearth worked their collective effects upon him. Brandon's eyes had long since closed when Annabelle laid a hand on her husband's arm, and nodded toward Brandon. "He's fallen asleep."

Brandon's head rested comfortably upon the chair's back—his eyes closed, lips parted ever so slightly, one arm resting upon the chair, his other arm extending limply over the chair's side. From this hand the little glass of half-finished brandy was about to escape his loosening grasp. Rising, Annabelle gently rescued the glass from Brandon's fingers before it could slip away and break. "Poor dear," she said softly, and set the glass on the side table.

Brandon moaned slightly and flinched gently in his sleep.

"Do you think we should wake him?" Annabelle asked.

"It's late. We should *all* go up to bed," William agreed.

Annabelle knelt by Brandon's chair and gently shook his arm, "Brandon ... Brandon...," she whispered.

Rousing from a deep, comfortable sleep, Brandon instinctively touched the hand resting upon his sleeve. "Mmmm ... Allison?" he murmured, drowsily opening his eyes. "Allison? ..."

"No, no ... it's Annabelle," she prompted gently.

Brandon squinted in the low firelight, his slumberous mind wakening to discover that the angelic face framed by a golden halo of tresses was not Allison's, after all, but her sister's, Annabelle's.

"Mmmm, Annabelle...," he yawned, and stretched slightly. "I'm sorry, I must have dozed off."

William rose from the sofa. "We'd best go up to bed. The children will be up early in the morning. We will need our strength!"

"Indeed," Brandon agreed.

As the three ascended the stairs, William leading the way with an oil lamp held aloft, Annabelle chided Brandon fondly, "No more working late nights until you leave for Washington. You need to rest a while, do you hear?"

"Yes, Ma'am," Brandon acquiesced good-humoredly.

Annabelle and William bid Brandon goodnight at the door to his bedroom. "See you in the morning. Sleep well."

No sooner had Brandon closed his bedroom door than he fell into bed too exhausted to even remove his shoes. There, sprawled upon the bedcovers, fully clothed, Brandon sank instantly into a sound, deep sleep. He scarcely stirred again, until well after dawn the next day.

CHAPTER 14

Washington Winter

Tender rays of morning sun barely glimpsed over the frosted rice fields as Brandon closed and latched his two large trunks, a carpetbag, and his satchel of sketching and writing materials. Although it was the day after Christmas, Brandon had decided that he should leave straightaway for Washington, D.C. It was decided that Jacob would drive Brandon by carriage over the miles of roads that spanned between Crawford Hill and Charleston's South Carolina Depot at the northeast outskirts of the city. From there, Brandon would depart from Charleston by train, traveling westward, and then northward through Richmond, Virginia before arriving in Washington. Looking out his bedroom window, Brandon was grateful for clear skies. Although a thin layer of ice caked the window panes, there would be no storms to delay his journey.

A knock sounded at Brandon's half-open door, and William entered. "Jacob has the carriage ready and waiting out front," he announced.

"Thank you. I'll be down in a moment," Brandon said as he finished buttoning his shirtfront and tucked the shirttails into his trousers. "Are the children up yet?"

"Yes, they're in the front room waiting to see you off. I'll send Jacob and Sabe up for your trunks."

Brandon nodded, and William went out. Within a minute or two, Sabe and Jacob arrived for the trunks.

Sabe, a young African in his early twenties, had been purchased by William just the day before—unexpectedly, on Christmas Day. Sabe was purchased cheaply, secondhand, from the Genovese plantation in North All Saints Parish. In conversation with William and Annabelle after the Christmas-morning church service, Mrs. Genovese was lamenting her husband's purchase of Sabe from the auction block in Charleston. She stood with the Crawfords in the back of the church, speaking quietly, but her words, nonetheless, pouring forth in a tizzy, "Sabe is good-natured, quiet, strong, and reportedly hardworking, but I really needed a female servant to help out. You see, my husband and I are expecting our fourth child in the spring, and … well, I need someone to help out with the mending, washing, the baby. I need help for myself and the baby, and Sabe simply isn't suitable." She sighed and all but rolled her eyes. "James *knew* I wanted a female, and we weren't in a hurry; regardless, Sabe's price was so low, James *couldn't* resist. But I said *no* and told James I cannot *possibly* make do with him." Mrs. Genovese gesticulated nervously. "… I simply *cannot!*" she told the Crawfords, as if apologetically. "I'm ever so anxious to sell him quickly and find a good Negress instead, but what am I to do?" she continued. "James just purchased Sabe and gave him to me last evening as an early Christmas surprise, a Christmas Eve present. You see, James had been in Charleston on account of the Convention and the vote, and he happened to see an advertisement for over fifty Africans to be sold at auction in Charleston's marketplace by a reputable broker, Alonzo J. White. Sabe's former owner asked for a low-ceiling price, apparently in need of a guaranteed sale. James was the highest bidder; and yet, Sabe was nonetheless a steal!" Mrs. Genovese sighed again, paused ever so briefly as if to catch her breath, then resumed, "Whatever am I to do? How can I tell James that Sabe won't do, especially when I have no idea on this *earth* who I could possibly sell him to? I'm sure we need to sell him for more than what James paid in order to find a suitable replacement for Sabe, at least a bit more. … How can I tell James that Sabe won't do?" Exasperated by her circumstances Mrs. Genovese fell silent, clearly beside herself and bewildered by the whole matter.

"Poor Mary," Annabelle consoled, with a gentle squeeze of Mrs. Genovese's arm, then whispered ever so gently in her ear, "Try not to upset yourself with such matters while you are with child, my dear."

"Perhaps *we* can purchase Sabe from you," William suggested. Mrs. Genovese started at this offer and looked up wide-eyed at William. "Mr. Crawford! Are you serious?" Perhaps she had heard wrong.

"Quite. If Sabe is suitable, we will purchase him from you for fair-market price."

Mrs. Genovese drew an audible gasp—she could still scarcely believe William's generous offer. "Oh, Mr. Crawford, that would be wonderful. Let me—..." She looked about the crowded church anxiously. "Let me just find James," she said hurriedly. "I won't be a moment. Oh, Mr. Crawford! ..." And with that, she rushed off to find her husband among the many clusters of congregation members visiting and chatting along the aisles and pews.

"William," Annabelle asked as she touched her husband on the arm, "are you sure?"

William considered the matter. "We need extra household help, someone to help Jacob. Since we took Cotta in from the fields, we've said it would be useful to have another male house-servant as well. I'd rather not bring in any of *our* male field hands. Besides, it's fair enough to pay a reasonable market price for Sabe; we'd have had to pay a bit more than the Genoveses anyway, I wager. No doubt Sabe's former owner simply wanted some quick Christmas cash—such a bargain price is an exception, not the rule."

Annabelle tentatively agreed, explaining, "It's just all so sudden."

After church, the Crawfords rode a few miles to the Genovese plantation. Sabe was introduced, and they found him to be of strong build, healthy, of sound wits, and intelligent, as well as strikingly handsome. His teeth were good and his manner quiet and respectful. William Crawford purchased him on the spot with a promissory note to be paid in full before the New Year. That very afternoon, Sabe came to live in a plain wooden cabin among the house servants' quarters just west of the Big House at Crawford Hill.

———⸎———

Now, while Jacob and Sabe carried the trunks downstairs, Brandon surveyed his bedroom for any item he might have forgotten to pack. Nothing was amiss.

Picking up the silver locket of Allison's, in which Brandon kept the few precious strands of her golden tresses, he slipped its chain about his neck letting the oval case slip down beneath his shirt. Cold to his skin, the silver case soon warmed where it rested near his heart. The locket's case sealed no picture of Allison, only the strands of treasured hair that Brandon had meticulously, and with trembling hand, salvaged from Allison's boar bristle brush during the disposition of her belongings five years before. Since then, Brandon was never without the treasured locket clasped fast about his neck, save for bathing and dressing. He wore it even at night, feeling Allison's presence within it warding off the loneliness of the shadows and darkness. Wearing the silver locket seemed a way of keeping Allison's spirit near to him. Closing the bedroom door behind him, the locket securely fastened about his neck, Brandon headed downstairs with his carpetbag and satchel in hand.

Barry did not seem to mind so much, this time, that he could not accompany his father to Washington. Perhaps it was the Christmas gift of his own horse, Lightning, that compensated for his being left behind. Nonetheless, Brandon had patiently explained to both his children, in practical terms, that there would be no one to look after them in Washington while he was occupied with working. "If your mother was still with us, we would all go together as a family. But it is best you stay here, continue with your lessons, and be with your cousins and Aunt Annabelle and Uncle William."

Only Mela had not seemed to understand that Brandon would be away for a very long time. No one could have explained exactly why, but Mela believed her father was going away for only a few days. Perhaps it was because his last and only trip away had been for such a short duration. Only now, while looking through the front-room window at Jacob and Sabe wrestling two great trunks into the waiting carriage, did Mela grow perplexed—it seemed that Father was going away for a *very* long time. Suddenly she wondered when she would ever see him again at all.

In a moment, Brandon entered the front room as the household gathered to say their farewells.

"Let's go out on the front verandah to see you off," Annabelle suggested. "The sun is already taking the chill off the morning."

Upon the verandah, Brandon first bid goodbye to the Crawford children with fond hugs and kisses for all—even feisty little Cooper. Next, Brandon turned to Barry. "Study hard when classes resume after the holidays," he admonished.

"I will, Father," Barry promised, and added that he would help to look after Mela.

Brandon gave Barry a final hug and tousled his hair, then turned to Mela.

Mela's worst fears were realized—Father was, indeed, going away for a very, *very* long time. As Brandon knelt down to tell Mela goodbye, her innocent young face screwed up, and she burst into tears. Hot streams poured down both her cheeks, drowning her bright-blue eyes. Wailing plaintively, Mela began to hiccup between sobs. "I . . .— don't *want* you . . .— to go . . .— away!" she wept, and clung fast to her father as if to never let him go.

"There, there," Brandon soothed. "Come now, there is nothing to cry about. Where's my brave little dear one? Where has she gone?" He tried, to no avail, to console her; his pocket-square was no match for her flood of tears. Mela sobbed and wailed in her father's arms for some minutes until she had quite exhausted herself with sorrow. Whimpering and hiccupping she accepted her father's pocket-square held to her nose. "Blow," Brandon prompted. Mela complied. "That's good. Again." Mela blew again. Brandon mopped Mela's nose and wet cheeks, then kissed her on the forehead. At last her tears subsided.

"I'll be home again soon, Mela," Brandon comforted. "Meanwhile, you'll have your cousins to play with, and Aunt Annabelle and Barry to look after you. And maybe Barry will take you for rides on Lightning; how would you like that?"

Mela only sniffled and, all the while looking down, gave a tearful shrug.

"I'll write to you often while I'm away, and I'll be back home before you know it," Brandon consoled. "Come on, let's see a smile now," he coaxed.

But Mela only looked downward and shook her head decisively.

"No smiles for me before I go, my little dear one?" he urged gently.

Mela slowly lifted her head and turned the corners of her mouth ever so slightly upward. All the while, she looked searchingly into her father's warm brown eyes.

"That's much better," Brandon smiled, and rewarded her with a kiss on each damp cheek. "You'll be my brave little girl now, won't you?"

Mela nodded dutifully, despite the great lump so tight in her throat that it ached.

"I love you," Brandon whispered.

At that, Mela turned abruptly and buried her face, sobbing, in her Aunt Annabelle's skirts.

Jacob called from the front of the carriage, "Massa Brandon, we bes' be goin', o' yer gonna miss de' first evenin' train."

In a final flurry of goodbyes, Brandon departed in the carriage down the front drive of Crawford Hill. All the while, Mela's sobs faded in the distance, muffled by the sound of hooves and wheels upon the tree-lined allée.

Stark branches lined the muddy streets of Washington beneath a slate canopy of winter sky. Despite the brisk winter air, the city retained its pervasive stench—a malodorous presence that seemed a crude insult to its architectural grandeur.

A new addition to the architectural grandeur of Washington was the nearly completed Capitol Building, which stood upon the east bank of the Potomac River. Scaffolding embraced the Capitol's inchoate dome, finished more in blueprints than in actuality. For now, the Capitol's dome resembled an oddly formed two-tiered layer cake above which protruded a strange crane-like structure. The dome's foundation, gaping vulnerably up at the threatening skies overhead, suggested—to Brandon, anyway—the rather forlorn and vulnerable state of the Union itself. Moreover, the land beneath the Capitol Building was no more majestic than its crowning scaffolding and crane. The building was set upon a hill that could only be described as muddy, desolate, and dreary. It was quite an inauspicious setting for so stirring an edifice as the nation's Capitol Building. "At least," Brandon thought as he looked out upon the distant unfinished dome from his hotel window, "the Capitol is some measure away from the city's insalubrious odors."

Upon the advice of a gentleman whom he had encountered on the northbound train, Brandon had booked a fourth-floor room at Washington's Morley's Hotel—a respectable, though modest, accommodation. Situated near the White House, yet inexpensive, it seemed practical and suitable enough for Brandon's purposes. Morley's Hotel was a locally renowned, older establishment—clean ... but in shabby repair. Location and price were its general advantages; and despite careworn appearances, the service was reputed to be impeccable.

Despite his surroundings—the bleak winter skies, rain-muddied streets, and less-than-first-rate lodgings—Brandon was excited to be in Washington and eager to begin work. After unpacking his trunks and cases at the hotel, Brandon set off on foot in search of a particular nearby restaurant called The President's Table that had been recommended to him by a member of the hotel staff. Both hungry and tired, Brandon decided the brisk walk to the restaurant would help revive him after his travels. En route to the establishment, he could not be sure which was least pleasant, the rather musty smell of his hotel quarters or the muddied stench of the city. Neither did much to pique his appetite, but the yawning growl at the pit of his stomach told him he was in need of a meal.

After partaking heartily of a bowl of beef-and-barley soup and a thick slab of bread accompanied by an ample glass of claret, Brandon withdrew a folded sheet of paper from his coat pocket. Opening the paper, he studied the name and address as well as the crude map drawn upon it. James Joyner, according to the unfolded paper, lived several blocks away. Mr. Joyner was a local journalist for *The Washington Dispatch*, a prominent Northern newspaper. Joyner's name had been supplied to Brandon by Alfred Cooke in Charleston. "Look Joyner up when you get to Washington," Alfred had suggested, "as it's always good to have connections, especially in a place like Washington." Rather than returning to his hotel room for a brief rest, Brandon decided to walk the several blocks to Joyner's residence. If Joyner was away at work, Brandon would leave a note; if he was at home, so much the better.

Paying his lunch bill, Brandon left The President's Table. Turning up his coat collar and pulling it snug about his neck, Brandon headed down the street on foot. The winter breeze had picked up in the afternoon, and its pleasantly bracing chill invigorated Brandon after the cozy, warm lunch at the restaurant had endeavored to engage the opposite effect of lulling him with drowsiness. Hands jammed in his coat pockets for warmth, his breath forming billows in the frigid air, Brandon strode down the sidewalk thinking of his children back home and everyone at Crawford Hill. Already, he missed them, although the excitement of being in Washington staved off any feelings of true homesickness. As he walked, he wondered what adventures lay ahead in these politically tumultuous times. Briefly he made a mental note to begin a letter to Alexandra in England to tell her of his new adventures and to tell her all about Washington. Maybe he could arrange for an interview with President-elect Abraham Lincoln—or even with President Buchanan. Yet, in these uncertain times, perhaps they would be inaccessible or unwilling to give their time to a foreign correspondent in a private interview; on the other hand, Brandon reminded himself that he had conducted interviews in his earlier journalistic days with Queen Victoria and the Prime Minister of Nepal. Possibly James Joyner would provide a door of assistance to him. Alfred Cooke's words echoed in his thoughts: "It is always good to have connections!"

"Stewart? Brandon Stewart?!" A buoyant voice called to Brandon from behind. Its owner had just strode past Brandon on the walkway, stopped, then turned abruptly. "Is that you, Stewart?"

Nonplussed, Brandon turned and eyed the stranger who addressed him. He in no way recognized this fellow who so unexpectedly accosted him, and he was further perplexed by the fellow's English accent.

"Well, I say!" the man laughed. "It *is* you, Stewart! Amazing!" he exclaimed heartily.

"I—I'm sorry—" Brandon shook his head in puzzlement and squinted at the gentleman. "Do I know you?"

"Ha, ha!" the man laughed in two bursts, a twinkle in his eyes. "I admit I've changed somewhat these past few ... what is it now?" He calculated quickly. "Twelve years, at least?"

Whoever it was who confronted Brandon was of a youthful complexion, but considerably gray and rather stout of stature. Although his eyes searched the gentleman's physiognomy for any sign of familiarity, it was to no avail—Brandon simply did not recognize the man.

"I still can't place you...," Brandon apologized.

"The university. London. Department of Literature...," the stranger hinted.

Brandon shrugged and shook his head, growing uncomfortably self-conscious that he could not place this individual who had so easily recognized and greeted him in mere passing along the street. Not even the voice was familiar.

Finally, the gentleman gave in. "Stanley ... Stanley Moore!" he grinned expectantly.

All at once recognition flashed in Brandon's eyes. "Stanley! My God! Stanley! What are you doing in Washington? Stanley Moore! I can't believe it! It's been—"

"Twelve years, at least!" Stanley beamed.

"Twelve years!" Brandon shook his head in wonderment.

"Remember Professor Barrow?"

"I try to forget!" Brandon laughed heartily.

"You look just the same," Stanley Moore observed. "I'll wager life's been pleasant to you."

Brandon only shrugged, and noted carefully, "I must say, you have changed a bit."

Chuckling, Stanley patted his round stomach. "I've put on a few stone." Then, indicating his graying temples and salt-and-pepper waves, he added, "I have quite a bit of snow on the roof as well. It's no wonder you didn't recognize me!" Stanley laughed again. "Besides, who would have thought we would meet again at all, let alone in Washington, D.C.!"

"It *is* quite a coincidence," Brandon agreed. Then he then explained the purpose of his stay in Washington and that he was visiting temporarily from the Charleston area. "Just now I was on my way to meet James Joyner of *The Washington Dispatch*."

"I know James Joyner! He's a good friend," Stanley said. "I'm writing for the *London Times* these days and have been in America just over a year, assigned to Washington. Fortuitous timing, politically. I met Joyner at last year's New Year's Eve celebration at the Tierny estate. If you don't mind, I'll accompany you to Joyner's house—haven't seen him in a while. It's about time I give him a ration of harassment." Stanley issued a mischievous wink and grinned.

"Yes, of course, come along. I would enjoy the company. And this evening, if you're not occupied, perhaps we could take dinner together."

"Splendid!"

Stanley Moore accompanied his friend for several blocks, all the while reminiscing, until they reached James Joyner's home. Climbing the front steps of Joyner's prosperous row house, Brandon clapped the brass door-knocker three times. In a moment, a prim young domestic in a black dress and white apron answered. She studied Brandon a moment, before recognizing Stanley who stood beside him on the landing.

"Mr. Moore, won't you and your friend come in?" She stepped back, opening the door wide to admit them. "Mr. Joyner is in the study. I'll summon him for you." She wasn't gone but a moment when an inner door was heard to open, and James Joyner appeared from around the entry-hall corner.

James Joyner, at forty-three, was ten years Brandon's senior. He was tall, trim, of lanky build, and possessed square-jawed, handsome features. His light-brown hair was just beginning to gray at the temples and thread his mustache. Dapper in dress, even in his at-home attire of comfortable trousers and rolled-up shirtsleeves, he commanded a distinguished appearance.

"Stanley! This is a pleasant surprise!" Joyner greeted his friend. Then he noticed Brandon whom Stanley introduced heartily, clapping Brandon fondly on the back.

"A pleasure to meet you, James," Brandon said as he extended his hand.

"Call me Joyner—everyone does."

"We were literature and journalism students together in London over twelve years ago," Stanley informed. With that, Stanley launched into the story of how he and Brandon had just unexpectedly encountered one another along the street. "In Washington, no less! What is the probability of such a thing?!"

"It *is* quite astounding," Joyner agreed.

"Actually," Brandon interjected, "I was on my way to meet you, Joyner, upon the advice of an acquaintance of mine from Charleston, Alfred Cooke, and—"

"Alfred Cooke?" Joyner interrupted. "You know Alfred as well? It *is* a small world isn't it?" Joyner smiled and shook his head. "Well, I'll be—Alfred Cooke. A decent fellow if there ever was one."

Stanley cleared his throat audibly.

"Second only to Stanley here, of course," Joyner jested. "Now, just what was this advice that Alfred gave you?"

"He suggested I should look you up, that you might be willing to show me the ropes of working in Washington and help me establish contacts," Brandon explained.

"Say!" Stanley interrupted, looking thoughtful. " 'The ropes.' Does that expression derive from circus acts? High wire acts?"

"I believe it stems from learning the systems of ropes used to control masts and sails on ships," Joyner said, indulging his friend's tangent with amusement. "But I will tell you one thing: Washington, lately, *is* a circus—the election of Lincoln, his impending inauguration, news of South Carolina's secession—" Joyner broke off and turned to Brandon, suddenly serious. "Are you living in Charleston?"

"Near Charleston—" Brandon began to explain, but Joyner enthusiastically interjected.

"I'll tell you what. You fill me in firsthand on the events of secession—the sociopolitical climate, anything and everything at all that you know of—and I'll help you learn all the ropes you need in Washington. Hell! I'll even get you interviews with Buchanan and Lincoln *both!*" Joyner was jubilant over his proposition. "What do you say, Mr. Stewart, is it a deal?"

Grinning, Brandon shrugged easily. "It's a deal," he said, and shook Joyner's proffered hand.

Yet Joyner grew serious again. "There is, however, one important stipulation," he cautioned.

Brandon felt his high hopes about to be dashed. "What stipulation would that be?" he asked, although he was not certain by Joyner's expression that he wanted to find out.

"You must accompany Stanley and me to the publisher Tierny's place tomorrow evening for the annual New Year's Eve dinner and dance. It is held every year for all local newspapermen—writers, editors, illustrators, photographers, publishers—and for visiting correspondents from around the world. It's—"

Stanley interrupted, waving him off from further explanation. "I've already invited Brandon along. I've told him all about it."

"Well, that's fine then!" Joyner exuded. "The more the merrier!"

"Why don't you join Stanley and me for dinner this evening at The President's Table?" Brandon suggested.

"The president's? ..." Joyner paused. "I don't quite understand ... *the* president? *Buchanan?*"

Brandon and Stanley laughed.

"No. The President's Table is a little restaurant near my hotel," Brandon explained.

Good-naturedly Joyner laughed at his misunderstanding and agreed to accompany them for dinner that evening.

The following evening, the three set off for Tierny's home for the New Year's Eve festivities.

———◇———

The Tierny home was nothing less than a regal mansion poised majestically on a wooded hill estate at the far edge of the city, overlooking the Potomac River. Although certainly smaller than Loxley House (or other such English country-estate homes), it was certainly more impressive than any plantation house that Brandon had yet seen. The home spoke of grandeur—and of a healthy fortune culled from the business of newspaper publishing. Towering Corinthian columns flanked a sweeping granite staircase that led from the cobblestone turnabout upward to two polished hardwood doors, each fitted with a gleaming brass knocker. Dangling from the eves and set upon the wide stonework railing of the expansive front-porch, numerous glowing lanterns lent a warm, fanciful atmosphere to the home. Beneath the twinkling nighttime sky, the soft light of the flickering lanterns illuminated the white of the mansion's exterior, which shone as alabaster, as if possessing a radiance of its own. Countless windows along the mansion's front beamed festive candlelight and lamplight from within, hinting at the inviting warmth and celebration taking place inside the estate home.

Horses' hooves clopped along the cobblestone turnabout as arriving carriages, one after the other, deposited guests at the foot of the broad front steps. Alighting from their own carriage, Brandon and his two companions, Stanley Moore and James Joyner, ascended the front steps along with the other arriving guests and entered through the open front doors.

Once inside, house servants checked the three men's invitations and politely relieved them of their cumbersome winter coats, hats, mufflers, and gloves. From the main threshold, they were ushered into the home's great entertainment hall where the night's festivities were well underway. There, a whirl of holiday spirit and gaiety dazzled their eyes as they entered the room.

"Old man Tierny's outdone himself this year!" Joyner noted pleasantly.

Brandon and Stanley could only nod in assumed agreement as they drank in the grandeur of the sights and sounds around them.

Crystal gaseliers, candle sconces, and an enormous fireplace at the rear of the hall bathed the room in radiance. Holly sprays, sprigs of mistletoe, and branches of evergreen tied with red ribbons adorned the hall along window ledges, table tops, archways, and wherever a touch of deep green and Christmas décor was needed to add holiday atmosphere to the enormous room. Amidst the decorations and bustling guests, crisply attired servants wended about offering Hors D'oeuvres and spirits served in crystal glasses and goblets perched upon large silver trays. Throughout, the hall was perfused with the aromas of soups, roast duck, stuffed goose, seasoned vegetables, spiced breads, puddings, pies, and trifles being prepared in the nearby kitchen. A string quartet assembled at the front of the hall had finished tuning and began to play a lively Haydn composition, which seemed to Brandon to suit the holiday atmosphere admirably.

Taking one of the small crystal glasses of claret from a proffered tray, Brandon sipped and looked about at the other guests around him. The women had dressed in their finest gowns of satin, lace, taffeta, and velveteen. Ample crinolines plumped their swaying skirts below tidy waistlines and swooning necklines. Hair was combed, curled, and pinned in the most elegant of coiffeurs and adorned with slivered combs, ribbons, and jewels. Far more subtly attired, the men were handsomely dressed in their traditional black wool suits, white shirts, and reservedly colored cravats.

For his own part, Brandon wore a black wool frock coat with matching trousers and a crisp white shirt beneath a pewter-gray vest of silk brocade. Accenting his attire was a starched cravat of burgundy silk surah, a gift sent to him from India by his brother, Jeremy, some years before. Despite a few remaining creases and wrinkles, due to not having been unpacked more than a day, the suit fit Brandon's trim build handsomely. Unassuming as ever, Brandon was not the least bit aware of the many prettily coifed heads that had turned to admire him, despite their arms crooked through those of their various escorts, fiancés, and husbands.

Close on the heels of Joyner and Stanley, Brandon threaded his way through the mingling guests who were gaily chatting, nibbling Hors D'oeuvres, and sipping from crystal glasses of claret and goblets of champagne. Here and there, ringlet-framed faces smiled charmingly as men smoothed Hors D'oeuvre crumbs from their mustaches. Now and again, the indistinguishable swell of conversations was punctuated with an abrupt eruption of laughter or a sudden exclamation. *"No! ... Really?"* "Have you heard?" "Did you see? ..." "Can you believe?" "Did she *really?!*" and "My *word!*" were among the snippets of conversation that Brandon heard as he wended his way across the great hall.

"There—there's our table," Joyner said, motioning for Stanley and Brandon to follow him. Joyner greeted a few of his colleagues from the *Washington Dispatch* who were seated at the table, then he introduced Stanley and Brandon all around. As Joyner, Stanley, and Brandon took their seats, the musicians struck up a lilting holiday tune. While the music played, the men began to chat and become acquainted amidst the din of surrounding conversation, clinking glasses, shuffling chairs, and nearby bows applied to strings. The table they occupied was one among the many other round white-clothed ones set with polished silver, cut crystal, and white china. In the center of each table stood a stout white candle of rolled beeswax wreathed in sprigs of pine and holly berries bound with a wide red ribbon. The particular table at which Brandon and his companions sat, however, was one of the few situated quite near the front of the hall, near the string quartet.

From his own vantage point, his chair's back to the east wall of the grand room, Brandon could look out upon the entire hall. Except for a large expanse of relatively open floor at the rear of the hall—where people could visit, have their glasses filled from oak wine casks and uncorked bottles, and dance—the room was an absolute sea of white-clothed tables, waiters balancing sliver trays, and mingling guests. As Brandon scanned the glimmering hall—flames lapping great yule logs in the cavernous hearth at the rear, elaborate crystal gaseliers glowing overhead, lit tapers nestled among winter greenery adorned with red bows upon the window sills, and flickering candlelight upon each silk tablecloth—his eyes came to rest on the lush evergreen tree at the front of the room. It was the same tree, framed in a west-facing window, that he had noticed earlier as he and his companions had first approached the house. Now he could see that the tree was decorated with glistening ornaments, shimmering ribbons, and flickering candles fastened to its sweet-scented boughs. No one yet occupied the extensive head table set near the great tree; the chairs were tipped to rest along the table's edge, signifying that it was reserved specially for someone other than the many guests. Brandon correctly assumed that it must be Mr. Tierny's table, and he glanced about the increasingly crowded room to see if he could perchance spot a gentleman who might present himself to be Mr. Tierny. This brief exercise proved to be in vain, and Brandon returned his attention to those at his table and to the string quartet that had commenced striking up another jaunty holiday melody.

As more guests arrived, the pleasant lilt of the musicians grew all but drowned out by the animated social chatter and din. Idly Brandon wondered what it must be for such refined and gifted musicians to play to no one's notice, to serve only as a token adornment of background atmosphere. Upon this thought, he could not help but smile to himself. After all, how many neglected articles of his published in *The Illustrated London News* had been used solely to line bird cages, make children's pirate hats, or wrap fish at the market! Brandon stifled a bemused grin at this thought and rejoined the conversation at his own table.

Thus, the cusp of the evening was pleasantly spent enjoying the elegant hall—the chattering guests, roaring hearth, pleasant social banter, sparkling gaseliers, flickering candlelight, melodious strings, as well as sipping spirits and nibbling Hors D'oeuvres—until, at eight o'clock, a bell was chimed, and Mr. Tierny addressed his many guests from the head table. Welcoming them heartily, Mr. Tierny invited everyone to be seated for "... a sumptuous feast that shall be served momentarily."

An exuberant man of perhaps sixty-five or so, Mr. Tierny was of stout build and pleasant nature. Aside from his wealth, he was not particularly noteworthy in appearance. His hair was mostly gray and his complexion ruddy. Although certainly not unattractive, he could not be considered the least bit handsome—merely of pleasant countenance. Intelligence, wit, excellent business acumen, and an amiable personality rounded out his better points. Within his profession, however, he was admired mostly for his strength of moral character. He had built his fortune through hard work and honest dealings, holding to the highest of ethical standards. Among Washingtonians, Mr. Tierny was both well-liked and well-respected. Only his stature as a wealthy man seemed to form a sort of intangible wall between him and others, even some of those whom he regarded as friends.

Immediately upon Mr. Tierny's announcement that dinner would be served, the guests took their seats as the waiters promptly bustled about wielding heavy-laden platters of soups, salads, side-dishes, breads, roasted duck, and stuffed goose. Accordingly, Mr. Tierny took his chair at the center of the head table, situated beside the decorated evergreen at the front of the hall, and commenced a friendly banter with those seated to each side of him.

The main course being served, Mr. Tierny rose once more and clanged his breadknife against his half-full wine goblet. "Ladies! Gentlemen! Everyone! May I kindly have your attention front and center—please!" The din of voices and clatter of cutlery grew hushed as Mr. Tierny raised his champagne glass to speak. "Once again, at the end of another successful year, I would like to propose a toast to the writers and editors of our *little* paper." He illustrated the word "little" between the index finger and thumb of his free hand. A roar of laughter arose throughout the hall—*little* paper indeed! As the laughter subsided, Mr. Tierny chuckled, "Well, I can see we are all of very fine *spirits* tonight!" He winked, lifting his wine glass to illustrate the double entendre. This elicited more good-natured laughter, which Mr. Tierny modestly waved down. The hall grew expectantly quiet. "Now then, I won't keep you any longer—" He paused, to quickly survey the sea of tables before him, then finished, "I see our chef has cooked your goose, so let's eat!" With that, he took his seat amidst a third chorus of merry laughter. Dinner was commenced.

No sooner had dinner begun, than the conversation at Brandon's table turned to politics, especially the secession of South Carolina just days earlier.

"Brandon, tell our friends here about the Ordinance of Secession—the signing and the vote," James Joyner prompted.

"Yes, do!" Stanley nodded emphatically. "I wouldn't mind hearing more about it myself." He stabbed a plump piece of goose meat with his fork and popped it in his mouth.

"You were in Charleston?" another asked.

Brandon nodded. "I was there."

"A first-hand account!" enthused another, leaning forward attentively.

All at the table listened with rapt attention as Brandon relayed the details of the vote, the signing, and the pandemonium and celebrations that broke out after secession had been officially declared. That his own dinner was growing cold—as he was hard pressed to swallow many bites between words—mattered little; he delighted in the retelling of the event, and enjoyed the wide-eyed attention of his small audience.

"Finally, the mayor declared that anyone lighting rockets after official celebrations would be fined ten dollars," Brandon informed. "The city prospered handsomely as a result."

As Brandon had relayed the story, one man began hurriedly jotting down notes on his pocket-square as two others scribbled notes on the linen dinner napkins. "Do you mind if we use any of this for our stories?" one asked.

"Not at all. Use anything you like," Brandon invited.

"Could I meet with you in the next day or two about some of the details?" another inquired.

Again, Brandon was willing.

At last one gentleman interrupted, "We'd better let Mr. Stewart finish his meal before they serve dessert!"

All apologized profusely for having kept Brandon from his dinner and let him commence eating without interruption. As Brandon ate, he listened to the others' banter, although most of the names and places in and about

Washington were foreign to him. Gradually his mind wandered as he ate and sipped his claret, until he found himself gazing in the direction of the decorated tree with its shortening tapers of wax and their flickering halos of golden light. He thought a moment of Crawford Hill and the children, and wondered if they were managing well enough without him—especially poor little Mela; how distraught she had been when he left her! An inadvertent elbow nudged Brandon from his musings as a waiter cleared the dinner dishes to make space for dessert plates. Silver trays laden with pies, puddings, and trifles were brought to each table for individual selection. Brandon considered the sweets for a moment, but he thought better of it and declined. Having finished dinner so late and so quickly, he felt no appetite for dessert as well.

As treats were served, Brandon's gaze was drawn again to the decorated tree by the front window, just to the left of Mr. Tierny's head table. Although, this time, it was not the glimmering tree that held Brandon's gaze—rather, it was a particular occupant at the Tierny table. All around Mr. Tierny's table, the chairs were occupied by older gray-haired men attired in fine black wool suits—including Mr. Tierny himself—save for one chair. That chair, its back to the decorated evergreen and facing Brandon from across the hall, was occupied by a young woman. Now it was far more the young woman who held Brandon's gaze than the tree. The evergreen, despite all its enchanting decorations and flickering candlelight, paled woefully beside the alluring young woman. Despite the engaging conversation at his own table, Brandon's attention returned again and again to the elegant and strikingly beautiful woman at the Tierny table, not a stone's throw away. Increasingly captivated, Brandon soon left off from paying any heed at all to the conversation around him as he studied the woman with whelming interest.

Conversing animatedly with an older gentleman seated to her left, the woman raised a crystal goblet of claret to her lips and sipped. Her thick waves of chestnut hair were pulled loosely back in a chignon, delicate ringlets framing the exquisitely chiseled contours of her face. High cheekbones arched gracefully below large emerald-green eyes. An intelligent, feminine brow beneath the chestnut coils of ringlets was set above an aquiline nose that suggested the grace of classic Grecian beauty. The cream-complected, heart-shaped face tapered to a perfect, tidy chin below generous lips of graceful curve. It would be purely a matter of opinion as to whether the woman was a classic beauty or uncommonly handsome—but that she was less than either of these would never occur to even the most critical observer.

Delighting in a comment by one of the gentleman at her table, the woman's melodic laughter mingled with the strains of the string quartet. Her manner was that of a proper lady of prominence in Washington society; however, she was not false. No artificial airs compromised her effusive genuineness and warmth. Her charm and grace owed nothing to her heritable fortune but everything to her apparent groundedness. She placed herself above no others—in contrast to other high-society women—but was refreshingly down to earth in both manner and attitude. Moreover, there was some aspect about her that, for all her poise, suggested ever so slightly a particular vulnerability, perhaps even a hint of fragility. It was this latter quality about her that intrigued Brandon all the more.

Brandon all but sighed as he gazed across the hall upon her. The woman smiled her consideration of something just said, then tipped her head sweetly to one side as if to ponder the comment further. Resting a green-sleeved elbow upon the table, she nestled her perfect chin in the cradle of her palm and contemplated the words just spoken. Her eyes seemed to take on a faraway look, and she gazed out upon the sea of white-clothed tables and guests before her. At that precise moment, her eyes by chance met Brandon's ... and lingered. The woman's gaze held Brandon's for longer than a mere moment, until Brandon, feeling embarrassed for having stared so, looked awkwardly away. Still, he sensed the woman looking in his direction. Scarcely daring to, he glanced ever so briefly back at the woman to find her gaze was still upon him. This time, however, it was her turn to look quickly and abashedly away—as a slight blush crossed her cheeks.

"What a bounder she must think me," Brandon thought, chiding himself.

"How forward he must think I am!" she regretted silently, but mused, "Yet he *is* so strikingly handsome."

"Kathryn Morgan is well beyond the likes of us," Stanley commented to Brandon, with a knowing nudge of his elbow.

"Kathryn Morgan?" Brandon asked—all the while, his eyes upon her.

"Kathryn Lissette Morgan," Stanley pronounced crisply.

"But ... who is she?" Brandon inquired, glancing briefly at Stanley.

"She is Mr. Tierny's only daughter, his only child."

With a confidential wink, James Joyner added, "Every year, I believe, half the men who attend this annual fete come only to see Kathryn. And if the other half lacks that purpose in attending, well ... I should be hard pressed to say who the sorriest lot is!" Joyner laughed.

Brandon grinned at his companion's humor. "She is not married, then?"

"No. No, she is not. Nor is she engaged," Joyner confided.

Brandon, puzzled by this, looked from Kathryn to Joyner. "But how can she *not* be married or at least spoken for? She is so—"

"Exquisitely beautiful?" Joyner suggested.

Brandon nodded.

"And," Joyner continued, "with a charming personality to match, as well as intelligence."

"Do you know her, then?"

"Good Lord, no!" Joyner laughed. "She is the well-protected only offspring of the city's most prominent publisher. No no no—not me!" He shook his head, then confidentially added, "But I would be sorely lacking in my journalistic talents if I had failed to have learned at least *something* of a woman with so compelling a presence." He grinned and winked.

Not wanting to violate her privacy, Brandon hesitated to inquire further of Kathryn Lissette Morgan, although he surmised Joyner knew much more of her that he could relay. Brandon did not wish to intrude in a way that would cause her displeasure. Nonetheless, no sooner had this consideration crossed his thoughts than Joyner continued.

"I believe Kathryn is in her early thirties," Joyner said. "She was married for several years to Kenneth Bradburn Morgan, a high-profile Washington lawyer. Unfortunately, he died the winter of 'fifty-seven ... or was it 'fifty-eight? ... of influenza. He developed pneumonia, I think. In any case, about two years before her husband's death, they lost their second son, Nicholas. He died in 'fifty-six of fever. Kathryn has one son now, Nathaniel. He's about seven years old." Joyner calculated quickly. "Yes, seven. He takes after his father, I am told." Joyner sipped the last remnant of claret from his glass.

Brandon glanced across the hall at Kathryn Morgan but found her chair now empty. Perhaps she was up and about, circulating among her father's guests according to her role as hostess. Dessert had long since ended, and guests were leaving their tables to mingle freely about the hall to visit with one another. Dancing would soon commence.

"Well! That is all I know of Kathryn Lissette Morgan, I'm afraid," Joyner concluded. "Not much else." He gave a slight chuckle, and said, "Except, of course, that not a man in this room would have any viable hopes for her."

Just then the string quartet had returned from a short break and reassembled at the front of the hall where they tuned their stringed instruments—violins, cello, and viola—and began to play a lilting waltz.

Gradually the occupants at Brandon's table excused themselves and set off in search of friends and colleagues, or for someone with whom to dance. Joyner excused himself to visit with acquaintances across the room. Just as quickly Stanley Moore disappeared—but not for long. He reappeared moments later with two women: one, an attractive blonde; the second, a rather plain woman, too thin, with raven-black hair and a longish nose—although it could not be fairly stated that she was unattractive. It was this second woman whom Stanley quickly introduced to Brandon as one having no companion to dance with for the evening. "She is the daughter of a French correspondent," Stanley explained. Feeling at loose ends himself, Brandon kindly obliged and asked the woman to dance.

Clearly the bookish sort, and not too lithe upon her toes, the rather plain-looking French woman quickly proved an awkward dance partner. Feigning tiredness, Brandon gallantly offered to escort the young woman to the wine tables at the rear of the hall where claret was being dispensed in abundance from large oak casks, and champagne bottles were being uncorked with loud pops. Perhaps there they could attempt to converse awhile and sip wine as they watched the others dance. Otherwise, Brandon felt certain that the poor woman would spend the evening alone; and he had no wish, after Stanley's efforts, to injure the woman's feelings unnecessarily. Nonetheless, after too many minutes of awkward glances, polite smiles, and suffering through the woman's broken English, Brandon could endure no longer. He politely escorted the young French woman back to her father's table. There, she sat alone with a brave and understanding smile as Brandon explained that it could not be helped, he must go and meet a friend.

"Do you understand?" he asked.

Looking uncertain a moment, the French woman's expression suddenly flashed comprehension. "Oui, oui, monsieur." She uttered something else unintelligible in French and smiled once more—this time, to conceal sorrowfully biting her lip as she nervously looked out upon the dancers.

Feeling as relieved as he did guilty for so abandoning the French woman, Brandon strode off toward the back of the hall. Perhaps he would simply enjoy a glass of claret alone and watch the couples waltzing. Besides, Brandon certainly had not asked Stanley to arrange any such company for himself; and so, he absolved his guilt.

Wending his way along the periphery of the hall, past the whirl of dancers filling the center of the floor, Brandon worked his way through the mingling guests toward the wine table. Inverted wine glasses arranged in pyramids were set out upon the large white-clothed table on either side of each oak cask. Servants' gloved hands dispensed the claret from brass spigots without spilling a drop. As Brandon reached a small clearing in the crowd before the wine table, he saw that several people were in line ahead of him waiting to be served in turn. He took his place patiently behind them and waited. Inching forward, one was served … then another … and another. Brandon would be served next.

Abruptly the person just ahead of Brandon turned away from the wine table, colliding with him as he stepped forward. Instantly two glasses of claret were spilled down Brandon's vest front.

"Oh, *dear!* I'm so terribly *sorry!*" an astonished young woman exclaimed, horrified at her blunder. She looked up wide-eyed from the red stain of claret upon the light-gray vest. "I'm so *very* sorry!" she uttered, and blushed crimson at the vestiges of claret in her two, nearly empty, glasses.

Brandon glanced from the swelling stain of red upon his silk brocade vest and the spatters upon his white shirt to meet the eyes of the woman who had so clumsily bumped into him. As he did so, he found himself looking into the upturned face and emerald-green eyes of Kathryn Lissette Morgan. For the briefest moment they shared an awkward, mutual recognition.

"I ... I am so *sorry*," Kathryn repeated, looking up earnestly at Brandon. "I should have watched where I was going."

"I'm afraid it was my fault," Brandon offered. Looking downward at his vest, Brandon brushed at the cold, wet stain with his hand. About to speak again—to explain that, after all, it was only wine and could do no real harm—Brandon looked up once more, merely to find that Kathryn Morgan had gone; only the two spilled glasses of wine stood empty on the serving table before him, leaving bright-red stains upon the exquisite white cloth at their bases. His brow knit in a mingling of annoyance and concern for his ruined vest, Brandon, nonetheless, glanced quickly about for any sign of Kathryn.

"This ought to help," Kathryn suggested. She had reappeared as unexpectedly as she had vanished, and this time, she held a glass of cold water and a clean dinner napkin that she dampened. "I really do apologize," she said, and pressed the damp cloth against the claret stain on the silk brocade.

"It's all right, really. You needn't bother so," Brandon assured.

"But it was so clumsy of me. And it's such a beautiful vest!" Kathryn dampened the napkin again and quickly dabbed at the vest.

Brandon stood uncomfortably, feeling the eyes of several guests turning to watch. "Please, it's all right," Brandon said. His voice held more of an edge than he intended. Suddenly he felt out of sorts, and he knew not why: perhaps it was the late hour, or the plain French woman, or the spilled wine upon his best clothes—or, no doubt, because his shirt was probably ruined as well as his vest!

Upon his sharp words, Kathryn's hand faltered and she drew back. "I'm sorry," she said, "perhaps *you* should—" She blushed once again and held out the sopping napkin for Brandon to take.

"Thank you," Brandon said, his humor returning somewhat. He accepted the damp wad of cloth and held it uncertainly, not quite knowing what to do with it.

"We have not met before. I am Kathryn Morgan." Her earnest emerald eyes searched Brandon's ruffled countenance expectantly.

"Brandon Stewart," he replied, managing a cordial smile. "And you are

Mr. Tierny's daughter?" He could have kicked himself—this was not at all the way he had hoped to possibly meet Kathryn.

"Yes, I am." She looked anxiously at the crumpled, damp napkin in his hand, prompting him to apply it to the purplish-red stain upon his vest. He dabbed perfunctorily at his vest and shirtfront to please her.

"I think your vest will be fine ... although it should be soaked in water tonight." Kathryn studied the fading stain, fearing that the vest was actually quite ruined. "I am truly sorry, Mr. Stewart." Inwardly she chided herself— this was not in the least how she had hoped to make this fine gentleman's acquaintance after she had first noticed him from across the room.

"Please, call me Brandon," he corrected easily, then quickly regretted that he might have spoken too familiarly. After all, if Joyner—who was at this moment surveying the scenario between the two from across the room—was correct, Kathryn Lissette Morgan's station in life was well above his. If she wished to address him as "Mr. Stewart," then perhaps it was not his place to invite her so forwardly to do otherwise. Nonetheless, it occurred to him that her manner and treatment toward him had, thus far, contained no false or formal airs common to so many of those born to wealth. Quite the contrary, she seemed genuine and unassuming, exactly as he had initially perceived her to be.

She looked up at him and smiled agreeably. "Brandon," she said, then put her hand out to receive the damp, crumpled napkin, which he carefully deposited upon her upturned palm.

Only then did Brandon notice the richness of her dress in stark contrast to the accessibility of her manner. Kathryn wore a forest-green gown of terry velvet trimmed in satin—fitting for the Christmas season. The neckline was broad and sweeping below a strand of gleaming pearls. Rich gathers of fabric descended from a slender waist. Bare shoulders glimpsed above puffed velvet, and below the puffs, the sleeves hugged the graceful contours of her arms. Buttons of satin rosettes fastened the sleeves as well as the low back of her dress. Although rich in its every detail, Kathryn's elegant gown paled compared to her own exquisite beauty and charming manner.

Still holding the damp, wadded napkin in her hand, Kathryn said, "I am pleased to meet you, Brandon Stewart." Her eyes looked deeply into his, and he looked meaningfully into hers. Neither spoke, and for a moment it seemed as if they stood alone in the great hall.

"Kathryn! There you are!" Mr. Tierny took his daughter's arm. "There are some people I would like you to meet." He turned to Brandon, and said cordially, "Excuse us, won't you?" He whisked Kathryn away through the clusters of guests, and in an instant, she was gone.

A friendly hand clapped Brandon on the shoulder. "Why, *Brandon*, I'm impressed," Joyner extolled, with a playful wink.

"Do you mean Kathryn?"

Joyner nodded with a knowing smile.

"She was only apologizing for spilling wine." Brandon blotted absently at his vest.

"Well, from where I was standing, I'd wager that one glass of claret spilled upon one's vest by Kathryn Morgan is far more intoxicating than consuming a whole bottle of claret oneself!" Joyner grinned and winked.

Brandon glanced down at his vest, but by now the damp stain was of no matter, and he couldn't help but grin as well. "It was *two* glasses," he corrected jokingly, then remarked, "She is quite something, isn't she?"

Joyner laughed. "Articulately expressed, my journalistic colleague—and *certainly*, she *is!*"

Both placed Kathryn on a pedestal, the heights of which Brandon believed he could not possibly ascend. The company of Joyner served to bring Brandon's fancies back down to earth. Perhaps he had misperceived her conduct toward him; perhaps he had read more into smiles and glances than was intended—perhaps, he concluded, she was not attainable after all. She was merely being polite, apologetic, and a good hostess to her father's party, nothing more.

"It's nearly midnight," Joyner's tone grew practical, "and it's a long way back into the city. Perhaps we should be going."

Brandon agreed, and at the mention of the late hour, he stifled a yawn.

"I'll go find Stanley," Joyner said, and was off on his errand.

Waiting for Joyner to return with Stanley, Brandon looked out upon the whirl of couples dancing. As the quartet played a lively waltz, Brandon could not help but tap his foot in time the music. How he suddenly longed for someone to dance with. It seemed like years since he had last danced—the rather bookish and awkward French woman had certainly not counted.

"I see your vest has nearly dried," a woman's voice remarked brightly.

"I'm sorry? Oh ... yes, it has," Brandon stammered, surprised to see Kathryn once again at his side.

"It's a lovely waltz, isn't it?" Kathryn commented.

"Yes, it is." Perhaps it was the late hour—he was not sure—but Brandon felt at an awkward loss for conversation. "It is a very fine waltz," he finished. With that most clever of responses, Brandon inwardly chided himself and suddenly felt self-consciously tense in Kathryn's presence. All at once he wished that she had some obligation to flit off to on her hostess duties, yet he dearly hoped she would remain a while at his side.

After a moment, Kathryn remarked, "I saw you dancing earlier. You dance quite well."

"Thank you." Brandon accepted the compliment easily, and added, "It's been quite some time since I've danced."

With that, the waltz ended, the last notes of the quartet muffled by the sound of hearty applause from all the guests.

"Perhaps you should dance more often...," Kathryn hinted.

"Perhaps so," he responded amiably as the musicians began to play a jaunty, melodic tune.

Kathryn cast an expectant glance at Brandon, but it was to no avail. Brandon merely looked out upon the guests that whirled about the floor before them.

Only then did the notion occur to Brandon that Kathryn might care to dance, and the realization that this might be the case at once daunted him—could one such as Kathryn really be hoping for *his* invitation?—and stirred him. "Would you ... care to dance?" Brandon asked.

Even as the overture left his lips, Brandon surmised that he surely must have misinterpreted Kathryn's words and her apparent interest in him. She could *not* have truly hoped for *his* invitation.

Surprisingly, however, Kathryn touched him lightly on the arm, brightened, and readily agreed. "I thought you'd never ask!"

Kathryn and Brandon danced three waltzes together until Brandon suddenly remembered his companions. "Good Lord! Stanley and Joyner!"

he exclaimed. "I nearly forgot!" He explained that he was to have left long ago with his two friends, and now it was almost one o'clock in the morning. "I'm sorry. I must look for them, and we must be going." Brandon thanked Kathryn for the dances, then turned to leave in search of his friends.

Kathryn watched after him as he walked away; and her heart fell, as she knew she would likely never see him again.

Soon after, Brandon returned to her.

"Kathryn—" Brandon hesitated, glanced downward, then met her eyes. "Would it be all right if I were to call on you sometime?" he asked. "How presumptuous!" he silently chided himself; nevertheless, he waited expectantly for her response.

"I would be most pleased if you *would* call on me." Kathryn smiled up at him, her eyes sparkling.

"When would it be convenient to call?"

Kathryn hesitated, nearly blushing at the promptness of her invitation. "—Tomorrow?" she offered.

Brandon's warm brown eyes engaged hers as before. He felt moved to lean down and kiss her cheek at that very moment, but he dared not. Instead, he confirmed, "Tomorrow," hesitated, then turned and walked away.

Brandon found Stanley Moore and James Joyner waiting patiently by the front door, and he apologized profusely for forgetting the time.

"It's quite all right," Joyner said.

"No one would blame you," Stanley grinned knowingly.

The three men retrieved their hats, coats, and scarves, then settled into the hired carriage that waited outside. As the carriage headed off from the Tierny mansion, Brandon announced, with a note of wonderment in his voice, "Kathryn said I could call on her—tomorrow!"

Stanley and Joyner—no less surprised than Brandon—nonetheless teased him about the spilled claret and his invitation to call upon Kathryn Lissette Morgan the entire drive back into the city.

CHAPTER 15

Kathryn Lissette Morgan

"I married Kenneth at a young age," Kathryn said with a trace of regret in her voice. Looking downward, she toyed with the handle of her dinner knife as Brandon listened intently.

The two were taking dinner together at The President's Table and sat before hearty portions of steamed vegetables, venison, seasoned rice, bread with fresh churned butter, and a shared bottle of wine between them.

"I wasn't yet eighteen when our fathers arranged the marriage. Our families had been acquainted for years," Kathryn explained, then met Brandon's eyes from across the table. "You see ... the Morgan's were upper-class, respectable, and Father was always overly protective of me. Before I could know my own heart well enough, Father had put it in my head that I should marry Kenneth—he was older, and I would be well looked after ... secure." Kathryn dropped her eyes, and confided quietly, "I thought that was what love was: security, reliability, having children together, making a home." She met Brandon's eyes once more, and finished, "But ... those things are not love. Love is something much more, isn't it?" She spoke rhetorically, yet her eyes seemed to Brandon as if seeking his confirmation.

"Yes, it *is* something *much* more," Brandon agreed, his tone reflective. For an instant, he thought of Allison; but Kathryn had resumed speaking, and he returned his full attention to her.

"Of course, I was quite fond of Kenneth—perhaps in the way a sister holds fond affection for her older brother and feels safe in his company. We believed love would grow with time, and it *did* ... but it lacked—" Kathryn paused and, blushing slightly, took a brief sip of her claret. She dared not be so bold as to utter the word "passion" this early in their acquaintance. "It lacked … something," she said. "Still, I grieved when Kenneth died, although his passing felt more to be the loss of a dear, beloved friend— nothing more." Perhaps the claret was affecting Kathryn more than she might have wished, as she further confided, "We were warm toward each other, and we conceived children … that is all." She took another small sip of her wine. "Ours was a life of social propriety, comfortable domesticity, practicality, and convenience. It was the loss of our second son, Nicholas, that I nearly could not bear. His passing was all but too much for me." For a moment Kathryn's eyes misted; nonetheless, she smiled warmly—partly to keep her impending tears at bay and partly to keep the social atmosphere from growing too grim for Brandon's sake.

"I am very sorry about Nicholas," Brandon consoled quietly. "I cannot imagine what it would be like to lose a child." He thought briefly of Annabelle losing her infant son, Charleston, and how very hard his death had been on both Annabelle and William—and he remembered many years earlier when Allison and he had lost their second-born to fever as an infant. Yet neither of these losses could have been as heart-wrenching as losing a grown child. "I am sorry, Kathryn," he repeated, his own eyes misting over her loss.

Sipping her claret, then hoping to turn the conversation to more cheerful topics, Kathryn invited, "Tell me about your children—Barry and Mela— and about Crawford Hill, where you live. I want to hear everything." All at once Kathryn leaned forward animatedly, the sparkle returning to her eyes.

As they dined Brandon decided that he would start from the beginning. He told Kathryn of his years at the university in London and of his brother Jeremy, of Allison—and her sisters, Alexandra at Loxley House and Annabelle at Crawford Hill—and of their married life together in both England and South Carolina, about the day that Barry was born in their stone cottage in Castleton years earlier, and then of Mela's birth. Only then, did Brandon grow somber, and his eyes brimmed as he spoke briefly of Allison's passing from childbed fever. Upon this telling, Kathryn clasped her hand upon Brandon's from across the table—they had each suffered the loss of a spouse, and Kathryn perceived correctly that Brandon's loss was felt far more profoundly than hers. She withdrew her hand as Brandon determined to smile despite damp eyes. Both resolving to brighten, they turned to more ordinary topics. As the hour grew late, they spoke together of Brandon's writing and illustrating, the newspaper business, secession, Lincoln's election, and slavery.

Although it was late and the restaurant nearly empty of patrons, Brandon and Kathryn lowered their voices upon their broaching the issue of slavery due to the few occupied tables around them.

"My father's grandfather actually lived in the South and held slaves. Louisiana, I believe it was," Kathryn confided. "On one hand, I certainly understand the moral imperative involved, while on the other hand, I understand the socioeconomic roots of the institution. Of course, I would love to see the system abandoned altogether. How does William justify slavery? What does he believe?"

"William would actually like to see slavery end one day. He is a strong proponent—some would say he is the *only* proponent—of reforms and a gradual, orchestrated plan to phase out slavery and assimilate former slaves into society as a whole while preserving the Southern economy and way of life. For William, slavery is an unfortunate practical imperative until one day it can be phased out. He views its end to be a moral imperative as long as slaves can be educated and trained for highly-skilled, advanced employment, should future jobs demand of them talents other than the skills they know from their current work."

Just then Brandon's eyes grew distant, his expression somber.

"What is it?" Kathryn asked. "What are you thinking about?"

"There was a young woman at the neighboring plantation to ours—the Davenport place," Brandon explained. "She was a young slave woman. Her name was Juliana. She was—" He stopped, not quite certain how to put the matter delicately. "She was ... violated ... and then whipped to death. She was only eighteen." Brandon's voice grew solemn. "To think that such atrocities go on within just two or three miles from home, from Crawford Hill—such grievous inhumanity." He shook his head as his eyes misted. "It goes on throughout the South. It is a wretched system, and I am hard-pressed to justify it despite the number of reputedly good plantations. The longer I am in the South, the more I learn of its vulgar atrocities against the African—as if enslavement, in and of itself, were not vulgar enough!"

Brandon had let his voice rise, drawing the attention of the few remaining restaurant patrons. However, none had discerned his words, and patrons' heads turned just as quickly and casually back to their own dinners and their own affairs.

"It's all right," Kathryn assured. "You are in Washington now, and if they *had* heard you, they would have all agreed with you." A brief silence passed between them, and she added softly, "I am sorry about Juliana."

Brandon nodded and sighed. "I just wonder how many more like Juliana must be tortured and murdered before slavery is abolished."

The two shared a moment of quiet commiseration, their empty plates and wine glasses before them.

"Shall we go out then?" Brandon suggested.

Kathryn nodded and ventured a smile.

Snow crunching underfoot, the two took a stroll along the frozen banks of the Potomac. They spoke little and quietly enjoyed the glistening stars overhead, the invigorating chill of the winter breeze, and the beacon of moonlight shining in splinters upon the inky blackness of the river. After nearly losing her footing on a patch of ice, Brandon let Kathryn take his arm for the remainder of their stroll. He liked keeping her safe, cozy, and close at his side; she liked feeling protected and warm beside him, and leaned gently upon his arm.

Their fingertips as well as the tips of their noses numb with cold, and their toes quick to follow suit, Brandon decided they had best return to their hired carriage and, given the late hour, that he should escort Kathryn home. Grateful for the blazing foot-warmer inside the carriage and its protection against the chill night breeze, Brandon and Kathryn reclined against the leather seatback as the driver lurched the carriage forward.

Before long, Brandon stood with Kathryn at the double front doors of the Tierny mansion.

"I enjoyed your company tonight," Brandon complimented. "May I call on you again?"

"I would like that very much," Kathryn consented.

"Would Saturday be all right? Perhaps we could spend the day—" Brandon stopped short, suddenly regarding his invitation too assuming and bold—a whole day *indeed!* How dare he be so presumptuous of Kathryn's time and intentions toward him!

Nevertheless, Kathryn smiled warmly. "Saturday would be fine. I shall look forward to it."

"Ten o'clock?" he asked.

"Ten o'clock," she confirmed. Then Kathryn's smile faded, and her eyes grew serious and longing. She looked up at Brandon, her heart full, wishing he would kiss her that very moment. Instead, he took her gloved hand and pressed it to his lips.

"Ten o'clock, Saturday. Until then," he said, then turned and headed down the front steps of the Tierny mansion to the waiting carriage.

———◇———

> *"Dear Alexandra,*   *January 19, 1861*
> *"There is so much to tell you, I scarcely know where to begin."*

Brandon set down his pen and gazed out his Morley's Hotel window. Outside, an unsavory sleet pelted the muddy streets below. Yet the weather hardly mattered, nor the disarray of the country as one Southern state after another threatened to secede—Brandon kept thinking only of Kathryn. He had called on her four times since he had first met her at the New Year's Eve fete, and he would see her again in a few days' time. Pen in hand, Brandon resumed the blank sheet of paper before him.

> *"I am sure you will have read, Alexandra, of the Federal garrison under Major Robert Anderson established on the island fort—Fort Sumter—in Charleston's harbor. Fort Sumter is roughly two and one-half miles from the city of Charleston—too close for comfort, I should say. I nearly think I should be in Charleston rather than in Washington, D.C., except that my colleague, Alfred Cooke, is sending me excellent reports from Charleston so that I may keep well informed. He tells me that the wives and children of the garrison have joined them on Fort Sumter and that they have brought along four months of rations as well as stores of medical supplies plus ammunition. I personally cannot*

understand the point of sending women and children into such a place—I can't suppose what the American Federal Government is thinking. I should not have wanted Allison and the children, nor Kathryn—"

Brandon lifted his pen from the page and stopped writing. Considering the matter quickly, he inked out Kathryn's name. He had not intended upon introducing Kathryn just yet to his sister-in-law—not quite yet. *"... nor any woman,"* he corrected, *"to even visit the fort."* Satisfied with his edit, he then resumed his writing.

"Some believe that all will proceed peaceably; however, many Charlestonians (Alfred Cooke included) believe that the fort's guns are aimed at Charleston and that the city may be bombarded at any moment. Citizens are climbing church steeples and rooftops armed with telescopes to verify the Federal forces at Sumter and to discern whether the fort's guns are in fact trained on the city. I dread to think of it, Alexandra, but I believe at this point that war is inevitable. After all, a Northern ship carrying reinforcements to Sumter was already fired upon by Southern units, forcing it to sail back to New York. Some say these were the first shots of war!

"By contrast, Washington is quite dull, even considering my recent interview with exiting President Buchanan. I would probably return to Crawford Hill, except that—"

Here, Brandon hesitated and carefully considered whether or not he should reveal his reason for staying on in Washington longer than originally anticipated. Gazing through the window beyond his writing desk at the gray and sleet outside, he mused that somewhere in the distance was the Tierny estate—and inside its gates, Kathryn. All at once he decided that he must confess to Alexandra his reason for not returning to Crawford Hill just yet. Besides, he would tell Annabelle and William soon enough as well.

"... except that I am courting a woman—Kathryn Lissette Morgan—and I hope to stay in Washington a while longer."

Perhaps "courting" suggested too serious of an intention. On the other hand, Brandon felt quite serious in his intentions toward Kathryn. Dipping his pen in the ink-bottle on his desk, Brandon resumed his letter.

"She is the only woman, other than Allison, whom I've ever truly felt drawn to. What I feel toward Kathryn is all quite difficult to sort out because my feelings for Allison still very much live in my heart—and yet, I want to be with Kathryn every moment of every day."

Brandon stopped writing and laid the pen aside. There it was, on paper—his admission of affection for Kathryn, despite Allison. How would Alexandra take the news of a new woman in his life, another in place of her dear departed sister? Fingering the silver locket tucked beneath his shirt, Brandon drew it out upon its chain and clutched the oval case—containing the precious golden threads of Allison's hair—in his palm. The hour was late, and suddenly weary, he rose to prepare for bed. Finishing the letter to Alexandra would wait until tomorrow. Then he would tell her all about Kathryn—how could that *not* endear Kathryn to her? Besides, he knew Alexandra's generosity of spirit; she would want him to find happiness with another, wouldn't she? He felt a pang of lingering doubt. Still, he dared not dwell on the matter, and extinguishing the lamps, he went to bed.

———◇———

"Sir, there is a telegram for you." The attendant at the front desk of Morley's Hotel held out an envelope for Brandon to take. Brandon had just finished a plain breakfast of eggs, boiled oats with jam, and tea in the hotel's dining room, and he was on his way past the front desk when the attendant had stopped him. "It's just arrived," the attendant informed.

"Thank you," Brandon said as he took the telegram, then he ascended the stairs to his second-floor room. Perhaps the telegram was about some urgent news from Alfred Cooke regarding further military actions—or even war! Once inside his hotel room, Brandon read the address on the envelope and saw that it was from not from Alfred Cooke but from Crawford Hill. Opening the envelope, he began to read the message inside:

January 20, 1861 STOP Dear Brandon STOP Return home at once STOP Barry and Mela were out riding Lightning STOP There was an accident STOP Barry was injured STOP Please return home at once STOP Love, Annabelle STOP

Brandon turned ashen, and for a moment, his heart stopped. How badly was Barry injured? It must be serious! And what of Mela? His blood chilled—what of Mela?! He scarcely dared to imagine the worst; however, the telegram had made no mention of how she was. And Barry's condition must be dire, or else Annabelle would have conveyed the extent of his injury and told him not to worry. Yet she had only wired for him to return home at once, with no mention of Barry's condition or any word about Mela at all.

Brandon stood as if transfixed, staring down at the telegram in his trembling hand. His eyes stung. How could he have been away for nearly a month?!

In a flurry, he packed. He would stop quickly by Kathryn's on the way to the train depot to explain his sudden departure. It was still morning, and he would catch the first-available southbound train.

Hailing a horse-drawn cab outside the hotel, Brandon bid the driver to make haste for the Tierny mansion. As the cab sped forward, his heart beat faster than the horse's hooves upon the street. "There was an accident … Barry was injured … Mela … Return home at once…," the telegram's words echoed in his mind as the carriage seemed to creep, despite its haste, down the long Washington streets.

At last the carriage deposited him at the bottom of the front steps of the Tierny mansion, and then stood waiting on the cobblestone turnabout. Brandon bounded up the granite steps by twos and pounded the brass knocker upon the door. Brandon paced anxiously, his breath clouding in the cold late-morning air. Presently the door was opened.

"I've come to call on Kathryn," Brandon informed the doorman.

"Yes, sir, Mr. Stewart. Come in, if you will. I shall see whether she is available to receive company." With that, the gentleman departed on his errand.

Brandon strode nervously in the drawing room for some minutes, then stood looking out the front window of leaded panes upon the Tierny grounds.

"Brandon, what a surprise this is. I had not expected you," Kathryn's voice lilted as she entered the drawing room.

Brandon turned from the window to meet Kathryn's eyes. "Kathryn," he said evenly, "I am sorry to have called on you so unexpectedly." His manner was distracted and ill at ease. He appeared pale and drawn.

Kathryn moved forward and pressed her hand upon his arm. "Brandon, whatever is the matter? Please, tell me."

"I received a telegram today, a short while ago, from Crawford Hill. Barry and Mela were out riding, there was an accident, and Barry is injured. There was no word sent regarding Mela."

"Oh, Brandon—I'm *so* sorry!" Kathryn said, her voice edged with concern. "I hope they are both all right. I'm sure they *must* be." She gave his arm a consoling squeeze as her eyes gazed worriedly into his.

"I must return home, Kathryn. I am on my way to the train depot just now. Before leaving Washington I wanted to stop and tell you that I was going, and—" He hesitated, his eyes meeting hers warmly. "I wanted to see you before I left," he finished softly.

"Will ... will you return?" Kathryn looked up questioningly at Brandon. The dreadful news and his going away came so abruptly, so very unexpectedly.

"Yes. Yes, I will," Brandon assured with decision. But he knew not when he would be back; he only knew that somehow he *would* return and see Kathryn once again, one day.

"I'll miss you," she said quietly.

"Write to me at Crawford Hill," he invited, and slipped a paper bearing the address in her hand.

Kathryn nodded. "I will write. And you must write to me here, at my father's."

"I will," Brandon assured.

For a moment neither one spoke. Only their eyes conveyed profound regret at parting. It was then that he gently tilted her chin upward and placed a warm, tender kiss upon her lips. "I will see you again," he promised, and he then turned and left, letting the front door close behind him.

Kathryn stood quietly in the drawing room for a moment, hardly believing Brandon was really gone. She placed the fingertips of one hand to her lips as if to seal his kiss upon them. In the other hand, she held the address of Crawford Hill—hundreds of miles away. Her eyes welled, then brimmed, until a warm tear spilled down from one eye, then the other.

Downstairs, Annabelle informed Brandon that Barry had been making jumps with Lightning in the field adjacent to the stables. After riding with Mela in tame circles around the roundabout of the front drive, he let her be his audience as he and Lightning practiced jumps in the tall grass. Mela had seen Barry's fall and quickly summoned a stablehand who then ran to the house to inform Annabelle of the accident. "Barry is upstairs. He is resting," Annabelle told Brandon quietly. Wordlessly she and Brandon ascended the stairs to Barry's room.

Entering Barry's bedroom, Annabelle touched Brandon on the arm. "He's asleep," she said softly.

Barry lay motionless upon two plump pillows. Wrapped about his forehead, strips of gauze bandages concealed the bruise to his temple and the several stitches needed to close the gash he had suffered. The two crescents of chestnut lashes upon his closed lids fluttered not the slightest. His complexion, white as cream, evidenced no pink stirring of life upon his cheeks. Pale and still, his lips uttered no sound.

Brandon moved toward his son's bed and sat upon its edge. Gently smoothing aside a lock of tawny hair from his son's brow, Brandon whispered, "Barry? . . . Barry, it's your father. I've come home. . . . Barry? . . ."

Annabelle placed a careful hand upon Brandon's shoulder. "He—" Her voice caught, and she swallowed hard. "He can't hear you," she managed, then bit her lip hard as her eyes welled.

"I . . . I don't understand." Brandon's eyes flashed bewilderment as he looked up at Annabelle. Seeing her tears struck panic in him. "Annabelle! What do you mean?!" Fear clutched his heart.

Brushing aside her tears, Annabelle explained, "He is asleep. He has been asleep for days. I've been sitting with him, and Ester and the plantation nurse care for him, and the doctor—Dr. Langford—comes when he can."

"What has Dr. Langford said?" Brandon's measured tone belied the trepidation underlying each syllable.

Annabelle drew an uneasy breath. "He said that Barry is in a coma, that he has a swelling of the brain—a concussion." Her voice thin and tremulous, she could not go on.

Brandon could barely take in all that Annabelle said. He looked upon his son lying so deathly motionless, save for the subtle rise and fall of the coverlets with each shallow breath. "Dear God," he uttered. A sensation of lightheadedness sought to overtake Brandon as his senses strained to comprehend the stark reality before him and of Annabelle's words. "*Christ*," he breathed, his eyes filling.

"I feel so responsible...," Annabelle blurted. Then, unable to choke back tears any longer, she bowed her face in her hands and quietly wept.

"Annabelle! ... *No!*" Brandon rose and swept her into his arms. "Annabelle, it's *not* your fault!"

Burying her face against Brandon's shoulder, she cried brokenly, "But I was watching over Barry and Mela while you were away. This is *all* my fault!" Whereupon she dissolved into heaving, disconsolate sobs.

Brandon pressed Annabelle closer to him and stroked her hair to calm her as he blinked back his own tears. "Shhh, shhh, now. Annabelle, please. ... No one is blaming you. It's not your fault," he soothed, his voice wrought with emotion.

"But how could this have happened?" she wept. "I love Mela and Barry as if they were my own." Hot tears spilled against Brandon's shirt.

"Here, now," Brandon intoned softly. "Let's go out. You can sit a while. We'll have Ester bring you some brandy to sip." Brandon's voice was calm and sure, belying the tremendous lump that welled in his throat.

Annabelle nodded her head tearfully against his shoulder.

Taking one more look upon his son lying still and quiet beneath the coverlets, Brandon led Annabelle out from the room and downstairs. He sat her upon the settee in the west sitting room and requested Ester to bring a glass of brandy to settle Annabelle's nerves. Offering Annabelle his pocket-square, Brandon sat beside Annabelle on the settee. Ester returned with the brandy in a stout glass. Setting it on the table before Annabelle, Ester looked anxiously from one to the other with an expression of sympathy that spoke volumes. "Massa Brandon ... c'n I bring you a glass o' brandy, too?" she asked quietly.

"No, thank you, Ester. We will be just fine. Thank you."

"Yessuh," Ester nodded, and cast another distressed look at her mistress weeping disconsolately into Brandon's pocket-square. "Po' Miss Annabelle! Po' Massa Brandon! Po' Massa Barry! Lawdy *Jesus!*" Ester whispered, lifting her damp eyes heavenward as she exited the room.

Brandon sat with Annabelle for some time, helping her sip the brandy and consoling her as best he could. Her tears gradually subsided, and she dabbed at her reddened nose and puffy eyes with the wadded pocket-square between sips.

"Are you feeling better now?" Brandon asked.

Annabelle nodded. "Yes, I think so." She gave Brandon's hand a heartfelt squeeze. "Why don't you go on up to sit with Barry, if you like. The doctor will come again this afternoon, and William will return home soon. I'll be all right now."

"I think I shall go up, then," Brandon said, whereupon he rose, giving Annabelle's shoulder a tender squeeze.

She placed her own hand upon his and looked up at him with stark, swimming eyes. "I am so deeply sorry, Brandon," she intoned, her heart breaking yet again with each syllable.

Kneeling before her, Brandon gently removed the glass from her hand and set it on the settee's end table. He took both her hands warmly in his and looked into her glistening pale-blue eyes intently, as if to speak from his very soul. "Annabelle, listen to me." His voice was gentle but firm. "Look at me."

Her damp eyes met his.

"None of this is your fault. I am not blaming you." He gave her hands a tender squeeze. "All right?"

Annabelle nodded. This time, something in her brother-in-law's words assuaged her concerns as the effects of the brandy quieted her upset.

Brandon caressed a stray tendril from Annabelle's forehead and rose. Then he went out and ascended the stairs once more to Barry's room.

———◇———

Dr. Langford spoke at length with Brandon the evening of his return to Crawford Hill.

"Will my son be all right?" Brandon asked.

"This kind of injury is difficult to assess," Dr. Langford explained. "Although I believe the swelling of his brain to be mild, the nature of the blow he sustained has nonetheless resulted in prolonged unconsciousness. We are fortunate that the swelling appears to be minimal, and surgery is not needed."

"Surgery?" Brandon exclaimed, aghast.

"On occasion, with head injuries, there is fluid or bleeding that necessitates a surgical means of relieving the pressure, draining the fluid."

Suddenly Brandon felt woozy. "But you say Barry does *not* require this surgery?" He wanted to be absolutely sure he was absorbing, carefully, every word the doctor uttered.

"Exactly. No surgery," Dr. Langford affirmed.

Brandon felt the color return to his cheeks. "What can be done for him, Doctor?" He scarcely dared to voice an expectation of hope.

Closing his black medical bag with a firm snap, Dr. Langford directed simply, "Keep Barry comfortable and warm. Continue with the nursing care—the throat-tube and rectal feeding, and the sponge bathing—that he has been receiving. Keep a close watch on him." Dr. Langford picked up his bag. "If there is any change, send for me. Meanwhile, I will continue to check on him when I can.

"Is that all? Is there nothing else?" Brandon asked as if disbelieving the doctor's spare instructions. Surely there was an answer, a remedy in the bottom of Dr. Langford's black medical bag—somewhere!

Dr. Langford clapped a sympathetic hand on Brandon's shoulder. "I am sorry I cannot give you a more definitive prognosis or more encouraging news." He sighed and added softly, "We always have hope. Barry could simply awaken at any time."

Brandon's eyes misted, and he nodded bravely, swallowing back tears.

"Let's give it time," Dr. Langford reassured. Giving Brandon's shoulder a consoling squeeze, he went out.

———————◇———————

Three days had followed since Brandon's return, and still, Barry had not stirred.

Now Brandon sat in a large wooden rocker at Barry's bedside and reflected on his meeting with Dr. Langford just three days earlier. The hour was late, and the room was illuminated by a single oil lamp upon the bedside table. Checking the time on his pocket watch, Brandon saw that it was nearly midnight. How hopeless it all felt. The night seemed eerily quiet.

Resting his head upon the rocker's back, Brandon lifted his eyes upward, and whispered into the night, "*Please!* ..." He sighed, and his eyes filled.

"Father?" a small voice whispered in the darkness. Brandon's heart stopped, and he looked down at Barry upon the bed.

"Father?" Little feet trudged across the wooden floor. Barry had not spoken; it was Mela who had called to her father from the doorway.

"Mela, my little dear one, what are you doing up so late?" Brandon asked softly.

"I couldn't sleep. I want to be with you," Mela whispered plaintively.

"All right, then, come here," Brandon offered, and lifted her easily up into the rocker to sit on his lap.

Mela nestled cozily in her father's lap, the hem of her flannel nightdress pulled warmly over her stockinged feet. Brandon's comforting arms encircling her, she rested her head of golden tresses upon his shirtfront and listened to the steady, reassuring beat of his heart. Brandon kissed the top of her head. The two sat in silence for some time, rocking languorously in the big oak chair, all the while their eyes fixed in the dim light upon Barry.

"Father ... will Barry ever wake up again?" Mela asked.

Brandon considered this carefully and fought the swelling lump in his throat. After a time, he spoke. "Yes, I am certain he will wake up again, little dear one." Kissing the top of Mela's head once more, he snuggled her warmly against him to sleep as he kept watch over his son.

The rails of the rocker creaked ever so quietly upon the wood floor. Beyond the darkened window, an occasional cricket chirped. No other sound pierced the silence of night. Even the flame of the oil lamp danced and fluttered silently upon its wick. To and fro, the rocker cheeped languidly, its rhythm and motion soon lulling Brandon to let his eyelids drift closed. The rocker crept to a stop as Brandon slipped into sleep, letting one arm fall limply away from Mela, the other held fast about her. The minutes passed and stretched into hours.

"Father? ... Father? ..." a weak voice called out in the darkness. "Father? ..."

The voice barely penetrated Brandon's consciousness as he drifted between sleep and wakefulness.

"Father? ..."

Roused, opening his eyes, Brandon found Mela still fast asleep in his arms.

"Father? ..." the small voice repeated plaintively.

Instantly Brandon lifted his eyes from Mela to where Barry lay upon the bed.

"Father ... I'm thirsty," Barry whispered.

Brandon's eyes widened, and his heart seemed to leap in his chest. For the briefest moment, Brandon wondered if he was not dreaming. Yet Barry's eyes shined up at him in the low lamplight.

"Father ... I'm thirsty."

Rising from the rocker, Brandon laid Mela carefully across the foot of the bed, and then he attended to Barry. With a trembling hand, Brandon poured water from the bedside pitcher into a small glass. Sitting on the edge of Barry's bed, Brandon placed the glass to his son's lips and helped him to drink in little sips. Joy and profound relief washed over Brandon in waves as his heart swelled and eyes teared.

"Where am I?" Barry murmured.

"At home, in your room," Brandon answered, his voice low with emotion.

"My head hurts," Barry complained faintly.

"You were out riding your horse, Lightning. You tried too high a jump ... the horse missed, and you fell," Brandon reminded quietly.

A vague puzzlement glimmered in Barry's eyes. "I don't remember," he murmured, then asked, "Is Lightning all right?"

Brandon had to swallow hard to answer. He cleared his throat. "Lightning is just fine," he said, and his eyes suddenly welled.

A tug on Brandon's sleeve diverted his attention. Unnoticed, Mela had waken and now stood at her father's elbow, a worried thumb in her mouth. "Is Barry awake now?" she asked blearily.

"Yes. Yes, he is," Brandon replied, with a heartened smile. Indeed, it was the first smile that had crossed his lips since he had first received the news of Barry's accident.

After giving Barry another sip of water, Brandon turned to Mela. "I want you to go to your aunt and uncle's room, knock on their door, and bring them here at once. Can you do that for me?"

Mela nodded emphatically and set off purposefully on her errand.

No sooner did Mela leave the room than Barry's eyes had shut again, and he lay still upon the bed. Panic seized Brandon.

"Barry! Barry!" he called to him, and shook him gently.

Instantly Barry's eyes fluttered opened.

"You must stay awake now, Barry. Do you understand?"

Barry nodded despite a haze of unnatural sleep seeking to consume him once more.

"Dear Kathryn,   *February 6, 1861*

 "By now, you should have received my first two letters, and I thank you ever so much for your letters to me and for your continued concerns. I assure you, everything is much better here day by day.

 "Barry is growing stronger. He is up and about; and although weak, his appetite has returned, as well as the sparkle in his eye and the color in his cheeks. Our physician, Dr. Langford, assures us that Barry is well out of danger and will soon be back at his lessons with the other children. Already, Barry is anxious to be well enough to ride Lightning again. I will let him ride again when he is able, but he is not to jump! Not for a long while yet."

Brandon sighed heavily, recounting the past many days, then resumed his letter.

"Kathryn, I cannot tell you what these past days have been. Having Mela near has helped to see me through—my having to be strong for her."

Brandon stopped again and ran a wearied hand across his brow.

"I hope this letter finds you and Nathaniel well. Crawford Hill seems a world away from Washington, D.C. just now. I have dearly missed your company since I've been home. It may be a while still before I can return to Washington. Meanwhile, I shall look ever so forward to seeing you again!

"By this time, every newspaper in the country must be spreading the word of the meeting of the Southern delegates in Montgomery, Alabama two days ago. Now that the Confederate States of America have been assembled and Jefferson Davis elected president of them, I hope to visit Montgomery briefly for Davis' inauguration on February eighteenth. Barry is excited for me to go so that I may tell him all about it. I, however, am reluctant to leave Barry in his convalescence for even such a short journey as that. Nonetheless, Dr. Langford assures me that Barry is 'out of the woods' and can only improve; he has reassured me that I should be free to go. I have yet to decide what I shall do. Meanwhile, I do plan to return to Washington by the first week of March."

Brandon paused from his writing and wondered if his anticipated schedule was perhaps too ambitious. Estimating the days needed for travel as well as time at home with the children, early March was just barely feasible. If he could not return to Washington until later, then that would have to do; he could prevail upon Stanley Moore or James Joyner for details of Abraham Lincoln's presidential inauguration—scheduled for the first week of March—to incorporate into his articles for *The Illustrated London News*. Similarly, if he felt compelled to remain at Crawford Hill as Barry convalesced—thereby missing Davis' Confederate inauguration in Montgomery in several days' time—he could certainly prevail upon Alfred

Cooke for information. For now, circumstances only afforded Brandon to patiently take one day at a time.

Business and politics aside, Brandon missed Kathryn and was truly anxious to return to her. He missed the radiance and warmth of her smile, the music of her laughter, her thoughtful intelligence, the exquisitely graceful curve of her cheeks, and the delightful sparkle in her gem-green eyes. These many days apart from her, he longed for the tender touch of her hand upon his arm once again and the soft scent of her thick waves of chestnut tresses. In short, he missed everything about her, as if a part of him was not quite whole without her near. A pang of affection stirred his heart, and he sighed longingly.

Through the few letters they had exchanged since Brandon's return home to Crawford Hill, both Kathryn and Brandon had been more candid about revealing their hearts to one another than they otherwise would have dared confess so early on in their acquaintance. Brandon checked his watch and decided he had best close the letter and head downstairs to dinner. He set pen to paper with a tender hand.

"Dearest Kathryn, your letters have brought me such solace and joy. Even though the miles part us, I have your letters to read. Although you cannot be here with me, nor I there with you, your letters bring you very near. Having the pages upon which your sweet hand has rested brings you closer to me. I miss you more with each passing day. If I dare confess it, I miss you beyond all earthly measure.

"Affectionately,

"—Brandon"

He folded the letter and sealed it in its envelope. It would go out in the morning post. How interminably slow the mails seemed.

After dinner, Brandon joined Annabelle and William for their customary brandy before the hearth in the east sitting room. Throughout dinner, he had already carefully pondered what he must confess to them. Any day, a letter might arrive from Alexandra in England disclosing what he had written to her of his affection for Kathryn, and so he dared not wait any longer. Still, Brandon felt some trepidation in telling Annabelle and

William of Kathryn—particularly Annabelle. It was easier to confess over the miles by mere letter to Alexandra the feelings he held for Kathryn; to do so face to face with Annabelle would be more difficult. Since Allison's death, either sister might not understand his having feelings for someone new, someone whom they did not know. Nonetheless, Brandon decided he must finally reveal the truth to Annabelle and William.

Settling upon the sofa with their glasses of brandy, Annabelle and William resumed a conversation they had been discussing more quietly at dinner, and Brandon took his usual chair to the left of the hearth.

"I still say it is arrogance," Annabelle said decisively to William.

"But it isn't attitude. It is belief," William put in.

Annabelle set down her glass of brandy, shot up, and paced. "Arrogance! Sheer arrogance!" she pronounced. Annabelle strode to and fro before the hearth, her arms folded firmly before her. She turned to face William, her eyes flashing, and exclaimed, "My God! How could *anyone* say such a thing?!" She lowered her voice and mocked the Confederate Vice President, Alexander Stephens, " 'The new government is founded on the great truth that the Negro is not equal to the white man.' *Humph!*" She punctuated her words with a stomp of her foot. "The sheer audacity to believe such a thing!" She snatched up her glass of brandy from the table and sipped three decisive gulps, then placing it firmly back down, nearly sending its contents sloshing over the brim. Unable to speak further, she turned and stared into the crackling flames upon the hearth.

William rose and stood at his wife's side. "But, my dear, that is what a majority of Southerners believe."

"But *you* don't believe the African is inferior, do you?" Annabelle intoned. It was a statement more than a question.

"No. Of *course*, I don't. You *know* I don't." He was exasperated—how could she think such a thing of him?

They stood in silence a moment as Brandon looked on. William and Annabelle were rarely at serious odds on anything. However, matters of slavery still could profoundly upset Annabelle. The formation of a Southern Confederacy and the stipulations of its Constitution were no exception.

William placed his arm around Annabelle, and added, "Besides, the

Confederate Constitution eliminates all further African slave trade. That is a step in the right direction."

"But it is only a reluctant concession to world opinion on the issue. It is not a moral choice in the least. It is only a political device to garner favor with other more civilized nations. Southerners are such hypocrites!"

William looked slightly wounded at this; and Annabelle, noting William's troubled countenance and her own uncontrolled agitation, apologized. "I'm sorry, William. I did not mean to imply that you are a hypocrite or even like most Southerners, for that matter. It's simply that this whole issue upsets me so."

"It's all right, Annabelle, I understand," William said gently, and planted a kiss on his wife's cheek. Looking across at Brandon, William jokingly confided, "She is still adjusting to Southern ways."

"As am I," Brandon said half-seriously. In particular, the atrocities committed against the young slave woman, Juliana, just two months before had remained fresh in his mind. He added, "Life in the South is an adjustment that I am not certain can ever be completed by anyone not born here."

"I dare say, you're right," Annabelle agreed.

Although hurt by this sentiment, William held his tongue as he was out numbered; besides which, he surmised that his wife and brother-in-law were likely correct in their various opinions. Nonetheless, an awkward silence followed and lasted quite some moments during which William, then Annabelle, resumed their seats upon the sofa. Sipping their brandies and avoiding one another's eyes, husband and wife gazed into the glowing hearth flames.

"Rather a mild winter this year," William noted, after a time.

"Ester says the roses out back should bloom early this year," Annabelle commented.

"I think you said it was cold up north, in Washington," William addressed Brandon.

"Yes, it was. Some snow, sleet—rather cold most of the time." Brandon remembered, just then, his evening stroll with Kathryn along the banks of the Potomac River—the snow crunching underfoot, her arm linked securely through his, the scent of her hair in the winter chill. So caught up by his reverie of Kathryn, Brandon did not hear the question put to him by Annabelle. He scarcely noted it the second time, but at last it penetrated his thoughts.

"Will you be home with us for your birthday?" Annabelle had asked.

"Hmmm? Oh … my birthday. Yes, I believe I will be … yes. The children are quite anxious that I should be here."

"We weren't sure if you would be able to return from Montgomery and Jefferson Davis' inauguration in time for your birthday celebration," William noted. "There is only one week between the two."

"Cotta is anxious to bake a spice cake for you—your favorite," Annabelle put in.

For a moment, Brandon said nothing but gazed into the amber pool of brandy in his glass. Then, lifting his eyes, his expression grew quite serious. Looking at William and Annabelle, he said, "There is something I must tell you." He studied their faces a moment, but their expressions only registered innocent anticipation.

"I have met someone … in Washington," he began apprehensively. Suddenly he regretted broaching the subject at all. Allison had been Annabelle's sister; perhaps Annabelle would find his attentions toward another woman insensitive or callous. After all, little more than five years had elapsed since Allison's passing. In all that time, even Brandon had not anticipated having room in his heart for another—not until Kathryn had entered his life and affections. Would Annabelle and William understand his possessing feelings for another?

Interpreting Brandon's consternation, Annabelle asked carefully, "You have met a woman acquaintance?"

"Yes … I have." Brandon spoke with reserve, unsure how to continue, uncertain whether or not he had noted disapproval in Annabelle's expression and tone of voice.

"Who is she?" William inquired with some curiosity.

"Her name is Kathryn Lissette Morgan, and—" Brandon stopped short and looked carefully from one to the other before admitting, "and … I find I am … quite serious toward her."

There! He had said it. He looked downward and swirled the brandy in his glass before taking two generous sips.

Annabelle's eyes widened, seeming to confirm Brandon's apprehension. Nonetheless, all at once she beamed joyously. "Why Brandon, that's wonderful news! Tell us, how did you meet her? What is she like? You *must* tell us *everything!*"

William, by his expression, was equally pleased with the news, and he eagerly leaned forward on the sofa to hear all Brandon had to tell.

Brandon stammered for a moment, unsure of what to say. "Do you ... do you mean that you ... you don't mind?"

"Mind? Brandon ... *why?*" Annabelle intoned, genuinely puzzled as to why such news should be received as the least bit objectionable.

Brandon spoke hesitantly. "I thought you might object because of Allison—" Here, he grew hushed and cast his eyes downward; for upon pronouncement of Allison's name, he felt a sudden qualm of misgivings in his own heart. However, his doubts were short lived as his feelings for Kathryn whelmed anew.

"Brandon, why should I object?" Annabelle's tone was tender.

"I was unsure whether to tell you about Kathryn." Brandon was clearly at a loss as to how to continue, and he fell silent.

"But Brandon ... don't you remember how I had told you about Miss Barton at church, that she had an eye for you? And Miss Simpson over the river, how she often asked about you? And, also, how I have encouraged you at times in the past to meet nice young woman to be your companion?" Annabelle's words fairly tumbled forth. She smiled encouragingly at her brother-in-law. His news warmed her heart.

"Yes. Yes, you did," Brandon admitted. Yet all of her previous coaxing and hints had fallen on deaf ears and a mourning heart. "I'm sorry, Annabelle. I remember now." He smiled at his needless fretting. "I suppose no one has affected me so until Kathryn."

"So! Do tell us all about her!" William prompted.

With that, Brandon embarked with delight upon telling them about Kathryn Lissette Morgan—or Lissy, as he was affectionately prone to think of her. As he spoke of her, Brandon vowed inwardly to court her in earnest upon his return to Washington and to learn her exact intentions toward him.

As the hour grew late, the three set aside their brandy glasses and headed upstairs for bed. As he bade Annabelle and William goodnight, Brandon felt a great joy and relief that his news had been taken so well, so hospitably. Brandon stopped by Mela's room, then Barry's room—both children were sound asleep, snug in their beds. One day, there would only be these two little ones left to tell about Kathryn.

Brandon anxiously counted the days before March and his departure north.

<hr />

Mela did not cry, this time, as Brandon left Crawford Hill for Washington. However, before he boarded the carriage to depart, Mela hugged him, kissed his cheek, and asked, "If Barry falls off his horse again, will you come home?"

Brandon could not help but break into a grin. "I will come home again, even if Barry does *not* fall from his horse," he assured.

Next, Brandon said his goodbye to Barry, who stood beside the carriage. "No accidents this time while I am away, do you hear?" Brandon admonished. "I don't want to receive any more telegrams."

"Yes, Father," Barry grinned sheepishly, then hugged his father goodbye.

Brandon had missed Jefferson Davis's inauguration in Montgomery, Alabama in mid-February—he could not bring himself to leave Barry as his son convalesced. Barry was disappointed for his father's sake and felt sorry about being the cause of his father's missing the historic event. Brandon, in turn, reassured Barry that Lincoln's inauguration in less than a week would be far more exciting. Besides, Alfred Cooke had been dispatched to Montgomery, and he wrote all the details of Davis's inauguration in a letter to Brandon at Crawford Hill. In return, Brandon would wire details of Lincoln's inauguration to Alfred Cooke as well as send him a letter about the event.

Brandon hugged each of his children once more, then stepped up into the carriage.

"It looks like a storm coming in," William noted, scanning the morning skies. "It's a good thing you are traveling today, before it rains."

Brandon nodded his agreement. "Yes, it is fortunate."

With that, he set off in the carriage for Charleston where he would catch the northbound train.

The next day, as Brandon traveled northward by train, he began to write rough notes on a pad of paper for an article he planned to draft for *The Illustrated London News*:

"The Southern Confederacy has been founded, in the words of its Vice President Alexander Stephens, on 'the great truth that the Negro is not equal to the white man.' The implication is not that the African is regarded as superior to the white man—but instead, is considered inferior in every way. Southern society—predicated on manner, propriety, and civility—stands as a hypocritical veneer over its bondage and mistreatment of the African. As a whole, Southerners treat their horses and chattel more humanely than that segment of their fellow man—the African."

Three weeks before Brandon's departure for Washington, two slaves on the neighboring Davenport plantation had dared to plan their escape. The two young Africans, a husband and wife in their early twenties, were quickly found out, however. Jack Davenport dispatched his overseer, a group of field hands, and a pack of hounds to track the couple through the woods. Caught, bound, and led by ropes back to the Davenport plantation, the two faced their punishment. His eyes burning with anger beneath his wild shock of fiery red hair, Jack Davenport paced and hurled orders to his white overseers, "Use the barrel on the woman. Use lots of nails. Take her to the hill."

"What about the buck?" the overseer asked coarsely, all but salivating in anticipation of what cruelty would be duly inflicted upon the man.

"Hmmm...," Jack Davenport mused as he stopped pacing and thought carefully. He ran a weathered hand over his rough beard, and his eyes narrowed. "I have something new in mind for him," he said as he broke into a satisfied grin. "By God!" he shot. "These two will be an example to *all* the other niggers! Not one of them will dare escape again! *Ever!*" He spat on the ground as punctuation.

That next morning, the woman was forced to climb into a wooden barrel that was hammered through with many long nails. The barrel, with the woman shut inside in utter darkness, was conveyed by wagon to a steep hill at the edge of the woods. Poised at the crest of the hill, the barrel was let go, and it rolled hundreds of feet downward into the thick of the woods. There, the barrel was abandoned, leaving the young woman to starve or bleed to death—whichever would come first.

Afterward, Jack Davenport had the African man's eyes branded shut with hot irons. The man was then taken deep into the woods and cruelly ordered to search for his wife. Abandoned there, the man was never seen again, and it was assumed that he had wandered aimlessly until he perished. The woman's body was left to rot in the barrel; her husband's remains were likely to be consumed by animals and stray dogs in the woodland.

The African was Jack Davenport's property to do with as he pleased. It was his constitutional right.

Within days of the torture and abandonment of the young man and woman, another young slave gave birth to a baby girl. Determined that her child would not become property of Jack Davenport, the young woman drowned her infant in a shallow pond. Hearing of this, Davenport chained her to a whipping post and issued fifty lashes to her bare back himself. No sooner was she unchained than she fell dead upon the blood-soaked ground.

As Brandon traveled northward by train, reworking the first draft of his notes, he paused and thought of the young slave woman, Juliana, and the likes of Jack Davenport. Setting pen to paper, he wrote, "Rebellion and yearning for independence have swelled in the hearts of Southerners. How long before rebellion and yearning for freedom strain beyond containment in the heart of the African slave?"

CHAPTER 16

A House Divided

The Davenport Plantation's Big House was roomy yet plain, a modest wooden structure of two stories. Its clapboards of peeling paint rose above a foundation of brickwork. A simple porch skirted the front of the house below a steeply peaked roof. Brick chimneys flanked either side of the house, between which two gabled windows gaped vacantly southward. A low white picket fence enclosed the front yard where Jack and Sara Davenport's son, Tom, had played as a child. The smokehouse and stables were each situated to one side of the Big House, not too great a distance away. In back of the Big House stood a carriage house and, behind it, a barn and various other outbuildings for farming equipment, grain and cotton storage, and for putting up the meager lot of rice that Davenport relentlessly determined to produce on a lower portion of untenable land. No grand canopy of moss-draped oaks shaded the pitted dirt drive leading to the house. Only a solitary magnolia stood near the home's eastern front corner, its branches shading the wood-shingled roof that jutted out over the front porch.

On this blustery winter night in late February of 1861, the Davenport Big House was quiet and pitch-dark, save for one oil lamp illuminating the front room. There, Jack Davenport sat alone before the flickering fireplace drinking from a bottle of whiskey.

Sara had retired for bed early, as was her habit. Her husband's penchant for drink—coupled with his brusque manner, bitter nature, harsh tongue, and abusive ways—was seldom conducive to Sara wanting to keep her husband company, especially not once evening fell.

Their son, Tom, age fifteen and bored that blustery evening, had taken a book upstairs to read for a while before blowing out his oil lamp to sleep. Only in the pages of a favorite book or the range of his imagination could Tom escape the oppressive and dreary existence beneath his father's roof. Not fond of school, Tom nevertheless devoured as many books of fiction as he could come by—and nearly all were tales of wild adventure.

As the hour grew late, and with Sara and Tom each asleep in their rooms, the house was still but for the crackling of flames upon the untended hearth and the occasional slosh of whiskey as Jack Davenport tipped the bottle to his lips to drink. Outside, in the distance, the crack of thunder echoed as the brisk winter night stirred in fitful gusts about the house. The sky pulsed light in far-off flashes, then grew pitch-dark. Roiling clouds eclipsed the quarter moon. After a time, the hearth flames dwindled as Jack Davenport, out cold with drink, lay slumped in his overstuffed chair before the dying embers, the whiskey bottle slipped from his hand, its remnants pooled upon the floor.

From an upstairs window, a candle's flame was drawn before the darkened panes in a large circular motion. A moment passed, and again the candlelight was drawn before the upstairs window in a broad arc. Then the candle was blown out, and dark fingers pinched the smoldering wick.

As Sara and Tom slept soundly, dark figures moved silently across the front yard in the chill nighttime breeze and tiptoed onto the porch. Ever so quietly, the front door was opened from within, and the shadowy figures entered the house. Some of those who entered stayed on the ground floor of the house while others quietly made their way up the staircase, now and again pausing nervously as the wooden steps creaked.

Upstairs, Sara Davenport awoke with a start to find a large dark hand clapped firmly across her mouth. Her frightened eyes darted as she struggled to breathe in her sudden panic. In the darkness, she could scarcely discern the faces of Jack's personal servant, Kitch, and her own servant, Hetty. It was Kitch's hand clamped tight upon her mouth as she struggled to speak or cry out. Neither Kitch nor Hetty spoke, but each stood determinedly over Sara as her heart beat in great thumps against her chest, and she broke out in a cold sweat.

From downstairs, there issued the sound of several pairs of footsteps moving about the house as more footsteps were heard upon the staircase in a great tumult of movement. At once there sounded a dull thud. Then the house grew ominously quiet.

Her breath issuing hard and shallow, Sara began to weep silently. Although her panicked tears wet Kitch's hand pressed hard upon her lips, he was not in the least prompted to loosen his grip.

From down the hall, Sara heard the sounds of her son, Tom, being roused. Anticipating trouble in subduing the fifteen-year-old son of Jack Davenport, three strong field hands were sent into his room to silence and hold him. They had armed themselves with field scythes and a pistol so that Tom would put up little struggle. Tom feared only for his mother; however, summarily gagged and bound, he was powerless to either call out or go to her. His eyes flashed anger and fear as he listened to the sounds of voices and footsteps downstairs.

Flanked by the three large field hands, Tom appeared in the doorway of Sara's bedroom. He was gagged with a handkerchief, and his hands were tied behind him with a length of coarse rope. Immediately upon seeing his mother frightened and weeping with Kitch's hand clamped over her mouth, Tom lashed out and kicked one of the field hands hard in the shins. Instantly a forceful blow struck Tom in the jaw, sending him reeling backward against the wall. At once the slave brandishing the pistol drew its barrel close to Tom's temple as a warning.

Sara went limp with fright, shut her eyes, and wept helplessly. She expected to hear a pistol shot ring out at any moment, killing her only child. Although no shot was fired, the anticipation was more than she could bear. Trembling and weeping, she struggled to cry out against the hand that was clamped roughly upon her lips.

"Hush, na', Miss Sara. Dey ain' gonna kill Tommy," Hetty promised quietly.

Sara's eyes darted from Kitch to Hetty, flashing abject fear.

Kitch bent near, and whispered in Sara's ear, "Don' cry out, o' we *is* gonna hurt Tommy." He waited a moment, then said, "Does you un'erstan'?"

Sara nodded, blinking back tears.

Ever so slowly, Kitch drew his hand away. Sara panted wide-eyed and turned her tear-streamed cheeks toward Hetty. Surely Hetty intended her no harm! After all, hadn't Sara risked beatings by her husband, and even sustained them many times, to protect and cover for Hetty?

"Where is Jack?" Sara whispered. Sitting up, she wiped the tears from her cheeks with the backs of her hands.

Although Hetty looked at her mistress with great sympathy, all she dared say was, "Please, Miss Sara, jus' do what we aks."

Obediently Sara fell silent. What else was she to do?

Two women, both field hands, entered the room, and with Hetty's direction, they began filling a large burlap grain sack with various articles of Sara's clothes and personal items.

Down the hall, two others hurriedly stuffed Tom's clothes into a second burlap sack, as well as a few of his favorite books. This latter detail had been seen to by Hetty's emphatic, prearranged instructions. Tom disliked and distrusted most slaves, but he abhorred his father's ways; he did not in the least condone his father's behavior or attitude toward the slaves who worked for him. In part, it was Sara who influenced Tom on this point, although even Tom knew the searing lashes of the bullwhip upon his own bare back delivered by his father's cruel hand. Never more than two or three such lashes at a time were administered as punishment, but it was enough for Tom to despise his father and his father's ways.

With the burlap sacks filled with clothing and personal items, then cinched closed, Sara and Tom were hustled downstairs. Kitch kept a firm grip on Sara's arm, pinning it painfully behind her. Hetty followed quickly behind. Tom, still gagged, his hands bound tight behind him, descended the stairs in turn, the three field hands close behind.

Downstairs, the harsh odor of kerosene permeated the house. Sara trembled so that she could scarcely walk as Kitch, Hetty, and the others led her and Tom out the front door and onto the porch. Sara fully expected to see her husband, Jack, on the porch, but he was not there. Instead, her eyes were met with the spectacle of hundreds of dark faces illuminated by torch light, assembled silently before the house in the pitch-dark of night. Overhead, a roar of thunder crashed, and flashes of lightning emblazed the scene before her. Fear gripped Sara. "Where's Jack?!" she cried. "What have you *done* with him?!" She looked wildly about. A rough hand slapped her, and she stumbled against Kitch.

"Hush!" Hetty warned.

Tom bolted in a violent flurry against the rough arms flanking him. A sound blow to his jaw and the glint of a brandished pistol quieted him.

Sara was nudged forward, directing her to descend the porch steps. Through her tears and the darkness, Sara nearly tripped upon the stairs. Steadying her, Hetty led her mistress downward and past the low white picket fence to the front drive. Close behind, Kitch and the others forced Tom to follow.

"What—what about Jack?" Sara stammered in a frightened whisper. "*Hetty!*" she pleaded.

Hetty's eyes flashed wide, but she turned abruptly away without a word.

"*Where* is *Jack?!*" Sara cried out, her voice shrill with panic.

Her plea was met only with silence and a dark hand clapped tight upon her mouth. Horror seized her as the band of field hands bearing torches approached the house.

At that moment, a wagon sped to a halt on the front drive, near Sara and Tom. The two burlap grain sacks filled with their clothes and other items were heaved into the wagon as Sara and Tom were forced to board. Hetty climbed up into the wagon's bed alongside Sara. Kitch and another field hand climbed in beside Tom.

At that instant, a massive blaze of light flashed. This time, it was not lightning. Churning flames began to engulf the Davenport house as mere tinder, then ignite the flower-bare magnolia beside it. The swelling flames swept hungrily about the house, fanned into a frenzy by gusts of the approaching storm. Sara stared at the house in horror as men ran toward the stables, smokehouse, carriage house, and other structures, setting each one ablaze with their torches.

With the crack of a whip, the driver sent the wagon lurching forward. Another stern crack sent the wagon quickly down the rutted drive and into the night.

"Where is *Jack?!* I don't understand!" Sara cried out, her voice hollow with abject fear, her eyes looking in terror at the familiar dark faces about her. "*Where is he?!*" she shrilled, her sensibilities bordering on hysteria.

A black fist silenced her and sent her reeling hard against the wagon's side. The fist rose again, but Hetty grasped it fast and shook her head. All at once Sara laid her head on Hetty's lap and sobbed. Helpless to protect his mother, angry tears crept down from Tom's eyes, wetting the handkerchief that bound his mouth.

As the wagon sped along the eastbound road, the red glow of the arson fire receded through the trees. By morning, there would be nothing left. Sara realized then that Jack had perished in the flames. He had, in effect, perished in a hell of his own making.

After a time, the wagon turned northward through a wood. Sara, gathering her composure as best she could, sat up and looked across at Tom. His eyes, imploring and fearful, met hers through the darkness.

"It's all right, son. It's all right," Sara said quietly, although she knew not what the night portended for either of them. She glanced at Hetty seated beside her for confirmation.

Hetty nodded solemnly.

Tom's eyes registered understanding—neither he nor his mother was to be harmed. Hetty had seen to that. Hetty had also insisted that their personal effects and changes of clothes be packed into sacks and brought along so as to not leave the two completely destitute. She would not have them turned out into the night with nothing but their night clothes.

"Please," Sara pleaded hesitantly. "Please . . . untie my son."

Hetty looked at the burly field hand seated beside Tom, and he removed the handkerchief from about Tom's mouth. Kitch insisted, however, that Tom's hands remain bound.

They rode on in silence for some time, until the wagon came to a sudden stop at the end of a long row of live oaks draped in Spanish moss. Pulses of lightning split the darkness, thunder crashed, and the scent of rain blew upon the frigid gusts that whipped about them. The canopy of moss-laden branches shut out the roiling nighttime sky above. In the far distance, a dim yellow glow of lamplight was barely discernible.

Kitch tossed the burlap sacks of clothes to the ground. Hetty and another house servant helped Sara down from the wagon. At gunpoint, Tom's hands were untied, whereupon he was ordered out of the wagon and made to stand some distance away.

"You make damn sho' dat boy o' yours don' say nothin'!" spat the slave holding the pistol.

Shuddering, wide-eyed, Sara looked over at Tom where he stood some distance away beneath the trees. "He won't say a word to anyone. I promise you," Sara quavered.

The slave fixed her gaze with steely eyes, then turned away. "Le's go!" he bellowed to the others.

Hetty lingered at Sara's side, her own eyes welling deep. "G'won now...," Hetty prompted, then turned to go.

"Oh, Hetty! *Hetty!*" Sara wept.

Hetty hugged Sara tight to her and fought breaking down altogether. Quietly, her voice strained with emotion, Hetty coaxed, "Miss Sara, you mus' *go* now." Hetty gave her mistress a final affectionate squeeze and turned to board the wagon.

A horse whinnied, the whip cracked twice, and the wagon lurched forward until its dim oil lamps were obscured by the darkness of the woods.

"Miss Sara, you mus' go now," Hetty had said. But where? Where could they go in the dead of night? Their only recourse, at least for now, was to head toward the distant glow of light that seemed to lie at the end of the long row of trees. Setting out, Tom slung his burlap sack over his shoulder and Sara dragged her sack along the road behind her.

At once a light rain began to fall beneath a rumble of thunder, threatening a downpour. The darkness pulsed white with bolts of lightning. All at once thunder snarled, cracked, then split the heavens. Suddenly the pitch-black skies above unleashed torrents of cold, stinging rain.

Crying quietly, Sara pushed back thin wisps of her sandy hair that clung damp to her forehead and cheeks. Dressed only in the night clothes in which they had been roused, Sara and Tom shivered as the storm's icy fingers cut through them.

"Are you all right, Ma?" Tom called out through the storm, his voice quavering.

For her son's sake, Sara nodded, yet she sniffled and the lump in her throat swelled. "Where ... are we?" she panted tearfully through chattering teeth as they sopped down the road toward the low, glowing light. She was not sure how much longer she could endure in the bitter cold and rain.

"I think ... it's ... the Crawford place," Tom managed, his lips numb and teeth clattering.

Out of breath, Sara stopped. She could no longer pull the heavy sack, weighted all the more from the rain that had soaked it through. She and Tom were obliged to abandon their belongings beneath the shelter of the trees along the roadside. Resuming their journey, Tom kept a watchful eye on his mother, staying protectively close to her side. Icy driving rain blew in sheets against them, pelting them, and drenching them through.

Nearing the house, its beacon of light was extinguished as William and Annabelle retired for bed. Seeing the house darken as they approached crushed Sara's spirit altogether. Weeping and shivering with cold, she stumbled blindly across the rain-spattered roundabout and sank down in her nightdress upon the front steps of the Crawford's verandah. There, she lay consumed with sobs in the pouring rain.

"Ma!" Tom cried out through the driving rain. He rushed to her side. "Ma!"

But Sara only lay prostrate upon the steps sobbing.

Pounding on the front door of the house with both fists, Tom shouted, "Mr. Crawford! Mr. Crawford! Help us! *Please!* Help us!"

An upstairs window opened. "Who is there?" William shouted. He could not see below the verandah roof, where Tom stood.

"It's Tom Davenport, sir!" Tom cried, his voice thinning, threatening tears.

Abruptly the upstairs window shut, and Tom gave into wrenching sobs. Sara lay whimpering upon the verandah steps, the rain lashing cold upon her drenched, shivering form.

Tom heard voices behind the front door and the rattle of the door latch. Quickly he stemmed his tears and ran the back of a wet hand beneath the tip of his nose. William opened the door, Annabelle fast at his side.

"Tom! Sara! What's happened?!" William exclaimed.

"Sara! Good Lord!" Annabelle rushed forward to where Sara Davenport lay weeping and helped her to sit up. "Please—come into the house," she urged.

William cradled Sara protectively next to him as he led her into the house, out of the storm. Annabelle followed with Tom close at her side.

Immediately Ester and Jacob were roused to see to warm blankets, dry clothes, and placing more logs upon the east sitting-room hearth. Cotta was awakened to make hot tea "a lot of it, quickly!"

William gently guided Sara to the sofa before the fireplace, and Tom sat attentively at his mother's side. Teeth chattering and distraught, Sara could not utter a sound but only wept. Tom, somewhat dazed, sat wordlessly and shivering at his mother's side, a protective arm about her heaving shoulders.

Annabelle sat upon a footrest before Sara, leaned forward, and took the latter's ice-cold hands in hers. "Sara, what on earth has happened?" she ventured timidly. "Has Jack thrown you both out?"

Instantly Sara buried her face in her hands and sobbed. Tom placed a consoling arm around his mother's slender shoulders once more and looked from Annabelle to William. "My Pa's dead," he said quietly, his lower lip quivering.

Annabelle and William's eyes widened.

"I mean ... I think so." Tom spoke slowly—all the while, his teeth chattering—to keep his voice from breaking. "He was ... still in the house ... when it caught fire." He stopped and swallowed hard.

Upon this, William retrieved two glasses and a bottle of brandy from the fireplace mantel. His hands shook as he decanted the dark amber liquid into each short glass. He handed a glass to Tom. "Here, take this. It will help."

Annabelle extended the second aliquot of brandy to Sara. "Please, Sara, drink some of this," Annabelle urged gently. Sara lifted her head, her tears streaming silently down and accepted the proffered glass, but her hand shook so that Annabelle was obliged to feed her the brandy in careful sips.

"I brung de tea," Cotta said, and placed it on the table before the sofa. "C'n I do an'thin' else, Miss Annabelle?" she asked as she looked earnestly from Tom to Sara.

"Make up beds in two of the spare rooms, please. Thank you, Cotta."

"Yes, 'm." Cotta hurried upstairs to see to her task. Upon the landing, the sounds of curious voices could be heard as Cotta shooed the children back to bed, "G'won now, o' y'all w'll be in big trouble!"

Ester passed Cotta on the landing and rushed into the sitting room with an armload of blankets that she deposited on the wingback chair near the hearth. "M'ybe let dem warm a bit by de fire," she suggested.

"Thank you, Ester," William acknowledged.

Ester hurried back upstairs to help ready accommodations for the two shivering upon the sofa.

Rekindling the fire upon the hearth, Jacob fanned the flames until they crackled and sparked, filling the room with warmth and a cheerful glow, then he went upstairs to help Ester and Cotta prepare the rooms for the Sara and Tom.

In the east sitting room, all was quiet. Only the sound of gentle rain and the echoing roll of distant thunder broke the silence.

"Sara, can you tell us exactly what has happened?" Annabelle coaxed softly. "It might help if you talk about it. We want to help."

Sara looked up mournfully from Annabelle to William. "We don't have anywhere to go," she quavered.

"It's all right," Annabelle comforted, and clasped the distressed woman's arm. "You and Tom will stay here tonight, with us."

"Now, please tell us … what on earth has occurred?" William encouraged.

Sara nodded as a stray tear crept down her cheek. "Our slaves revolted," she said quietly. "They burned the house, the stables … everything. *Everything*. And they … they killed Jack." She fell silent and glanced at Tom, her eyes confirming what he had suspected, then she looked downward at her cold, nervous hands fidgeting upon her lap. "Now … there is nothing left," Sara finished, her voice scarcely audible.

Just then William retrieved the warmed blankets from the wingback chair and draped them about Sara's and Tom's shoulders.

"Sip your tea while it's hot," Annabelle urged.

Some moments passed as Sara and Tom drank the hot, soothing liquid from their teacups, and their shivering gradually subsided.

"I can't believe everything is gone." Sara whispered, once again near tears. She swallowed hard, then looked up. For the first time, her eyes were clear and her voice steady. "God forgive me," she pronounced quietly, "Jack was my husband, and I loved him once … I mean, I loved the man I had once married years ago, but … in time … he came to love drink more than he loved either Tom or me. He inflicted so much abuse, not only toward our slaves but toward us both as well. It is tragic—" Sara shook her head and tried to keep from breaking down once again, determined to collect herself. "It is tragic," she continued, "that he perished as he did ... but—... please forgive me—it was in a hell of his own making." Sara hesitated, then admitted, in a voice scarcely above a whisper, "I can't believe he is gone. ... Despite this ... I am ... *relieved* he is gone." Her eyes welled deep, and she gave Tom's arm an assuring squeeze. "We are safe now. We are safe," she uttered. Upon this pronouncement, she fainted dead away upon the sofa.

Quick at her side, William carried Sara upstairs to the spare room that Cotta and Jacob had prepared. Promptly Ester was dispatched to bring the smelling salts.

At Sara's bedside, Annabelle reassured Tom, "Your mother will be feeling better by morning," then added, "You had best try to get some sleep now." Yet she wondered how *any* of them could sleep.

William showed Tom to the spare room they had prepared for him.

"Our things ... our clothes ... they are in sacks under a tree along the drive ... near the house," Tom said, near tears. "It's all we have left."

"We'll send Jacob out, now that the storm is easing. He can take a lantern with him. Don't worry; he will find them," William encouraged.

"There are two burlap sacks...," Tom said as a tear crept down one cheek, and he ran the back of his hand across the tip of his nose.

"It's all right, Tom; we'll find them," William soothed.

A short time later, warm and sheltered once again in William's arms beneath the winter woolens and quilt coverlets, Annabelle looked wide into the darkness of their bedroom. Outside, the storm had abated. A pleasant sprinkling of rain pattered the ground outside and the roof above. Suddenly Annabelle wished Brandon were at home and not northbound by train to Washington on this night of all nights. She would feel safer with an extra man in the house! Images of revolt, arson, and murder haunted her thoughts until, at last, her eyes fluttered closed, and she slept.

Brandon looked all about his hotel room for the letter and notes that Stanley Moore had sent to him at Crawford Hill. There had been direct quotes from President-elect Lincoln on slavery and abolition as well as regarding the dissolution of the Union. "Damn!" Brandon sighed, then riffled yet again through his trunks and carpetbags; nonetheless, the paper and letter simply weren't to be found. Perhaps he had accidentally thrown them away, or perhaps he had left them behind in his desk at Crawford Hill. Either way, they were of little use to him now. The article he had hoped to write for *The Illustrated London News* about Lincoln would have to wait. If he didn't finish unpacking, he would never get to Kathryn's—and he was most anxious to see her. From all of her letters to him at Crawford Hill, she had equally anticipated his return to Washington.

Finding a fresh change of trousers and a not-too-rumpled shirt among the disheveled contents of his trunks, Brandon washed, changed, and set off straightaway by hired cab to the Tierny mansion.

It had been over a month since he had last seen Kathryn, and he felt oddly nervous now as the cab rolled down the city's streets. What if Kathryn was out? He would leave a note informing her of his arrival and his stay at Morley's Hotel. And he would leave her the flowers he had bought. Flowers were a difficult item in Washington this time of year—the last day of February—but with the help of the cabby, he managed to find a dozen white and pink roses from a florist on Pennsylvania Avenue. They were not as fresh a bouquet as spring flowers would have been, but Brandon was determined to bring Kathryn something both lovely and exquisite as a token of his deep regard for her. The roses had cost him a dear amount, but that was of no matter. His heart was buoyant simply upon his return to Washington—hence, his chance to see Kathryn. Little else mattered, not even the lost notes quoting Lincoln.

Before long, Brandon found himself, roses in hand, before the great oak doors of the Tierny mansion. How much grander and more intimidating the house seemed now, after he had been away for a month! He lifted the brass door-knocker and clapped it three times. For a moment, no one came, and Brandon looked out upon the grounds and city beyond. Despite the brisk weather, it had not snowed in some time, and patches of turquoise shone brightly between the thickets of somber clouds drifting overhead. Brandon knocked again. Presently, the door opened.

"Mr. Stewart! A pleasure to see you, sir," the doorman greeted with a note of surprise. "We received your wire, but we weren't sure what day you were arriving. Please, won't you come in?" The doorman stepped back and opened the door wide.

Brandon thanked the doorman and entered, grateful to be in from the cold. "Is Kathryn in?" he asked.

"Yes. Certainly." The doorman glanced at the bouquet of roses in Brandon's hands. "I am afraid, however, that she is with someone at the moment." He indicated the closed drawing-room door. "However, if you would care to wait."

"Perhaps I should return later—," Brandon began. But at that moment, the drawing room door opened, framing Kathryn and a dapper young gentleman, his hand upon the knob.

Kathryn's eyes sparkled up at the man. He was strikingly handsome, perhaps in his late thirties. He wore a finely tailored suit and black wool coat. His deep-blue eyes gazed affectionately at Kathryn as he smiled at her.

"Thank you for today," Kathryn said, "and for staying for tea. I enjoyed it *ever* so much."

"It is always a pleasure, Kathryn," the gentleman said, then bent and kissed Kathryn's upturned cheek. "Look after yourself. Tell Nathaniel goodbye for me."

"I will, John. We shall miss you," Kathryn said as her eyes misted. She gave the man's arm a gentle squeeze, then turned and went into the drawing room. She had not taken even the slightest notice of Brandon.

With that, the gentleman went out, bidding the doorman a fond greeting of farewell and briefly, yet politely, acknowledging Brandon as he left. Brandon stood as if transfixed before the scene he had just witnessed. He watched the gentleman, John, descend the steps as the doorman, once again, closed the front door.

"I'll inform Kathryn that you are here, Mr. Stewart."

Brandon's heart fell, and the bouquet of roses seemed to wilt in his hands. What a ridiculous and pointless token the flowers now seemed. He thought of Kathryn's letters of increasing endearment written to him while he was at Crawford Hill. But now his eyes had *not* deceived him. It was plainly evident that she held strong affections for another. In an instant, Brandon felt hurt and betrayed. He scarcely knew what to think.

"Brandon!" Kathryn swept forward in her skirts. "How nice to see you!"

she said, smiling warmly. "We received your telegram, but we were not sure which day you would arrive."

"Evidently not," Brandon said tersely. He scarcely knew whether to feel betrayed, jealous, or hurt. He concealed each of these and held forward the roses for Kathryn to take. "I brought these for you," he said unceremoniously. Then the hurt he felt inside betrayed itself in his expression. Seeing Kathryn practically in the arms of another man was hardly what Brandon had expected to witness upon his return to Washington. It was as though the brilliant-blue patches in the Washington sky had suddenly grown ashen.

"Why, thank you, Brandon. That was so very kind of you!" Kathryn accepted the pretty bouquet and inhaled the roses' scent. "They are just *lovely*. Why don't you take a chair in the drawing room, and I'll take these to Mary to put them in water." She turned to go, then stopped and looked up at Brandon, her eyes sparkling warmly. "It is *so* good to see you again, Brandon."

"Is it?" he returned flatly.

Kathryn regarded him quizzically for a brief moment, then departed down the hall with the flowers toward the kitchen. "Mary! Mary!" her voice sang out as she sought after the housemaid.

Brandon took a seat in the drawing room and set his hat upon the side table, inwardly chiding himself for his terseness and ill manners. Before him, on a low table, were the used tea things. Kathryn's pale lip pomade stained the rim of one cup; the second cup had been John's. Brandon resolved for his humor to return, despite the circumstances. Obviously, he had assumed too much about Kathryn's affections for him. Being an American, she was probably less reserved or demure in her demonstrativeness than he was accustomed to—perhaps her previous overtures held less weight than he had perceived. He decided that he would visit briefly, make his excuses, and then leave. He sat soberly, his gaze fixed on the shared tea service before him as Kathryn entered the room.

"Brandon, it is *so* wonderful to see you again. I am so glad you are here. It feels like ages," Kathryn effused. She set the vase of roses on the side table, then sat on the sofa opposite him, the low table of tea things between them.

"It is good to see you, Kathryn." Brandon's tone was polite, nearly formal—belying the welling hurt he felt inside. He managed a wan smile, then looked aside as if surveying some detail of the room.

"Brandon … are you feeling all right?" Kathryn intoned solicitously.

"Yes. Quite. Of course. And you—how are you?" Brandon inquired, his words all but stilted.

"I'm fine," Kathryn said, then paused. Brandon's manner perplexed her. "Would you care for some tea?" she offered. "I can ask Mary to prepare some if you like—it's no trouble."

"No." Brandon absently surveyed the used tea service before him. "No, thank you. It isn't necessary." He would be leaving soon anyway.

An awkward silence passed between them before Kathryn spoke. "Nathaniel is upstairs resting; otherwise, I would bring him down to say hello. We went to lunch with John, and Nathaniel ate too much cake for dessert. His tummy is a bit upset."

"John?" Brandon asked.

"Yes, his Uncle John, my late husband's youngest brother. He's been practically a father to Nathaniel since Kenneth passed away."

"John … the gentleman who just left a short time ago … is your brother-in-law?"

"Why … yes," Kathryn affirmed simply.

Upon that pronouncement, all of Brandon's doubts fled. Although, he *did* feel sorely chagrinned that he had mistrusted her.

"He is Nathaniel's uncle."

"Yes." Kathryn nodded her affirmation.

Brandon sighed. "I thought he was … perhaps … a gentleman caller of yours," he reluctantly admitted.

"John?" Kathryn laughed. "Heavens, no, Brandon. Is that what has troubled you since you got here? He is a part of the family, but nothing more—not as you imagined."

"Then, please forgive me my ill manners, Kathryn. I saw you with John before he left, and I assumed—" He didn't finish. What a fool he had been, and how unkind, upon his reunion with Kathryn—his Lissy, as he thought of her—to doubt her sentiments toward him, especially on the heels of their many heartfelt letters.

"Kathryn Lissette!" A booming voice entered the drawing room. "Why didn't you tell me that Mr. Stewart was here?" Mr. Tierny came forward and greeted Brandon heartily with a firm handshake and a sound clap on the shoulder. "You *are* staying for dinner, aren't you?" he invited robustly.

"Well ... I hadn't actually thought about it." Brandon was caught off guard.

"Please, *do* stay Brandon," Kathryn encouraged warmly. Her eyes pleaded for him to stay.

"Then, thank you, yes. I shall stay," Brandon accepted happily.

Dinner passed pleasantly around a polished antique cherrywood table in the family dining quarters. Mr. Tierny headed the table, with Kathryn seated opposite him. Brandon sat to Kathryn's right, opposite little Nathaniel who was feeling well enough by now to eat his dinner.

"But no dessert," Kathryn admonished her son.

Nodding forlornly, Nathaniel consented, "Yes, Mother."

The roses that Brandon had given Kathryn graced the table's center, surrounded by white china, sparkling silver, and cut crystal. After appetizers, a main course of rabbit was served with nutted rice, steamed vegetables, freshly baked rolls, and a fine red wine decanted into crystal goblets. Dessert followed—a rich hazel-nut cake imbued with liquor—and afterward, coffee.

Mary, the house maid, attentively served water throughout dinner from an ornate silver pitcher. Impeccably the kitchen staff worked in perfect orchestration to bring each course in its turn and unobtrusively remove finished plates. Unlike Southern hospitality, all of the hands that serviced the dinner were free and white.

Throughout dinner, conversation centered on Crawford Hill as well as on Kathryn and Nathaniel. Mr. Tierny listened with interest and amusement as Brandon and Kathryn, mutually rapt, caught up on one another's news since being apart. Over dessert, topics turned to the newspaper business, and eventually, over coffee, to politics and secession. Nathaniel, for his part, had been sent up to bed as coffee was being poured, for it was, by then, past his bedtime.

"You see," Mr. Tierny explained, "since about 1789 until ... oh, about 1825, the Southern state of Virginia provided all the nation's presidents but one. By now, however, the South has lost its dominant position in the country. The election of Lincoln is a hard thing for Southerners to take."

"Lincoln wasn't even on the ballot in ten Southern states," Brandon noted.

"Exactly! Southern rancor runs deep. They say Lincoln is a moderate," Mr. Tierny guffawed, "but that depends on whose perspective we're speaking of!"

Brandon and Kathryn laughed and exchanged amused glances.

Mr. Tierny continued. "Lincoln detests slavery, but his plan only proposes to halt the extension of slavery. For many Northerners, myself included, that measure does not go far enough. Most Northerners, in fact, want immediate abolition. But Southerners see Lincoln's election and platform on slavery to be a death knell—a lethal threat, as it were. Without any future expansion of slavery into new territories and states, the South will become outvoted in Congress. Southerners would consequently see their political power atrophy. They fear losing their 'property'—their slaves—and they fear that they will, therefore, ultimately face abject ruin due to massive economic upheaval and loss, and God knows, a major social readjustment. If I were a Southern plantation owner, I dare say, I might be pro-secessionist myself!"

"Yet Lincoln said he would rather be assassinated than see a single star removed from the nation's flag," Kathryn interjected soberly.

"Yes, he did; that's true," Mr. Tierny acknowledged. Then he addressed Brandon specifically, "I can't say I envy your brother-in-law ... is it 'Crawford'?"

"Yes. William Crawford," Brandon affirmed.

"How do his views fit into all of this?" Mr. Tierny asked.

"His stance is pro-secession," Brandon began, "but for rather more complex reasons than either the popular abolitionist or secessionist extremes." With that, Brandon explained in detail William's idea of a gradual phasing out of slavery over several years' time while concomitantly implementing and enforcing a program of regulations and reforms to standardize a humane system until slavery could be ended. "His impetus is morality—to free the slave. Slavery is a system he has inherited. Admittedly, he enjoys the Southern way of life, but he acknowledges the sheer inhumanity and evil of the system as it now exists—the immorality of slavery as a whole. By William's plan, he believes that the Southern economy and way of life could have been preserved while averting secession and the potential for war, and while averting what he sees as a national socioeconomic calamity should all slaves be immediately freed without any practical plan of assimilation into the nation's socioeconomic fabric. It is for this latter reason that William is reluctantly pro-secession—freeing all slaves abruptly, according to the current Northern populist agenda, would shatter the Southern economy and way of life. An independent South could potentially allow for William's proposed series of reforms and gradual abolition, since the Union no longer exists to possibly embrace such reforms and a gradual phasing out of slavery—if it ever could have, given so much Northern abolitionist extremism. Unfortunately, however, William—although wealthy and influential—has made little headway with such a notion as this. He is seen as not extreme enough to suit either side." Indeed, Brandon had grown to champion William's thoughts on the matter to such a degree that he felt his own cheeks flush with the emotional charge of the issue.

"And now we may be on the brink of war," Mr. Tierny said soberly. He sipped his coffee, and added, "They are already bringing knives and pistols into Congress."

"Who is?" Brandon asked.

"Why, our noble elected officials!" Mr. Tierny exclaimed with a dash of sarcasm. Then he elaborated. "A few years ago, Representative Preston Brooks of South Carolina savagely beat Senator Charles Sumner—an abolitionist—with his cane! Consequently, Southern abolitionists sent Senator Brooks new canes!"

"Yes, I did read of that incident in the *Charleston Mercury*," Brandon said, adding, "If the government is so torn at its very core, what does that portend for the country?"

"War," Mr. Tierny stated simply.

"I dare say, you're right," Brandon agreed soberly.

Kathryn sat in silence. She could not bear talk of war, although such talk was increasing all around Washington. Surely the whole matter could be resolved peaceably. Certainly Lincoln, a moderate, could peaceably restore and preserve unity!

Upon return to his hotel room that night, Brandon found the letter and quotes of Lincoln's in his coat's breast pocket where they had been all the while. Now he remembered—he had expressly put them in his coat pocket upon departure from his bedroom at Crawford Hill so they would be safe and not become lost on his journey north. Why was it when he put anything valuable in a special place for safe keeping, it was precisely then that he was most prone to forget just where he had left it? He smiled to himself and shook his head—he would have to be more mindful in the future.

Brandon sat on his hotel bed, unfolded the page of Lincoln's quotes that Stanley Moore had sent, and began to read in the bright glow of the gaslamps: "Those who deny freedom for others deserve it not for themselves; and, under a just God, cannot long retain it. ... As a nation, we began by declaring 'All men are created equal.' We now practically read it, 'All men are created equal except Negroes.' Soon it will read, 'All men are created equal except Negroes, and foreigners, and Catholics.' When it comes to this, I should prefer immigrating to some country where they make no pretense of loving liberty. To Russia, for instance, where despotism can be taken pure and without the base alloy of hypocrisy ... I believe this government cannot endure, permanently, half slave and half free. I do not expect the Union to be dissolved, I do not expect the house to fall. But I do believe it will cease to be divided. It will become all one thing or all the other ... A house divided against itself cannot stand."

———◊———

Annabelle sat at her writing table in the bedroom and put pen to paper to compose a letter to her sister in the wee hours of the morning, by the light of a flickering oil lamp.

"Dear Alexandra,

I hardly know where to begin. Brandon has left again for Washington, D.C. We celebrated his thirty-fourth birthday on February 25th, before his departure. President-elect Abraham Lincoln is to be inaugurated in a few days. Although, as Brandon mentioned he had written to you,

*Lincoln was not his only interest in returning to Washington—he was
also looking forward to seeing Kathryn Lissette Morgan.*

*"Meanwhile, the children are all growing by leaps and bounds—in
little Cooper's case, the metaphor can be taken literally! I wonder what
the future holds for each of them.*

*"Our state of South Carolina has seceded, and now others have
followed . . . and there is talk of war. I mean to tell you about all of
these and more, dear Alexandra, but first I have to tell you of the most
dreadful occurrence."*

Annabelle paused and thought of her older sister an entire ocean away
in Derbyshire, England. *"How I miss you, dear sister!"* Annabelle wrote, and her
eyes misted. With that, in the predawn hours, she again set pen to paper and
began to relay the story of the previous days' events regarding the Davenport
plantation. She told of the slave revolt, the arson, Jack Davenport's murder
as he perished in the flames, and about how she and William had taken in
Sara Davenport and her fifteen-year-old son, Tom.

*". . . They will stay with us for however long is necessary, under the
circumstances. Poor souls! I dare say I've hardly slept the past two nights
since we first found Sara and Tom troubled and upon our doorstep."*

Annabelle stopped writing and lifted the oil lamp toward the clock
upon her writing table; it was not yet sunup. She sighed and, setting pen to
paper, resumed her letter to Alexandra, continuing with news of the children
and brighter tidings.

———✦———

As Annabelle wrote upstairs, Sara Davenport had long since risen and
was now sitting downstairs, alone, in the west sitting room. She sat upon the
settee working on a bit of embroidery in the dim lamplight, a needlework
that Annabelle had supplied to occupy her. The wooden hoop, needle,
and floral pattern occupied Sara's hands but little else. Her thoughts were
concentrated on the night of the rebellion and coming to Crawford Hill. It

was Sara Davenport's third morning at Crawford Hill, and although Ester brewed her a strong tea of valerian root and chamomile each evening, Sara, nonetheless, slept fitfully and rose well before sunrise each morning.

Now, while Sara sat upon the settee embroidering and dabbing at stray tears with a damp handkerchief, dawn's tender rays peered through the window, softly illuminating the shelves of colored glass vases, bowls, pitchers, and plates. Sara found comfort in the bright colors of the glass items, reminding her of the stained glass windows of the All Saints Church. She found solace each morning in the quiet solitude of the west sitting room.

Of slight frame, Sara could have easily been mistaken for a young woman of just twenty in the dim lamplight. In spite of this, as the sun crept in through the glass panes, Sara's face bore the burdens and lines of a woman much beyond her years. At thirty-four, Sara was Brandon's age, but she appeared roughly ten years older. Slender and frail of limb, Annabelle's borrowed dress fit loosely about Sara. Dark, haunting circles framed her exquisite pale-blue eyes. Though fair of complexion, lines of life's miseries and trials etched her brow, chin, and framed her lips. Her blond hair—thin and the color of wheat—although hurriedly pinned up on this morning, framed her face delicately in tender wisps. Beneath the pale eyes, her nose was narrow, straight, pretty, and delicate at its tip. Her mouth was thin but nonetheless appealing by virtue of its contours. The cheeks and chin were ordinary and unnoteworthy for their part, but they by no means detracted from Sara's delicate attractiveness. Sara's countenance was at once vulnerable yet stoic, delicate yet strong—and no less could have been said of Sara herself. The recent trauma and upheaval of the previous few days had only etched deeper the lines about her face and darkened the circles about her pale-mist eyes; regardless, she was determined to prevail—if not for her own sake, then for Tom's.

Laying the embroidery in her lap a moment, Sara turned to gaze upon the carnival of colors lining the shelves before the window. It seemed there were items of every hue—among them, there was a vase of deep ruby red; a plate of brilliant cobalt blue; bud vases of emerald green, deep violet, and honey yellow; as well as a pitcher of etched crystalline glass that refracted the sunlight as prisms. As Sara's eyes drank in the deep, rich colors coming to life in the early-morning light, she heard the pleasant, muffled sounds of the household beginning to stir upstairs and in the kitchen. She wondered if Tom had yet risen, though she hoped he still slept. If it weren't for Tom, she mused, she would not have endured these past sixteen years nor, most assuredly, the horror of the revolt just three nights earlier. Upon this thought, her eyes, already damp and swollen from crying, filled once more until the radiant tints of glass blurred before her. Turning from the rainbows of brightness upon the sun-streamed shelves, Sara resumed her needlework. She occupied her mind with thoughts of Tom as she busied her hands with the needle and thread.

Lost in her thoughts and intent on the embroidery hoop before her, Sara did not hear anyone enter the sitting room that she alone had occupied. Then, inexplicably, she sensed another's presence standing near her, watching her. Ill at ease, Sara lifted her eyes from her embroidery. "Sabe!—you *startled* me." Sara's casual manner was betrayed by a rising note of unease in her voice.

Sara Davenport had been introduced to the household staff the previous morning, in particular to Ester, Jacob, and Cotta, as well as to Sabe, who had been presented as the new house servant. Although Sabe had regarded Sara with civility before the Crawfords and the other household staff, he secretly glowered at her with a calculated coldness when, on occasion, she had passed by him alone about the house or yard.

At this moment, Sabe, tall and muscular, stood squarely before her, his fists clenched at his sides. His eyes shot daggers as he glowered down at Sara upon the settee.

Bewildered and seized by fear, Sara swallowed hard but found her voice. "What is it, Sabe?" she ventured, her voice edged with constrained panic.

Sabe uttered no sound but drew near Sara until she was trapped between him and the settee.

Her heart pounding in fear, Sara tried to cry out, but her voice eluded her.

Sabe's eyes narrowed menacingly, his fists tightened. He stood trembling with anger, unable to find his own tongue.

Her knees all but turned to water, Sara rose gingerly from the settee. Praying she had not lost her ability to speak altogether, she would feign casualness in excusing herself from the room, she would flee before—

In an instant, Sabe lashed out, striking Sara hard across the face with the back of his hand, knocking her downward onto the settee. At once, in a blind rage, he lunged at her, lifted her up by the shoulders, and hurled her against the shelves of colored glass. A number of objects toppled wildly to the floor, shattering in loud crashes as splinters of color scattered across the hard floor. Sara struck her head against a shelf, and she slipped half-dazed to the floor, a rivulet of blood trickling from the corner of her mouth where Sabe's hand had struck.

In an instant, Sabe was upon her. He shoved her roughly down upon the hardwood floor. Sara elicited a sharp cry silenced by the sharp blow of Sabe's hand. The room spinning wildly about her, Sara only saw Sabe leaning over her, his eyes flashing rage, and felt his rough hands upon her throat.

"Sabe! *No!*" Sara uttered a frantic cry, her eyes wide with fright.

Quickly Sabe's grasp tightened as Sara labored for breath, flailing and clawing at his hands. Scarcely able to draw but choked gasps, Sara's struggles diminished as the crush of Sabe's fingers about her slender neck threatened to extinguish the very life from her. No longer able to struggle, Sara's vision went black—and she lay limp upon the floor.

All at once Sabe's grasp loosened. His eyes grew wide with alarm. What had he just done?! Tears sprang to his eyes as he looked down upon Sara as she lay motionless before him. What *had* he just *done?!* He stood stock-still in horrified disbelief. His blood ran cold.

"Lawdy! God a'mighty!" Ester shouted as she dashed forward and grabbed one of Sabe's arms with all her might, pinning it behind him.

Sabe offered no resistance.

Without delay, Cotta was fast beside Ester, grasping Sabe's other arm and holding it as best she could. "Massa Willem! *Massa Willem!*" she shrieked.

"Get off me!" Sabe cried out, pushing Cotta roughly aside—with far greater force than he had intended—sending her reeling backward onto the floor.

Sabe stood with welling eyes, looking down upon Sara lying motionless upon the floor. Yet neither Ester nor Cotta realized the expression of abject regret and defeat he wore as his heart beat wildly against his chest.

Cotta picked herself up from the floor strewn with shattered glass and regained a hold of Sabe's free arm.

A single tear coursed its way down Sabe's cheek.

"*Massa Willem! Jacob!*" Ester cried, keeping her hold of Sabe's arm pinned painfully behind him.

Jacob charged into the room, William quick at his heels. In an instant, Jacob and William were fast upon Sabe, shoving him to the floor as Jacob landed a fist squarely against Sabe's jaw.

Curious kitchen servants clustered in the doorway, then quickly withdrew, gasping and chattering over what had just transpired.

"Get my overseers! Get help!" William barked to Cotta.

"Yessuh!" Cotta—her heart pounding wildly, her eyes streaming tears—ran to the front verandah to ring the bell for help to come.

Sara had regained consciousness and, quivering so that she could hardly move, she crept into the corner where she sat huddled in her skirts, whimpering and shaking, and blotting the blood upon her swollen lip and chin with her hand. Ester was quick at her side.

"Good *God*, William! What is going *on* here?!" Annabelle stood aghast in the doorway. She saw before her Sabe pinned steadfastly upon the floor by William and Jacob, Ester in the corner of the room tending to Sara, blood spatters, and broken glass scattered all about. "William—what's *happened?!*" Annabelle's voice was hollow with alarm.

"See to Sara," William said curtly.

Annabelle flew to the corner and, with Ester, helped Sara to her feet, then led her from the room.

An overseer and three slave drivers arrived, Cotta following close behind them and wringing her hands. Quickly the men bound Sabe until he could wrestle against them no more, then brought him to his feet. Sabe no longer struggled but complied with the hard chains about his wrists and ankles.

Before Sabe was led away, William faced him squarely, his eyes narrowed, deadly serious. "You will pay," he said tersely, and then nodded for the overseer to remove Sabe. "Lock him away. Three days. No food," William pronounced.

As Sabe was led away, William could not have imagined the profound remorse that now welled within the young slave's heart and flooded his eyes.

As Sabe was led roughly across the yard to the seldom-used plantation prison house, he lifted his eyes beseechingly heavenward, then he bent his head and wept.

"I was in the study writing a letter to Alexandra when I heard noises downstairs. I thought it must be the children up early and roughhousing ... or the servants being clumsy in the kitchen. It wasn't until I heard Ester and Cotta call out for help that I knew something was wrong." Annabelle was clearly distressed. She paced in William's study, her voice tremulous, her eyes welling.

William, standing at the edge of his desk, held out a hand to Annabelle and drew her safely to him. He held her gently and kissed her temple.

"But I don't understand! I simply don't understand!" Annabelle exclaimed as she pulled back and paced some more.

William sighed heavily. "For the life of me, Annabelle, I don't understand either. Sabe has been good up until now."

"I just don't *understand*," Annabelle muttered, and paced.

A light tapping sounded on the study door. "Massa Willem ... c'n I have a word wit' you?" It be mighty impo'tant," Cotta asked, then waited anxiously in the hallway.

William opened the study door to see Cotta standing with her hands clasped nervously, her brow furrowed, eyes urgent.

"Yes, Cotta, what is it? Come in." William held the door wide and gestured for Cotta to enter.

"Miss Annabelle, Massa Willem ... I is here 'bout Sabe." Cotta spoke hesitantly and looked from Annabelle to William. "I know why Sabe's done what he done to Miss Sara." She stood nervously before them.

"Here, Cotta. Sit down," William said kindly.

Cotta sat down in the proffered chair. "Thank you, Massa Willem." Looking down at her folded hands upon her lap, Cotta gathered her thoughts, then began carefully, "Massa Willem ... you 'member dat young woman on de Davenport place call'd Juliana,?"

"Yes, yes we do," William and Annabelle each affirmed.

"Well ... Sabe ... he be Juliana's brother."

A stunned silence passed between the three.

"Sabe is Juliana's brother?" William's brow arched. He had not expected any such news as this, not in his wildest considerations.

Cotta nodded emphatically and wide-eyed up at William.

"Cotta, how do you know this?" Annabelle prompted gently.

Quietly Cotta confessed. "I been talkin' t' Sabe through de bars on de jail-cabin door. I brung him water t' drink, an' he tell me he be Juliana's brother, dat ol' Jack Davenport sold Sabe fo' cheap in Charl'ston, for de low'st price he c'n git so dat he be rid o' Sabe. Dat way Sabe don' cause no troub'l aft'r Davenport—" Cotta hesitated uncertainly, then continued, "... aft'r he had his way wit' n' killed Juliana. So, Davenport, he done send Sabe off on a task, but it turn'd out t' be a trap instead. De overseer, he put Sabe on a wagon fo' de Charl'ston market. Davenport needed de money anyhow, so he sol' Sabe—dat way Sabe don' cause trouble, an' Davenport gits de money he wants." Cotta went on to explain how Sabe had only heard of Juliana's death since he had come to live at Crawford Hill—through talking with others as the story was retold among various field hands and house servants. Sabe was profoundly enraged by Jack Davenport's rape and beating to death of his sister; consequently, a consuming rage had built up inside him. Finished with what she had come to say, Cotta looked up imploringly at Annabelle and William. "Sabe ... he be eber so sorry!" Cotta intoned, with large swimming eyes. She toyed nervously with her hands upon her lap and continued, her brown eyes glistening. "He say he can't take back what he done, but he been mournin' de whole day inside his self. He say ... he say you bot' is *good* people, an' treat him fair, an' he want to do right by you an' fo' his self." Cotta paused again, then explained quietly, "De problem be dat Miss Sara come to lib here, an' Sabe be so angry at Massa Jack Davenport dat he done taken his hatred out on Miss Sara. He say he got all 'nraged inside his self an' couldn' help his self ... and den he—" Cotta didn't finish; there was no need. Sabe had brutally attacked Sara Davenport and nearly strangled the life from her with his own two hands.

William and Annabelle had listened with rapt attention. Without question, Cotta's account of the circumstances was true. It was evident in her manner, her emphatic tone, and her tearful eyes; and ever since coming to live in the Big House, Cotta had always been a sweet, genuine, trustworthy member of the household. Nothing in what she had relayed about Sabe rang false.

"Good Lord above," Annabelle uttered, her voice nearly a whisper. "Sabe is Juliana's brother. No wonder!" As horrified as Annabelle had been about Sabe's assault on Sara Davenport, her heart was tempered with a wealth of sympathy for him. "No wonder!" she repeated quietly.

Cotta rose from her chair. "Massa Willem ... please fo'giv' me fo' speakin' so plain like ... but Sabe ... he be ever so sorry 'bout hurtin' Miss Sara, an' he *knows* she's a good woman. He says he's good at perseverin' in intolerable times, dat he neber made no trouble fo' Davenport, an' dat he's sorry dat he caused trouble here, an'—" Cotta's eyes filled with tears and her voice grew tremulous. "... Sabe tell me he feared o' de whip. Dat he seen Davenport fiel'hands whipped to death, jus' like Juliana." Cotta shook her head, her hands clasped fast together at her chin, and looked beseechingly at Annabelle and William. "Den ... den he break down and weep, beseechin' God to fo'giv' him." Cotta's eyes welled deep. "Lawdy, Miss Annabelle, Massa Willem, I ain' *never* heard a growd man cry an' weep so b'fore." A single tear spilled down Cotta's cheek, and she bowed her head, her hands clasped tight before her.

A moment of silence passed between the three, and Cotta collected herself. Annabelle handed Cotta her lace handkerchief to dry her eyes.

"Thank you, Cotta, for coming to me and telling me of this. You were right to do so, and I appreciate it," William said. "You may go now," he finished.

Cotta turned to leave, but William stopped her. "Cotta—"

"Yessuh, Massa Willem?"

"You may take an extra half-day free this week."

"Thank you, Massa Willem," Cotta said, then hesitated at the door. "Massa Willem?" Her voice was meek and barely audible. "Please show Sabe mercy. He ain' meant to do no wrong, an' he be pr'foundly sorry—"

"Cotta," William cut her off firmly, but not unkindly, "you were right to tell me about Sabe, but it's not your place to ask for leniency in this matter. Do you understand?"

"Yessuh, Massa Willem." Cotta nodded and quietly went out, closing the door behind her.

After Cotta had gone, Annabelle asked quietly, "How *will* you deal with Sabe?"

William heaved a troubled sigh. "I'm not sure yet. I'm not sure." He ran a weary hand over his face. "Ethically, I cannot sell him after what he has done. Morally, I can't kill him."

"*William!*" Annabelle uttered, aghast.

"I'm not sure yet, Annabelle," he sighed, and with that the discussion was ended.

That afternoon, Annabelle wrote a long letter to Brandon in Washington. In it, she wrote about the rebellion on the Davenport plantation and about the incident regarding Sabe. The detail and length of the letter was as much a catharsis as it was to simply to inform her brother-in-law of all that had transpired in so short a time—it helped to have his strength to lean on as well as William's. And Annabelle realized that she felt more of a kinship or bond with Brandon over these matters as they both haled from England— their homeland, where current notions of slavery, uprisings, and whippings of another human being were regarded as utterly foreign and horrifically evil. Dipping her pen in her ink well, she resumed writing.

> "*Over a week has passed since Sara and Tom have been here with us at Crawford Hill, and William and I have welcomed them to stay indefinitely if they like. They have nowhere else to turn, no family to go to.*
>
> "*Sara is quite nice—a very sweet person, I must say. She is such a slight, almost fragile thing; notwithstanding, she has born up remarkably well under the circumstances. She even confided in me that her husband, Jack—the devil incarnate, I dare say—had abused her many times in the past! Poor thing! Sara insists on helping mind the children, mending, polishing the silver, and even a little baking. She feels uncomfortable accepting charity, even from the willing kindness of close neighbors. 'I want to do my part,' she says. William has assured her it is not charity but*

our genuine concern for her and Tom's welfare, as well as our growing fondness for her and Tom, that moves us to look after them. We have told them to regard Crawford Hill as their new home, and Sara has consented gratefully.

"Tom, thank heaven, is not at all like his father. Even in appearance he takes rather after Sara, though his hair is brown and not fair and blond as hers. According to Sara, Tom likes his new surroundings—a clean, bright house; a cheerful atmosphere; and especially, a new friend in Barry to go to school and spend leisure hours with. Although Barry is only twelve (three years Tom's junior) the two are becoming fast companions. Both seem glad, at long last, to have someone as a companion who is near his own age to share adventures and trade secrets.

"Brandon, I hope you will not mind (and I do not believe you shall), but we have decided to let Tom share Barry's room. When William asked Barry if he would mind sharing his room with Tom, Barry was ecstatic, saying, 'It will be almost like having a brother!' He beamed and was excited at the prospect of a roommate—as you once had at the university in London! As you are aware, Barry revels in the stories you tell of your days at the university and the carousing about with your buddies (when not diligently studying, of course!).

"The only concern about having Sara and Tom live at Crawford Hill regards what we must do about Sabe. William still feels it would be unethical to sell Sabe without disclosing his assault upon Sara. Despite Sabe's avowed remorse and that his assault was out of character, William feels a prospective buyer will only say that Sabe could become violent again.

"And so, after three days in our seldom-used plantation jail cabin, Sabe is now confined to his own cabin in the servant quarters, down the hill behind the Big House. Cotta and the kitchen help take him food and water, but Sabe has yet to see the light of day other than through the cabin window. Hearing that we probably will not sell Sabe, Sara expressed her concerns to William about Sabe staying on at Crawford Hill. William told her, 'Don't worry about Sabe, I'll take care of him.' His assurances and affable manner have put Sara at ease. (Sara had not previously recognized that Sabe was from the Davenport plantation—given so many field hands—nor had she known that Sabe was Juliana's brother,

until now.) Meanwhile, Sabe cannot stay forever confined to his cabin,
and so I wait to learn what William will do to exact a penalty on Sabe.
William said that he feels he must do something, otherwise the others in
our keep may see any exhibition of poor or violent behavior as excusable."

Annabelle reviewed her last few lines to Brandon. "Exact a penalty" sounded a bit contrived, but the word "punish" only conjured horrific images of bullwhips, stocks, chains, and beatings—if not worse tortures. William would not resort to these methods of punishment, she was sure; but instead, perhaps, a brief demotion to the fields after his confinement, and then a return to house-servant duties—after a firm talking to—would be in order.

As Annabelle closed her letter to Brandon, she silently thanked her lucky stars that William was not at all like Jack Davenport or numerous other slave holders, but instead, was kind, humane, sensitive, and capable of genuine empathy toward all others on this earth—no matter their color. With that, she dripped sealing wax onto the envelope and smiled— everything would work out fine. As the pastor had said that past Sunday, all things were providential—what one perceived as ill at any moment could yet bear fruit, if one remained hopeful.

Yes, everything would work out fine.

CHAPTER 17

Inauguration day

Brandon blew repeatedly through his black woolen gloves to warm his fingers from the chill morning air. March fourth, 1861—Abraham Lincoln's inauguration day—had dawned blustery and cold. Rain-laden clouds hung heavy over Washington, D.C. Despite the cold, Brandon would have at least enjoyed the fresh scent of rain upon the air but for the typical stench of the city. On this early morning, he had decided to walk the several long blocks from his room at Morley's Hotel to the Capitol Building for Lincoln's inauguration ceremony—despite unavoidably passing along the many fetid dirt streets en route. Stray pigs snorted through the garbage-strewn streets adjoining Pennsylvania Avenue. Nearby, sewage marshes wafted a pestilent odor upon the cold March wind, unequaled in its repulsiveness save for a malodorous drainage ditch north of the Washington Mall through which a putrid soup of city waste—and an occasional dead rat, cat, or dog—wended. Adding to this less-than-salubrious atmosphere was the ample presence of livery stables and saloons.

Surely Brandon's familiar London had its rank sections of habitances too, but the worst that could be said of London regarded the persistent sky of coal soot that hung over the city during the cold autumn and winter months. Yet London was a city of centuries-old tradition and the royal seat of a vast empire that boasted subjects of the British Crown numbering nearly one quarter of the world's population. By contrast, the city of Washington— the ragtag capital of a fledgling and now faltering America—could not, arguably, be expected to exist on the same level of refinement and civility as London. Brandon reflected upon this as he blew once more upon his icy gloved fingers and gazed up at the Capitol's unfinished dome.

Flexing the stiffness from his fingers, Brandon again took up the drawing pencil and sketch pad he had carried with him from Morley's Hotel. His plan so far, it seemed, had been successful: to wake before dawn and reach the Capitol shortly thereafter in order to secure the absolutely best vantage point before the Capitol Building and the four-poster canopied podium where Lincoln would soon speak and be sworn in as president. Few others were up and stirring so early; the city was just waking. Only small gatherings of would-be onlookers had begun to emerge from various pockets of the city and mill about.

Nearby, on a low hill, stood a row of manned howitzer cannon poised and ready to fire upon the streets in the event of assassins or general unrest. Federal Artillery and Cavalry clattered noisily down Pennsylvania Avenue's cobblestones. They seemed present as much for political pomp as for Lincoln's protection, should there be an attempt on his life. Already, plainclothes detectives wandered about the early morning's gathering crowds as trained sharpshooters took up strategic positions atop the Capitol Building and lined the rooftops of various businesses flanking the long stretch of Pennsylvania Avenue.

Despite the gathering commotion about him, Brandon concentrated upon the sheet of sketching paper before him, lifting his eyes intermittently in order to faithfully execute the lines of what he surveyed before him. Skillfully his woolen-gloved hand drew the Capitol's east wing with its majestic portico of Corinthian columns. Above the portico, the Capitol's dome rose abbreviated, just as it had stood upon Brandon's first visit to Washington. Incomplete, the dome remained in its two-tier state, crowned by a towering crane and ensconced to the right by scaffolding. Along with the slate skies and chill air, Brandon wondered if the unfinished dome was also, perhaps, an ominous sign on this occasion. The sharpshooters taking their posts on the Capitol's roof punctuated this thought.

Below the inchoate dome, at the foot of the Capitol's steps and dwarfed by the towering marble columns behind, the sprawling inauguration platform had been erected. The platform included seating for cabinet members, congressmen, and various dignitaries. Centered in this arrangement protruded the focal point of the platform, the four-poster canopied inauguration stage and podium. From Brandon's vantage point, how very tiny the temporarily erected stage seemed—fragile and insignificant before the towering colonnades behind it. As Brandon sketched, lifting his eyes from his paper to the canopied podium, he idly wondered if it had been wise to subject Lincoln—though tall of stature—to such a backdrop of towering magnificence and solidity. Surely Lincoln, the congressmen, and the countless dignitaries to be seated before this grand backdrop would appear, by comparison, to be ant-like and inconsequential in both their scale and innate human vulnerability. Undoubtedly, these men, including Abraham Lincoln, would seem more as the inchoate dome above, rather than as the grandeur and substance of Grecian heritage behind them. America was no empire. Perhaps a less presumptuous setting would have suited the occasion more proportionately, what with America being on the verge of tatters. Upon these musings, Brandon smiled wryly to himself— although not at all unsympathetically toward his foster country—as he began to illustrate the nearby bare-branched trees and dreary sky in swift shadings of his pencil.

Gradually, as time passed, the crowds behind Brandon began to thicken. Inadvertently jostled, Brandon turned to survey the growing throngs behind him and lining Pennsylvania Avenue. Stanley Moore and James Joyner would join him later, as well as Kathryn, her father, and little Nathaniel. Meanwhile, Brandon would be careful to save them space near him in the front row of onlookers. Only a short expanse of ground lay between the Capitol Building's platform podium and where Brandon stood; they should be able to catch Lincoln's every word and view all of the proceedings with ease, despite the swelling crowds.

After a time, Brandon drew out his pocket watch to see that it was yet only midmorning. Lincoln was not due until well after twelve o'clock noon. In the meantime, Stanley Moore had arranged to post himself outside of Lincoln's Hotel room, suite six of Willard's Hotel. James Joyner similarly stationed himself near President Buchanan's whereabouts at the White House. Together, the three journalists would share notes on all aspects of the occasion and, consequently, write full accounts of the day from every perspective for each of their respective papers. Additionally, Brandon would send Alfred Cooke, in Charleston, all the details of the inauguration for his stories in the *Charleston Daily Courier.*

Time passed slowly, and as hunger began to gnaw pleasantly, Brandon drew out a handkerchief-wrapped buttered muffin from his overcoat pocket and ate it, washing it down with a flask of tepid coffee extracted from his coat's breast pocket.

By noon, Pennsylvania Avenue and the east plaza of the Capitol was a sea of people—men bundled in black wool overcoats and top hats; women wrapped snug in their warmest winter cloaks, bonnets, and muffs; sturdily bundled children prattling at their parents' sides; and wee ones held cozily in their mother's arms. Among the sea of onlookers, Kathryn and her father, Mr. Tierny, had joined Brandon with little Nathaniel in tow. Presently, James Joyner and Stanley Moore also arrived, their cheeks ruddy with March's bluster, their breath clouding in the air.

At the appointed time of Lincoln's arrival, all eyes were trained on the approaching procession down Pennsylvania Avenue—a parade of floats, military bands, cavalrymen upon skittish horses, infantrymen, and coaches. From the surrounding rooftops, the eyes of the sharpshooters were trained in equally intense anticipation upon the crowds below.

"Keep your muffler up about your ears," Kathryn recommended, then bent and adjusted Nathaniel's woolen scarf snugly. "Let me know if you are too cold."

"There!" Brandon pointed, his arm extended so Kathryn could see where to look. "There comes Lincoln now!"

"Where? I can't see." Kathryn stood on tiptoe and placed a hand on Brandon's shoulder for balance.

"He's there, in the open carriage with President Buchanan."

"Yes! Yes, I see now!" Kathryn beamed.

"*I* can't see! *I* can't see!" Nathaniel complained. At only seven years of age, he felt small and all but swallowed up by the press of black wool coats all about him.

"Here, Nathaniel," Brandon offered as he leaned down and hoisted Nathaniel up upon his shoulders.

"There now, is that better?" Brandon asked, grinning.

"Wow!" Nathaniel exclaimed. He ran a small hand over his forehead to clear away a lock of sandy-brown hair that the stiff March wind had blown over his eyes. "I see Lincoln! I *see* him!" Nathaniel gaped in open-mouthed wonder as the carriage, flanked and followed by cavalry, approached the Capitol.

"I can see *everything!*" Nathaniel extolled.

Kathryn beamed up at her son with sparkling eyes.

"I'm even taller than *Lincoln* now!" Nathaniel cried. At this, Kathryn, Brandon, and all those around them burst out in amused laughter.

"All right. Down you go." Brandon let Nathaniel down, promising, "I'll let you up again when Lincoln speaks." He gave Nathaniel a wink and rumpled the boy's hair. Nathaniel was duly pleased.

"The crowd isn't as large as I had expected," Joyner commented.

"I'd expected more people to come, as well," Mr. Tierny added.

"Lincoln was only elected by about forty percent of the pre-secession Union," Stanley Moore reminded them, explaining the modest crowds. "Ten Southern states omitted him from their ballots altogether!"

"But certainly more local people would have come—," Mr. Tierny began.

"If it weren't for the weather?" Joyner interjected.

"Perhaps," Kathryn suggested, "there is such a low turnout because of the rumors of assassination. Perhaps people are afraid and have stayed indoors."

"Given human nature," Stanley noted, "people are likely *more* prone to attend when there *is* the threat of an attempt on a president-elect's life!"

Kathryn winced at the thought.

"A little bloodshed, eh?" Joyner put in, with a wry grin.

Kathryn looked helplessly at Brandon, her eyes inviting his defense. How she disliked being teased!

Evasively Brandon only grinned and facetiously warned her off. "Shhh—I'm taking notes." He showed Kathryn his open notebook.

"Why, your fountain pen isn't even *out!*" Kathryn gave his arm a playful slap.

Brandon merely chuckled, then directed Kathryn's gaze with a pointed finger. "They are here. Lincoln has arrived at the front steps."

Kathryn looked to see the open carriage, a short distance away, roll to a stop before the Capitol's steps. As armed soldiers kept watch from the windows of the Capitol Building, and the sharpshooters upon its roof were poised to fire if necessary, Lincoln, alongside President Buchanan, disembarked from the carriage. In a moment, they both were lost in the sea of black coats and tall hats about them.

"How odd for Lincoln to ride in an open carriage when there are threats of assassination," Kathryn commented to Brandon. "It seems foolhardy!" Yet her tone was less composed criticism than that of heartfelt concern.

"It seems foolhardy given the *weather!* Brrrr!" Stanley jested, with a grin.

Brandon chuckled but nonetheless nodded his agreement with Kathryn. "It *does* seem unnecessarily risky," he said, then took out his pen and began to work, making notes in his book.

As he wrote, he remembered what had been written in the *Charleston Mercury* about Lincoln: "Abraham Lincoln is a horrid-looking wretch and a blood-thirsty-tyrant who has sent abolitionist spies into Southern lands to circulate 'Lincolnisms,' and goad the slaves into rebellion." Indeed, with the nation so torn as to Lincoln's becoming president, inauguration day could very well hold some as-yet-unforeseen tragedy by day's end.

At that instant, Nathaniel squirmed from between the black wool trouser legs about him and darted beneath the low rope cordoning the crowd of spectators from the inauguration platform and Capitol's steps. Quickly he scampered across the short expanse of intervening walkway in the direction of Lincoln.

"Nathaniel!" Kathryn cried out, her voice near panic.

Instantly Mr. Tierny clambered over the rope as his stout frame hurried after his wayward young grandson.

Kathryn's hands flew to her mouth as her eyes darted wide from Nathaniel and her father to the sharpshooters poised upon the Capitol Building's rooftop. Scarcely drawing a breath, her countenance pale, Kathryn stared wide-eyed as her father caught Nathaniel by the arm.

Nearly as alarmed, Brandon lowered his focus from the Capitol's roof and watched intently as Mr. Tierny pulled Nathaniel quickly in tow, back toward the crowd. All the while, Nathaniel, as he dutifully trudged along, stared back in the direction of Lincoln and the cluster of gentlemen about him as the president-elect ascended the Capitol's steps to the platform.

Having retrieved Nathaniel, Mr. Tierny stepped over the rope balustrade and mopped his brow with a large white pocket-square as Brandon hoisted the boy over the rope. Instantly Kathryn knelt down and hugged Nathaniel to her, feeling as relieved as she was angry at his mischievous escapade. Holding her son at arm's length and looking him evenly in the eye, Kathryn scolded, "You are *never* to run off like that again, *ever!* Do you hear me?"

Nathaniel nodded comprehension.

"What do you say, Nathaniel?" Mr. Tierny asked firmly, looking down at this grandson.

Nathaniel tilted his head upward and squinted at his dear old grandfather, then faced his mother once again. "I'm sorry, Mother."

Kathryn, still feeling shaken, said nothing but rose, keeping a firm grasp on Nathaniel's small hand.

"It's all right now, Kathryn. There wasn't any danger. He's just a boy," Brandon consoled.

His words calmed Kathryn considerably. Up on the roof, the sharpshooters reconnoitered their aims away from a small boy and stout gentleman who had caused a brief flurry of concern near the Capitol's steps.

Before long, Lincoln filed out onto the inaugural platform along with nearly three hundred dignitaries. Tall and somewhat lanky of build, Lincoln stood out distinctively from the rest, his brand-new stovepipe hat adding to his impressive stature. Distinguished in appearance, Lincoln was dressed in a new black wool suit and glistening boots, and he carried a bright gold-headed cane. At fifty-two, his physiognomy bearing a somewhat weathered and learned intensity, Kathryn surmised that Lincoln looked his age. But she found him handsome, in his own way, and of compelling presence. His deep-set, piercing eyes possessed gentleness, and even at a distance, she felt their allure. In the cold March afternoon, Lincoln looked pale but by his demeanor—even if he felt nervous upon this momentous occasion in his life—appeared collected, if not calm. Absently Kathryn wondered how he might have looked if he smiled.

Feeling a furtive tug on his coat-sleeve, Brandon turned and lifted Nathaniel up momentarily to see. Satisfied after some minutes, Nathaniel conceded to be let down again.

"This is history. Remember it," Mr. Tierny bent and whispered into the boy's ear.

Truly, it was historic. And even as Brandon took notes and studied this singular man—Abraham Lincoln—upon the inaugural platform, his own heart swelled with the profundity of the moment.

As Lincoln squinted out over the sea of people before him, the crowd drew to a hush. Patches of sunlit blue sky crept out from between the scattering clouds as the crisp afternoon wind ruffled the tails of his suit coat. Lincoln doffed his stovepipe hat, but there seemed no place handy to store it; Senator Douglas, seated nearby, thoughtfully took it from him. After leaning his gold-headed cane against the platform railing and gently clearing his somewhat-nervous throat, Lincoln unrolled his speech upon the podium. Donning his steel-rimmed spectacles, Lincoln began to speak.

Brandon's, Stanley's, and Joyner's pens scratched quickly across their respective notebooks as Lincoln orated. From Lincoln's words it was clear he did not regard the seven seceded states as actually having left the Union. They were rather more cast as wayward children who, although run away from him, were still bound by the rules under their parent's roof. Lincoln declared secession unconstitutional and pleaded for the separated states to return to the Union. To some of those listening it seemed a vain and lofty appeal because Confederate President Jefferson Davis had already called for the creation of a military force of one-hundred thousand Southern volunteers. Still others in the crowd held out a profound hope that Lincoln's appeal would strike a chord of peace and reconciliation that would move the South to surrender their foolishness and rejoin the Union. Kathryn, decidedly, was among those who held such a hope.

As Brandon listened and penned his notes, he could not help but observe that for all Lincoln's physical stature, fine suit of clothes, and aura of presence, he definitely appeared dwarfed by the backdrop of immense, towering Corinthian columns behind him. As Brandon had anticipated, the inaugural stage and canopied podium, and all the seated dignitaries flanking Lincoln, seemed insignificant in bearing before the grand marble edifice. However, as Lincoln spoke, his words increasingly magnified his presence and his convictions of purpose. Gradually the gleaming marble columns of the Capitol's east portico grew superfluous beside the sheer scale and import of Lincoln's oration. Near the speech's end, Brandon's hand almost forgot to write, so taken was he by the poetry of Lincoln's words and the convictions of his heart. Riveted, the crowd scarcely stirred or uttered a sound as Lincoln spoke, hanging onto his every syllable.

"Can aliens make treaties easier than friends can make laws?" Lincoln appealed. "Can treaties be more faithfully enforced between aliens than laws can among friends? Suppose you go to war, you cannot fight always; and when, after much loss on both sides and no gain on either, you cease fighting, the identical old questions as to terms of intercourse are again upon you. ... In *your* hands, my dissatisfied fellow countrymen, and not in mine, is the momentous issue of civil war. The government will not assail you. You can have no conflict, without yourselves being the aggressors. You have no oath registered in heaven to destroy the government, while I shall have the most solemn one 'to preserve, protect, and defend' it.

"I am loath to close. We are not enemies, but friends. We must not be enemies. Though passion may have strained, it must not break our bonds of affection. The mystic chords of memory, stretching from every battlefield and patriot grave to every living heart and hearthstone all over this broad land, will yet swell the chorus of the Union when again touched, as surely they will be, by the better angels of our nature."

Here, Lincoln closed, and turning, he faced Chief Justice Taney—renowned architect of the Dred Scott Decision—who was about to administer the presidential oath of office. Lincoln's hand placed steadily upon the Bible, he solemnly pledged to preserve, protect, and defend the nation. Sworn in as the nation's sixteenth president, a volley of cannon fire from the howitzers posted on the nearby hill heralded his inauguration, reverberating in thunderous celebration. Below, the crowds cheered and hats were tossed buoyantly in the air. A military band struck up a celebratory tune, and Lincoln filed off the platform, taking his stovepipe hat and carrying his gold-headed cane at his side. It was, most memorably, a historic moment!

Brandon only wished that Mela and Barry could have been there with him to witness it.

CHAPTER 18

The Better Angels of Our Nature

"Dear Alexandra,

"I have missed you so, dear sister. There is so much I want to write, to tell you. And I have received your latest letter. I am so happy that all is well with you and Loxley House. No longer do I fret about you being all alone, rattling about in your big country house; your life sounds wonderfully gay with one round of house parties, dances, excursions, and picnics after another. I remember springtime in Derbyshire, especially at Loxley House—the roses in the front garden, the labyrinthine hedges and sundial, the stone bridge over the pond and stream where William and I first met. Oh, but Alexandra, when I think of Loxley House I grow homesick, even still. And I still miss our sister, Allison."

Annabelle paused from her writing as her eyes misted and sentimentality swelled in her throat. She sighed, blinked back tears, and continued her letter.

"I agree, Alexandra, it is good that Brandon has found a companion in Kathryn Lissette Morgan ... although I fear the possibility of his moving with the children to Washington, D.C. to be near her. You see, I believe Brandon is quite serious in his intentions toward Kathryn. Nonetheless, I believe Allison will always be a part of him, an inseparable part, as if their very souls are eternally bound. Still, what a new spirit for life Kathryn seems to afford him!

"Now I must catch you up on the children. There are so many little

ones in the house, I nearly lose track! Needless to say, there is never a dull moment with three six-year-olds in the house—Cooper, Mela, and Cinda can be quite a handful! (Although, I dare say, our mischievous little Cooper is handful enough on his own. My heavens, the things he gets into!) Thank goodness for Ester and Cotta to look after the children, to help with them all. Barry turned twelve last month, in March, and is now quite grown up, it seems. Where has the time flown? And Carolina, just a year behind Barry, is becoming quite the young lady—a true Southern Belle. Ashley, already eight, is as a porcelain doll with her head of fair curls—William says she takes after me in looks, and I dare say she does. She is such a good, quiet child. I hope by Christmas we can send you a daguerreotype of the family and whole household staff, including Ester and Jacob with their little ones, Cinda and Quash—Quash is nine now, can you believe it?—and the other household servants, including Cotta and Sabe."

Here, Annabelle reflected a moment as she contemplated exactly how to broach the next subject—updating Alexandra on the matter regarding Sabe—and then set pen to paper and continued writing.

"Alexandra, do you remember in my last letter to you that I wrote of Sabe's assault on Sara Davenport? I still do not know what William intends to do with Sabe, either by way of reprimand or future employment. I really do not want Sabe sent into the fields; he had served so well as household help until the unfortunate incident with Sara Davenport. I must say, William seems in a quandary as to what to do about Sabe. Even so, we cannot keep him 'imprisoned' in his cabin indefinitely. And, Alexandra, I truly believe what Cotta had relayed to us—that Sabe was simply traumatized over the brutal assault upon and death of his young sister by the wicked hands of Jack Davenport, and that Sabe is now racked with remorse over his blindly—ever so blindly— taking his rage out upon poor Sara Davenport! Surely William will see this as well, and—"

A soft knocking sounded on Annabelle's bedroom door. Laying her pen aside on the writing table, Annabelle rose and opened the door to find Sara standing there.

"Annabelle ... may I please speak with you?" Sara asked.

"Why, of course, Sara. Please come in." Annabelle stood aside and gestured for Sara Davenport to enter.

"It ... it's about Sabe...," Sara began tentatively. Her pale-blue eyes looked into Annabelle's intently. "I ... want to thank you for all your generosity and hospitality, for opening your house to us. Tom and I are ever so grateful to you and William." She looked nervously downward, her hands clasped uneasily at her waist.

Perceiving that Sara's errand to speak with her was of a quite serious nature, Annabelle's brow furrowed as she listened with due interest.

Sara sighed and met Annabelle's gaze. "I hope to repay your kindness one day, but for now ... I have decided that ... Tom and I must leave."

This declaration, so completely unexpected, took Annabelle aback. "Leave? ... Leave Crawford Hill?"

Sara nodded, clenching her jaw to keep from crying.

Annabelle knit her brow harder and gave her head a little shake. "But ... where will you and Tom go?"

Sara could not answer, for a flood of tears suddenly threatened as sorrow swelled and ached in her throat. She looked abruptly downward. All at once Sara Davenport buried her face in her hands and wept. "But ... we can't stay here ... we've no right to impose on you ... Sabe is yours. There was no trouble until we came here ... and as long as Tom and I *are* here—" Sara broke into sobs, unable to continue.

"There, *there!*" Annabelle placed an arm consolingly about Sara's shoulders and sat with her on the edge of the bed. "Come, now, Sara. You mustn't cry. You need not leave. We want you and Tom to stay with us for as long as you like."

Sara required some moments to compose herself. She swallowed her tears and, gratefully accepting Annabelle's proffered handkerchief, mopped her eyes. Sniffling, her voice tremulous, Sara explained, "But now Sabe is your house servant; he's no longer a Davenport field hand. I hadn't meant to cause trouble by being here. You and William have every right to keep

Sabe and employ him in your house. But now, because of my presence here he is banished, confined to his cabin—" Sara's voice faltered, and more tears streamed silently down her cheeks.

"Sara, dear," Annabelle intoned, "truly, we will decide something about Sabe. It will all work out absolutely fine. Really it will. You mustn't feel any blame at all. We want you to stay here with us."

"Are you ... sure?" Sara's red-rimmed eyes looked earnestly into Annabelle's.

"Yes, absolutely sure," Annabelle said as she gave Sara a consoling squeeze.

Sara dried her eyes and swallowed. "I understand now why Sabe did what he did—it was because of what my husband had done to Sabe's sister, Juliana. Sabe simply took his rage—his understandable rage—out on me. He had never treated anyone poorly before, not when he was ours. I did not know Sabe, among so many on our plantation, but of course he knew me, that I was Jack's wife. Had Sabe presented trouble for us, I definitely would have heard of it. But he never did; Sabe never caused trouble. I dare say, I don't want him punished on my account." Sara wiped away a stray tear with the back of her hand.

"William said he will decide what to do about Sabe since you and Tom have come to live with us, and it will be an amicable plan for all, I am certain. I know that Sabe is deeply remorseful for his wrongdoing. Our main concern has been that you feel safe here; otherwise, William and I would never forgive ourselves if we were to let you and Tom leave!" Upon this utterance, Annabelle's own eyes filled, and the two women embraced.

"I ... I'll be all right now," Sara said. "I'm sorry for being so upset. It's simply that I have been through so much these past many days—I am not quite myself. Tom and I will stay." She managed a faint smile.

Annabelle embraced Sara a second time. "I'm glad you are staying, and everything will work out fine—you'll see."

After Sara went out from the room, Annabelle resumed her chair at the writing table to continue her letter to Alexandra—between intermittent thoughts regarding Sabe and Sara as well as William's intentions about resolving the matter.

Finding where she had left off writing, Annabelle reread the part of her letter that had been interrupted.

> "*...and that Sabe is now racked with remorse over his blindly— ever so blindly—taking his rage out upon poor Sara Davenport! Surely William will see this as well, and—*"

"And what?" Annabelle paused a moment, then set pen to paper, assuring herself that all would ultimately be well.

> "*—and I am sure he will be lenient and humane in his handling of Sabe.*"

To dash these matters from her thoughts, Annabelle then wrote to her sister of the inauguration, drawing from Brandon's latest letter and the local newspaper accounts.

> "*I should have liked to have been at the inauguration. Brandon's letters to us make me feel as if I had been there, and I am so intrigued by Lincoln. I dare say, I think of him as our president too, but Alexandra— we have seceded! Our Southern president, Jefferson Davis, abhors the 'Negro,' and I wonder that he doesn't abhor the North as well! What times we live in. Will this nation be irrevocably torn apart by secession—even by war? I pray, Alexandra—as Lincoln so eloquently expressed it— that we are instead ruled by 'the better angels of our nature!'*"

<hr />

The days passed placidly as springtime approached. Tom and Sara began to feel more at home, and the household seemed to be in good order.

In the rice fields, harrowing, plowing, and trenching had commenced in preparation for the spring's rice planting. With better weather, and less rain and cold, the Crawford Hill overseers were up before dawn, assigning tasks earlier in the morning; that way, if the slaves finished their tasks soon enough, they and the overseers would have the rest of the day off to enjoy the good weather. Although many plantation owners used the task system as a way to have work accomplished more quickly, some insidiously assigned additional work when tasks were completed ahead of schedule so that the slaves were not free for the remainder of the day but were simply overworked to a scathing degree. However, William did not approve of this ploy—he made sure that his overseers let his slaves have free time off during this rare time of year when the weather was tepid, not icy or sweltering, and the humidity low; he reasoned that this would refresh his workers and his overseers so that the rest of the year they would be in better health for their own sakes as well as more productive for the good of all at Crawford Hill.

William also believed—as many Waccamaw plantation owners did—that Saturdays should be half-task days so that the slaves could have some time to themselves for washing, cleaning, gardening, and tending to their own livestock. On Saturday evenings, during spring and summer, one could sometimes hear the distant sounds of banjo, fiddle, and harmonica music wafting across the fields on the breeze toward the Big House as the slaves partied, socialized, and danced.

Sundays were considered a full day of rest. On Sundays, the slaves would oftentimes request passes from their overseers to visit friends or relatives on neighboring plantations. Other slaves would use this time to hunt in the woods, which were abundant with prey. Still others would use this as a spiritual time, a time of worship.

On this particular Sunday morning in late March, only Sabe remained confined, unable to go out and socialize, tromp through the woods hunting, or share in worship—let alone resume his household tasks. For his part, Sabe remained imprisoned in his cabin, all but cut off from the light of day. His only socializing was when Cotta would come to bring him food and water three times a day, when the overseer would bring water for him to sponge bathe with, and when a young slave child would be ordered to remove his chamber pot twice a day and replenish it with a clean one.

As Sabe remained confined on this Sunday morning, the Crawfords bustled about readying themselves for their weekly carriage ride to the All Saints Church.

"The better angels of our nature," Annabelle mused silently as she pinned up her hair in preparation to leave for church. What an inspiring phrase it was. "How poetic," she thought as she pinned a ringlet into place. "The pastor could title a sermon with just those words: 'The Better Angels of Our Nature.'"

"Mother? . . ." Carolina sashayed blithesomely into her mother's dressing chamber.

Fastening a pin to her curls, Annabelle turned. "Yes, sweetie?"

"Cooper says he isn't going to church—*again!*" Carolina pirouetted in her hoops and flounced upon a chair where she sat idly kicking her legs.

"And why isn't Cooper going to church *this* morning?" Annabelle all but rolled her eyes.

It had become an all-too-familiar game on Sunday mornings. If Cooper wasn't purposely slow at dressing in order to prevent everyone from leaving on time—or until it was too late to go at all (which never worked to his advantage anyway)—then he would, at intervals, complain of aches or a fever in order to stay at home. These imaginary ailments seldom worked as he had planned.

Carolina stopped kicking her legs and rose from the chair. "*This* time Cooper says his stomach feels bad, so he is not going."

Annabelle smiled, shook her head before the looking glass, and secured another ringlet. "Tell Cooper I'll be there to look in on him in a minute."

Carolina nodded. Pirouetting again, her hoops swaying, Carolina walked on tiptoe to the door and hesitated. "Isn't Father coming to church this morning?" She particularly liked sitting by her father in church when he wasn't either away on business or tending to work in his study.

"No, angel. He said he has a lot of business to catch up on this morning—a lot of bookkeeping and paperwork. He said it simply can't wait."

Issuing a little frown, Carolina nonetheless chirped, "I'll go tell Cooper you're coming to look in on him." And she went out.

"William . . . I think Little Cooper's tummy is really out of sorts this time." Annabelle stood at William's desk in the study where he sat before stacks of papers, files, and account books. "Maybe he shouldn't go to church this morning. Maybe I should stay home with him."

"Oh, Cooper's fine," William said, with a casual wave of his hand. "He's always concocting some excuse to stay home from church. He just has too much energy to sit still in a pew all morning long, that's all. He gets bored."

"But church is important—"

"Yes, dear, I know it is," William interjected.

"Then, won't you please go in and look at Cooper yourself? I'm just not quite sure, this time, if he is really ill or not," Annabelle asked, her eyes pleading her husband to heed her request.

"Of course, in a minute." William resumed sorting the papers before him upon the desk.

"It can't wait, William. We'll soon be late as it is, if we are to go at all."

"Very well." William rose, and noting his wife's exasperation, he apologized. "I'm sorry, dear. It's just that I seem to be preoccupied this morning with business." He gave Annabelle a peck on the cheek and went out, down the hall to Cooper's room. Following behind her husband, Annabelle stood at Cooper's open door as William entered the room and sat on the edge of the bed to examine the boy. Father and son spoke quietly, then William probed the boy's tummy and felt his forehead. "Now, I want you up, dressed, and ready for church as quickly as you ate your breakfast this morning," he admonished, with a cheerful wink.

Lying back upon his plumped pillows, Cooper nodded dutifully.

William met Annabelle at the door.

"Is he quite all right, then?" she asked.

"Sure—he's fine," William said. "His stomach may be a little upset, but he ate breakfast so fast, then he had lain down again right after eating. Doesn't Ester say it isn't good to lie down directly after eating a meal, that it's bad for the digestion? All Cooper needs is to be up and about, and he will feel better in no time."

Still, Annabelle looked doubtful. "Perhaps I should look at him again, perhaps we should stay home and—"

"Cooper is *fine*, Annabelle. Go to church. Don't worry. If you don't leave soon, it *will* be too late to set out at all, and *everyone* will miss church."

Seeing Cooper out of bed and beginning to dress himself, Annabelle sighed. "Perhaps you're right. I *do* tend to worry too much about the children." With that, she went in to Cooper's room and helped him on with his Sunday clothes.

Minutes later, Annabelle set out with all of the children—Jacob driving them in the family carriage—along the north road to All Saints Church. Annabelle sat up front with Jacob. The children—Mela, Barry, Carolina, Ashley, Cooper, and Tom Davenport—sat in the rear.

Sara would have accompanied them, but she decided to stay home and nurse a mild headache. This afforded both a not-too-crowded carriage and a quiet morning with most the children out of the house so that Sara could rest.

Only Cinda and Quash remained home, and Ester was busy with their morning reading-and-writing lessons upstairs in their turret quarters. Every Sunday morning, Ester taught Cinda and Quash how to read and write. As some plantation owners were prone to do, William and Annabelle believed in educating their house servants on how to read and provided them each with a Bible for this purpose. This was of particular importance to Annabelle who impressed upon William that the All Saints Church pastor had always prevailed upon the slaveholders to treat their slaves well and that teaching Cinda and Quash to read and write was a part of treating them well.

Not long after Annabelle and the children departed for church, and while Ester and her two children were busy with lessons, William set his papers aside, descended the stairs, and went out of the Big House. Behind the house, near the willow tree at the edge of the pond, William met with one of his overseers and two African slave drivers. One driver—of large powerful frame—held a coiled fifteen-foot bullwhip.

The bullwhip was constructed of braided rawhide leather secured at one end around a ten-inch wooden handle with the remaining plaited length ending in a knot from which the leather ends splayed as a tassel. It was this knotted splay of leather at the whip's end that had come to be known as the "cracker," for it was what split the skin when used for whipping slaves.

After a brief exchange of words, William and the three men walked down the gentle slope of grass toward the short rows of wooden cabins that the kitchen and household staff occupied. In this small neighborhood of simple one-room cabins lived the household cooks, blacksmiths, stablemen, coachmen, seamstresses, and other slaves of similar occupations. It was a short distance beyond this where William, the overseer, and the two drivers stopped before a cabin—its windows boarded up save for a narrow slit, and its entry latched. Unfastening the door's lock, William entered, whereupon the cabin door creaked open, letting in a bright stream of morning light.

Sabe sat up on his bed, a single mattress of carded-lint cotton on a wooden frame crossed with leather straps. Raising a hand to his brow, Sabe squinted toward the open door and the sudden flood of morning sun.

"Massa Willem? ..." Sabe uttered.

Summarily Sabe was shackled and led to a remote meadow just east of the pond. There, Sabe's hands were bound with a length of rope, the end of which was slung high over the limb of a tree and pulled taut. Stretched so that his toes barely scraped the ground, Sabe all but dangled from the branch. As the overseer and drivers secured Sabe into position, William remained silent; he did not relish what he was about to do, but he deemed it necessary—unavoidable.

Sabe simply had to be disciplined—to be punished—; to do otherwise would set a dangerous precedent. For days, the slaves' tongues had wagged over Sabe's attack on Sara Davenport and that his only retribution was to be sent to the jail-cabin for three days followed by confinement to his own cabin for an indefinite length of time. Surely not administering a more harsh punishment as an example to others would be foolish. In any event, this is what William had at long last reasoned. Despite Sabe's deep remorse, his assault upon Sara was heinous and squarely deserving of stronger disciplinary action. Even though William had neither the heart nor stomach for whippings, Sabe, he decided, had left him no choice.

William would find a way to tell Annabelle of Sabe's whipping later. She would understand, in retrospect—at least, he hoped she would. Although, historically, whippings had rarely ever been meted out at Crawford Hill— and no whippings had been administered since William's inheritance of the plantation—now it was for the best. It had to be done. There was simply no alternative. William would explain this to Annabelle—she would recognize the necessity of it.

William, the overseer, and the slave driver who had bound Sabe stood at a safe distance from the burly slave driver wielding the bullwhip as he positioned himself a measured distance from Sabe.

Overhead stretched a crisp blue sky of white billowing clouds. The cool late-March breeze feathered the new spring grass and ruffled William's shirt. Not far off, roses of pale pink and white at the edge of the pond had begun to blossom.

"When you're ready," William called to the slave driver brandishing the bullwhip, his voice flat.

"Jesus, Lawd … God A'mighty," Sabe uttered a desperate plea, raising his eyes heavenward past the huge billows of white that crept overhead, above the budding branches and coarse ropes that cut into his wrists. His eyes welled deep. "Lawdy Jesus, I's sorry!" he whispered. Sabe concluded that he was first to be whipped before he was hung. The bare and budding branches intertwined overhead would serve as his gallows.

"One!" the driver called, hurtling the bullwhip's plaited length through the air.

Recoiling, the splayed end of the whip then cracked forward, tearing sharply through Sabe's dark-skinned back. Sabe's stomach heaved with the pain as his flesh erupted in rivulets of blood. He dug the nails of his hands, above his bound wrists, hard into his palms to keep from flinching or crying out.

"Two!"

The whip cracked again, sending blood in streams down Sabe's back. Still, he did not flinch or cry out.

"Three!"

CRACK!

The rawhide splay seared Sabe's flesh with riveting pain. Warm torrents of red flowed downward. "Jesus, Lawd!" Sabe uttered, tears catching in his voice.

"Four!"

CRACK!

"Five!"

CRACK!

"Six!"

The driver's whip tore repeatedly, mercilessly into Sabe's bare back, crosshatching his flesh with rivers of blood. Again and again, Sabe's stomach heaved with pain as he writhed in helpless agony.

"Seven!"

CRACK!

Sabe convulsed upon the rope and cried out, his anguish echoing through the nearby woodland.

"Eight!"

CRACK!

"Nine!"

William's eyes stung with each crack of the whip. Yet as much as his eyes stung, William told himself that Sabe must be dealt with—however unfortunate, it simply had to be done. He clenched his jaw and willfully hardened his heart.

"Ten!"

CRACK!

Sabe's body convulsed with pain as his blood rained down upon the tender blades of spring grass below.

Sara Davenport, a light-knit shawl about her shoulders, had ventured out of the Big House for a morning walk about the pond to enjoy the roses beginning to bloom and the pleasant early-spring morning. Her headache had abated considerably after a brief rest and a cup of herbal tea administered by Cotta. Now Sara felt that the fresh morning air and a walk outdoors would do her good as well. Passing by the willow tree at the pond's edge, she heard a reverberant crack split the air and a man's tormented cry. "What on *earth?*" she wondered as she looked about her.

"Eleven!"

Another crack split the air.

In the distance, down the gentle slope of grass, at the edge of the meadow beside the woods, Sara saw the small assembly of men—Sabe among them, all but dangling from his wrists bound to the tree limb.

"Twelve!"

CRACK!

Sabe's agonized moan reverberated in the silence. His body flinched upon the rope.

Sara's heart stopped. "No! ... *No!*" she breathed, her hands clasped trembling before her lips, horrified at the scene that had so rudely and unexpectedly met her eyes.

"Thirteen!" The whip cracked again.

Writhing, Sabe bit his lip until it bled to keep from crying out as the blinding pain of the bullwhip coursed through him.

"*Fourteen!*"

CRACK!

Instantly Sara dropped her shawl and fled down the hill toward the gathering of men. Drawing near, she skirted the range of the bullwhip and ran to where Sabe was tied. There, she stood but a few feet away in the shadows, panting to catch her breath.

"*Fifteen!*" the driver called out. Focusing on his aim and on his target, the driver scarcely paid any heed to the spectator who had apparently wandered down from the Big House to watch.

William, his beleaguered conscience piqued by witnessing the rivulets of blood and welts emerging upon Sabe's back, had looked away for the last several lashes of the whip. He was not aware that anyone had drawn nearby to observe.

"*Stop! Stop!*" Sara shouted, her eyes wide with alarm.

But the driver had already cast the whip forward toward its target. The bullwhip recoiled in midair, then sailed forward, its splayed tassel in an earnest trajectory toward Sabe's torn and bloodied back.

CRACK!

Sabe convulsed wildly upon the rope. Sara winced and averted her eyes.

"Get back!" William shouted to Sara as he motioned for the driver to hold off.

Her heart pounding and her thoughts whirling, Sara reeled back several paces and labored to catch her breath.

"Continue," William signaled the driver.

"*Seventeen!*"

CRACK!

The bullwhip's splay struck Sabe's back, spattering fresh blood. Horrified, Sara clasped a hand to her mouth as her eyes filled. Then she darted in front of where Sabe all but hung from the tree branch.

"Sara! Stand away *now!* Go back to the house!" William ordered.

Sara did not move.

Purposefully William set out in long strides across the grass toward Sara.

THE BETTER ANGELS OF OUR NATURE

Near tears and trembling, Sara moved backward.

Satisfied, William also moved to the side, out of range of the whip's trajectory.

"*Eighteen!*" the African driver called out, raising the bullwhip again. Fifteen feet of rawhide recoiled in midair ready to strike.

"*No!*" Sara cried out as she darted forward, then held herself squarely against Sabe, her breast heaving upon his lacerated back.

CRACK!

The rawhide splay struck Sara. Crying out, Sara stiffened in pain as she felt her own blood seep wet and fresh through the white cotton lace of her spring frock. Nonetheless, she clung to Sabe protectively, the blood of his wounds, warm and liquid, absorbing into the fabric of her bodice, soaking it through.

"*Christ!*" Aghast, William sprinted down the grassy slope and roughly pulled Sara off of Sabe. "*Christ, Sara!*" William rebuked her as he slipped his arm about her slender waist. "Continue!" William ordered the driver as he began to guide Sara away, out of range of the whip. Sabe was due his twenty-nine lashes, and William was *not* going to stop now—no matter how much he detested the heinous punishment—it simply had to be done!

"*Nineteen!*" the driver shouted.

At once Sara pulled free of William's grasp, and as the whip's plaited end hurled downward she intervened a second time between its leather tassel and Sabe.

CRACK!

The leather slashed her dress, welting and slicing her smooth, fair skin in a ribbon of red. Her arms fast about Sabe, Sara convulsed and uttered a sharp cry, the pain of the whip searing and racking her body in waves. Nearly swooning, she rested her cheek against Sabe's bloodied back, her arms still protectively encircling him.

"Lawdy Jesus ... Lawdy *Jesus,*" Sabe half breathed, half wept.

William, consternation etched deep upon his brow, motioned for the driver to stop, and he strode toward Sara as she clung tenaciously to Sabe, her silent tears mingling with the blood upon his back and staining the stark white cloth of her frock. She lifted her head upon Sabe's bleeding back, her tears cleansing his wounds, and looked up beseechingly at William as he drew near.

Defeated, wearied, William could think of little to say. His own eyes stung with tears. "Sara!" he breathed, and laid a gentle quivering hand upon her shoulder.

"He's just ... he's just a boy!" she wept plaintively. "It's wrong ... it's wrong, William." She spoke quietly, earnestly. Her eyes had witnessed enough inhumane atrocities committed by her now-deceased husband's hands; she was not about to witness more, even if purportedly on her behalf. Her heart broke for Sabe.

William sighed heavily and glanced downward. "Come away," he urged softly.

Sara did not move, and William knew what she wanted, what she first had to be assured of.

"No more!" he shouted across the meadow to the slave driver, his voice weary and defeated. "It's over! No more!" William's eyes welled. "It's over," he said quietly to Sabe and Sara, as much as to his own heart.

Upon that, Sabe bent his head and sobbed piteously, his tears streaming down his face and falling in glimmering droplets upon the blades of grass below.

Just then Sara swooned. Quickly William caught her up in his arms, then reclined her carefully upon the lawn. Ordering Sabe untied, William turned and walked wearily up the slope toward the Big House. He would dispatch Ester and Cotta to tend to Sara's wounds and to care for Sabe until Dr. Langford could arrive and attend to them both.

Treading up the grassy slope, his eyes brimming so that he could hardly see, William cursed himself. He cursed slavery, he cursed the whole damned South! Disgusted, he wanted no more of it. He wanted—

"How *dare* you, William! How *dare* you!" Annabelle cried out. She appeared suddenly before him.

William looked up, startled. "*Annabelle!*"

"*How dare you!*" Instantly she flew at him in a rage, her eyes flashing, pummeling him with her fists, venting the anger and indignation that pounded in her chest. "How *dare* you!" she shouted, socking William hard in the ribs with a clenched fist. "You *brute!* You *liar!*" Annabelle spat, striking him forcefully with a final blow.

William merely stood and suffered her clouts. There was nothing he could say—no excuse or adequate reason. His eyes brimmed fuller as the ache in his throat welled.

"How *dare* you!" Annabelle's voice shook with tears. Abruptly she turned and, gathering her skirts, she ran sobbing up to the house.

William sighed, his mouth bent in a frown, his eyes brimmed to spilling. Overhead, in the bright blue sky a billow of white eclipsed the sun, casting him momentarily in its shadow. William wiped the stray tears from his cheeks with the cuff of his shirtsleeve and walked down the low hill to where Sabe lay upon the grass. Sara, now roused, knelt attentively at Sabe's side.

William knelt beside Sabe, opposite Sara. He looked at the latter with red-rimmed eyes, and asked quietly, his voice rough with emotion, "Are you all right?"

Weeping silently, Sara nodded and gazed down upon Sabe.

William laid a tentative hand on Sabe's arm, his damp eyes surveying the crosshatchings of welts and raw, bloody gashes along Sabe's back. With effort, William's lips struggled to form the words he wanted to say. "Sabe—" William broke off and swallowed hard. "Sabe … I'm sorry," he whispered, his heart anguished. How utterly inadequate and hollow his words sounded—yet how very deeply he meant them.

Sabe, too tortured in mind, spirit, and body, could not speak—only his tears flowed silently, wetting the tender blades of spring grass where he laid shivering and convulsing with pain.

William rose and ran a trembling hand over his brimming eyes. Heavy hearted, he trudged up the hill toward the house, tersely dismissing the overseer and drivers as he went. As he approached the pond and the willow tree at its edge, Ester and Cotta rushed past him in long angry strides. Ester, for her part, could not look William in the eye, while Cotta surveyed her master with a mixture of fright and indignation. William, however, scarcely had the heart to look either of them in the eye. He noticed only that Ester carried a basket of cloth bandages and tinctures of salves, and that Cotta carried a bottle of whiskey.

Inside the Big House, William found Annabelle standing at the west sitting-room window, looking out beyond the stained-glass items that lined the window shelves.

"Annabelle...," he called quietly from the doorway.

Turning from the window, Annabelle faced William from across the room. Her eyes cold, she studied him as she drew in deep angry breaths, her lips tight. For a moment, neither spoke, only the sounds of the children playing upstairs could be heard.

William understood that he had been wrong to inflict physical punishment upon Sabe—he realized it thoroughly. Sabe's raw and bloodied back told him this, the lash marks on Sara Davenport's back and the blood staining her dress told him this, Annabelle's hurt and anger told him this— and William's own heart told him he had been horrifically wrong. Now, as he stood facing Annabelle, his head fairly swam to grasp at ample reason for his actions, for his decision to put Sabe to the whip. All he could think was that it had seemed warranted and prudent at the time, despite his better nature, and he had not known what else to do. Now he was piteously sorry.

Finding his voice, William uttered, "Annabelle—"

"How *dare* you do such a thing!" Annabelle's eyes flashed. "*My God,* William! Are you so arrogant? Who do you think you *are?!*"

"I was wrong," William admitted solemnly. His eyes and his heart implored her understanding and forgiveness.

"You lied to me, William. And you had Sabe whipped—*whipped!*" All at once Annabelle's words tumbled forth as she paced before the window, gesticulating angrily. "I was on my way to All Saints Church—to *church,* William—and you said you could not go. You *said* you had to stay here and attend to paperwork. And I *believed* you!" she shouted, her voice filled with rage. She crossed her arms angrily and protectively before her and faced William. "You said you had paperwork to do, but instead you had a hidden agenda. You could not be direct with me and discuss it with me. No! You had to do this ... this *hideous, heinous* thing—let alone, behind my back!" Annabelle punctuated her anger with a stomp of her foot upon the hardwood floor.

"I felt it had to be done—"

"What—whipping Sabe at *all?* Let alone nearly to *death?*" Annabelle shrilled. "And you call yourself a *reformer!*" Her eyes flashed daggers that cut into William's very heart. "You hypocrite! You—you arrogant *hypocrite!* Why—why you are *no* better than Jack Davenport!"

William knew not what to say. He felt with full force the guilt due him; nonetheless, his heart felt crushed by being compared to the vile Jack Davenport. Finding his tongue, his voice pained, he said quietly, "I only did what I had thought was best—" He left off wearily, his eyes filling.

Wiping away tears of infuriation with trembling fingers, Annabelle looked hard at William. "What was best? You did what you thought 'was best'? ... You *lied* to me, and you had our new house servant—our new family member—*whipped!* Good Lord, William, even Sara understood what prompted Sabe to lash out at her and has forgiven him. You urged me to go to *church* and to take our son with me, even though I suspected he was ill. And do you know *what*, William? Cooper *was* ill! *That* is why I returned early. *That* is why I caught you so by surprise out by the pond. Cooper was sick, and we had to turn around and come home. But you didn't care, did you! You didn't mind about lying to me, or about little Cooper! You only had it in your head to have Sabe brutally punished."

Annabelle fell silent. The many wounds upon her heart had been spoken and laid out bare for William to face. She stared damp-eyed, almost with loathing, at William. Her hair, in all its pretty ringlets, had loosened from its pins, wisps clinging about her damp brow and cheeks. Her head swam with condemnations of his abject wrongdoing.

William said quietly, his voice thick with emotion, "I'm sorry, Annabelle. I wish I could take it back ... but I can't."

"I can hardly look at you right now," Annabelle said. With that, she pushed past William and strode from the room.

At the banister at the foot of the stairs, Annabelle stopped a moment, then burst into sobs. William heard the rustle of her skirts and her shoes clatter up the stairway, and an upstairs door slam. He pictured her flounced upon their bed, consumed with sobs, and he wanted to go to her to explain, to comfort her—but he dared not. Every word she had spoken to him so sharply rang true. He had been wrong, hideously wrong. "Reformer!" Annabelle's pointed sarcasm echoed starkly in his mind. William sat wearily upon the settee of the west sitting room. No amount of remorse would erase the bloody gashes upon Sabe's back, none would heal Sara's wounds, none would repair his breach of trust with Annabelle, and none would compensate for his casual disregard for little Cooper. No amount of remorse would atone for the wrongs he had committed that morning. William's eyes brimmed, then spilled over.

⸻◇⸻

Cooper's stomach ailment was short-lived. Sabe was placed in Dr. Langford's care and given, for the time being, Brandon's room in which to recuperate. Dr. Langford prognosticated that Sara Davenport's wounds would be quick to heal; merely a few stiches were required in her case.

Only the gulf between Annabelle and William persisted. Determined not to cry—determined to keep up appearances for the children's and household's sakes—Annabelle kept her tears buried just below the surface; yet the wound of William's actions and falsehoods weighed on her heart as if upon her very soul.

On the afternoon following Sabe's whipping, William had come to Annabelle to try to make amends. "I would like to respond to what you said to me yesterday ... if you want to listen," he offered.

Looking downward, Annabelle considered carefully before giving her answer. "I'll have to think about it," she said, and went out.

The pain upon her heart was so great, she had felt so betrayed and invalidated, that she wondered if she and William would ever make amends.

CHAPTER 19

A Proposal

"On the day following his election, Republican President Abraham Lincoln informed reporters, 'Well, boys, your troubles are over now; mine have just begun.' Indeed, this simple, prophetic insight has proven true in the span of just one short month since Lincoln's inauguration—and more so than he may well have imagined upon first uttering it."

Brandon paused from his writing and reread the paragraph. Satisfied, he gazed momentarily out his fourth-floor Morley's Hotel window. Leaden skies over Washington had threatened rain for days; but as yet, not one drop had spilled. Collecting his thoughts, Brandon reviewed the notes before him from his morning interviews—one with Secretary of State Seward and one with President Lincoln. With the details of his interviews still fresh in his mind, Brandon continued writing his latest article for *The Illustrated London News*.

"Poised uncomfortably between two slaveholding states, Washington, D.C. is in a state of increasing alarm as rumors of the potential for war continue to swell. Meanwhile, in the face of growing alarm, Secretary of State Seward complains that Lincoln is myopic, incompetent, and without any policy whatsoever, foreign or domestic—and this may, arguably, be the case. Nonetheless, Seward's questionable, if not audacious, proposal for the reunification of North and South is for Lincoln to declare war on Spain, France, and England as a mandate against European intervention in Mexico and the continent. If Seward believes such foreign policy is superior to none and that it would avert war between North and South—and spawn their reunification—then someone had best inform Seward that some

Southerners want an ideological clash with Washington precisely to help unite the Confederacy!

"Appalled at Seward's April-first communiqué to this effect, Lincoln's terse reply was a resounding 'No!' resentful of Seward's apparent play for administrative power. Furthermore, Lincoln declared, 'Whatever policy we adopt, *I* must do it.' By this simple statement, Lincoln has asserted that *he*, not Seward, will make the policy decisions in his Administration. Abraham Lincoln, after all, *is* president, and one cannot help but wonder if Seward's April-first communiqué—entitled 'Some Thoughts for the President's Consideration'—would not have been more fittingly regarded as a mere All Fools Day jest!

"As if Lincoln's troubles over Seward were not difficult enough, they seem to pale in comparison to Washington, D.C.'s precarious position between the two slaveholding states of Virginia and Maryland. However, even this geopolitical predicament seems to pale almost to utter disregard considering another matter presently plaguing Lincoln this first week of April, 1861—the matter of Fort Sumter."

Here, Brandon laid down his pen and leaned back in his chair in serious reflection. Earlier that morning, Lincoln had confided to Brandon in the course of their interview that all the troubles and anxieties of his life, so far, could not equal the current Fort Sumter imbroglio. Although tempted to include this rather personal comment of Lincoln's in his article, Brandon thought better of it, respecting Lincoln's confidence in him and the privacy of their interview. Further, he rather liked Lincoln, and such a comment in the press might make Lincoln sound weak or overwhelmed by current circumstances. Instead, as Brandon continued writing, his fountain pen scratched upon the page a rather more objective paragraph.

"Sumter is a fort occupying a small manmade island at the mouth of the Charleston harbor in South Carolina. Construction of the fort, begun in 1829, remains incomplete owing to a lack of financial enthusiasm for the project on the part of the Federal government."

Brandon set his pen aside to shuffle through the masses of interview notes and papers strewn across his desk in order to find a recent letter from Alfred Cooke in Charleston. Drawing from this letter, which Alfred Cooke had so generously and thoughtfully provided, Brandon would be able to explain the nature of the fort as well as the potentially volatile political issues surrounding it. Unfolding the letter and reviewing its contents, Brandon again set pen to paper.

"Sumter had been designed to accommodate two tiers of guns in casemates and one in barbette, but few of the guns are, as of yet, mounted properly. Much work on the fort remains to be completed before it can be ready to sustain a prolonged siege. Still, its pentagonally shaped walls tower nearly sixty feet high and rest upon two and one-half acres of sandbar. Centered at the mouth of Charleston harbor, the fort also boasts the strongest of the harbor's defences—blocking, as it does, passage to the sea. Furthermore, surrounding shorelines, and even the city of Charleston itself, stand within range of Sumter's cannon. Despite, then, its inchoate state, the fort, nevertheless, could serve to the Confederacy's distinct advantage, with the exception of one minor problem—Fort Sumter was recently occupied by a Federal garrison under the command of Major Robert Anderson.

"Major Robert Anderson had decided to move his garrison into Sumter with the idea of reducing the potential for bloodshed. Additionally, the rationale for Federal occupation of Sumter seems based on President Lincoln's earlier statements that he would recapture any and all Federal forts and arsenals the Confederacy has taken. Consequently, it seemed logical for a Federal garrison to occupy the heretofore empty Sumter, despite its incompletion, to prevent a Confederate move to occupy it. A Confederate strike against a Union-held Sumter seems, arguably, less likely than a Union strike to reclaim a Confederacy-held Sumter. Upon this reasoning, and in accordance with Republican Federal Policy, Anderson occupied Sumter.

"In actuality, Major Robert Anderson might well be the perfect benign liaison to be posted at Sumter to avert bloodshed. A distinguished officer of the Federal army from West Point, with strong Federal loyalties, Anderson is also, however, a Kentucky slaveholder with strong Southern sympathies—a unique combination of North and South in one man that could effectively assuage the potential for bloodshed.

"Why, then, is Federal occupation of Fort Sumter by Major Robert Anderson a trouble for Lincoln? The Federal garrison at Sumter is now surrounded by Southern batteries established along South Carolina's regional coastal shores, and Anderson's supplies are quickly dwindling;

he will need resupply from the North in order to maintain his garrison at Sumter. Because Sumter is surrounded by Southern rebel batteries, this could prove a tricky maneuver, and there is some question as to whether resupply is worth the risk of provoking Southern hostilities.

"On one hand, Lincoln is being petitioned to remove Anderson and his garrison from Sumter, relinquishing the fort to the Confederacy to ensure peace—the Federal flag flying proudly above the mouth of Charleston harbor is aggravating to the Confederacy, to say the least! On the other hand, Fort Sumter has become a powerful symbol of the Federal government; politically and strategically, Federal withdrawal would only weaken the Republican Party, bolster Seward's accusations of Lincoln's incompetency, and lose a strategic Union stronghold should war inevitably prevail rather than peace.

"Within the coming days, it will be Lincoln's decision either to hold Sumter and maintain Major Anderson's garrison by Federal resupply ships or abandon the fort altogether.

"Lincoln's troubles, it would appear, have just begun; and those troubles, for the moment, are not centered upon a tiny capital city perched precariously between two slaveholding states but rather upon the volatile situation concerning a tiny speck of an island in the mouth of the harbor of the first American state to secede from the Union."

Brandon stopped writing. The article was finished. Although it was a short draft, the writing of it seemed more arduous and tedious than usual. Perhaps this was due to the flood of facts and notes strewn upon his desk from which he drew to write it. Furthermore, he had been pressed for time. He had promised Kathryn an early dinner out followed by the theater, and these plans had markedly shortened the afternoon hours for researching and writing. Now, as he sat back at his desk, fairly satisfied with his afternoon's work, he pulled out his pocketwatch—less than one hour before he must leave for the Tierny Estate to collect Kathryn.

Instantly Brandon bolted up from the desk chair, yet to bathe, dress, and hire a cab. Reviewing the article for finishing touches would have to wait, and such final polishing would clearly be necessary. While writing, not only had Brandon been deluged with new facts, figures, quotes, and scribbled notes, as well as working under a time constraint—his mind had also, all the while, been distracted by something of importance he meant to speak to Kathryn about before his various obligations might not afford him the chance. Brandon was not certain how much longer he would remain in Washington with the inauguration well over with and Charleston—specifically Fort Sumter—becoming the focal point of Northern and Southern concerns. Soon, very soon, he would need to return home to Crawford Hill, Mela and Barry, and the work that awaited him there. Dressing to go out, he considered that he could scarcely dare broach the subject of his impending departure on this night; he could not bear the thought of leaving Kathryn for an indefinite period of time—perhaps forever—and he was not sure how she would respond to the news of his leaving. He *would* have to tell her soon, but he wasn't sure quite when or how.

***

Mr. Tierny kept Brandon company in the front room while Brandon waited for Kathryn to come downstairs. Mary, the housemaid, poured them each a glass of claret, then departed.

"What is playing at Ford's Theater tonight?" Mr. Tierny inquired, with a jovial arching of his eyebrows. Then he sipped his claret.

"It's called *The Colleen Bawn*. It's a melodrama that first opened in ... I believe it first opened in New York, nearly a year ago, in March of 1860. I don't know much about it," Brandon said, then added, "I do hope that Kathryn has not seen it yet."

"Melodramas—" Mr. Tierny reflected a moment. "Melodramas have been a favorite of Kathryn's since she was younger, maybe sixteen or seventeen. Good heavens, where does the time go? Is my little Kathryn nearly thirty-five?" Mr. Tierny mused with a disbelieving shake of his head and a sip of claret.

"No wonder, then, that Kathryn had mentioned that she had her heart set on seeing this play tonight, since melodramas are her favorite." Brandon swirled the dark purplish-red in the bowl of his glass, then took a sip.

Brandon had wondered about Kathryn's age. Due to Mr. Tierny's minor conversational slip of propriety (and perhaps due to the effects of the claret), he had casually disclosed his daughter's age—something not typically announced in polite society. Kathryn was roughly two years older than Brandon, although she certainly appeared young for her years. That she was slightly beyond him in years bothered Brandon not one wit—he was content enough that they were of nearly the same age.

"Oh, yes," Mr. Tierny chuckled fondly. "I can't recall how many times she must have read a particular book of melodramas I had given her for her eighteenth birthday—over and over, until the pages were all dog-eared."

"I'm sorry I'm so late!" Kathryn breezed into the room, her skirts rustling. "A button tore and it seemed easier to stitch it up instead of beginning dressing all over again," she explained. "I had Mary sew it on for me ... I haven't made us too late, have I?" She looked anxiously at Brandon.

Rising from his chair, Brandon drew out his pocketwatch to survey the time. "Seven minutes late. Had it been eight minutes, I'd have been off without you," he pronounced with a theatric air. He summarily placed the watch back in his pocket.

"Somehow I don't quite believe you!" Kathryn laughed, her green eyes twinkling.

Brandon broke into a grin. "It is becoming increasingly difficult to tease your daughter," Brandon quipped to Mr. Tierny.

Just then little Nathaniel appeared from around the door and entered the room. Slowly he trudged in, his young countenance of a dejected humor. "I want to go too, Mother," he complained.

"You wouldn't like it, dear," Kathryn consoled. "It's a play about a young girl who marries someone, but her husband's family does not care for her ... and ... well, it is a bit too frightening a tale for innocent young ears."

Nathaniel wrinkled his nose. Predictably, tales about young girls and marriage did little to pique his interest. "If you already know how the story goes, then why are you going to see it?"

"Yes, Lissy, we had best not go, since you already know the story," Brandon teased.

Kathryn cast Brandon a playful look of mock warning and turned back to Nathaniel. "I'm going to see it because I like the storyline, and—"

"Can I *please* go too?" Nathaniel piped. Despite the tiresome mention of young girls and marriage, he nonetheless did not want to miss out on an adventure out of the house.

"I'm sorry, Nathaniel. You stay home tonight with Grandpa and keep him company. All right?"

Resigned, Nathaniel nodded his downcast head of sandy locks.

"We will—all three of us—do something special together one afternoon. Perhaps tomorrow, Saturday," Brandon promised. "How would you like that?"

"I would like that very much!" Nathaniel grinned. He rather liked Brandon and had grown quite fond of him.

"Does that meet with your approval, Mother?" Brandon asked Kathryn with mock formality.

"Yes, of course," she agreed, and smiled brightly at Nathaniel as she knelt down to hug him goodbye and receive his promise to be good for Grandpa while she was out.

"We'd best go," she said to Brandon.

Glancing at his watch, Brandon noted, "We still have roughly two and a half hours for dinner before the play at eight o'clock. But yes, we had best be going." He took one more sip of his claret, then turned to escort Kathryn to the front door.

"Have a delightful evening," Mr. Tierny said as he gave Brandon a friendly pat on the shoulder.

"We will," Brandon smiled.

"Goodnight, Father," Kathryn said, then she took Brandon's arm.

Descending the front steps of the Tierny mansion with Kathryn, her gloved hand upon his arm, Brandon complimented, "You look ravishing tonight."

Kathryn dropped her eyes modestly. "Thank you," she said, then noted shyly, "... and you look quite handsome tonight as well."

"Only tonight?" Brandon quipped.

Kathryn giggled and gave his arm a little slap.

Brandon and Kathryn dined not at The President's Table that night but at a far more elegant establishment—The Golden Partridge—near Ford's Theater, where the play was to be performed. The restaurant was an enchantment of elegance, replete with polished mahogany paneling adorned with grand mirrors in gilt frames; Baccarat chandeliers imported from France; round tables draped in white-linen cloths and sparkling with cut crystal, gleaming silver, and flickering candlelight; and a wandering violinist softly playing sweet, romantic melodies. Exotic orchids from London decorated the center of each table. The glow of two crackling, cavernous stone fireplaces filled the room with warmth. Flanking the stonework chimneys, windows of beveled leaded-glass panes looked out onto a garden lit with lanterns. Threading his way through the dining room, pausing now and again at each table, the violinist played a delightful accompaniment to the pleasant chatter of conversation, the tinkling of glassware, and the occasional clatter of silver.

Seated by a window at a cozy candlelit table, Brandon and Kathryn shared a feast of claret, roast duck with seasoned rice, steamed vegetables in wine sauce, and hot buttered rolls. Their desserts of chocolate and peach meringue would come later.

Initially, as appetizers were served, Brandon and Kathryn commented on the weather—how March had ironically rolled in like a lamb with warm, sunny spring-like days, only to have rolled out like a lion with a few bouts of snow and temperatures in the low twenties in mid-March. Both agreed that they were happy for the spring-like weather of April to finally be arriving—despite vestiges of snow on the ground.

Throughout dinner, they spoke mostly of Brandon's morning interviews with both President Lincoln and Secretary of State Seward. Kathryn listened with rapt attention as Brandon spoke of his meeting with Lincoln. Brandon had found him to be warm, hospitable, eloquent, and ever at the ready with a keen sense of humor. Far less intrigued by Brandon's interview with Seward, Kathryn nonetheless sat politely as he delighted in relaying the squabbles between Lincoln and his wayward subordinate.

Over dessert, mutually tiring of politics and rather more serious matters, they turned to talk of the latest news from Alexandra at Loxley House, of Nathaniel (that he liked his school master and that they hoped he was behaving at home this evening), and of Nathaniel's Uncle John who was in the process of moving to New York to become a partner in a law firm. "I don't know when we shall see him again," Kathryn said, her eyes misting—she had never imagined that her brother-in-law would ever leave Washington. Finally, conversation turned to news from Crawford Hill and of the children, particularly Mela and Barry.

"You must miss your children terribly," Kathryn said.

"Yes. Yes, I do—" Brandon abruptly stopped himself. He had nearly mentioned his plan to return home soon to Crawford Hill, perhaps as early as the next week. However, he wanted to tell Kathryn of his plans later— he did not wish to trouble her with pressing issues just now, spoiling their evening. The matter of his imminent departure would have to wait. "Well, we had best head for the theater," he advised, changing the subject as he opened his pocketbook to pay the bill. "We don't want to be—" He was about to say "late"; instead, he exclaimed, "The tickets! *Blast!* I've forgotten the theater tickets!" The fold in his pocketbook, where he was sure he had placed them, gaped up at him empty. "They must be back at the Hotel," he said with dismay.

"Do we have time to go and get them?" Kathryn asked.

Quickly Brandon pulled out his pocketwatch. "If we hurry." Snapping the watchcase shut, he tucked it back into his pocket. Hurriedly he paid the bill, not waiting for change to be made. Outside the restaurant, Kathryn quick at his side, Brandon hailed a passing hansom cab that rushed them off the many long blocks toward Morley's Hotel.

As the horses' hooves clattered and clopped along the rough road, Brandon asked, "You already know quite a bit about the play tonight—have you seen it before?"

"No. I've not seen it. But I had read several excellent reviews this past year. And, I must admit, I had read the book that the play is based on—*The Collegians*, by Gerald Griffith—when I was younger. It was my very favorite novel. Father misremembered—it was not a book of melodramas that got all tattered and dog-eared, it was *The Collegians*; I overheard father telling you when I entered the front room this evening."

"And here I thought I was treating you to something new." Brandon sighed and shook his head with some disappointment. Not only had he misplaced the tickets, but it was a play based on a novel Kathryn already knew inside out. Perhaps the evening was not going quite as smoothly as planned. "Believe it or not, I don't know much about the play at all. But the advertisements for *Colleen Bawn* near the hotel looked intriguing," Brandon admitted.

"Tragically, the novel and the play are based on a true story—" Kathryn laughed. "You are a writer, so I had best rephrase that. It is not tragic that the novel and play are based on a true story—it is the true story that is quite tragic!"

"Ten demerits!" Brandon teased.

Kathryn light-heartedly slapped Brandon's arm. "Do you want to know what it's about, or don't you?" she giggled.

"Do tell," he encouraged.

"Ellen Scanlan, a fifteen-year-old girl, had married young. But when her husband saw that she would not be accepted into his family, he had his servant kill her—murder her! Perhaps the play will allude to certain details. You see, the servant killed her with a musket, stripped her bare, and dumped her body in a river tied to a stone. I won't tell you the rest, as I don't want to spoil the ending."

While Brandon knew what melodramas were, he had not assumed this one would be so bleak a tale—especially in light of what he had hoped to tell Kathryn that night. Glancing at his pocketwatch once more, he asked the driver to stop the open carriage along West Potomac Park, on the riverfront.

"Brandon ... do we have time to stop?" Kathryn asked, puzzled.

He glanced at his pocketwatch. "Yes, a short while."

As the horses came to a halt, Brandon alighted from the carriage, then helped Kathryn down. "Please wait," he asked the driver, who nodded his agreement, his hands dutifully on the reins, keeping the horses from proceeding.

"I thought you said that we might be late ... the tickets ... you're sure we have time?" Kathryn queried as she walked briskly at Brandon's side. She briefly cast a look back at the waiting carriage.

"Ford's Theatre is not very far from Morley's Hotel ... and the tickets," Brandon began, then slowed his pace. How could he say what he was about to say to Kathryn? But it could not wait. He would be leaving Washington D.C soon. And now that Brandon knew the tragic, mournful story of the melodrama they were about to see at Ford's Theatre—let alone that it was a true story—this had changed his mind about waiting to tell Kathryn what he had to say until after the play. The mood set by the melodrama simply would not be right for what he had to tell her—nor for what he *wanted* to say. "I thought a short stroll by the river would be nice before the theatre," he commented, then chided himself for speaking so lamely. After all, it was here where they had walked after their first night out—and given what he planned to tell her, walking here, with snow crunching under foot as on that first evening together, would make this evening special, memorable.

"It *is* a nice evening," Kathryn remarked, allowing herself to dispel her worries about the time and stroll with Brandon along the riverfront.

A half-moon reflected on the inky black ripples along the water's surface. Here and there, starlight glinted from behind sailing clouds shrouded in gray. Crickets chirped along the grasses and reeds near the river's edge. Melting patches of snow glittered in the moonlight. A cool breeze wafted strands of Kathryn's hair loose from their pins along her cheek, which she delicately combed back with her gloved fingers. All the while, Brandon was silent, thinking of the words he intended to say.

"Brandon? . . ." Kathryn prompted quietly. This unexpected amble along the river still had her perplexed, yet it was certainly a pleasant diversion.

"Do you remember the first time we walked along the Potomac when we first met?" Brandon gave Kathryn's gloved hand a tender squeeze.

"Yes, I do." She smiled and snuggled closer to Brandon as they strolled.

At that moment, in the shadows cast by a flickering gaslamp, a bench appeared, as if providentially, situated along the river's edge.

"Would you care to sit a moment?" Brandon asked.

Kathryn nodded, looking up into Brandon's soft brown eyes—eyes that reminded her of the sweetness of chocolate. "Yes . . . that would be fine." She only hoped they would still have time to retrieve the tickets and make the play on schedule.

Brandon escorted her to the bench and took his place beside her. He knew what he had designed to tell her, but it would not be quite so easy as he had earlier supposed. While he did not want to tell her of his imminent departure to return to All Saints Parish, he did want to tell her what was pent up in his heart for her—and to broach a question. Surely playhouse actors had it easier somehow; Brandon had silently rehearsed the words he had wanted to say all afternoon, to the point of having trouble concentrating on his article about Lincoln and Seward . . . but now . . . now it seemed nearly impossible to speak at all.

"Brandon? . . ."

His expression seemed far off as he gazed across the river to the distant shore.

Brandon turned to face Kathryn, and his eyes drank her in—each delightful contour of her delicately chiseled face, the wisps of chestnut hair that quivered in the breeze about her cheeks, the sparkle of her emerald-green eyes in the moonlight. He reveled in the warmth of her gloved hands held in his.

"Kathryn," he began, "I've something I have been meaning to tell you . . . something I am not certain you will wish to hear . . . but there is so little time . . . and it can't wait. I cannot wait any longer."

In that instant, Brandon longed to gently sweep a stray tendril from Kathryn's cheek, then kiss and embrace her as if to never let her go.

Kathryn listened attentively, not sure that she should dare anticipate what she thought she was about to hear.

At that moment, Brandon's hand rummaged in his coat pocket for something.

"Are the tickets in your pocket?" Kathryn wondered.

"Um . . . no," Brandon said absently. He withdrew a small sterling-silver box. For a moment, he held it in his hands, wondering what the future would hold if she should say no.

As Kathryn sat gazing out at the moonlight that glittered on the river's lapping surface, she took no notice of the small box he held.

Brandon cleared his throat somewhat nervously, then he began to speak. "Kathryn . . . I never thought I would know love again. And then . . . you came into my life." He had not wanted to sound so trite, but he could not stop himself—his heart was full. As Kathryn returned her attention to him, he sank down on one knee before her, the proffered silver box in one hand. "You are my miracle," he said, his eyes misting, "a miracle I thought I would never again know. I love you with all my heart." He paused, glanced down at the box in his hands, then looked upward into Kathryn's questioning eyes. "And . . . if you would have me . . . I would be most honored if you would consent to be my wife. Kathryn Lissette Morgan . . . will you marry me?"

The crickets chirped, and the wavelets of the Potomac slapped along the riverbank. Somewhere in the distance, a night-bird twittered. Kathryn turned her head and shifted slightly away from Brandon on the park bench. Not far off, the horses whinnied by the waiting carriage. Overhead, the gaslamp flickered nervously.

Brandon's heart fell. This was not at all the response he had so longingly hoped for. He gazed down at the proffered box in his hand, the lid of which he had forgotten, in his nervousness, to open. Tucked inside was a modest emerald gemstone exquisitely framed upon a filigree band of white gold.

Before he could reluctantly place the box back in his coat pocket and apologize for his inappropriate boldness, if not his utter foolishness, Kathryn wheeled about on the bench, her eyes welling deep, her lips quivering.

"Kathryn—what is it?" Brandon breathed. "Have I upset you?" His eyes welled.

"Oh, Brandon! I love you. You are *my* miracle too! Yes, of course, I will marry you!"

Instantly Brandon sat upon the bench next to her, his arms enfolding her, holding her close. "I love you," he whispered.

"I love you, too," she returned as she wept warm tears of heartfelt joy.

Neither could scarcely believe the moment they had just shared. The misplaced theatre tickets were of no longer of any paramount importance.

"Do you want to see the ring?" Brandon asked eagerly.

Kathryn nodded, smiling and wiping the tears from her cheeks.

"Here … here's a handkerchief," Brandon said, his own eyes welling deeper as he handed her his pocket-square.

Dabbing at her eyes and cheeks, Kathryn collected herself, eager to see the ring.

"It's a bit dark out to seek it properly," he said as he opened the box. "It's an emerald. I chose an emerald to match your eyes."

Kathryn's hand trembled as she removed her glove and while he slipped the ring on her finger.

"It's beautiful," she said quietly. Although she could barely make out the emerald-green color in the darkness, the white gold glinted in the moonlight.

"Does it fit well enough?"

Kathryn nodded. "Quite," she said, then her arms flew about Brandon's shoulders, and she kissed him on the cheek.

"Do you still want to see the play?" he asked, being at once practical and yet sentimental. He wanted to punctuate their night with the entertainment they had so looked forward to sharing together.

"Yes, if there is still time."

Brandon did not bother to glimpse at his pocketwatch this time; his spirits were so buoyant, he was absolutely sure there was still time. Telling Kathryn of his need to return to Crawford Hill would have to wait—he did not want to spoil this moment.

They rushed hand in hand back to the waiting carriage, glad for the heat of its foot-warmer, then they proceeded to Morley's Hotel to retrieve the tickets.

For an early-April evening the weather still held the crisp bite of winter, and Kathryn gratefully entered the hotel with Brandon to keep warm. As Brandon hurried up the stairs, Kathryn waited near the front door of the hotel, opposite the reception desk. Adjoining the small lobby, where Kathryn stood waiting, was a pub and reading room crowded with formally attired men apparently assembled after some convention or business meeting. Cigar and pipe smoke choked the air, thick with men's voices and the occasional eruption of bellowing laughter. Tankards of ale were served in proliferation from the bar. Two men, red-faced with drink, emerged from the pub and eyed Kathryn provocatively as they passed by her in order to make some inquiry or other at the front reception desk. Kathryn dropped her eyes and stood bashfully by the door. The two men turned to glance at her and caught her eye as she timidly looked up. Nervously she gazed toward the pub. Just as she had sensed, she was the only female in the establishment. A group of men standing near the entry to the pub noticed Kathryn, each surveying her from head to toe as they spoke quietly among themselves. Increasingly uncomfortable, Kathryn felt her cheeks redden, and she grew anxious for Brandon to return.

Just then the front door opened, jangling a little bell, and Kathryn was inadvertently jostled as three boisterous, inebriated men strode in upon a blast of chill air. Each, in turn, glanced the length of Kathryn with more than mere casual interest or curiosity as they stepped inside the lobby. The third of these dared to wink at her, his eyes roaming her liberally.

Kathryn felt herself blush to her core. Without hesitation she strode to the staircase next to the reception desk and climbed upward in quick steps. Uncomfortable to be alone in the thick of so many unfamiliar men and their intruding glances, she wanted only to be near Brandon, to feel safe and chaperoned at his side. Only when she reached the fourth floor, Brandon's floor, did Kathryn realize two things: it was considered unseemly for an unmarried woman to visit a man alone in his room, and—she did not know Brandon's room number.

Quietly she stole down the carpeted hall and finding a door open just a crack, she gingerly peered inside. To her relief it was Brandon's suite—she saw him standing at a desk across the room. Lightly she tapped upon the door frame.

"Lissy!" Brandon turned, surprised to find her standing in the doorway. He had been engaged in a search through the stacks of books, notes, letters, and various papers that cluttered the small desk looking for the misplaced theater tickets. Not having found them, he was about to start the whole process over again just as Kathryn had arrived. "The tickets weren't on the bureau, and I thought I must have left them on the desk," he informed her.

"Shall I help you look for them?" Kathryn inquired somewhat timidly from the doorway.

Brandon gratefully accepted the suggestion, and Kathryn entered the suite, her sense of propriety prompting her to carefully shut the door behind her to keep out any prying eyes that might pass by along the hall.

The suite, cozy and papered, looked comfortable and clean, though well-worn. To the right gaped a modest hearth, and flanking it, two sets of double-pane windows. A small sofa stood along the wall opposite the hearth, and beside it, a hall tree and umbrella stand. At the far end of the suite's front room, a set of doublewide doors were open to the bedchamber. Before the bedchamber's desk and east-facing windows, Brandon stood reexamining the mass of papers and books for any sign of the lost tickets.

Kathryn approached Brandon. "Which papers should I look through?" she asked as she glanced down at the desktop.

"Try these." Brandon indicated a stack and sighed. "I'm sorry Kathryn. It's my fault if we're late." Brandon frowned, displeased with himself. "The play is sold out. We won't be able to buy replacements." This was *not* how he had wanted to celebrate their engagement. He had wanted the night to be perfect.

"It's all right, really. I don't mind that you forgot the tickets. I understand that you had a busy day," Kathryn said, though she was disappointed for both their sakes.

Not finding the tickets among the papers that Brandon had given to her, Kathryn stopped to look out the window, beyond her own translucent reflection in the panes, to admire the city lights and, above, the star-dappled night sky. Then she set her gaze upon the panes of glass to study Brandon's reflection. How very handsome he was, she mused, and how intelligent, decent, responsible, and kind. How very much she had grown to care for him. She issued a heartfelt sigh and dropped her eyes.

"What is this?" she asked as she happened to glance down at a number of handwritten pages held by a paper weight.

"That is the article I was working on this afternoon," Brandon said absently. "*Damn!* They aren't here either!" Disappointment and exasperation mingled in his tone, and he all but scowled. It wasn't generally like him to go about misplacing things.

Lifting the paperweight and the pages of Brandon's article, Kathryn exclaimed with a laugh, "Brandon, look! They're here! They've been under your article this whole time!"

As she laughed, Brandon had to consent to grin as well. The tickets safe in her hand, Kathryn felt relieved to have discovered them, as Brandon had been growing pressed about the matter for her sake, and it troubled her to see him even the least bit distressed about anything at all.

"Let's see...," Kathryn said, then began to read aloud the printing on the tickets, "*Colleen Bawn,* Ford's theater, eight o'clock ... Thursday—*Thursday!* April *fourth?!* Brandon!" Her eyes wide, she exclaimed, "Why, these tickets were for *last* night! Today is Friday, April fifth!"

"No!" Brandon stopped cold. "No—you're *not* serious!"

Kathryn broke into laughter and held the tickets out to Brandon. "I'm only joshing you!" she giggled, her eyes sparkling mischievously. "You are *so* fun to tease!" she chuckled, pleased with her little jest.

Brandon reached out to take the tickets from Kathryn, but she snatched them away and held them behind her back. "Do you ... want them? ... " Playfully she smiled and batted her eyes.

"Kathryn—come on now, or we *will* be late," Brandon protested.

In mock surrender, Kathryn pouted and held the tickets out for Brandon. But as he went to pull them from her hand, she would not let go.

"Kathryn, please. We're running late," Brandon warned, though not unpleasantly.

Brandon's hands upon hers, her fingers unyielding, Kathryn grew quiet and looked upward into Brandon's serious, warm brown eyes. Her eyes traced his dark waves of hair, his handsome brow, the arc of his cheekbones, and the blush of his lips beneath his handsomely groomed mustache. All at once she ached for him to kiss her, to feel his lips warm and soft upon hers. She longed to feel his arms encircle her, to feel his warmth next to her, engulfing her.

"Kathryn...," Brandon whispered softly. He had stopped the game too and looked with matched earnestness into Kathryn's eyes. "Your hands are cold," he murmured.

Kathryn did not speak but gazed longingly into Brandon's eyes. Then, for the first time in all their acquaintance, his warm, tender lips met hers in an ardent kiss, and she melted to his touch. Gently he held her close, pressing her to him as she tenderly returned his embrace, letting the two theater tickets flutter, forgotten, from her hand. Drawing back ever so slightly, Brandon's eyes caressed Kathryn's sweet upturned face, then met her eyes as if to see into her very soul. He sighed and bent his mouth to hers, letting his lips barely brush against hers. "Oh, Kathryn...," he murmured, his voice barely audible. Tenderly he kissed her again and yet again, Kathryn responding with equal ardency until Brandon gave way to a flurry of kisses upon her lips, brow, cheeks, and chin. His lips brushed against an earlobe, then caressed the warmth of her neck. "Dear Lissy...," he breathed.

At once Kathryn averted her head and rested her cheek upon Brandon's shoulder, her arms fast about him. He placed a tender kiss upon the part in her chestnut locks, his arms secure about her. Looking up at Brandon once again, tears welled deep in Kathryn's eyes.

"Kathryn ... what is it?" Brandon asked with alarm. "Have I done something wrong? Have I been too forward?" He drew back ever so slightly.

Silently she gave her head a little shake and searched his gaze with damp, earnest eyes.

"Lissy, why are you sad?" Brandon asked quietly, his brow duly troubled. "Please, don't be sad. Tell me what is wrong. ... You're sure I haven't done anything?"

Kathryn shook her head as a hot tear spilled from one eye, then the other, each silently coursing down her cheeks.

"Lissy, *please*. ... I can't bear to see you cry."

"Oh, Brandon!" Kathryn abruptly averted her gaze downward.

"Lissy! ..." Brandon murmured, heartfelt concern knitting his brow.

After a moment, she lifted her eyes to meet his, and whispered, "Brandon, I ... I love you so!"

He gathered her to him and held her close. "Dear Kathryn—and I love you. *How* I love you!"

Lifting her chin to meet his, they kissed in earnest, even as Kathryn's tears flowed silently downward.

"Why, Lissy ... you're still weeping." Brandon caressed aside a stray chestnut tendril from her dampened cheek. "You *must* tell me what is troubling you," he prompted gently.

Kathryn hesitated, then said quietly, "I've grown to love you, Brandon, with all my heart ... and you will return home one day to Crawford Hill, perhaps soon, and ... I don't know when I will ever see you again. Perhaps with time and distance you will forget or regret our engagement." Kathryn looked up at him with swimming eyes.

"*Kathryn*," Brandon intoned, embracing her as if to never let her go. "I *love* you, Kathryn. We won't be parted. Please, don't trouble yourself so— not tonight. I nearly told you earlier that I must soon return to Crawford Hill—when we were by the Potomac, and I said that there was something I didn't want to tell you—but I decided to wait. I didn't want to spoil things ... not when I was about to ask you for the honor of your hand in marriage." Brandon drew back and searched her swimming eyes. "How could you think that I might forget or regret our engagement—my love for you and my commitment to you?" he asked softly.

Kathryn could only issue a bewildered shrug, and she fell to covering him in warm, wet, ardent kisses—her fingertips caressing the arc of his cheeks, his brow, his chin, then tracing the warm curve of his throat and tenderly exploring his lips.

Pressing her close, Brandon responded in kind, kissing and caressing her upturned face. "I love you, Kathryn," he murmured.

"I love you, Brandon . . .," she breathed softly, and swooned against him.

Quickly Brandon caught her up in his arms, all the while kissing her, as Kathryn, all but overcome with desire for him, murmured her proclamations of love.

"Kathryn. . .," Brandon whispered as he slowly ceased his stream of kisses. "Kathryn. . .," he repeated, looking tenderly down at her, gathered in his arms. "Please tell me once more . . . please say you will consent to be my wife. . . . Please say yes once more. . . ."

Kathryn's eyes glistened up into his in the low lamplight. "Yes—I will be your wife—with all my heart."

With Kathryn held snug in his arms, Brandon hesitated a moment, then drew back slightly. His eyes searched hers earnestly. "Kathryn . . . Lissy . . . I *want* you so."

Taking his meaning, Kathryn melted in his arms. "Yes," she consented softly. "And I want you. . .," she breathed.

Brandon adjusted the flame of the desk's oil lamp to a low flicker, and Kathryn let him carry her toward the room's stately bed in the dim light of the bedchamber.

Gently, reverently, Brandon reclined Kathryn upon the large four-poster bed, then he carefully lay beside her. He caressed her cheek and her waves of hair. "Are you sure, Lissy?" he asked ever so softly, ever so tenderly.

Kathryn's eyes shone up at his in the flickering lamplight, and she nodded. "Yes, I'm sure," she answered, her voice scarcely audible.

———◇———

Afterward, once still, they quietly lay together for some time. At last Brandon spoke, his voice tentative, "Kathryn, perhaps I was too forward . . . perhaps I shouldn't have."

"Oh, no, Brandon," Kathryn affirmed quietly, "I wanted this. I wanted this so *very* much." She turned and kissed him generously on the lips. Drawing back, she smiled at him in the low light.

At that instant something glinted about his neck, catching her eye.

"What is this?" she asked, fingering the slender strand of silver chain at his open shirt collar. "May I see?" Whereupon she pulled the silver locket out from beneath Brandon's loosened shirt. Cradling the oval locket case in her upturned palm, Kathryn tilted her head in curiosity. "What is it?"

Utterly caught off guard, Brandon knew not what to tell her. His eyes fell from hers to the treasured locket lying in her hand.

"Was it … Allison's?" Kathryn asked, her voice rather more sober now.

"Yes … yes, it was Allison's," Brandon conceded softly.

A brief silence passed between them.

"May I open it?"

Reluctantly Brandon nodded his consent.

Kathryn opened the oval locket, revealing the few tender strands of golden hair tucked inside.

"Allison's?" she asked softly.

"Yes, Allison's," he said quietly, and closing the case, he withdrew the locket from her hand and tucked it beneath his shirt.

Consternation clouded Kathryn's brow as she gazed upon the place where the locket case lay, once again hidden beneath Brandon's shirt.

Turning on the bed to face Kathryn, Brandon took her hand in his and held it at his heart. Then, drawing her hand to his lips, he pressed a warm kiss to her slender fingers and, meeting her eyes, reassured her. "I love you, Kathryn. You must know that."

In response, Kathryn's eyes only searched his in the dim light as doubts plagued her. She knew not what to say. The unanticipated locket had caught her up in unexpected confusion.

Kissing her brow tenderly, Brandon pressed her gently to him, nestling her beside him upon the bed, then sighed. "Lissy, I love you with all my heart. Here—" Brandon rose from the bed and deftly slipped the chain from about his neck. Glinting in the low lamplight, the oval locket dangled upon its chain. "I shall only keep it in the bureau from now on," he said as he placed the locket carefully in the corner of a top drawer.

This gesture, though truly from Brandon's heart, only vaguely comforted Kathryn as the fear loomed that perhaps Brandon was not ready to marry her after all. Slowly Kathryn sat up on the bed, her knees drawn up beneath the coverlets with her arms hugging them to her as if protectively, her countenance distinctly troubled. She had surrendered herself to him willingly, passionately, and unabatedly—but now she felt hollow and uncertain. Kathryn feared that in spite of their proclamations of love, in spite of Brandon's proposal of marriage, and despite their shared intimacy, she would only ever share him with his memory of Allison.

Troubled by her somber expression and discerning her heavy heart, Brandon sat gently beside Kathryn on the bed, then took her hands from about her knees and held them in his. He glanced downward, then met her eyes with a look that sought to speak the utter sincerity of his heart. "Kathryn," he said softly, earnestly, "I love you with all of my heart. I want to share my life with you. I love you more that I can say—you *must* believe that."

Deathly afraid he was about to lose her to doubt, Brandon cast his eyes downward upon her hands held in his—her one hand bearing the emerald-and-gold ring he had just bestowed upon her as a symbol of his love, of his commitment—and he felt a weight steal upon his heart. Then his eyes met hers once more. "I love you, Kathryn. *Please* believe me," he implored, his eyes welling.

Kathryn interrupted him by placing her finger tips gently to his lips. "Ask me again," she whispered, drawing her hand away to let him speak.

Looking puzzled, his eyes searched hers.

"Please, Brandon," she entreated, "please, ask me again."

Taking her meaning, he tenderly pushed back a few stray chestnut strands from her cheek and smiled, though his eyes had welled to nearly spilling. "Lissy, please marry me ... please say you will be my wife," he asked gently.

"I will," she assured him. "I will."

CHAPTER 20

A Wedding

A letter and a parcel arrived at Crawford Hill on Saturday, April twenty-seventh, 1861. Brandon had sent them from Washington, D.C. As Annabelle sat for her afternoon tea in the west sitting room with Sara, she read Brandon's letter silently while Sara embroidered. Only the ticking wall clock punctuated the quiet.

> "*Dearest Annabelle and William,*   *April 20, 1861*
> "*I apologize profusely for not having written to you or the children these past few weeks. Time got away from me, I'm afraid, but not without very good reason. I had thought to telegram, but under the circumstances, a letter seemed best.*
> "*Kathryn Lissette Morgan and I were married at her father's estate on Sunday, April fourteenth.*"

Annabelle stopped short and, eyes wide, reread the latter line of Brandon's letter. "Oh, my *Lord!*" she breathed.

"What is it, Annabelle?" Sara looked up from her embroidery hoop. "Is anything wrong?"

"Brandon and Kathryn ... they've married!" Annabelle uttered, stunned by the suddenness of the unexpected news. For the moment, her expression registered neither joy nor disappointment, merely the shock of the news— nearly two weeks ago, by now—that left her all but nonplussed.

"Married! Have they *really?*" Sara leaned forward with due interest. "What does he write?"

"Wait ... please ... let me read further." Annabelle waved Sara off distractedly. Patiently Sara returned to her needle and thread as, settling back on the settee, Annabelle intently read on.

> *"I hope with all my heart that this comes as happy tidings to all, especially to the children—Barry and Mela. Please, Annabelle, tell them of the good news in a way that they can understand. I regret so much that I cannot yet tell them myself.*
>
> *"Kathryn's son, Nathaniel, is seven, a year older than Mela—and so, she will have a new little brother roughly her age to be her companion. Nathaniel is quite eager to meet his new little sister and his new older brother, Barry.*

Annabelle stopped reading. Her tea, quite forgotten, stood idle and growing cold on the table beside her. Suddenly her thoughts seemed all in a muddle, and she hardly knew quite how to feel about Brandon's revelation. True, she had hoped Brandon and Kathryn might one day marry; she and William had quite encouraged the idea, even recently supporting Brandon wholeheartedly in his intentions toward Kathryn. But Annabelle had assumed that marriage—if at all—would be in a year or two, that Kathryn and the children would be able to become acquainted first, and that there would be a proper wedding that everyone could attend as a family. Desultorily Annabelle's thoughts swirled as she resumed Brandon's letter.

> *"The wedding was small and informal. It was held in the front room of the Tierny estate. Stanley Moore (my old friend from the university in London of whom I wrote to you) and John Morgan (Kathryn's former brother-in-law) were our witnesses. Stanley served as my Best Man. John Morgan happened to be in Washington from New York where he has joined a law partnership. Otherwise, there was not enough time for invitations to be extended to friends or family outside of Washington, D.C. Mr. Tierny, Kathryn's father, gave the bride away. Nathaniel served as the ring bearer, although he seemed rather bored with the entire proceeding. (I do wish Mela could have been our flower girl!)*

"We both deeply regret that we were unable to extend proper invitations, and we both hope you will understand.

"I had intended to return home to Crawford Hill by last week, but once Kathryn and I planned to marry, my schedule was inevitably delayed.

"With war apparently imminent, Kathryn simply would not be parted from me during our engagement. I dare say, I relished the thought of our being apart no more than she. Just last week there were rumors that angry Maryland mobs were on their way to burn the Capitol. As well, there have been rumors of rebel attack, assassination, and abduction attempts. Northern troops and supplies have been sent for, as it is feared the government might otherwise fall!

"Accordingly we decided to marry straightaway, leaving no time for a formal wedding or for sending invitations to any but those nearby in Washington. You both must know that I hope this is not a source of disappointment for you; and of course, it is my main concern that Mela and Barry understand. Truly, under the circumstances it could not be helped. Enclosed is a letter to the children to that end, and inside the parcel that accompanies this letter is a daguerreotype of Kathryn and me on our wedding day for you and the children before we arrive home.

"It does seem that war is close at hand or, indeed, even upon us. Alfred Cooke, at the Charleston Daily Courier, has been excellent about sending news regarding the bombardment of Fort Sumter on April twelfth, and the newspapers here are filled with the stories as well. I do wish I could have been in Charleston during the week of the bombing—on April twelfth, particularly. Apparently, the day after I interviewed President Lincoln—on April sixth—he decided that Major Anderson's garrison should be resupplied at Sumter. I know the Sumter issue has been a torturous one for the president, and I wonder now if it is not one that he regrets. According to the Washington papers, the Confederacy fired upon Fort Sumter for two and one-half early-morning hours before Major Anderson returned fire. It seems the Confederates were greatly relieved when Anderson's troops fired back, as they had felt guilty firing upon a man who would not defend himself.

"Alfred wrote that he was one of the many spectators crowding

Charleston's White Point Gardens and the wharves along the peninsula's tip in order to see the bombardment of Sumter in the harbor. He wrote that the windows and houses in Charleston were shaken by the blasts! After the garrison's barracks on Sumter caught fire, Sumter looked like a volcano erupting and spouting smoke. Alfred further wrote that the consequent explosions of munitions were so strong that they shook the wharves! Can you imagine? The newspapers here are full of accounts of Major Anderson's surrender from Fort Sumter on April fourteenth—incidentally, the very same day Kathryn and I were married! Alfred says that everyone in Charleston celebrated the victory, that the harbor was filled with boats, and that ferrymen were conducting fifty-cent tours past the still-smoldering fort—not to mention a jubilant parade down the city streets by the Charleston Citadel Cadets. How I wish I could have been there!

"I should be home again soon—perhaps a week or so after you receive this letter. Kathryn is looking forward to meeting everyone. Please remember to share the enclosed note with Mela and Barry, and also the daguerreotype portrait of Kathryn and me on our wedding day.

"I have missed each of you so unbearably much these past few weeks, but there has been much to attend to with the wedding, work, and now arrangements for Kathryn and Nathaniel to travel southward with me to Crawford Hill.

"Look after yourselves. You are ever in my thoughts no matter how distracted my hand is from corresponding.

"~With warm affection, Brandon"

Annabelle sighed. She felt a mixture of joy for her newly betrothed brother-in-law and consternation due to having been taken quite suddenly aback by the unexpected news. Carefully she folded the letter and replaced it in its envelope. She would save the note for the children along with the parcel containing the daguerreotype for later.

"What was the wedding like? What does Brandon write?" Sara asked.

"He only wrote that it was a small and informal wedding at the Tierny estate, and he was sorry we could not attend given the shortage of time. Most the rest of his letter was about the bombardment of Fort Sumter.

"Isn't that just like a man?" Sara laughed lightly. "They would rather talk of politics and war than of matters of the heart and weddings!" Smiling, bemused, Sara poked her needle through the cloth stretched across her embroidery hoop and gave a little shake of her head.

"Yes ... it is rather how men are," Annabelle said idly, her voice sounding stunned and far off.

Granted, Annabelle was happy for the news of Brandon's marriage to Kathryn. After all, Brandon clearly cared for Kathryn, and from everything he had conveyed in his letters to Crawford Hill, she was personable, charming, sensible, and enviably well-bred. But most of all, Brandon loved Kathryn, and it was upon this fact that Annabelle, at least momentarily, put aside her lingering misgivings about the suddenness of their betrothal.

The only immediate problem Annabelle saw was how to impart the news of their father's marriage to Mela and Barry. Although Brandon had written previously to tell them of "a very nice and grand lady" he had met in Washington, Brandon's consideration to perhaps one day marry Kathryn had not previously been made known to the children. Now, sipping her tepid tea and contemplating how to approach the children on the matter of their father's seemingly impetuous marriage, she suddenly resented Kathryn for causing this uncomfortable assignment. She issued a slight frown, and draining her cup of tea placed it back upon its saucer. This unexpected news made her momentarily cross, and she sighed with annoyance. Then she inwardly reprimanded herself, recognizing that her brief resentment of Kathryn was really due to her harsh mood as of late toward William. She had been feeling distinctly out of sorts for quite some time, and it wasn't fair to take it out on Kathryn nor on any other difficulties imposed upon her.

Annabelle was still deeply hurt and angered by William's severe punishment of Sabe and his dishonesty about it—waiting until she and the children had gone to church to have Sabe whipped, let alone having the poor young man whipped at all! Though nearly a month had passed since their altercation on the matter, her heart was still plagued by William's falsehood and his harsh sentence upon Sabe. She found it difficult to look William in the eye or speak to him, save for the sparest civility for the children's sakes.

For his part, William was torn with both remorse for his decision about Sabe and his deceit toward Annabelle. He wanted very much to talk with her, to clear the air and apologize, to explain—but Annabelle, feeling betrayed and wounded to the quick, had not the heart to hear him out. She refused his every earnest overture for discussion and amends until he gave up trying.

Annabelle had not intended to be mean-spirited or unfair in not hearing William's words; it was simply that her hurt ran so deep, she feared incurring further hurt by listening to what else he might have to say—perhaps he would reveal other such goings on about which she had not previously been made privy to or consulted about. Even though she sensed a trace illogic about her troubled suppositions and wounded emotions, this realization was not sufficient to lead her to speak to her husband in order to come to an understanding and dissolve the growing rift between them. She could simply manage no more than to carry on as normally as possible for the household's sake, all the while feeling engulfed by a hurt and a distance from William that she had not invited from the start and from which she knew not how to escape. Each night Annabelle would wear her brave front until long after William fell asleep on his side of their shared bed, whereupon Annabelle would silently cry herself to sleep, her tears sinking into her pillow. It seemed to her that her marriage to William was now hanging by a thread, and she knew not what to do to mend things—or even if she should mend things.

And now, as Annabelle sat upon the settee, having drained her cup of lukewarm tea, she realized that despite the joyous news of Brandon's marriage to Kathryn, she felt a compounded hurt because her own marriage had gone abruptly, disconcertingly awry. Annabelle turned her head to look out the window at the fading afternoon sun. Silently she mused that she and William were as distant now as when they were first acquainted at Loxley house years before, when he was a stranger and she had abhorred him for his slaveholding. That was nearly as remote and estranged as she felt from him now, and the feeling tore woefully at her heart.

Idly Annabelle turned her gaze to the empty teacup on its saucer upon the table beside her. Her eyes misted, and she said to Sara, "I think I shall go have a brief lie-down before dinner."

Sara nodded knowingly, and encouraged quietly, "Things will get better, Annabelle."

"Yes ... of course," Annabelle replied, though without heart. She gathered up Brandon's letter, the parcel containing the daguerreotype, and the note to his children, then she went out. Climbing the stairs, Annabelle consoled herself that at least Brandon would be home soon, and although Kathryn's addition to the household was both sudden and unexpected, it would be nice to have yet another new woman friend at Crawford Hill.

After dinner, Annabelle called Mela and Barry into the west sitting room and closed the doors to the adjoining rooms and hallway. Mela and Barry sat in each of the two wingback chairs that stood flanking the hutch and facing the settee. Having closed the doors, Annabelle took her place on the settee—Brandon's letter to the children in her hand.

"Are we in trouble?" Mela whispered to her brother.

Annabelle smiled to herself, pretending not to hear.

Barry only shrugged, and admonished Mela to be silent with a stern, "Shhh!"

Collecting her thoughts a moment, Annabelle addressed the children. "Your father has written to your Uncle William and me that he is sorry for not writing to us all sooner. But now he has sent a very special letter for you as well as a picture." She paused a moment and mulled over what she had rehearsed all afternoon to say to Amelia and Barry. Then she carefully continued, "Do you both remember the lady your father has written to us of before? The woman he met in Washington, D.C.—Kathryn Lissette Morgan?"

Mela nodded.

"Yes," Barry said.

"Yes," Mela dutifully echoed.

"Well—" Annabelle hesitated again. Her carefully rehearsed words seemed so inadequate now. She glanced from Barry to Mela and back again as each child looked expectantly up at her. "Your father has sent some *very* good news," Annabelle said, contriving a smile. Then she brightened—putting as joyous a face on the disclosure as possible would help ameliorate any abrupt shock or upset the message might cause. She cleared her throat and broadened her smile. "He and Kathryn Morgan have wed," she pronounced. Annabelle beamed encouragingly, looking anxiously from one young attentive face to the other.

"Father's ... *married*? ... When?!" Barry asked incredulously, not quite absorbing his aunt's words. To Barry's sensibilities the news might as well have been unexpected cannon fire from Fort Sumter!

"The wedding was two weeks ago," Annabelle informed quietly—no longer smiling.

All of a sudden Mela looked as though she might cry. "Isn't ... isn't Father coming home?" Her eyes grew round and swimming.

"Of course, he is coming home." Annabelle sprang up from the settee and knelt before Mela who sat all but swallowed up in the great wingback chair. "Of course, he is coming home again, Mela," she comforted.

"Why ... why didn't Father want us at the wedding?" Mela's damp, flooded eyes blinked up at her Aunt.

"*Oh*, Mela," Annabelle intoned, then hugged her young niece and kissed her cheek. "Your father wanted us all to be there very much, but there wasn't enough time. He misses us all terribly—most of all, he misses you and Barry."

"But ... why didn't he want us there?" Mela persisted, hot tears beginning to brew. At not quite six, her upset over the matter outweighed her comprehension of her Aunt's words.

"It couldn't be helped, Mela!" Barry snapped in annoyance, his sharp tone betraying his own disappointment and resentful bewilderment.

"Mela, dear, your father is very sorry about it," Annabelle gently explained, "but it couldn't be helped." With her thumb, she stroked away the large globe of a tear that had rolled down Mela's cheek. "Some things simply do not go the way we would like them to," she soothed.

Mela calmed somewhat and swallowed her tears.

"Here," Annabelle said as she rose and held out the letter in her hand to Barry, "this is specially written from your father. Why don't you read it for Mela and me?"

Barry took the letter, unfolded it, and read aloud, halting only now and again at places where his father's handwriting was unclear.

"Dear Barry and Mela,

"I am sorry to have been away from you both for so much longer than expected, and I am anxious to return home to you very soon. I am sorry I am not home with you now to tell you in person of the news I have asked your Aunt Annabelle to share with you.

"Kathryn Lissette Morgan has consented to be my wife, and we were wed on April fourteenth. I wish so very much that you could have met Kathryn and her son Nathaniel before our marriage and that you could have been here for our wedding—everything has happened so quickly these past few weeks that it could not be helped. I am very sorry you could not have been here. I have missed you both tremendously, and I missed you even more on that day. Kathryn and Nathaniel are both quite eager to meet you.

"Barry, Aunt Annabelle wrote to me your lessons at school continue to go well, and I am pleased and proud of you as always.

"Mela, you are, as always, my little dear one.

"I have sent with this letter a daguerreotype of Kathryn and me on our wedding day for you both to see before you meet her.

"I will close now and post this letter. I promise that I will be home again very soon.

"Be good. All my love,

"Father"

"Where is it?" Barry asked—regarding the daguerreotype—as he carefully refolded his father's letter.

Sitting on the settee, Annabelle opened the parcel Brandon had sent and extracted the daguerreotype wrapped in paper and bound with string. "Here it is," she said as she pulled out a slender hinged Molded Union case of silver with flowers embossed in relief upon its cover. "Come and sit by me," Annabelle invited. With Mela seated at her right and Barry at her left, she showed them each the silver case. "Isn't it beautiful?" Annabelle exclaimed, running her fingers over the exquisitely embossed blossoms.

Mela nodded as Barry looked on silently.

Annabelle opened the case to find a single sheet of paper written upon in Brandon's hand from which she read aloud.

"You must wait to see what Nathaniel looks like, as he could not manage to stand still long enough to pose for a portrait. He is, nonetheless, most eager to meet his new brother and sister."

"Is Barry and me going to be his brother and sister?" Mela tilted her head quizzically up at her Aunt.

" 'Are Barry and I,' " Annabelle corrected. "And, yes, Nathaniel will be your stepbrother, and Kathryn will be your new mother," Annabelle explained.

Mela looked thoughtful a moment. "But ... our mother is in heaven—"

"She's not going to be our *real* mother," Barry clarified somewhat impatiently. "She's just our stepmother."

"You mean like Ester?" Mela asked.

Annabelle laughed heartily at this. "Yes, dear, somewhat like Ester."

Even Barry had to consent to a grin upon Mela's prattling deduction.

"Well," Annabelle lilted, "shall we see the picture, then?"

Both children nodded in unison.

Annabelle drew away the sheet of paper written in Brandon's hand to reveal the wedding portrait. Because the daguerreotype photograph was only visible from certain angles, Annabelle tilted the case so that she, and then Barry and Mela, could each discern the image.

"Oh, she's *lovely!*" Annabelle pronounced in a whisper.

"She *is* beautiful, isn't she?" Barry noted quietly, his voice tinged with a trace of awe.

"Is she a *princess?*" Mela piped.

"Good heavens—I dare say, I think she *must* be," Annabelle said. Finding herself warming to the reality of Brandon's unexpected betrothal, she added, "I believe we shall all like her very much."

By midmorning of the following day, Kathryn's daguerreotype had been viewed by the entire household at Crawford Hill. Annabelle had it passed around the table before breakfast with the admonition that no one spill preserves on it. Afterward, Annabelle took it around for all the domestic servants to see as well. "Lawdy," Ester had exclaimed, "she look jus' like a young queen!" "My—*my!*" had been all Jacob could utter before issuing a loud complimentary whistle. "She's jus' *lovely!*" Cotta had declared, her jaw dropping in awe. All were duly impressed with the image of Brandon's bride and with how handsome and dapper Brandon looked posed at her side. The daguerreotype threw the household into a flurry of excitement and preparation for Brandon's return as well as Kathryn's imminent arrival at Crawford Hill.

Despite the gaiety and fluster of activity about the house, Barry found himself bearing mixed feelings in anticipation of Kathryn's arrival. Sitting at his desk, Barry looked out from his upstairs window as the late-afternoon sun stretched shadows across the side yard, gilding the carpet of new spring grass first golden then tawny in hue. Desultorily working at his school studies, he could not concentrate, having slept roughly the night before. Tom Davenport lay upon his bed in their shared room reading an adventure book loaned to him from William's personal library. Marking his page with a finger, Tom half-closed the book and looked across at Barry. "She looks nice enough from the picture," Tom said of Kathryn, in an effort to assuage Barry's apprehensiveness. "I'm sure it will all work out fine," Tom encouraged, then turned back to his book.

"I suppose it will," Barry answered idly. At age twelve it would be difficult to suddenly have a new mother. The news had come so unexpectedly, he hardly knew *how* to feel about the matter. He remembered his own mother so well—her long, cascading ringlets of golden hair; the stories she read to him when he was small; her pretty, musical laugh; how she had comforted him when he fell and skinned a knee or grew afraid of the dark; her sweet, angelic face; and her magical sky-blue eyes. He recalled her strolling hand in hand with his father, stealing a kiss before sitting at breakfast, and the two of them playing childhood games with him. Lastly, Barry reflected upon the voyage the three of them had taken as a family to come to America and Crawford Hill. How very strange it would be now, Barry mused, to have a new mother, to see someone else at his father's side. How very hard to imagine it was. However, as Tom had said, Kathryn did seem nice enough from the daguerreotype.

Rust and pinks tinged the clouds' edges beyond the panes of glass. Barry sighed heavily and closed his school books. All at once he missed his father with a profound ache. At least Father would return home soon—any day now. But Barry's heart fell again when he realized his father would likely be just as distant upon his return as he was now in miles—for Kathryn, his new wife, would by rights receive nearly all his undivided time and attention. A knot formed tight in Barry's throat, and the yard and trees beyond the window dissolved in a watery blur.

Tom paused from his reading again, sensing that his young friend remained troubled. At age fifteen, Tom felt the role of big brother to his new companion. Now, playing older brother, Tom sought to distract Barry from his unease. "Hey, let's go out riding, Barry. What do you say? It's still early—we have at least an hour before dark, before dinnertime."

Barry pondered the exuberance in Tom's voice and decided that he needed the diversion to take his mind off his father's long absence and the impending major change in his life. "Let's go!" he said, breaking into a smile.

"Race you to the stable!" Tom challenged, whereupon the two boys dashed quickly down the hall.

"No running on the stairs!" Annabelle shouted after them as they passed her in the hallway. "No running in the *house!*"

"Yes, Aunt Annabelle! Sorry Mrs. Crawford!" they acknowledged, slowing their gait.

Continuing down the hall, Annabelle heard the younger children at play in Mela's room. Standing by the open door, she stopped to listen a moment.

"I do!" Mela trilled.

"And does you, Cooper, take Mela fo' yer 'awful wedded wife 'til death o' distance does you part?" Cinda chirped.

"I *do!*" shouted the rambunctious little Cooper.

"I now 'nounce you huzbin an' wife," Cinda pronounced—whereupon Mela shrieked, and Ashley, Cinda, Quash, and Cooper broke into gales of laughter.

Annabelle smiled to herself, bemused that Cooper must have planted a sloppy kiss on Mela's cheek, much to her little-girl horror. And of course, Annabelle mused, horrifying Mela would have been Cooper's only motive, as there is no other way on God's green earth whereby he would have been compelled to actually *kiss* a girl! Still smiling, Annabelle continued on her errand, the children's laughter receding down the hall.

Leaving the house by the back door, Annabelle walked down the footpath—bordered with Barry's and Quash's round white-painted stones— toward Brandon's studio. In one hand, she clasped the daguerreotype case and, in the other, the studio's front-door key. She had imagined that Brandon might like to keep the wedding daguerreotype on his writing desk and would delight in finding it placed there upon his return home.

Fitting the key in the lock, Annabelle entered the studio. She stood a moment near the open door and looked about at the several framed charcoal sketches of her sister, Allison, that adorned the walls. Her eyes misted as she recalled how, just five years earlier, Brandon had drunk himself half-mad in his abject grief and destroyed nearly every last image that his loving, artistic hand had created of Allison. Only a few renderings had survived—drawings that had somehow escaped his intoxicated anguish—and these, he had reverently matted, framed, and hung to grace his studio walls.

In the far corner of the studio, Annabelle's eyes rested on the oil painting of Allison posed at Loxley House in her green taffeta gown. This canvas was a replacement of the first that Brandon had so disconsolately destroyed on that troubled night five years before—and this rendition was, without a doubt, more radiant than the first. Quite some time had elapsed between the destruction of the first painting and the creation of this one—a beautiful life-size image lovingly set upon a special carved-wood studio easel that Brandon had purchased in Charleston. For Brandon, painting the second canvas had been a labor of both love and healing.

Annabelle crossed the floor of the studio to gaze more closely upon the oil painting of her sister, the early-evening light sifting down from the studio's northern skylights casting it in soft hues of rose. For a moment Allison's eyes seemed to twinkle, and she appeared to smile at her sister in the gathering twilight.

"Allison...," Annabelle whispered, "I still miss you so." She touched a tender finger to her sister's image, and her eyes welled deep, a single tear spilling from one eye ... then the other. Collecting herself, Annabelle dashed the tears from her cheeks, then she turned and crossed the studio in the half-light toward Brandon's desk to complete her errand.

There, upon Brandon's desk, lay his familiar papers, books, pencils, and pens, including a favorite fountain pen, just as he had left them. Annabelle pressed her hand affectionately to the sheaf of writing paper placed upon the desk before Brandon's empty chair. "We have all missed you, as well, dear Brandon," Annabelle said quietly. Casting a brief sigh, Annabelle stood the open daguerreotype with care upon Brandon's desk, its silver case glinting in the settling darkness.

Annabelle went out and locked the studio door behind her. Any day now, Brandon and Kathryn would arrive. What changes there were yet to be at Crawford Hill.

"Miss Annabelle! Miss Annabelle!" Cotta, the skirts of her plain cotton frock gathered in her hands, ran pell-mell down the sloping lawn toward the studio. "Miss Annabelle!"

"Cotta, what is it? My word!" Annabelle turned from the studio door, slipping its key in her pocket.

"Miss Annabelle!" Cotta exclaimed, panting for breath where she stood opposite Annabelle on the stone-bordered footpath. "It's Sabe!" Cotta's eyes flashed joyously. "He done aks'd me t' marry him!" she beamed, adding, "Dat is if Massa Willem say it be aw'right wit' him, an', o'course, wit' *you*, Miss Annabelle!"

* * *

After dinner, Annabelle broached the matter of Cotta's marriage to Sabe with William. She found him alone in the east sitting room pouring his customary evening brandy from the familiar decanter on the mantelpiece. He took his evening brandy alone now—now that Brandon was away in Washington and Annabelle, apparently still upset with him, no longer shared their usual evening time together. Surprised to see Annabelle enter the room, William hoped that perhaps she had come to talk with him, to make amends together—but declining even to sit, she came quickly to the point of Sabe's marriage to Cotta. William agreed wholeheartedly, adding, "We will plan the wedding for any day they choose."

"There is another matter," Annabelle began. "Yesterday, before tea, Sara confided in me that she misses her servant—I think she is called Hetty. At the very least, Sara is concerned about Hetty and wants to know where she has gone, if she is all right. Hetty had fled with the other slaves from the Davenport place the night of the rebellion. Sara hopes that Hetty could be found and might be persuaded to return to her and live here with us at Crawford Hill. It has been only two months since the night of the rebellion; perhaps Hetty is still in the area, somewhere near All Saints Parish."

"Or perhaps she has gone north," William surmised.

"You won't even try to find her, then?" Annabelle's presumptive tone held a hard, nearly accusatory edge.

"Annabelle, that's not what I meant." William sounded wounded. "I will do all I can to locate Hetty," he assured.

"Then, I'll tell Sara." She hesitated only a moment before turning on her heel and striding out.

William could not see the tears that welled, so familiarly as of late, in his wife's gentle pale-blue eyes. Nor did she hear his troubled sigh or see the frown that crossed his brow and drooped the corners of his mouth downward. How William detested the remoteness between them! And how he lamented his poor judgment of several weeks before—both in his disregarding little Cooper's tummy upset and, most of all, in deciding to have Sabe put to the whip. Troubled to the very core of his soul over the whole of it, William took a sip of brandy, scarcely tasting it, and sat alone in the darkened, empty room. Somehow, he and Annabelle *must* reconcile—but as yet, he knew not how.

A telegram arrived the next day from Washington, D.C. To everyone's disappointment, Brandon and Kathryn would be delayed at least one week, perhaps two. Not only had little Nathaniel taken ill with a slight cold due to the inclement April weather, but the streets of Washington had become, by turns, muddy rivers of swirling eddies, then muck and mire hard-pressed to dry out in the brief sun. Early to mid-May would, no doubt, prove more suitable for travel, and Nathaniel—the Tierny's personal physician inferred—would be well over his fever in a week or so. Furthermore, this would, by happenstance, afford Kathryn more time to prepare and pack for the journey south.

Somewhat daunted by the prospect of moving to the South—a place Kathryn had never visited even once—she fretted and fussed over just what clothes to pack, what would be suitable for the weather as well as appropriate for the new social culture she was about to encounter. But what piqued her misgivings the most was the prospect of living among slaves. Although concerned about her son's fever and the inclement weather, Kathryn felt some degree of relief upon the dispatch of the telegram regarding their delay to All Saints Parish—at least the inevitable would be postponed by some days until she could rally herself to embrace the uncertain future that loomed ahead. All that gave her comfort was knowing that she would have Brandon at her side, that they were forevermore to be husband and wife.

Upon hearing the news of the telegram—that Brandon, Kathryn Lissette, and Nathaniel Stewart were to be delayed—Cotta and Sabe decided to postpone their wedding until Brandon's return home. Cotta, being especially fond of Brandon, wanted him to be present on that most special day. Becoming husband and wife would simply have to wait until the Stewarts' arrival at Crawford Hill.

CHAPTER 21

The Wisteria

As soon as little Nathaniel's fever abated; his reddened, chafed nose ceased to be a nuisance; and he felt like playing again—and as soon as Washington's mid-May weather cooperated—Brandon booked three southbound train accommodations. After traveling from Washington, D.C. to Charleston's North Eastern Railroad Depot, Brandon, Kathryn, and Nathaniel spent three days visiting the city of Charleston, taking a suite at the elegant Charleston Hotel. This hotel was undeniably considered to be the most fashionable accommodation in all the city, and Mr. Tierny had insisted upon footing the bill as a portion of his wedding present—he was resolute that they have the very best the city had to offer. These three days in the city of Charleston were to serve as Brandon and Kathryn's honeymoon— political and secessionist times precluded an exclusive, intimate honeymoon; and given the climate of impending war, a brief stay in Charleston simply had to suffice for the occasion. Nonetheless, they took in all that the city had to offer. All the while, Nathaniel seldom complained but looked in awe at the plethora of new sights and sounds around him.

Kathryn was instantly charmed by Charleston—its fresh sea breezes; the scenic and charmingly named White Point Gardens park with its promenade along the city's peninsula tip; the regal grandeur of the distinctive Southern architecture, which figured most notably among the many fine mansions that overlooked the harbor; and nearby, stately homes that bordered the city's small pleasure lake, understatedly dubbed "The Pond." And all around, fresh bursts of springtime blossoms of every hue brightened each nook and corner of the city with gaiety and seasonal fragrance. All of Charleston's architectural and landscaping aesthetics—replete with verandahs, front-porch rockers, stately white columns, wooden shutters, gabled roofs, wrought-iron fences with elegant gates, spreading shade trees draped in Spanish moss, prim side yards, and lush oleanders—seemed to Kathryn to resonate deep within her very soul. Having never traveled to the South before, she was—to her complete and utter surprise—increasingly loath to leave Charleston. What a charming contrast the city was to Washington, D.C.!

Throughout the Stewart's short stay in Charleston, the weather was, in a word, perfect. The chill of winter had long since fled, and summer's oppressive humidity had not yet descended. Overhead, magical billows of clouds glided silently in a sea of brilliant blue as gentle breezes tousled the harbor waters into ruffles of white and as seagulls glided and perched upon the promenade's railing.

Only the shouts of a barker—walking along the promenade near the Cooper River wharves and touting sailing tours past the bombardment-ruined Fort Sumter—interrupted the pleasant springtime ambiance of the city and reminded Brandon and Kathryn of the looming reality beyond their newly wedded bliss.

Finally, on the evening of the Stewart's third day in Charleston, it came time for Brandon, Kathryn, and Nathaniel to depart for Crawford Hill— and Kathryn was, by far, the most reluctant to leave. She would not only miss the delightful time she had enjoyed in Charleston, but she still secreted misgivings about arriving at Crawford Hill and meeting everyone there for the first time—let alone coming to live on a slaveholding plantation. The thought of meeting Brandon's children, Mela and Barry, and of being introduced to Annabelle—Allison's own sister—put a tumult of butterflies into her stomach. How would she be received, she wondered, as the new Mrs. Stewart—as Brandon's new wife and the new mother (albeit, stepmother) to his children? Nervously her thoughts fluttered about the play, *Colleen Bawn*, that she and Brandon had finally seen in Washington—when the newly wed husband of Colleen saw that she would not be accepted into his family, he had her killed! Decidedly, it was better not to dwell on such ponderings for any length, and so Kathryn bravely endeavored to swallow her misapprehensions, even as her trunks and cases were boarded onto a northbound steamship called *Wisteria*. Just as accommodations in the elegant Charleston Hotel had been arranged by Mr. Tierny for his daughter, grandson, and his new son-in-law, so too, he had generously booked their northbound passage on the steamship *Wisteria*. Sailing would certainly prove more comfortable and accommodating for traveling from Charleston to All Saints Parish than horse-and-carriage.

The *Wisteria* was an elegant, but older, steamship—a wooden-hulled vessel, coal fueled, and driven by a combination of two great paddlewheels flanking her hull. Because the *Wisteria* regularly navigated inland, upriver into shallow waters, as well as along South Carolina's coast, the steamship could not be fitted with a modern screw propeller; screws were apt to entangle brackish growth and run the ship aground in rivers' silt beds. Although not able to travel at as many knots as her cousins—steamers outfitted with both propellers and paddlewheels—the ship was nonetheless capable and considered soundly seaworthy. At over one hundred thirty feet in length, the *Wisteria* was able to accommodate roughly seven hundred fifty passengers and crewmembers plus two thousand tons of coal. Above deck, sails and masts stood tall alongside two towering smokestacks. Masts, spars, and sails were to be used only should the ship's engines break down or in the event of irreparable damage to the paddlewheels sustained in stormy seas.

Boasting various amenities, in addition to her quaint-but-sturdy reliability, the *Wisteria* was equipped with cozy cabins as well as large staterooms that included the *Wine and Spirits Bar* lounge; three dining saloons serving French cuisine and fine wines for dinner, continental fare for breakfast, and light midday meals of sandwiches with tea; and a handsome promenade deck for passengers to walk along outdoors and breathe in the fresh salt-sea air. Oil lamps and candles illuminated the inhabited bowels of the ship, brightening otherwise gloomy berths and staterooms. Steam heat, channeled to every room, provided comfort against the chill of cold harbor waters and icy seas.

With great coal furnaces heating boilers unavoidably positioned near wooden planks, as well as reliance upon candles and oil lamps for light, the risk of fire or explosion on a steamer such as the *Wisteria* was always a possibility. Despite this, the *Wisteria* had survived nearly twenty years thus far without incident, and so her passengers invariably felt safe within her cramped wooden confines, assuming the probability of disaster to be next to nil.

Putting out to sea from Charleston's harbor in the wee hours of the morning, the *Wisteria's* journey northward to Georgetown typically took ten to twelve hours. Given this grueling schedule, most travelers slept aboard the steamer the night before departure, waking after already seabound. This was the sensible course of plan that Brandon and Kathryn had decided upon as well; and Nathaniel, for his part, was exuberantly thrilled to sleep aboard a ship for the first time ever. If the sunrise and bustle aboard the ship did not wake its passengers, then the rough seas usually did. Sailing as early as seven o'clock in the morning, the *Wisteria*, piloted by Captain Hanford, would typically arrive in Georgetown by early evening.

The Stewarts occupied a modest family stateroom below deck. Upon struggling to fit their luggage into the cabin, Brandon lost his usual good humor, and grumbled, "It would be *far* easier to pass an *expecting elephant* through the eye of a needle!" At this, Nathaniel emitted a burst of laughter, whereupon Kathryn and Brandon could not help but good-naturedly join in. Dark wood paneling all about the stateroom lent the accommodation a more cramped air than its actual dimensions warranted. Even the beds, narrow and thin of mattress—railed on one side and situated against the wall on the opposite side to prevent tumbling out during the ship's sway— seemed far too short for all but Nathaniel. A single porthole, granting a view of the harbor and sea beyond, provided the only relief for the feeling of claustrophobia inherent to such quarters. A small writing table, two chairs, and a narrow sofa also occupied the small room. Brandon groused that he would rather have done without the furnishings for the want of more space.

After a dinner of fresh meat and fowl, sauces and sautés, steamed rice, and freshly baked breads in one of the three dining saloons—a feast sumptuous enough to quell Brandon's complaints about their stateroom— Brandon, Kathryn, and Nathaniel strolled for a short time on the ship's promenade deck, then returned to their cabin to turn in early for the night.

------⋄------

Brandon rose before dawn and moved quietly about their cramped berth until his stirrings roused Nathaniel. Rumpled hair combed, dressed, and faces washed, in hushed whispers, Brandon and Nathaniel decided to let Kathryn sleep as they tiptoed out, quietly closing the stateroom door behind them.

As Brandon and Nathaniel climbed the stairs to the lower deck, the *Wisteria* had just crossed the sandbar of Charleston harbor and was heading out to sea. Standing together at the starboard railing of the ship's bow, Nathaniel's hand tucked in Brandon's, they looked eastward across the slate-blue seas tinged with copper glints as the morning sun peeked over the horizon. A fresh breeze of salt air whipped gently about their shirtsleeves and trousers, and ruffled their hair. Slowly the gray sky blushed with the radiance of swelling sunlight. A seagull glided before the bow, landed on the banister's top railing ever so briefly, then flapped easily and soared off toward land.

Together, the steady rhythm of the steamer's engines, cascading water streaming from her dipping paddlewheels, the light slapping of waves against the hull, sharp cries of gulls in the distance, fresh breezes of sea air, and the emerging golden rays of morning sunlight filled Brandon with a sense of complete and utter wellbeing. It was one of those rare moments when all the senses breathed in a harmony of nature and one's place in it—a moment that felt transcendently tranquil. For Brandon, this sense was heightened further by two things—he was headed for home, and Kathryn was accompanying him. Nothing could have improved the moment more but to have had her next to him as he stood at the railing with Nathaniel beside him, each looking eastward at the warming rays of crimson light flecking the ocean's undulating surface.

For his part, Nathaniel stood rapt at the vastness of the ocean that lay ahead of the ship's pushing prow, his hands clasped about the lower deck's banister. At once he imagined he felt quite small and yet quite singularly significant standing at the ship's bow, taking in the enormity of the ocean and the sky that stretched, as if infinitely, ahead. His young eyes scanned the arc of the horizon, and he squinted ever so briefly at the melon-like sun, now whole and as though floating upon the horizon's edge. Overhead, a single star glistened in the fading blush of dawn. Nathaniel's young mind, unable to translate the profundity of his impressions and feelings into articulate thoughts, turned his musings to more tangible and practical matters. Standing at the railing, at Brandon's side, his eyes fixed upon the sea, he hesitated a moment before speaking.

"Father? ..." he asked.

Upon hearing this, Brandon's heart swelled, for it was the first time Nathaniel had called him "Father." Turning his eyes from the fading star nestled between hues of rose and blue, Brandon tousled the boy's sandy hair and smiled, giving Nathaniel his full attention.

"Are you hungry?" Nathaniel's hazel eyes looking up with anticipation.

"I dare say, I am. Let's go find out what the captain is serving, shall we?"

Nathaniel nodded, and putting his hand in Brandon's, the two set off across the deck to inquire about breakfast, then they stopped at the aft railing of the steamer to watch the city of Charleston as it receded from view.

Presently, the gentle rocking of the steamer upon the open sea roused Kathryn from her sleep. She woke to find Brandon and Nathaniel long since risen and out from their shared stateroom. Quickly she set about her morning toilet, dressing in a new spring frock that Brandon had purchased for her in Charleston that was, as little Nathaniel had observed, "the color of cantaloupe." Nimbly her fingers platted, coiled, and pinned her long chestnut tresses in a stylish arrangement with wisps of curls framing her face. Seeing that it was already eight o'clock, she set off to find Brandon and Nathaniel above deck.

An hour later, the steamer was well put out to sea as Brandon, Kathryn, and Nathaniel took a simple breakfast of fresh oranges, buttered muffins, coffee, and jam, along with a number of the other passengers in one of the three dining saloons. As Nathaniel had finished only half his plate, Brandon confessed to Kathryn that he had let Nathaniel eat an orange and two muffins earlier "as the poor boy had been famished." Relieved that Nathaniel's spare appetite was not due to illness, Kathryn did not insist that he clean his plate as usual. While Brandon and Kathryn finished their breakfast at leisure—chatting animatedly, observing various details of the dining saloon, and surveying the other passengers assembled there—Nathaniel grew, at turns, bored, restless, and fidgety. Presently, Kathryn felt a tug at her sleeve.

"Can I go play with the other children?" Nathaniel asked in a whisper.

" 'May I?' " Kathryn corrected. "And, yes, you may."

Upon that, Nathaniel scampered off to embark on a game of follow-the-leader with a number of other children upon the ship's deck.

After breakfast, and after briefly acquainting themselves with some of the other passengers, Brandon and Kathryn decided upon a stroll about the steamer's deck, coming to a quiet spot along the portside railing. Side by side, they stood in quiet conversation together, leaning their elbows on the ship's banister and gazing out upon the distant coast of wooded green beyond the lapping sea.

"It is a splendid day, isn't it?" Brandon remarked.

"Yes, it is," Kathryn agreed, "—lovely!"

The *Wisteria* swayed languidly upon the water in rhythm to the little waves slapping her wooden hull. Great plumes of sooty black smoke spewed from the steamer's funnels, trailing over the ship's ruffled wake as her two immense paddlewheels dunked into and churned the water below. The banister where Brandon and Kathryn stood bobbed and dipped—meeting the distant shore, and then dropping seaward. The midmorning's breeze had warmed somewhat and pleasantly caressed Kathryn's cheek.

"Did you sleep well?" Brandon inquired.

"Yes ... yes, I did," Kathryn reflected, then, stopping short, she looked up at Brandon. "And you, did you sleep well?" she asked with a note of concern.

"Yes, quite comfortably."

"Yet you and Nathaniel were both up and about quite early, it seems," Kathryn noted, her tone and manner holding an edge of solicitation, not unlike that of any bride concerned for the wellbeing of her husband. "You two must have risen before sunup."

"We *men* are heartier souls than you *women!*" Brandon pronounced—his handsome, noble nose poised aloft in an attitude of mock superiority.

"Mr. Stewart! You take that back this *instant!*" Kathryn gave her husband's arm a spirited slap.

"So—it's 'Mr. Stewart' now, is it?" Brandon countered with a wry smile. Absently rubbing his arm where Kathryn's hand had struck with a thwack of greater force than she had intended, he gazed out upon the water, his smile fading, his eyes holding a serious countenance.

Kathryn studied her husband's expression a moment, and her own grew serious. "Brandon ... I'm sorry, I didn't mean—"

"What? Oh … no, Lissy … it isn't you," Brandon assured, though his expression remained reflective.

"What is it, then?" Kathryn placed a hand tenderly upon Brandon's arm and cocked her head to one side, all at once solicitous again.

"Just now, when you called me 'Mr. Stewart,' it reminded me—this morning, while Nathaniel and I stood on the bow watching the sunrise together, he looked up at me and called me 'Father.'" Brandon shifted his gaze from Kathryn to the receding horizon. "… 'Father,'" he repeated, a warm sentimental smile crossing his lips.

Locking her arm about Brandon's, Kathryn clasped his hand in hers with a gentle squeeze. "That is *just* wonderful," she said, silently hoping that Barry and Mela would just as easily accept her as their new mother.

Brandon bent and bestowed a tender kiss on Kathryn's lips, then tucked her hand in both of his.

Together they shared some moments of pleasant silence, hand in hand, standing before the railing as the wind-swept sea slapped the wooden hull and the steam engines chugged and belched. The not-to-distant coastline passed by dipping and bobbing—the steamer's handrail cresting and falling, meeting the horizon of wooded land, then plunging seaward. Now and again, Brandon remarked on some aspect of the land in the distance, pointing over the bobbing-and-dipping banister. Attentively Kathryn's eyes followed his gaze each time, and she remarked appreciatively in kind. All the while, the steady lolling of the steamer side to side and gentle bobbing from bow to stern pleasantly rocked Kathryn beneath the warm late-morning sun.

"That must be the Isle of Palms and Dewees Inlet," Brandon said as he pointed over the dipping portside. "And up ahead is Bull Island, I presume."

"Where?" Kathryn sidled up close to Brandon—at heart, far less concerned with the precise location of Bull Island than as a convenient excuse to stand affectionately near her new husband. "Where? Around that bend?"

"Where the shore curves—there," he pointed.

"Yes, I see," Kathryn answered dully—for just then a lilt of queasiness overcame her that she determined to ignore.

As Brandon lowered his arm, Kathryn's eyes remained fixed on the low curve of land in the distance as it languidly rose and fell above and below the larboard railing.

Instantly Kathryn's color drained as her hands clutched the ship's railing, and she emitted a low groan.

"Kathryn?" Brandon studied her with a measure of concern.

"Oh, my!" she uttered, her eyes wide, complexion white. "Oh! ..." One hand flew to her stomach as the other hovered near her lips. "I think—" She swallowed hard. "I think I'm going to be sick—" Stifling her stomach's sharp impulse to heave, she clasped one hand to her mouth, the other gathering up her skirts as she quickly turned and all but ran, trembling, toward the stern of the ship.

"Kathryn!" Brandon was quick beside her, his arm protectively about her as she trotted toward the rear of the *Wisteria*.

Urgently she waved him off and shook her head. "Leave me," she uttered, stifling another contraction to heave, her hand again clasped fast to her mouth.

Heeding her plea, Brandon reluctantly let her go.

Kathryn fled past the strolling onlooking passengers toward the aft of the ship where she hoped to be out of view. There, she promptly leaned over the railing—and all sense of ladylike propriety was dispensed with, as were the contents of her complaining stomach. All of the morning's delicious muffins, coffee, orange wedges, and jam—now an unidentifiable sludge— merged in the white roiling wake of the steamer. Tremulous, eyes watering, her stomach hollow and achy, Kathryn leaned hard against the railing's banister, her fingers clasped fast about it. Hearing the sounds of a man retching nearby, she realized she was not alone at the steamer's aft suffering the very same affliction—seasickness. Dizzy and nauseous, she dropped her eyes once more to the frothing wake, her hands tight upon the banister for support.

"Kathryn?" Brandon drew close beside her, his arms protectively about her. "Kathryn, come along, now," he coaxed gently.

"Thank God, you're here." Kathryn let him nestle her to him. Resting her cheek against his shoulder, she let her eyes close. "I'm so embarrassed," she bemoaned quietly.

"Shhh ... it's all right," Brandon comforted, escorting Kathryn swiftly along the deck, past several sympathetic onlookers.

"I'm so sorry, Brandon." Kathryn held a hand to her stomach. "I feel so sick—"

Brandon kissed the waves of hair at her temple. "Shhh, now," he soothed. "We'll put you below deck where you can rest and lie down."

Stifling her tears, Kathryn nodded.

"Didn't I tell you that we men are heartier souls than you women?" Brandon jested gently.

In spite of her embarrassment and discomfort, Kathryn could not help but smile at this, and her humor returned somewhat. She did not bother pointing out that there had been a gentleman at the aft railing as sick as she.

Kathryn remained below deck in their stateroom for the remainder of the voyage—a lidded ceramic pot near the small bedstead where she lay, should she again feel ill. Shortly past noon, a lunch of finger sandwiches, fruit, and tea was served in the dining saloons, but Kathryn remained upon her mattress. She felt too motion sick to do much but lie still and wait for the seeming eternity of time to pass before they would all, at long last, arrive in Georgetown. After telling Brandon and Nathaniel to take lunch without her, Kathryn settled back on her pillows with an achy moan.

"A few sips of tea would do you good," Brandon urged Kathryn, by midafternoon. He and Nathaniel had whiled away the time by strolling the decks—Brandon visiting with the other passengers, and Nathaniel playing with their children. Occasionally Brandon would slip below deck, as he did now, to check on Kathryn and sit with her some moments before she would shoo him off to "enjoy the beautiful day." Now Kathryn finally did sit up upon her bed and, with Brandon's prompting, sip from the teacup he held for her, grateful for the warm, soothing liquid to quench her tongue and calm her stomach.

"I'm sorry you are so ill." Brandon frowned as Kathryn handed the teacup back to him to replace in its saucer. "I had absolutely no idea that sailing would have affected you so, or I would have troubled William for us to travel up from Charleston by carriage—by land." He sighed heavily, displeased with the outcome of their choice to sail by steamer as Mr. Tierny had planned as a wedding gift.

Kathryn reclined on her pillow. "But ... I didn't suppose that I would become seasick," she said, her voice weak and unsteady.

"Yet you said you had never been seasick before." Brandon reminded, his brow knit with puzzlement.

"I didn't know there was a difference between the *Wisteria* and rowboats on our pond or small sail boats on a lake. I thought it was all the same." She admitted her naiveté with a due measure of chagrin.

"Oh, Lissy! ..." Brandon sympathized, though not without a degree of humor at her plight. "Rowboats on ponds and sailboats on small lakes are altogether different from sailing in ships or steamers on the ocean—being out to sea. You've never been out to sea before? At all? Ever?"

Her hands folded upon her stomach, Kathryn shook her head upon her pillow and looked apologetically up at Brandon seated on the edge of her bed. Her cheeks colored, and she suddenly felt quite foolish. "I'm sorry, Brandon," she uttered, and her eyes teared.

Brandon broke into a kindhearted grin and shook his head. "Poor Lissy." He leaned over and kissed her forehead. Drawing out his pocket watch, he noted, "It's three o'clock now. We should reach Georgetown by five or six o'clock. It won't be much longer."

Kathryn nodded, letting her eyes close, and in a moment she drifted off to sleep.

Brandon sat with her a while, her hand held in his as his eyes studied her sleeping countenance with love and concern. Gently he leaned forward and tenderly kissed her temple whereupon she murmured quietly in response, then he let go of her hand. "Poor Lissy," he thought. Rising, Brandon yawned broadly and went out.

Above deck Brandon sought out Nathaniel among the other children and passengers who had not yet succumbed to seasickness. Perhaps he and Nathaniel should also have a lie down before the *Wisteria* docked in Georgetown; they had, after all, arisen quite early that morning. Catching a wink or two of sleep would do them good.

An abrupt tempest sent the *Wisteria* wildly pitching side to side just as she approached the inlet to Winyah Bay, near Georgetown. *BOOM!* The sudden tumult and resounding claps of thunder roused the steamer's passengers from their activities and naps in short order. Another riveting explosion—*BOOM!*—echoed like canon volleys splitting the sky as large wet drops spattered onto the steamer's deck, then drenched downward in a windblown torrent. *BOOM!* Another resounding volley thundered overhead.

In the gloom of their stateroom, Brandon bolted awake from his short nap to see Nathaniel sitting up on his bed, his eyes wide with alarm. Kathryn, nearly as frightened as Nathaniel, listened intently as rain pelted the decks overhead, her watchful eyes fixed upon the dark ceiling above.

Glancing briefly at Brandon as he struggled to light an oil lamp with a stubborn match, she returned her gaze to the rocking ceiling above, her hands pressed to her stomach. "Where are we, Brandon? What is happening?" she asked, unable, even for Nathaniel's sake, to keep the edge of concern from her voice.

"It seems we've hit a squall." He pulled his pocketwatch out and, steadying himself against the pitch of the ship, read its face in the flickering glow of the swaying oil lamp that hung overhead. It was precisely five o'clock. They must, by now, be near Winyah Bay, he surmised, then snapped the metal watchcase shut. "I'll go up and inquire as to where we are and how much longer we are to be at sea."

Kathryn nodded anxiously as Brandon opened their stateroom door. "Be careful," she entreated, then sank back down upon her thin bed, holding its side rails as if for dear life against the ship's wildly undulating pitches. "Nathaniel, come here," she urged, and extended an arm out as Nathaniel joined her upon her bed—each grateful for one another to share the cacophony of booming thunder and pelting rain, the violent pitching and creaking of the *Wisteria* upon the wind-tossed sea, and the eerily flickering lamplight. Holding Nathaniel close and praying not to be sick to her stomach once more, Kathryn silently vowed never to sail again anywhere—*ever!*

Up top, upon the steamer's deck, Brandon, dressed in only his shirtsleeves and cotton trousers, braved the warm squall winds and stinging rain that drove as nails from the thick charcoal clouds roiling overhead in the evening sky. Above, the blanket of dark, tumultuous clouds seemed to issue from the *Wisteria*'s sooty smoke that belched forth in great black billows from her two immense funnels.

Relaying his message through crew members, Captain Hanford informed his passengers that they would be delayed and put farther out to sea in order to try to steer clear of the storm—the waves were far too rough to navigate the harbor and proceed up the Waccamaw River. Captain Hanford hoped for no more than an hour or two delay. Upon hearing this, Brandon's heart fell as he thought of poor Kathryn.

Nonetheless, Brandon had wanted to assess the storm himself, and having ventured above deck, he squinted against the winds and rain to see the coast and Winyah Bay just beyond the railing of the *Wisteria's* stern, in the near distance. What a frustration to be so close yet have to put farther out to sea! Looking upward, rain wetting his shirt in warm sopping drops, the skies overhead loomed dark as far off as the eye could see. The only glimmer of sunlight that was evident was to the north, beyond the horizon.

Without warning the *Wisteria* rolled violently, and Brandon held fast to the ship's railing for support. A great wave lashed across the bow of the steamer, and Brandon descended once again to his cabin below.

———◇———

Fireflies flitted in the dark, damp night-air as a sea-weary Kathryn and a slightly queasy Nathaniel at last descended from the *Wisteria* onto a Georgetown wharf. Brandon, admittedly queasy as well, soon followed behind, after first seeing to the matter of their collective trunks and luggage. Thankfully, the rain had let up. Overhead, stars and a round moon shone brightly in a black cloud-mottled sky.

Sensibly Brandon had predetermined that they should spend the night at a Georgetown hotel before continuing on to Crawford Hill. Given the storm and rough seas as well as the late hour—a half past nine—he was doubly glad for having preplanned a night's stay.

"What about our luggage, my things?" Kathryn turned in a sudden panic once they were upon the dock.

"It has all been taken care of, Lissy," Brandon said, then explained, "William wired that it would be easier to transport everything on a flat boat to his wharf at Crawford Hill on the Waccamaw. Jacob will see that everything reaches the Big House safely. William has arranged everything.

We have only to look for Jacob to take us to Crawford Hill in the morning. We will meet him down by the *Wisteria's* wharf so that he can arrange for the transport of our things. For now, I have brought only what we need for tonight."

"I … I don't understand. William has a wharf? A wharf like this one?"

Brandon nodded. "He has several wharves, Lissy."

"Like a city? Like Georgetown?"

"Quite. The wharves are necessary for postharvest rice transport upon flat boats. Actually, much travel between plantations is by boat upon the Waccamaw." He paused reflectively, then noted, "William has nearly one thousand slaves, while Georgetown's population numbers roughly one-thousand five hundred. And, although not entirely contiguous, his holdings comprise twenty-five thousand acres."

"I didn't realize William's plantation was so large!" Kathryn exclaimed, awestruck. Despite the late hour and a gnawing hunger at the pit of her hollow stomach, she was duly impressed—but then, her expression changed.

"What is it, Lissy?" Brandon peered at her in the glow of moonlight and oil lamps with due concern. "Are you feeling ill again?"

Absently Kathryn shook her head, her gaze fixed out upon the inky black waters of the Waccamaw. Then her eyes met his, and she commented uneasily, "I was just thinking of something you had said."

Brandon's eyes prompted her to continue.

"You said much travel from plantation to plantation is by boat, upon the river. … I don't think I will ever set foot upon any boat again as long as I live!" Her tone was serious and measured, her eyes round and earnest in the soft moonlight.

All at once Brandon broke into a grin and good-humored laugh. "Poor Lissy!" he intoned, giving her an affectionate squeeze.

Calling for Nathaniel to stop scampering about the wharf and the disembarking passengers, Brandon suggested they head for their hotel. Hiring a carriage and a driver to load their few pieces of luggage into their transport, they headed to their night's establishment and the promise of warm, soft beds on a nonundulating floor in serene quiet and stillness. After a room service order of hot ginger tea—laced with a spare dash of brandy for all but Nathaniel—the three slept soundly until dawn.

CHAPTER 22

New Arrivals

Across the fields, by word of mouth, plantation to plantation, the message was discreetly spread—the Crawfords were seeking the whereabouts of Hetty Washington, a former house servant on the Davenport plantation. By careful inquiry and a measure of patience, the vast network of slave community associations that threaded the whole of All Saints Parish had finally supplied Jacob with the closely guarded information as to where to find Hetty. At last, after several days, Hetty had finally been discovered; but she was wary that her former mistress sought her only in order to punish her for fleeing and, most of all, for her part in the rebellion.

"How does I know dis ain' no trap jus' t' ketch me?" Hetty looked up at Jacob, her eyes searching his as much with fear as with hope.

"Jus' come wit' me, Hetty," Jacob entreated.

Hetty had tried to flee North with many of the others through the Underground Railroad, but her plan had failed. For weeks now, she and a handful of runaway Davenport slaves, Kitch among them, lived in-hiding deep in the woods that bordered the Waccamaw River, west of All Saints Parish. Hetty would not tell Jacob where she was hiding out, but through messengers, she had agreed to meet Jacob at a prearranged rendezvous point at the edge of the woods, near the vestiges of an old burnt-out chapel beside the main road. Now she stood warily in the shadows of the ruined chapel, amidst the tall spring grass and wildflowers, squinting up at Jacob in the midmorning sun. Uneasily she considered William Crawford's conveyed offer that she reside with her former mistress, Sara Davenport, at his home—at Crawford Hill. Although Hetty and Sara had always been as close as any mistress and house servant could hope to be, Hetty held back uncertainly now, fearful of what change her part in the rebellion might have wrought in Sara's heart. Yet the woods loomed large and foreboding behind her as an abyss of tangled wilderness.

Black as pitch, the thick of the woods were most terrifying at night. Bats swooped erratically through the moss-draped trees as all manner of creatures scurried and crept below. The woods were home to raccoons, possums, foxes, as well as black bears, and the swamps that flanked much of the Waccamaw River's course harbored alligators and venomous water moccasins. Bed was the cold, hard ground shared by creeping spiders, biting ants, and large scuttling cockroaches. Only the magical glow of lightning bugs flitting in the night from early spring to late autumn offered any comfort in the bleak, dark woodlands.

Without sufficient firearms with which to hunt, food consisted mostly of fish; turtles, called 'cooters'; rabbits or possums caught in makeshift traps; as well as wild berries and grasses. Cooking fires, started with flints, served to boil river water for bark tea and for cooking what little meat the renegade slaves were able to come by. Hunger was nearly constant for Hetty and her companions as they lived in hiding in the woods.

"Are you comin' wit' me o' not?" Jacob asked. It was his final plea.

Squinting up at Jacob, Hetty stood poised—unsure of what to do.

Jacob turned to go.

"No! Wait! I's comin' wit' you!" Hetty looked up at Jacob, her eyes shining.

———◇———

"Massa Willem! Miss Annabelle!" Cotta rang the plantation bell that faithfully hung at the west side of the front verandah. "De carriage is comin'! It be Jacob! De carriage is comin'!"

William, Annabelle, and Sara Davenport hurried out of the house and stood on the verandah alongside Cotta as Jacob drove the open carriage up the tree-lined allée and brought it to a halt in the roundabout.

Descending the front steps and squinting in the noonday sun, a hand held to shade her eyes, Sara surveyed the thin, bedraggled slave woman seated beside Jacob in the carriage. "Hetty? ..." Sara inquired tentatively. Surely this gaunt, wasted frame of a woman could not be her personal house servant, Hetty.

"Go on ... it's all right," Jacob coaxed Hetty.

Slowly Hetty descended from the carriage. She stood silently, her large wide-set eyes cast downward. About her head, her kerchief was smudged with dirt. The hem of her dress hung in muddy tatters about her bare, callused feet. The elbows of her sleeves were worn through, and the spare cotton shawl tied about her shoulders was equally threadbare. Although nearly forty, she now looked to be at least ten years older, and her once stout-and-sturdy build was now diminished to a thin, waiflike countenance. Still, her face held its familiar physiognomy of warmth and common-sense practicality about the round, full cheeks; the large doe-like eyes; wide pug nose; and broad, full lips. Her head bowed, Hetty stood silently—her voice, deep and smooth as thick honey, now resided as a knot in the pit of her throat—she scarcely dared breathe! As mistress and servant, Sara and Hetty had grown close through the years under Jack Davenport's cruel domineering; but now Hetty was uncertain of Sara's regard for her. Had Sara truly forgiven her for her part in the rebellion?

"Hetty? ..." Sara repeated as she drew forward, a step closer.

Tremulously Hetty stood but a few feet from her mistress across the short span of gravel roundabout. She remained quietly by the carriage, her kerchiefed head bowed, hardly looking up, scarcely daring to meet her mistress's eyes.

"Hetty! It *is* you! Thank God! *Hetty!*" Sara's voice caught, and she rushed forward with open arms.

At once Hetty's fears were dispelled, and the two women embraced as long-parted sisters at last reunited, weeping and kissing one another on the cheek.

In an instant Hetty sank to her knees and sobbed. "I's so sorry, Miss Sara. I's so terribly sorry!" She wept bitterly, her face cradled in her hands.

Jacob moved forward to aid Hetty, but Sara motioned for him to stand back. Kneeling in her skirts upon the gravel drive, Sara hugged Hetty to her. "It's all right, Hetty," Sara soothed, her eyes filling. "It's all right. *None* of us could take it much longer. Master Jack's gone now—we're all going to be all right."

"I's so sorry," Hetty wept quietly.

Sara held her fast and kissed her tear-streamed cheek. Swallowing hard, Sara tried to no avail to choke back her own tears that flooded hot and silently downward. "God help me, but he brought it upon himself," Sara said. "He brought it upon himself. We're safe now, Hetty. We're safe now!" Sara and Hetty clung tight to one another and wept silently.

William descended the front steps and knelt beside the two women. Placing a hand on each woman's shoulder, he whispered some gentle words, and presently Hetty and Sara rose. Withdrawing his pocket-square, William offered it to Hetty to mop her eyes while Sara dabbed at her own eyes with her lace handkerchief

"Cotta!" William called toward the verandah. "Have Sabe draw a warm bath, then please make some tea and prepare a plate of food—plenty of it!—for Hetty."

"Yessuh," Cotta nodded, then turned upon the verandah to go inside.

"Oh—and, Cotta! Have Ester find some fresh clothes for Hetty."

"Yessuh, Massa Willem!" Cotta disappeared into the house on her errands as Sara and Hetty, each with an arm tucked about the other's waist, walked up the front steps of the Big House.

———◊———

Jacob had been issued a pass by William the morning that he had driven out by carriage to search for Hetty several miles from Crawford Hill. Passes were essential for a slave to carry when visiting other plantations or when traveling on errands of business for one's master. Any slave caught wandering without a pass was regarded as a runaway, and severe punishment inevitably followed.

Customarily, William would write out Jacob's errand upon a paper and sign it, then Jacob would fold the note and carefully slip it in a leather pouch slung about his neck on a lace, wearing it securely tucked beneath his shirt. Jacob had determined long ago that there was simply no way he would *ever* risk losing a pass again—as he once had—not with the patrollers out looking for runaway slaves or those off their plantation grounds without their master's permission.

Slave Patrollers were out on their rounds especially at night, and it was on an evening ten years earlier—when Jacob was twenty-six and out visiting another plantation—that he was caught without a pass. The pass that William had issued was lost through a hole in Jacob's trouser pocket. While returning to Crawford Hill late that evening, Jacob was stopped and questioned by two patrollers. Reaching into his pocket to retrieve his signed pass, Jacob discovered to his horror that it was missing.

Quickly the patrollers threw Jacob to the ground and positioned him over the trunk of a fallen oak tree in a clearing alongside the road. In the light of the full moon, the patrollers laid five lashes of the whip across Jacob's bare back—the only whipping he had received in his life—before one patroller thought better of administering further lashes. Perhaps it had been Jacob's adamant protestations and pleadings that had piqued the patroller's doubts about Jacob being a runaway, or perhaps he reasoned that if Jacob was in fact out with permission and his pass really was lost, then there would be hell to pay with prominent plantation owner William Crawford.

Roughly they escorted Jacob home and apologized profusely to William for the misunderstanding, all the while under William's stern gaze.

Now, on an early predawn morning in mid-May, just one day after Hetty's arrival at Crawford Hill, Jacob again stood in William's study as the latter wrote out and signed a pass for Jacob to carry with him into Georgetown.

"Don't lose the pass!" William admonished in a playful tone.

"No, suh. No, suh!" Jacob grinned, slipping the leather pouch containing the pass beneath his shirt.

William's familiar warning and Jacob's rote reply had become a fond banter between them over the past ten years—it not only solidified the ever-growing bond of affection between them, but it helped to ameliorate their memories of Jacob returning home with his back lacerated by the whip as well as Ester's grave upset over finding her husband so bloodied and wounded.

On this particular morning, Jacob was being dispatched with his signed pass to nearby Georgetown in order to meet Brandon, Kathryn, and Nathaniel, and convey them by vis-à-vis to Crawford Hill.

———⟡———

Georgetown lay around the bend of Winyah Bay, upon the banks of the Waccamaw River. The modest town of one and one-half thousand residents was situated inland, fewer than ten miles northeast of Crawford Hill, and provided the next-closest approximation to urban life in the region aside from Charleston, roughly sixty miles to the south. Special trips and matters of business were usually conducted in the larger city of Charleston, while Georgetown served a mere provisional and practical function in the lives of All Saints Parish landowners.

The town, nestled against a backdrop of thick green woods—cypress, pine, magnolia, and oak—and fronted by the broad, wending Waccamaw was, at least upon initial impressions, quite pretty in its provincial, rustic charms. However, upon closer inspection, the town was largely discovered to consist of weathered residences, decrepit outbuildings, a malodorous turpentine distillery, two noisy lumber mills, a shoe factory, hotels, stables, and various taverns and beer shops. This is not to suggest that Georgetown was without its share of aesthetic attributes—constituted by a number of proper homes and old-wealth mansions boasting regal Southern architecture, as well as two majestic churches—that graced the otherwise wanting urban landscape. But even these glories of architecture held but little relief for the eye and sensibilities; for overall, the town could be described, in fact, as little more than utilitarian, pedestrian, and dull.

While the hotel that Brandon, Kathryn, and Nathaniel had stayed at for the night was clean—and from a distance, possessed gorgeous architectural flares—it's peeling paint, creaking floors, and cracked window-glass spoke of its utilitarian purpose. Nonetheless, the hotel's service was prompt and courteous, and the three had spent a much-needed restful night in its bland, albeit comfortable, accommodations.

Arguably, the true charms of Georgetown had less to do with the town itself and more to do with its lush wooded setting along the banks of the Waccamaw. Yet even its riverfront lacked pristine, unadulterated, natural beauty inasmuch as the river's banks were spoiled by a clamor of wharves where ships and steamers from along the whole of the East Coast would routinely arrive, dock, and depart—loading and unloading rice, lumber, and other goods, as well as visitors from afar. From far-off ports, sailing ships and passenger steamers—such as the *Wisteria*—all found their way to Georgetown's noisy, bustling wharves.

It was here, among the teeming Georgetown wharves, where Jacob was to meet Brandon, Kathryn, and Nathaniel, then escort them by carriage to Crawford Hill. The three stood on a wharf flanked by the *Wisteria* on one side and a cargo steamer on the other. Kathryn and Nathaniel looked about them at their strange new environment—surrounded by the clatter of carts, disembarking passengers, shouts and whistles, and winging insects—while Brandon kept a watchful eye out for Jacob. Before them, the backdrop of forest green, below crisp blue skies, grew illuminated by the rays of the rising sun.

There, at the end of the wharf, Jacob raised an arm and waved broadly. "Massa Stewart!" he called, breaking into a welcoming grin.

"Jacob!" Brandon greeted, then gently nudged Kathryn. "He's here."

Jacob strode down the wharf to gather their luggage, then see to their trunks and carpetbags.

"Jacob, this is Kathryn and … Nathaniel." Brandon had nearly said "her son, Nathaniel" but refrained, remembering how Nathaniel had called him "Father" as they stood on the deck of the *Wisteria*. Although Brandon was not the boy's natural father, he would have to acclimate himself to remembering that he was now, for all intents and purposes, Nathaniel's parent.

"Pleased t' meet you," Jacob greeted as he tipped his cap and gave a little bow before Kathryn.

"Nice to meet you," Kathryn said, suddenly feeling shy and foreign. She gave Nathaniel's shoulder a squeeze, prompting him to remember his manners.

"Nice to meet you," Nathaniel echoed quietly, squinting up in the morning sun at Jacob. He had heard of slaves but had never met one before, and it rather daunted him; indeed, it rather daunted Kathryn as well.

Jacob turned to Nathaniel. "Der be lots o' chil'n yer age t' play wit' at

Crawford Hill," he informed, remembering that Nathaniel was said to be seven years of age. Granted, Tom and Barry, at ages sixteen and thirteen, were too old for Nathaniel; and Ashley and Carolina, at ages nine and eleven, were not only too old for Nathaniel, but they were girls. Jacob hoped that at least Nathaniel and his own son, Quash, at age ten, would have some interests in common. And although they were girls, Cinda and Mela, each at nearly age six, might also offer some companionship to the boy in his new home.

"Y'all wait here, an' I's gonna carry yer luggage to de carriage," Jacob instructed. "Den I's gonna see dat yer other tunks 'n things git loaded on a flatboat headed fo' Crawford Hill."

"I'll help," Brandon offered, and immediately pitched in, leaving Kathryn and Nathaniel standing at the wharf's edge amidst the commotion and bustle of Georgetown's waterfront activity.

After a time, Jacob and Brandon returned. Brandon had paid for a flatboat to transport the trunks and other luggage upriver to Crawford Hill. Next, the two men loaded the remaining lighter luggage into the waiting vis-à-vis. Brandon and Kathryn settled into the back seat of the carriage, Nathaniel seated snuggly between them. Jacob sat on the raised driver bench, gave the reins a gentle slap, and urged the horses forward with a gentle clicking of his tongue.

Brandon suggested that perhaps they might travel southward along the main road a few miles in order to afford a view of the Crawford Hill plantation and its surrounding environs from a low hilltop. A narrow dirt road would direct them to the hilltop lying just south of the spill of the Waccamaw into Winyah Bay. From there, they could cross the river's south bridge and join the main road homeward. Brandon broached the plan tentatively—he supposed that due to her previously feeling ill, Kathryn might prefer to travel directly from Georgetown to Crawford Hill; and for his own part, Brandon was anxious to return home straightaway to see Mela and Barry again. Nonetheless, the locally renowned view from the southern knoll was superb, and the journey would help Kathryn to acclimate to her new home and surroundings—for those reasons he simply could not have avoided mentioning the detour.

Understandably, Nathaniel was as excited at the prospect of yet another adventure as any young boy would be. He looked up at Kathryn with round, anticipating, pleading eyes. "May we, Mother? May we?" he asked, anticipation edging his voice.

To both Nathaniel's and Brandon's surprise, Kathryn—who, although well-rested from the comfortable night's lodging, was still feeling a bit piqued from the ordeal of her unseaworthiness the previous day—accepted the plan in short order.

"That is a *wonderful* idea!" she exclaimed, eagerness brimming in her otherwise pale countenance. Inwardly she concealed the real reason for her marked enthusiasm; increasingly she felt uneasy about meeting the Crawfords, and she was particularly worried about meeting Brandon's children, Mela and Barry—let alone living surrounded by slaves. The short diversion to the hilltop vantage point would delay their arrival at least a little longer, and perhaps by then, the nervous butterflies that swirled in her stomach would be still.

"Is that all right with you, Jacob?" Brandon called to Jacob as he drove the carriage along the Georgetown street—the *Wisteria* and the wharves receding in the distance.

"Dat be fine wit' me. It means m'ybe bein' later gitt'n home dan anticipat'd, but dey shan't worry none," Jacob returned. Then he chuckled, "Although, Massa Willem might think I done los' my pass ag'in!" He laughed heartily at this. Surely an hour or two of sightseeing for Kathryn and Nathaniel's sakes would be well worth the little side trip.

Leaving behind the tree-shaded streets of Georgetown, the carriage wheels creaked pleasantly along the wooded, rain-puddled road leading south. Overhead, the morning's pristine skies promised a beautiful day for traveling. Detouring slightly inland, they entered a low flatland threaded with waterways and marshes where, after a time, they headed southward once again. Along their route, great spans of rice fields flanked the river and hugged the road. Through the sparse rows of trees and beyond the rice fields, Brandon pointed out to Kathryn the many neighboring plantations. First was Rose Hill, with its moss-draped live oaks and a broad green lawn extending down to the river's edge. Here, tame geese strutted as ducks waddled and splashed along the Waccamaw's east bank. Next, they passed by the Alderly, Marietta, Friendfield, and Calais plantations as the carriage rounded the contours of the Waccamaw and Winyah Bay. All the while Kathryn's eyes drank in the strange and foreign surroundings.

As it was now mid-May, the low flatlands flanking the muddied road had all been planted with new rice by the first of the month. Several days previously, the sprout flow had been drained from the fields. Now, while Jacob conveyed Brandon, Kathryn, and Nathaniel southward, they could see regiments of slaves moving in rows across the fields, hoeing the troughs of newly sprouted rice plants,.

"What are they all doing?" Kathryn asked Brandon in a whisper, indicating the distant legions of dark-skinned workers with their heads kerchiefed, cotton shirt-sleeves rolled up, and trouser-legs cuffed high.

"They are preparing the fields for a flooding," Brandon explained. "The new rice plants have just sprouted, and now the fields must be cleared and prepared for what is called the 'long water,' which is to submerge the rice fields to kill insects and grasses that sprout alongside the rice." Then he added, "Water snakes can be an issue—they are *not* killed by submerging the rice fields. The water moccasin, also called the cotton mouth, lives in wetlands such as South Carolina's swamps, marshes, rivers, and streams— all too often in All Saints Parish a rice-field worker loses his life to the venomous bite of the water moccasin or some other poisonous water snake while working in the rice fields."

"I see…," Kathryn said distractedly, looking all the while in awe at the passing landscape so very foreign to her urban Washington, D.C. sensibilities. Suddenly uncertain of her strange new surroundings, she found the lush green setting to be all at once as foreboding as it was enticing. Brandon's mention of water snakes—particularly of insidious water moccasins that inhabited the nearby brackish marshes and flooded rice fields—did not serve to ease Kathryn's misgivings about her new environment.

However, the reference to snakes piqued Nathaniel's interest as he sat in his less-than-optimal vantage point, nestled low in the seat between Brandon and Kathryn. Nearly dozing, this subject had roused his full attention. "Snakes?" he piped with a stifled yawn, and sat up tall, eager to hear more.

After sensibly warning Nathaniel of poisonous snakes in the region that "one has to be very careful of," Brandon proceeded to regale Nathaniel with regional folklore about snakes historically spread among the slave communities. Aside from tales of snake charmers, as one had heard of from faraway lands such as India, there were magical powers that the snakes in lower All Saints Parish exclusively possessed—there were small green snakes that could turn water sweet, garter snakes that could break themselves into pieces and put themselves together again, snakes that could travel by holding their tails in their mouths and roll like hoops, as well as snakes that could eat eggs out of hens' nests and milk cows dry. Nathaniel listened with rapt attention, intrigued and mesmerized by such stories. However, Brandon refrained from telling the tale of the so called "coach-snake" that could kill a victim by coiling its body around a person and whipping him to death with its tail—that would be far too much for Nathaniel's vulnerable young imagination!

Nonetheless, Kathryn admonished Brandon to stop filling Nathaniel's head with such unsettling ideas with a stern, "*Shhh!*"

Casting Kathryn an apologetic glance, Brandon fell silent for a moment—then a mischievous twinkle filled his eyes. "*And*, Nathaniel, there are the snakes that crawl inside people's mouths and turn their tongues into snakes that hiss, 'Shhh!'" he chuckled. Even Jacob laughed aloud at this as he guided the carriage onto a side road. Kathryn, for her part, was not amused—at least not until the contagion of their humor and her son's delight prompted even her to turn up the corners of her mouth in an amused smile.

At last Brandon requested that Jacob turn off from the narrow road and follow a ribbon of carriage tracks along a grassy slope to nearly the top of a windswept knoll. This was Picnic Hill, the same vista—just south of All Saints Parish and the Waccamaw rice plantations—where Allison, Barry, and he had first glimpsed their home eight years earlier. Bringing the carriage to a stop near the crest of the hill, Jacob set the brake as Nathaniel scampered down and set off to explore, much as Barry had once done years earlier. As Brandon helped Kathryn down from the carriage, he called after Nathaniel with a fatherly admonishment, "Don't wander too far. Stay where you can see us."

Brandon and Kathryn walked a short way through the grass and wildflowers to admire the view while Jacob waited by the horses and carriage.

In the distance, the burnt ruins of the Davenport Big House—now little more than a foundation of charred brickwork—and its surrounding grounds stood out among the patchwork of fields and densely wooded land as a black gaping wound. Weeks earlier, word of the Davenport revolt and the Crawford's new boarders, Sara and Tom, had been conveyed by mail to Brandon in Washington.

Now Brandon and Kathryn quickly turned their attention away from the scorched spot of land and, together, viewed brighter aspects of the springtime landscape before them. Overhead, Ester's enormous clusters of "cauliflower clouds" loped slowly across the sky, promising springtime rains before the week was out. A light breeze ruffled Kathryn's skirts and blew in gentle waves against Brandon's shirt.

Kathryn inhaled deeply. "The air is so fresh here!"

"Yes, it is, Lissy," Brandon agreed, happy to be away from the stench of Washington, D.C. "However," he cautioned as he surveyed the vast earthworks of rice banks that stretched along the coast, "you've not been here yet when they drain the rice fields at harvest time. Come autumn you shall wish we *were* in Washington."

Kathryn was not sure whether Brandon was jesting or quite what he meant. "Why do you say that?" she asked with a sidelong tip of her head.

"When the wind wafts up from the east and blows toward the house, it can carry, shall we say, a rather indelicate fragrance—rather like rotting fish ... or raw sewage."

"Oh, Brandon!" Kathryn exclaimed, dismayed and aghast.

"Not to worry, Lissy. The wind rarely shifts *that* direction; and, in any case, the smell is not quite so bad as Washington!" He smiled and winked.

"Brandon! You're incorrigible!" Kathryn scolded, and gave his arm a playful, admonishing slap.

Scanning the horizon, Kathryn's eyes traced the contours of gleaming rivers and wending waterways that all seemed to have as their ultimate home the wide, yawning Winyah Bay. Eastward stretched the seemingly infinite Atlantic. In the foreground lay the gently undulating landscape of rice fields, croplands, salt marshes, and woodlands. Despite the orderly rows of cabins comprising slave neighborhoods, as well as various barns, stables, and other outbuildings—and especially in spite of the neatly manicured yards and gardens that surrounded the elegant Big Houses dotting the landscape—Kathryn found the place to be wild and all but civilized.

"As with many plantation owners' properties," Brandon was saying, "William's holdings are not contiguous. His lands extend on either side of the Waccamaw River and its tributaries, and they include a portion of woodland. What you see before you are the richest rice plantations in all the South, and of these, William's is by far one of the largest."

They stood in silence a moment, taking in the view of rice fields and, inland, lush emerald woods of magnolia, cypress, oak, and pine.

"Regional historians say that the earthworks built here by the slaves rival the architecture of the pyramids in Egypt. Those are the long, broad mounds of earth you see built up to flood and drain the rice fields." Brandon traced the forms with his hand for Kathryn to see. The network of rice banks extended for miles, as far as the eye could discern, standing at least eight feet tall and spanning some several feet across at the breadth of their tops. It was truly an impressive sight.

"These and the pyramids in Egypt were built with slave labor," Kathryn mused solemnly.

"Indeed," Brandon acknowledged. "And it is due to the sheer expertise and labor of the slaves that these are some of the wealthiest lands in all the South. That the rice produced here is called 'Carolina Gold' is not without its implied meaning or its due credit to native African expertise. A majority of the workers hail from African rice plantations—without them and their proficiency in rice planting and harvesting, these lands would never have flourished as they have."

Both silently reflected upon this fact and the simple irony that slaves living in such harsh and meager conditions were responsible for the astounding wealth of so many plantation owners.

"Can we see Crawford Hill from here?" Kathryn raised a hand to shield her eyes from the sun and squinted into the distance.

"Absolutely. We should have Nathaniel come and see."

Kathryn called out to Nathaniel to join them. Hearing his mother's voice, Nathaniel reluctantly let go of the grasshopper he had so carefully stalked and captured, then he ran up to the crest of the knoll where Brandon and his mother stood.

"Would you like to see where your new home is?" Brandon asked his stepson.

The boy nodded. "Yes, Father."

Brandon knelt down and extended his arm toward the horizon. "Now, just look down my arm and ... see where my finger is pointing?"

Nathaniel nodded.

"Do you see that long row of trees there? And the Big House just beyond that with the cluster of trees close about it?"

Nathaniel nodded. "Uh-huh. ..."

"That is Crawford Hill." Standing, he turned to Kathryn and asked, "Did you see?"

"Yes ... yes, I did. It is quite impressive." Kathryn smiled despite the nervous butterflies beginning to dance again in the pit of her stomach.

"Kathryn, are you feeling all right?" Brandon looked at her with a measure of concern, for he found she had placed a hand to her stomach once again.

"Oh ... I'm all right. ... Really, it's nothing." Still, she stared straight ahead as the patch of landscape called Crawford Hill seemed to loom ominously nearer.

Brandon studied her preoccupied countenance a moment, and at once sensing her concerns, he took up her hand in his. "Don't worry, Lissy. They will all adore you."

"Will they like *me*, too?" Nathaniel chirped.

Brandon laughed. "Of course they will like you! They will like you best of all!" He affectionately rumpled the boy's sandy locks.

CHAPTER 23

Homecoming

"Father's home! Father's home!" Mela shouted, jumping up from the front verandah steps. Waiting since breakfast—her anticipation of her father's return prompting her to eat scarcely a morsel—she was the first one to see the familiar carriage turn up the long canopy of live oaks. Instantly she dashed inside the house to alert the household of her father's arrival, and called excitedly for her brother Barry to, "Come quick!" Then, just as urgently, she returned to the verandah. Eagerly she watched as the carriage made its steady approach beneath the long arbor of moss-laden boughs streamed through with ribbons of early-afternoon sun.

"Father! Father!" Mela flew to Brandon.

Jacob had scarcely stopped the horses with a gentle "Whoa!" when Brandon bounded down from the carriage, catching Mela up in his open arms.

"Father! Father!" Mela piped.

"Mela, my little dear one! How *good* it is to see you! I've missed you so!" Brandon gave his daughter a heartfelt squeeze and planted a sound kiss on her rosy cheek. "Here, let me have a look at you," he said, letting her down and setting her feet upon the ground. "Good heavens! Why, I think you've grown at least a foot since I have been away!" Brandon studied her with mock surprise.

"No I haven't!" Mela giggled. "You're only teasing!"

At that moment, Barry emerged from the house and ran down the steps to greet his father.

"Barry!" Brandon's voice caught with emotion as he looked from Mela to Barry—he had been away *far* too long.

Barry embraced his father soundly. "I'm glad you're back home, Father." Brandon squeezed his son's shoulder affectionately. "I've missed you, Barry."

Annabelle appeared on the front steps and strode forward to welcome Brandon. By now the entire household was assembled about the verandah to greet Brandon and meet his new bride plus little Nathaniel.

Jacob, by this time, had helped Kathryn down from the carriage, then hoisted little Nathaniel down. Quietly Kathryn and Nathaniel stood near the carriage. Nathaniel felt shy yet intrigued by all the new faces before him. For her own part, Kathryn felt somewhat timid about meeting Brandon's children for the first time, and she was particularly daunted about encountering Annabelle Crawford—the younger sister of Brandon's first wife, Allison. The butterflies began to stir nervously.

Embracing Brandon snugly, Annabelle greeted him with sisterly affection. "We are *all* so glad to have you home again!"

"It is good to *be* home!" he beamed.

William stepped forward, and in an instant the roundabout became a bustle of introductions, reunions, scurrying children, and busy household staff.

"Sabe and Jacob can help with the luggage," William said. "The trunks arrived at the wharf a short time ago. We expected you earlier ... I trust you had a good trip from Georgetown?"

"It was fine," Brandon assured. "We took the detour to Picnic Hill."

"And here I'd thought Jacob had lost his pass!" William joked.

Jacob, unloading a piece of light luggage from the carriage, only grinned at his master's friendly jest and shook his head.

Next, Brandon introduced William and Annabelle to his new wife, Kathryn Lissette—no longer Morgan, now Stewart—and her son, Nathaniel. William was as jovial and welcoming as ever, and Annabelle was as warm and accepting of Kathryn as the latter could have ever hoped for.

At least upon this initial acquaintance, Kathryn surmised that the Crawfords could not have been more cordial and hospitable toward her— and her butterflies, at least for the moment, began to settle down. William was a true gentleman—affable, kind, respectful—and he possessed a quick wit. Annabelle seemed equally warm, considerate, and personable; and she was quite attractive, in an ordinary, accessible sort of way. Kathryn supposed that if Annabelle possessed any second thoughts about Brandon's choice of a wife, then she left those feelings well concealed, as she had extended a welcoming smile and heartfelt embrace. However, first impressions are just that—first impressions; Kathryn supposed that only time would tell just how welcomed and accepted she would truly be. Upon that thought, the butterflies in Kathryn's stomach began to flutter once more.

In a moment the Crawford Hill children, scampering and chattering, were quickly rounded up and introduced to Kathryn and Nathaniel. Carolina, Ashley, and Cooper—who somehow managed to be on his best behavior—came first, followed by Mela and Barry. The latter two, coached earlier by Annabelle on the proper way to present themselves, put forth their very best manners—Barry cordially extending his hand, and Mela offering a little curtsey and a cluster of daisies she had picked.

Next, the principal household staff was introduced, including Ester with her two little ones, Cinda and Quash, as well as Cotta and Sabe, and the recently arrived Hetty. Thoughtfully, Hetty offered to take the daisies from Kathryn and put them in a vase for her.

Lastly, Sara Davenport and her son, Tom, came forward to be introduced to Brandon, Kathryn, and little Nathaniel.

"I'm very pleased to meet you," Kathryn smiled, offering Sara her hand. Kathryn knew not how she would ever keep everyone's names straight!

Despite having served as hostess for both her father and her former husband in Washington's high society for a number of years, along with the concomitantly acquired skill for instantly learning names and faces, Kathryn now felt all her former poise and confidence vanishing. She suddenly felt overwhelmed. Perhaps it was the heat or her tiredness from the journey or due to not having eaten much since her bouts of seasickness on the *Wisteria* the day before, but now she felt she would forget everyone's names by evening. Already, she had called Jacob "Joshua" and complimented Annabelle on what an adorable boy little Tom was when she had meant to say Cooper. The butterflies in her stomach began to flutter dizzily.

"Why don't you all come in for tea and something to eat," Annabelle invited, "and then you can rest a while. I know it has been a long journey up from Charleston, especially due to last evening's storm."

Brandon gave Kathryn's hand a squeeze, and she nodded. "Thank you, yes. We'd love to," she said.

"Let's all go inside, then" William invited, extending his arm for Brandon and Kathryn to lead the way. He and Annabelle, along with Sara Davenport, would follow.

As they crossed the short gravel span of the roundabout toward the front verandah steps, Jacob turned away to lead the horse and carriage back to the stables. For their part, Cotta, Ester, Hetty, Sabe, and the other domestics were already inside the Big House conveying the luggage upstairs and readying a light meal of iced tea, finger sandwiches, biscuits, and mint juleps. Meanwhile, Carolina and the other children, including Nathaniel, had already dispersed, playing and chattering about the roundabout, verandah, and nearby lawn. Tom and Barry, far too old to frolic with the other children but too young to find much amusement in tea and sandwiches, took off on their own adventure—to explore the nearby fields or perhaps whittle upon a river bank and talk of secession and rumors of war. Brandon and Kathryn, followed by William, Annabelle, and Sara would be left to enter the house and become better acquainted, taking tea and a light meal in the sunlit west sitting room.

Approaching the Big House, Kathryn paused a moment to survey it. "What a *lovely* house you have," she complimented, her eyes taking in the rose-threaded verandah that ran about the periphery of the house, the three stories crowned by gables, the enchanting turret, and the gleaming white wood siding of the Big House. "Just beautiful!" she said, her hand resting on Brandon's arm as they neared the verandah.

"It looks like we'll have more rain before the week is out," William mentioned to Brandon.

"I say, it does," Brandon agreed pleasantly as he and Kathryn reached the front verandah steps.

In an instant Kathryn sank in her skirts, her hand tight upon Brandon's arm for support.

"Kathryn! . . ." Brandon knelt quickly at her side. "What is it, Kathryn?!" he asked with alarm.

Wavering where she knelt, Kathryn leaned against Brandon to steady herself. "I ... I don't know ... everything is spinning!" she uttered, her voice tinged with panic. She closed her eyes, her hand clutching Brandon's arm as if for dear life.

"Shall we send for Dr. Langford?" Annabelle asked worriedly.

Cradling Kathryn where she knelt, Brandon nodded silently, his complexion pale, his eyes wide with concern.

"Yes, send for Dr. Langford!" William instructed.

Annabelle flew into the house and dispatched a servant to summon Dr. Langford "—double quick!"

Sara followed, quick on Annabelle's heels, to fetch the smelling salts, "—just in case they are needed!"

William knelt down beside Kathryn. "Are you able to stand?" he asked gently.

Slowly Kathryn opened her eyes. She gave a slight nod.

"I ... I think I'll be all right now," Kathryn said. With Brandon at her side, his arm fast about her waist, she rose uncertainly, holding the verandah's wooden banister as William stood attentively close by. "I'm so sorry...," she said with feigned casualness as she stood, despite the world shifting crazily about her and the ground swirling and undulating beneath her feet.

"Oh! ... *Brandon!*" she suddenly cried, her knees buckling once more as the ground seemed to slip out from under her. Crumpling in her skirts, she sank down in a half-swoon upon the ground.

"Kathryn! *Kathryn!*" Brandon held her as she leaned upon him.

She placed the back of one limp hand to her forehead. "Everything's ... spinning...," she whispered.

"We had best carry her inside," William instructed, his brow knit with concern, belying the calm of his voice.

His expression grave, Brandon's heart pounded as he swept Kathryn up in his arms and entered the house. William followed close at hand, consoling that the doctor would surely arrive "as soon as he is able" and suggesting that "perhaps some cool tea with honey and biscuits might help."

"I'm ... so sorry ... I'm so ... scared...," Kathryn murmured as Brandon carried her up the stairs to their bedroom. Then, closing her eyes to keep the room from spinning, she let her tears flow hot and silent.

"Your wife will be just fine," Dr. Langford said as he snapped his black medical bag closed.

Kathryn lay atop the bedcovers, against three plump pillows. Tea with honey, finger sandwiches, and a fresh peach had quelled her bout of dizziness even before Dr. Langford had arrived—it had been too late to cancel the doctor's visit once he had already been sent for. Besides, as even Dr. Langford himself pointed out, one couldn't be too careful about such things!

Brandon felt a profound wave of relief upon Dr. Langford's pronouncement of Kathryn's wellbeing.

"She only needed to take some sustenance, to eat a little and rest a while," the doctor explained to Brandon, then gave a comforting wink to Kathryn.

"I feel so utterly foolish, Doctor," Kathryn apologized from her place upon the bed. "I am so sorry to have made you come all this way."

"Nonsense!" Dr. Langford replied. "The important thing is that you rest a while and take regular meals." To Brandon, he added confidentially, "I would like to have a few further words with you before I leave." Turning to go out, he reminded, "Remember, Mrs. Stewart, rest and regular meals."

Kathryn nodded. "Thank you again, Dr. Langford."

As the doctor opened the bedroom door to go out, Brandon followed, telling Kathryn, "I won't be a moment."

Once in the hallway, the bedroom door shut behind them, Dr. Langford took Brandon aside.

"What is it, Doctor?" Brandon asked, half-afraid of what the doctor might say.

"Your wife will be just fine, Mr. Stewart," the doctor began, then explained, "Upon being summoned here, and upon the description of her ailment as relayed to me, I had thought that perhaps she had suffered a seizure or possibly a mild stroke or some similar impairment. I am relieved, as we all may be, that she was only suffering the after-effects of her previous bout of seasickness and, despite a small breakfast very early this morning, lack of proper sustenance." Dr. Langford hesitated, then added, thoughtfully, "There is, however, one other point of some concern."

"What is it?" Brandon asked, his manner grave once more.

"I don't mean to alarm you," Dr. Langford brightened, and clapped a friendly hand on Brandon's shoulder.

"Good Lord!" Brandon breathed, scarcely daring to guess the doctor's news. "Are you ... are you telling me that Kathryn is ... with child?" Brandon's heart pounded anticipation. Kathryn's dizziness, her need for rest, and perhaps even the severity of her seasickness—it all seemed to make sense.

Nonetheless, Dr. Langford shook his head. "No, Mr. Stewart, I'm afraid it is a rather more minor issue than that," he informed. "It is only that your wife mentioned to me her deep concerns about coming to Crawford Hill, to this house, and to the South. When I first examined her, she asked me if a fit of nerves could have caused her collapse. It seems the matter of her arrival here has been of quite some concern to her, it has quite upset her."

Upon this pronouncement, Brandon recollected the conversation he had with Kathryn that very morning as they stood upon Picnic Hill overlooking Winyah Bay, with All Saints Parish to the north as well as Crawford Hill. At the time, he had not thought her concern to be of any considerable importance, simply a mild case of nerves as anyone might have upon coming to a new home. "I knew she had a concern about coming here ... but I don't quite take your meaning...," Brandon said.

"It appears that Kathryn's concerns about coming to live here have been greater than she has let on. I won't say that her nervousness about coming to Crawford Hill—and in particular, meeting your children and Allison's sister, Annabelle—was the sole reason for her episode, but I also would not rule it out as a contributing factor. Overall, I believe her seasickness and consequent lack of sustenance to have produced the effect of her present condition. Regardless, it is well worth being safe and trying as best you can to put her mind at ease about her new surroundings, to help her feel at home here as soon as possible."

Listening intently, Brandon nodded, adding only that he had previously possessed no idea as to the depth of Kathryn's concerns and that, in accordance with Dr. Langford's advice, he would speak with her immediately. "Thank you so much, Dr. Langford, for coming all the way out here on such short notice. How much do I owe you?" Brandon finished, pulling out his pocketbook from his trouser pocket.

Dr. Langford waved him off. "Please, regard it as a courtesy call. I'm just heading north to Bellefield on a call; this was on the way. Besides," he clasped Brandon's shoulder warmly, "consider it my wedding present until I can send something more suitable. I hadn't received word of your marriage while you were away in Washington, D.C. Congratulations!"

With that, Dr. Langford went out, and Brandon returned to the bedroom to find Kathryn as he and the doctor had left her—obediently resting upon her bed of coverlets and plump pillows.

"I rather like Dr. Langford," Kathryn said, when she saw Brandon re-enter the bedroom. "He seems capable enough."

"Quite. One of the best," Brandon agreed, remembering the doctor's attendance at Allison's side the day she died and his regrets that Dr. Langford had not been called upon to deliver Mela—Allison would have never contracted childbed fever had Dr. Langford attended the pregnancy and birth; yet she had received his excellent care and comfort as she had breathed her last. "One of the best," Brandon repeated quietly. Sitting beside Kathryn on the bed, Brandon took up her hand in his and kissed the curve of her fingers. "How are you feeling?"

"Much better, I think ... quite well. ... Brandon, I'm so very sorry."

"Shhh...," he cut her off gently, then laid a finger to her lips.

Obediently Kathryn fell silent.

"Now, what is all this I hear about you being so frightened of coming to live at Crawford Hill and to the South that you mentioned it to Dr. Langford?" Brandon kissed Kathryn's hand again and nestled it in his.

Kathryn lowered her eyes and thought a moment; it was hard to know quite how to begin. She sighed, then admitted, "I've been afraid all along, I suppose ... especially that Barry and Mela would reject me because ... because I am not their mother." She lifted her eyes to meet Brandon's. "I'm not ... Allison—" She broke off, and her eyes welled to spilling. Then, all at once, her words and worries poured forth. "I'm not Allison, and I don't know whether the children can accept me as their new mother. ... I didn't know how Annabelle would receive me, let alone William or *any* of the children. ... I felt so out of place coming to live here, not knowing how I would fit in, not knowing if I would have a place here. ... And to top it all off, I am a Northerner, and the South is so ... so terribly different than what I am used to. It feels as though I have landed in a different country ... and I didn't know how William, in particular, would regard me, and—" Her voice grew thin and tremulous, and she swallowed hard. Kathryn had felt her confident high-society poise begin to vanish the instant she and Nathaniel had departed from Washington, D.C. to head southward. "And now ... now I have caused all this trouble!" she wept. Her composure completely shaken, she let her hot tears flow unchecked. She bent her face in her hands and sobbed quietly, letting Brandon gather her to him and hold her close.

"Oh, Lissy!" Brandon soothed, stroking her hair and rocking her against him. "I had simply no idea you were so very worried about coming here," he said softly as he nestled her against him, her tears liberally dampening the collar of his shirt. "I'm so sorry, Lissy. I didn't realize."

"I suppose you think I am being silly." Kathryn sniffled and looked damp-eyed at Brandon.

"No, I don't. Not at all! ... I only wish I had known how troubled you were about coming here." He hesitated and thought a moment. "How did Barry and Mela greet you when we first arrived? ..."

Kathryn mopped her eyes with her handkerchief and managed a faint smile. "Mela curtsied and introduced herself ... she gave me some daisies she had picked ... and she hugged me and gave me a kiss on the cheek. I had one of the house servants take the daisies ..."

"Hetty," Brandon reminded.

"Yes, Hetty. She took the daisies and put them in water for me. They're in a vase on the bureau," Kathryn said as she waved her tear-dampened handkerchief toward the small vase of flowers.

Brandon smiled, proud of his little girl's thoughtfulness. "And Barry? ..."

"Barry was friendly. ... He welcomed me to Crawford Hill, gave a little bow, shook my hand. He said that he was pleased to meet me."

Brandon grinned, pleased that his son was so gentlemanly and welcoming. "And William and Annabelle?"

Kathryn at last broke into a smile that prompted more tears—this time, happy tears. "They have both been as kind and welcoming of me as I ever could have hoped for. In fact, Annabelle embraced me and told me—" Kathryn stopped and swallowed hard, composing herself lest she break down all together again.

"What did Annabelle tell you?" Brandon urged gently.

Swallowing again, Kathryn continued, her voice thin. "She told me she was happy for our marriage—happy that I had come to live at Crawford Hill." Kathryn mopped at her damp eyes.

At that moment, a light rapping sounded on the bedroom door.

"Come in," Brandon called.

William opened the door and stood just inside. "How is our patient doing?" He beamed encouragingly.

"I'm feeling much better thank you," Kathryn replied, her emerald-green eyes sparkling as prettily as the wedding ring she absently toyed with upon her finger.

"The doctor said it was nothing serious," Brandon explained. "Simply an upset from the voyage and lack of proper meals."

"I see!" William said, adding, "Some women will do *anything* to be carried over the threshold!"

He was joking, of course—and it was a silly jest, but just the thing to ease Kathryn's spirits. She and Brandon laughed heartily along with William. Perhaps Kathryn would feel at home at Crawford Hill after all.

CHAPTER 24

Aftermath

For dinner, Kathryn changed into a spring dress trimmed with ivory lace. This particular evening, in mid-May of 1861, would be her first at Crawford hill. Revived from the earlier snack of tea, sandwiches, and fruit, and after a long late-afternoon nap, the color had returned to her cheeks, and she felt quite herself again. The relative cool of the spring evening nonetheless retained the day's humidity, leaving damp wisps and tendrils of Kathryn's chestnut tresses clinging to her neck, cheeks, and temples despite the numerous pins applied to arrange her thick waves of hair. She brushed aside these renegade strands with her fingers and studied herself a moment in the bureau's looking glass.

"You are simply stunning!" Brandon complimented, then bent and kissed her neck and set about tucking the tails of his white cotton shirt into a fresh change of khaki trousers.

Kathryn smiled. "I am feeling much better now."

"Here, help me with this—" Brandon indicated the limp ends of a brown tie threaded through his collar.

"*Honestly.*" Kathryn feigned complaint. "Why ever do men wear ties if they can't even tie them?" Her fingers worked nimbly to loop the ends.

"We only ask for women's help as an excuse."

"An excuse?" She knotted the tie, pulling on its ends to straighten the bow. "An excuse for *what?*" She patted the finished bow's ends against Brandon's collar.

"An excuse for this!" Brandon swiftly embraced her, his arms fast about her, and bending her back, he planted a warm, encompassing kiss upon her unsuspecting lips.

Kathryn let out a muffled cry and gave his arm a light-hearted slap. "Brandon! ... Behave!" she scolded playfully.

"By all means!" Brandon struck a gentlemanly pose, offering her his arm. "Shall we?"

After glancing in the looking glass to be sure her hair was not too mussed up from her husband's theatrics, Kathryn cast him a wary glance, then she took his arm to go downstairs.

Seated beside Brandon at the dining-room table, Kathryn took in the conversation, chatter, and pleasant bustle of the household, as well as the distinctive aromas and ambiance of Southern plantation dining. The dining table—with a new leaf added and mismatched chairs borrowed from other rooms to accommodate everyone—was occupied all around. A fresh white-linen tablecloth edged with lace had been spread out upon the table with matching napkins at each place setting. Annabelle had instructed the servants to set out the finest plates of white china, polish the best silver, and light fresh tapers in the table's candleholders. She wanted Brandon's return home and Kathryn's welcome to Crawford Hill to be celebrated as specially as could be managed. Low crystal vases held summer bouquets arranged by Cotta's skillful hand and artistic eye. Aromas of smoked meats, corn bread, black-eyed peas, peppered corn, steamed collard greens, and gingered carrots wafted through the dining room as servants stationed nearby fanned the room to cool the air and as the door to the adjoining kitchen swung wide, to and fro, while the bustling kitchen help served the various dishes.

About the extended table sat Sara Davenport and her son, Tom, paired opposite Brandon and Kathryn near the table's head, occupied by William. Beside Kathryn sat Nathaniel and, next to him, Mela and Barry. Facing Nathaniel, Mela, and Barry, sat the Crawford's three children—Carolina, Ashley, and Cooper—the latter of whom was strategically seated nearest to Annabelle, who occupied the far end of the table, where she could keep a watchful eye on him. Usually, William and Annabelle sat catercorner at the table's head, near one another; but Brandon surmised that the new seating arrangement placing them far apart, at opposite ends, was both a formality due to Kathryn's arrival and to practically afford a more convenient seating arrangement for everyone.

After a brief silence of gratitude for what they were about to receive and for the safe return of Brandon to Crawford Hill, William clanked his bread knife against the stem of his wine glass. "Here, here!"

All attention turned to William. "A toast to the happy couple!" William beamed. Glasses of wine were raised (water glasses for the children, of course), and congratulations were voiced all around. Then it was time to enjoy the feast.

Conversation flowed pleasantly as dinner commenced. The dining-room atmosphere was charged with merriment in the spirit of reunion for Brandon's return home from Washington and, notably, in celebration of Brandon and Kathryn's marriage. Not even Annabelle's intermittent stern-but-hushed admonishments to Cooper to stop kicking his heels against the chair rungs dampened the buoyant atmosphere.

After words of welcome to Kathryn were reiterated, William, Annabelle, and Sara Davenport were anxious to hear how she was feeling now. Grateful for their concern, Kathryn assured them that she was just fine and to please not worry.

Nathaniel, for his part, was elated to have so many new playmates about since having lived the entire span of his seven short years all but alone in his grandfather Tierny's huge estate house in Washington, D.C. He now had several children for companionship—Mela, Cooper, and Cinda, each age six; Ashley, age eight; and Quash, age nine. Carolina, Barry, and Tom Davenport were, of course, too old to become new playmates; but Nathaniel was nonetheless fascinated by all the new young faces about him. In spite of his initial shyness, he was eager to get to know each one. What games they could play! He imagined foot races and games such as tag, hide-and-go-seek, blind-man's buff, as well as sailing paper boats on the pond.

"Remember to eat your dinner," Kathryn whispered to Nathaniel, as he had nearly forgotten his plate, letting it grow cold while he intently observed the other children, imagined the fun they could have, and sought to join in their quiet banter. Obediently, albeit slowly, Nathaniel began to eat, not even minding the plethora of vegetables before him—especially the mound of wilted collard leaves. The excitement of his arrival at Crawford Hill outweighed his pickiness.

"Chew with your mouth closed," Kathryn whispered into her son's ear, apologetically interrupting her conversation with Sara Davenport.

"My extended family—the Kohler's—originally settled in Woodbridge, Virginia, near Washington, D.C.," Sara continued. "They have lived in that area for generations now."

"I don't believe I have ever been to Woodbridge," Kathryn replied. "Have you?" she asked Brandon.

"No ... no, I don't believe I have."

"The name is quite charming," Kathryn noted.

"In Washington, did you really see President Lincoln, Mr. Stewart?" Tom Davenport asked.

"Tom, you're interrupting," Sara admonished gently.

"It's all right," Brandon allowed, then continued, "I not only saw Lincoln, but I interviewed him as well."

Tom Davenport was duly impressed, despite his political leanings; and Barry's heart swelled with pride on his father's behalf. His father's articles from the interview with Lincoln had been published in *The Illustrated London News* and read internationally, around the world.

As Brandon recounted details of his interview with Lincoln, Tom Davenport listened with rapt attention. Even if Abraham Lincoln was a "Yank," he *was* the president of the Northern states and, by all accounts, a tall, charismatic, imposing figure of a man. Had Brandon mentioned the unexpected, rather high pitch of the man's voice, it is doubtful that Tom or any of the other's listening would have been any less impressed with Lincoln. Even if one's political views clashed with President Lincoln's, one could not deny that he was a leader and a powerful force to be reckoned with.

Carolina pictured her Uncle Brandon's meeting with Lincoln in her mind's eye. "Uncle Brandon is undoubtedly *far* more handsome than the Northern president, Lincoln," she speculated silently, with a little sigh.

Midway through dinner, conversation around the table evolved from talk of Lincoln to a myriad of other topics. Amidst the various conversations, William and Brandon talked together, catching up on the latest news—in part, about local events in the environs about All Saints Parish that Brandon had missed while away but primarily about Washington, D.C. and the North. That led the conversation between the two men to politics and secession.

"The way I see it—the way the *South* sees it—," William was saying, "America is a voluntary union of states. Therefore, any state has the right to voluntarily secede from the Union at any time. It is the North and Lincoln who are pressing for war. Why, only late last month—April twenty-ninth or thirtieth, I believe—President Davis addressed the Confederate Congress to say that the Confederacy does *not* seek war but seeks the right to go its own way in peace. Not three days afterward, Lincoln called for more than forty-thousand Union volunteers. Given that, it is more than understandable that President Jefferson Davis has officially recognized a state of war between the Confederate States of America and the North."

"War is no longer a prospect. War is upon us," Brandon noted solemnly, then added, "Word has it that Queen Victoria will proclaim neutrality in the American war."

"Well, the South sure as hell won't proclaim neutrality. If the North wants to provoke a war, then the South will give them what they are asking for!" William asserted, punctuating his words with a pound of his fist on the table that caused the silverware to rattle.

Kathryn dropped her eyes and grew quiet.

"William—*please!*" Annabelle admonished, facing her husband across the long table. "Let's not have talk of war at the dinner table!"

Half a moment of awkward silence passed.

"I think I have the right to discuss war or any other subject at my own table, in my own house, if I have a mind to," William declared, his words measured beneath a veneer of patient amiability.

Annabelle fixed William with a hard stare. "War is not a fit subject for the dinner table nor for the children!"

William said nothing, took a sip of wine from his glass, then set the glass down thoughtfully. He had at the ready an arsenal of replies to wage against Annabelle, and she had certainly provoked him. But he knew she was right; he had gotten carried away—and most of all, he had not been sensitive in the least to the presence of Kathryn, who looked helplessly to Brandon, then self-consciously at her plate.

Being from the North was one aspect of assimilating at Crawford Hill that Kathryn had considered earlier, among her host of other concerns about arriving. Her previous unease now returned, compounded by William's talk of Southern retaliation, as she was a Northerner. Her cheeks flushed scarlet. Beneath the table lace, Brandon gave her hand a supportive squeeze.

The dinner table was now deadly quiet. William, feeling somewhat chagrined, cleared his throat and issued a genuine apology—though not directed nearly as much to Annabelle as to the others, especially to Kathryn. "I'm sorry. I was speaking inappropriately." He cast Kathryn a shamefaced glance, and said to Brandon, "Sorry."

"My fault, I'm afraid," Brandon said—as much to Annabelle as to anyone. "I had asked William about the Union-prompted rioting in Saint Louis last month."

The table remained quiet for some time as the meal resumed in uncomfortable silence, not even the children daring to speak among themselves. Only the conspicuous clatter of silverware punctuated the quiet. Then, gradually, Sara Davenport sought to put things right with cheerful conversation about the ducks she saw on the pond that afternoon, the pretty sunset that evening, and how nicely the flowers in the garden out back were blooming in the springtime air. Mending things over and paving rough ways smooth were acquired skills Sara had learned under the violent hand and harsh tongue of Jack Davenport. And now, almost effortlessly, Sara's means of smoothing things over had restored the dining room's atmosphere to its former sociability, nearly reaching its previous lightheartedness by dinner's end. Only Annabelle seemed a bit more reserved and quiet than before, and anyone seated at the table might well have attributed that to little Cooper's intermittent fussing.

After dinner, the dishes were cleared, and a regal two-tiered cake slathered with swirls of white icing was brought out on a silver tray. Decorating the cake were lavish patterns of garlands, flowers, and doves, and an exquisite array of pink peach blossoms adorned the top. Two kitchen servants set the tray upon the center of the table as Cotta and Hetty brought out dessert plates and fresh settings of silverware.

"Isn't it just lovely?" Sara exclaimed.

"It is absolutely *beautiful!*" Kathryn complimented.

"It be a spice cake," Cotta informed in a half-whisper to Brandon, knowing that spice cake was his favorite.

"Brandon and Kathryn—this cake is in honor of your betrothal," Annabelle announced, her pale-blue eyes twinkling above a warm smile.

Kathryn's earlier nervousness about being a Northerner coming to live in a Southern plantation household eased once again upon seeing this grand wedding confection set before her. The cake was a heartfelt gesture on the part of the Crawfords; consequently, Kathryn now truly felt that her marriage to Brandon had been accepted and that her welcome to Crawford Hill was indeed sincere. "Thank you both so very much," she said to both Annabelle and William, her eyes misting. Beneath the table cloth, she gave Brandon's hand a heartfelt squeeze.

The glinting blade of a cake server dipped beneath the thick froth of white icing, making the first cut for the cake to be served as a dark hand set aside a fallen peach blossom.

Upon Kathryn's request to save the clusters of blossoms adorning the cake, Cotta was dispatched with a wire basket containing the collected flowers to the water pump to rinse them. Afterward, they were to be arranged in a in a crystal bowl of water and carried up to Brandon and Kathryn's room.

It was then, while Cotta departed upstairs with the bowl of flowers, that Carolina informed her Uncle Brandon and her new Aunt Kathryn that "Sabe and Cotta are to be married on June first. They were waiting for you to return home, Uncle Brandon."

"Cotta and Sabe are to marry? Why, that's *wonderful* news!" Brandon beamed.

"They ought to have a cake as fine as this one!" Carolina enthused. "May they, Mother?"

Little Ashley nodded her head up and down emphatically, her blond curls bobbing.

"Of course, they may," Annabelle happily agreed.

"Oh, goody! More cake!" Cooper chirped, kicking his heels against his chair rungs.

"Cooper—mouth closed while you chew," Annabelle reprimanded quietly, "and please stop kicking—Cooper!"

"I am planning the grandest wedding for Sabe and Cotta that this plantation has ever seen!" William boasted jovially. "A truly *grand* wedding!"

Contending with Cooper's rambunctiousness at the table's far end, Annabelle nonetheless looked up sharply. "It will take much more than a grand wedding, William," she admonished. Her tone was hard. "It will take more than some *grand* celebration to make up for what was done!" she all but spat.

The table grew quiet.

Sara Davenport flushed scarlet and nervously looked down at her half-finished serving of cake.

The table fell silent.

"Children, you may be excused—go on now. Go outside and play. Mela, Barry—you too." William directed his voice gently toward the children, yet his tone held a stern, no-nonsense edge.

Mela regarded her father quizzically.

"Go on," Brandon prompted.

Leaving her cake half eaten, she clambered down from her chair with a sigh and obediently followed the other children out.

"If you will excuse me—" Sara Davenport rose abruptly and strode from the room—her cheeks red, tears brimming, and her heels sounding a swift staccato on the hardwood floor.

"Ma? . . ." Tom called after her as he got up from the table, then rushed after his mother.

Annabelle dismissed the two young servants who had stood faithfully fanning throughout dinner. Then she sharply addressed William. "You needn't have sent the children away," she said pointedly, her tone more accusatory than constructive.

William sighed. "Apparently I should *not* have done any number of things that I have done!" he said wearily, an edge of anger to his voice.

Annabelle flinched. She took William's meaning as a declaration of regret for ever having married her. Coloring deeply, she rose from her chair. Her hands trembling upon the table's edge, she faced William squarely across the table's length. "Apparently you should *not* have!" she pronounced, determined not to break down altogether, and finished brutally, "Apparently a grand wedding means *nothing!*" With that, Annabelle turned and strode from the room.

Kathryn looked with urgency at Brandon, her eyes wide and round— could they excuse themselves and leave?

Brandon, dumbfounded at the conversation's sudden and unexpected stormy turn, acknowledged Kathryn silently, his eyes and a slight nod conveying to wait but a moment.

"I'm sorry," William apologized, running a weary hand over his face and sighing heavily. The room was now empty but for himself, Brandon, and Kathryn. His eyes red-rimmed, William slowly rose from his chair. "If you will excuse me...," he uttered, and went out.

———◇———

Later, after the children were put to bed, Kathryn pleaded exhaustion from two long and eventful days, and she retired early as well. Annabelle, for her part, had remained confined to her and William's room since dinner, the door latched shut. Sara Davenport also remained alone in her quarters, assuring Tom that she would be all right in a while and telling him to go on to bed. As the hour grew late, the house fell quiet and dark, save for the dim glow of a few oil lamps, and Brandon ventured to seek out William, supposing to find him in the east sitting room sipping his customary evening brandy.

William sat upon the sofa opposite the cold, empty hearth in the looming shadows cast by an oil lamp. An open bottle of brandy on the round side table, William swirled the amber liquid in the bowl of his glass and looked solemnly into the yawning black of the fireplace.

After a while, Brandon entered the room and set down his flickering lamp. Hesitating a moment, he asked, "William—mind if I join you?"

"Not at all ... please." William motioned desultorily, indicating the bottle.

Brandon retrieved an empty glass from the mantelpiece and poured himself a modest drink. Setting the bottle aside, he took his usual wingback chair to the left of the hearth.

Silently William sipped from his glass. "I'm sorry about this evening."

Brandon shrugged dismissively, but he knew not what to say. He was troubled for William, and for Annabelle, but he did not know what had transpired while he was away in Washington that could have caused such disharmony between them.

Brandon took another sip of brandy, and asked, after a time, "Annabelle won't be joining us, then?"

William shook his head with a slight frown. "And Kathryn?" he inquired, brightening slightly.

"She is worn out from the journey, I'm afraid. And she wants to rest, as Dr. Langford advised this morning. She conveys her apologies."

"Of course," William said kindly. He poured another long draught of brandy into his glass, then held the bottle out for Brandon.

Shaking his head, Brandon waved him off, indicating that his glass was still half-full.

For a time, the two sat in silence.

"William . . . would you care to talk about it?" Brandon asked quietly.

Upon this, William's eyes welled, and tilting his head back, he drained the remaining brandy from his glass in two great gulps. Swallowing, he said softly, "I think I'm losing her, Brandon." William's eyes welled deeper, and he clenched the brandy glass.

Rising, Brandon frowned thoughtfully and poured himself more brandy, then he aliquoted a fresh portion into William's glass. He sat solicitously upon the sofa alongside his brother-in-law. "William, you can't be serious," Brandon said, his tone hushed.

William's eyes met Brandon's, the latter seeing the profound heartache in them. "I think I *have* lost her," William pronounced solemnly.

The two men sat in silence for some time. Then, with Brandon's prompting, they talked until well past midnight. William recounted in detail about Sabe being the brother of Juliana, the young slave woman who had been whipped to death by Jack Davenport. "None of us knew when we had purchased Sabe from the Genovese's in northern All Saints Parish that Sabe was Juliana's brother," he explained. "When Sara and Tom came to live here . . . after a short time, Sabe's anger welled." William continued, relaying how Sabe had lashed out at Sara and all but strangled the life out of her. "Jack was dead. He had burnt to death in the rebellion. So, Sabe took his anger out on Sara." William sighed. "It wasn't like Sabe to do such a thing—I see that now—and he was *profoundly* remorseful." William paused and took a long sip of brandy. Next, William told of the day of Sabe's whipping and how Sara had intervened between the splays of the bull whip and Sabe's bloodied back. "I'd had Sabe confined for days and days, and I didn't know what else to do. .... I just didn't know. A slave has not been put to the whip nor withstood corporal punishment on this plantation since my father's death, years ago. I just didn't know what else to do!" William again shook his head sadly, then resumed quietly, "Annabelle arrived home from church early." He continued, telling Brandon the events of that day and, in detail, how Annabelle unexpectedly witnessed the final blows of the whip as well as Sara's desperate intervention to protect Sabe. He ended the account with a heavy sigh and lifted his eyes to meet Brandon's. "She hasn't been the same toward me since, growing more distant with each passing day. I've tried to speak with her, to explain, to somehow make amends—" He broke off and cast his eyes downward, dejectedly gazing into the amber liquid in the bowl of his glass. "I still love her, Brandon. I love her as much as when we first met at Loxley house in England all those years ago, but now ... now it's as if—" He swallowed hard. "It's as if she wants to leave me, to take the children and return to England." He bit his lip hard, but it was no use. The late hour, the brandy, the pent up regret, and the welling heaviness of his heart all these past months culminated and took their collective toll. William set his brandy glass aside, then bent his head into his hands and wept.

Brandon gently clapped a comforting arm about William's shoulders. He had never before known his brother-in-law to display such emotion. "It can't be as bad as all that," he consoled.

In a moment, William regained his composure and mopped his eyes with his pocket-square.

By this point, Brandon's own eyes had welled. "Would you mind if I try and speak with Annabelle?" he offered quietly.

It seemed no harm could be done by Brandon's intervening. And so, William agreed—he felt he had nothing left to lose.

Brandon resolved to speak with Annabelle at the first opportunity. For now, yawning broadly, he went upstairs, reluctantly leaving William alone in the dim lamplight of the east sitting room.

Once upstairs, Brandon looked in on Mela, asleep under a thin layer of coverlets. Bright moonlight streaming past the curtain lace illuminated her innocent face and soft blond curls. Sitting on the edge of the bed, he kissed her forehead and stroked her hair. "Pleasant dreams, little dear one," he whispered.

Down the hall, Brandon next looked in on Barry, who was soundly sleeping on the far bed in the room he shared with Tom. Brandon was glad that Barry finally had a companion near his own age at Crawford Hill to spend time with. Both boys fast asleep, Brandon went out, leaving the door slightly ajar as he had found it.

After washing his face and brushing his teeth, Brandon tiptoed into his bedroom and put on his night clothes. Gently slipping into bed beside Kathryn, Brandon nestled her sleeping form next to him and kissed her hair where her thick chestnut tresses were plaited in a long braid at the nape of her neck.

Quietly Kathryn stirred. "Brandon?" she asked blearily.

"Were you expecting someone else?" he whispered.

Although sleepy, Kathryn gave his arm a light-hearted slap. "You fool," she yawned. Then she grew serious. "Is everything all right?"

Brandon knew she was referring to William and Annabelle, given their earlier altercation.

"It's all right, Lissy. Go to sleep now. We'll talk in the morning," he said softly.

Kathryn let her eyelids drift closed.

His arm resting comfortably about her, Brandon nestled his cheek against his pillow. Sleepily he mused about the children—Barry and Mela, plus the children that he and Kathryn would, undoubtedly, one day have together. Slowly his eyelids drifted closed as soft moonlight, a cool spring breeze, and the sweet scent of peach blossoms lulled him gently to sleep.

CHAPTER 25

Amends

"A Union cannot long endure that differs profoundly over basic moral principles and over which negotiation, diplomacy, compromise, and trust no longer prevail. The inevitable consequence that follows is separation—absolute, irrevocable separation.

"It is precisely such a wrenching separation that presently divides the remaining United States of America from her dissenting sister states—the United Confederacy of America. As in the words of Abraham Lincoln, the Union must remain all one thing or all the other; it cannot endure half slave and half free—the strains of divisiveness are too great otherwise.

"By virtue of his office, President Lincoln's constitutional duty is to preserve, protect, and defend the government of the United States of America; for the Southern states to secede is unconstitutional. Southern states have countered that secession was induced by the government's denial of certain of their constitutional rights, arguing that the doctrine of states' rights versus federal power remained an open issue; and Southern states further demanded that Congress protect slavery throughout the United States. Southern secessionists assert that since colonial America had been justified in severing its ties to England, the South is similarly justified in severing its ties to the North. Contrary to this view, the North rebuts that while slavery was commonplace in colonial times, the founding fathers of the United States of America expressed the desire that slavery eventually die out, that *all* men should be free: 'We hold these truths to be self-evident, that all men are created equal, ...' The South yet maintains that it is their constitutional right to hold slaves—noting the apparent hypocrisy that the founding fathers, Washington and Jefferson among them, were slave owners themselves. Negotiation, diplomacy, compromise, and trust no longer prevail in the face of argument, counterargument, secession, and rumors of war.

"Could cooler heads prevail, the South might have weathered President Lincoln's first year in office while availing itself of American political processes—with as much enthusiasm and determination as it is now mustering for war—in order to stave off an immediate or gradual abolition of slavery as, respectively, Northern abolitionists and Lincoln are proponents of. Together, North and South might have engineered a Federal system of regulations to modulate slavery until a gradual program of dissolution of slaveholding could be carried out while preserving the Southern economy and way of life sans the need for slave labor. After all, the North, the Abolitionists remind us—however stridently—manages well enough *without* the institution of slavery. However, cooler heads have not prevailed over the profound, basic moral principles that divide North and South, and consequently, argument is escalating into war!

"Whether North and South coexist amicably is a question now rendered moot by the firing upon Union-held Fort Sumter in the Charleston, South Carolina harbor by Confederate batteries last April. In point of fact, a key catalyst to war has been the issue of the United States of America's military property in the South, within the boundaries of what are now the seceded states of the Southern Confederacy. As in any divorce, the settling up of property—property being key to power and quality of life—becomes the catalyst to aggression in a process in which peace and amicability are the first casualties.

"Sadly, the first human casualty in this divorce of South from North concerns Union Colonel Elmer Ellsworth, killed this month while removing a secession flag in Federally occupied Alexandria, Virginia. Some say the war has, in effect, begun; but many on both sides—North and South—are convinced the war will be brief, swifter than the process of secession. For Colonel Elmer Ellsworth, the war has been tragically brief. How brief will the war be for others? A review of Northern and Southern capabilities can lend insight.

"In the face of imminent civil war, the North, by all appearances, possesses the upper hand at the outset, by virtue of its sheer force in available manpower and its strategic capabilities in terms of industrialization— attributes that the South surely lacks. When diplomats abroad and the foreign press liken the South to David going up against Goliath, it should give the South pause; however, Southerners scanning these same headlines remind us of the outcome of *that* story.

"Notwithstanding, the facts are plain: the population of the Northern states numbers roughly 22,000,000; the population of the South boasts a mere 9,000,000—of which approximately 3,500,000 are slaves! Furthermore, the South is an agrarian society, not equipped with great centers of manufacture and possessing far less developed rail systems. Three quarters of America's wealth lies in the Northern unification of states, holding more than 80% of bank deposits. Northern manufactured goods are valued at $1,730,000,000 versus $155,000,000 in the Confederacy. And while strong industrially, we are reminded that the North also remains self-sufficient in agriculture, holding 65% of the former Union's farmlands. Northern crops of wheat and corn alone produce a revenue of $845,000,000; that is nearly 3.5 times greater than the Southern economy of cotton that—supplying three quarters of the world's cotton—is worth just $235,000,000.

"Augmenting the North's strengths in terms of her industrial, material, strategic, and manpower forces, is foreign sympathy for the North founded upon an abhorrence of slavery. A Southern adage, 'Spare the whip; spoil the [Negro],' is seen with extreme distaste, at the very least, among foreign heads of state. Aside from Queen Victoria's declared neutrality in America's civil squabbles, foreign aid favoring the Southern Confederacy would seem highly unlikely."

Here, Brandon paused from his writing and reviewed the drying ink on the page. He wondered if perhaps he should draw a more detailed parallel between the Southern Confederacy waging war against the Union and the Patriots of the American Revolutionary War revolting against the British—the meager forces of the Patriots had been greatly outweighed by the British "redcoats" in manpower and equipment; in spite of that, albeit with the foreign assistance of the French on their side, the Patriots had won.

Brandon mused that without substantial foreign assistance, the South would surely lose to the North in the event of a full-scale war. The notion was unsettling. In many respects, the South—at least the region of All Saints Parish and the city of Charleston—had begun to feel like home to Brandon. The mere notion of a civil war between the North and South was unsettling—*whichever* side was to prevail. He leaned back in his desk chair and drummed his pen against his fingers, deep in thought.

A light tapping sounded on the open door of Brandon's studio. Roused from his contemplations, Brandon half expected that it must be Kathryn. But it was still early morning, and he had left Kathryn sound asleep, as she was spent from their long journey the day before.

"Brandon ... may I come in?" a hesitant voice asked from the open doorway.

Turning in his chair, Brandon found Annabelle standing in the sun-streamed entrance of his studio. As she stood in a pale cotton frock, her hair pinned up prettily about her face, the play of light upon the waves and curls casting a halo about her—she looked for a moment like Allison.

"I hope I'm not disturbing you...," Annabelle said as she stepped just inside the studio.

"Not at all—please come in." Brandon rose, setting his pen aside. "Please, sit down." He indicated the empty chair opposite his desk. "You are up early, too, I see."

"I ... I couldn't sleep."

Annabelle approached the desk and the indicated chair but remained standing—her manner quiet and subdued. "I've come to apologize for yesterday evening." She glanced down at the floor, then lifted her eyes to meet Brandon's. "I'm afraid I made quite a scene at dinner's end. It especially must not have been very pleasant for Kathryn on her first night here ... and it wasn't a pleasant homecoming for you—" Annabelle stopped short, her buried tears threatening.

Brandon studied Annabelle's wan, troubled countenance. "It is *you* who I am concerned about," he said, his expression pensive.

Quickly Annabelle looked away, her eyes suddenly welling.

"I spoke with William last night ..." Brandon said, his voice low and gentle, "and ... I know things haven't been well between you both as of late."

Annabelle dropped her eyes, and admitted quietly, "No … no. Things have *not* been well between us for some time." She dashed aside a stray tear.

Brandon rose from his chair. "Annabelle," he began solicitously, "if there is anything—"

"I'm sorry, Brandon. I didn't mean to burden you with all of this. I only meant to apologize for my inappropriate behavior at dinner. I do not mean to trouble you further … and spoil your homecoming … and—" All at once she bent her face in her hands and wept.

Just as quickly Brandon stepped around his desk and drew near her. "Come … let's sit by the window." He led her, a caring arm about her waist, to the window seats below studio's northern skylights.

As they sat together in the window nook, Brandon pulled out a fresh pocket-square from his trouser pocket and offered it to her.

"I'm so sorry," Annabelle wept, her voice thin and tremulous. Sniffling, she applied the pocket-square to her eyes, then the tip of her nose.

Overhead, a flood of soft morning light filtered downward through the boughs of a magnolia. The twittering of songbirds broke the silence, save for Annabelle's sniffles and quiet bouts of weeping as she sought very hard to compose herself.

"Do you want to tell me about it?" Brandon encouraged softly.

Annabelle swallowed hard, mopping her tears, her eyes cast down at the hardwood floor. "I hardly know what to say," she quavered, her voice scarcely audible. With trembling fingers, she dabbed at stray tears, then clutched the pocket-square nervously upon her lap.

"Annabelle, I want to help if I can," Brandon whispered. His arm about her, he gave her shoulders a tender squeeze.

"I'm not sure things *can* be helped." She brushed a tear from her cheek. "William and I have seldom quarreled. But last night was by far our worst row ever. Still … at least we were *speaking*," she finished, an edge of sad sarcasm tingeing her voice. She looked up at Brandon. "I suppose William has told you all about it."

"A great deal, yes. But only from his point of view. I would like to hear your side of things," Brandon prompted.

"I'd never seen a slave whipped before—*ever*. Not in all my years in the South. Can you believe it? I had only ever seen the aftermath of whippings when I used to go with Jacob to the Davenport plantation to tend to slaves whipped or beaten at the hand of Jack Davenport."

"You and Jacob would go to the Davenport plantation to nurse the slaves?" Brandon was taken aback. "Was William aware of this?"

Annabelle shook her head. "No ... actually, I never told William why. What I mean is ... I told William that, on occasion, Jacob would drive me to visit Sara Davenport. I swore Jacob to secrecy." Annabelle hesitated, then confided, "I never told William about one rather more difficult visit ... my last visit to the Davenport place."

"What do you mean?"

"The last time I set foot on Jack Davenport's property was actually the spring—in fact, the very day—when you and Allison had arrived to come and live with us here at Crawford Hill. Jack Davenport found us that day—Jacob and me—tending to a slave woman in her cabin, whip marks crosshatching her back, blood everywhere it seemed. ... Anyway, there was quite a scene." Annabelle paused and toyed nervously with the tear-dampened pocket-square on her lap.

"Go on...," Brandon coaxed gently.

Annabelle reflected carefully, "I remember Jack Davenport aimed his rifle and threatened us. Then, as I would not leave, he swung the butt of the rifle at Jacob, and I intervened—"

"Were you *struck*?" Brandon interrupted, alarm in his voice, his eyes wide.

"No, no ... nor Jacob. But then Davenport hurled the rifle aside and shoved me. I fell, striking my temple against the wall, I believe it was. As Jacob and I left, Jack Davenport fired a shot in the air, then he reloaded and fired again. At first I thought he had shot Jacob, and I was *terrified*—absolutely *terrified*! But Davenport had only fired in the air. When William saw me later that evening—after you and Allison had arrived—I told him that I had injured my head from tripping as Ester and I were preparing your and Allison's room in anticipation of your stay here. I never told William of that visit to the Davenport plantation or of the other such visits. He only ever believed that I was paying the rare social call to see Sara." Annabelle dabbed at her eyes with the pocket-square. "I never went back, afterward."

"And ... you never told William of this ... of *any* of this? ..."

Annabelle shook her head. "Never."

The two sat in silence for some moments—Brandon, deep in thought, reflected on all Annabelle had confided as she mopped at silent tears that had sprung anew beneath damp lashes.

At length, Annabelle sighed, and concluded, "I suppose William and I were each trying to protect the other in some way—for my part, by not telling him the true nature of my visits to the Davenport plantation, which I knew would only cause him worry and which he would certainly have disapproved of, and for William's part, by not telling me that Sabe was to be whipped, because he knew it would upset me and that I would staunchly disapprove."

"Do you plan to tell William now . . . about your visits to the Davenport place?"

"Yes," Annabelle nodded. "Although, I dare say, he will feel as betrayed and lied to about the matter as I have felt over his decision to have Sabe put to the whip. I felt that William was deeply wrong and hypocritical. And . . . I told him . . . in a flash of anger . . . that he was no better than Jack Davenport." Upon this utterance, hot tears flowed down her cheeks as she recollected William's own eyes welling in response to her comparing him to such a sick, vile creature.

Brandon could not begin to imagine how William must have felt by being compared to such a horrid man. "Go on," he prompted quietly.

Dabbing at her tears, Annabelle collected herself and continued, "Since I first met William in England—at home, at Loxley house—I remember he used to say, 'If I could free every slave, I would! All I can do is the very best I am able by my own slaves and by encouraging humane treatment for those slaves belonging to others.'" Annabelle paused and sighed heavily. "After Sabe's whipping, I said terrible things to William, and for days I felt anger—anger over the whipping, over William's not discussing the matter with me, and then lying to me . . . and over his blatant hypocrisy. But I see now . . . he was torn between being raised a Southern slave owner on one hand and yet having a good, caring heart. As he has said, he simply did not know what else to do."

Brandon listened with rapt attention. The growing divide between

North and South had seeped its way into the Crawford Hill plantation household and threatened to divide William and Annabelle.

As Annabelle continued, her voice grew increasingly thick with emotion. "As time passed, I saw, more and more, William's remorse—his profound remorse and hurt. It became evident that he knew he had made a mistake—a grievous, unspeakable error—by having Sabe whipped." Annabelle toyed with the damp pocket-square in her lap, thinking of how to word what she had to say. Her eyes met Brandon's. "I've realized, while I've had time to reflect, that William had not waited until I had left for church the day of Sabe's whipping in order to be deceitful ... but rather, he waited until I had left in order to do what he thought was best at the time. He knew I would never have supported such an act, and ... I know that he deeply regrets it now—that he regrets *both* having Sabe whipped and lying to me."

"I dare say he *does* regret it—quite profoundly," Brandon said softly.

Annabelle cast her eyes downward. "William didn't set out to be deliberately cruel or deceitful—but it simply turned out all wrong. And now it is my stupid pride that has ruined everything between us. I have seen the hurt in his eyes, his profound regret ... and ... yet ... due to my stubborn pride, I've done my level best to thwart all of his efforts to make amends and put things right between us." A great tear spilled down Annabelle's cheek as she spoke. "By the time I did want to go to him and apologize, to explain that I was wrong, it was too late ... he seemed to shut me out, and now ... *now?*" Annabelle gazed disconsolately out the window at the distant rice fields beyond.

Brandon's heart ached for her. "And now ... what, Annabelle?" Brandon prodded gently, his arm consolingly about her, his hand kneading her gently heaving shoulder to calm her.

"And now," she quavered, "... now he regrets that he ever married me, and ... and I dare say, I believe he wants to leave me!"

With that, Annabelle fell against Brandon weeping as though her heart would break, his damp pocket-square clutched in her hands upon her lap.

"Now, now, Annabelle," Brandon soothed, gently rocking her to him, "William wants no such thing. Far from it."

"Are ... are you sure?" Annabelle sniffled as she worked to stem her tears and sit up once again.

"Quite sure. William told me last night that he thought he had lost you ... that *you* were planning to leave *him*. He has the notion that you want to leave and take the children to England, to Loxley House."

Annabelle sat up attentively and stifled her tears. She looked at Brandon as if scarcely daring to believe him. "He told you *that*? ..." She sniffled, her swimming eyes searching Brandon's.

"Annabelle, I have known William for quite some years now—"

Annabelle nodded.

"And ... I have never known William to so utterly break down and weep ... not even when baby Charleston passed away. He mourned then, but—" Brandon stopped and searched for the right words. "He *does* love you, Annabelle, and this is *killing* him—it is ripping him apart." Brandon looked down at the floor. He knew not what more he could say; his heart felt the weight of both Annabelle's and William's sorrow.

Annabelle gave Brandon's shoulders a gentle squeeze. "Thank you, Brandon," she said, a glimmer of a smile upon her lips. She gave him a peck on the cheek, then she rose and went out of the studio, into the sunlight— toward the Big House.

———◇———

William sat pouring over his accounts in his upstairs study, although his mind was hardly focused on the columns of credits and debits upon the ledger pages. Heavy hearted, unable to concentrate, his mind flitted disconsolately over the events of the past few months—in particular, the previous evening. What could he possibly do to put things right—especially as Annabelle had increasingly shut him out? And, he reasoned, even if Brandon *would* talk to Annabelle, what could he possibly say to help right things between them? He concluded that Annabelle had simply experienced a change of heart, that was all; she could no longer bring herself to love him, and all that they had shared and built together—*their* union—was unraveling before his very eyes. It was as if the ever-widening gulf between them was becoming as irreparable as that between the North and South.

Unable to concentrate, William closed the ledger before him and ran a weary hand over his brow. Sadness and an inexplicable, sudden anger seized him. Rising from his desk, he picked up the ledger and hurled it across the room—it splayed open, struck the wall, and slid to the floor in a flutter of pages. Grabbing his pen, he paced to the window and stood rigidly, both hands gripping the pen behind his back as if to break it. As he stared, clench-jawed, out upon the rice fields beyond, he heard a quiet knocking at the door.

"Come in," he answered somewhat gruffly. He remained tense, his hands clasped behind his back as he looked out past the leaded panes.

The door opened, and someone entered, but he heard no further sound or any indication of who had come to call. Perhaps it was one of the children.

"Yes? . . ." William turned abruptly.

Instantly his manner changed, and it seemed a thousand emotions swirled within him.

Annabelle stood just inside, having quietly closed the door behind her.

Why had she come to his study, he wondered. Was she about to announce her plans to leave him and Crawford Hill—to return to England with the children? His heart could not bear it. Slowly his eyes welled deep.

"Annabelle. . .," he uttered.

She wanted to speak, to apologize, to make amends, but she scarcely knew how to begin. For a moment, she only looked downward, toying nervously with her hands, missing the tears that welled deep in William's eyes.

"William . . . I . . . I don't know what to say . . . how to begin," she said quietly, her eyes downcast. Then, looking up, she met his gaze from across the room.

William did not speak, but his heart swelled as he noted a change in Annabelle's manner and about her countenance that gave him a glimmer of hope. "You don't have to say anything," William said gently as a great tear coursed its way down his cheek.

"William . . . I am *so* sorry!" Annabelle rushed forward into William's heartfelt embrace. "I am *so* very sorry!" she wept, her arms fast about him.

"I am sorry, too," he whispered, kissing the tears from Annabelle's cheeks and letting his own tears fall in a flood of reconciliation.

CHAPTER 26

A Welcoming, a Farewell

Kathryn awoke late the morning after her arrival at Crawford Hill as cooing songbirds outside the window glass eased her from her dreams. Upon on bathing, dressing, and finishing a late breakfast, Kathryn accompanied Brandon on a brief tour of the house, yard, and nearby grounds of the sprawling plantation. It was a beautiful, sunny spring Saturday in May—a perfect day for Kathryn to become acquainted with her new surroundings.

Annabelle and William did not accompany Brandon and Kathryn; having reconciled over the matter of Sabe's whipping, and Annabelle having at last confessed trips of mercy to the Davenport plantation to assist whipped and beaten slaves, they wanted to spend some time alone together to reconnect. William suggested an early-afternoon walk along the allée—flanked by moss-draped oaks, it would offer shade from the midday sun and quiet from the hustle and bustle of the Big House. Without a myriad of house servants about or children underfoot, perhaps there they could find some private, uninterrupted time. And so, by noon, hand in hand, William and Annabelle set out from the front verandah on their afternoon stroll.

Meanwhile, Barry and Mela, were eager to show their new stepbrother, Nathaniel, around Crawford Hill. Accompanied by the other children—Carolina, Ashley, Cooper, Cinda, and Quash—they first toured the yard, then they visited the stable where they fed carrots to the horses, especially to Endeavor and Lightning. Afterward, they headed down the sloping back lawn to the pond where they skipped pebbles upon the water, barely missing the ducks that cruised upon the water's lapping surface. Soon the children were wildly scampering about the grounds, inventing one adventurous new game to play after another. Only Carolina, finding such silliness beneath her at the ripe age of eleven, scarcely participated in their frolics, and instead supervised them as a self-appointed nanny, playing the role of Ester.

By early afternoon—as William and Annabelle walked beneath the moss-laden trees, and the children scampered about the plantation grounds—Brandon and Kathryn set out to visit Brandon's studio.

"How quaint!" Kathryn remarked as they approached. "The stone-lined footpath is so charming! Who whitewashed the stones?"

"Barry and Quash. The chore devolved into a race between them, each trying to see who could paint the stones the quickest. Barry and Quash ended up with more paint on each of them than on the stones!" Brandon chuckled, remembering when Quash and Barry were younger and tussling over who could complete the chore the fastest.

"I can't imagine!" Kathryn pictured the two boys doused in paint, grateful for Nathaniel's rather more refined upbringing.

"Boys will be boys, I suppose," Brandon quipped.

"And I presume Barry takes after you? . . ." Kathryn teased.

"Like father, like son," Brandon grinned, with a mischievous wink.

Kathryn gave his arm a playful slap. "Now, behave."

Opening the door to the studio, Brandon let Kathryn enter first.

"It *is* a bit musty in here, isn't it?" Kathryn commented as Brandon crossed the room to draw back the curtains and open the windows. Light and fresh morning air streamed in, and beyond, the northern view of the backyard with its pond and willow tree was perfectly framed by the glass panes.

"This should help," Brandon said as he raised a window sash. "It *has* been some time since the windows were opened. This morning, it was still a bit nippy out, so I had kept them closed. I quite agree; it *is* musty."

Just then Kathryn noticed the large canvass upon Brandon's easel. The painting of Allison—so endearingly lifelike, posing in her green taffeta at Loxley House—quite dominated the studio. By comparison, the daguerreotype of Brandon and Kathryn on their wedding day that Annabelle had placed on Brandon's writing desk was dwarfed to the point of scarcely being noticed. Slowly Kathryn walked toward the painting and stood solemnly before it. She seemed to no longer be listening to anything Brandon was saying—indeed, she seemed to nearly forget that he was in the room with her.

Noticing the sudden attention Kathryn was paying to the canvass, Brandon chided himself. He should have thought to wire ahead to have Jacob remove the painting and various portraits of Allison to the attic before Kathryn's arrival. Unsure of quite what to say, Brandon began somewhat awkwardly, "That … that's a painting … it's, um—"

"She was *beautiful*, Brandon. It *is* Allison, *isn't* it?" Kathryn interjected quietly, a catch in her throat,

Brandon nodded. "Yes … it is." He drew near Kathryn to view the image.

"You painted it?"

"Yes, from memory and from a few portraits I had sketched of her … years before she passed away."

"It's just lovely, Brandon. I had never seen any of your finished works until now."

They both stood before the painting, neither speaking, each feeling suddenly awkward.

As Allison smiled placidly down at them, Brandon felt the familiar ache and emptiness in his heart over his loss of her. It was a forlorn and hollow feeling of sadness that had scarcely visited him even once in the months since he had met Kathryn. Now the sense of loss loomed full and pulled deeply at his heart strings. His eyes welled as he looked up at Allison's sweet, angelic gaze.

While Kathryn had no longer felt threatened by Brandon's memory of Allison—after all, he had stopped wearing the sliver locket containing the treasured strands of her hair—she nonetheless felt crowded by the painting, as if she were no longer alone with Brandon in the studio, and as if being his new wife was somewhat superfluous.

Blinking back his welling tears, Brandon suppressed the familiar ache that had surfaced from the depths of his heart. To cure their mutual awkwardness over the moment, he reached up and plucked the painting from its easel. "I know Annabelle would like to keep this one," he said, feigning a casual air.

Kathryn did not know quite what to say. Although she felt it would be appropriate to comment that Brandon need not take the painting down from its easel for her sake, she remained silent.

Brandon clasped each edge of the oil painting of Allison, nearly feeling her presence draw near to him as he did so, and with one last look, he drank in the pale-blue eyes that smiled back at him. "Here ... I will set it here for now," Brandon said, barely able to conceal the catch in his throat as he placed the canvas upright upon the floor—facing the wall.

"Yes, I am sure Annabelle would appreciate it. ... It will be a lovely present." Kathryn watched as he placed the painting away, Allison's image now hidden.

With the canvas removed from the easel, the sunlight that streamed in through the open windows seemed somehow less vibrant, less robust to Brandon. The studio appeared to him to be more ordinary, more stifling and plain. To Kathryn, however, the room, bathed in midday sun, felt more airy and open—more welcoming.

By the end of the day, the few remaining portraits of Allison in the studio were stored neatly in the Big House garret, and the oil painting of Allison in her green taffeta was hung in William and Annabelle's room. Upon receipt of this present, Annabelle nearly wept as she embraced Brandon and tenderly kissed him on the cheek. "Brandon, are you quite sure you want to give it up?"

Brandon smiled, although Annabelle detected a distinct sadness about his manner. "Yes, Annabelle, quite sure. I want you and William to keep it. ... I had always intended it for you and William one day."

Annabelle gazed at the painting, and said very quietly, "If you ever change your mind, you know where it is." Then she looked up at him and smiled gratefully. "Thank you, Brandon. We will treasure it."

———✦———

After dinner that evening, Brandon, Kathryn, William, and Annabelle sat on the front verandah sipping mint juleps. Fireflies flitted as the sun sank below the western horizon of pine woods. The humidity was low for a May evening, and the temperature was pleasant, not oppressively hot—perfect weather for sipping mint juleps outdoors on a Saturday evening.

"Tomorrow, you and I—as well as Jacob and some of the others—should go turkey hunting," William suggested to Brandon. "It's the perfect time of year. Hens have laid their eggs for the season, and the gobblers are at their peak—no hens to get in the way of hunting now that breeding is over with. What do you say?"

"I'd like that," Brandon said, adding, "If *you* don't mind, Lissy."

"Not at all." Kathryn smiled her approval.

"Then, it's settled!" William grinned. "We'll get Jacob to come along, and my gunkeeper, Brister—some of the others."

"*After* church," Annabelle put in.

"Of course, after church," he said, then leaned over and gave her a peck on the cheek.

"I can't believe it's already Sunday tomorrow. Nathaniel starts school with the other children on Monday," Kathryn noted, adding, "This was Nathaniel's choice, even though there are only a few weeks of school remaining before summer."

"He didn't want to be at home alone while all the other children are in class," Brandon added.

"Do Cinda and Quash go to school too?" Kathryn asked.

"Quash is nine, but aside from learning to read and write a bit—Ester teaches him from the Bible—he is mostly beginning to learn certain chores and tasks from Jacob that will allow him to become a house servant or skilled laborer one day," Annabelle explained. "And Cinda—although the same age as Cooper and Mela—is not in school either, but she is being taught to read and write by Ester as well. And she will soon be learning cooking and certain housekeeping tasks."

"I know it is quite different here from what you are used to," Brandon said to Kathryn. "It will take some time to get used to it. I know it did for me and—" He nearly said "Allison" but stopped himself. Instead, he said, "—and I am sure you are concerned about Nathaniel's education here, in the South."

"I dare say, I am a *bit* concerned," Kathryn admitted, looking apologetically at William and Annabelle.

"Concerned about what?" Sara asked as she opened the front door and joined the others on the verandah, a cool mint julep in her hand.

"She is a bit concerned about Nathaniel's education here," Annabelle said. "I imagine it must be different than in the North?" she asked, looking toward William for some clarification.

"Not to worry!" William began. "You see, schools in the South are developed according to available resources as well as according to whom to instruct, who will comprise the student body. Where funds are not sufficient—on poorer plantations—much of the children's schooling is derived from their parents, particularly the father. Obviously, you won't have that issue here in Lower All Saints Parish—we have quite a robust economy here. That's why the rice crops are called 'Carolina Gold.'" He smiled and winked.

"William is leaving out an important point on that matter," Sara said, a note of gratitude in her voice.

William cleared his throat modestly. "Oh, now." With a dismissive shake of his head, he waved her off.

"What point is that?" Kathryn asked, intrigued.

"There have been a few plantations in All Saints Parish that have struggled a bit. My late husband, Jack, was not wealthy by any means—not like most in these parts. William donated money to allow Tom and other children who are less well-off to attend the finest schools in All Saints Parish."

William blushed slightly, looked down at his silver goblet, and took a sip of his mint julep. "I just believe that a solid education is the foundation of a solid people—a solid community."

"Well, we can *never* thank him enough," Sara finished.

After a shared silence between them, Kathryn spoke up. "What subjects will Nathaniel be taught?" Kathryn was relieved to know that because William was one of the wealthiest plantation owners in All Saints Parish— perhaps, she imagined, in all the South—Nathaniel would have a first-rate education, and this put her nerves somewhat at ease. Still, she wondered exactly what subjects he would have the opportunity to learn.

"Boys are expected to become learned, studying Latin and Greek along with the curriculum they share with girls and young women in science, English, philosophy, history, mathematics, geography, and religion," William explained.

Quickly Annabelle interjected, "The content of formal education here is generally devised so that girls are able grow into cultivated young women, directing them into the responsibilities of their future station in life. While they share the same basic curriculum as the boys, their studies are perhaps less rigorous, as they are trained to become proper ladies of high society."

"Some families opt for private tutors," William said.

Annabelle added, "In communities where financial resources are abundant, such as All Saints Parish, children can afford to have either private tutoring or attend classes away from home at a day school. The choice of whom to instruct and what to teach them is a community decision, while adhering to a basic, preparative curriculum."

"When our children are older, we may hire tutors for them as well," William noted.

Upon hearing this, Kathryn's nerves were now fully at ease. She felt assured that Nathaniel would receive as thorough and rigorous an education in the South as he would have received in upper-class Washington, D.C.

Nonetheless, moving to the South remained foreign and strange to Kathryn in many ways, including certain conventions of the education system. As they talked further, Kathryn learned that because teaching for salary was still not considered a fit occupation for women, most of the children's school teachers were men. It was acceptable for women to teach Sunday School or to teach their own children and slaves but not to teach formally for pay, unless out of necessity due to widowhood or absolute financial need. In the North, on the other hand, women were trained for careers as teachers in institutions developed for that purpose. Common schools were widespread throughout the North in a more standardized system—that is what Kathryn had known growing up, and it is what she had envisioned for Nathaniel. Nonetheless, her nerves had been calmed about the matter, and she could now explain to Nathaniel more precisely what to expect on Monday when he and the other children would head off to school.

Soon the conversation turned to other topics—church the next morning, how to keep Cooper from generally misbehaving, the turkey hunt the following afternoon, and how mild the late-spring weather had been so far this year.

As the hour grew late, Brandon stifled a yawn. Taking a final sip of his mint julep, he said that he had best be heading in. Kathryn followed, then Sara. Sitting alone together on the porch swing, only William and Annabelle remained a short while on the verandah.

"I hope you don't mind my mentioning it ... but—" Annabelle paused and looked down at her hand clasped lovingly in William's; she did not want to spoil this day, this moment—their reconciliation.

"But what, my dear?" William asked solicitously.

"You had mentioned Cotta and Sabe marrying ... that you were planning a wedding."

"Ah, yes." William gave his wife's hand a gentle squeeze.

"I am sorry, William, about what I said—about how that wouldn't make up for—" She didn't finish—perhaps she ought not to have brought it up.

"Shhh," he whispered, giving her hand another tender squeeze. "It's all right now; I understand." He paused, then cleared his throat. "I thought in a week or two—perhaps even by next weekend—we should have enough turkey meat put up for a *fine* wedding feast."

"That would be wonderful. Why don't you invite Sabe along on the turkey hunt tomorrow?"

William nodded and smiled. "Why, I believe I *will*."

They shared the pleasant quiet of the late evening for a moment as they listened to the crickets chirping all around and watched the fireflies flit in the night. Above, the moon was full, beaming down a pristine glow of light in the surrounding darkness.

"And what are you and the children, and Sara and Kathryn, going to do tomorrow afternoon while we are out turkey hunting?" William asked.

"I'm not sure. Perhaps a picnic before the weather gets too hot and damp—before summer stifles us all with heat and humidity."

"A pignic?" a little boy's voice chimed in from the front doorway. "Are we gonna have a pignic?!"

"Cooper, you go to bed this instant!" Annabelle warned her son, an authoritative tone in her voice. "You should have been in bed *hours* ago."

"But I wanna catch fireflies!" he chirped.

"Cooper! That's enough," William admonished. "Now, get upstairs to bed! On the count of three: one … two … three—"

With that, the staccato of Cooper's bare feet on the wood floor could be heard receding into the night.

"We'd best be turning in too," Annabelle suggested.

"Yes, we'd *better*…," William said, a mischievous lilt to his voice.

"I *meant* so that you are not overtired for your hunting tomorrow," Annabelle retorted playfully.

"But … it's been so long…," William entreated, his tone now serious and tender.

Annabelle looked into William's longing eyes in the moonlight. How relieved she was that their quarreling and estrangement was ended, that they were once again as one. "Yes, it has been—a very long time," she said softly. Then she rose, William's hand in hers, the mint-julep goblets left forgotten. William opened the front door, and they ascended the stairs together.

After church on Sunday, William and Brandon had a quick bite to eat, then hurried to brush their teeth and change into clothes suitable for hunting. Khaki trousers and plain cotton shirts would do, as the weather was warmer in midspring than for wintertime hunts. Kissing their wives on the cheek, they headed out the back door to meet Jacob; Sabe; Brister, the gun keeper; and a few other slaves—a blacksmith, Yao; a carpenter, Cuffee; and an engineer, Bilah—who often hunted with William and Brandon. Along with them, the slave in charge of the kennels, Cato, brought the hunting dogs—Caesar, the alpha dog of the pack, was William's favorite. The five dogs—all feists—anxiously meandered about, sniffing the ground and air for the scent of imagined prey, their pointed ears erect, their long snouts probing the breeze. William and Brandon carried their rifles with them as Brister distributed rifles to the others. No sooner had Cuffee distributed hand-whittled turkey calls than the air was filled with the manufactured sounds of turkeys gobbling.

Annabelle, Kathryn, and Sara stood on the back verandah to see the men off as Tom and Barry whisked past.

"Are you going too?" Sara asked her son nonchalantly.

"Yep!" Tom grinned. At sixteen he was certainly old enough to hunt, and he had been hunting since he was at least Barry's age—thirteen.

"Just be careful," Sara reminded.

"And you—you're going too?" Kathryn asked Barry with some degree of concern.

"Yep." Barry beamed ear to ear with excitement—this was to be his very first hunt!

"It's all right," Brandon called out from amidst the sounding turkey calls and the dogs meandering and sniffing anxiously about.

"I'm gonna go too!" Cooper piped up, scampering past the women's skirts.

Without delay, Annabelle bent and grabbed her wayward son by the shoulders. "Oh, *no* you're not!" she admonished.

With that, the men and boys were off with a final wave to the women on the back verandah and to little Cooper who stood pouting against his mother's skirts.

Just then, as the springtime sun beamed directly overhead, Cotta rang the work bell on the front porch, announcing that the noontime meal was ready to be served in the dining room. Platters of food were brought out from the kitchen and placed on the table as everyone gathered about the white-linen tablecloth. Mela, Cinda, Ashley, and Carolina rushed downstairs behind Quash and Nathaniel. Ester soon followed along with Hetty as Cotta came in from the front verandah to help with serving.

Lastly, Cooper wandered in and quietly stole up to his mother. "Mother, I wanna go hunting," he whispered, tugging on her sleeve.

"Why, Cooper—you know you aren't old enough to go hunting!" She indicated for him to please obediently take his place at the table.

Happily he skipped around the table and took an empty chair between Ester and Nathaniel. "Can we have a pignic?" he piped gaily. "Last night you said we were gonna have a pignic!"

Annabelle corrected, "It's pronounced 'picnic' not 'pignic,' and it's pronounced 'going to have' not 'gonna have.'" She added, "And yes, I did say that we might." Besides, she mused to herself, a picnic would cheer Cooper up since he was too young to go hunting with the older boys and men—plus, keeping Cooper of good cheer meant keeping him better behaved. "All right, then—are we all agreed? Shall we have a picnic?" she asked those seated about the table.

The vote was unanimous.

As the men, along with Tom and Barry, headed out on their hunt, the women and children set off for the shade of the willow tree down by the pond with quilts, baskets of food, and pitchers of cider to drink. It was such a fine day—there remained the vestiges of a cool spring breeze outside and no threat of rain beneath cloudless blue skies. It was a perfect afternoon for both hunting and picnicking.

As the women spread patchwork quilts upon the grass beside the willow tree, the children scampered about playing. "Don't go off too far!" Annabelle reminded. "It's nearly time to eat!"

"We won't!" they chorused, and ran off to play follow-the-leader on the footbridge over the pond, Carolina leading the way. At age eleven, she often led the games; she felt too old to simply follow the childish whims of the others. The children dutifully followed along as she tromped down the footbridge and around the pond, then chased the ducks that waddled nearby.

"Gobble! Gobble! Gobble! I'm a turkey!" Cooper piped.

"No you're not!" Carolina turned and all but rolled her eyes.

Cooper crouched down imitating how a turkey walked, his hands on his hips, flapping his folded arms, and jerking his head to and fro. "Gobble! Gobble! Gobble! Yes, I am—look!"

"Cooper, that's silly!" Ashley blurted. But she soon joined in.

Within seconds, all the children—Cinda, Quash, Mela, Nathaniel, Ashley, and Cooper—were strutting about the lawn gobbling like turkeys. Carolina simply shrugged and strode toward the picnic blankets to join the women—such frivolous, childlike conduct was far beneath her. After all, if she was to grow up to be a proper Southern lady, she *certainly* couldn't strut about the yard imitating a turkey!

"Come now, children! It's time to eat!" Sara called out.

"I done brought de peach pie, an' if you all don' come and eat yer lunch, ain' none o' you's gonna get dessert!" Ester warned.

"Same goes fer de pecan pie!" Cotta added.

With that, the children stopped their strutting and ran up the sloping lawn toward the shade of the willow tree and the picnic baskets.

"Here, Nathaniel, come sit by me." Kathryn patted the patchwork quilt beside her.

Obediently Nathaniel sat down beside his mother while Cinda and Quash took their places near Ester and Cotta, and as Ashley, Carolina, Cooper, and Mela situated themselves next to Annabelle, Sara, and Hetty. In no time, the baskets were opened, and plates and silverware were handed out as biscuits, rice, steamed vegetables, fried fish, and fruit were served. Pewter cups were filled nearly to the brim with cold cider, then passed around carefully to avoid spilling.

"Ouch! My tooth is loose!" Mela whined and stopped eating.

"Here, let me see," Annabelle asked, setting down her plate.

Mela dutifully opened her mouth wide for her Aunt to inspect.

"It's only a wee bit loose. Simply bite down on the other side," she advised.

"I don' like fish—it smells!" Quash complained.

"You's gonna eat it anyhow!" Ester prompted. "How else you's gonna become a strong growed-up y'ung man?"

"Yeah! Like me!" Cooper boasted as he stood up, spilling his plate from his lap, and made a muscle to show off.

"Now see what you've done, Cooper!" Annabelle shook her head.

"Here, I'll clean it up and fix him a new plate," Sara offered.

"I c'n help, Miss Sara," Hetty said.

"Thank you, Hetty. Thank you, Sara."

"May I please have the cider, Cotta?" Kathryn reached out her hand to take the pitcher. "Nathaniel would like a bit more."

"Me too!" Ashley put in.

"Der's gonna be 'nough fo' y'alls t' git some. Don' worry none." Cotta handed the pitcher across the quilt to Kathryn.

"I want some more too," Carolina said.

"May I please have more?" Mela held out her half-empty cup.

"Certainly," Annabelle said, setting down her plate to pour some.

"Nathaniel, are you looking forward to your first day of school tomorrow?" Sara asked.

Feeling shy, Nathaniel shrugged.

"Go on, answer," Kathryn prodded, giving her son a little nudge.

"I suppose so." Nathaniel had no idea what to expect in his new school, but he certainly did not want to be left at home while all the others were off attending their classes.

"I hear Mr. Carson is a wonderful teacher," Kathryn said. Then she confided to Nathaniel, "Don't worry. I hear that your new school is going to be just wonderful—lots of interesting classes, new children to meet and play with. Why, it'll be a new adventure, won't it?" She gave her son an encouraging smile. Yet she could only hope that Nathaniel would not find his new school as foreign and daunting as she had felt upon first coming to Crawford Hill.

Nathaniel nodded. His spirits seemed lifted somewhat—at least for company's sake.

"I'm almost finished with my embroidery," Carolina announced.

"Who cares!" Cooper rolled his eyes, then coughed, nearly choking on a bit of biscuit.

"What have I told you about talking with your mouth open?" Annabelle admonished.

This sent the other children into gales of laughter, with Cooper laughing the loudest.

"What—what did I say?" Annabelle looked puzzled.

Kathryn leaned over to explain. "You said '*talking* with your mouth open,' but you meant to say '*eating* with your mouth open.'"

"Oh! So I did!" and with that, Annabelle joined in the laughter around her.

Cheerily the picnic banter progressed about the blankets and quilts, baskets and pitchers, glasses and plates, until the rice, vegetables, biscuits, and fish had been quite "gobbled up!" as Cooper had put it—imitating a turkey once again.

It was now time for pie.

"I'm too full for pie," Mela complained.

"Me too," Cinda added.

"Me three!" Ashley giggled.

"Ha! Me four!" Nathaniel quipped.

"Me five!" Quash shouted.

"Me six! Me seven! Me eight! ... Me *one-hundred!*" Cooper bellowed.

All the children called out numbers at random until they were rolling over in side-splitting gales of laughter.

"Oh, to be young again!" Sara mused.

"Where has the time gone?" Annabelle smiled sadly and shook her head. Such silly, trivial, innocent days were long behind her and the other women—their lives had taken on more challenging and responsible roles than when they were once children. Afternoons such as this were a rare treat and provided a way for the women to revisit their own youth, if only vicariously through the pranks, play, and prattling of their little ones.

"Okay! Okay, now!" Annabelle clapped her hands. "Why don't you all go play for a while, run around a bit and work off some of that energy you have—then, when you have worked up an appetite, you can have some pie. How does that sound?"

"Okay! Yippee! All right! Yea! Yes Aunt Annabelle! Yes, Miss Crawford!" they chorused and leapt to their feet.

"I know! ..." Cooper jumped up and down. "Let's play hide-and-go-seek! I'll be blindfolded, and you all hide from me. Then I'll look for you!"

"Hide where?" Nathaniel looked around—all that was nearby was the willow tree, the footbridge over the pond, and in the near distance, the woods.

"Let's go up by the house," Carolina directed. She led the children as they all scampered up the sloping lawn toward the back of the Big House. "There are *lots* of places to hide there!" she called out as she ran.

Only Cooper remained behind. "Can I ... I mean, may I have a bandana?" he asked Ester.

"I don' have no bandana, but here ... dis napk'n should make a fine blin'fold," Ester said. "Jus' don't put it 'round yer eyes 'til you is up by the house wit' de other chil'un," she warned as she held out the proffered cloth.

Taking the napkin, Cooper half ran and half skipped toward the Big House, calling back over his shoulder, "Thank you, Ester!"

The women, relieved to have some peace, drew closer on the quilts and set about serving themselves thin slices of fresh peach and pecan pie.

"I hope the men are having a bountiful hunt," Annabelle said.

"I's sure dey is," Ester nodded. "Dis mornin', Jacob done tol' me dat dis has been one o' de mos' 'bundant turkey seasons dat der's been in many a year."

"Sabe tol' me de same," Cotta added.

Hetty agreed, "Dat's what I done heard tell of."

"I just hope they stay safe," Annabelle said, always mildly fearing an accidental shooting in the thick of the woods. Memories of the tragic hunting accident near Loxley House that claimed Benjamin's life and left Alexandra widowed so many years earlier still haunted Annabelle.

While the children scampered off to play, the women savored their pie and enjoyed the beautiful spring day—and the quiet.

As the children gathered at the back of the Big House, Cooper jumped up and down, and piped, "Hide-and-go-seek! I'm it! I'll give you thirty seconds to hide!"

"Only thirty seconds?!" Carolina challenged, her hands on her hips.

"That's not enough time for us to try and hide!" Mela complained.

Ashley pouted, "Yeah! We need more time!"

"Thirty seconds! Thirty seconds!" Cooper shouted, jumping adamantly about.

"Okay ... thirty seconds," Carolina grumbled.

With Carolina's help, Cooper tied the cloth napkin around his eyes. "A thousand one, a thousand two, a thousand three," he began counting.

"Y'all go an' hide!" Quash commanded excitedly.

"Hurry up! *Hurry!*" Cinda shouted as she darted across the lawn.

With that, the children dashed off to nearby places about the back— the verandah, woodshed, barn, stables, nearby trees, an old wheelbarrow— anywhere they could think of to hide.

"No fair peaking!" Carolina called out as she ran.

Finally, Cooper reached thirty—to him it seemed an eternity! He took off his blindfold and looked toward the house, various outbuildings, and all around him. The other children had definitely hidden well—he could not see *any* of them from where he stood. But instead of looking for them, his mischievous young mind had another idea. Rather than trudging all over to seek them out, Cooper skipped off in the opposite direction—he was already bored with the game of hide-and-go-seek.

As Cooper had scampered off toward the creek, to the west of the Big House, William, Brandon, Barry, Tom, Jacob, and Sabe had finished their turkey hunting. However, Brister, Cato, Yao, Cuffee, and Bilah wanted to hunt just a bit more to be sure to have plenty of meat for their families and neighbors. Accordingly, William agreed to let them use Caesar and the other hunting dogs a while longer.

William bent down and affectionately ruffled Caesar's ears and patted his head. "Good boy!" he said. "Good boy!" Then he stood, pointed toward the woods beyond, and ordered, "Go on now, get!" With that, the dogs headed off toward the thick of the woodland—Caesar leading the yelping pack. Brister, Cato, and the others, followed close on the dog's heels.

As for William, Brandon, Barry, Tom, Jacob, and Sabe, it was now late afternoon, and having bagged nearly one plump gobbler each, it was time to head in and take the turkeys to the cooks at the plantation smokehouse. Once plucked and smoked, some of the meat would be used for the evening's dinner, and the rest would be stored in the cold cellar far below the house—a portion of that meat would be served at Sabe and Cotta's upcoming wedding. Complimenting each other on their successful hunt, the men strode up the lawn from the southern range of the woods toward the Big House carrying their rifles and their prey.

Nearly an hour had passed, and the women began to wonder if the children were ever coming back for their pie or not. A slight chill set up in the late-afternoon breeze. "Where can they be off to?" Annabelle wondered.

At about that same time, Brister, Cato, Yao, Cuffee, and Bilah retired from their hunt. The last hour had paid off—they bagged another two healthy, fat gobblers. As they returned from the woods, Brister let the dogs drink and frolic on the west side of the creek near his cabin. The heat of the spring day and entire afternoon spent hunting had clearly worked up a thirst in the dogs. Caesar and the other feists lapped up cool creek water as Brister said his goodbyes to his fellow hunters, then went to his cabin a short distance away. With a final wave, the others dispersed with their gobblers to their own cabins deep in the slave neighborhoods.

In his cabin, Brister set his rifle aside and checked on his ailing elderly father, then happily showed him his one fat bird to be plucked and cleaned for cooking. Then, while the dogs splashed and drank in the creek, Brister rummaged for some leftover bones from the previous day's stew to give to the dogs as a treat, a reward for their diligent hunting.

Meanwhile, the children had long since grown tired of waiting for Cooper to find them. They had emerged from their various hiding places and decided that he had given up looking for them. After playing among themselves for some time, Carolina decided that Cooper had probably returned to the picnic for some pie. Following Carolina's lead, the children skipped and ran to back to the picnic—slowing as they approached.

"Where's Cooper?" Carolina cocked her head quizzically. "We thought we'd find him here."

"Isn't he with you?" Annabelle wondered.

"No, he's not with us," Ashley and Carolina answered in unison.

"You sure you ain' seen him about nowhere?" Ester asked.

Cinda shrugged. "No, we ain' seen him nowhere."

"We got tired of waiting for him to find us," Mela put in. "We reckoned he must've come came back here for pie."

"Please don't say 'reckoned,'" admonished Kathryn—the word offended her Northern sensibilities. "Please say 'supposed' or 'thought.'"

"Yes, please say 'supposed' or 'thought,'" Annabelle agreed.

"We *supposed* he came back for pie," Mela corrected.

"Cooper ain' *nowhere!*" Quash finished with an edge of exasperation and shrugged.

"O' m'be he thought y'all was gonna look fo' him 'nstead o' him lookin' fo' you," Hetty suggested.

Cotta nodded. "Dat could be."

"Or he must have gone into the house and not told you," Annabelle concluded. But she felt an unease she could not quite put her finger on. Perhaps it was just a mother's needless worry about her absent child. Yet . . . she felt unsure.

"I'm certain he's about somewhere," Kathryn said. "Little boys don't just disappear!"

"Of course," Sara said, then added, "Perhaps, as Hetty said, he thought that *he* was supposed to hide from *you*—rather than the other way around."

Little did any of them suspect that Cooper was down by the creek, near the edge of the woods and the slave cabin neighborhoods. He had trudged through the long grass and spring wildflowers, strutting and flapping his bent arms like a turkey and making gobbling sounds. As he happened near the feists drinking and frolicking in the cool water of the creek, he stopped and picked up stones and sticks to hurl at the dogs—he was still upset at not being able to go hunting and took it out on the dogs, teasing them. After all, they were *only* dogs, and *they* got to go hunting! "Gobble! Gobble! Gobble!" he yelled, provoking the dogs, then laughed as he hurled a handful of pebbles at them.

At once Caesar growled and barked, setting off a cacophony of barking from the rest of the pack just as Cooper let go another handful of sticks and pebbles.

Ester, Cotta, and Hetty were busy gathering up the picnic things as a violent, frightening din of yapping and barking sounded from the edge of the woods. Immediately they froze, staring into the distance. What on earth could be going on?

Instantly Annabelle sprang to her feet. "*Cooper!* ..." she breathed, her eyes wide and fixed in the direction of the harsh, discordant clamor—her heart pounding.

Cooper's fistful of pebbles and sticks rained down upon the frothing, snarling dogs. Bolting, Caesar splashed across the creek and lunged at Cooper. The boy turned to run, but it was too late; Caesar's teeth caught on his shirt at his shoulder. Cooper shrieked, dropping a fistful of stones, his eyes wide with terror as Caesar lunged again—this time the dog's teeth clamped on the boy's neck, Cooper's jugular spouting rivers of bright-red blood. Another dog lunged and latched onto Cooper's leg, felling him to the ground. Cooper screamed until spewing blood choked off his echoing cries. All about him, the dogs circled, viciously growling, snapping, and baying, trying to vie for a piece of their prey along with Caesar and the other feist—but the tumult was so violent that they were all but unable to join in the assault. Then, at once, the barks and growls eerily stopped.

Annabelle wordlessly fled across the lawn, down the sloping hill, and toward the woods as Kathryn swiftly followed after her.

"Children, come to the house with me!" Sara commanded.

Hurriedly Sara, Ester, Cotta, and Hetty left the picnic things behind and rushed toward the Big House, shepherding the children ahead of them. Each of them scarcely dared to fear the worst. Surely it wasn't a small boy's screams they had heard amidst the growling, yapping dogs—least of all Cooper's screams. It simply couldn't be.

Brister rushed from his cabin, rifle in hand, to see the snarling pack of feists madly vying to attack little Cooper. There was no time to call to the dogs to stop—Brister's only viable option was to get a clean shot. Aiming several times, beads of sweat sprouting upon his brow, he scarcely dared to pull the trigger—it was imperative that he get a clean shot at Caesar without accidentally hitting Cooper.

A shot rang out, its staccato reverberation echoing ominously over the fields.

In mid-jump, Caesar's body blasted upward into the air, then sank down, lifeless, amidst the windswept grasses and wildflowers. Startled, the other dogs backed off, the last dog finally letting go of the boy's lacerated leg. Desultorily the dogs cowered back in fear, tails tucked beneath them.

"Cooper!" Annabelle shrieked, her voice choked with terror and panic as she fled down the hillside toward the creek, the fading echoes of the dogs' growls, and the rifle shot.

Kathryn's heart pounded in fear as she chased after Annabelle.

Oblivious to everything else, only yearning desperately to see her son safe and sound, Annabelle ran blindly down the incline of spring grasses and blossoms to where the gunshot had rung out. "Cooper! *Cooper!*" she cried, abject panic rising in her voice.

Both women were terrified at what they might find at the edge of the wood, by the glistening waters of the babbling creek.

Brister's discarded rifle lay among the wildflowers, next to Cesear's inert carcass. His eyes welled deep as he bent down and scooped Cooper's limp body into his arms.

Just then Kathryn noticed Annabelle abruptly slow to a halting walk. Something about Annabelle's manner frightened Kathryn, and she paused a moment before rushing down the gentle slope of grass. Annabelle stood motionless as Kathryn cautiously approached. Both women stood panting, trails of perspiration matting wisps of their hair about their reddened cheeks. Nearby, a songbird twittered among the tree branches. A mild breeze wafted across the rice fields and grasslands. Beyond, the westward sun loomed bright and warm.

Squinting in the sunlight, Annabelle and Kathryn gazed upon the horrific scene beyond.

In an instant, Kathryn's mind reeled—it could not be, it simply could not be! She turned and fled in a panic up the sloping hill toward the Big House. It simply could not be! It *couldn't!*

Annabelle moved down the gently sloping hill as if in a daze. Her knees felt weak as she discerned Brister approaching her and carrying a disheveled bundle in his arms.

"*Cooper!*" Annabelle cried out, aghast, and rushed forward toward Brister who strode up the sloping hill of tall grass to meet her. It was, indeed, Cooper's still, lifeless body that he carried in his arms. Both Cooper's and Brister's clothes were sopping with blood.

Not far behind Brister lay Caesar, William's favorite hunting dog, shot clean through, lying dead among the springtime petals. The other feists— quiet now, and bewildered by Caesar's inert body—sniffed and licked at the lifeless dog as if trying to somehow rouse him.

As Brister drew near, Annabelle's mind reeled, barely able to absorb the surreal horror before her. Wordlessly she sank to the ground and knelt in her skirts as tears silently streamed down her cheeks.

Kathryn stood breathless at the foot of the back verandah steps. Clutching the railing, she cried out, "William! William! ... *William!*" The back door of the Big House squeaked on its hinges as William emerged onto the verandah.

"What is it? Have you found Cooper?" he asked anxiously. Surely the tumult down by the creek that had echoed across the grasslands had nothing to do with his son's going missing.

Kathryn could only point with a quivering hand toward the woods as tears cascaded down her cheeks. Startled, William looked in the direction of her trembling hand. At once Kathryn crumpled in a dead faint upon the ground at the foot of the verandah.

"Brandon!—Brandon!" William called out over his shoulder. Then he trod down the steps, his gaze fixed on the two figures approaching across the back lawn, dappled in early-evening sunlight that sifted through the magnolia trees.

Brandon emerged from the back door and quickly knelt at Kathryn's side.

Hetty, Sara, Cotta, and Ester shooed the children away from the back door and ordered them to go up to their rooms "at once!"

William squinted, puzzling over what he was seeing. Annabelle had been wearing an ivory frock that afternoon—what were the bright-red floral patterns on it now? It was a pattern he had never seen before. And what was the bundle in Brister's arms—could it be a plump gobbler that he had shot in the woods? Why were the two of them walking up to the house together? ... His mind reeled as they drew near, as he finally absorbed the macabre reality of what he was seeing. Blood spatters covered Annabelle's bodice where she had hugged her son's dead body to her chest. Brister held in his arms William's dead son, Cooper—not a plump offering of prey from the hunt.

William's eyes welled, blurring the grizzly and tragic scene before him. He walked slowly to meet Brister, who wept as he transferred Cooper's lacerated, lifeless body over to William's extended arms.

Annabelle, trembling, in a state of shock, pronounced softly to her husband, "Cooper's *dead*."

———◊———

White rose and magnolia petals jostled loose and fell from the tiny casket as the hearse-wagon's wheels creaked along the rutted road. A light splattering of spring rain gently pelted the gleaming wood of the casket beneath gray mottled skies. On the rear bench of the wagon's bed, William sat with welling eyes, Annabelle nestled against him, quietly weeping. Seated beside their parents, Carolina and Ashley simply stared bewildered through damp lashes at the somber scenery beyond. It was still hard for them—for anyone—to truly believe that Cooper was dead.

The ride to the All Saints Churchyard's graveyard seemed interminable that Sunday. There was no lighthearted wedding scheduled for Sabe and Cotta that day as originally planned; instead, the day was reserved for mourning and remembrance.

Brandon rode with Barry, Mela, and Nathaniel in a vis-à-vis that followed behind the hearse-wagon. His own eyes misting, Brandon endeavored to comfort Mela who had flounced across his lap whimpering. Barry sat silently next to his father, staring straight ahead, his own eyes brimming. Silently watching the Big House recede from view, Nathaniel stoically strove to swallow the tears that threatened over the loss of his new little playmate.

Only Kathryn was not among the mourners that day. She could not bear witnessing Cooper's burial after seeing his blood-soaked body carried limp in the arms of Brister just a week earlier. Instead, Dr. Langford had administered a mild dose of laudanum and advised her to rest.

Dr. Langford joined the funeral procession, along with Sara and Tom, many friends from the nearby All Saints Parish plantations, and those who regularly shared the Sunday church services with the Crawford family. Jacob and Ester, along with Quash and Cinda, as well as Cotta, Sabe, and Hetty, also attended.

Finally, as the light spattering of springtime rain diminished to a heavy mist, the hearse-wagon and carriages halted before the wrought-iron gate of the graveyard. Brandon lifted Mela down from the vis-à-vis as Barry and Nathaniel stepped down. At the hearse's side, Brandon helped Carolina and Ashley down while William and Annabelle—damp-eyed and clinging to one another—alighted. As the funeral workers removed the casket from the hearse-wagon's bed, the mourners walked slowly toward the freshly dug grave. Nathaniel followed behind, wishing desperately that his mother, Kathryn, could have been there.

Slowly Cooper's tiny casket was borne through the wrought-iron gateway to the gaping rectangle dug in the earth, alongside which generations of Crawfords had been laid to rest in years past. Standing before the mourners, the pastor opened the Bible and began to speak in solemn, yet reassuring, tones—Cooper was going to be with God in heaven for all eternity. More tears fell from swollen red-rimmed eyes as the spring drizzle once again descended from pregnant billows overhead.

Her ears scarcely taking in the pastor's words, Annabelle stood in the protective embrace of William's comforting arms as they both gazed down at the white rose and magnolia petals that shivered on their son's casket in the warm springtime breeze. Still scarcely able to comprehend their sudden, tragic loss, their tears flowed unabated.

The mahogany casket was slowly lowered into the ground—next to the tiny grave of Cooper's infant brother, Charleston—as a final hymn was sung. Urged by the pastor's soft words and a whisper, Annabelle stooped in her skirts and clutched a fist of damp raw dirt. Casting it into the grave, Annabelle then turned and buried her face against William's chest, sobbing—whereupon she sank to her knees, disconsolate. William knelt beside her, weeping. Instantly Carolina and Ashley joined them, both kneeling in their black mourning frocks and sobbing as if their tender young hearts would break.

Brandon stood solemnly next to the grave and cast a small bouquet of spring wildflowers into the gaping abyss. "Goodbye, Cooper," he whispered as his eyes flooded, then spilled.

Overhead, a break in the clouds sent a glimmer of sunlight downward through the sober skies as if to suggest to all the mourners that springtime would resume, that life would somehow go on. The rain would not last forever.

CHAPTER 27

A Month of Sundays

Mela twirled gaily about on the hardwood floor in the west sitting room as she pretended to be a ballerina—a ballerina just like the ones Kathryn had seen on stage in Washington, D.C. She felt the warmth of the early-August Sunday-afternoon sun filter through the window panes as it illuminated the bright carnival of glass items lining the shelves. She imagined that looking at the sunlight glinting on the bowls, vases, plates, and pitchers was like looking through a stained-glass window or—as she twirled—like looking through a kaleidoscope. As she spun, she closed her eyes, wondering what it would be like to be blind—to not be able to see the summer sun casting a rainbow of brilliant hues across the room.

All of a sudden Mela bumped into something. Immediately a loud crash sounded as splintered glass scattered across the hardwood floor. Horrified, Mela opened her eyes and gasped. Standing still, her mouth agape, she saw fragments of broken glass strewn about her feet—cobalt blue, emerald green, crimson red, and golden yellow—all in glittering in bits and shards flung across the hardwood.

Instantly Kathryn strode into the room.

"Mela? What on *earth* are you doing?!" Kathryn shot as she stared down at the splinters of glass.

"I didn't mean it...," Mela quavered, taken aback by the sudden harsh tone in Kathryn's voice.

"You must be more careful!" Kathryn scolded. "What were you doing?! Tell me this *instant!*"

"Nothing! I wasn't doing anything *wrong*. It was an accident," Mela sniffled.

"Don't talk back to me!" Kathryn shot. Whereupon she spied a long-handled pewter spoon on the tea-service tray kept on the west sitting room's hutch. Kathryn picked up the spoon and clenched it tightly. "Hold out your hand," she ordered.

"It was an accident...," Mela whined.

"Don't disobey me. *Hold* out your *hand!*" Kathryn's green eyes flashed abject anger.

"No!" Mela countered. Desperately she wished her father was there to rescue her.

"*Do* as you're told!" Exasperated, Kathryn tugged at Mela's arm and roughly turned her palm upward.

Crying, Mela reluctantly kept her arm outstretched, her vulnerable palm obediently exposed.

Kathryn raised the spoon upward into the air, then thrust it forcefully downward.

Thwack!

The bowl of the spoon landed hard against Mela's upturned palm.

Mela cried out, instinctively jerking her hand away and tucking it behind her back as her eyes welled deep.

"Again!"

Mela shook her head.

"This is for your own good!" Kathryn scolded.

Whimpering and blinking back tears, Mela slowly stuck her palm out once more, wincing at the thought of being struck again.

Thwack!

All at once Mela shrieked with pain and broke down sobbing. Her eyes shut tight, she massaged her wounded hand, which was already welting from the blows.

"Again! You have to learn your lesson to be more careful!"

Tremulous and sobbing, Mela reluctantly held out her other hand—she could not endure any more pain inflicted on the hand that had already been struck.

Kathryn stood with the pewter spoon poised, ready to strike.

"*Kathryn!*" Annabelle exclaimed from the sitting-room doorway. She rushed to Mela's side and instantly knelt down amidst the pieces of broken glass, hugging the sobbing child to her. Annabelle glared at Kathryn. "What on earth are you *doing*?!"

Kathryn indicated the bits of broken glass strewn across the floor. "She was playing with these when she shouldn't have been. She broke several, let alone the fact that she could have cut herself as well!" Then she addressed Mela. "You know these are not playthings, don't you?!" she asked sharply.

"I know," Mela quavered and nodded, hot tears pouring down from her innocent blue eyes.

Handing a lace handkerchief to Mela to dry her eyes and blow her nose, Annabelle rose. "As this is *my* glassware," she said sternly, "I should think Mela's punishment—if *any*—would be mine to mete out." Annabelle felt as a mother to Mela, and she had certainly known the child for many years more than Kathryn had. Annabelle knew that Brandon would *never* have sanctioned a corporal punishment under any circumstances.

"As I am Mela's mother now, it is my duty to discipline her as I see fit," Kathryn countered. She stood defiantly, her arms folded, the pewter spoon clutched tight in her hand, and her lips pursed, all but glaring at Annabelle.

Annabelle was nonplussed. She smoothed back Mela's blond curls, then bent and whispered gently in her ear, "Why don't you run along to your room. Your father will be there soon."

Mela, whimpering and cradling her injured hand, began to shuffle toward the hallway door.

Beside herself with indignation, Kathryn called out, "Amelia Stewart! Don't you dare leave this room until *I* give you permission!"

"Go on, Mela, dear. It's all right," Annabelle prodded gently.

Upon her Aunt's permission, Mela fled from the room. Her footsteps receded up the staircase, punctuating the stark silence.

"Kathryn … Brandon has *never* struck his children—there has never been cause to, nor does he *believe* in it. I dare say, William and I have never struck *our* children *either*—"

"Perhaps if you *had*, then Cooper wouldn't be—" But Kathryn didn't finish—the word "dead" failed to escape her lips.

A look of abject disbelief and shock registered in Annabelle's expression. Her face grew ashen, and turning on her heels, she rushed from the room and ran up the stairs sobbing.

Kathryn's own eyes welled. How could she have said such things to Annabelle and to Mela? How could she have been so harsh and heartless? She looked down at the pewter spoon in her hand. She simply had not felt herself since witnessing Cooper's death—nor, it seemed, since coming to Crawford Hill. This was not her home, it was not the Tierny estate where she had lived most her life. So much of the South—the many enslaved dark faces around her, the cultural differences, the ruralness, and the climate— seemed so increasingly foreign to her. Rather than acclimating during the previous four months since her arrival at Crawford Hill, she felt increasingly as though she was losing control over the very foundation of her life. As she replaced pewter spoon onto its tea-service tray, she wondered how she would now face Brandon.

Upstairs, Mela sat on her bed crying, waiting a seeming eternity for her father to arrive and somehow make everything better.

Finally, a tapping sounded on her bedroom door, and Brandon entered, closing the door behind him. "Now, what's all this about?" he asked, sitting on the bed beside her. "Your Aunt Annabelle seemed quite upset. Can you tell me what happened?"

"I didn't mean to do anything wrong...," Mela whined, then dissolved into tears, consoled that at least her father was there to be with her.

"Annabelle said that your mother—"

"She's *not* my mother!" Mela spat through her tears.

"No, she's not your *real* mother, Mela; she's your stepmother. But you must respect and obey her as if she *were* your real mother."

Mela sniffled and kicked her feet nervously against the bedrail.

"Now, can you tell me what you were doing?"

"I was pretending." She mopped at her damp cheeks with her uninjured hand.

"Pretending what?"

"That I was a ballerina ... and then ... I closed my eyes."

"You were dancing? ..." Brandon prompted.

Mela nodded, stemming her tears. "I was dancing in circles and pretending I was blind," she said matter-of-factly.

Brandon didn't know whether to laugh or cry. It seemed so sweet, so empathetic that his little girl, while playing, would want to put herself in the place of someone who was disabled and could not see. He put his arm around her tiny shoulders and gave her a gentle squeeze. "Why were you pretending to be blind?" he asked softly.

"'Cause I heard Hetty talking about an old man on the Davenport place who couldn't see ... and ... and I wanted to know what it would be like ... what it would be like to be him."

"So, you weren't playing with the bowls, vases, and plates on the shelves as Kathryn had said?" For now, Brandon determined that he would avoid referring to Kathryn as "Mother" so as not to further upset his daughter.

Mela shook her head emphatically. "No, I *wasn't*! It was an accident," she finished, giving a helpless shrug, her tiny arms outstretched.

Just then Brandon glimpsed the red welts on Mela's right palm.

"What is this?!" he asked, taking her little hand in his.

"That's where she hit me," Mela said quietly, her eyes welling once more.

"This is where your ... where Kathryn ... *hit* you?" Brandon enunciated, his brow knit with concern.

Mela nodded emphatically and sniffled as she withdrew her injured hand.

"Kathryn, I don't understand! ..." Brandon paced, perplexed, in front of Kathryn as she sat nervously on the edge of their bed.

"I ... I haven't felt myself lately ... since Cooper's death."

"Did you *really* tell Annabelle that if she and William had corporally punished Cooper, then he wouldn't have *died*?" Brandon asked, in utter disbelief.

Kathryn nodded, then buried her face in her hands and wept. "I'm so sorry, Brandon! I didn't mean to say it—it just came out! I ... I don't know *what's* gotten into me lately."

In the three months since little Cooper's death, none of the Crawford Hill household had felt quite the same. Still, as summer lengthened, at least some degree of normalcy, humor, and cheer had returned to Crawford Hill. Only Kathryn seemed particularly out of sorts. Dr. Langford had kept her on a prescription of laudanum for nearly two weeks after Cooper's mauling, as Kathryn had complained that visions of his dead, lifeless form covered in blood continually cropping up in her mind's eye was more than she could bear. Since then, she had seemed more on edge than usual.

Brandon sighed and sat on the edge of the bed next to his new wife. "Kathryn, please ... don't upset yourself so." He offered her his pocket-square, which she took as she tried to stifle her tears. "Now, tell me ... why did you take it upon yourself to *strike* Mela?"

Kathryn froze. What would Brandon think of her? Everything seemed to be falling apart. "I struck her ... because she was misbehaving." she admitted, her words barely audible. Then Kathryn straightened and, looking Brandon in the eye, offered, "I simply did not know that you had never struck your children or spanked them ... or given them the belt." She knew not what else to say. She dared not admit that the incident was more than a mere matter of disciplinary action, that it was also a way to vent her pent-up frustration over coming to live at Crawford Hill and that little Cooper's macabre death had only made the strange new surroundings seem all the more unfamiliar and foreboding. "I'm sorry, Brandon." she said, looking up at him as though her heart would break. She only hoped that he could forgive her—and that Annabelle and Mela could forgive her as well.

Brandon could not imagine Mela, about to turn six, having her tiny hand struck by a large pewter serving spoon. As his eyes teared, he put his arm around Kathryn's shoulder. He kissed the waves of chestnut hair at her temple, and said quietly, gently, "I know you're sorry, and I forgive you, Lissy, but ... it must never happen again. Never. Do you understand?"

Kathryn nodded, dabbing at her nose with the pocket-square. "How will I *ever* look Annabelle in the eye again?" She desperately hoped Brandon would have some magical answer.

"We have all been through a lot since Cooper's passing. Annabelle and William have had a hard time of it. But in recent weeks, I think they are rising above it, coping with their immediate grief. ... I am sure Annabelle will understand if you simply apologize and explain," he soothed.

———※———

Before dinner that evening, Kathryn tearfully apologized to Annabelle, and the latter perfunctorily accepted the apology—although she was still sorely wounded and deeply insulted at the implication that some failure of hers and William's to physically discipline Cooper was somehow the reason for his tragic death. After all, Ashley and Carolina were well-behaved and very much on their way to becoming educated, poised, fine young ladies. Cooper had simply been innately rambunctious and mischievous since birth—that had always been his inherent constitution.

William also accepted Kathryn's earnest apology—although hearing even secondhand the implied meaning regarding Cooper's fate that had come from Kathryn's lips *stung*. Her harsh, impulsive words conjured the sorrow and difficulty of the last few months—as he tried to blot from his mind the sight of his young son's body lacerated with dog bites, blood everywhere. Nevertheless, he decided to forgive Kathryn's unfortunate words and to put them in the past—at least for Brandon's sake.

As Kathryn made her rounds of apologies, Brandon was in his studio beginning the first draft of a new article for *The Illustrated London News*. Sifting through notes from Alfred Cooke in Charleston, telegrams from contacts in Washington, and a recent piece in the *London Times*, he set pen to paper and began writing.

"The first major battle of the war between the states—the Battle of First Manassas—commenced in near Manassas Junction in Virginia, only thirty miles south of Washington, D.C., on July 18, 1861. The Northern newspapers had pressured President Lincoln to quickly resolve the rebellion of the Southern states. Adding to this pressure was Lincoln's awareness that the ninety-day enlistments of Northern recruits who had responded to his call to arms after the Confederate attack on Fort Sumter were about to expire—Lincoln needed to engage these recruits again, and soon, to apply pressure to quickly bring the rebellion to a definitive end! Lincoln pressed for action, and consequently, Union General Irvin McDowell hatched a plan: he would march his army of 35,000 (inadequately trained) troops thirty miles south and attack the Confederate army of 22,000 troops, commanded by General Pierre G.T. Beauregard, defending the vital railroad junction at Manassas, Virginia. Beauregard's troops were well entrenched behind a meandering stream called Bull Run. Regardless, 22,000 Confederate troops versus 35,000 Union troops did not bode well for a Confederate victory!

And a Union victory would open the way to the Confederate Capital at Richmond—securing an end to the war and reunification of the states.

"Given the magnitude of the plan and the significance of the potential outcomes for either side, several hundred spectators turned out to view the battle—including Senators and Representatives—bringing with them picnic baskets and field glasses. Citizens traveled from regions as distant as the town of Centreville some seven hours away. In holiday spirit, they set out in carriages, wagons, and hacks to view what they believed would be the climactic end to a brief rebellion—the end to a short war. The majority of spectators camped out along Centreville Heights, some five miles from the battle, although some, including Governor Sprague of Rhode Island, ventured into the thick of the battle.

"*London Times* correspondent William Howard Russell observed that '… a lady with an opera glass … was quite beside herself when an unusually heavy discharge roused the current of her blood—'*That is splendid, Oh my! Is that not first rate? I guess we will be in Richmond to-morrow.*'

"However, by Sunday, July 21ˢᵗ, the Battle of First Manassas was decidedly a Confederate victory. The current casualty figures number 2,700 Union to 2,000 Confederate troops killed—a numbing shock to both sides! An officer rode up to the cheering crowd, 'We have whipped them on all points!' Shortly thereafter, many of the curiosity-seekers got caught in a stampede of retreating Union troops—some fleeing in panic, others sauntering away—yet escaped unharmed.

"In the several days since that battle, there has been immense apprehension that the Confederates will follow up on this victory and seize Washington, D.C.! This is indeed the desire of the Confederacy in Richmond."

A light knocking sounded upon Brandon's studio door. He stopped writing and looked up to see Kathryn. After making her apologies to William and Annabelle, Kathryn had come to talk alone with Brandon in his studio. There was a request that had been pent up in her heart for weeks, and she had not wanted to voice it until now. As she entered the studio, Brandon rose from his desk to greet her.

"Are you feeling better, Lissy?" he asked, and kissed her on the cheek.

Kathryn nodded. "Yes … somewhat. How is Mela feeling?"

"She's feeling better, as well. I told her she could have some extra dessert if she promises never to pretend to be a blind ballerina again." He broke into a smile, shook his head, and chuckled. "Mela's always had such a curiosity about things." He paused, remembering her cheeks slathered with shaving cream and testing the sharpness of his razor by sawing a linen towel draped over her hand. At least *this* time she was only pretending to be blind. "Children can do the darnedest things," he remarked, with a grin.

His sense of humor about it put Kathryn a bit more at ease. But then her eye fell on the empty easel where the painting of Allison once stood, and she grew serious once more. She did not belong here—neither in the rural South nor in the shadow of Allison's memory, near so many who knew and remembered her.

Noticing Kathryn become pensive and somewhat distant, Brandon urged, "What is it, Lissy?"

Kathryn took her gaze from the empty easel and the rural Southern landscape beyond the window panes, and looked into her husband's endearing brown eyes. "I ... I've been wanting to ask you something."

"What about?" he prompted.

"Can we sit?" She indicated the window seats along the north wall of the studio.

Brandon grinned. "Is *that* what you wanted to ask me?" he joked. "If we can sit?"

Kathryn endeavored frivolity and gave his arm her token playful slap, although her mood was not light. "No, that's not what I wanted to ask," she chastised, issuing a wan smile.

Sitting on the window seat beside her husband, she wrung her hands, and stated quietly, succinctly, "I want to leave Crawford Hill."

Behind them, beyond the glass panes, a rose hue tinged the early-evening the sky.

Brandon drew back and studied her a moment. "What ... what do you mean? ... *You* want to leave Crawford Hill? Do you ... do you mean you want to ... leave *me?* ..." For a moment, time seemed to stand still.

"Oh, no ... *no,* that's not what I meant," she said, lovingly clasping his hand in both of hers. "I mean ... can *we* leave Crawford Hill ... perhaps move to Charleston? I know the paper, *The Illustrated London News,* needs you in the South, especially with war imminent ... and with Fort Sumter securely in Confederate hands, Charleston should be a safe place to live. There is talk of Washington, D.C. possibly being attacked—even my father is considering leaving for New York for a time, until things settle down. Certainly, we can't go there—to Washington, D.C. Yet I feel so out of place here ... still. And since Cooper's passing—" Here she stopped short and averted her gaze. She so desperately wanted a change of scenery, a new place where Brandon, the children, and she could settle—to have their *own* home, a fresh start, to escape the foreignness of plantation life and build happy new memories of their own.

Brandon took in her words but did not know quite what to say. It was a lot to absorb all at once—and so unexpectedly. This was the only home Mela had known and nearly the only home Barry had known, aside from spare memories of Derbyshire, England. Moreover, Crawford Hill had become home to Brandon—he could not imagine leaving his best friend, William, and Allison's sister, Annabelle, not to mention his two nieces, Ashley and Carolina. He would also miss Jacob, Ester, and their little ones, Cinda and Quash, as well as Cotta. Brandon knew not how many seconds passed as he looked at Kathryn, nonplussed. Clearly, leaving Crawford Hill was a matter she had given considerable thought to—but Brandon was quite taken aback.

"I ... I'm sorry, Brandon. I know it is so terribly much to ask," Kathryn said quietly. She cast her eyes downward and absently toyed with the emerald engagement ring that had, just months before, become the wedding ring on her finger.

"No ... no, I understand. ... I'll give it some careful thought." Yet Brandon felt unsure as to whether he could live up to that promise. "It will take some time to consider." He stood and walked to his desk, then put his pen aside, too distracted by Kathryn's request to continue his article. "I can work on this some other time," he said. "Let's go up to the house for dinner, all right?"

Kathryn nodded.

Dinner passed pleasantly amidst platters of roasted turkey, fried catfish, steamed rice, vegetables picked fresh from the garden, whole grain biscuits, and glasses of claret and cider. Although not quite fully recovered from the stinging blow of Kathryn's words, William and Annabelle both endeavored to be cordial with Kathryn, and the latter had gratefully accepted their proffered forgiveness. The dinnertime banter of the children further helped to ease any tensions that had been caused earlier.

Only Mela seemed a bit more quiet than usual and did not eat with much appetite. At least Kathryn's earlier apology to her, and kissing the inflamed welts on her palm to "make it all better," helped to reassure Mela somewhat. Brandon's serving Mela an extra slice of dessert to cheer her had at last put a smile on her face as her pale-blue eyes, framed by spirals of blond curls, sparkled lovingly up at her father. She knew that everything would always be all right as long as Father was near.

———◇———

"You're it!"

"You're it!"

"You're it!"

"You're it!"

"Why am I always it?" Ashley sulked.

"Because!" Nathaniel laughed.

Ashley frowned. "But I don't *wanna* be it! I'm *always* it!"

"Don't be such a baby." Carolina rolled her eyes. At nearly age twelve, she was beginning to tire of such childish trifles.

"I c'n be it," Quash volunteered.

"Good!" Ashley said, and a glimmer of a smile returned to her face.

"Giv' us a head start!" Cinda shouted as she began to run, the others quickly following, scattering in all directions.

"I ain' giv'n *no one* a head start!" Quash threatened as he began to chase the others pell-mell around the yard—dodging trees, wicker lawn furniture, and rope swings.

"Catch me if you can!" the children laughed and giggled.

Unsuspectingly Cotta walked down the back verandah steps only to find herself nearly colliding with a breathless, scampering Ashley. "Sorry!" Ashley gasped as she regained her footing and streaked across the yard.

"Good Lawd!" Cotta shook her head and giggled. She hoped that one day she and Sabe would have children of their own, only she hoped it would be when the war would soon end—*and* when the North might prevail and they could be free. At least the sight of the children frolicking about was a sign that their grief over Cooper was ebbing near summer's end—that things were finally returning to normal. Still, Cotta regretted that she and Sabe had never been able to enjoy a real wedding celebration and feast. Shaking her head as another scampering child nearly ran headlong into her, she set out her errand to pick berries in the garden, careful to avoid any more careening children as they ran and giggled, shouting "You're it!" about the yard.

As the children played their game of tag, Barry and Tom had gone horseback riding—their favorite pastime. Tom, at sixteen, still felt that he could outride Barry any day. But on this particular day, Endeavor was being shod by the plantation blacksmith; consequently, Tom was loaned a mere workhorse while Barry got to ride his own horse, Lightning. Given a workhorse to clomp along on, Tom had suggested that they pretend they were on a battlefield—the battlefield at Manassas. The large expanse of fields at the far end of the front drive was a perfect make-believe Manassas for them to playact upon.

"You're dead!" Tom declared, grinning.

"No I'm not! You missed!" Barry swung around on Lightning to confront Tom.

"I shot you! You're dead!"

"Do I *look* dead?" Barry laughed and wheeled about on his horse.

"How can we practice at being soldiers if you're going to *horse* around!" Tom challenged, and laughed at his play on words.

"Okay, I'll be serious."

"Now you are a Union soldier at the Battle of Manassas, and you've been given the command to charge, and I—"

"You mean the Battle of Bull Run!"

"*Manassas!*" Tom retorted, with a grin.

"But I am a Union soldier, and the Northern forces call it the Battle of Bull Run." Barry sat up high in his saddle and looked down his nose at Tom, whose workhorse was decidedly shorter.

"Aw, get off your *high horse!*" Tom laughed.

"Hey, I'll race you to the main road!" Barry challenged, with a slap of his reins.

There was no opportunity to argue. Tom slapped the reins of his workhorse and followed, his horse's hooves kicking up dust from the fields as he chased after Barry.

Slowing to a stop near the main road, along the oak-lined allée to the Big House, Tom called out to Barry to double back and pull up alongside him.

"We should join the Confederate forces—for *real,*" Tom said.

Barry was not quite sure if Tom was joking or not, but his countenance was quite serious. "Yeah?"

"Yeah. You up for it? If the war spreads to these parts, to South Carolina, to Charleston, to Lower All Saints Parish—anywhere around these parts—lots of Confederate troops will be needed. You up for it?"

Barry weighed Tom's words and demeanor carefully. "Yeah, I'm up for it."

"You swear? It's a pact? We will enlist if the war comes this way."

"I said *yes,*" Barry confirmed.

"Ha! No, you didn't. You didn't say yes; you said '*yeah.*'" Tom laughed and slapped his old work horse with his reins. As gravel scattered up from the long drive, he galloped beneath the canopy of moss-laden trees toward the Big House, calling out, "Race ya!"

With that, Barry slapped his reins and dug his heels into Lightning's side. "Hya! Hya!" he yelled, to spur the horse on. He was not going to let Tom win just because Tom was a few years older, especially not when he was riding some lumbering old workhorse! As he closed in on his friend, Barry pondered his agreement to join in the fighting should the war come near—Tom was his best friend, and it was a vow he would not break.

———— ✦ ————

That afternoon—as Barry and Tom vowed to enlist should the war reach All Saints Parish—William stood discussing a serious wartime matter with Brandon.

"I have pledged a few hundred of my field hands to the Confederacy to help with construction of coastal and harbor defenses," William informed as he chatted with Brandon in the studio. "Lots of plantation owners are doing the same around these parts," he explained.

Brandon sat at his desk sketching a pen-and-ink illustration to go with his latest article about the Battle of Manassas. He glanced up at William. "A few hundred? Can you spare that many?"

"For now. I will need them back in the autumn for the rice harvest."

"Let's hope the conflict does not last that long," Brandon pronounced solemnly, then resumed his drawing representing the massive conflict and casualties at Manassas. Deep down, he knew the war would last beyond the autumn months, but no one could say for certain when it all might end.

"At least Barry and Tom are too young to join up," William noted.

"Fortunately," Brandon acknowledged as he surveyed the nearly finished drawing before him.

"Do you have the reported casualties? Losses?"

Brandon rifled through some notes on his desk. "Let's see ... at Manassas, the Union suffered nearly three thousand casualties—killed, wounded, and captured or missing—and the Confederates suffered about two thousand. It is said that no photograph by journalist Matthew Brady or anyone else survived the battle; we only have rough sketches—such as this one, sent to me by Alfred Cooke's contacts, that I am referring to for my article's illustration." He shook his head as his eyes traced the macabre images before him. "I can't imagine what it would have been like, to actually have been there."

"Nor I." William paused. "Ashley and Carolina told Annabelle last night that they want to become nurses to help the wounded soldiers."

"Is that so?" Brandon drew back in his chair. "I don't suppose they have any idea as to the blood, the carnage, the abject suffering of the wounded ... the myriad amputations." Brandon's recent reading of newspaper reports as well as letters and telegrams from his fellow colleagues and contacts had painted a thorough picture in words of the horrors at Manassas. It seemed incomprehensible to think that future conflicts could be even worse. Thinking of William and Annabelle's two innocent young girls—Ashley, at age nine, and Carolina, at age eleven—wanting to have any part of it was even more incomprehensible.

"Annabelle wants to shelter them as much as possible from those sorts of details, although she *is* impressing upon them the tragedy of war—the 'inherent evil in it,' as she puts it."

"As I am doing with Mela," Brandon noted.

"Apparently, Sara confided in Annabelle that Tom wants to join the Confederate forces one day when he is older—should the war prevail for some time."

"Thank God, Barry is not of that attitude," Brandon said, oblivious of Barry's pact with Tom to join the Confederate forces one day.

William nodded. "Well, I'd best be getting back to my study. I have some financial records to go over, and then I have to meet with other plantation owners regarding helping one another while we parcel out our workers to assist with the construction. The owners of smaller plantations in All Saints Parish are bound to struggle more with a reduced work force. But it's not yet harvest time, and maybe the war will be over by then."

"We can only hope."

"We always have hope," William said, then walked out of the studio and up the stone-lined path toward the Big House.

Cotta and Sabe's wedding celebration had been planned for the following Sunday. William determined it was just what Crawford Hill needed to end the summer on a lighter note—in the wake of Cooper's passing and with matters of war swirling about everywhere. Besides which, it was a promise made to Sabe and Cotta that was long overdue.

Slave weddings were a matter that was new to Kathryn. William and Annabelle explained that wedding cards would be sent out to all their friends, and the day would be commemorated by both slaves and plantation families alike. There would be feasting with ham, turkey, beef, chicken, a plethora of vegetable dishes, Carolina Gold rice spiced with saffron, coffee, wine, cakes, pies, and bowls of fresh berries. The ceremony would be held outdoors—in the backyard of Crawford Hill's Big House, down by the pond. The pastor from the All Saints Parish church would preside, with Sabe and Cotta standing on the footbridge over the pond. Slaves who played music in their off times would serve as the musicians for the reception—fiddles, banjoes, mouth harps, and washboards would all be welcome to provide festive, celebratory melodies for dancing and singing.

On the day of the wedding, in mid-August, everything proceeded as planned. Fortunately, the few days of summer thunderstorms had passed just in time. This particular afternoon was perfect—a clear blue sky without any trace of Ester's billowing "cauliflower clouds."

Annabelle had given Cotta a hand-me-down dress of ivory silk that was slightly worn but nonetheless quite elegant. Sara had sewn a veil of sheer lace for Cotta that flowed from the flowered garland crowning Cotta's hair down to her heels. Together, Annabelle and Sara explained to the bride that a white dress was a new tradition begun when Queen Victoria in England wore a white wedding dress for her betrothal to Prince Albert in 1840, just twenty-one years earlier. In the Big House attic, flanked by Annabelle and Sara, Cotta whirled about in her white dress and veil, and beamed, "Thank you, *so* much Miss Annabelle and Miss Sara! I ain' neber worn such pretty clothes b'fore!" With that, Cotta hugged each of them as her eyes sparkled.

Meanwhile, William and Brandon had rummaged through their old clothes to see what they could attire Sabe in for the special day. Black trousers, a white shirt, and an old black jacket with tails were scrounged from the attic. Together they explained to the groom that those were the only clothes they could find. They did, however, gift Sabe with a burgundy cravat of silk and new suspenders "for luck." But Sabe instantly countered, "With a gem of a woman—a Queen o' de Nile like Cotta—no man need' any extra luck!"

As bride and groom put the finishing touches on their wedding attire, Carolina, Ashley, and Mela gathered summer wildflowers and verandah roses for Cotta's bridal bouquet.

Finally, with the guests from throughout Lower and Upper All Saints Parish assembled on the lawn near the pond's willow tree, it was time for the afternoon wedding ceremony to begin. Ester and Hetty served as bridesmaids as Jacob and Brister served as best men. Once the little fieldworker quartet—banjo, fiddle, mouth harp, and washboard—began to play, William escorted Cotta to the crest of the footbridge where Sabe stood, a spring rose in his lapel. Cinda, as flower girl, skipped happily ahead of William and Cotta, tossing petals from a sweetgrass basket that Hetty had woven as a wedding gift. Below the footbridge, exquisite white magnolia blossoms floated among the paddling ducks.

Cotta and Sabe's eyes glistened as they gazed at one another. Motioning for the quartet to hush its tunes, the pastor spoke a few words of scripture. Quash, standing near the pastor happily served as the ringbearer. When the vows were concluded, Sabe slipped the ring of simple steel on Cotta's finger and pledged his eternal troth. Cotta, too, pledge her everlasting devotion. Then they embraced and kissed. Wedding guests—slave and white alike— let out a grand cheer. Hats were tossed in the air, and pistol shots rang out as everyone hollered, hooted, and whooped their hearty congratulations.

Yet the ceremony was not quite considered complete until Cotta and Sabe carried out the long-held tradition of "jumping the broom." Hand in hand, they walked joyfully down the footbridge to a clearing in the crowd where Hetty had placed two brooms that she had decorated with ribbons and flowers tied about their handles. Often, branches from a shrub or tree were used as brooms, but Hetty insisted that they have proper brooms. Hetty and Ester set the brooms three feet apart on the ground—one in front of Sabe and the other before Cotta. The crowd grew hushed as everyone vied for a view—the children positioned in front so that they could see too. As the quartet struck up a lilting melody, Sabe and Cotta each stepped over their brooms and joined hands to signal that they were truly married. Again, a tremendous cheer arose from the throngs of guests. At once the quartet struck up a jaunty tune, and everyone began to dance and feast. Cotta and Sabe were truly man and wife—the reception had begun!

The celebration continued until well after dark when it was suddenly realized—with a wink, a nod, and a smile—that the bride and groom had slipped away to savor some time alone together. Drawing out their pocket watches, guests decided that they too should be heading back to their respective homes. The hour was indeed growing late. Thanking William and Annabelle Crawford for the invitation, all agreed that it had been a joyous, uplifting, *glorious* Sunday that would not soon be forgotten.

For Mela, however, the fairy-tale splendor of Sabe and Cotta's wedding was soon eclipsed—its memory overshadowed. It was the following evening when Mela found herself, once again, out of Kathryn's good graces. This time the purported offense was quite minor, and the punishment—according to Brandon's previous wishes—was not nearly as severe. Nonetheless, the incident pained Mela even more greatly than before.

"Mela, please don't put your elbow on the table," Kathryn admonished in a hushed voice, at dinner that evening.

Barry, sitting beside Mela, had just handed her a pitcher of water for her to pour some into her glass. It was while Mela was pouring the water into her glass that she was so remonstrated for her ill manners. Brandon had not seen the supposed infraction, as he was busy talking with William about the war effort.

Mela finished pouring her water before promptly setting down the pitcher. She had *not* put her elbow on the table!

"Mela! ..." Kathryn warned in a hushed tone.

"I didn't *have* my elbow on the table," Mela timidly asserted back at her.

Kathryn dabbed her lips with her napkin, glanced at Brandon and William, then redirected her attention toward Mela. "I saw you," she insisted, this time her voice louder than she had intended.

"What is it?" Annabelle asked, from the far end of the table. William and Brandon stopped their conversation, interrupted by the quiet commotion.

"I was reminding Mela of her manners," Kathryn said.

"What did you do?" Brandon asked Mela.

Before the child could answer, Kathryn stated, "She had her elbow on the table."

Barry, for his part, had not paid attention to Mela and had no idea whether she had or had not committed the accused "dire offense," as he sarcastically thought of it.

"I did *not!*" Mela pouted, and frowned. In truth, she had not set her elbow on the table while pouring water from the pitcher—her elbow had been at least one inch *above* the table.

"Mela," Kathryn said, trying to maintain her composure, "I saw you. Now, don't talk back to me. If you are finished, please go to your room."

"But I didn't *do* it!" Mela protested heatedly.

"Go to your room—*now*," Brandon ordered.

"No! I didn't put my elbow on the table!" Mela insisted, her eyes flashing at both Brandon and Kathryn. It wasn't fair. Her father had not even been paying attention—he could not have witnessed one way or the other if she had put her elbow on the table. She sat sullenly, near tears.

"Go to your room," Brandon repeated. He said it more quietly this time but more firmly as well. Brandon got up from his chair and walked around the table as everyone sat stock-still, forks and spoons held idle, watching the contentious scenario unfold.

Only Nathaniel dared to whisper, in a teasing sing-song, "Mela's ... in ... trouble!"

"Nathaniel! ..." Kathryn warned.

Mela sulked down from her chair.

"Come along," Brandon said.

Brandon followed Mela up the stairs as the cheerful dinnertime banter and clinking of silverware on plates resumed. The familiar sounds emanating from the dining room made Mela's unwarranted punishment seem all the more unfair.

"But I didn't *do* it!" Mela whined plaintively as she trudged up the stairs, her father close behind.

"Your mother says you did," Brandon asserted as they stepped onto the landing.

Mela all but stomped up the stairs, indignation stewing in her young heart.

All of a sudden she stopped and turned. Brandon paused, standing a few steps below Mela—at eyelevel with her. Mela's eyes narrowed in defiance. She drew back her tiny hand and slapped Brandon hard across the cheek. "I didn't *do* it," she enunciated clench-jawed.

Brandon did not move. As he looked into his young daughter's defiant eyes, his own eyes welled. "All right ... perhaps you didn't. ... But for now, go up to your room. We will talk later," he said quietly.

Mela's heart ached for having struck her father. She loved him dearly, more than she could ever say. She only resented that Kathryn had so stubbornly insisted that she had misbehaved when she hadn't and that Kathryn had made her father disbelieve her. Now, because his tone was gentle, wounded, and reflective, and because he looked at her with brimming eyes, she perceived—correctly—that he had simply felt caught in the middle. It was evident from his manner that he had likely believed Mela but felt he must, nonetheless, send her to her room to appease Kathryn. Mela blinked back tears and marched up the stairs to her room as Brandon turned and slowly descended the staircase to return to the dining room. He could only surmise that perhaps Kathryn was still not quite feeling herself.

———◈———

After dinner, Brandon checked in on Mela—bringing her some fruit pie to cheer her. "How is my little dear one?" he asked. He set the plate of pie on the bureau and sat on the bed beside Mela.

"I ... I'm sorry I hit you." She looked deep into her father's brown eyes as if to convey the depth of her apology.

Brandon's eyes misted. "I know you are. But you must learn never to strike me—or anyone—when you are upset. ... Do you remember long ago, when I thought you had misbehaved by visiting the pond without my permission? Do you remember that you had struck me then, too? ..." His eyes welled.

At once Mela dissolved into tears. The memory—and her current action—tore at her heart. "I didn't mean to hit you. I *love* you, Father. And I ... I didn't have my elbow on the table—"

"Shhh, shhh," Brandon soothed, hugging her to him as she heaved with sobs. "I know, I know; it's all right. Shhh." After a moment, helping Mela dry her eyes, he coaxed, "How about that pie, now?

Mela nodded, her blond curls bouncing.

Brandon rose, retrieved the plate from the bureau, and handed it to Mela. "I love you, too, little dear one." He ruffled her hair, smiled, and gave her a wink.

Mela looked up at him, her expression lighter. "Thank you, Father," she said, indicating the pie.

With that, Brandon headed downstairs to rejoin Kathryn, William, Annabelle, and Sara on the front verandah. There, after-dinner conversation had turned to talked about Cotta and Sabe's recent wedding, the news of the new baby born on the Hagley place, that the weather had been unusually clear lately, and about what Lincoln's next move might be with regard to the war.

Already, in August, it was growing evident that the war was far from over. On August tenth, there were skirmishes in Missouri at Wilson's Creek with over two thousand five hundred dead, wounded, and missing. And there were rumors that battles would soon reach West Virginia and the shore of Cape Hatteras in North Carolina.

"Word has it that by August second, Lincoln had approved a plan to attack the South coast of the Confederate States," William said, with regard to the Cape Hatteras rumors.

"I heard that there are two Confederate forts that are under construction at Hatteras Inlet," Brandon mentioned as he resumed his porch rocker. "I can't imagine those two fledgling forts withstanding an imminent Union invasion."

"Indeed," William said. "I imagine that Union victories at Hatteras Inlet and Roanoke Island could place the region under Union control and perhaps extended a blockade of the whole southern coast."

"Good Lord, let's hope not," Sara gasped.

As a Northerner, Kathryn ventured her perspective as politically tolerant as the conversation might allow. "Whether Union forces should prevail or not, I suppose a blockade would prevent or at least curtail shipments of goods to the South, making it hard on families."

"And driving up prices," Annabelle added.

While the others talked of the day's war news, Brandon grew increasingly distant, caught up in his own thoughts of his children and Kathryn. As war loomed near, Brandon knew he could not return to England; his job was as foreign correspondent specializing in the various economic and sociopolitical issues of the Confederate South—and now becoming a foreign war correspondent as well—was too vital and, admittedly, too exciting to simply abandon. Plus, with the war simmering, the pay he would earn from *The Illustrated London News* would become far greater due to his promotion as foreign war correspondent than the relative pittance he could earn back home, in England, covering more mundane, pedestrian stories. He had to stay in the South, but maybe not in All Saints Parish and Crawford Hill. Perhaps Kathryn had been right about relocating to Charleston.

CHAPTER 28

Absence of Light

If Kathryn had been right about relocating to Charleston—as Brandon decided she indeed was—he would have to tell William and Annabelle of his plans that night. Meanwhile, he listened distractedly while the others talked about all manner of things on the front Verandah.

As the hour grew late, long overdue rain clouds shrouded the moon and sparked lightning flashes. Consequently, it was decided that they had all best go inside. Kathryn, on her way in, gave Brandon a peck on the cheek, stifled a yawn, and said that she was going up to bed. Sara also decided it was past time to turn in. Before William and Annabelle could say the same, Brandon confided to them, "I need to have a word with you."

"Why certainly. Of course" William said.

"Is something the matter?" Annabelle asked.

Brandon scarcely knew how to answer. It seemed woefully difficult to tell them what he was about to.

As Annabelle and William sat on the sofa in the east sitting room, Brandon paced—he did not take his usual wingback chair near the hearth.

"Brandon, is something the upsetting you?" William asked. "You seemed rather withdrawn earlier, out on the verandah."

Brandon stopped his pacing and faced William and Annabelle. He sighed. Annabelle—Allison's sister—was as dear to him as his own flesh and blood. And William was as a close brother to him. How could he tell them what he was about to say?

"There is no easy way to put this...," he began.

William and Annabelle sat attentively, waiting for what words would come next.

"Kathryn and I ... well, I ... I have decided that we must ... I mean, Kathryn, the children, and I ... we must leave Crawford Hill." Brandon grew quiet and looked downward; he could not bear the stunned expressions on their faces.

"Leave Crawford Hill? ... But ... why?" Annabelle asked.

"What is this all about?" William puzzled.

Brandon did not want to put all the blame on Kathryn—her need for city life; her disdain for the foreignness of rural plantation life; and least of all, the trauma she suffered witnessing Cooper's tragic death that past spring.

"We have decided to take a house in Charleston. I wired Alfred Cooke a week ago, just in case, and he located a house on Bull Street, on the central west side of the peninsula."

"But why? What's changed?" William and Annabelle exclaimed.

Brandon paced a few steps, then sat in his customary wingback chair to gather his thoughts. "It is in part due to Kathryn not feeling at home here." Before they could protest or query as to why not, he quickly clarified, "It's not that she doesn't care for Crawford Hill—and for you both, as well as for Ashley and Carolina. It's plantation life that she has felt unsettled with all these months. She misses city life. But that is only a small part of it. She feels ... we feel we should have a place of our own, a house we can call our own—our home. We would move to Washington, D.C., but the paper—*The Illustrated London News*—needs me in the South. The paper has me contracted in the South ... and they recently wired that if I continue to work as a foreign correspondent in the South, with war brewing, they will promote me and greatly increase my salary as a foreign war correspondent. With a wife and three children and, undoubtedly, wartime likely making the cost of living much higher, it seems practical, even warranted, that we move to Charleston and that I accept the post as foreign war correspondent."

"But—," William interrupted.

"No—please let me finish," Brandon waved him off. "And we feel, at least for the foreseeable future, with Fort Sumter in Confederate hands—guarding the harbor to Charleston—we will be safer there than most anywhere else in the South."

William and Annabelle were dumbstruck. It came as a tremendous shock. Tears welled deep in their eyes as they sought to comprehend the stunning news.

Brandon's own eyes welled deep. He held so many fond and treasured memories of Crawford Hill—as well as profoundly meaningful remembrances that would forever be etched deep in his heart.

"It seems your mind is . . . made up, then," William concluded, his voice taut with sadness.

Brandon nodded, blotting a tear from his cheek with the cuff of his shirt. "I'm afraid it is. We have decided," he said softly.

"Excuse me." Annabelle rose from the sofa. She wanted to say more, she wanted to embrace Brandon and plead with him to please stay—but she could tell that his mind was made up. Swiftly she strode from the room, her skirts rustling with each step as she unsuccessfully fought to stave off a torrent of tears.

William cleared his throat to keep his emotions at bay. "When will you go?" he asked, his voice gruff.

"Soon," Brandon said. "Soon."

———◇———

Annabelle, barely able to sleep that night, got up to pen a letter to her sister, Alexandra, at Loxley House, in Sheffield, England. Although the letter would not reach her sister for some time, it at least provided Annabelle an outlet for pouring out her emotions, of venting on the sudden, wholly unexpected turn of events. Setting pen to paper, by the light of a flickering oil lamp in William's study, she began to write.

> *"Dear Alexandra,*   *August 19, 1861*
>   *"By the time this letter reaches you, we at Crawford Hill shall have suffered still another loss—Brandon intends to leave us, taking his family to live in Charleston. Oh, Alexandra . . . it is so sudden, unforeseen, and sad—especially on the heels of losing our little Cooper. So much is*

changing with war, the loss of Cooper—and now Brandon, Barry, and Mela leaving.

"Do you remember when Brandon first came to visit us with his brother Jeremy at Loxley house that Christmas so long ago? Do you remember the snowball he threw that accidentally struck Allison? Those were such simple times. Now the world is changing so. And Crawford Hill will change as well—we shall all feel such a loss.

"Brandon truly feels like a brother to William and me. I dare say, William and I were both quite shocked and saddened to learn that he is leaving. It is still hard to believe, to absorb, as I write this to you—we learned of the news only tonight.

"I hold such fond and special memories of Brandon's time with us these past several years. And I shall miss Amelia—little Mela has been such a gift in our household. And Barry, what a fine young man he is becoming! He and Tom Davenport have become best friends in such a short time. I wager Tom will miss his favorite companion considerably, just as Barry will miss Tom.

"As for our daughters, Ashley will soon be ten and is such a well-behaved little thing. She is the shy one in the family, although she enjoys playing with the other children. They all have such energy and such great times running about the yard—making up games, playing on tree and rope swings, netting butterflies, and catching fireflies in the evening. Their lives here on the plantation are quite different than our lives were in Sheffield—there is so much open space and free time for them.

"And Carolina—at age eleven, she is already becoming a young lady. She is at that age where she is caught between childhood games of make-believe on one hand and yearning to be a grownup young lady on the other hand. I dare say, she has a bit of a crush on her Uncle Brandon! She tries to conceal it from us, but it has been apparent for a few years now—very sweet. Sadly, she will surely miss him.

"I don't know how William and I are ever going to break the news to Carolina and Ashley that the Stewarts are leaving. Our two girls have even grown quite fond of Nathaniel, Kathryn's son, who is about one year older than Mela—he is nearly seven, I believe.

"I suppose it will be up to Sara Davenport to break the news of their leaving to Tom. I am sure he will be devastated.

"And Cinda and Quash—how they enjoy Mela and Barry! Cinda and Mela, who are the same age, were born just days apart—in September, just six years ago. They are best friends—dear friends. Cinda is such a sweet child, so intelligent and creative, just like Mela. They play so well together—dress up, dolls, tea party, all manner of games—they are as close as sisters. I believe both their little hearts shall break when they are given the news that they are to be parted—perhaps forever.

"So much has changed these past several months—from the Confederate forces taking Fort Sumter in the spring to the Battle of Manassas a month ago. In between ... Cooper's tragic death, mauled by our hunting feists. The only thing that gives me any consolation in his passing is in trying to believe that it was divine providence—that he was to join his twin brother Charleston in the hereafter; there is no other way I can wrap my mind around it or cope with the loss. His passing still weighs on my heart beyond what I can express.

"The brightest spot this summer was the wedding for Sabe and Cotta. Oh, I wish you could have been here to enjoy it, Alexandra! There was music, flowers, a fine feast. All our neighbors came, from near and far! Cotta looked so pretty in her ivory gown (it suited her tall, slender figure so well!). And Sabe looked so handsome in his suit with tails and silk cravat! (It seems a miracle, a blessing beyond measure, that Sabe and William have forgiven one another and even grown close—just as William is to our Jacob.) You should have seen the sun glinting on the pond adorned with floating magnolia blossoms below the arc of the footbridge where Cotta and Sabe exchanged their vows. It was such a joyous, beautiful day!

"William and I pride ourselves on allowing, as much as possible, for our field hands and house servants to find love in its natural course and not—as many slaveholders do—force slave men and woman into marriage for the sole purpose of begetting more slave children! That is unconscionable to me! On some plantations, girls as young as twelve are forced into wedlock simply to become 'with child' in order to provide

more slaves for the plantation owner! Treating human beings as mere
chattel—and even worse!

　　"Writing of weddings . . . makes me wonder. Dear Alexandra,
forgive me, as I know it is not my place, but I have wondered in recent
days . . . if Brandon did not marry Kathryn too soon. I only mean that
he and Kathryn did not have a long courtship, and their time together
was interrupted when Barry had his horse-riding accident, and Brandon
had to return home to Crawford Hill for a time. Kathryn is in so
many ways such a fine woman—cultured, city bred, well educated,
well mannered, and certainly elegantly beautiful beyond measure. But
I venture to say . . . that she seems a bit delicate or fragile in some way
that I cannot quite yet surmise."

As the hour was getting late, Annabelle placed the letter in the writing-
table drawer and went to bed. She would finish writing perhaps the next
day. For now, sleep was finally having its way with her, despite her worries
over Brandon and the children moving away from Crawford Hill.

———◇———

The next morning, after breakfast, Brandon broached the subject of
leaving Crawford Hill to his children—first to Barry, then to Mela.

Upon hearing the news, Barry was understandably indignant. "I'm *not*
going to Charleston!" he huffed.

"Barry, I know it's difficult—you have school friends here, plus you
and Tom are best friends—"

"Why do we have to go at all?" Barry shot. Clearly, he was as puzzled
as he was angry and downhearted over the matter. His question was more
rhetorical than inquisitive—he knew he would not have a choice in the
matter, whatever the purpose for leaving Crawford Hill.

"There are many reasons, Barry—"

But Barry's eyes had welled, and he walked briskly away. Feeling too
grown-up for his father to see him shed tears over the matter, he strode
out of the house and went for a long ride on Lightning—galloping over
the fields, far from the Big House, where no one could see his anguish over

having to leave. Barry loved the fields, woods, and streams, the rural life that the plantation living afforded—he could not imagine living in a city, especially not a small, cramped peninsula city like Charleston. And he would miss his friend, Tom. "Perhaps Tom and I should sign up with the Confederate forces *now!*" he thought as he galloped Lightning over fields and creeks to vent his anger and heartbreak.

Mela, for her part, did not fare much better upon hearing the news. "Charleston? *Why?*" she frowned.

"There are many reasons, my little dear one," Brandon explained. "For one thing, we will have a house of our very own, and—"

"I like it here! I *like* the Big House!" And with that, Mela began to cry. "I don't wanna leave Aunt Annabelle and Uncle William," she whined, "or Cinda!"

"Mela, now, don't cry," Brandon comforted. "It will be all right. You'll see."

But even Brandon did not know for certain if everything *would* be all right. Moving to Charleston—making a major change—was something that naturally filled one with both anticipation and at least some degree of trepidation.

———◇———

For the final evening of the Stewarts' stay at Crawford Hill, a special dinner was prepared. Afterward, everyone gathered on the front verandah to visit and reminisce—William and Annabelle with their two daughters, Ashley and Carolina; Sara with her son, Tom, and her personal assistant, Hetty; newly married, Cotta and Sabe; Ester and Jacob, as well as their two little ones, Quash and Cinda; William's hunting comrades, Brister, Cato, Yao, Cuffee, and Bilah, along with some of the other longtime field hands; several house servants; and Brandon and Kathryn with their children, Nathaniel, Barry, and Mela.

As conversation drifted into grown-up topics, the children grew bored and restless. Tom and Barry suggested that they all catch fireflies, whereupon Ester, Cotta, and Hetty went into the house to fetch some mason jars to put the insects in once caught. As the children ran about the front yard and the roundabout trying to cup fireflies in their hands, a distant field slave struck up a sweet, slow tune on his fiddle. Melodic notes sailed out into the night on the late-summer breeze as those sitting on the verandah quieted their talk and looked out upon the children happily playing together one last time. Lightheartedly the children scampered about giggling and yelling, trying to trap the winging glints of light. It was a magical evening of the sort that one wishes would never end. Yet, as the hour grew late, the children were finally urged to "Come in now, and get ready for bed," particularly the Stewart children due to the long journey ahead of them the next day.

Later, that final evening at Crawford Hill, Brandon stopped by Mela's room to tuck her in and wish her goodnight. But upon approaching her doorway, he heard the muffled sounds of her crying alone in her bed. Knocking softly and opening Mela's bedroom door, the light from his oil lamp illuminated her tear-stained cheeks as her pale-blue eyes stared up at the ceiling. Setting the oil lamp down on the bureau, Brandon sat on the edge of the bed. "Hey, now, ... what's all this about?" he asked quietly.

"Nothing." Mela quavered.

"It doesn't sound like 'nothing' to me. . . . Come on, now, little dear one, tell me what's wrong." Brandon ran a tender hand through her blond tresses.

Mela turned her head on her pillow to look up into her father's questioning, soft brown eyes. "I don't ... want to leave ... Crawford Hill," she sniffled.

"But there will be so much to look forward to in Charleston," he prompted. "We won't be so very far away from here. And one day, perhaps we can visit." Although with war looming all about, he was not sure if or when they ever *would* be able to visit.

Mela tried to stem her tears as she lay looking up at the ceiling.

"Can you be a big brave girl for me, now?" Brandon asked softly.

Nodding unconvincingly, a large tear crept down Mela's cheek.

"You had so much fun this evening," Brandon reminded, indicating the mason jar of twigs, leaves, and several glowing, flitting fireflies on the nightstand next to her.

Again, Mela nodded, though she still silently wept.

It broke Brandon's heart to see his little dear one so upset; even so, he felt at his wits' end to know what else to say to console her. "Is there anything else the matter?" he coaxed quietly.

Mela turned her head on her pillow and looked up at him in the flickering shadows of her room. "I don't want to die," she whispered as another great tear spilled down.

Brandon was taken aback. This was not in the least an answer he had expected. He had imagined that she would say that Barry had teased her, that perhaps she had another loose tooth that was hurting her, or that she had a tummy ache from too much pecan pie after dinner—*anything* but the words she just had uttered. Brandon cleared his throat to quell the knot that had formed and to take a moment to think of how to respond. Seeing his young daughter distraught over the notion of death, let alone after such a wonderfully pleasant evening, tore at his heartstrings.

"Nobody wants to die," Brandon whispered. "And you're not going to die for a long, long, *long* time," he assured her, hoping he was summoning the right words to console her.

"Everyone dies," Mela said. "I heard you and Aunt Annabelle and Uncle William talking about all the men dying in the war … and Jacob and Ester were talking about the baby in the slave cabins that died last week … and Cooper's dead … and … mother died—" Mela's voice caught, and she looked up at the ceiling, weeping as if her young heart would break. "Mother's dead … and it's all my fault! … She died because of me! … *Everyone* dies!" Mela sobbed as if her tears could wash away the confluence of hurt and looming fear she felt.

"Shhh … Shhh … now. Mela, please don't carry *on* so," Brandon soothed, comforting her as best he could. "It is certainly not your fault that your mother is no longer here. Whoever put such a horrid notion in your head?" Brandon's eyes welled as he gazed down at his little dear one.

"Barry told me that Mother died after I was born," Mela pouted, and looked helplessly up at her father.

Brandon stroked her forehead and, for lack of a handkerchief, dabbed the tears from her cheeks with the bedsheet. "Now, Barry had no business telling you that."

"It was at the graveyard … when we put Cooper in the ground … he told me after that. It's not his fault he told me. I asked him why Mother died. He didn't want to tell me, but I made him tell."

Brandon's eyes welled deeper. He loved his children dearly, and he could only imagine the solemn brother-sister talk they must have shared on that day.

"I'm scared of dying. When you die, everything is dark. There isn't anything else—it's just dark," Mela whined. She knew that at nearly age six she was expected to think of death as angels sitting on clouds or as devils with pitchforks raging over lost souls—mere storybook images. But her concept of death was far more abstract—a black void of eternal darkness—no more seeing, no more hearing, no more feeling, no more being. Only darkness.

Brandon sighed, wondering what to possibly say to console his daughter as she sniffled up at the ceiling. All at once the jar of fireflies and the flickering lamplight seemed to inspire the right words. "Darkness is merely the absence of light," he said quietly. "If you look for it, you can always find light. Even at night, the stars and the moon shine light down. And when you close your eyes and it's dark, you can imagine light." He gave her a tender nudge and pointed to the mason jar of fireflies on her nightstand. "See the fireflies? See how they make their own light? There is always light, even in the darkest night, if we want there to be—we just have to make our own light from within—just like the fireflies."

He leaned over and kissed Mela's forehead as she gazed wonderstruck at the flitting dashes of light in the jar beside her bed.

"I'll tell you what," Brandon comforted. "Let's think about all the fun you will have in Charleston—The Pond downtown, the grand houses along the harbor, the shops where I can buy you pretty new dresses, the flowers in White Point Gardens, the new house on Bull Street we will have to live in, and all the new friends you will make. Let's think about that. All right?"

Mela had stopped her flow of tears and nodded.

Brandon smiled, his heart full. "Now, count some sheep, and go to sleep," he prompted gently.

Mela nodded again and managed a little smile for her father's sake. "Can I count fireflies instead?" She gazed up at him quizzically.

"Yes, you certainly may." Brandon tucked her in, kissed her forehead, and picked up the oil lamp. From the doorway, he whispered, "Goodnight, little dear one," then went out and closed the door softly behind him.

As Mela lay beneath the coverlets and gazed at her jar of fireflies glowing in the night, she still harbored misgivings about going to live in Charleston, a place she knew almost nothing about. It was not counting fireflies that finally led to her closing her eyes and dreaming—it was the satisfaction she felt that out of profound love for her father she had stoically pretended to give up her distress about leaving Crawford Hill and about death. She realized that he was simply trying his best as a father to comfort her and that he could not have possibly realized the abstract notion she had, at nearly the mere age of six, about death, which she was far too young to adequately articulate.

Nonetheless, his words—"darkness is merely the absence of light"—echoed in her thoughts and comforted her. Whispering goodnight to her jar of flitting fireflies, Mela turned onto her side, nestled warmly against her pillows, imagined light, and let her eyelids flutter closed.

———◊———

With the children all put to bed and their parents upstairs getting ready to turn in, Brandon stood on the front verandah and looked down the long allée flanked by dark silhouettes of moss-draped oaks. On this final night at Crawford Hill, crickets chirped in the long grass, frogs issued guttural grunts, fireflies glinted in the sultry air, and starlight glittered overhead in the darkness as the sweet scent of jasmine and magnolias wafted on the night breeze.

This was where his daughter Amelia was born. It was the house where his dearly beloved wife, Allison, had passed away. It was here where so much of life and death had transpired over so very many years. And it was the home he had once hoped to share with Kathryn Lissette and her son.

Now, as war loomed closer with each passing moment, the opportunity for Brandon to gain a higher salary as a foreign war correspondent in order to better provide for his family during what would undoubtedly be hard times—as well as Kathryn's deep desire to leave All Saints Parish—meant that there was no alternative but to move away. Brandon's eyes welled as he gazed out upon the darkened land. Would he ever be able to return, he wondered.

Just then a warm hand clapped down on his shoulder. Startled, Brandon turned to see William.

"Tomorrow morning, then?" William said quietly.

Brandon looked at William, the latter's eyes also welling, and nodded. "Yes, tomorrow morning."

William gave Brandon's shoulder a heartfelt squeeze, then turned and went into the house. The two men had become as brothers—parting would be hard, a profound loss for each. Brandon took one last look down the tree-lined drive and across the darkened grounds about the Big House, then sighed and went in.

All was packed and ready for the morning's departure. Kathryn had once mused that it seemed like a month of Sundays before they would at last leave Crawford Hill. But now it was only a matter of mere hours.

CHAPTER 29

Departure

In the early-morning haze, Brandon strode along the narrow path that led to the All Saints Churchyard's graveyard. Nearby, Endeavor whinnied as Brandon's boots crunched upon the gravel underfoot. Lifting the wrought-iron gate's latch, he reverently slowed his step as he threaded his way past the various headstones until coming, at last, to Allison's. There, he knelt and tenderly offered a bouquet of summer wildflowers, laying them upon the gentle mound of her grave. Then he placed a kiss upon the arc of her headstone and stood. Solemnly he gazed down upon the engraved slab of marble in the blush of mist, and—in spite of vowing not to shed any tears at his final visit to her gravesite—his eyes welled deep.

"I still miss you, dear one," Brandon murmured, then bit his lower lip to try to keep his tears at bay—but it was of no use. Upon this utterance, he dropped to his knees and wept. "I will always love you, Allison—*always*," he promised softly.

Mopping desultorily at his damp cheeks, he silently reminisced about their early days at Loxley house in Sheffield; their first home together in Castleton, England; the birth of their son, Barry; their voyage to America—to South Carolina; their time together at Crawford Hill; and lastly, their shared joy when they learned that little Amelia had been conceived.

All but stemming his flow of tears, Brandon spoke quietly. "You should see Amelia—our little Mela. She is so sweet and bright, just like you, dear one. Her sixth birthday will be celebrated any day now. And Barry—he's grown so much. He just turned thirteen—can you imagine? He's becoming such a fine young man—" More tears clutched at his throat, and Brandon fell silent—for he realized that Allison would never see their two little ones grow up.

As Brandon knelt at Allison's graveside, he reflected upon his grief-stricken northbound train journey six years earlier to desperately—*somehow*—seek her out in the wake of her death. He recalled how Allison's apparition had appeared to him that one night at the roadside inn where he had stayed in Castleton-on Hudson. "I had *implored* God to *please* send you back to me, Allison," Brandon whispered, blotting the dampness from his cheeks with his shirt cuff. "I had a vision of you that night, dear one. Do you remember? You said to me, 'I will always be with you.' Sometimes I imagine that I *do* feel you near to me ... so *very* near to me."

On this early morning at Allison's gravesite, however, Brandon only felt the chill breeze and the solemn quiet of the churchyard. He longed to feel her presence as before, to hear her whisper to him as before, and to once again behold a vision of her. Nevertheless, he reminded himself that it must have simply been his imagination that night at the inn—his imagination merely swayed by a night of intoxication.

Brandon dabbed at his eyes as Endeavor whinnied softly and songbirds chirped in the canopy of branches above. He placed a tender kiss on his fingertips, then extended his hand to the bright summer flowers at the base of Allison's headstone and gently pressed the kiss upon their petals. "I love you, Allison—my dear one. Please—always be with me and our little ones," he whispered. Dashing a tear from his cheek, he rose to his feet and gazed downward, one last time, at his dear one's headstone.

Hesitantly Brandon turned and walked from Allison's grave, then closed the wrought-iron gate behind him and shut its latch. There, he turned to look once more upon the wildflowers and the marble headstone marking Allison's final resting place. His eyes filled once more. At that moment, just as Brandon turned to leave, hushed words—"Look to the future"—seemed to rustle in the leaves.

Who was there? Another mourner? Or in the desolate quiet of early morning, was he simply imagining things?

Brandon glanced back in the direction of Allison's gravesite—whereupon he gasped, his eyes all at once wide with disbelief and yet squinting to be certain that what he was seeing was real.

There, at the graveside, in a glistening white gown and cast in the mist of early-morning sun, shimmered Allison's ethereal apparition—her very spirit. Sweetly smiling, she whispered, "Look to the future—I will *always* be with you."

As Brandon's eyes welled, blurring her delicate image, her ghost slowly faded into the sunlight.

"*Allison!*" Brandon uttered as he stared past the wrought-iron gate toward the graveyard—but she was gone.

It was then that Brandon felt a sense of profound peace envelop and comfort him—a feeling of unearthly calm, unlike any solace he had ever previously known. For a moment, he stood as though transfixed, the morning sun showering a warm golden light all about him. "*Allison,*" he breathed, sensing her sweet presence at his side. He knew, in that instant, that somehow she would always, indeed, be with him.

A songbird twittered overhead, reminding him that the hour was getting late. Reluctantly he turned from the gate.

Mounting Endeavor, and giving a gentle slap of the reins, Brandon headed back to Crawford Hill. There, breakfast would be waiting—and it would be time for final goodbyes before heading southward to Charleston.

———◊———

"Good heavens, we wondered where you had gone to. Where were you?" Kathryn asked, consternation knitting her pretty brow. She stood upon the front verandah where she had been waiting for nearly an hour. "We held breakfast for you."

"I'm sorry, Kathryn. I was up early and thought I would be back sooner," Brandon said as he climbed the front steps.

Kathryn looked into his eyes. "Were you at All Saints Churchyard?" She detected the slight puffiness about her husband's eyes and construed that he had been to visit Allison's grave.

Brandon had neither the heart nor the frame of mind to discuss his errand. It was with a deep reverence and profound love that he had visited Allison's resting place; and on this day of all days, he wanted to treasure the experience and memory of it unscathed by others' remarks—even if such comments *were* those of his new wife. Brandon simply nodded. "Shall we go in?" Putting his arm around Kathryn's waist, he proceeded toward the front door.

"But Brandon—" Kathryn hesitated.

Brandon paused, his free hand on the door knob. "Kathryn," he said softly, yet firmly, "please."

Kathryn searched her husband's eyes, suddenly feeling as an old tea towel—as second choice, at best.

Brandon detected a trifle of insecurity in Kathryn's expression and turned toward her. He placed both hands upon her shoulders. "Lissy, sweetheart, I love you." His eyes welled with this pronouncement, and in an instant, he drew her to him and held her close. "I *do* love you," he assured her—perhaps nearly as much to reassure himself. Then he pulled back and looked into her emerald-green eyes as if to ask, "Do you understand?"

Kathryn's eyes misted, and she nodded—her lips forming a glimmer of a smile.

"Then, let's go in, shall we? I am famished." Brandon swung the front door open for Kathryn to enter.

With that, the two walked arm in arm into the dining room to join the others—all of whom had patiently waited breakfast for the Stewarts. It would be their last meal with everyone together at the Crawford Hill Big House.

———✧———

After breakfast, Jacob and Sabe had the carriages and wagons loaded with trunks and luggage, then waiting in the roundabout. Larger trunks and pieces of luggage would be sent by river barge down the Waccamaw, then shipped to Charleston by steamer.

While Kathryn and the three children—Mela, Barry, and Nathaniel—waited momentarily in the east sitting room, Brandon made one last trip upstairs to be sure they had not forgotten anything. At least that is the reason he had presented before dashing up the stairs one final time. Instead, he simply wanted to walk the halls once more, to take in the cozy familiarity of the Big House and ponder the long-held memories of events that had happened within its walls—the first day he and Allison arrived at Crawford Hill, with Barry in tow; the nights spent with Allison cuddled next to him in their bed as the moonlight glinted through the curtain lace upon her soft skin, golden waves of hair, and pale-blue eyes; the delightful sounds of the Crawford children playing in their rooms, Cooper always the loudest and most mischievous; the somber late-afternoon of Allison's passing and the sorrow that pervaded the house upon word of her death; the sounds of baby Amelia—his little dear one, Mela—prattling quietly in the nursery; the night Brandon returned home from Washington when it was telegrammed that Barry had suffered a riding accident, that he had fallen from Lightning; and finally, bringing Kathryn and Nathaniel to share his life at the Big House. As Brandon peered into each room, the memories—both treasured and tragic—surfaced one by one, and his eyes grew damp with each recollection. Memories of ordinary happenings of daily life and of major life-changing events seemed to echo through the rooms and hallways, and infuse the very walls of the Big House.

Lastly, Brandon happened upon William and Annabelle's room—and the large oil painting of Allison that he had gifted to Annabelle upon Kathryn's arrival at Crawford Hill. Serenely Allison gazed down upon Brandon in her green taffeta gown—pink roses all about her, matching the soft blush of her cheeks and the delicate hue of her lips. Quickly Brandon turned away to head back downstairs, for if he lingered even a moment longer, he would give in to sentimental tears—as even now, his eyes brimmed to nearly spilling.

As Brandon stood upon the upstairs landing, he did not want to leave—he nearly dared announce to Kathryn that they would stay after all, unpack the luggage and trunks, and *stay*. Yet he knew they must leave, that it was best for everyone as previously discussed and ultimately decided upon.

Downstairs, Brandon made one last glance into the various quarters—the kitchen where the aromas of so many savory meals had been prepared by talented servants' hands; the dining room where the cheerful banter of adults and giggling of little ones filled each meal time; and the west sitting room, with its shelves of colorful glass items glinting in the sun. Finally, he came to the east sitting room and his favorite wingback chair near the hearth where he would spend late evenings sipping brandy and visiting with

William and Annabelle—and where, now, Kathryn and the children waited to depart southward.

As Brandon approached the east sitting room, he hesitated a moment at the doorway, his eyes taking in the familiar comforts of that room and the memories—memories of the night he had come home drenched in rain after William had tried to stop him from visiting Allison's grave in the thunderstorm; the letters regarding Jeremy's death in Lucknow, India; sipping Brandy and talking politics with William and Annabelle by the crackling wintertime hearth—

"Brandon? ... Are we ready?" Kathryn asked.

Collecting himself from his reflections, Brandon nodded. "Yes, we are ready."

And with that, Kathryn, Barry, Mela, and Nathaniel rose from the sofa to head out to the waiting carriages.

The entire Crawford Hill household was assembled before the front steps of the verandah. Fortunately, the recent good weather was still holding, and it would not rain until at least the next day. William and Annabelle stood with their two daughters, Ashley and Carolina, alongside Cotta, Sabe, Ester, Jacob, Cinda and Quash. Beside them were Sara and Tom Davenport, and Hetty. Also assembled nearby to bid farewell were Brister, Cato, Yao, Bilah, Cuffee, the various household servants, cooks, and groundskeepers. Each stood fondly by to see the Stewarts off to their new home and new lives in Charleston.

As Brandon, Kathryn, Barry, Mela, and Nathaniel walked down the verandah steps, there were hugs and kisses all around. Ester wept openly, and Annabelle clung to Mela until the last possible second. Damp-eyed, Carolina hugged her Uncle Brandon—the profound crush upon him still brewing in her heart—and gave him a shy peck on the cheek. Barry and Tom clapped each other on the back and said their final goodbyes, vowing to stay in touch. Brandon and William shook hands solidly, as men will do at such times; but then, caving in to sentiment, their eyes brimmed as they embraced soundly, clapping each other heartily on the back.

"Write and visit when you can," William said.

"Our door is always open when you make it down to Charleston," Brandon returned.

William nodded. Although with war brewing, neither knew when or even if such future visits would be feasible.

Just then Annabelle rushed forward and clasped Brandon to her in a final, tearful embrace. "We shall all miss you more than I can say. Please write when you can," she entreated, then drew back for fear of breaking down all together.

"I will write often," Brandon promised. Then, to cheer her, he quipped, "After all, I am a writer." He winked and smiled, despite the profound sorrow that weighed on him. Then he added, "And I will write to Alexandra at Loxley House in England, as always. I have her address."

Attempting a smile through damp lashes, Annabelle managed, "She will greatly appreciate you staying in touch—" Whereupon, her voice faltered, and she swallowed hard to hold back tears.

"We bes' be goin'," Jacob gently reminded.

Brandon nodded, his heart heavy.

"We is gonna miss you, Massa Brandon," Cotta called out.

Ester could only wave from where she stood on the front steps of the verandah, as the lump that swelled in her throat prevented her from calling out her final farewell.

With Kathryn, Mela, Barry, and Nathaniel at last seated in the carriage, Brandon climbed in and put an arm around Kathryn's shoulders. On command, the nearby wagon drivers slapped their reins, prompting their horses to head southward, down the familiar long allée of oaks hung with Spanish moss. In turn, Jacob gave his reins a slap and clicked his tongue until Endeavor and Lightning slowly lurched the Stewart's vis-à-vis carriage forward.

Hands waving farewells and tearful shouts of goodbye faded into the distance as the carriage proceeded toward the main road. As the wheels creaked forward, Mela and Barry turned in their seats to watch the Crawford Hill Big House recede until it was a mere speck of white.

Although Kathryn savored the relief she felt inside—that she would finally be delivered from the harsh and foreign rural surroundings as well as the social deprivations of plantation life—she sensed that Brandon's emotions were quite mixed upon departing.

Indeed, Brandon felt at least as sorrowful and sentimental about leaving

Crawford Hill as he felt intrigued about his new role as a foreign war correspondent for *The Illustrated London News* and beginning a new family life in a home of his own.

As the vis-à-vis and small caravan of wagons turned onto the rutted main road—Crawford Hill disappearing from view—Charleston awaited. Meanwhile, war swelled in the distance, ushering in a new and uncertain era. Brandon wondered what the future would hold. Only time would tell. Life would surely never be the same.

About the Author

Marsha J. MacDonald has edited a wide range of genres of novels and short stories. The inspiration for writing her first historical novel, Absence of Light—Crawford Hill, came from the years she lived in Charleston, South Carolina. In 2011, the novel ranked among the top three in both the San Diego Book Awards and nationwide Mensa uRGe contests for unpublished novels.